This book was set in Sabon by DEKR Corporation and printed and bound in the United States of America.

Library of Congress Cataloging-in-Publication Data

Global accord : environmental challenges and international responses / edited by Nazli Choucri.
    p.   cm.—(Global environmental accords)
Includes bibliographical references and index.
ISBN 0-262-03200-7
1. Environmental policy—International cooperation.
2. Environmental protection—International cooperation.
I. Choucri, Nazli. II. Series.
HC79.E5G5915   1993
363.7′0526—dc20   92-35201
                                                                CIP

Global Accord
Environmental Challenges and
International Responses

edited by
Nazli Choucri

The MIT Press
Cambridge, Massachusetts
London, England

Global Accord

Global Environmental Accords
Nazli Choucri, editor

Global Accord: Environmental Challenges and International Responses, Nazli Choucri, editor

Institutions for the Earth: Sources of Effective International Environmental Protection, Peter M. Haas, Robert O. Keohane, and Marc A. Levy, editors

Contents

Foreword

The unprecedented increase in human numbers and activities since the industrial revolution, and particularly in this century, has given rise to a deterioration of the environment and depletion of natural resources that threaten the future of the planet. The transboundary and systemic nature of environmental issues and the globalization of the economy that gives rise to them are making international interdependence an inescapable reality.

Effective international responses can be achieved only on the basis of cooperation among nations, and effective cooperation must be based on common interests. There is widespread acknowledgment, at the level of principle, of the need to achieve a sustainable balance between environment and development. But it should be no surprise that the perspectives of developing countries on the issues differ substantially from those of industrialized countries.

The gross imbalances that have been created by the concentration of economic growth in the industrialized countries and population growth in the developing countries are at the center of the current dilemma. Redressing these imbalances will be the key to the future security of our planet in environmental and economic terms as well as in terms of traditional security. This will require fundamental changes in both our economic behavior and our international relations. Effecting such changes peacefully and cooperatively is, without doubt, the principal challenge of our time.

The challenge is all the greater because it demands of decisionmakers a new approach that is more complex and participatory. Environmental problems are systemic in nature, and important linkages must be taken into account in formulating policies to tackle them. Furthermore, today's leaders must make decisions on some issues in the face of a high degree of scientific uncertainty. The transition to sustainable development will require fundamental changes in the behavior of government, the private sector, and citizens alike. The environment and development priorities of developing and industrialized nations differ, and they must be reconciled on the basis of a common but differentiated responsibility. International responses must reflect the responsibility of the industrialized world for the majority of the global environmental risks that have accumulated to date. They must also take into consideration the means and abilities of the developing countries to develop along paths less damaging to their own environments and resource bases, as well as to the global environment.

A New Approach

As we deplete the earth's natural resources and approach its capacity to assimilate our wastes, it is increasingly dangerous, and indeed difficult, to ignore the linkages between issues. A purely sectoral approach to the analysis of environmental problems and to devising policies to combat them is inadequate both in terms of understanding the issues and in terms of implementing the necessary actions. At the same time, given the magnitude of the risks that we face, decisionmakers will have to adopt the precautionary principle and be prepared to incur expense for which there is no predictable return.

A feature of successful management of environmental problems as we enter the twenty-first century will be an integrated approach to planning that takes into account the major linkages, such as the relationship between environment, economics, and public policy. The 1992 United Nations Conference on Environment and Development (UNCED) has articulated the importance of the linkage between environment and development and gives practical effect to this in its "Agenda 21." It recognizes the important reality that environmental impacts arise as a result of our economic behavior and can be effectively addressed only by changes in that behavior. Thus the main task of the 1992 conference is to move the environment issue into the center of economic policy and decision making.

Fundamental Change

The changes we must make in our economic life and our international relations to effect the transition to sustainable development are fundamental in nature and will be extremely difficult to achieve. For they will entail changes in economic, energy, transport, industrial, and urban policies that will have major impacts on the economic interests and competitiveness of nations and of industry as well as on the lives of people.

This transition will require an extensive review and reorientation of the system of incentives and penalties that motivates our economic behavior. Environmental costs must be internalized and the measurement of economic growth reexamined. While governments must set a macroeconomic framework conducive to sustainable behavior, it will be essential to secure the full engagement and cooperation of business and industry as the primary agents through which we conduct our economic affairs.

If the key to sustainable development is economic change, then industry, as the prime instrument of economic change and development, of technological innovation and the environmental and social consequences that follow, is at the center of the transition to sustainable development. Multinational corporations conduct the bulk of the world's economic activity, and their influence on national policies and international agreements cannot be ignored. This book considers their impact on the environment and argues for a close relationship between the crucial triangle of government, industry, and the universities. In a world in which knowledge is the primary basis of competitiveness, this will be essential for sustainable development. Developing countries are often compelled to overexploit the natural resources on which their development future depends, as they are presently unable to compete in an international marketplace in which the principal sources of added value and comparative advantage are technology, capital, management and marketing skills, and scientific knowledge.

To achieve these societal changes will require the active involvement of people and the nongovernmental organizations through which they act from the grassroots to the national and international levels. It will involve significant changes in lifestyles as more people in the industrialized world opt for lives of sophisticated modesty and people of developing countries receive greater support in their attempts to achieve livelihoods that do not undermine or destroy the environment and the resource base on which their future livelihoods depend. And there will be basic changes in consumer preferences and practices, the portents of which are already visible in the move toward green consumerism.

International Cooperation: Reconciling Differences in Priority

International institutions and systems must also respond to the need for change. The linkage between environment and development highlights the second challenge for the nations of the world as they devise global responses to global problems: the challenge of reconciling the different priorities of developing and industrialized countries. This volume examines institutional responses to global climate change, focusing on the challenge of building a collective regime to address the problem and the obstacles to agreement posed by its intergenerational aspects. Implementing the convention to limit climate change, which was signed at UNCED in June 1992, will test the ability of North and South to reconcile the different priorities arising from diverse stages in development and agree upon an equitable apportionment of the costs associated with meeting the new obligation. This negotiating process over a global environmental threat neatly illustrates the interdependence of developing and industrialized nations.

Interdependence is not an unmitigated blessing, particularly when it serves to exacerbate the vulnerability of the weak and increase their dependence on events they cannot control. The international economic environment has clearly contributed to the gross imbalances between North and South that have weakened the economies of developing countries during the past decade. These imbalances continue to present a primary barrier to the revitalization of the economies of these countries and to their prospects for effecting the transition to sustainable development.

The primary responsibility for the future of developing countries, after all, rests with them, and their success will depend largely on their own efforts. But these countries deserve and require an international system that lends strong support to their efforts to develop along sustainable paths. The common need for global environmental security requires a substantial and sustained increase in the flow of financial resources to support the broad development needs of developing countries. It will also require a concerted international effort to remove barriers to trade, to provide access to markets and, crucially, to strengthen the technological and professional capacities in the developing world.

Next Steps

It is clear that international responses to environmental problems must deal with a complex web of environmental and social processes: natural systems, economics, politics and international relations. The complexity and novelty of the issues demand an appropriate intellectual framework to facilitate their analysis and to identify the changes necessary in our economic behavior and international relations. This volume sets out to provide such a framework. It explores some crucial linkages, such as those between the social and environmental processes and between generations. It considers countries with different profiles of growth and reviews the international legislative framework and institutions for global management. Finally, it analyzes some methodologies for measuring our progress in combating environmental problems. The theoretical concerns of this volume should be of great interest to the international community as it faces the challenge of devising effective international responses to global environmental problems. The time has now come to translate sustainable development from theory into action.

Maurice F. Strong
Secretary General
United Nations Conference on
Environment and Development

Preface

By now everyone recognizes the dangers of environmental degradation caused by human activities. Both causes and consequences may pose serious problems for all countries—from the most developed to the least—despite differences in extent and implications. For the first time in human history, there are the beginnings of concerted efforts to understand the nature of these issues and to embark on programs and policies to remedy the most serious of these effects.

At the heart of the efforts is the need to resolve an essential intellectual problem. The problem is this: The body of scientific and social knowledge that we have developed over the centuries has been based on a clear differentiation between humans and nature—between natural and social conditions. This differentiation has allowed us to parcel social problems in small pieces and to place these under analytical and empirical scrutiny.

This strategy of differentiation has been successful in large part because it was supported by commensurate institutional mechanisms in the scientific and academic communities. Such mechanisms consisted of fragmentations in the organization of knowledge into different and discrete disciplines, supported by individual academic departments, in which both the standards of excellence and the nature of recognition and rewards reinforced and sustained this strategy of intellectual and analytical fragmentation. The growing appreciation of profound interconnections between social and natural conditions and between social and natural systems—each responding to its own "laws"—has seriously challenged conventional intellectual practices as well as the basic policy predispositions guided by such practices.

Equally if not more compelling is the evolving recognition by the international community that prevailing norms should be reassessed and that new policies and practices at the global level need to be developed. The long record of international environmental agreements—over 140 in all—framed between 1920 and the present time stand as testimony to the gradual shaping of new global accords on management of both social and natural environments, at all levels of social organization.

This book is part of a series that addresses both the intellectual and the policy challenges posed by this evolving understanding of environmental degradation due to human activities. The *intellectual* challenge is to contribute to the development of the appropriate analytical and theoretical underpinnings relevant to a changing appreciation of evolving realities. This means that we will focus on synthetic interconnections of the two complex systems within which we exist—the natural system, operating according to the physical laws of nature, and the social system, operating according to the legislated laws of humans. Stated differently, the challenge to which this series is directed is to develop an integrated perspective on social action that reflects the real and profound interconnections between humans and nature.

In this book, and in the series as a whole, the global system is conceived as encompassing individuals, collectivities, and the international system—and their interactions. Consisting of the planet and its surroundings (including the sun), its geological and geographical features, flora, fauna (human beings included), natural processes, and human enterprises, the global system encompasses the biosphere—a unique and indispensable environment for life as we experience it.

The *policy* challenges follow directly: if humans are to improve their relations with nature and moderate the conventional and prevailing patterns of environmental degradation, this must be done with some degree of coordination worldwide. No one can influence the global environment alone; if there is to be global protection for the natural environment, then strategies must be coordinated.

If there is a simple way to view the global policy problem, it is this: a wide range of normal and legitimate human activities are generating patterns of effluence and creating dislocations that produce serious ecological imbalances. These imbalances may be setting in place fundamentally unalterable environmental outcomes. In what *way* and to what *extent* are such alterations created is a matter of great controversy. While on scientific grounds there may be little danger of imminent collapse of the globe—from whatever source of pressure envisaged—the contending and more powerful hypothesis is for a gradual, imperceptible erosion of environmental viability, straining life-supporting properties.

It seems increasingly probable that *social impacts* on environmental processes may be stressing the resiliency of *ecosystems* at various levels of complexity. But there are many uncertainties. What *is* predictable is that the future holds many surprises. And the linkages between individuals operating in local contexts and the global system, encompassed by a global, planetary environment, are likely to contain many surprises as well, as are interconnections between local and global environments.

These basic considerations—as simple as they are complex—render environmental issues intensely political at all levels of social organization. This book, as well as others in the MIT Series on Global Environmental Accords, are devoted to international levels of analysis—to the cross-border and cross-jurisdictional cross-purposes and priorities. In so doing, however, we cannot neglect any level of social action. Our particular focus is with the community of nations, the transnational and international governmental and nongovernmental institutions, the private and the public firms—all forms of coordinated action across borders—that define the very fabric of the international community as we know it.

It is our hope that with a dual focus on *intellectual* development and improved *policy* perspectives, we would enhance the quality of the knowledge base as well as the types of political interventions designed to the global context within which we exist—the natural as well as the social environments.

Part I is on conceptual and empirical dimensions of environmental change.

Chapter 1: Nazli Choucri provides a brief statement of the late twentieth century environmental challenge, a conceptual framework encompassing some of the main processes leading to global change and a basis for policy formation and implementation.

Chapter 2: Thomas Homer-Dixon examines the impacts of the absence of corrective dynamics and the lack of a coordinated policy of intervention to constrain anthropogenic emissions, effluents, and consequences—with special attention to the potentials for conflict and violence inherent in environmental issues and global change.

Chapter 3: Nazli Choucri and Robert C. North present a global view of environmental processes and issues (including inherent stresses between growth and development, on the one hand, and ecological sustainability, on the other).

Chapter 4: Hayward R. Alker, Jr. and Peter M. Haas trace the intellectual evolution of environmental ideas and the transition of ecological issues from peripheral to central concern. As an essay in the sociology of knowledge, the chapter defines characteristic features of the ecological perspective.

Part II is on actors and processes.

Chapter 5: Francisco Sagasti and Michael E. Colby focus on contentions and implications in the study of eco-development—and frame an alternative perspective that draws attention to different strategies, policy instruments, and expected outcomes.

Chapter 6: Nazli Choucri looks at the collectivity (the entity and institution) of multinational corporations as producers and distributors of effluence and agents of environmental degradation within institutional, organizational, and global contexts.

Chapter 7: Eugene B. Skolnikoff examines the multiple consequences of technological change and the ways in which knowledge and skills serve to generate degradation but also to enhance prospects for cleanup, prevention, perhaps mitigation, and even abatement.

Chapter 8: Garry D. Brewer addresses the subject of managerial responses to emerging environmental problems, tendencies, and vital challenges and some of the ways in which these responses are impeded by institutional factors, dormant concentrations, and sometimes even "good" management practices.

Part III is on economics and law.

Chapter 9: Jerome Rothenberg reviews the analytic propensities for the conventional economics of intertemporal and intergenerational valuations schemes—juxtaposing the (known) characteristics of global environmental change against traditional economic theory and analytic perspectives.

Chapter 10: Edith Brown Weiss frames a legal perspective for managing social equity across generations and argues for bringing the future back into the present in policy responses to global concerns and managing the legacies of these interventions across time.

Chapter 11: Jerome Rothenberg draws on critiques of time comparisons and the legal basis for broadening that perspective and then proposes alternative principles for the conception and computation of intertemporal and intergenerational time comparisons.

Part IV is on international institutional responses.

Chapter 12: Peter M. Haas and Jan Sundgren examine the evolution of international environmental law and provide an empirical basis for the proposition that international responses require recognition of outstanding problems, adequate scientific knowledge about those problems, and acceptable institutions reflecting environmental science.

Chapter 13: Oran R. Young calls attention to institutional bargaining pertaining to the rules according to which negotiations over substantive issues of the environment are to be resolved and draws upon the Montreal Protocol for evidence of procedures involving political exchange, rule-making, and strategies.

Chapter 14: David G. Victor, with Abram Chayes and Eugene B. Skolnikoff look at possible pragmatic institutional responses to international environmental management and put forward a series of organizational proposals for practical implementation.

Part V addresses imperatives for the twenty-first century.

Chapter 15: Nazli Choucri and Robert C. North present a synthesis of the major intellectual and policy issues and empirical interactions addressed in previous chapters—along with an indication of the requisites, conditions, and processes for management of the global environment in the twenty-first century.

Effective management of the global environment may well become the most significant institutional challenge for the twenty-first century. Each chapter in this book points to the importance of articulating global norms for environmental management. These norms derive from the realities created by highly dispersed sources of environmental degradation. The development of global accord on environmental management will be facilitated to the extent that sound theoretical orientation is coupled with realistic strategies for international cooperation.

Acknowledgments

I am grateful to many colleagues, friends, and associates at MIT and elsewhere for advice, commitments, critique, and review of this manuscript—in whole and in parts. Special thanks are extended to: Lincoln P. Bloomfield, Joshua Cohen, Marcus Feldman, Vincent Ferraro, Robert O. Keohane, Richard Locke, Mario Molina, John Montgomery, Craig Murphy, Kenneth A. Oye, Brian Pollins, Thomas C. Schelling, Marvin Sooros, Charles Stewart III, Arild Underdal, and Carl Wunsch.

The research assistance of Danaue Aitchison, Rebecca Berry, Daniel Froats, Walid Hazbun, Raun Kupiec, Jan Sundgren, and Jason Wittenberg is acknowledged with appreciation.

I am grateful to the Center for International Studies for support of this project through its grant from the MacArthur Foundation and to the Department of Political Science for support of the MIT Faculty Seminar on Global Change: An Interdisciplinary Perspective, which served as an intellectual forum for many of the discussions that led to this book.

The assistance and organizational skills of Elizabeth McLaughlin at every phase of this project were invaluable—both to the editor and to the contributors.

Contributors

Hayward R. Alker, Jr.
Department of Political Science
Massachusetts Institute of
Technology
Cambridge, MA 02142

Garry D. Brewer
School of Natural Resources and
Environment
University of Michigan
Ann Arbor, MI 48109

Abram Chayes
Harvard Law School
Cambridge, MA 02138

Nazli Choucri
Department of Political Science
Massachusetts Institute of
Technology
Cambridge, MA 02142

Michael E. Colby
Eco-Development Associates
732 Ballentine Street
Raymond, WA 98577

Peter M. Haas
Department of Political Science
University of Massachusetts, Amherst
214 Thompson Hall
Amherst, MA 01003

Thomas F. Homer-Dixon
University College
University of Toronto
Toronto, Ontario M5S 1A1, Canada

Robert C. North
Professor Emeritus
Stanford University
Stanford, CA 94305

Jerome Rothenberg
Department of Economics
Massachusetts Institute of
Technology
Cambridge, MA 02142

Francisco R. Sagasti
The World Bank
1818 H Street, NW
Washington, DC 20433

Eugene B. Skolnikoff
Department of Political Science
Massachusetts Institute of
Technology
Cambridge, MA 02142

Maurice F. Strong
Secretary-General
UNCED-Geneva
160 Route de Florissant
P.O. Box 80
CH-1231 Conches, Switzerland

Jan Sundgren
Department of Political Science
Massachusetts Institute of
Technology
Cambridge, MA 02142

David G. Victor
Department of Political Science
Massachusetts Institute of Technology
Cambridge, MA 02142

Edith Brown Weiss
Georgetown University Law Center
600 New Jersey Avenue, NW
Washington, DC 20001-2022

Oran R. Young
Institute of Arctic Studies
Murdough Center
Dartmouth College
Hanover, NH 03755

1

Introduction: Theoretical, Empirical, and Policy Perspectives

Nazli Choucri

The growing scientific consensus that human beings are altering the global environment in potentially significant ways poses important challenges for the study and implementation of national policies and international relations. Despite scientific controversy and continuing uncertainty, there is an increasing recognition that the composition of the earth's atmosphere is changing. This recognition is based on observed trends as well as projected increases of greenhouse gases generated by human activities that are altering atmospheric balances and affecting global climates in new and uncertain ways.

The possibility of such changes raises new questions about the analysis of national and foreign policies throughout the world, as well as the formulation and conduct of such policies. Much of the debate on global change and associated environmental threats—together with the pursuit of global accord on these issues—has been informed by scientific analyses (and controversy) without comparable "scientific" attention to social (human, behavioral) aspects of resource depletion and degradation. The possibility of global change induced by human action, for example, is a relatively new factor in the formulation and implementation of national and international environmental policies. It is now increasingly recognized, however, that human knowledge and skills (technology) interacting with population trends and demands for resources (and derivatives therefrom) have generated environmental problems worldwide. But social science approaches to such issues are only now beginning to come into play.

In the course of intellectual development over recent generations, the social sciences have been predicated on the investigation of motivations, attitudes, decisions, behaviors, and other phenomena from philosophical, historical, psychological, anthropological, sociological, economic, and political perspectives.[1] Only rarely, however, have these disciplines been systematically directed toward human interventions in nature or to anthropogenic responses to the intended or unintended consequences to nature resulting from human action taken in pursuit of narrowly defined human interests. The tendency has been to abstract humanity from nature and reinforce the separation by withholding formal recognition of our total dependence on the planet and its resources for day-to-day survival.[2] Even the behavioral sciences—identifying, formally quantifying, and analyzing regularities in human behavior—have only in very specialized circumstances combined the "laws" and behaviors of nature and the "laws" and behaviors of people within the same equations. The whole issue of global change lies at the frontier of the social sciences as they are conventionally viewed.[3]

Yet even a cursory purview indicates that interactions between social and natural environments involve issues of economics and politics at the very least. Potential, if not inherent, contradictions between economic growth (and stability) and environmental sustainability immediately come to mind, as do forest preservation, jobs/property rights, and population growth balanced against available resources.[4] In fairness, increasing numbers of economists and other social scientists have taken environmental issues seriously in recent years, especially in terms of international trade, investment, and multinational corporations as mechanisms and agents in the diffusion of polluting technologies and products.[5] But a considerable proportion of the economic literature is concerned with the possible effects of environmental regulation on economies without comparable attention to the effects of economic growth on the environment.

The time-worn problem is that the assumptions, concepts, theories, and methodologies of the various social science disciplines frequently serve as what amount to "protectionist" barriers that shut them off from one another, with the result that findings do not circulate widely in a common marketplace of ideas. In any case, the search for better understanding of the sources and consequences of anthropogenic impacts on the natural environment will by necessity constitute a major challenge to the social sciences.[6] Since the need for policy responses worldwide is increasingly felt, moreover, the conventional modes of policy delibera-tion may also be put to the test. Already the possibility of global change has injected scientific evidence, influences, and uncertainties into national and international policy domains.

A major purpose of this book is to develop an integrated conceptual framework linking natural and social systems within which basic (and dynamic) social and natural "actors," behaviors, and interactive pro-cesses can be identified and analyzed from some optimal range of dis-ciplinary perspectives. An underlying premise is that the effective management of global environmental change requires coordinated action among sovereign states in the international system and the cooperation of all other relevant actors—at all levels.

The fact that human activities within one jurisdiction can alter envi-ronmental conditions in another—and possibly over the planet as a whole—suggests both that there is a new form of politics in the making and that the theoretical foundation for the study of politics among nations must necessarily address a range of interstate and transnational interactions bearing on the management of environmental transforma-tions generated by social activities.

The interdependence among states that had been conceived in eco-nomic and political terms is now regarded in environmental terms as well. And environmental conditions do not respect the sanctity of na-tional boundaries. By definition, the very pervasiveness of environmental alteration due to human activities contributes to the globalization of these concerns.

Of the many conceptual challenges posed by possibilities of global environmental change, three are central to the design of this book. First is the *linkage challenge:* the challenge of relating environmental variables and processes to social activities, national characteristics, and interna-tional relations. The concerns of this volume bear directly on the intel-lectual core of the social sciences that have developed over the better part of two centuries as the disciplines designed to improve knowledge of social interactions. None of the social sciences is currently directed to address human interventions in nature or the responses to intended and unintended consequences to nature due to human action. Indeed, the whole issue of global change lies at the frontier of the social sciences as they are conventionally viewed.[7] Understanding the sources and consequences of anthropogenic influence will, of necessity, also constitute a major challenge to the social sciences.[8] Since the necessity for policy response worldwide is becoming increasingly salient, the conventional modes of policy deliberation may also be put to the test. Already the possibility of global change has injected scientific evidence and uncertainties into the policy domain—national and international.[9]

The second conceptual challenge is the *policy challenge:* the challenge of defining appropriate concepts for, and approaches to, decisions about managing the global environment. This challenge emerges from the recognition that the ecological balance of the globe is inadvertently affected by how individuals behave and how institutions, groups, and, most important, countries manage their environments. Such behavior inevitably generates cross-border patterns of effluence that under certain conditions could threaten both the social and the natural environments.

The third conceptual challenge is the *institutional challenge:* the challenge of identifying the appropriate framework for international responses to global environmental alterations due to human action. The international nature of emissions and effluents all but ensures the need for alteration in the behavior of individuals, collectivities, corporations, and nations, and, in all likelihood, for coordinated international response. In these terms bargaining and negotiation become central to the formulation of global environmental policy. At issue is whether the global environmental problems can be reduced to questions of scale (requiring only existing modes of international coordination of environmental processes of planetary proportions) or, alternatively, whether there is something generically different about matters pertaining to the global environment (necessitating adjustments in prevailing international approaches and institutional responses).

The increased visibility of environmental degradation—irrespective of the scale, scope, or uncertainties—politicizes global environmental issues as well as the processes shaping international responses. At issue, then, are the types of responses, their characteristic features, and their prospects for effectiveness. Given the fact that environmental processes do not respect national borders, the international community finds itself in a condition in which countries hold one another hostage: Very little can be effectively done on a unilateral basis, and one nation cannot effectively insulate itself from the actions (and environmental degradations) of others.

The Logic of this Book

According to the underlying premise of this book, effective management of the global environment requires the development of an appropriate intellectual framework within which human-environment interactions affected by, and affecting, global environmental change can be addressed. Given the logic of global processes and the need for coordinated environmental action, it is necessary on both conceptual and empirical grounds to systematically articulate the linkages between natural and social processes and the conditions that generate effective international responses.

This chapter and those that follow are designed to articulate the elements of a framework for the international politics of global environmental management. Together they proceed from the recognition of the three challenges identified above: the ambiguities about the linkages between natural and social systems, the great uncertainties in both causes and effects of global change and about policies and decisions, and the remarkable absence of systematic institutional analysis of linkages between local and global commons, and local and global levels of action.

The contributors to this book have jointly developed an organizational plan to address differences in both dimensions and perspectives. By *dimension* is meant the substantive focus of concern or the problem at issue. By *perspective* is meant the nature and extent of departure from the status quo with respect to political orientation. It is that clue that provides added coherence to our joint effort.

Environmental conditions can no longer be taken for granted. Natural systems can no longer be viewed independently of human action. The contributors to this book tend to believe that growth is environmentally degrading, but the extent of degradation is not inevitable. It is contingent on government policies, on perceptions of the environmental problems, and on the management of environmental variables.[10] Development, if managed effectively and appropriately, can be set on a path that may minimize hazardous consequences. Sustainable development, a new objective of the international community, is intended to be holistic. Later in this book we will consider the ambiguities inherent in the notion of sustainable development and, based on an analysis of these ambiguities, we will propose a concept of sustainability (and its empirical manifestation) that is more robust than the original formulation of the World Economic Commission in its report, known as the Brundtland Report.

The organizational plan of this book is summarized in table 1.1. The dimensions of inquiry addressed in each chapter bear on intellectual orientations, policy concerns, and institutional responses. In other words, we consider ideas, actions, and organization. The perspectives put forward in the book refer to the political (and ideological) orientations and beliefs of the actors (encompassing individual firms and other collectivities, states, and international groups). Simplifying devices are always necessary to facilitate parsimony; therefore, we consider three modalities of political orientation underlying action. First is the *conservative modality*, which minimizes departure from the status quo. Second is the *reformative modality*, which adopts strategies of gradual departure from current conditions. Third is the *transformative modality*, which is characterized by a substantial break or departure from traditional (status quo) perspectives.

It is this attention to political perspective and resulting policy action (conservative, reformative, or transformative) with reference to dimension of inquiry (intellectual orientation, policy concerns, and institutional responses) that constitutes the organizational plan. There are also some efforts to link environment to contemporary policy priorities. For example, poor countries manage their economic problems and are not willing to impose stronger policies on the use of the environment.

While the nature of political deliberations will continue to be affected by scientific assessments and by interpretation of the evidence—often of a very conflicting nature—it is the bargaining and the negotiation among planetary players and among local groups affecting these players that will shape actions. The political processes—national and international— will marshal concerted strategies for the management of global issues and will ultimately legitimize the responses to evolving scientific evidence and concerns and corresponding policy options. Deliberations around negotiation for a Framework Convention on Climate Change illustrated the dramatic politicization of environmental factors. In this process the

Table 1.1 Dimensions and perspectives of global environmental management: An organizational device[1]

Dimension[2] of inquiry	Political perspective[3]		
	Conservative	Reformative	Transformative
Intellectual orientations	Geopolitical view Conformist view	Incrementalist view Gradualist view	Society-nature interaction Ecological paradigm (local/global commons)
Policy concerns	Broadening technological options Adopting a market solution	Developmental alternatives Managing growth processes	Legal measures Judicial resources
Institutional responses	Pragmatic moves Specific institutional adjustments	Strategies for international equity Institutional bargaining	Intergenerational valuation Novel equity calculations

Notes:

1. This matrix is for organizational purposes. It has been developed jointly by the contributors to this volume. Entries are illustrative only. The theoretical implications and further delineations of the concepts in each box will emerge in the individual chapters.

2. *Dimension* refers to the substantive concerns at issue. *Intellectual orientations* refers to epistemological and theoretical concerns. *Policy concerns* refers to discrete "moves" in the policy context. *Institutional responses* refers to changes in the "rules" of the game within which "moves" are made.

3. By *perspective* is meant the nature and extent of departure from the status quo with respect to political orientation.

roles of science, scientific information, uncertainties, and attendant controversies continue to assume major political proportions.

In due course we might expect bargaining among states to reach agreement on policy across forms of environmental degradation. This could lead to a practice of trade in concessions on behavior modifications designed to reach a more comprehensive accord on global environmental issues.[11]

Levels of Analysis

Central to the intellectual challenges addressed in this book are four interconnected levels of systems, decision, and analysis: (1) individual humans and their decisions; (2) major collectivities and social organizations (states, firms, corporations, nongovernmental institutions, and so forth) and their decisions organized within (3) a competitive international system, with institutional mechanisms for decision making and encompassed by an increasingly (4) global system and (natural and social) components—all interconnected within a complex of dynamic feedback relations (North 1990: 11–20). Ultimately what is needed is a better understanding of interconnections, linkages, and feedback relations both within and across levels as well as their social and environmental implications.

In this connection *globalization* refers to the prehistorical and historical tendency of the human species to grow, develop, and expand (North 1990: 183–85, 212–13). Viewed retrospectively and understood in terms of the intense interactivity and interdependence of human population growth, technological advancement, and pursuit of resources, the globalization of the planet that has proceeded for millennia emerges as a logical and compelling anthropogenic process. Presumably it began with the prehistoric migration of our remote ancestors from their region(s) of origin (Africa?) throughout the other land masses. As the story line unfolds, they gradually learned to use untried resources at hand and, even more gradually, how to obtain resources that for one reason or another were not originally available to them. Their learning rate was exponential, however, as were their numbers and the resources they demanded and "consumed." For hundreds of millennia their population growth, learning, and consumption curves were nearly flat, but over the last dozen generations or so all three have climbed spectacularly. The world is rapidly "filling up" with human beings, along with their organizations, machines, weapons, and other "works."

Superficially the *global system* is easily defined. It consists of the planet, its "envelope," and the totality of its features and processes—continents and all their features, oceans (including depths and floors), the biosphere, ecosystems, flora, fauna, and all the species except for *Homo sapiens*. Admittedly, human beings constitute one of the many mammalian species belonging to the natural environment, but for analytical convenience we treat them, their organizations and institutions, and their works as a distinct social environment. By taking this liberty we divide the global system into two large, complex, and interacting systems—one "natural" (characterized by ecological processes, ecosystems, and geophysical, geochemical, and biogenic processes) and one "social" (characterized by human knowledge and skills, organizations and institutions, technologies, processes of production, and other activities and behaviors). In closely interconnected, interactive ways individuals (together with their families, communities, and others with whom they have essentially face-to-face relationships), states (and firms, corporations, and comparable organizational components), and the international system can be envisaged as fitting into the encompassing global system.

The Individual in Natural and Social Environments

To investigate interactions and relationships between social and natural environments, we need to find ways of identifying and analyzing connections or linkages within and between the two systems. Such a linkage occurs whenever an action on one side of an organizational or other systemic boundary affects conditions in another system, subsystem, or environment (Rosenau 1969). On the side of the natural environment, we accept such systems and subsystems as the scientists make them available, but on the social side we need to make our own definitions reasonably explicit.

The most fundamental unit in all human social systems is the individual human, the dominant thinking, organizing, and deciding actor who, like other living creatures in the natural system, responds to felt needs, wants, and desires by making demands and acting upon natural and social environments in order to obtain the sustenance without which he/ she cannot long survive. In coping with these environments, individuals make demands, reach decisions, and act upon many organizational levels from the family, neighborhood, and community to large corporations, the state, and the international and global systems. This means that each individual—each of us—bears responsibility for and may also suffer from outcomes at all levels of social aggregation and in all parts of the natural environment.

Human decisions yield tight interconnections (direct and indirect) among individual and social actors, activities, and outcomes: Each individual, through his or her central nervous system, translates internally generated needs, wants, and desires into demands, which may or may not be met. Demands combine, in turn, with capabilities to produce decision and action. A decision (and consequent action) represents an application of energy (and other resources) in order to narrow or close a discrepancy or gap between a "fact" (an individual's perception of "what is" and his or her perceptions of "what ought to be") (Boulding 1956: 11, 20–22, 84–85, 99–100; North 1990: 36–38).

An important aspect of decision is feedback, which in effect amounts to the actor's sensitivity, conscious or reflexive, to the consequence of the act that he or she has undertaken. Feedback is an essential element in the ability of a person to learn from experience and to adapt to changes in social and natural environments. Thus, through action and positive and negative feedback processes, each individual "learns" and "adapts" to changing circumstances (including outcomes of his or her own behavior)—and thus contributes to collective learning or sociocultural evolution. To a large extent actions are guided and knowledge and skills (technologies) are "learned" through positive and negative feedback—that is, the perception and interpretation by the actor of the favorable or unfavorable consequences of his or her actions. Here a brief interpretation from prehistory and history may be useful.

Dating from primeval times, human beings—through bargaining, leverage, and coalition building—have maintained, expanded, and developed organizations and institutions of increasing complexity. The earliest human institutions appear to have been hunting and gathering bands (essentially extended families), followed, as a consequence of population growth and the development of more advanced knowledge and skills, by tribes and chiefdoms. Membership in these institutions is thought to have been based on birth and voluntary association. Concepts of authority, governance, and legal sanctions emerged with the first pristine states—either because a stronger tribe conquered and learned to rule over a weaker one or possibly because a number of weaker communities combined to protect themselves against a more powerful neighbor.

From bands and tribes to modern states, organizations have made it possible for individuals to manage their activities in order to obtain what they demanded from the natural environment (and for security against rival communities). All such organizations can be viewed as coalitions (or coalitions of coalitions) resulting from interpersonal (and intergroup) bargaining, leveraging, and other exchanges (Riker 1962). Repetitively, in historical times such interactions within states have given rise to networks of "horizontal" and "vertical" linkages that have been more or less persistent and, not uncommonly, have contributed to new, more complex organizations, institutions, and modes of activities.

The State as "Sovereign" Actor
Organizations and institutions—states included—enable people to accomplish collectively what individuals could never achieve by themselves. Such collectives are often referred to as making decisions and acting. Strictly construed, however, the real decisionmakers and actors are individuals working in concert. This is to say that individuals in organizational or institutional settings reach collective decisions and undertake collective actions by establishing a coalition in support of particular options. This tends to be true even though some "bargainers"—as in a dictatorship—may possess vastly greater power than others (Cyert and March 1963).

Among the many organizations and institutions that constitute social environments, the state is the only one that is accorded "sovereign" power domestically and is franchised to act independently and "legitimately" in the international and global systems. As such, it contributes to, encompasses, and in a sense presides over all the resource expansion and resource depleting and degrading that occurs within its boundaries. In this and succeeding chapters, therefore, the entity and institution of the state requires special attention.

In historical writing and in the formulation of theory, more attention has often been focused on the meaning and exercise of sovereignty than on the driving forces that have contributed to the sociocultural evolution of states and to their undeniable impact upon human life and upon the natural environment. There are, of course, many forces driving the state, but demographic, technological, economic, and political growth and development are surely among the most powerful.

Social functions performed by states (through their institutions) include resource extraction (taxation or some equivalent indispensable for the maintenance of power), resource allocation (a major source of investment and of power as influence), the maintenance of some measure of security (economic, political, and strategic), value formulation and socialization of the young, and the regulation of domestic activities (North 1990). These activities contribute to the growth and development of states, but over time they cannot succeed unless the underlying growth and development processes are functioning in proper balance.

Growth, as we define it, refers to incremental increases (or expansions) in the quantities, sizes, levels, or "prices" of things—numbers of people, aggregates of territory, resources, products bought and sold, and so forth. By *development* we mean quality or qualitative changes, tendencies, or trends. Chapter 3 examines these processes in greater detail.

Growth and development processes are highly interactive, with growth contributing (sometimes, but not always) to development, and development leading (sometimes, but not always) to growth. Included in the concept of development are enhancements of the technological, economic, social, political, and other capacities of a state or other organization (public or private) resulting from the interactions among the growth variables (North 1990: 48–49, 62–63). From this perspective, the three master variables—embedded in a network of human communications and social actions—constitute a dynamic nexus as they interact among themselves and with the many and varied intervening and dependent variables and types of feedback to which they contribute and respond—and by which they themselves are partially shaped.[12]

Constraining these growth and development processes and adding to their complexities are two "natural" laws: According to the first law of thermodynamics, basic energy cannot be "consumed" or destroyed; but according to the second law, no "work" can be performed (no action can be taken) without some measure of energy denigration from more to less usable forms. This means that some form of resource degradation (effluents, emissions, toxics, and other wastes) accompanies all uses of energy and other resources.

The implications of the thermodynamic laws have often been overstated, but all too frequently they have also been prematurely dismissed or wholly ignored. What they reveal is a paradoxical relationship between unrestrained anthropogenic growth and development, on the one hand, and environmental economy and sustainability on the other. It is well known that a certain amount of economic growth and development is necessary for social and political stability—and for a long time that appeared to be all we needed to know. In the latter decades of the industrial age, however, it became increasingly evident that exponential population growth and exponential technological (and economic) development—in combination—were overburdening the natural environment and creating policy dilemmas.

In human affairs, paradoxes—real or perceived—commonly translate into decision and policy dilemmas. In community, national, and international affairs decisionmakers and the public in general, when confronting a policy dilemma, tend to take positions around (or near) one or the other of its horns—the growth and development horn, in this instance, or the environmental sustainability horn. Internalizing both horns, individuals may be immobilized or alternatively deny that any contradiction exists. Much the same can often be said of organizations as collective actors, but there is also a high probability that factions, interest groups, or political parties will rally around one or the other of the horns as a policy position.

Both within and across states, population, technology, and resource access tend to grow and develop unevenly and to interact in ways that are critically relevant to their relative capabilities, dispositions, and impacts upon social and natural environments. To the extent that a country's population growth accelerates more rapidly than its technological development, for example, demands for energy and other resources may be expected to increase, but development will be constrained, and damage to the environment may remain relatively localized and low.

Insofar as technology accelerates in advance of population growth, however, development will be enhanced, resource availabilities will ex-

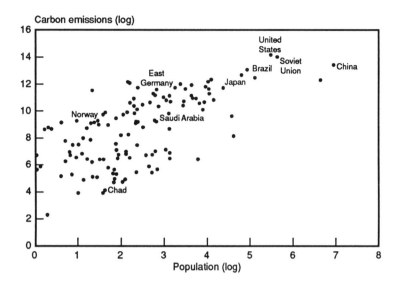

Figure 1.1
Carbon emission and population
Note: Laos (CO_2/cap.: 23 tons) and Côte d'Ivoire (CO_2/cap.: 10 tons) are extreme outliers due to heavy deforestation and are not included.
Sources: Based on data from Marland et al. 1989; World Bank 1988; Central Intelligence Agency (various years).

pand (through exploration, "discovery," and/or trade), and the demand for resources will further accelerate—as will resource depletion, pollution, and other forms of degradation. But new technologies may include the development of machines and the identification of resources that are more resource-efficient and/or "environment-friendly."

There are other implications and qualifications deriving from these propositions, which will be discussed in chapter 3. As a prelude some basic patterns are presented in figure 1.1 (carbon emission and population size) and figure 1.2 relating carbon per capita and GNP per capita.

Limits of State "Sovereignty"

Institutionalized sovereignty does not imply that states are the only (or necessarily the most important) agents or institutions responsible for transforming (depleting or degrading) social and natural environments.[13] Quite the contrary. Emerging from barter exchanges in prehistoric times, markets have provided some of the most powerful driving forces behind the location, transportation, transformation, and redistribution of re-

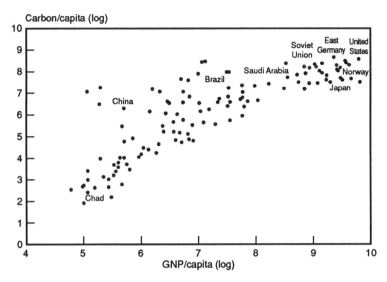

Figure 1.2
Carbon per capita and GNP per capita
Note: Laos (CO_2/cap.: 23 tons) and Côte d'Ivoire (CO_2/cap.: 10 tons) are extreme outliers due to heavy deforestation and are not included.
Sources: Based on data from Marland et al. 1989; World Bank 1988; Central Intelligence Agency (various years).

sources (and manufactured goods) among states and must be recognized, therefore, as playing a major role in determining relationships between natural and social environments. In many respects markets made states possible and contributed to their development into the complex institutions we know today. Closely associated with markets, moreover, are private firms (companies, corporations) servicing them and at the same time benefiting from their ubiquitous functions. Like markets, these organizations and institutions have played historically important roles in technological and economic growth and in development and political stabilization.

Many, if not most, of the more powerful human impacts on the natural environment are exerted by private firms, corporations, and comparable organizations and institutions. In this regard multinational corporations play an increasingly significant role. Because of their uniquely "sovereign" roles in the global system, states are the cognizant and ultimately responsible aggregators and record keepers for their populations, their economies, their military establishments, their governmental accounts, and increasingly their performances on environmental issues. But markets, firms, and corporations provide mechanisms of production and exchange that are critical to economic stability and the ability of the state to apply leverages domestically and externally and to effectively implement its policies.

Activities Generating Emissions and Effluents

Contemporary anthropogenic activities as diverse as industrial production (i.e., the production of cement, refrigerants, etc.), the burning of fossil fuels, stock raising, rice paddy culture, deforestation, and landfilling generate effluents and emissions that affect the global climate and other aspects of the global system in various ways.[14] In this section of this chapter we are concerned primarily with the sources of such materials, whereas the next section deals with modes of transmission and their implications for state, international, and global environments. In the aggregate the greater the level of production (and associated technological and economic activity), the more rapid will be the expansion of emissions and effluents.[15]

The generation of carbon dioxide (CO_2), a major gas contributing to global effects, is an inescapable consequence of nearly all social processes. Carbon emission is "produced" principally by energy use (74 percent), industry (cement and gas flaring) (3 percent), and deforestation (23 percent) (Marland et al. 1989; Houghton et al. 1987). These estimates are rough at best, given the uncertainties, controversies, and difficulties associated with estimating, let alone computing, indirect effects (see, for example, Stern, Young, and Druckman 1992), as well as interactive effects. By contrast, methane is generated largely by activities in developing regions—the raising of rice (29 percent) and ruminant domestic animals (20 percent), burning of biomass (15 percent), creation of landfills (15 percent), and use of fossil fuels (21 percent)—as well as by the solid industrial wastes of developed societies (25 percent). Methane produced in developing areas is closely tied to subsistence and to activities necessary for the poor to survive day to day.

The chlorofluorocarbons (CFC 11 and CFC 12) are man-made and are used strictly in industrial manufactured products and industrial processes. Although CFCs are currently produced mainly in advanced societies—for refrigeration, cooling, electronics, etc.—the fastest-growing markets for these products are the developing countries. And nearly 80 percent of the world's population resides in developing areas. CFCs contribute significantly to the erosion of the ozone layer, and their residence time is among the longest of the effluents. For these reasons—and others that will be discussed later on in this volume—CFCs have been acknowledged early as crucial outputs. We will show how the international community has been effective in framing a response to this environmental challenge. Relative to the other effluents, the nitrous oxides are the least understood of the greenhouse gases. Such effluents are produced largely by fossil fuel use, biomass burning, fertilizer use, and the contamination of aquifers. Since almost every country in the world uses fossil fuels and fertilizers, the sources of nitrous oxide are distributed globally, as are the activities producing these effluents.

The relevant considerations for subsequent chapters are the major differences in the volume, intensity, and productivity of greenhouse gases—and attendant effluents—across nations and over time.[16] These differences provide important parameters as well as key variables in the formation of strategies for global management. In some cases they may even serve as multipliers, interacting with other social or ecological issues and thereby showing the ubiquity of human-nature interconnections. These differences are created by the differences in distribution of actions and activities worldwide that produce various effluents. Figure 1.3 provides an approximate distribution of effluents by activity. It is approximate because it draws only on first-order consequences at the point of measurement. More than that would be a foolhardy exercise indeed. (See the notes to table 1.2.)

The scope of the global problem is illustrated by the fact that current emission rates of the major greenhouse gases—in conjunction with past emissions—may be in excess of the capacity of the tropospheric, oceanic, and terrestrial sinks to absorb them, creating the ecological imbalances or "deficit." This outcome provides a nearly perfect illustration of the complexities in interactions of social and natural processes. Measurement and observations on these individual gases—carbon dioxide, methane, chlorofluorocarbons, nitrous oxide, and others—vary significantly

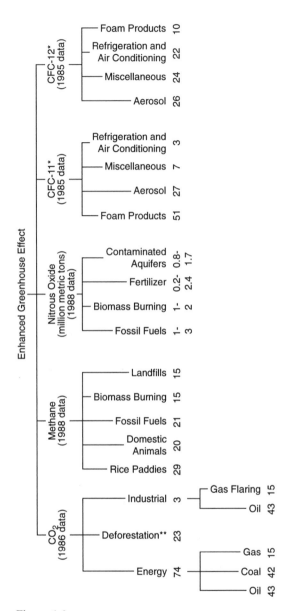

Figure 1.3
Enhanced greenhouse effect: Effluents and activities in terms of approximate percent contribution of various activities to each gas

Notes:
[1]Reporting countries only. For Communist countries CFC 11 is estimated at 12% and CFC 12 is estimated at 18%. An earlier version was presented in Choucri and North 1990.
[2]1980 figure.
Sources: Based on data from the following sources: CO_2: Marland et al. 1989; Houghton et al. 1987. Methane and nitrous oxide: EPA 1989. CFCs: Hammit et al. 1986.

Table 1.2 Properties of major anthropogenic greenhouse gases

Property	CO_2	CH_4	N_2O	CFC-11	CFC-12
Pre-industrial atmospheric concentration	280 ppmv	0.8 ppmv	0.288 ppmv	0	0
Current (1990) atmospheric concentration	353 ppmv	1.72 ppmv	0.310 ppmv	0.000280 ppmv	0.000484 ppmv
Current rate of atmospheric accumulation	1.8 ppmv (0.5%)	0.015 ppmv (0.9%)	0.0008 ppmv (0.25%)	0.0000095 ppmv (4%)	0.000017 ppmv (4%)
Atmospheric lifetime	50–200 yrs (see caption)	10 yrs	150 yrs	65 yrs	130 yrs
Direct global warming potential	1	11	270	3400	7100
Indirect global warming potential	none	positive	uncertain	negative	negative

Notes: CO_2, carbon dioxide; CH_4, methane; N_2O, nitrous oxide; CFC-11, chlorofluorocarbon-11 (CCl_3F); CFC-12, chlorofluorocarbon-12 (CCl_2F_2). Other chlorofluorocarbons are not shown. Several precursors to formation of tropospheric ozone (a strong greenhouse gas) also are not shown; these include carbon monoxide, various hydrocarbons, and oxides of nitrogen. Concentrations are expressed in parts per million by volume (ppmv). Concentration and rate of accumulation data are from globally averaged *in situ* measurement and are well known. Atmospheric lifetimes are computed from observational data and models and are less certain. The "lifetime" of CO_2 reflects a range of model estimates of the rate at which atmospheric CO_2 concentrations would adjust to changes in emissions—CO_2 has no permanent sinks but rather is transferred between atmosphere, ocean and biota through complex and not fully understood processes. The global warming potential (GWP) is an index used to compare the greenhouse effects of sources (and sinks) of different gases in common units (on a mass basis). By definition the GWP of CO_2 is 1. Direct GWPs shown here account only for the direct radiative effects of emissions (or absorption) of these gases. Some greenhouse gases also yield indirect effects, e.g., by altering the chemistry of the atmosphere and thus the concentration of other greenhouse effects. Indirect effects are very uncertain and thus not quantified. Sources: after table 1.1 Houghton et al. (1990) and table 3 of IPCC (1992). (Compiled by David Victor.)

in extent and reliability in terms of both quality and quantity; but with allowances for interactions, feedback, and substantial uncertainties, a rough indication of both the sources and the impacts of these effluents can be gauged.

The distributions in table 1.2 show relative contributions of select greenhouse gases to temperature change (global warming), residence time in the atmosphere for the 1980s, and annual growth rate (see Hansen et al. 1988 and Graedel and Crutzen 1989 for slight differences in estimates). While there are many ambiguities, the table shows the differences among the greenhouse gases for each of these factors and provides the basis for propositions about the linkages of these gases to human action.[17] Since these gases are generated by different types of human actions (and hence decisions), we can begin to develop hypotheses about society-ecology linkages.

Differentiating among the greenhouse gases provides an initial entry point into identifying the relative sources of emission and action as aggregated within the institution of the sovereign state. Then, too, differentiating among gases in terms of hypothesized relative contributions to climate alterations—in conjunction with distribution by state source—helps shape assessments of relative impacts on global environmental alterations.

The time element remains critical: The residence time in the atmosphere of the individual greenhouse gases all but ensures that past human effects cannot be eliminated—however effective either present policies or future commitments might be. At issue is modulating present and future effects of present and future actions. In a very real sense, therefore, the broad contours of global accord for environmental management are illustrated by the distribution of the variables in table 1.2, as are the uncertainties and complexities. Because all countries generate these gases, but in different amounts and in different proportions, differences in residence time make it especially difficult to account with any precision for who does what and how much—and whether it matters and how much. To illustrate linkages between human action and types of effluents, in this section we will further highlight the significant connectives between gases and action. Figures 1.4 and 1.5 provide an approximate distribution for CO_2 emissions.

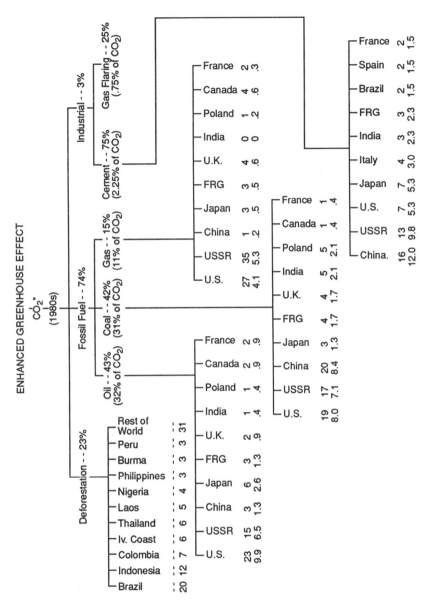

Figure 1.4
States' contributions to activities generating select trace gases
Notes: The first row in each series indicates % contribution of states to uses of oil, coal, gas, and cement, respectively. The second row in each series indicates % contribution of states to deforestation, fossil fuel use, and industrial activity from oil, coal, gas, and cement use.
N.B.: All numbers are in % and have been rounded. Countries listed under each subheading are the top 10 for total contributions to deforestation, fossil fuel use, and industrial activities, respectively.
Source: Based on data from Marland et al. 1989: Houghton et al. 1987.

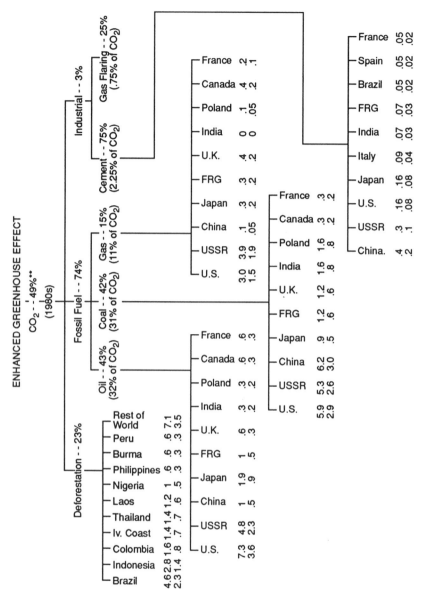

Figure 1.5
State activities and global effects[1]
Notes:
[1]In % and rounded.
[2]Note the inherent statistical inconsistency: 49% of *current* greenhouse effects is the product of all *past* as well as *current* emissions.
The first row in each series indicates % contribution of each state, by activity, to global CO_2 emissions. The second row in each series indicates % contribution of each state, by activity, to enhanced greenhouse effect. Countries listed under each subheading are the top 1 for total contributions to deforestation, fossil fuel use, and industrial activities, respectively.
Source: Based on data from Marland et al. 1989; Houghton et al. 1987.

The fact that human activities within one jurisdiction can alter environmental conditions in another—and possibly for the planet as a whole—suggests both that there is a new form of politics in the making and that the theoretical foundation for the study of politics among nations must necessarily address a range of transnational and interstate interactions bearing on the management of environmental transformations generated by social activities.

With respect to activities and effluents, according to their respective roles and functions, we can view actors in the global system in two broad categories: (1) those that are "full-time" resource depleters and degraders (individuals, firms, corporations, and states) that function as environmentally oriented negotiators and/or regulators in particular circumstances; and (2) those that negotiate and/or regulate environmental and related issues on a more or less sustained basis (agencies of the United Nations, regional or functional regimes, et al.). Beyond that broad differentiation, however, the differences within each group are considerable.

Transmission Mechanisms: Natural Forces and the International System

At this point we turn to two modes of transmission that move emissions and/or effluents—directly or indirectly—from their countries of origin into global space: the natural and the social. The natural modes are illustrated by emissions or effluents that move directly from the site of generation and are "captured," so to speak, by natural forces—updraft, wind, large rivers, ocean currents, and the like—through biogeochemical and related cycles and processes. Among the social modes of transmission are the effluents and degradation materials embedded, moreover, in products that are produced in one country and used in another (automobiles and/or fossil fuels, for example)—from the United States, perhaps, to Germany, Brazil, or possibly Bangladesh. When such transfers are completed, there are almost certain to be at least three mechanisms of social transmission to be accounted for: one at the primary production site in the United States, where emissions or effluents are released into the global environment and moved by natural forces; one accomplished by social means of transport (railway, trucking, maritime shipping, air freight, pipeline, or whatever); and one associated with product use, where emissions or effluents are again released to natural forces of the global environment.

From the point of view of human societies organized into "sovereign" states in an international system, the interactive effects of natural and social (ecological and anthropogenic) modes of transmission affect—and are affected by—organizational and institutional arrangements of the international system. Shaping both structure and process in the international system are driving forces traceable to uneven growth, development, and competition among the states (and their components)—phenomena of considerable complexity, paradox, and potentials for contention. The discussion here will be limited to the distributional (and essentially competitive) functions of the system, whereas a growing concern among the nations for environmental sustainability—and a measure of global accord—will be considered in the next section. The dynamics of the natural forces of the global system are even more complex (and uncertain), and a more detailed discussion of them is reserved for a subsequent section.

States and their component institutions differ substantially in terms of the levels ("sizes") and rates of change of their populations, technologies (knowledge and skills), and resource availabilities. For this and related reasons their economic, political, and military (strategic) bargaining and leverage capabilities also differ substantially, as do their respective levels and rates of resource depletion and degradation.

Interacting with each other diplomatically, economically, militarily, and otherwise, states constitute the international system. Just as bargaining and leveraging within states contribute to domestic distributions of attributes, resources, capabilities, influence, and agents of environmental depletion and degradation, so bargaining and leverage between states of different profiles (basic structures) and capabilities contribute to the production and distribution of resource-depleting and degrading resources, goods, and technologies across each others' national borders.[18] Through such largely unintended distributions (driven by more or less legitimate economic forces), states create for themselves and for other states conditions of environmental interdependence which none of them intended to impose.

Private and Public Activities

Among the most powerful social distributive mechanisms are the activities (and facts) of production; but once goods are produced, the transport mechanism, the utilization of goods, and their dispersal for intermediate or final use are processes that are generally emission-based. The "normal" practice of international trade best illustrates this simple fact: Effluence is endemic to production; effluence is a necessary corollary of transportation; and effluence is a byproduct of consumption and utilization. As noted below, the complexity of transmission internationally also contributes to significant uncertainties about the sources and consequences of global change and, by extension, to the difficulties of framing appropriate international responses.

Entailing both public and private activities, trade and other commercial and financial exchanges between states can be either binational or multinational within the international system and may involve either state or nonstate actors. In effect, by exporting resources, goods, services, and technologies across national boundaries, countries also export the growth-development/environmental sustainability paradox by the inclusion of depleting, degrading, or polluting actions or agents. The characteristics and outcomes of such transactions are influenced, intentionally or unintentionally, by the profiles of actors on both sides of the relevant border(s).

Additionally, insofar as markets, firms, foreign trade, and other economic ventures (investment, for example) facilitate the production, distribution, and consumption of energy and other resources across state frontiers, these institutionalized transactions often allow the effluents and other residuals to flow back into common property areas of both internal and external environments, thus exacerbating domestically generated pollutants that were domestically distributed and contributing to environmental interdependence (Choucri and North 1990).

Crossing Borders

State borders compound complexities—and derivative uncertainties—because (1) they are man-made and partly protected but also fallible; (2) they delineate jurisdictions of states, indicating where one jurisdiction begins and others end, thereby delineating the legitimate exercise of political authority; (3) and states, in principle, are autonomous in the exercise of authority within their jurisdictions—even though the impacts may be felt elsewhere. In practice, moreover, (4) states are seldom able to exercise their internal authority over external consequences as effectively as they desire; (5) they are generally unable to control access across their boundaries (of people, goods, and services) entirely—if at all; (6) they cannot regulate flows of environmental effluents across their borders, even if they desire to; and (7) they cannot insulate or protect themselves effectively from actions of states in other jurisdictions (as when deforestation in one state affects carbon balances, and potentially environmental conditions, elsewhere).

Viewed in an international context, it is apparent that no single state can individually control the direction or alter the distributions of effluents, but neither is any one state insulated from the effluents of others. The conjunction of indirect social transmissions of emissions and effluents (through use in one location of products and processes produced in another) and the vagaries of transmission by natural forces give rise to a peculiarly pervasive gridlock of "complex" interdependence[19] wherein all are potentially hostage to all. And the reality of national borders—delineating limits of "sovereign" jurisdiction—is the defining factor of the international system at any point in time.

International Pursuit of Sustainability and Accord

International growth, development, and economic exchange and competition, together with the attendant transmission and diffusion of environmentally degrading agents (including assistance from natural forces) helps to frame the paradoxical relationship between growth and development and environmental sustainability. One horn of the consequent policy dilemma represents economic and political stability, profit, and jobs now (at uncertain environmental cost); the other horn stands for the preservation of environmental assets (at uncertain economic cost) with future generations in mind. The debate is worldwide and is attracting attention at local, national, regional, and international levels.

We view the individual human being as the only true decision- and policymaker in any organization or other collective body—family, community, firm, state, or international or global system. Hence when we assert that any one of these collectives has decided, we mean that through some kind of bargaining and leveraging process, however equal or unequal and however conscious or unconscious, a coalition of individual human beings has been established in support of some particular option.

We put forward another stipulation: The state is the only organization, institution, or collective actor that is recognized as sovereign or successfully operates in ways that meet the (mythical?) criteria of sovereignty. This means that private firms—including multinational corporations—are not sovereign, nor are any international agencies or the United Nations. There is no world (or global) government. If there were, it would be sovereign by definition, and the status of "sovereign" states would be called into question. This aspect of the sovereignty "myth" helps to explain why there is no world government—down to this day, at least. We cannot conclude, however, that various agencies of the international system, or the United Nations, have little power. On the contrary, they have as much power (which can be considerable), as a sufficient number of powerful or at least influential "sovereign" nations are willing to accord them.

In recent decades numbers of international agencies—and notably the United Nations—have exerted unprecedented power and influence with respect to environmental (as well as security and related) issues. Additionally, several states in the international system, including the United States, have on numerous occasions demonstrated their ability to limit the influence of the United Nations and other international agencies. Such demonstrations remind us that states remain sovereign and are therefore qualified, in effect, to bring as much influence, power, and/or naked force to bear as other nations in the system are willing to allow.

Given these imperatives, how much substance is available in support of the reality that global environment is the encompassing, overarching system on which all social systems and our very existence as a species are irrevocably dependent? Few would deny that the substance is total. At the same time the logic of our status brings us back to our starting point: Only individuals make decisions; only states (for now, at least) are sovereign. And the natural system is the only possible source of everything we need or want. Every action we take has an environmental cost.

We have seen how our power to generate effluents and inflict environmental damage beyond state (and other) borders makes each state (or other actor) interdependent—almost hostage—to others. Subsequently we will reveal some of the complex ways whereby damage we create in the global (natural) environment is thrown back against us in ways that are likely to remain outside our direct control. Within this complicated (and uncertain) context, bargaining and leveraging define our social relationships, and coalitions determine our "power," influence, and possibilities for pursuing accord.

Viewed within an international (or global) context, clearly no single state can individually alter the global distributions of effluents and none is insulated from the effluents of others. International collaboration is thus a necessary element of effective environmental management both to influence present trends affecting the global environment and to provide both the necessary and the sufficient interventions in prevailing patterns of "individual" and "systemic" human activities.

Because of the long lead time, the complex feedback dynamics within and between social and natural systems, and the irreversibility of many environmental changes, policy interventions set in place now will have impacts only in the longer range. In those terms international coordination becomes a necessary condition for influencing future trends of global environmental deterioration.[20] Although the issue of environmental alteration is relatively new in international forums, there has been a discernable trend toward the regulation of environmental degradation.[21] Already the international community has concluded some 140 environmental treaties.

As indicated in several chapters of this book, the record suggests that accord on the global environment involves a dynamic policy process revolving around bargaining, negotiation, and leveraging among relevant actors. That process begins with recognition of the problem; agreement on goals and principles, identification of specific procedures, and formulation of policy alternatives; and—finally—a decision on policy. Matters of implementation and compliance emerge at a subsequent stage. One of the most important achievements in this entire process is the building of consensus between scientists and policymakers in the development of a flexible framework designed to avoid obsolescence in the face of new scientific evidence.[22]

The basic differences and unevenness among states on either side of the growth-development-sustainability ledger—whether generating patterns of effluence or contributing to their management—help shape the contours of responses to global responses to environmental change. Industrial societies are expressing concern over the developing countries' reluctance to engage in environmental deliberations.[23] And developing states are countering with the charge that since it is the industrial societies that have polluted the environment, they must bear the costs of management. These concerns begin to frame the bargaining dimensions of global accord for environmental management. So, too, while there is an appreciation of the distinctive environmental problems for industrial and developing countries, the common predicaments are not agreed upon, nor is there consensus on the salience of environmental problems—on priorities and policy.

While the nature of political deliberations will continue to be affected by scientific assessments and by interpretation of the evidence—often of a very conflicting nature—it is the bargaining and the negotiation among actors and among local groups affecting these actors that will shape actions. The political processes—national and international—will marshal concerted strategies for the management of global issues and will ultimately legitimize the responses to evolving scientific evidence, concerns, and corresponding policy options. Deliberations around negotiation for a Framework Convention on Climate Change and a Framework Convention for the Preservation of Biodiversity illustrate the dramatic politicization of environmental factors. In this process the role of science, scientific information, uncertainties, and attendant controversies will continue to assume major political proportions.

The Encompassing Global System

The earth and its features might be envisaged as a massive incubator of life—all flora and fauna, including our own human species, and their needed resources—heated by the sun and tempered by winds, clouds, rain, and other natural forces. The whole system—geological, chemical, climatic, biological et al.—has always been undergoing change, but throughout most of the planet's history, such changes have been attributable primarily to the amount of solar radiation reaching the earth's surface and to alterations in the planet's orientation to the sun (Hileman 1989, 40), which is not only the "prime mover of the earth's climate" but also "the source of its life" (Schneider 1989a; Schneider 1989b, 13). Only during comparatively recent times (no more than a few ticks of nature's clock) have human beings emerged as agents of disruption of the global equilibrium.

From this perspective, if the nested social systems discussed in previous pages are "fitted into" and intensely interact with nature's encompassing system—thus completing the global system as we have defined it—individuals on all levels (all of us) continue to function as the ultimate anthropogenic actors. Like other living things, humans remain sensitive to myriad events in the natural system, which is sensitive in turn to a wide and ever-broadening range of anthropogenic activities. They demand products that contribute to soil erosion, deforestation, and flooding. The fossil fuels we burn generate carbon monoxide, carbon dioxide, sulfur dioxide, and methane. Our refrigerators, aerosol sprays, and foams combine with other effluents to deplete the ozone layer, and on and on. These are all elements of what Westerners have defined as the "good life," one to which people in other parts of the world increasingly aspire.

In guiding us through the formulation of theory and making of policy, an integrated perspective relating social and natural environments to global change is less a luxury than a necessity. Figure 1.6 centers on the interactions of ecological systems and decision-making systems as they are shaped by natural processes (on the environmental side) and by action and decision-making processes (on the social side). It is this connectivity between the two types of processes that defines the essence of global environmental problems, and it is the distinctiveness of the respective processes that enables identification of potential policy alterations or interventions.

Seeking to penetrate what casual observers might perceive as enigmas of the universe, scientists address the top part of figure 1.6. These seeming mysteries emerge from the nature of planetary processes and sources of change within and between ecological systems. Social scientists, by contrast, are concerned with the remaining elements of the diagram—the core interactions between decision-making and ecological systems and the underlying social processes (or process variables). These variables are presented in bold type in the lower part of the diagram. In all their complexity, multidimensionality, and intense interactivity, these

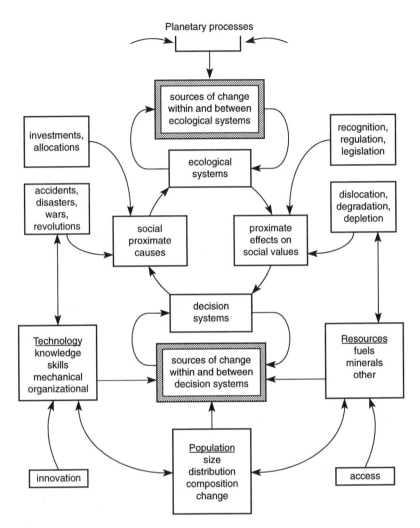

Figure 1.6
Integrated global perspective: social and natural environments
Source: Extended and adapted from Stern, Young, and Drukman 1991.

master variables contribute to the variables of human outcomes and effects on ecological balances.

For scholars of international relations the conception of a global system as distinct from an international system is especially challenging.[24] Conventionally the study of international politics has focused almost exclusively on social interactions across national jurisdictions.[25] It becomes increasingly apparent, however, that the interactions between social and natural forces exert strains on the global system, calling into question the global system's capacities to adjust, accommodate, or absorb dislocations thrust upon it and lies beyond the bounds of the field as traditionally conceived.

The political problem worldwide derives from the consideration that in all societies population demands must be managed and basic needs met. To the extent that such demands are met, managed, postponed, diffused, or mitigated, the essential conditions for ecological security may be met for the short term. But if the demands of a population exceed the carrying capacities of resources, land, and the economy, environmental security is threatened. And if populations, in conjunction with prevailing technologies and social adaptation techniques, place pressures on resources in excess of the prevailing resource base or its capacity to meet or "absorb" pressures, the viability and environmental conditions for social systems may be threatened—in the sovereign state, in the international system, and in the global system.[26]

This means that the individual—each of us—bears responsibility for and may suffer from outcomes that occur at all levels of social aggregation in all parts of the world. Concurrently, to the extent we individuals buy, sell, invest, produce, or otherwise operate through privately owned and managed manufacturing, commercial, or financial institutions, we find many of our internationally and globally oriented activities mediated by our respective firms or corporations and also, directly or indirectly, by governmental agencies in ways that have political and economic as well as environmental implications.

For both analytical and policy purposes figure 1.6 depicts a significant challenge: the need to distinguish among global processes and outcomes in terms of those which for all practical purposes are, and are likely to remain, outside human control (such as cloud formation and solar radiation); those over which human control is partial (such as the buildup of carbon dioxide levels through fuel use); and those which are entirely under human control. The global processes and outcomes that are entirely under human control are those for which human beings are primarily, even wholly, responsible as "producers" and which, in principle, they distribute globally.

Added purposes of figure 1.6 are to (1) help frame the logic for international action, (2) identify the junction at which policy interventions may be crucial, and (3) highlight the need for consistency on conceptual grounds and for a definition of international policy responses. Figure 1.6 depicts highly complex processes in a highly simplified form. To read the figure as it is intended, one views each component itself as composed of complex nonlinear and highly complicated processes fraught with uncertainty. This mental exercise, applied to the distribution in figure 1.3, should yield a sense among the state entities in the international system with respect to the scale and scope of the dynamics of figure 1.6.

Also embedded in figure 1.6 are the major intervention junctions, i.e., the points at which alterations in human action due to policy changes, different types of interventions, and different types of actors are salient in each phase. Government performance everywhere is shaped to administrative capabilities, political stability, and support of the population, all of which directly bear on its capacity to act. Different governments have different tools and policy preferences for meeting demands.[27]

Complicating the problem from a policy perspective is the fact that from an ecological perspective—at the top center of figure 1.6—there is a generic dilemma that underlies all social processes: Activities undertaken in the pursuit of legitimate ends (i.e., economic growth, industrialization, etc.) can be ecologically dislocating and environmentally threatening. Defining the global predicament, this policy dilemma is by now both recognized and to some extent accepted in industrial societies. But it is especially controversial—and compelling—in those developing countries in which the demands of a rapidly growing population must be met.

In the parlance of dynamic feedback processes, the central proposition of figure 1.6 is the necessity for joint action: The persistence of unconstrained human activities that are degrading to the environment and unabated patterns of effluence may substantially disturb the interaction and relationship between two complex environments, the natural and the social. The disturbances induced by human activity could exceed nature's adaptive and absorptive abilities. They could also effectively transform conditions for life on earth on an aggregate basis (for example, the prevailing temperature) as well as regionally, if not locally. Central in this connection is the fact that most patterns of environmental degradation are basically due to actions and investments that are viewed as normal and legitimate and are entirely in keeping with the most routinized social processes worldwide. These are the actions we encourage, uphold as valuable, and seek to emulate. And people everywhere have defined these as "growth" and "development."

Clearly there are also sources of environmental degradation that are considered to be not normal and which we would all view as pathological and not always legitimate—such as nuclear warfare—with potentially potent impacts on the global environment. But for the most part it is "normal" human behavior—and its underpinnings of social legitimacy—that emerge as root "causes" of deleterious effluence and environmental degradation.

A wide range of environmental alterations and the increased patterns of environmental interdependence shape the parameters for coordinated institutional responses. Under certain circumstances these pressures may even be articulated as "demands." The obvious fact that environmental effluents do not respect the sanctity of territorial boundaries defines the character of environmental interdependence. The diffusion of effluents across territorial borders and the inability of states to control their diffusion or destination place states in a bargaining stance in which managing effluents—their sources and consequences—is the central issue of deliberations that may shape the choice of targets, of strategies, and of expected outcomes.

In the context of figure 1.6, the outliers in the diagram, on both sides of the figure, represent the intervention points—through normal processes (such as regulation, legislation, allocations, investments, and so forth)—as well as processes considered less normal, or at least socially undesirable (such as war, violence, dislocating conflicts, and the like). Both types of processes are generic features of social practice and of social systems. The policy sector in figure 1.6 points to the problem inherent in striving for global accord. In the absence of changes in human action, prevailing patterns of human activities may seriously stress the resiliency of ecological systems. Inducing behavior changes could alter current trajectories; without alteration, however, we can envisage greater environmental strains. Therefore, devising approaches to alter behavior amounts to an imperative. And since alterations may be needed in all social contexts, the challenge (originating "locally") is inherently one of individual decision, international politics, and global impact.

Uncertainty, Policy, and Risk

Unavoidably a presumption of pervasive uncertainty accompanies any discussion of resource-depleting or -degrading activity, the generation of emissions or effluents, and possible global consequences. The gross immeasurability of uncertainty on both sides of the ledger—in terms of both ecological systems and social systems—and the unknowns of "cause" and "effect" are nearly overwhelming. In this connection types and sources of uncertainty can be roughly categorized as follows. First, while the basic biogeochemical characteristics of global environmental change are broadly recognized, uncertainties about the *feedback effects* on both the physical and social processes are compelling.

Second, environmental as well as social processes operate in multiple, unequal, and sometimes overlapping *time frames*. Variability in time increments complicates assessments of the underlying processes. Fundamentally the long lead times in both social and environmental processes—and the separation of "cause" and "consequences"—themselves amount to major sources of uncertainty. Third, there are uncounted uncertainties associated with intertemporal effects. In particular, there are *intertemporal and intergenerational impacts* of environmental change whereby future generations incur the environmental costs of the actions of past and present generations, which reflect the complexities associated with long lead times.

Fourth are uncertainties due to *irreversibility*. It may well be that some patterns of environmental alterations cannot be "undone" and that the underlying sources cannot be eliminated either wholly or in part—at least not within the frame of historical rather than geological time.[28] Finally, given a major unevenness in the sources and consequences of environmental perturbations, the differentials in the determinants of greenhouse gas emissions and in their effects both regionally and worldwide raise crucial issues of *equity* related to intertemporal (over time) and intergenerational (across generations) effects. Not all countries contribute the same way to the global balances, nor are they uniformly affected. Some will benefit from climate alteration.[29] This unevenness may be a significant constraint on the development of international responses.

These features characterize some crucial uncertainties associated with global environmental change. Because human activities are incremental in historical time and therefore minuscule in geological time, they confound assessments of complex feedback, time frames, and differentials in sources and in consequences.[30] Together these factors bear on the political issues and on the policy responses of the international community, as they serve also to frame analyses of the constituent components of the global issue—in terms of both sources and consequences.

The more illusive uncertainties in the natural environment derive from our limited knowledge of climatic and other processes of change affecting human and other forms of life on the planet. Uncertainties in social environments are shaped in considerable part by the fact that whereas individual human beings are the only real decisionmakers on any level of organization, competing states with grossly unequal power and influence are the sole sovereign and legal decisionmakers in the international and global system. And firms, also with unequal capability, scope, and influence, are the major producers and distributors of effluents and agents of environmental degradation. It is the conjunction of these uncertainties in both natural and social systems that confounds a simple policy prescription for environmental management—at any level of decisionmaking.

The climate focus is particularly important as it highlights, par excellence, the salience of uncertainty—in both cause and consequence—and the sensitivity of climate to levels, rates, and perturbations of atmospheric conditions. Because the climate's mechanisms are highly sensitive to a set of trace gases, labelled the "greenhouse gases," the role of humans in "producing" these gases is of critical concern.[31]

The most frequently cited pattern of climate change is the record of global temperature, which shows a distinctly upward slope over the span of a century. The attendant trend in carbon emissions also shows a notable increase. The concentration of carbon dioxide in the atmosphere today is roughly twenty-five percent higher than a century ago. And it is generally agreed that with increases in carbon concentrations, the temperature of the earth's surface will also rise. In this sense climate serves as a dependent variable to be "explained" by patterns of human activity, and the effluents attained (carbon dioxide in this case) serve as intervening variables to be altered by conscious policy intervention in order to respond to the change in climate.

To the extent that the environmental and ecological systems are perturbed by human action, both the sources and the consequences are fraught with uncertainty.[32] The climate system illustrates some compelling complexities. In physical terms the climate system is a complex process governed by intricate feedback interactions among biota, air, sea, land, and ice components.[33] The system, driven by solar radiation, is "regulated" by natural feedback processes, such as changes in the earth's position in relation to the sun and changes in the gaseous composition of the atmosphere.

Because of the complex interactions among the underlying natural processes—and given uncertainty about the effects of social interactions of the distinctly human element—separating out these effects is exceedingly difficult, if not impossible. The oceans and the biosphere, for example, play major (and highly uncertain) roles in the climate system,[34] and the conclusions we reach depend on how we approach the extensive uncertainties about these interactions.[35] The ubiquity of the underlying sources of global environmental change shapes, in principle, the nature of the interactions depicted in figure 1.6. So, too, figure 1.6 highlights the generic processes of linking "local" and "global."

These and associated imponderables are often put forward as a rationale for political indecision. How can we mount a full-blown program of environmental sustainability when we cannot assess the risks and other probabilities involved? There are two simple answers. First is insurance: If there were no uncertainties and risks in life (no fires, shipwrecks, automobile and aircraft crashes, floods, hurricanes, or earthquakes), there would be no need for insurance companies. Programs of environmental sustainability can be viewed as insurance programs. Second is the logic of local-global linkage: To the extent that global depletions and degradations originate locally (and nearly all of them do), clean, healthy, and reasonably safe local environments will ensure clean, healthy, and reasonably safe global environments—at no additional cost.

Notes

Collaboration with Robert C. North in framing the theoretical issues of this volume, and of this chapter, is especially acknowledged, as are contributions to the logic of this chapter and the joint research that shaped inquiry into underlying analytical and empirical issues. I am grateful to Hayward R. Alker, Jr., Kenneth A. Oye, Thomas Homer-Dixon, Peter Haas, David Victor, and Oran Young for comments on an earlier version, to the members of the Harvard-MIT Seminar on International Institutions and International Cooperation for insightful discussion of the political issues and, especially, to the MIT Faculty Seminar on Global Change: An Interdisciplinary Perspective for a critical review of parts of this chapter.

1. Exceptions to this generalization reflect the increased recognition of the importance of environmental issues and their integration into disciplinary frameworks. See, for example, the development of economic analysis to address environmental issues as a distinct subfield of economics. For an analytic perspective, see Arrow and Fisher 1974.

2. Among the most relevant analyses of this issue is that of Young 1989a. See Krasner 1983 for alternative approaches to the problem of converging expectations and norm development.

3. For valuation of environment and for analysis of pollution, for example, see Dorfman and Dorfman 1972.

4. With relevance to such issues, Paul and Anne Ehrlich have quoted economist Kenneth Boulding to the effect that anyone who believes that exponential population growth "can go on forever in a finite world is either a madman or an economist" (Ehrlich and Ehrlich 1990, 159).

5. See, for example, Rubin and Graham 1983, and Walter 1975.

6. On the role of knowledge and issue linkage in international politics, see, for example, E. B. Haas 1980.

7. For valuation of environment and for analysis of pollution, for example, see Dorfman and Dorfman 1972.

8. On the role of knowledge and issue linkage in international politics, see, for example, E. B. Haas 1980.

9. See Skolnikoff 1990 for a discussion of political obstacles to domestic response to global environmental issues.

10. For a detailed analysis in the context of the Mediterranean region, see P. M. Haas 1990a.

11. The literature on bargaining and negotiation is rich with propositions and directives for cross-issue bargaining. For background and strategic analysis, see especially Raiffa 1982 and Fisher 1981. See also Young 1975. See Oye 1990 for a theoretically important and useful distinction between tactical and substantive cross-issue bargaining. On the issue of self-binding commitments, see Maoz and Felsenthal 1987. For a useful overview of approaches to regime analysis, see

Haggard and Simmons 1987. Already there are efforts to articulate a viable transfer of technology to the developing countries in return for their compliance with pollution abatement measures.

12. See the dynamic representation in figure 21.2 in Choucri and Bousfield 1978 (p. 314) for an operational model.

13. In chapter 6 we show the conceptual (and empirical) relationships between expansion of state behavior outside national boundaries and expansion of firm behavior, extending markets, and market share (North 1990; Fligstein 1990).

14. See, for example, Keyfitz 1989, 1990, and 1983.

15. See Keyfitz 1989. See also Mathews 1990.

16. See, for example, Graedel and Crutzen 1989.

17. For a more recent analysis of the residence time issue, see Victor 1990.

18. Somewhat similar outcomes can result when large numbers of migrants move from their own countries into densely populated urban areas of other countries.

19. Peter Haas has suggested a related perspective, namely temporal, spatial, and functional transmission.

20. The alternative hypotheses are (1) that coordination among the most significant actors is sufficient to generate significant outcomes (in terms of imposing the corrective measures in figure 1.2); and/or (2) that spontaneous, uncoordinated action could generate behavior modifications; and/or (3) that effective bilateral exchanges on a generalized scale could generate requisite behavior alterations.

21. See Thatcher 1989 for a brief survey of institutional responses.

22. For examples of technological change and more scientific evidence, see Manzer 1990.

23. With the exception of the United States, the countries of the Organization for Economic Cooperation and Development (OECD) appear to be willing to engage in the search for interventions and policies to induce alterations in human activities and reduce greenhouse gas emissions.

24. North 1990 provides a detailed argument for separating "global" from "international," defining *global* as the Fourth Image, and thus extending the original Waltz formulation (Waltz 1959). See Choucri and North 1990 for an explicit articulation of the environmental linkages at each level/"image."

25. A nascent literature on the global dimension of world politics is emerging. See Pirages 1989 and North 1990. The intellectual debt to Aron 1973; Renouvin and Duroselle 1967; and Sprout and Sprout 1962 must be acknowledged.

26. See Keyfitz 1989 and Mathews 1990.

27. From a methodological perspective, this statement is best illustrated by the way in which different macroeconomic models rely on different types of "closure rules." For a detailed analysis of this issue, see Taylor 1983.

28. For an analytical perspective, see Arrow and Fisher 1974.

29. For example, global warming could alter the Siberian climate, enhancing agricultural prospects.

30. The broad scientific task involves improving understanding of the underlying forces for each of the greenhouse gases as well as interactions with gases that are not themselves greenhouse gases but can significantly alter the chemistry of the atmosphere and hence affect the concentration of greenhouse gases.

31. In the absence in the atmosphere of the greenhouse gases—which absorb heat that radiates from the Earth's surface and emit some of the heat downward, heating the earth—the earth would be about thirty degrees centigrade colder than today. This downward emission is a basic natural process governing the earth's "thermostat." But human activities are not increasing the atmospheric concentration of these gases on a global basis and, therefore, apparently intensifying the greenhouse effect. See IPCC 1992 for a recent synthesis of assessments and a scenario of effects.

32. Most of the hypotheses about climate alterations are derived from atmospheric general circulation models exercised to date largely in terms of exploring the effects of doubling atmospheric carbon dioxide—a fairly dramatic intervention. For a discussion see Schneider and Rosenberg 1989.

33. For a summary of key processes, see Schneider 1989a and Graedel and Crutzen 1989.

34. The ocean's ability to absorb carbon dioxide and heat is a major determinant of the rate and the extent of climate change. The oceans today absorb 45 percent of annual fossil fuel emissions. While the elementary chemistry is well understood, complex ocean/atmosphere feedback is not; further, the effects of the oceans can change as well, (possibly) due to climate change. Thus one of the most important pieces of the global climate puzzle is largely unknown, and it is unlikely that scientific closure could be achieved in the foreseeable future.

35. See, for example, Wunsch 1984.

I

Theoretical and Empirical Dimensions

2
Physical Dimensions of Global Change

Thomas F. Homer-Dixon

This chapter addresses the question "What will the world environment be like in the next decades if we continue with business as usual?" The answer depends, in part, upon our knowledge of the physical processes in the global environment. The answer also hinges on what we mean by "business as usual." Here this phrase refers to the consumption patterns, social practices, institutions, technologies, and individual attitudes prevailing in a given society. Differences in our starting assumptions about such factors—about the specific nature of, and flexibility inherent in, "business as usual"—may lead to very divergent predictions of eventual environmental damage.[1]

We begin with what we know and can predict about changes in the physical features of the global human-ecological system until the year 2025. Several factors are highlighted that affect the degree of uncertainty surrounding predictions of these physical features. For some features, uncertainty is largely a function of weaknesses in our knowledge about certain physical processes. For others, it is more a function of our uncertainty about possible variations in social processes. In these cases, our starting assumptions about the nature and flexibility of "business as usual" are particularly important, since humankind may face very different environmental outcomes depending on prevailing institutions, social relations, technologies, and individual attitudes. This chapter then describes two plausible worlds in 2025, one optimistic and one pessimistic, and proposes how the differences between these worlds could be, in part, a function of human social choice.

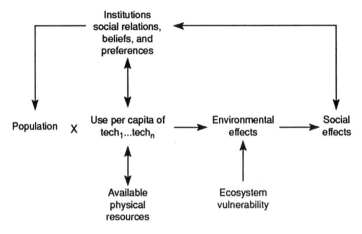

Figure 2.1
Main variables and causal relationships

Main Variables and Causal Relationships

The environmental problems facing humankind might seem overwhelming. They are large-scale, long-term, and inadequately understood. They strike directly at our most intimate links to the biosphere, such as our ability to obtain the food and water we need for survival and social stability. But we must avoid slipping into simple-minded environmental determinism: There are numerous intervening factors that often permit great variability, resilience, and adaptability in human-environmental systems.

Some of these factors are identified in figure 2.1.[2] It shows that the total effect of human activity on the environment in a particular ecological region is a function of two main variables: first, the product of total population in the region and of the use per capita of each of the range of technologies (*Tech*$_1$ . . . *Tech*$_n$) available to the population; and, second, the vulnerability of the ecosystem in that region to those particular technological activities. The use per capita of each technology, in turn, is a function of available physical resources in the region (which include nonrenewable resources such as minerals and renewable resources such as water, forests, and agricultural land) and "ideational" factors, including institutions, social relations, preferences, and beliefs.[3] Over the short and medium terms, the *n* in *Tech*$_n$ does not vary much.

It is a function of the economy's current capital stock, which embodies the society's prevailing level and type of technological development. Over the long term, as this capital stock turns over, n varies as a function of certain ideational factors and available physical resources.[4]

The figure goes on to show that environmental effects (for example, the degradation of agricultural land in a particular region) might cause certain types of social effects (such as the large-scale migration of people out of the region). There are important feedback loops from social effects to the ideational factors and thence back to activity per capita and population (thus, migration could alter class and ethnic relations in a society and thereby its economic activity).[5]

Particularly important are the ideational factors at the top of the diagram. This social and psychological context is immensely complex: It includes patterns of land distribution; the social distribution of wealth; the economic, political, and legal incentives to consume and produce material goods (including the system of property rights and markets); family and community structures; perceptions of the probability of long-term political and economic stability; historically rooted patterns of trade and interaction with other societies; the distribution of coercive power within and among nations; and metaphysical beliefs about the relationship between humans and nature. Without a deep understanding of these factors we cannot begin to grasp the true nature of the relationships between human activity, environmental change, and its social effects.

Sources of Uncertainty

This chapter focuses on the physical dimensions of global change listed down the left column of table 2.1. The first variable, population size, is explicitly identified in figure 2.1. The second, energy consumption, is a reasonable surrogate measure of general material consumption in human societies and therefore of the figure's "use per capita of technology" variable. The other variables in the column are all encompassed by the "environmental effects" category of Figure 2.1[6]

The next section of the chapter will show that the future values of all the variables in table 2.1 are uncertain, sometimes highly uncertain. Across the top of the table, four factors are identified that affect the

Table 2.1   Factors contributing to the severe unpredictability of selected environmental variables

	Quality of theory	Quality and quantity of data	Uncertainty about capacity for human response	Chaotic processes
Population size				
Energy consumption	X		X	
Climate change	X	X	X	X
Ozone depletion	X			
Deforestation		X	X	
Degradation of agri-cultural land		X		
Reduction in water supply and quality		X	X	
Depletion of fish stocks				
Decline of biodiversity		X	X	

degree of uncertainty accompanying predictions of these future values. The Xs within the table indicate the factors likely to be severe sources of uncertainty the each variable. The table shows that for some variables, such as population size and depletion of fish stocks, few (if any) of these factors will be serious sources of uncertainty. For other variables, such as decline of biodiversity and climate change, two or more of the factors are very important. This suggests that for some physical variables the degree of uncertainty surrounding predictions of their future values is much higher than for others.[7]

Reading from left to right across the top of the table 2.1, the first factor affecting the degree of uncertainty is the quality of our theories about the physical and social processes that determine the values of the variables. Demographic theory, for instance, gives us a fairly firm grasp of the determinants of fertility rates and population growth; yet, in contrast, the timing, rate, and climate impacts of global warming are largely unknown, mainly because of serious gaps in knowledge about the roles of clouds and the oceans.

The second factor is the quality and quantity of the data available that describe the processes determining the values of the variables. A review of material published by the World Resources Institute shows, for instance, that reasonably detailed data are available on the annual catch and sustainable yield of regional marine fisheries, but data for degradation of agricultural land, especially erosion, are, for the most part, either unavailable or highly uncertain. Similarly, our estimates of the number of plant and animal species on the planet range from five to thirty million, and this makes our predictions of the future decline in biodiversity highly imprecise.

The third factor is our degree of uncertainty about both the ability and the willingness of humans to change the social, economic, techno-logical, and physical processes that contribute to environmental stress. For some variables, this uncertainty is low. For example, world popu-lation size in 2025 will be strongly influenced by the population's present size and age structure; in particular, the momentum of population growth is sustained by the large number of young females still to reach reproductive age. Demographers know that this limits the potential influence of family planning measures, which in turn narrows the range of uncertainty accompanying population estimates.[8] In contrast, there is great uncertainty surrounding both the extent to which energy con-sumption can be reduced through conservation and new technologies and the extent of people's willingness to accept such reductions.

The fourth and final factor contributing to the level of unpredictability of these variables is the degree to which the physical and social processes influencing the variable are chaotic. A chaotic system has nonlinear and feedback relationships between its variables that amplify small pertur-bations, thereby rendering accurate prediction of the system's state in-creasingly difficult the further one tries to project into the future. In chaos (not to be confused with randomness), deterministic causal pro-cesses still operate at the microlevel and, although the system's state may not be precisely predictable for a given point in the future, the boundaries within which its variables must operate are often identifiable. (See Crutchfield, Farmer, and Packard 1986; James Gleick 1987.)

Until recently environmental systems, in particular the earth's climate, were regarded as relatively resilient and stable in the face of human insults. But now scientists widely believe their behavior is chaotic and therefore often quite unpredictable, because these systems have many nonlinear relationships between the huge number of variables describing them. This means it may be much easier than previously thought to push an environmental system from one equilibrium state to a very different equilibrium state. In 1987, for example, geochemist Wallace Broecker (1987) reflected on recent data on polar ice cores and ocean sediment: "What these records indicate is that Earth's climate does not respond to forcing in a smooth and gradual way. Rather, it responds in sharp jumps which involve large-scale reorganization of Earth's system. . . . We must consider the possibility that the main responses of the system to our provocation of the atmosphere will come in jumps whose timing and magnitude are unpredictable."

William Clark (1985, 41) has made a similar point about interlinked physical, ecological, and social systems: "Typically in such systems, slow variation in one property can continue for long periods without noticeable impact on the rest of the system. Eventually, however, the system reaches a state in which its buffering capacity or resilience has been so reduced that additional small changes in the same property, or otherwise insignificant external shocks push the system across a threshold and precipitate a rapid transition to a new system state or equilibrium."

Physical Dimensions of Global Change

This section summarizes some current trends and projections for the physical variables in Table 2.1. For most environmental variables, the absolute range of change of the variable's value has increased sharply this century. Thus, while the annual increment to the world's population in 1900 was about 10 million people, today it is nearly 90 million. This population increase has combined with dramatically increased per capita material consumption to produce staggering jumps in energy consumption, carbon emissions, water consumption, fish consumption, land degradation, and deforestation.

The figures below are highly aggregated and obscure important regional differences. Moreover, societies tend to differ in the values they assign to various environmental resources and services, and therefore some societies will be more severely affected than others by an equivalent physical change in the environment. However, the figures and trends discussed here provide a quick, heuristic overview of the extent and nature of human activity and its environmental effects today and in 2025.[9]

Population Growth

Figure 2.1 shows that population size can be a key force driving environmental change. Sometimes population growth does not damage the environment, but often this growth—in combination with prevailing social structures, technologies, and consumption patterns—makes environmental degradation worse.[10] During the 1970s and early 1980s, family size dropped dramatically in many countries from six or seven children to three or four. But family planners have discovered that it is much more difficult to convince mothers to forgo a further one or two children to bring family size down to replacement rate. As a result, the growth rates of some of the world's most populous countries—including India and China—are hardly declining at all (Sadik 1990; Feeney et al. 1989). India's rate has leveled off at around 2.0 percent (about 17 million people) per year, while China's has stalled at around 1.3 percent (14.8 million) per year.[11] These developments have recently led the United Nations to revise upwards its mid-range estimate of the globe's population in 2025 from 8.2 to 8.5 billion (Sadik 1990, 1991). The UN has also raised its estimate of the globe's population when it stabilizes (predicted to occur towards the end of the twenty-first century) from 10.2 to 11.3 billion, which is more than twice the size of the planet's current population.

Demographers have long assumed that developing countries would pass through a "demographic transition" similar to that exhibited by currently developed countries in the nineteenth and twentieth centuries, during which a decline in death rate was eventually followed by a compensating decline in birth rate. This transition is thought to have resulted from increased material prosperity and certain social changes, such as higher literacy rates and the emancipation of women. However, if some developing countries cannot maintain a steady growth in social and economic prosperity, their demographic transitions may be in doubt.

Energy Consumption

Total human commercial energy consumption in 1988 was roughly equivalent to 8 billion metric tons of oil (WRI et al. 1990, 142). This was an increase of 3.7 percent over the 1987 figure. During the past two decades, energy consumption's steady climb has been broken only in 1980, 1981, and 1982; and the U.S. Department of Energy expects the rate of growth to continue at 1.5 to 2.1 percent annually through the year 2000 (U.S. Department of Energy, 1989, 10). As industrialization, electrification, and transportation networks expand in developing countries, their energy consumption may grow up to twice as fast as that of the developed world.

Currently, oil makes up 38 percent of global commercial energy consumption; coal, 30 percent; natural gas, 20 percent; hydropower about 7 percent; and nuclear power, 5 percent. As the cheapest and most accessible petroleum reserves are depleted, these percentages will change significantly. In the first decades of the next century, many experts predict that oil consumption will decline, while natural gas, nuclear power, nonconventional sources (such as solar power), and perhaps coal will have to fill the gap (Lee 1989).

The level of global energy consumption in 2025 will depend on a huge array of factors, including whether energy prices are adjusted so they reflect environmental and other external costs, whether technological innovation permits greater efficiency in energy production and consumption, and whether international agreements are achieved to restrict releases of carbon dioxide. Despite this uncertainty, experts have tried to estimate future primary energy demand.[12] In 1981, for instance, the International Institute for Applied Systems Analysis published low and high estimates suggesting that global energy demand in 2025 would be between 16 and 26 billion metric tons of oil equivalent. In 1985, Jose Goldemberg and other researchers proposed that a dramatic effort at energy conservation could cut this to less than 9 billion tons.

Climate Change

As is now widely understood, human activities release a number of gases (mainly carbon dioxide, chlorofluorocarbons, methane, and nitrous oxide) than impede the escape of infrared radiation (heat) from the surface of the earth to space. In the crudest terms we can say that (given a certain amount of incoming solar radiation) the more of these gases present in the atmosphere, the higher the mean temperature at the surface of the planet.[13] In fact, if it were not for the naturally occurring greenhouse effect, the current average temperature of the planet would be about 33 degrees Celsius lower than it is now, and the earth would not be able to support most of the life currently present. However, the scientific story is much more complicated than this, because there are countless ill-understood positive and negative feedbacks that may accentuate or diminish human perturbations of the global heat balance. For instance, scientists are uncertain to what extent increased cloud cover caused by global warming will trap further heat (a positive feedback) or reflect sunlight (a negative feedback).

Over the last few years, though, a number of experts have reached a rough consensus: Assuming no major changes in the trend of human emission of greenhouse gases, we will likely see a global warming of 1 degree Celsius by 2025 and 3 degrees by 2100.[14] This may not seem like much of an increase, except when we realize that the earth has warmed only about 5 degrees since the coldest period of the last ice age, about 18,000 years ago. Moreover, the predicted rate of increase during the next 100 years will be about 0.3 degrees per decade, which is far faster than rates following the ice age.

What could be the impacts of such a warming? At the moment, the three-dimensional computer models of the atmosphere used to estimate global warming trends have insufficient resolution to give us confidence in predicted changes in precipitation patterns, storm frequency, and soil moisture for specific regions. However, we can say that temperature increases in high latitudes will be much greater than the mean, that sea levels will rise about 6 centimeters per decade (principally from thermal expansion of sea water), and that coastal areas will generally receive more precipitation than currently while interiors of continents will become drier. For instance, by 2030 central North America is predicted to warm from 2 to 4 degrees in winter and 2 to 3 degrees in summer and to experience a 15 to 20 percent decrease in soil moisture (Houghton et al. 1990, xxiv). This could have a major effect on grain production in the United States and Canada.[15]

Ozone Depletion

A dramatic example of the above-mentioned nonlinear (or "threshold") effects in complex environmental systems was the discovery of the Antarctic ozone hole in the mid-1980s. The scientific models of ozone depletion used to that point had, for the most part, assumed a rough linear relationship between chlorofluorocarbon (CFC) emissions and ozone depletion. Atmospheric scientists had not even remotely anticipated the ozone-destroying catalytic process that occurs on the surface of stratospheric ice crystals when certain temperature and light conditions interact with particular concentrations of water, nitrogen compounds, and CFCs. If the conditions are right, it turns out, this destruction can occur at lightening speed, stripping the ozone from multikilometer layers of the stratosphere in a matter of days. (See Toon and Turco 1991.) The Antarctic ozone hole was startling evidence of the instability of the environmental system in response to human inputs, of the capacity of humankind to significantly affect the ecosystem on a global scale, and of our inability to predict exactly how the system will change.

The Antarctic ozone hole contributes to the general depletion of ozone over a wide area of the southern hemisphere. Each southern spring, the hole forms inside a circular pattern of wind called the "circumpolar vortex"; as summer approaches this vortex breaks up, and ozone-depleted air moves northward from Antarctica. During the past several years scientists have found very disturbing evidence that rapid depletion may eventually occur in the Arctic too. In addition, while the situation over the Poles is perhaps the most urgent, stratospheric ozone depletion is occurring around the planet as CFCs move into the upper atmosphere. In early 1991, the U.S. Environmental Protection Agency (EPA) announced that satellite data showed an ozone decrease of 4.5 to 5 percent in the last decade over the United States and 8 percent over northern Europe; losses in the Southern Hemisphere (outside Antarctica) were on average 2 percent higher than those in the Northern Hemisphere (Stevens 1991).

Humankind has already released immense quantities of CFCs into the atmosphere. It takes on average about ten years for CFC molecules to migrate from the ground to the middle stratosphere. Once these molecules are there, sunlight breaks them down, and the liberated chlorine can catalyze the destruction of ozone molecules for decades before precipitating back into the lower atmosphere. Thus, with the CFCs released to date, we have probably already committed ourselves to a dramatic thinning of the ozone layer over the coming decades. It is extremely difficult to give precise estimates of future depletion; current mathematical models, based on existing principles of atmospheric science, have generally underestimated the rate of ozone loss. However, the EPA currently predicts worldwide depletion of 10 to 12 percent by 2010 (Stevens 1991), and we can speculate that depletion of 15 to 20 percent by 2025 is not implausible. Recent estimates suggest that a one percent decrease in stratospheric ozone produces about a 1.6 percent increase in the incidence of carcinogenic ultraviolet radiation on the surface of the earth, which in turn produces about a 2.7 percent increase in non-melanoma skin cancer rates (Kelfkens, de Gruijl, and van der Leun 1990). The deleterious effects of increased ultraviolet radiation on crops, forests, ocean phytoplankton (which are at the bottom of the ocean food chain), and human and livestock health may also be severe (Worrest et al. 1989; Longstreth 1989). Research results on these effects are still preliminary.

While greenhouse warming and ozone depletion have caught the public's attention over the last few years, certain terrestrial and aquatic environmental problems—such as deforestation, soil degradation, depletion and degradation of water resources, and depletion of fish stocks—deserve equal consideration. Such problems may, in fact, interact with and multiply the effects of atmospheric change; and they merit immediate concern because they are already seriously threatening the well-being and cohesion of many developing societies.

Deforestation

Estimates of tropical deforestation vary widely, since there are different kinds and degrees of forest degradation, and it is often unclear whether a particular hectare should be included in the category "deforested." Furthermore, forests frequently recover through planting and natural regeneration, which also tends to blur category boundaries. Finally, satellite images are far less precise than commonly thought in allowing researchers to determine the extent of forest damage. The images usually have to be supplemented with detailed ground inspections. (See Smil 1987, 231–37).

Despite these difficulties, recent estimates by the World Resources Institute (WRI) et al. (1990, 101–20) suggest that there has been a sharp increase in the rate of tropical forest depletion since the 1970s. Whereas the UN Food and Agriculture Agency estimated in 1980 that the world was losing 11.4 million hectares of tropical forest annually, the new WRI study says the figure may be as high as 20.4 million hectares.[16] Particularly affected by these increased rates, according to the WRI, are the forests of Brazil, Costa Rica, India, Myanmar, the Philippines, and Vietnam. However, the Brazilians have credibly responded that the WRI figures are inflated in Brazil's case because the rate of deforestation in Brazil has dropped dramatically since 1988 due to changes in domestic policy. Given the unreliability of the data and the susceptibility of deforestation rates to policy decisions, it is hard to predict the state of the world's forests in 2025. But it seems safe to say that most of the remaining virgin tropical forests in Southeast Asia, South Asia, and Central America will be gone and the remainder will be concentrated in Zaire and Brazil.

A closer look at the Philippines reveals the speed and extent of forest loss. As recently as the Second World War, about half the area of the Filipino archipelago was forested. Since then, logging and the encroachment of farms have reduced the virgin and second-growth forest from about 16 million hectares to between 6.8 and 7.6 million hectares (Porter and Ganapin 1988, 24). At the turn of the century, the Philippines had about 10 million hectares of virgin forest; now less than 1 million hectares remains, and it seems certain that almost all of this will be gone by early in the next century. The logging industry boomed in the 1960s and 1970s and, following the declaration of martial law in 1972, President Ferdinand Marcos handed out concessions to huge tracts of land to his cronies and senior military officials. Pressured to make payments on the foreign debt, the government encouraged log exports to the voracious Japanese market. Despite the regime change in the Philippines and the more aggressive concern for the environment of the Aquino government, the recent WRI estimates suggest that the rate of deforestation remains very high.

Degradation of Agricultural Land

Currently, total global cropland amounts to about 1.5 billion hectares. Optimistic estimates of potentially arable land on the planet range from 3.2 to 3.4 billion hectares, but nearly all the best land has already been exploited. What is left is either less fertile, not sufficiently rainfed or easily irrigable, infested with pests, or hard to clear and work. Experts generally describe a country as "land scarce" when 70 percent or more of the potentially arable land is under production. In Asia about 82 percent of all potential cropland is cultivated. While the percentages are lower in Africa and Latin America, the poor quality of the remaining land and its inequitable distribution in these regions suggest that the previously high rates of cropland expansion cannot be maintained (WRI, et al. 1990, 5).

For developing countries in general, during the 1980s the amount of cropland grew at just 0.26 percent a year, less than half the rate of the 1970s. More important, arable land per capita dropped by 1.9 percent a year (Sadik 1990, 8). In the absence of a major increase in the amount of arable land in developing countries, experts anticipate that the world average of 0.28 hectares of cropland per capita will decline to 0.17 hectares by the year 2025, given the current rate of world population growth (WRI, et al. 1990, 87).[17] Large tracts of land are being lost each year to a combination of problems, including urban encroachment, erosion, nutrient depletion, salinization, waterlogging, acidification, and compacting. The geographer Vaclav Smil, who is generally very conservative in his assessments of environmental damage, estimates that 2 to 3 million hectares of cropland are lost annually to erosion, with perhaps twice as much land going to urbanization and at least 1 million hectares abandoned because of excessive salinity. In addition, about one-fifth of the world's cropland is affected by desertification. Taken together, he concludes, the planet will lose about 100 million hectares of arable land between 1985 and 2000.

Smil gives a particularly startling account of the situation in China. From 1957 to 1977 the country lost 33.33 million hectares of farmland (30 percent of its 1957 total), while it added 21.2 million hectares of largely marginal land. He notes that "the net loss of 12 million hectares during a single generation when the country's population grew by about 300 million people means that per capita availability of arable land dropped by 40 percent and that China's farmland is now no more abundant than Bangladesh's—a mere one-tenth of a hectare per capita!" About 15 percent of the country's territory is affected by erosion. Severe erosion on the Loess Plateau "makes the region the area with the lowest grain yields and the poorest standard of life," while the Huanghe River annually carries 1.6 billion tons of silt to the sea (Smil 1987, 231–37).

Reduction of Water Supply and Quality

Experts now recognize that the scarcity and degradation of fresh water supplies will be one of the chief resource issues of the twenty-first century. At the moment, humans withdraw about 3,500 cubic kilometers of freshwater a year from various sources (mainly rivers), and about 1,400 cubic kilometers are returned to these sources, often in a polluted condition (WRI et al. 1990, 170–71). This consumption is growing at a rate of 2 to 3 percent a year. Total river resources at any one time amount to about 2,000 cubic kilometers, but because of the constant cycling of water between the atmosphere and surface of the earth, the annual quantity available from rivers is probably closer to 40,000 cubic kilometers. But while these aggregate figures might seem to indicate abundance, there are great differences in water availability between regions, and many areas—including much of Europe, large parts of the United States, the Ganges basin in India, and the northwestern provinces of China—are using virtually all of their locally generated river runoff. In many arid developing countries, quick population growth threatens to reduce per-capita water availability to levels below those required to meet minimum household, industrial, and agricultural needs. If greenhouse-induced climate change causes large shifts in precipitation patterns, some of these regions may no longer face water shortages, while others may suffer ruinous drought.

We can identify certain regions where water crises are a virtual certainty by the year 2025. Table 2.2 shows that the Middle East and certain parts of Africa are particularly vulnerable because these regions' populations are expanding rapidly, because water is already extremely scarce, and because water has long been a source of contention between certain groups and societies. For instance, the Nile River runs through nine countries, and downstream nations—Egypt and the Sudan, for example—are especially vulnerable to upstream pollution or water diversion because of their dry climates and dependence on irrigated agriculture. Other African rivers shared by several countries deserve close attention, including the Zambezi and the Niger, which flow through eight and ten countries respectively, and the Senegal, which has been at

Table 2.2   Water availability in 1990 and 2025 (selected countries)

Country	Cubic meters of water per year per capita 1990	Cubic meters of water per year per capita 2025
Africa		
Algeria	750	380
Egypt	1,070	620
Ethiopia	2,360	980
Kenya	590	190
Libya	160	60
South Africa	1,420	790
Middle East		
Israel	470	310
Jordan	260	80
Lebanon	1,600	960

Source: Gleick 1991

the center of a recent serious dispute between Mauritania and Senegal. Depletion of aquifers may also be a source of disputes: Egypt and Libya, for example, see the Nubian aquifer as a vital future source of water for huge agricultural zones. In the Middle East, there is strong disagreement between Syria and Turkey over Euphrates water. Some experts contend that the desire to secure the waters of the Jordan, Litani, Orontes, and Yarmuk rivers contributed to tensions preceding the 1967 Arab-Israeli war. Access to extremely limited underground water resources is also an extra source of stress in the Israeli conflict with the Palestinians over the future of the West Bank and the Gaza Strip.[18]

Depletion of Fish Stocks
The UN Food and Agriculture Organization (FAO) estimates the sustainable yield of the world's marine and freshwater fisheries to be 100 million metric tons. Since 1950, total fish landings have increased fivefold, from 19.8 to 97.4 million tons in 1988 (WRI et al. 1990, 180). As we approach the limit of sustainability, there is widespread evidence of regional overexploitation. In 1987, the FAO commented, "The time of spectacular and sustained increases in fisheries catches is over. . . . Almost all important stocks of demersal species are either fully exploited or overfished. Many of the stocks of more highly valued species are de-

pleted. Reef stocks and those of estuarine/littoral zones are under special threat from illegal fishing and environmental pollution" (FAO 1987, 6).

By the year 2000, demand for fish is predicted to rise to between 113 and 125 million tons (Peterson and Teal 1986, 133); assuming a relatively modest growth rate (in historical terms) of 15 percent every ten years, annual demand will exceed 160 million tons by 2025. Some of this additional demand will be met by expanding aquaculture, using nonconventional species, switching to human consumption fish now caught for animal feed, and increasing the exploitation of currently discarded fish. But as the limits of sustainability are exceeded, the collapse of regional fisheries is likely; artisanal and small-scale fishermen, especially in developing countries, will be most severely affected.

Decline of Biodiversity

As noted above, the estimates for the number of species on the planet cover a wide range, from five to thirty million. This is because of great uncertainty about species diversity in the tropical forest regions. Experts assume that these forests contain a vast repository of genetic information, the majority of it in insects and microbes not yet identified or catalogued. As these forests are destroyed, this genetic information is lost.

In the last 600 million years, five great episodes of extinction have afflicted life on the planet. The most severe occurred at the end of the Permian period, 240 million years ago, during which between 77 and 96 percent of all marine animal species vanished (Wilson 1989, 111). The more famous episode of extinction occurred when the dinosaurs disappeared at the junction of the Cretaceous and Tertiary periods, 65 million years ago. In all five cases, animal species were more severely reduced than plant species. Recovery to the preexisting level of biodiversity took from 10 to 100 million years.

Today, with the rapid loss of tropical forests and with the destruction of other species' habitats around the planet, both plant and animal species are disappearing at an extraordinary rate. E. O. Wilson has conservatively calculated that the global loss from tropical deforestation alone could be between 4,000 and 6,000 species a year, a rate 10,000 times greater than the natural background rate prior to the appearance of human beings (Wilson 1989, 112).[19] If we add the stress of fast climate change, a 25 percent reduction in planetary biodiversity over the next 100 years is plausible. Such a loss would rival those of four of the five previous mass extinctions on earth.

Two Scenarios

We will now briefly sketch optimistic and pessimistic scenarios for the world's human-ecological system in 2025 if we continue with "business as usual." One can be optimistic or pessimistic about either the predicted process of the system's evolution or about the predicted result of its evolution. As we sketch scenarios for a "business-as-usual" future, it is important to ask three questions. First, if there is great uncertainty surrounding either the theory or data that characterize a given environmental problem, how likely is it that the problem in the future will be much better or much worse than current theory and evidence indicate? Second, what is the likelihood of significant surprises or threshold effects? And third, how much social flexibility is inherent in "business as usual"?

With respect to this third question, an optimistic prediction must assume that "business as usual" will permit significant international and domestic cooperation, institutional flexibility, technological innovation, and change in people's values. Such a sanguine view of "business as usual" assumes there is a vast reservoir of human adaptability and creativity available to be tapped as environmental problems emerge. It further assumes that constructive responses to challenge will be endogenous to the social system; they will tend to be incremental, technocratic, and diffuse, not sudden, heroic, and centered on key individuals at key historical junctures. Effective human response to environmental challenges will be truly "business as usual."

In such an optimistic scenario, cooperation in a world of sovereign states may be propelled by the threat of environmental catastrophe, and a sense of a global "we" could develop because of the perception of a common threat. As suggested by the first question above, an optimistic prediction may also assume that environmental problems will turn out to be less serious than current evidence and theory indicate. Optimists may claim, for example, that experts and specialists consistently exaggerate environmental damage and underestimate the resilience of natural systems. Moreover, optimists will probably downplay the possibility of negative surprises in the human-ecological system.

The world may well have to support a human population of at least eight billion by 2025, and economic output in real terms may more than triple (World Commission on Environment and Development 1987, 4). Optimists might argue, however, that the energy consumption of that population could be kept within a doubling of current levels. Furthermore, this doubling does not necessitate a doubling of carbon emissions, because much of the new energy could be generated using nuclear power and natural gas.[20] Reductions in energy consumption per unit of the gross national product (GNP) (i.e., reductions in energy intensity) will require a concerted shift from material-intensive to service-intensive and labor-intensive economic growth and to energy-efficient technologies. And if this shift is to be achieved in the developing world, optimists must assume that there will be by large transfers of capital and technology from North to South. China and India alone could scuttle international agreements on carbon dioxide and CFC emissions simply through nonparticipation, since their future emissions of these gases could swamp any reductions in the developed world.

An optimistic scenario might suggest that deforestation and the decline in biodiversity will be slowed by international conventions that govern trade in forest products and endangered species and by novel financial mechanisms such as debt-for-nature swaps and tradable permits for carbon emissions. Optimists may also assume that social and technological innovation will produce alternatives for the large portion of the world's population that still uses wood as a main source of energy.[21] Aquaculture and careful management of marine and freshwater fisheries could sustain fish stocks, but it seems unlikely that these measures alone will prevent permanent damage to wild stocks should the rapid growth of consumption seen over the last decades continue.

Even in the optimistic scenario, though, the predictions for agricultural land seem gloomy. First, the processes resulting in the degradation of land in the developing world occur largely at the levels of communities and smallholders, often in ecologically and politically marginal areas (such as uplands), and these processes are therefore frequently not easily accessible to intervention by central government. Second, previous sustained increases in crop output during the green revolution depended on the development of high-yielding grains and on the substitution of petroleum-based fertilizers for poor or degraded land. However, old green revolution technologies are now producing diminishing returns, and compensating technological improvements (such as drought-resistant, salinity-resistant, or nitrogen-fixing grains) will not be widely available in the field for many years, even in the best circumstances. And if the real price of petroleum rises sharply, as is quite possible before 2025, the option of increasing fertilizer inputs will be constrained. Third, in many poor countries, land scarcity is driven not by degradation, but by population growth, which—as was noted above—is rarely susceptible to rapid change. Even in an optimist's "business-as-usual" world, therefore, by 2025 humankind will be living on a planet with significantly degraded ecological resources. The remaining resources will have to be husbanded and carefully managed through creative procedures of international and domestic cooperation.

A pessimistic answer to the third question posed at the beginning of this section would assume more inherent conflict within and among societies, serious institutional inertia, a lower rate of technological innovation, and little change in people's values. This gloomier view of "business as usual" asserts that there may be limits to human creativity, adaptability, and cooperation in response to emerging environmental problems. There are several reasons for holding this view. First, most people are cognitively conservative: They change their simple theories of reality and the "good" only when confronted with evidence that dramatically contradicts these theories in a very direct and personal way. Unfortunately, because of the timelags exhibited by most environmental problems, at the moment there is little evidence that is sufficiently dramatic to convince people that action is needed. Second, the vast numbers of competing interest groups with powerful economic and political constituencies in modern societies have produced a social sclerosis and impotence that paralyzes creative economics and politics.[22] And third, emerging environmental problems might actually decrease the social creativity societies need to respond effectively, because these problems will increase the complexity of the decision-making process for policymakers and will also increase "social friction" as elites and interest groups struggle to protect prerogatives affected by environmental change.[23]

Pessimists argue that environmental change is unlikely to induce a new era of harmony and human concord. History, they say, suggests that the outcome will be otherwise: Widespread calamities from plagues to economic depression have usually produced more conflict, not less. The United States may use its power to block environmental agreements and preserve the status quo of inflexible and often counterproductive international economic and political institutions. And while structural adjustment and effective markets in developing countries may inspire some resource conservation and technological innovation, there is as yet little commitment by any one to internalize environmental costs.

Pessimists might also contend that if the demographic transition stalls in several of the large developing countries, as appears to have occurred in China and India, the world's population will push toward nine billion by 2025, with an eventual number of fourteen or more billion by the end of the twenty-first century. Assuming only moderate economic growth in poor countries, carbon dioxide emissions from the developing world will therefore probably exceed those of the developed world in the first decades of the next century (Smil 1990, 18). Not only will this give an extra push to global warming, it will mean that a larger and more diverse group of countries will be the principal emitters of carbon dioxide, which could make negotiating and sustaining a climate change regime much more difficult.

If rising petroleum prices make fertilizers more expensive, it will become more difficult to compensate for the declining productivity of land, while in many countries population pressures will be simultaneously pushing the amount of agricultural land per capita well below one-tenth of a hectare. A pessimistic scenario would probably also assume that there will be little progress in controlling deforestation (or, as a result, declining biodiversity), because states will defend their sovereign interest to extract timber and because appropriate technologies that could serve as alternatives to fuelwood will prove hard to develop.[24] Fish stocks will be exploited to the point of exhaustion, since aquaculture will not be able to satisfy steadily increasing demand. And management of entire water basins, a prerequisite to controlling water degradation and over-use, will remain politically impossible in many areas.

For pessimists much depends on whether humankind encounters negative surprises or threshold effects in either the physical or the social components of the global environmental-social system. A warming of a degree might change ocean current regimes, monsoon paths, and the climate patterns that world agriculture has been built around. A breakup of the Gulf Stream, for example, could have dire effects on European crop output (Broeker 1987, 124).[25] Unforseen dynamics of atmospheric chemistry might cause ozone depletion to jump, both over the Arctic and more generally. Although the ultimate impacts of sharply increased ultraviolet radiation on ocean phytoplankton are as yet unknown, beyond certain thresholds plankton productivity may drop precipitously along with fish harvests. And social systems stressed by environmental change may exhibit similar nonlinearities with, for instance, sudden and dramatic migrations out of overcrowded or environmentally devastated areas and civil strife and social collapse within the developing world (Homer-Dixon 1991b).

In conclusion, we should be cautious in our assumptions about the resilience of our natural environment. We should not invest much faith in "business as usual," even if such a path permits considerable cooperation and social flexibility. Even the optimistic scenario above places immense demands on the global ecosystem, and this raises the probability of harsh surprises. Moreover, although serious uncertainties surround many aspects of global environmental change, in light of this genuine risk of negative surprises, uncertainty should not become an excuse to avoid investigating alternatives to "business as usual." Humankind should consider some of the more reformative or transformative social options outlined later in this volume.

Notes

Portions of this chapter have appeared in Homer-Dixon 1991a, 1991b. The author would like to thank in particular Nazli Choucri, Jerome Rothenberg, and David Victor for their helpful suggestions.
1. The phrase "business as usual" has recently been given prominence in discussions on global change by the working groups of the Intergovernmental Panel on Climate Change (IPCC). For the IPCC, business as usual means that "few or no steps are taken to limit greenhouse gas emissions"; it is little more than an extrapolation of current trends into the future. The interpretation of this phrase

that is used here is broader and offers more scope for optimism, since the IPCC usage refers only to patterns of greenhouse gas emissions and assumes that human societies have little natural ability or willingness to respond to environmental problems with mitigative strategies. The complete report of Working Group I has been published as Houghton et al. 1990.

2. Ehrlich and Holdren (1971) introduced a product formulation similar to that in figure 2.1. They proposed that $I = P \times F$, where I is the total negative impact on the environment, P is the population, and F is a function that measures per capita impact on the environment. For a more recent formulation, see Ehrlich and Ehrlich 1990.

3. Technological activity can have feedback effects by changing the "ideational factors" and by reducing the availability of physical resources. The adjective *ideational* emphasizes that institutions, social relations, preferences, and beliefs are products of the human mind.

4. The ideational factors include beliefs about the nature of physical reality held by particular knowledge-oriented groups in the society and also the society's general propensity to invest in new capital.

5. Numerous writers, especially those considering the social impact of climate change, have generated similar diagrams. See in particular the excellent survey article by Warrick and Riebsame (1981). Note first that there are many ways figure 2.1 could be made more accurate, but at the cost of greater complexity; it highlights the variables and causal linkages most important to our discussion. Also, each variable in figure 2.1 aggregates many subvariables. For instance, "use per capita of technology" encompasses subvariables ranging from the extent of cattle ranching to the rate of automobile use. Consequently, an arrow in Figure 2.1 may represent either a positive or a negative correlation, depending on the specific subvariables considered. Finally, the time frames for the different arrows in the diagram may not be the same.

6. This selection is intended to be illustrative and is therefore somewhat arbitrary. Other environmental issues, such as dispersal of toxic wastes and acid deposition, are not listed because they are less prominent in literature on global change and because their effects are generally less pronounced or widespread than those listed. Readers interested in technical background on the issues in the table should consult *World Resources 1990–91* (New York: Oxford University Press, 1990) and *World Resources 1988–89* (New York: Basic Books, 1988).

7. Readers may disagree with the placement of some of the Xs in Table 2.1. It is intended not as a rigorous and final classification of the sources of uncertainty for each physical variable, but rather as a first effort to develop a method for understanding and managing the often serious problems of uncertainty surrounding discussions of global change.

8. One qualification: If many countries were to adopt "one child" policies such as China's, population growth would decline markedly. However, it is unlikely that such measures will be widely adopted, and even in China the desired fertility reductions have not been fully achieved. See Feeney et al. 1989, 315–17.

9. This chapter intentionally avoids providing great statistical detail, since that would imply an unjustifiable and misleading level of precision. Given both extensive uncertainty and the wide variance in researchers' methodologies of estimation and prediction, policymakers should not seek precise quantitative predictions as a basis for making decisions about global change problems.

10. Experts vigorously dispute the effects of population growth on the environment, economic well-being, and social organization. Simon (1981) is optimistic, while Paul and Anne Ehrlich (1990) reiterate their pessimism. The question is surveyed by McNicoll (1984).

11. The global population growth rate is about 1.7 percent per year. Countries range from a high in Kenya of 4.2 percent to a low in Hungary of −0.18 percent.

12. The following figures are estimates based on the summary material provided in Keepin 1986, 357–92.

13. Global mean temperature is also affected by such factors as changes in the amount of radiation released by the sun, in the earth's orbital parameters, and in global volcanic activity.

14. The consensus on the likely magnitude, rate, and timing of human-induced greenhouse warming is summarized in the reports prepared by Working Groups I and II of the Intergovernmental Panel on Climate Change under the auspices of the World Meteorological Organization and the United Nations Environment Program. For the complete report of Working Group I, see Houghton et al. 1990.

15. See Parry et al. 1989 on climate change and agriculture. The most important result of a change in the average value of a variable (such as temperature, pressure, or soil moisture) in an environmental system is often the change it induces in the probability of "extreme" environmental events. Thus, while a mean global warming of 2 to 3 degrees Celsius might not seem too significant for agricultural production, it might produce a large increase in the probability of crop-devastating droughts, floods, heat waves, and storms. See Parry 1986.

16. The total area of closed tropical forest on the planet is estimated to be around 1.2 billion hectares.

17. Nearly 73 percent of all rural households in developing countries are either landless or nearly landless. Using this figure, Leonard estimates that "935 million rural people live in households that have too little land to meet the minimum subsistence requirements for food and fuel. These data exclude China, which could add as many as 100–200 million more people to the category." See Leonard 1989, 13.

18. For a thorough and alarming review of the potential for water conflicts in the Middle East, see House of Representatives, Committee on Foreign Affairs 1990.

19. Wilson estimates that current tropical deforestation at about 1 percent per year is producing a yearly decrease of 0.2 percent to 0.3 percent in the number of species in these regions.

20. Nuclear options include "inherently safe" reactor designs that minimize the risk of meltdown and breeder reactors that provide an essentially limitless supply of plutonium fuel. Even optimists would agree that fusion power will probably not be providing large amounts of electricity by 2025. Natural gas is attractive because it produces less carbon dioxide per unit energy than other fossil fuels.

21. The FAO (1983) estimates that up to 2.5 billion people in the developing world will face acute fuelwood shortages by the year 2000.

22. See Olson 1982.

23. For a discussion of environmentally induced "social friction," see Homer-Dixon 1991b, 102–104.

24. On the difficulties of developing fuelwood alternatives for cooking, see Manibog 1984.

25. Broecker points out that the "Earth's climate system currently works in a way beneficial to northern Europe. This region is warmed by heat released from the surface waters of the North Atlantic. The amount is a staggering 30 percent of that received by the North Atlantic from the Sun!"

3

Growth, Development, and Environmental Sustainability: Profiles and Paradox

Nazli Choucri and Robert C. North

From an environmental perspective the terms *growth* and *development* are often used interchangeably with reference to advances in a country's technology and/or increasingly productive economy. Conventionally, they are also used interchangeably in typologies of and comparisons across countries. This chapter proposes that this conventional practice, while useful for some purposes, is inherently misleading, both in providing effective comparisons among countries and in yielding predictable indices of environmental degradation. In this chapter an alternative approach is presented that is based on fundamental differences between growth (expansion of size) and development (transformation of structure and processes). As defined here, *growth* refers to incremental increases (or expansions) in the quantities, levels, or sizes of particular variables relevant to the processes, issues, and outcomes under scrutiny. *Development,* by contrast, is construed as qualitative change, adjustment, adaptivity, organizational transformation toward improved quality of life, and, in the long run, sociocultural evolution.

For states in the international system—the focus of this chapter—successive and differential levels and rates of change of any society's population, technology, and resource availabilities tend to play central roles in shaping its profile, that is, its structure, and behavioral relations with other societies—and its impacts (positive and/or negative) upon natural as well as social environments (Choucri and North 1975, 14–16; 1989, 292–94). As indicated in chapter 1, the variables of consequence for the growth and development of states and their environmental relationships are population, technology (applied knowledge and skills, mechanical and organizational), and resources, together with a wide range of "conditioning" (largely derivative) variables such as agriculture and industry, trade, and so forth.

Three propositions summarize the relevance of these variables to environmental issues on all four organizational levels—individual, national, international, and global—as put forward in chapter 1: (1) through time, growth and development tend to be uneven on all four of these levels; (2) these differentials contribute to different manifestations and patterns of resource depletion and degradation; and (3) growth and development differentials also affect social and natural environments—locally and worldwide—in many different and complex ways. The challenge is to identify why these differences occur and how they lead to particular economic, political, strategic, and environmental linkages and outcomes.

Growth and development processes are uneven and highly interactive, growth contributing (sometimes, not always) to development, and development leading (sometimes, but not always) to growth. Included in the concept of development are enhancements of the technological, economic, social, political, and other capacities of a state or other organization (public or private) resulting from the interactions among the growth variables (North 1990, 48–9, 62–3). From this perspective, the three master variables—embedded in a network of human communications and social actions—constitute a dynamic nexus as they interact among themselves and with the many and varied intervening and dependent variables and feedbacks to which they contribute and respond—and by which they themselves are partially shaped.[1]

Translated into acceleration (growth) and "steering" (development), the three master variables may be expected to interact in ways that are critically relevant to the contradiction between environmental sustainability and technological and economic growth and development: (1) To the extent that population growth accelerates more rapidly than technological advancement, demands for energy and other resources will increase, but development will be constrained, and damage to the environment will remain relatively low and localized; however, (2) insofar as technology accelerates in advance of population growth, development will be enhanced, resource availabilities will expand (through exploration, "discovery," and/or trade), and the demand for energy and other resources will accelerate—as will resource depletion, pollution, and other forms of degradation.

In the first instance, prevailing qualities of life will remain low and subject to further deterioration. In the second instance, many of the negative qualities of life will be reduced or eradicated. At the same time, moreover, accelerations in technological growth and development will be reflected by alterations in the distributions of resources and benefactions (advantages, general welfare, and the structures of social, economic, and political institutions). And new challenges relative to quality of life may be expected to appear as new technologies emerge. This means that individual or collective policies and actions that change the (normally) uneven rates of growth and/or development among the three master variables (second difference changes in first difference rates) can be conceptualized as steering functions constraining population growth relative to technological advancement and resource availabilities, for example—or, down the line beyond that, constraining energy-inefficient technologies and resources through the "discovery" of more energy-efficient technologies and resources.

Population is viewed here as an aggregate of individuals on any organizational level (local community, state, international, or global). Technology gives people—and derivative organizations, including the state—new resources (and new uses for old resources). Historically, the more advanced the technology, the greater the amount and range of resources in demand and the greater the amount and range of resources that people think they need and increasingly define as necessities. A crucial issue for the future is the extent to which technological change enables increased efficiency in resource extraction, processing, and use. Resources in various forms, including energy, are the sine qua non for human existence and social enterprise. Without access to basic resources (air, water, food, fabrics, and the like) our species obviously could not survive.

In line with the second law of thermodynamics, neither energy nor other resources are entirely consumed or destroyed, but each transformation or application involves a reduction from more usable to less usable form. In general, the larger the amount and the wider the range of resources used, the greater will be the production of such wastes (garbage, trash, junk) and the greater the risk—direct or indirect—of toxic consequences. Additionally, the greater the use of natural resources in any given environment, the greater is the likelihood that costs (local depletions, pollution and/or other degradations) will increase, and the greater will be the inclination to find more affordable substitutes (often requiring new technologies) or to pursue lower-cost resources in other environments.

Regardless of its geographical location, any country may be expected to supplement the domestic resources available with imports from other countries, either to substitute for resources that have not been found (or not yet exploited) at home or because they can be obtained less expensively from abroad. These considerations are accounted for in the profiles by including trade (imports and exports) as a conditioning or qualifying variable (among many such variables) augmenting a country's resource availabilities in major ways. In this connection, when a powerful state interacts intensely with a state that is weaker economically, politically, or strategically, the stronger state is likely to penetrate (and possibly exploit, intentionally or unintentionally) the weaker state economically and politically in terms of new techniques, higher standards of living, energy consumption—and attendant environmental impact. This indicates that states can become hostage to environmental deterioration due to the actions and investments of others. Thus "environmental invasion" is gradually becoming recognized as another mode of invasive interaction.[2]

Profiles and Paths of Growth and Development

Along with natural forces (or as an aspect of them), human beings— both individually and through bargaining, leveraging, and coalition formation—can be envisaged as primary extractors, producers, multipliers, and distributors of resources (including information), goods, services, power, and authority both "vertically" and "horizontally" within their respective local and national societies. All of these activities, in turn, exact costs from the natural environment by means of various types of resource depletion, pollution, and other forms of degradation. Aggregated on a national level, these intensive activities, along with population increases (and decreases), contribute to the structures (or profiles) of individual states.

By drawing on specific interactions among the master variables and a wide range of intervening variables, we hope to bring the capabilities and dynamic characteristics of each country into sharper focus. Such differentiation is needed for policy—as well as analytic—purposes. Unless there are effective "diagnostics," effective strategies for solutions will be obscured.[3] We begin with the following questions: What are the expected outcomes if resources and technology are held constant and population is allowed to spiral indefinitely? What if resources are held constant and population and technology increase exponentially? What if population is constrained and access to resources is systematically developed? In each case, what are likely to be the consequences for social and natural environments?

It goes without saying that number of inhabitants is a key indicator of population. But growth in numbers is not the only indicator, and a host of other demographic factors are often used (and are useful) as indicators of population (Choucri 1974). With respect to growth and development, each state's progress along its path (or at any specific "milestone") is measured by its gross national product (GNP), an indicator of growth, and GNP per capita an indicator of development. Again these are conventional indices, but not the only ones (Choucri, North, and Yamakage 1992).

Measuring access to (or availability of) resources involves a problem that is difficult to resolve. Most analysts assume that a nation's resources are more or less randomly distributed and that the larger a country's territory, the less specialized its resource base is likely to be. Kindleberger (1962, 23) added a qualification to the effect that a nation is likely to have greater resource diversity in its north-to-south territory than in its east-to-west territory, particularly insofar as such a resource base includes territory in both temperate and tropical zones. (Trade—imports and exports—serves as an important conditioning or qualifying variable, among many such variables, augmenting the availability of a country's resources in major ways.) We recognize the limitations of using area as a surrogate for resources. If we use known resource reserves of one type or another, we improve realistic measurement but contaminate conceptual underpinnings in the sense that for reserves to be "known," some technological investments and applications must have been made.

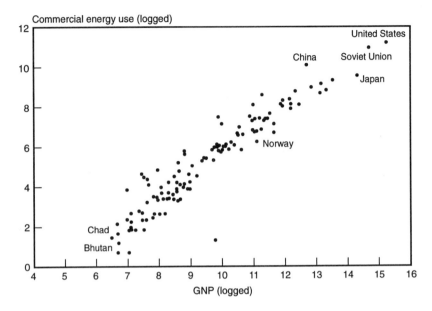

Figure 3.1
GNP and commercial energy use
Source: Based on data from Marland et al. (1989); World Bank (1988); Central Intelligence Agency (various years).

The indicators of technology are especially controversial. Patents, licenses, inventions, innovations, and increases in efficiency are all plausible indices and also plausible indicators of economic performance, such as GNP. Each, however, has some fundamental flaws. Nonetheless, a strong positive relationship can be seen between GNP and energy use (figure 3.1).

A schematic illustration of interactions among the master variables that define the profiles (table 3.1) is presented in figure 3.2 in the form of a three-dimensional space. In principle, all countries within each profile can be located in their relative and appropriate positions in this figure. Although the profile of any given country is determined by the configuration of its population/technology/resource-access indicators, these indicators (and the master variables they represent) are generally conditioned, constrained, or qualified by intervening and/or dependent variables (or feedback linkages therefrom).

The major types of intervening variables—linking the master variables

Table 3.1   Profile definition

Group I:	Resources > population > technology
Group II:	Population > resources > technology
Group III:	Population > technology > resources
Group IV:	Resources > technology > population
Group V:	Technology > resources > population
Group VI:	Technology > population > resources

Note: For operational purposes each group is defined as follows: Each master variable for every country is computed as a share of the global total for that variable. The variables in each group definition are thus framed in proportional relative terms, and the group profiles are in terms of relative shares. This simple method provides information about relative sizes of master variables within states and relative constraints among the master variables within states. The same information is provided across states within each profile and across states and across profiles. With respect to indicators, for illustrative purposes, following Kindleberger (1962), we use area for resources. As an indicator of technology, following Kuznets (1966), we use GNP. See text for further explanation.

in their raw form to their socially meaningful contexts—are the following: (a) Population/area/domestic resource base conditioned by agricultural production, manufacturing activity, energy consumption, and imports and exports, among others. (b) Population density and per capita levels of GNP, agricultural production, manufactures, energy consumption, imports, and exports. Potentially, there are many more intervening variables; their relative importance is an empirical question.

In both the (a) and (b) configurations, it is apparent that the master variables and their combinations are treated as independent variables; all other variables—including agricultural production, manufactures, energy consumption, imports, exports, and so on—are treated as intervening or dependent variables (contingent on the specific questions under investigation). In a fully specified, completely interactive dynamic system, however, the simple independent/dependent variable designation loses its meaning. The real world must be viewed in terms of its inherent complexities, with everything related to everything else. Intensely interactive among themselves, the master variables (and their indicators) "link up" with and are affected by these (and other) intervening and dependent variables. The use of the core or master variables as independent variables in this analysis is undertaken for empirical analysis and conceptual clarity.

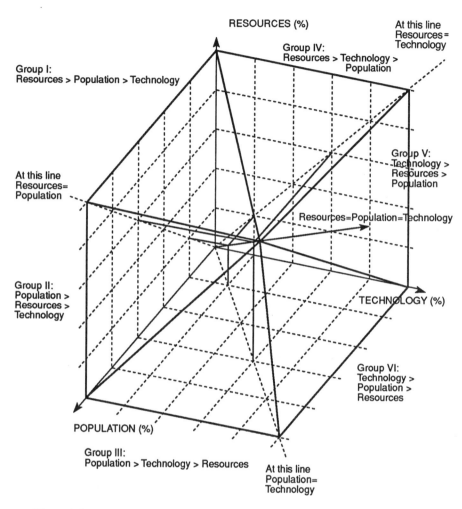

Figure 3.2
Profiles in three dimensions. In this figure we see six profile types in relationship to each other. Each profile type is the set of points contained in the 3-space defined by a triangular pyramid formed by the triangle drawn in bold and the point (0, 0, 0).
Source: MIT Project on Global Environmental Accord, Center for International Studies, prepared by Waleed Hazbun, MIT, Cambridge, Mass., 1992.

At a minimum, each country profile draws upon and includes the five conditioning variables listed under (b). There is nothing magic about the number five, however; other factors are certainly at work. Certainly, the master (or core) variables affect and are themselves conditioned by a host of other variables, some domestic, others external, and by allocations and devices of national governments. These allocations, which involve decisions as to how much money is given to health, how much to education, how much to the military, and how much to basic research, for example, may affect (and be affected by) birth and death rates, the availability of resources (including territorial size and usable land), and the technologies that are favored in principle and in practice.

The central proposition of this chapter is that different patterns of growth and development generate different forms of lateral pressure and that different modes of lateral pressure generate different types of effluence and patterns of environmental degradation. A corollary to the proposition is that there are both qualitative and quantitative differences in the relationship between growth and development, on the one hand, and patterns of lateral pressure and effluence on the other. The next step is empirical measurement and the respecification of these propositions into hypotheses to be submitted to empirical testing.

Determination of Profile Groups

To the extent that the possible variable-size combinations are exhausted, six profile clusters or groups—predicated on master variable-size relationships—emerge. Although we compiled and explored relevant data for nearly all countries of the world (a few are so newly established that adequate data are not yet readily available), we selected a limited number (130) for the initial construction of profiles and profile groups. The data are for one cross section of time only—1986. The larger research program, of which this chapter is only a segment, involves analysis of cross-national state attributes and behavior since 1950. This more inclusive conjunction of intertemporal, cross-national, and interstate approaches to data analysis should provide multidimensional views of international relations through time. Only at that juncture will we observe how the profiles (cross-section snapshots) begin to "move" along their respective paths of growth, development, and possible transformation. And only then will the full measure of the pattern of development become apparent.

Empirical Perspective: Problem and Procedure

The main criterion for selecting the 130 countries was representation—that is, we chose countries which, overall, would be representative of variations in size, levels of development, geographical location, forms of government, and the like. Very small countries are underrepresented, in part because the variables of many of them, expressed in percentages of global totals, required so many decimal places that the tables would have become unwieldy for presentation. Also underrepresented at this time—because of the rapid changes that were occurring among them—are the East European and other former Communist Bloc nations, for which much data from 1986–87 might be misleading for the 1990s. Such uncertainties were already evident with respect to the former USSR, as well as Yugoslavia, both of which are included in this set. In fact, at this writing (early 1992) the current areas, populations, GNPs, resource availabilities, and other critical dimensions of these two countries (and of their constituent components) are beyond calculation. But eventually the countries of Eastern Europe will be included in the time series analysis. The overall quality of data used is notoriously uneven. Our only defense is that we have drawn upon the most acceptable sources available—the World Bank, for example, and the United Nations and more or less comparable publications. In short we, like these institutions and other enterprises, must do the best we can.

Each profile is derived from the relationships between the key indicators, which are presented in descending order by variable size. (The choice of indicators is obviously crucial, as is the mode of measurement.) In terms of the levels and rates of change of its population, technology, and access to resources through time, every country of the world can be located somewhere within one of the six groups. The complexity of the international and global systems thus becomes evident. Neither states nor their encompassing systems stand still: To one degree or another, all are changing all the time, however unevenly; all are interacting, however differentially; and, within its own profile group, each is pursuing its own growth and development path. Viewed from this perspective, every state, every locality, every community, and every individual is an active component within a global network of intensely dynamic social and natural environmental change. The profile groups are both consequences and determinants of these changes.

The 130 nations were sorted according to the relationships between their respective master variables. The countries in each *A* table are ranked according to their respective GNP levels ("sizes") from "low" (small) at the bottom to "high" (large) at the top. In these terms those countries located at the lower left side of figure 3.1 are less "advanced," engage in less economic activity, generate less effluence, have lower institutional and organizational capabilities, and influence global environmental conditions less than do the "more advanced" countries at the top right side of the diagram.

In each case size is measured in terms of shares relative to the global total. In this way we can bypass some of the difficulties of comparing apples and oranges (people, technology, resources)—and remain consistent with the basic objective of using profile delineations to clarify ranges of interaction among social and natural environments. This suggests that a reading of national GNP values from bottom to top will provide an overview of countries at different locations along the growth pathways that characterize their respective groups, from Chad (or Bhutan) to Brazil in group I, from Lesotho to China in group II, and so on.

The size tables indicate rough positive relationships between GNP levels and levels of carbon dioxide (CO_2) production. (Below we present the correlation coefficients.) But there are notable anomalies that point to the importance of ratio indices, such as density and per capita values. The *B* tables may suggest strong population and/or resource-access influences work in shaping national profiles. The *C* tables provide added information on variations across and within profiles.

Clearly, such numerical comparisons will not substitute for the rigor of formal statistical or more complex quantitative analysis, but an understanding of what the distributions of relative shares in the tables reveal may provide valuable clues for the design of the most appropriate strategies for analytical and quantitative inquiry. These profiles are broad, ideal types. They are not meant to reflect all conceivable historical possibilities or future prospects; they are designed to guide our understanding of interactions among social and natural environments in different contexts. If GNP is admitted as an indicator of growth and if

GNP per capita is accepted as a rough indicator of development, then even a cursory comparison of the rank orderings in the *A* tables, *B* tables, and *C* tables should empirically reveal some of the reasons for distinguishing between unevennesses in growth and development processes and some of the consequences to be expected within the six growth and development profile groups and along the attendant pathways through process and over time.

But an examination of the tables also reveals some seeming idiosyncracies that casual scanning of the data may not elucidate—or that may even be obscured by complex inquiry. Looking at group II, for example, we see that the People's Republic of China generates a remarkably high GNP (eighth in the world in 1987) and a correspondingly high level of carbon dioxide. But since the country's population is also large (the largest in the world), the Chinese GNP is transformed into a low (typically Third World) GNP per capita (level of development) and its high level of carbon dioxide production into a relatively low (typically Third World) per capita value. Thus, compared with a U.S. resident, an individual in China is not a serious threat to the environment. But in the aggregate China's remarkably high level of carbon emission obscures the per capita differences. What growth and development (or other) variable(s) would need to be altered in order to reduce China's overall carbon emission? Do these differ from what would need to be altered for the U.S. or other states? The tables effectively expose such issues but often fail to clarify them. The high ratio of coal use to total energy use and the extensive decentralization in coal use—down to individual households—partly explain the seeming anomaly of the China case. Therefore, it would be only from a close look at the composition of the master variables and their change over time that one could find additional information.

It will be evident that the levels of carbon emission by some countries are higher (or lower) than their per capita GNP and/or energy consumption values might lead us to expect. As in the case of China, clarification in such instances is likely to require formal analysis in order to uncover the potential influences of intervening variables (such as agricultural production, value added by specific manufactures, imports of polluting agents, and the like) which may condition or qualify the impacts of the master variables on natural and social environments.

Exploring the Logic of Development

The distribution of countries according to relative global share presented in these tables is a useful device for framing hypotheses about developmental trajectories. For example, the tables may suggest that, despite unevenness in the growth among the three master variables, all individual countries appearing in any one of the six groups may be envisaged as proceeding along the same broad path of growth and development. But there may be contending hypotheses. First, there are undoubtedly variables of importance (some of them difficult or impossible to quantify) that may help to explain anomalies in the tables and suggest alternative developmental paths. The quality-of-life indicators of several former colonies, for example, or the levels and other particulars of trade, may vary according to the policies of the former imperial power (England, France, Belgium, Germany, the Netherlands, or whatever) of which these now independent countries were once colonial components.

A second type of hypothesis can be derived from the fact that a given table represents only one cross section of time, thus obscuring a distinctive trend among countries within it. Therefore, within-group differences might be as significant as across-group differences, since variations in rates of change may be shifting countries toward other groups. A third set of hypotheses emerges from a consideration of investment decisions. Investments in certain directions (such as toward advanced technology) may accelerate change and help transform the profile of a country in short order. If the change is both rapid and sharp enough, it may result in a cross-group shift without a country's going through the sequence of within-profile development.

In assessing the dynamics inherent in the (uneven) levels of variables, rates of change (first differences), and changes in rates of change (second differences), formal time series analyses (beyond anything covered in this chapter) will require measurement of the continually changing widths or gaps (through time) between paired master variables (and intervening variables where relevant). Used in conjunction with a body of time series data that are sampled in the *A, B,* and *C* tables, these gap measurements should provide information that will be useful for ascertaining the variables within each group that might be "throttled up" in one country or "throttled down" in another in order to maneuver the whole society along a new pathway leading to lower levels of carbon dioxide emissions and other more sustainable environmental outcomes, at the same time adjusting other second differences in order to minimize impediments to economic growth and development. Among intervening variables, we would expect energy-efficient technologies and resources to be essential for environmental sustainability as well as for maintaining a country's position within a profile—given growth in population.

Transgroup clusters emerge to the extent that countries in two or more groups share compelling characteristics that set them apart in distinctive ways. The Middle Eastern oil-producing countries constitute one such cluster. Five Scandinavian nations—Norway, Sweden, Finland, Denmark, and Iceland—form another. And a number of small, low-lying Pacific Island states share the possibility of submergence as a consequence of global warming—a rare, if dubious, distinction.

Toward Profile Measurement
The profile groupings presented here are defined in terms of relative size and relative constraints. In the discussions below we will also consider investment allocation variables and indices of political behavior, namely degree of "political liberty." In each case it is essential to stress the difference between size and profile.

Group I is defined as: $[R > P > T]$,

where R = resources, P = population, and T = technology.

Countries in group I possess more resources relative to their populations and more resources relative to their levels of technology. Resource availability is constrained by the low level of technology. Conditioning and intervening variables include climatic and topographical factors exemplified by the tropical rain forests of Brazil, the slopes and high plateaus of Bolivia, and arid regions in Chad. The less developed among these countries may provide the closest modern approximations to the agrarian-based states of the past. Agriculture, grazing, mining, lumbering, or other forms of exploitation of basic resources may be expected to predominate as compared with manufacturing. Group I countries tend to rely heavily on exports of raw materials in exchange for manufactured products from more developed countries, and a single product such as coffee, sugar, hemp, tin, timber products, or other resources often predominates.

Among the "bottom" cases in group I is Chad—one of the world's least developed countries with its population density of four persons per square kilometer, a per capita GNP (1986) of $180, and per capita energy consumption of 10 metric tons (oil equivalent). The country is also one of the world's lowest producers of carbon dioxide emissions. Despite significant differences in endowments of known resources, Sudan, like Chad, also ranks low in resource availability. The country has vast known oil reserves but, in large part because of violence in the south and weakness in its infrastructure, these resources are largely unexploited. The compelling tragedy of the "bottom" states of group I is that their low levels of knowledge and skills deprive them of ready access to their territorial resources. Skilled labor is generally in limited supply, the number of specialized professionals falls far short of the critical mass required to stimulate growth or development, and educational possibilities remain extremely limited. Potentials for development also tend to vary according to the proportions of each country's national territory that is arable and the availability of water and other vital resources that can be acquired, processed, and distributed among the populace.

Modes of environmental degradation (natural as well as social) include over-grazing, slash-and-burn agriculture, deforestation, soil erosion, and desertification. The introduction of insecticides, defoliants, internal combustion engines, and comparable products from more developed countries contributes to these processes. Thus, limited by their natural and social environments, the bottom states in group I commonly suffer from famine, and diseases tend to be endemic. However threatened (or constrained) these countries may be by local environmental phenomena, their contribution to carbon emissions and other forms of globally significant effluents and degradation seems almost minuscule. But aggregated with global levels, their low-level resource depletions, pollutions, and other degradations cannot be discounted—especially to the extent that such countries are justifiably encouraged to grow and develop.

Several countries in group I are borderline in population density relative to GNP—that is, the number of inhabitants per square kilometer (20 to 30) as compared with more typical group I densities (from two

Table 3.2A Dimensions of growth: Ranked by GNP

Group I: Area > population > GNP

	Population % global	Area % global	GNP % global	MnVA % global	AgVA % global	CEC % global	Exports % global	Imports % global	Carbon emissions % global
Brazil	2.837	6.469	1.655	2.433	3.298	1.142	1.075	0.716	5.882
Iran	0.935	1.252	0.571	0.752	1.275	0.573	0.645	0.535	0.472
Argentina	0.635	2.103	0.481	0.465	0.461	0.584	0.329	0.217	0.398
South Africa	0.662	0.928	0.395	0.258	1.064	1.151	0.886	0.598	1.401
Algeria	0.459	1.810	0.383	0.442	0.643	0.309	0.378	0.468	0.234
Venezuela	0.365	0.693	0.343	0.233	0.841	0.652	0.481	0.440	0.400
Colombia	0.594	0.866	0.236	0.143	0.262	0.247	0.245	0.178	2.056
Peru	0.406	0.977	0.143			0.115	0.120	0.130	0.769
Chile	0.250	0.575	0.106			0.122	0.203	0.158	0.091
Ecuador	0.197	0.216	0.074	0.099	0.245	0.068	0.105	0.083	0.661
Cameroon	0.215	0.361	0.063	0.040	0.361	0.033	0.099	0.070	0.025
Côte d'Ivoire	0.219	0.245	0.052	0.037	0.380	0.023	0.154	0.093	1.549
Sudan	0.463	1.904	0.048	0.021	0.378	0.016	0.024	0.052	0.014
Kenya	0.434	0.443	0.042	0.026	0.254	0.018	0.058	0.076	0.017
Tanzania	0.471	0.718	0.038	0.016	0.340	0.010	0.016	0.048	0.009
Uruguay	0.061	0.134	0.038		0.088	0.020	0.052	0.038	0.013
Jordan	0.074	0.074	0.037	0.021	0.048	0.041	0.035	0.112	0.037
Zimbabwe	0.178	0.297	0.036	0.055	0.081	0.063	0.062	0.052	0.053
Ethiopia	0.892	0.929	0.034	0.021	0.345	0.009	0.022	0.051	0.009
Panama	0.045	0.059	0.034	0.018	0.069	0.016	0.116	0.136	0.012
Zaire	0.650	1.782	0.034	0.002	0.250	0.023	0.088	0.068	0.545
Angola	0.184	0.948	0.031			0.010	0.086	0.050	0.009
Bolivia	0.135	0.835	0.026	0.034	0.146	0.024	0.027	0.033	0.017

Table 3.2A (continued)

	Population % global	Area % global	GNP % global	MnVA % global	AgVA % global	CEC % global	Exports % global	Imports % global	Carbon emissions % global
Paraguay	0.078	0.309	0.025	0.021	0.139	0.010	0.011	0.027	0.007
Gabon	0.020	0.204	0.020		0.046	0.014	0.050	0.044	0.011
Afghanistan	0.316	0.492	0.020			0.018	0.026	0.065	0.012
Mozambique	0.291	0.609	0.020	0.020	0.216	0.005	0.008	0.022	0.005
Senegal	0.139	0.149	0.019	0.033	0.120	0.010	0.030	0.047	0.009
Nicaragua	0.070	0.099	0.018	0.009	0.093	0.011	0.012	0.035	0.009
Papua New Guinea	0.070	0.351	0.016		0.123	0.011	0.050	0.052	0.009
Madagascar	0.217	0.446	0.016		0.165	0.004	0.016	0.018	0.003
Zambia	0.141	0.572	0.014	0.021	0.026	0.021	0.033	0.033	0.012
Congo	0.041	0.260	0.013	0.005	0.025	0.009	0.032	0.029	0.007
Niger	0.135	0.963	0.011	0.002	0.137	0.004	0.016	0.020	0.003
Guinea	0.129	0.187	0.011	0.002	0.114	0.005	0.021	0.016	0.004
Mongolia	0.041	1.189	0.011			0.036	0.000	0.000	0.034
Somalia	0.113	0.485	0.010	0.006		0.006	0.004	0.020	0.005
Mali	0.156	0.942	0.009	0.003	0.192	0.002	0.018	0.020	0.002
Burkina Faso	0.166	0.208	0.008		0.079	0.002	0.005	0.015	0.002
Liberia	0.047	0.084	0.007		0.061	0.004	0.019	0.011	0.003
Yemen, People's Democratic Republic of	0.045	0.253	0.007	0.002	0.053	0.017	0.000	0.000	0.015
Botswana	0.023	0.456	0.006	0.002	0.006	0.000	0.000	0.000	0.005
Chad	0.105	0.976	0.005			0.001	0.006	0.009	0.001
Central African Republic	0.055	0.473	0.005	0.002	0.053	0.001	0.006	0.010	0.001

Table 3.2A (continued)

	Population % global	Area % global	GNP % global	MnVA % global	AgVA % global	CEC % global	Exports % global	Imports % global	Carbon emissions % global
Mauritania	0.037	0.783	0.005		0.037	0.003	0.020	0.017	0.002
Laos	0.076	0.180	0.004			0.001	0.000	0.000	1.288
Bhutan	0.027	0.036	0.001			0.000	0.000	0.000	0.000

Notes: Data is for 1986, except where otherwise noted.

All percentages are of the global total. The global total is the sum of data for all countries listed.

Within each group countries are listed in descending order in terms of the percentage of the world GNP.

MnVA: Total value added in manufacturing. MnVA data (from World Bank 1988) is for 1985.

AgVA: total value added in agriculture.

CEC: Commercial energy consumption.

Carbon emissions: Carbon dioxide emissions from energy, cement, and deforestation. Deforestation figures are for 1980.

Sources: Population, GNP, area, exports, imports, MnVA, AgVA, exports, and imports: World Bank 1988. For countries with missing data: Central Intelligence Agency (various years).

Commercial energy consumption: World Resources Institute 1989.

Carbon emissions from energy and cement: Marland et al. 1989.

Carbon emissions from deforestation: Houghton et al. 1987.

or three people per square kilometer up to eighteen or nineteen). In some of these countries the level of population is increasing relative to resource access and the rate of technological advancement. Table 3.2B suggests that bottom countries like Afghanistan and Ethiopia will be both economically and environmentally vulnerable to further population growth, thus increasing pressure on available resources, unless the rate of their technological development accelerates faster than the number of their people. Furthermore, *rates* of population growth are often high.

The more developed "top" countries of group I include Brazil, Venezuela, Argentina, and Algeria, with per capita GNPs (1987) of between $1000 and $5000. These countries play significant regional and international roles in terms of their production, energy consumption, exports, imports, and production of carbon and other environmental impacts. In Brazil, especially, intensified deforestation, loss of biodiversity, and effects on global carbon balances have exerted economic, political, and social impacts internationally as well as at home—as have the illegal production and international distribution of illicit materials originating in these countries and elsewhere. To the extent that their populations are allowed to grow faster than their technologies advance, these and other more developed group I countries may be expected to exert increasingly intense pressures on available resources and to generate higher levels of carbon dioxide and other forms of environmental depletion and degradation.

The governments of some (but not all) group I countries allocate larger budgetary shares to military expenditures than to education or health. Chad has followed this pattern, as have North Yemen, Bolivia, Ethiopia, and Mali. Data from Afghanistan have not been available. Tending to correlate with the GNP and energy consumption per capita, quality-of-life indicators such as infant mortality and life expectancy generally leave much to be desired in group I countries—as do political rights and civil liberties.

Compared with highly industrialized societies, most group I countries produce relatively low levels of pollutants, but contributions to local resource depletion and global effluents (carbon emissions and other gases and effluents) by some of the top states of group I are substantial. In response to population growth, early stages of industrialization, and intensifying urbanization, Brazil, for example, has tended to squander a

Table 3.2B Dimensions of development: Ranked by GNP per capita
Group I: Area > population > GNP

	GNP per capita ($/pers.)	Government expenditure			Life expectancy (years)	Infant mortality (per 1000)	Political rights	Civil liberties
		Military % global	Education % global	Health % global				
Gabon	3,080	0.015	0.021	0.010	52	105	6	6
Venezuela	2,920	0.095	0.457	0.222	70	37	1	2
Algeria	2,590	0.130	0.479	0.207	62	77	6	6
Argentina	2,350	0.128	0.174	0.173	70	33	2	1
Panama	2,330	0.011	0.035	0.041	72	24	6	3
Uruguay	1,900	0.017	0.023	0.010	71	28	2	2
Iran	1,895	1.899	0.375	0.231	59	109	5	6
South Africa	1,850	0.303	0.405	0.064	61	74	5	6
Brazil	1,810	0.273	1.128	0.516	65	65	2	2
Jordan	1,540	0.065	0.027	0.012	65	46	5	5
Chile	1,320	0.068	0.110	0.052	71	20	6	5
Colombia	1,230	0.043	0.140	0.048	65	47	2	3
Ecuador	1,160	0.020	0.051	0.018	66	64	2	3
Peru	1,090	0.176	0.049	0.037	60	90	2	3
Paraguay	1,000	0.004	0.006	0.002	67	43	5	6
Congo	990	0.009	0.012	0.006	58	75	7	6
Cameroon	910	0.019	0.035	0.011	56	96	7	7
Botswana	840	0.003	0.013	0.005	59	69	2	3
Mongolia	835	0.021		0.003	64	47	7	7
Nicaragua	790	0.054	0.023	0.030	61	65	5	6
Côte d'Ivoire	730	0.010	0.048	0.012	52	96	6	5

Table 3.2B (continued)

| | GNP per capita ($/pers.) | Government expenditure | | | Life expectancy (years) | Infant mortality (per 1000) | Political rights | Civil liberties |
		Military % global	Education % global	Health % global				
Papua New Guinea	720	0.004	0.018	0.013	52	64	2	2
Zimbabwe	620	0.034	0.061	0.021	58	74	4	6
Bolivia	600	0.010	0.011	0.002	53	113	2	3
Angola	522	0.138	0.044	0.016	44	139	7	7
Yemen, People's Democratic Republic of	470	0.023	0.007	0.003	50	142	6	7
Liberia	460	0.003	0.007	0.003	54	87	5	5
Mauritania	420	0.005	0.006	0.002	47	127	7	6
Senegal	420	0.002	0.005	0.001	47	130	3	4
Sudan	320	0.061	0.047	0.003	49	108	4	5
Kenya	300	0.019	0.055	0.021	57	74	6	5
Zambia	300	0.010	0.015	0.009	53	82	5	5
Central African Republic	290	0.002	0.006	0.001	50	134	7	6
Somalia	280	0.008	0.012	0.000	47	134	7	7
Guinea	270	0.007	0.008	0.003	42	148	7	5
Niger	260	0.001	0.009	0.002	44	135	7	6
Tanzania	250	0.026	0.037	0.012	53	108	6	6
Madagascar	230	0.008	0.012	0.008	53	130	5	5
Mozambique	210	0.008					6	7
Afghanistan	200	0.031		0.011	48	120	7	7

Table 3.2B (continued)

	GNP per capita ($/pers.)	Government expenditure			Life expectancy (years)	Infant mortality (per 1000)	Political rights	Civil liberties
		Military % global	Education % global	Health % global				
Mali	180	0.004	0.005	0.001	47	144	7	6
Laos	178		0.001		50	146	7	7
Chad	160	0.005	0.002	0.001	45	134	7	7
Zaire	160	0.018	0.003	0.007	52	100	7	7
Bhutan	150				45	139	5	5
Burkina Faso	150	0.004	0.004	0.002	47	140	7	6
Ethiopia	120	0.052	0.029	0.008	46	155	7	7

Notes: Data is for 1986, except where otherwise noted.

All dollar amounts are in 1986 U.S. dollars.

All percentages are of the global total. The global total is the sum of data for all countries listed.

Within each group countries are listed in descending order in terms of percentage of the world GNP.

GNP/cap: GNP per capita, stated in terms of dollars per person ($/pers.).

Political rights and civil liberties are on a scale from 1 (most free) to 7 (least free); See Gastil 1988, pp. 7–8.

Sources: Population, GNP, area, life expectancy, and infant mortality:
    World Bank 1988.

    For countries with missing data: Central Intelligence Agency (various years).

Government expenditure: Sivard 1989.

Political rights and civil liberties: Gastil 1988.

Table 3.2C Per capita dimensions: Ranked by GNP per capita
Group I: Area > population > GNP

| | GNP per capita ($/pers.) | Population density (pers./km²) | Government expenditure | | | MnVA $/person | AgVA $/person | CEC (petajoules/ mil. pers.) | Exports $/person | Imports $/person | Carbon emissions (thous. metric tons/ mil. pers.) |
			Military $/person	Education $/person	Health $/person						
Gabon	3,080	4	124	155	65		323	37	1,052	951	747
Venezuela	2,920	20	46	194	79	593	251	99	563	537	1,483
Algeria	2,590	9	50	161	58	275	330	37	352	454	690
Argentina	2,350	11	35	42	35	579	286	51	221	152	849
Panama	2,330	29	43	120	117	191	218	19	1,096	1,343	357
Uruguay	1,900	17	47	58	22		205	18	363	273	286
Iran	1,895	28	355	62	32			34	295	255	684
South Africa	1,850	26	80	95	12	344	99	96	571	402	2,864
Brazil	1,810	16	17	62	24	420	166	22	162	112	2,807
Jordan	1,540	37	155	57	21	137	92	31	204	676	684
Chile	1,320	16	48	68	27			27	346	282	490
Colombia	1,230	25	13	36	10	192	202	23	176	133	4,684
Ecuador	1,160	34	18	40	12	247	178	19	227	189	4,547
Peru	1,090	15	76	19	12	173	92	16	127	143	2,566
Paraguay	1,000	9	9	13	4	135	254	7	62	152	118
Congo	990	6	41	44	18	64	87	12	337	315	231
Cameroon	910	22	15	25	7	91	239	8	196	144	159
Botswana	840	2	23	91	29	45	41	45	502	1,276	293
Mongolia	835	1	91		11			48			1,123
Nicaragua	790	26	134	51	56	231	191	9	73	226	168
Côte d'Ivoire	730	33	8	34	7	83	247	6	299	189	9,562
Papua New Guinea	720	7	10	41	24	60	252	9	304	332	171

Table 3.2C (continued)

| | GNP per capita ($/pers.) | Population density (pers./km²) | Government expenditure | | | MnVA $/person | AgVA $/person | CEC (petajoules/ mil. pers.) | Exports $/person | Imports $/person | Carbon emissions (thous. metric tons/ mil. pers.) |
			Military $/person	Education $/person	Health $/person						
Zimbabwe	620	22	33	53	15	151	65	19	150	130	406
Bolivia	600	6	13	13	2	124	154	10	85	108	172
Angola	522	7	131	37	11			3	199	120	69
Yemen, People's Democratic Republic of	470	7	91	25	8			20	72	222	451
Liberia	460	21	10	22	7	21	160	4	176	102	79
Mauritania	420	2	22	27	8		141	4	233	202	89
Senegal	420	35	2	6	1	70	123	4	90	150	85
Sudan	320	9	23	16	1	22	116	2	22	50	40
Kenya	300	36	8	19	6	30	83	2	57	78	54
Zambia	300	9	12	17	8	74	26	8	100	103	115
Central African Republic	290	4	5	16	3	20	138	1	48	81	16
Somalia	280	9	13	17	1	25	243	3	16	80	54
Guinea	270	26	9	9	3	7	126	2	71	56	42
Niger	260	5	2	10	2	9	144	2	50	66	29
Tanzania	250	24	10	12	3	17	103	1	15	46	24
Madagascar	230	18	6	9	5		108	1	31	37	20
Mozambique	210	18	19		5		106	1	11	34	23
Afghanistan	200	24						3	36	91	51
Mali	180	6	4	5	1	11	72	1	50	58	14
Laos	178	16		3				1	498	402	22,988
Chad	160	4	8	3	1			1	24	40	11
Zaire	160	14	5	1	1	2	55	2	58	47	1,135

Table 3.2C (continued)

	GNP per capita ($/pers.)	Population density (pers./km²)	Government expenditure Military $/person	Education $/person	Health $/person	MnVA $/person	AgVA $/person	CEC (petajoules/mil. pers.)	Exports $/person	Imports $/person	Carbon emissions (thous. metric tons/mil. pers.)
Bhutan	150	28						1			7
Burkina Faso	150	30	5	4	1		52	1	14	40	14
Ethiopia	120	36	10	5	1	11	55	1	10	25	13

Notes: Data is for 1986, except where otherwise noted.
All dollar amounts are in 1986 U.S. dollars.
Within each group countries are listed in descending order of GNP.
MnVA: Total value added in manufacturing. MnVA data (from World Bank 1988) is for 1985.
AgVA: Total value added in agriculture.
CEC: Commercial energy consumption.
Carbon emissions: Carbon dioxide emissions from energy, cement, and deforestation. Deforestation figures are for 1980.
Sources: Population, GNP, MnVA, AgVA, exports, and imports:
  World Bank 1988.
  For countries with missing data: Central Intelligence Agency (various years).
Government expenditure: Sivard 1989.
Commercial energy consumption: World Resources 1989.
Carbon emissions from energy and cement: Marland et al. 1989.
Carbon emissions from deforestation: Houghton et al. 1987.

critical element of its environmental assets. Tropical rain forests, in effect, have been harvested—or cleared and burned—partly in order to obtain what often turns out to be shallow grazing and farm lands. Effluents from this burning, in turn, have produced clouds of gases which may be transmitted by atmospheric processes over the spaces of other countries.

A number of group I countries possess domestic resource bases that could allow them to grow, depending on the levels and rates of advancement of their respective knowledge and skills. Vividly highlighting some of the potential contradictions between environmental sustainability and economic growth and development, however, the World Bank and other financial and development institutions, national and international—for a time, at least—in effect underwrote excessive Brazilian timber cutting. This policy was designed not only to support badly needed economic expansion, but also to facilitate the repayment of the loans that these same institutions were making available. The debt/environmental paradox is defined by this type of often deleterious trade-off.

Overall, the conclusion to be drawn from the group I country profiles is clear. Despite a number of exceptions, the major trends are strong: From bottom to top, economic and quality-of-life indicators (including political rights and civil liberties) tend to improve somewhat—and per capita energy consumption and carbon emissions tend to increase. The challenges are to promote energy-efficient technologies and expand access to energy-efficient resources, domestic and foreign, in pursuit of some dynamic equilibrium between growth and development on the one hand and environmental sustainability on the other.

Group II is defined as: $[P > R > T]$

With populations that are "large" relative to area (however large such an area may be) and with GNPs that are "small" relative to both population and area, the countries in group II can be characterized as having populations that have grown—and still may be growing—relative to levels of technology and rates of resource access. As with many bottom countries of group I, Malawi, Bangladesh, and Bhutan have often been identified as among the world's most dire cases.

Characteristically, group II countries (somewhat like those in group I) tend to possess relatively large territories and resource bases but are

Table 3.3A Dimensions of Growth: Ranked by GNP
Group II: Population > Area > GNP

	Population % global	Area % global	GNP % global	MnVA % global	AgVA % global	CEC % global	Exports % global	Imports % global	Carbon emissions % global
China	21.602	7.266	2.089	3.982	11.997	8.052	1.495	1.986	8.393
India	16.015	2.499	1.497	1.491	9.272	2.278	0.563	0.749	2.685
Mexico	1.644	1.499	0.986	1.826	1.649	1.408	0.779	0.552	1.614
Indonesia	3.410	1.458	0.539	0.479	2.794	0.515	0.711	0.615	3.333
Nigeria	2.113	0.702	0.436	0.309	2.870	0.183	0.317	0.207	1.099
Turkey	1.055	0.594	0.378	0.514	1.380	0.531	0.383	0.507	0.520
Thailand	1.078	0.391	0.281	0.322	1.001	0.256	0.422	0.422	1.643
Iraq	0.338	0.331	0.264			0.121	0.000	0.469	0.139
Egypt	1.019	0.761	0.250	0.207	1.179	0.365	0.222	0.438	0.301
Pakistan	2.033	0.611	0.229	0.337	1.058	0.278	0.162	0.247	0.198
Philippines	1.174	0.228	0.212		1.154	0.149	0.229	0.248	0.995
Malaysia	0.330	0.251	0.195			0.181	0.666	0.498	0.139
Syria	0.221	0.141	0.112	0.056	0.503	0.141	0.064	0.124	0.127
Bangladesh	2.115	0.109	0.109	0.084	1.043	0.070	0.042	0.124	0.047
Morocco	0.461	0.340	0.088		0.451	0.079	0.118	0.175	0.076
Viet Nam	1.297	0.251	0.082			0.079	0.000	0.000	0.622
Tunisia	0.150	0.125	0.055	0.041	0.175	0.056	0.084	0.133	0.050
Guatemala	0.168	0.083	0.050	0.028		0.017	0.050	0.041	0.015
Burma	0.779	0.514	0.050	0.034	0.561	0.035	0.014	0.028	0.799
Sri Lanka	0.330	0.050	0.043	0.022	0.219	0.021	0.058	0.090	0.015
Ghana	0.271	0.182	0.034	0.029	0.290	0.014	0.041	0.036	0.011
Dominican Republic	0.135	0.037	0.031		0.131	0.031	0.034	0.066	0.027

Table 3.3A   (continued)

	Population % global	Area % global	GNP % global	MnVA % global	AgVA % global	CEC % global	Exports % global	Imports % global	Carbon emissions % global
Yemen, Arab Republic	0.168	0.148	0.030	0.011	0.180	0.013	0.001	0.048	0.012
Costa Rica	0.053	0.039	0.025		0.127	0.014	0.054	0.053	0.009
Uganda	0.312	0.179	0.023	0.005	0.363	0.005	0.019	0.016	0.003
Honduras	0.092	0.085	0.022	0.018	0.116	0.010	0.041	0.040	0.008
Albania	0.061	0.022	0.018			0.043	0.000	0.000	0.040
Nepal	0.348	0.107	0.017	0.005		0.005	0.007	0.021	0.004
Haiti	0.125	0.021	0.013		0.105	0.004	0.018	0.023	0.003
Rwanda	0.127	0.020	0.012	0.011	0.058	0.002	0.009	0.016	0.002
Malawi	0.152	0.090	0.008	0.005	0.076	0.003	0.012	0.012	0.002
Sierra Leone	0.078	0.055	0.008	0.003	0.091	0.003	0.007	0.007	0.002
Burundi	0.098	0.021	0.008	0.004	0.094	0.001	0.008	0.010	0.001
Benin	0.086	0.086	0.007	0.002	0.046	0.002	0.009	0.018	0.002
Togo	0.064	0.043	0.005	0.002	0.007	0.002	0.013	0.017	0.002
Lesotho	0.033	0.023	0.004	0.001		0.000	0.000	0.000	0.000

Notes: See table 3.2A.

defined as lacking the technologies needed for locating, extracting, and otherwise exploiting many of the raw materials that would facilitate growth and development. China, for example, was considered resource poor (with only limited availabilities of low-grade coal and oil) until (under the Maoist regime) new technologies and expanded exploration located wholly new reserves. But group II countries suffer additionally from constraints imposed by their relatively large populations.

With improved health services and better nutrition, death rates in many group II countries have fallen sharply in modern times, often without corresponding reductions in birthrates. Some countries, including India and China, have made efforts to curb birthrates, but with varying success. Not without high costs in terms of human rights, China's draconian measures have been relatively successful, but in view of the country's huge population base, it is not surprising that the numbers of people continue to increase, albeit at considerably lower rates.

A number of group II countries have undertaken strong modernization programs calculated to reduce the economic gaps between themselves and the industrialized West, with varying degrees of success. Despite measures imposed to reduce birthrates, however, the wide gap between population levels and rates of growth and technological development has remained a stubborn obstacle. Continuing population increases in several of these countries threaten to further constrain the effects of technological infusions and economic expansion on per capita income levels. High fertility rates, in short, combined with weak economies, reduced mortality rates, and impaired access to vital resources, have exacerbated the poverty already prevailing. By the year 2025 the population of India is expected to reach 1.445 billion—almost overtaking China, whose population, despite powerful fertility control policies and the effects of nascent industrialization, is projected to reach about 1.49 billion.

As in the past, burning vegetation on jungle slopes in India and many other group II countries still releases various effluents—carbon dioxide, hydrocarbons, nitrogen oxide, nitric acid, and so forth. Over recent decades a number of developing group II countries have made notable progress toward industrialization combined with continuing population growth, yielding many of the standard environmental consequences (see tables 3.3A, B, and C). With the addition of many of the same pollutants resulting from modern technologies, expanding urban areas in many of these countries—Shanghai, Bombay, Calcutta, and Mexico City among dozens of others—are shrouded by industrial and vehicular emissions.

For the most part, the production of effluents among the countries of group II tends to be low relative to that of industrialized countries, but— in spite of (and partly as a consequence of) population densities— somewhat higher than that of group I states. Bangladesh, a state with one of the densest national populations in the world (and one of the lowest GNPs per capita) is also one of the lowest producers of carbon emissions. As if that were not enough, the country regularly receives the brunt of disastrous floods (exacerbated by soil erosion and deforestation), typhoons, and tidal waves it cannot control. While these events are frequently labelled "natural disasters," they are also the product of human alterations of ecological balances in conjunction with "normal" ecological processes (see figure 1.1).

Among the group II countries the distinction between population/ territorial size and level of development (as indicated by GNP per capita, at least) is not always taken into sufficient account. In general, the smaller countries in the group tend to be the least developed, whereas several middle-sized to medium/large but relatively less densely populated countries (Tunisia, Jordan, Turkey, Egypt, Mexico, and Iraq) are the more developed—and also among the higher per capita producers of carbon. It is the largest states (China and India) that best demonstrate the constraints on technological and economic development exerted by high population levels. But note that these two large but somewhat less developed states (as measured by GNP per capita) rank with the others in carbon dioxide emissions. Again, these are important differences that help us distinguish between size and profile.

Countries in group II that spend more on military development than on education or health include Yemen, Burundi, India, Pakistan, China, Jordan, Turkey, Egypt, and Iraq. The reasons vary, as do the predispositions, but this pattern is strong. In the absence of a persuasive theoretical explanation for the differences, an operational hypothesis might relate to the type of regime and to the priorities of the regime derived from their own conceptions of security.

Overall, per capita GNP levels for group II countries are somewhat—

Table 3.3B Dimensions of development: Ranked by GNP per capita
Group II: Population > area > GNP

	GNP per capita ($/pers.)	Government expenditure			Life expectancy (years)	Infant mortality (per 1000)	Political rights	Civil liberties
		Military % global	Education % global	Health % global				
Iraq	2,424	1.426	0.186	0.048	63	71	7	7
Mexico	1,860	0.158	0.798	0.586	68	48	4	4
Malaysia	1,830	0.210	0.309	0.085	69	27	3	5
Syria	1,570	0.341	0.150	0.024	64	50	6	7
Costa Rica	1,480	0.003	0.025	0.034	74	18	1	1
Tunisia	1,140	0.060	0.055	0.036	63	74	6	5
Turkey	1,110	0.416	0.200	0.059	65	79	3	4
Albania	933	0.020		0.015	71	41	7	7
Guatemala	930	0.015	0.025	0.011	61	61	3	3
Thailand	810	0.192	0.222	0.083	64	41	3	3
Egypt	760	0.380	0.234	0.060	61	88	5	4
Honduras	740	0.024	0.023	0.014	64	72	2	3
Dominican Republic	710	0.009	0.011	0.012	66	67	1	3
Nigeria	640	0.085	0.136	0.048	51	104	7	5
Morocco	590	0.031		0.011	60	85	4	5
Philippines	560	0.066	0.075	0.039	63	46	4	2
Yemen, Arab Republic	550	0.040	0.034	0.009	46	152	5	5
Indonesia	490	0.244	0.386	0.087	57	87	5	6
Sri Lanka	400	0.044	0.031	0.013	70	29	3	4

Table 3.3B (continued)

	GNP per capita ($/pers.)	Government expenditure			Life expectancy (years)	Infant mortality (per 1000)	Political rights	Civil liberties
		Military % global	Education % global	Health % global				
Ghana	390	0.007	0.030	0.003	54	89	7	6
Lesotho	370	0.002	0.003	0.002	55	102	5	5
Pakistan	350	0.278	0.103	0.011	52	111	4	5
Haiti	330	0.004	0.004	0.003	54	119	5	4
Sierra Leone	310	0.002	0.005	0.001	41	154	5	5
China	300	2.215	1.126	0.699	69	34	6	6
India	290	0.881	0.961	0.315	57	86	2	3
Rwanda	290	0.004	0.007	0.002	48	116	6	6
Benin	270	0.003	0.005	0.001	50	117	7	7
Togo	250	0.003	0.006	0.002	53	96	6	6
Burundi	240	0.005	0.004	0.001	48	114	7	6
Uganda	230	0.037	0.011	0.002	48	105	5	4
Burma	200	0.026	0.020	0.012	59	64	7	7
Viet Nam	196				65	47	7	7
Bangladesh	160	0.029	0.049	0.016	50	121	4	5
Malawi	160	0.004	0.006	0.005	45	153	6	7
Nepal	150	0.005	0.011	0.004	47	130	3	4

Notes: See table 3.2B.

Table 3.3C Per capita dimensions: Ranked by GNP per capita
Group II: Population > area > GNP

	GNP per capita ($/pers.)	Population Density (pers./km²)	Government expenditure			MnVA $/person	AgVA $/person	CEC (petajoules/ mil. pers.)	Exports $/person	Imports $/person	Carbon emissions (thous. metric tons/ mil. pers.)
			Military $/person	Education $/person	Health $/person						
Iraq	2,424	38	737	85	18			20	107	618	555
Mexico	1,860	41	17	75	46	544	143	47	202	150	1,329
Malaysia	1,830	49	111	145	33			30	862	673	572
Syria	1,570	58	269	105	14			35	123	250	779
Costa Rica	1,480	51	9	72	82		324	14	433	441	237
Tunisia	1,140	45	71	57	31	134	340	21	241	396	452
Turkey	1,110	66	69	29	7	238	167	28	155	214	667
Albania	933	103	56		32		186	39	0	0	885
Guatemala	930	75	16	23	9			5	127	110	123
Thailand	810	102	31	32	10	146	132	13	167	174	2,063
Egypt	760	50	65	36	8		165	20	93	191	400
Honduras	740	40	45	38	20	93	179	6	190	194	121
Dominican Republic	710	135	11	13	11	106	138	13	109	217	272
Nigeria	640	112	7		3	72	194	5	64	44	704
Morocco	590	50	12	10	3	89	140	9	109	169	223
Philippines	560	191	10	10	4	140	140	7	83	94	1,148
Yemen, Arab Republic	550	42	42	31	7	32	153	4	2	126	100
Indonesia	490	87	12	18	3	69	117	8	89	80	1,323
Sri Lanka	400	244	23	15	5	50	95	3	75	121	63
Ghana	390	55	5	17	2	40	153	3	65	59	55
Lesotho	370	53	9	14	6	16	31	118	550	1,688	0
Pakistan	350	123	24	8	1	50	74	8	34	54	132
Haiti	330	218	5	4	3			2	61	82	31

Table 3.3C (continued)

	GNP per capita ($/pers.)	Population Density (pers./km²)	Government expenditure Military $/person	Education $/person	Health $/person	MnVA $/person	AgVA $/person	CEC (petajoules/ mil. pers.)	Exports $/person	Imports $/person	Carbon emissions (thous. metric tons/ mil. pers.)
Sierra Leone	310	53	4	10	2	19	139	2	37	41	39
China	300	110	18	8	4	90	79	21	30	41	526
India	290	238	10	9	3	46	83	8	15	21	227
Rwanda	290	238	5	9	2	42	118	1	30	56	16
Benin	270	37	6	10	2	10	155	1	43	92	35
Togo	250	54	8	14	4	16	103	2	89	122	39
Burundi	240	171	9	7	2	18	133	0	35	43	9
Uganda	230	64	21	5	1	9	166	1	26	23	14
Burma	200	56	6	4	2	18	103	3	8	16	1,389
Viet Nam	196	192						3			649
Bangladesh	160	717	2	4	1	13	70	2	9	26	30
Malawi	160	62	4	6	4	17	55	1	33	35	20
Nepal	150	121	3	5	2	6		1	8	27	15

Notes: See table 3.2C.

but not much—more favorable than those of group I nations. Several bottom states with low (but not the lowest) per capita GNPs are also among the more densely populated. By contrast, most of those with the higher per capita GNPs have relatively lower population densities. Although somewhat lower than in group I, quality-of-life indicators (including political rights and civil liberties) again improve with increases in per capita energy consumption and carbon emissions, but again there are important exceptions. Despite its high growth levels, per capita GNP, energy consumption, and carbon dioxide emissions, the People's Republic of China ranks near the middle among group II countries, and its quality-of-life indicators are mediocre at best. Its political rights and civil liberties are close to the bottom.

Insofar as we look to the future, China is the developing state par excellence, with the world's eighth largest GNP (in 1986) and the world's third highest level of carbon dioxide production (contrasted with its low per capita GNP, low per capita energy consumption, and low *per capita* production of carbon dioxide). A large part of the national product is attributable to agriculture, though it is increasingly generated by industry and supported by vehicular traffic. Consider, therefore, the environmental consequences insofar as China's industrialization advances ("modernizes") and its level of carbon emissions rises commensurately. Many of the same considerations can be applied to India, where industrialization proceeds; trucks, buses, and passenger cars already jam the highways, and the atmosphere yellows or darkens despite low per capita levels of carbon emissions.

Group III is defined as: $[P > T > R]$

With large populations relative to GNPs and large GNPs relative to areas, group III nations are also subject to constraints on their resource bases and levels of technology. In contrast with group I states, however, they have technologies that have advanced relative to their resource bases. Countries with group III profiles can generally be distinguished according to their respective responses to these constraining dimensions.

The most spectacular demonstration of the potentials of group III countries for success and failure is attributable to Japan from the Meiji Restoration to the termination of World War II. Beginning in the last quarter of the nineteenth century, Japan undertook a developmental transformation that moved it from something approaching a group II profile to a group III program of growth and technological (and economic) development. Responding to that country's population growth and consequent pressure on a limited resource base, Japanese leaders imported technologies from Western nations; "modernized" the country's production, military, and naval forces; and undertook a strategy of territorial expansion (guided by their interpretation of the successes of European and U.S. expansionism). Their expectation was that colonial raw materials (and markets) would compensate for the insufficiencies of Japan's domestic resources.

In the wake of the Japanese Empire's World War II defeat and occupation, a new Japanese leadership—under the strategic umbrella of the United States—undertook a second transformation that moved Japan from its pre-war group III profile to its late twentieth century group VI profile. As a consequence, through further development (scientific, industrial, economic, and political), the Japanese were able to compensate for their limited domestic resource base by substituting high domestic production, effective but competitive exports of goods and services to foreign markets, and the peaceful importation of energy and other resources from abroad (Choucri, North, and Yamakage 1992).

Are there candidates for transformations of this order among today's group III states? Characterized by years of internecine warfare, two bottom states, El Salvador and Lebanon, defy such analysis at this writing. The less developed of the two, El Salvador, has spent almost twice as much on its military as on education and four times more than on health. Comparable data (1986) are not available for Lebanon, whose GNP per capita is reported as relatively high, largely due to its commercial capabilities. Characterized by ethnic and religious contention, Yugoslavia has formally disintegrated. Portugal, a major imperial power in the past, seems to be relatively stable today, with modest levels (for a marginal industrial power) of per capita GNP, energy consumption, and carbon dioxide production.

Four of the eleven countries listed for group III—Korea, Cuba, Syria, and El Salvador—allocated more funds per capita to military expenditures than to education or health, and Yugoslavia was only slightly better. El Salvador (lowest ranking in per capita GNP, energy consumption, and carbon dioxide emissions) and Lebanon were generally low on

Table 3.4A Dimensions of growth: Ranked by GNP
Group III: Population > GNP > area

	Population % global	Area % global	GNP % global	MnVA % global	AgVA % global	CEC % global	Exports % global	Imports % global	Carbon emissions % global
South Korea	0.851	0.074	0.650	1.025	1.737	0.739	1.666	1.453	0.687
Poland	0.769	0.238	0.513			1.910	0.579	0.531	1.885
Yugoslavia	0.478	0.195	0.354		1.034	0.617	0.497	0.541	0.527
Portugal	0.209	0.070	0.152		0.279	0.147	0.348	0.444	0.123
Hungary	0.217	0.071	0.141		0.562	0.433	0.440	0.442	0.320
North Korea	0.428	0.092	0.126			0.627	0.000	0.000	0.608
Cuba	0.209	0.087	0.124			0.156	0.000	0.000	0.136
El Salvador	0.100	0.016	0.027	0.025	0.116	0.010	0.036	0.042	0.008
Jamaica	0.049	0.008	0.013	0.017	0.021	0.028	0.029	0.044	0.025
Lebanon	0.055	0.008	0.012			0.030	0.024	0.101	0.027
Mauritius	0.020	0.002	0.008	0.008	0.026	0.005	0.032	0.031	0.004

Notes: See table 3.2A.

Table 3.4B Dimensions of development: Ranked by GNP per capita
Group III: Population > GNP > area

	GNP per capita ($/pers.)	Government expenditure			Life expectancy (years)	Infant mortality (per 1000)	Political rights	Civil liberties
		Military % global	Education % global	Health % global				
South Korea	2,370	0.616	0.653	0.043	69	25	4	5
Yugoslavia	2,300	0.398	0.430	0.578	71	27	6	5
Portugal	2,250	0.105	0.154	0.241	73	18	1	2
Poland	2,070	0.734	1.129	1.197	72	18	6	5
Hungary	2,020	0.182	0.329	0.331	71	19	5	5
Cuba	1,833	0.174	0.164	0.101	75	14	6	6
Mauritius	1,200	0.000	0.006	0.004	66	35	2	2
North Korea	909	0.301		0.041	68	25	7	7
Jamaica	840	0.004	0.017	0.010	73	19	2	3
El Salvador	820	0.017	0.012	0.006	61	61	3	4
Lebanon	667						5	4

Notes: See table 3.2B.

Table 3.4C Per capita dimensions: Ranked by GNP per capita
Group III: Population > GNP > Area

| | GNP per capita ($/pers.) | Population density (pers./km²) | Government expenditure | | | MnVA $/person | AgVA $/person | CEC (petajoules/ mil. pers.) | Exports $/person | Imports $/person | Carbon emissions (thous. metric tons/ mil. pers.) |
			Military $/person	Education $/person	Health $/person						
South Korea	2,370	423	127	119	7	590	291	48	837	761	1,094
Yugoslavia	2,300	91	146	139	157		309	72	444	504	1,494
Portugal	2,250	111	88	114	149		190	39	710	946	797
Poland	2,070	120	167	227	201			138	322	308	3,319
Hungary	2,020	114	146	234	197		368	110	865	906	1,995
Cuba	1,833	89	145	122	63			41			881
Mauritius	1,200	500	3	44	24	185	178	13	675	684	265
North Korea	909	173	123		12			81			1,922
Jamaica	840	218	14	55	28	170	62	32	248	402	679
El Salvador	820	233	30	18	8	122	165	6	154	184	109
Lebanon	667	270	952		95			30	185	816	651

Notes: See table 3.2C.

quality-of-life indicators, Syria surprisingly high, and Portugal slightly higher. Each of these patterns represents different sociopolitical conditions shaped and influenced by profile configurations. (The link to policy preferences still remains to be made explicit.)

The strongest candidate for a Japan-style transformation to group VI status is probably the Republic of Korea, a high-density country (denser than Japan) with a per capita GNP which (in 1987) was higher than that of any group II country listed (or any group I or group II country except Algeria or Iraq) and substantially higher than that of any other group III country except Portugal. Korea's per capita energy consumption has been moderately low, its quality-of-life indicators mediocre, and its carbon emissions moderately low for the level of its per capita GNP. If we set aside the Korean Republic's relationship with communist North Korea (which raises a host of analytical and empirical difficulties), the country's challenge for the twenty-first century is likely to be three-fold: to stabilize population growth; to pursue the most efficient technologies, fuels, and other resources that can be made available; and to stabilize (if not reduce) its current generation of carbon and other effluents.

Group IV is defined as $[R > T > P]$

Group IV countries are characterized by relatively small populations possessing relatively well developed knowledge and skills and with large amounts of resources occupying a spacious resource base. In developmental terms, group IV countries—typified by Australia, Canada, and the former USSR (data is from 1986)—could be viewed as one-time group I countries with profiles transformed by technologies that have accelerated relative to their populations and national territories. On the face of it, we might expect a country with this profile to be almost ideally situated, but the obvious differences among the seven group IV countries listed here raise empirical and analytical issues that require close scrutiny.

In particular, three countries—Oman, Saudi Arabia, and Libya—require special attention. What sets these countries apart is the nature of their resource endowments which, while extensive relative to their population levels, are limited in two fundamental respects: First, their territories are generally arid (in large part desert), but they are rich in one extraordinarily valuable resource—petroleum; second, their populations are not only sparse (as sparse as those of group I countries), but also dependent in large part on technologies that have been imported from industrialized countries of the West, but not well integrated into their respective societies. Further, a large fraction of their populations has been imported to help apply the new technologies that were, and continue to be, imported.

In order to implement and manage the extraction and shipping of oil, these countries have also introduced technical and managerial expertise from the West (and from India and other developing countries), as well as skilled and service labor (from India, Pakistan, and other more populated countries) to perform lower-level functions. For purposes of analysis, these special factors amount to intervening variables that in particular and influential ways condition the master variable profiles of these nations. Over time, foreign populations settle and remain in these countries. Through changes in fertility/mortality dynamics they endogenously alter the master variables. On theoretical grounds these three cases highlight an important generic issue. Changes in the master variables occur in three ways: (a) gradually, through "normal" processes of growth due to investments, budgetary allocations, dynamics of births and deaths, etc.; (b) sharply through importation of technology, people, resources, or all three; and (c) as a combination of (a) and (b).

Although the per capita GNPs of all three countries are higher than any manifested in the listings for groups I to III, Libya's is the most outstanding. Primarily due to the domestic availability of oil, this apparent affluence and related characteristics make these countries appear anomalous—not only in terms of the master variables, but also in terms of the interplay among intervening variables (imported knowledge, skills, equipment, expertise, and service labor) that derive from the basic characteristics of the master variables and, in turn and over time, alter them in potentially fundamental ways. Also notable is the consideration that although Oman's per capita levels of energy consumption and carbon dioxide emission are the highest we have encountered so far, the other two oil-producing countries (Saudi Arabia and Libya), while roughly comparable energy consumers, are not high-level producers of carbon dioxide. With allowance for faulty data, this discrepancy may be attributable to differences in technological and/or resource use efficiencies.

If oil and the knowledge and skills associated with its exploitation and processing can dominate—but fail to be sufficiently integrated into—

the profiles of Saudi Arabia and Libya, it is not surprising that vast expanses of open space (with only two and three persons per square kilometer), combined with sophisticated technologies, go a long way toward defining Australia and Canada. With allowance for geographic and related factors (deserts in Australia and frozen tundra in Canada), these two countries—and especially the former USSR—have ample space (literally and figuratively) for growth over generations to come. Against this background, the former USSR, Australia, and Canada seem to emerge as ideal manifestations of the group IV profile—all three typified by sparse populations, high levels of indigenously developed knowledge and skills, and expansive and generally rich territories and resources. Of these three, the former USSR's population, while sparse relative to those of most major countries, is denser than those of Australia and Canada.

Canada stands out as the group IV country with the highest GNP per capita, the highest consumption of energy per capita (8,945 kilograms of oil equivalent, in 1986 the highest in the world), and a comparably high level of per capita carbon dioxide production. In assessing these levels we must keep in mind the sparsity of Canada's population relative to spatial factors (driving per capita values upward arithmetically). We must also remind ourselves of the environmental responsibility of each individual Canadian as an ultimate source of anthropogenic depletion, pollution, and other forms of resource degradation. (The same is true of all of us.)

Another sparsely inhabited country, Iceland, is by far the smallest on the group IV list. Roughly the size of Ohio, but nudging the Arctic Circle, Iceland has the highest per capita GNP among the seven countries. Its energy consumption per capita is low compared with U.S. levels but not remarkable among industrialized nations. The country's production of carbon dioxide is relatively low, however. If Iceland is notable for its high per capita productivity, the former Soviet Union (given its spectacular resource base and low population density) was productively mediocre—a consideration that is much more evident now than it was in 1986 when the data were compiled. To a large extent, countering this low level of productivity is the challenge that newly independent components of the "new Russia"—an entity well advanced along the group IV path of growth and development—confront at this writing.

Table 3.5A Dimensions of growth: Ranked by GNP
Group IV: Area > GNP > population

	Population % global	Area % global	GNP % global	MnVA % global	AgVA % global	CEC % global	Exports % global	Imports % global	Carbon emissions % global
Soviet Union	5.761	17.024	15.571			19.481	4.671	4.089	15.303
Canada	0.525	7.581	2.388	2.465	1.560	2.700	4.328	3.914	1.593
Australia	0.328	5.842	1.260	1.287	1.202	1.155	1.086	1.201	0.928
Saudi Arabia	0.246	1.634	0.551	0.318	0.495	0.540	0.964	0.879	0.469
New Zealand	0.068	0.204	0.163	0.253	0.426	0.142	0.282	0.278	0.083
Libya	0.080	1.337	0.132	0.051		0.146	0.288	0.208	0.126
Oman	0.027	0.228	0.043	0.011		0.117	0.121	0.110	0.083
Iceland	0.005	0.078	0.022	0.026	0.053		0.074	0.063	0.007

Notes: See table 3.2A.

The former Soviet Union's per capita GNP in 1987 (roughly $8,670) provided a somewhat different perspective. Despite advancements in many dimensions, Soviet technological development had always been notoriously uneven, in part because of the country's highly centralized and regimented economy, but also for other reasons. Overall, the structured economic, political, planning, and managerial bureaucracies in the country discouraged individual initiative and committed serious errors in allocating critical materials, knowledge, and skills within technological enterprises (sufficient for the support of heavy industry and the military, for example, but not enough for basic science and management). As a consequence, within the former USSR craftsmanship and sophisticated technological and economic control systems have often suffered. (Such inferences must remain tentative, however, until time series analyses have been completed).

Group IV countries that allocated more to military expenditures than to education or health included Oman, Libya, Saudi Arabia, and the USSR. (The same caveats noted earlier with respect to other groups pertain.) Quality-of-life indicators at the bottom ranged from those of Oman (103 infant deaths per 1000 births and a life expectancy of 54 years) to Saudi Arabia (64 deaths, 63 years) to the industrialized former USSR (30 deaths, 70 years) to oil-rich Libya (85 deaths, 61 years). These countries also scored low on political rights and civil liberties. At the top, Canada, Australia, and Iceland scored high on all measures (more favorably than the group V U.S. on infant mortality and life expectancy measures). If allowances are made for national territories that are relatively resource poor, the potentials for growth and development—through the introduction of more advanced (or appropriate) technologies—of nations on the group IV path including those not listed here (those "behind" as well as those "ahead") should be relatively positive.

Group V is defined as: $[T > R > P]$

Characteristic of group V countries is the consideration that their technologies are dominant, their domestic resource bases (areas) are larger than their populations, and their GNPs are larger than either their populations or their resources. Or, from a slightly different perspective, their population densities are relatively low, and their GNPs per capita are relatively high. In principle, at least, this means that—on average—

Table 3.5B Dimensions of development: Ranked by GNP per capita
Group IV: Area > GNP > population

| | GNP per capita ($/pers.) | Government expenditure | | | Life expectancy (years) | Infant mortality (per 1000) | Political rights | Civil liberties |
		Military % global	Education % global	Health % global				
Canada	14,120	0.951	3.569	3.800	76	8	1	1
Iceland	13,410		0.019	0.030	77	5	1	1
Australia	11,920	0.627	1.348	1.614	78	10	1	1
Soviet Union	8,384	31.782	16.344	11.959	70	30	7	7
New Zealand	7,460	0.002	0.010	0.005	74	11	1	1
Saudi Arabia	6,950	2.050	1.078	0.492	63	64	6	7
Libya	5,128	0.293	0.278	0.099	61	85	6	6
Oman	4,980	0.218	0.059	0.035	54	103	6	6

Notes: See table 3.2B.

Table 3.5C Per capita dimensions: Ranked by GNP per capita
Group IV: Area > GNP > population

| | GNP per capita ($/pers.) | Population density (pers./km²) | Government expenditure | | | MnVA $/person | AgVA $/person | CEC (petajoules/ mil. pers.) | Exports $/person | Imports $/person | Carbon emissions (thous. metric tons/ mil. pers.) |
			Military $/person	Education $/person	Health $/person						
Canada	14,120	3	317	1,053	936	2,299	424	285	3,523	3,323	4,110
Iceland	13,410	5		593	770	2,588	1,550		6,337	5,638	1,984
Australia	11,920	2	334	636	636	1,921	523	195	1,414	1,632	3,829
Soviet Union	8,384	13	964	439	268			187	346	316	3,596
New Zealand	7,460	12	5	23	9	1,830	897	116	1,782	1,828	1,652
Saudi Arabia	6,950	6	1,457	678	259	632	287	122	1,674	1,593	2,584
Libya	5,128	2	641	539	160	312		101	1,540	1,157	2,142
Oman	4,980	4	1,430	343	172	205		243	1,944	1,847	4,229

Notes: See table 3.2C.

each person in each of these countries has access to more resources, contributes to greater productivity, and has the possibility of gaining more advantage therefrom than his or her numerical counterparts in many roughly comparable countries with quite different profiles.

As exemplified by the United States over the course of its history, nations with group V profiles—with allowances made for the size and richness of their respective resource endowments—have had unique potentials for growth and development, with populations "moderate" relative to their resource bases areas, and rated "high" on technology. Insofar as their areas remain stable, their population increases, and their technologies continue to advance, however, such countries, under the pressure of increasing demands for resources, are likely to reach out for new resources. This reach tends to be made through trade, discovery of new domestic resources, or territorial acquisition.

The United Arab Emirates (UAE) appears as a bottom country on the group V list. Like Oman, Saudi Arabia, and Libya on the group IV list, the United Arab Emirates owe their level-of-development indicators to the oil in their respective resource bases which, as an intervening variable, exerts strong effects on their master variable profiles. The UAE also ranks high—remarkably high—in per capita energy consumption and production of carbon dioxide.

With low population densities relative to those of most industrialized countries, group V Finland, Sweden, and Norway (a developed oil-producing state), along with group IV Iceland, have reputations as peaceful and effective trading and welfare-producing countries with high qualities of life, and their per capita energy consumption and carbon dioxide production are "moderate," if still relatively high. To a large extent, the low population densities of these four Scandinavian states result from early migrations (to the United States in particular), demographic transitions, strong family planning programs, and advancing technologies.

Altogether, such considerations seem to speak well for the potentials of a high-technology, low-density, favorable-resource-access profile—if the issue is viewed in a strictly national context. But there is a caveat. For example, through its corporate activities overseas, Norway is one of the largest fertilizer producers of the world. Carbon emissions associated with such activities are "counted" as part of some other (host) country's balances, not those of Norway. While this is true as a general

Table 3.6A Dimensions of growth: Ranked by GNP
Group V: GNP > area > population

	Population % global	Area % global	GNP % global	MnVA % global	AgVA % global	CEC % global	Exports % global	Imports % global	Carbon emissions % global
United States	4.952	7.115	27.902	33.642	12.866	24.695	10.428	17.809	18.192
Sweden	0.172	0.342	0.730	0.874	0.552	0.443	1.788	1.504	0.246
Norway	0.086	0.246	0.427	0.332	0.371	0.298	0.875	0.934	0.135
Finland	0.100	0.256	0.394	0.511	0.723	0.299	0.785	0.706	0.225
United Arab Emirates	0.029	0.064	0.136	0.114		0.105	0.475	0.343	0.083

Notes: See tables 3.2A.

accounting procedure, it raises some qualifications about the environmental soundness of the Norwegian-type profile. In 1991 the Norwegian government imposed a ceiling on carbon emissions for industrial enterprises within Norway, not a ceiling for all Norwegian enterprises operating outside its territory. The same type of qualification is generally applicable to other countries of this group.

To the extent that populations in group V countries grow faster than their technologies advance, however, pressures on their domestic resource bases are likely to increase (access to new resources will be more costly to acquire) and per capita shares in the economy may be expected to diminish—unless they are compensated for by exports and imports and/or increasingly efficient knowledge and skills (transformable from more knowledgeable and skillful populations).

Although it is clearly the "top state" on the group V size list, the United States drops to third place (after Norway and Sweden) in the development table. Compared with the Scandinavian countries, the United States ranks high on military expenditures, energy consumption, and involvement in warfare—and somewhat lower on education, health, and other quality-of-life indicators. Responsible for generating more than 22 percent of the (1987) global level of carbon, the United States can be characterized as a state that, conceived in resource abundance, "learned" environmental profligacy during its earliest formative years. (In Chapter 6 we will show evidence of "learning" environmental responsibility as reflected in the trends of U.S. environmental legislation over time.)

Group VI is defined by: $[T > P > R]$

Countries in group VI are characterized by higher GNPs relative to their populations and resources (areas). These countries have relatively high per capita levels of GNP, energy consumption, and carbon dioxide production. Greece and Spain are clearly among the lowest. Middle states include Israel and Singapore.

A number of group VI nations—notably Japan, Britain, West Germany, France, Italy, the Netherlands, Belgium, and Spain—are the developed cores of former empires stripped of their overseas colonies. What is notable about all of them is the extent to which—relative to the United States, which is more industrialized ($17,480 per capita GNP), and much

Table 3.6B Dimensions of development: Ranked by GNP per capita
Group V: GNP > area > poulation

	GNP per capita ($/pers.)	Government expenditure			Life expectancy (years)	Infant mortality (per 1000)	Political rights	Civil liberties
		Military % global	Education % global	Health % global				
United States	17,480	32.948	29.667	29.970	75	10	1	1
Norway	15,400	0.233	0.569	0.550	77	9	1	1
United Arab Emirates	14,680	0.220	0.063	0.034	69	33	5	5
Sweden	13,160	0.389	1.156	1.455	77	6	1	1
Finland	12,160	0.118	0.474	0.573	75	6	2	2

Notes: See table 3.2B.

Table 3.6C Per capita dimensions: Ranked by GNP per capita
Group V: GNP > area > population

| | GNP per capita ($/pers.) | Population density (pers./km²) | Government expenditure | | | | | CEC (petajoules/ mil. pers.) | Exports $/person | Imports $/person | Carbon emissions (thous. metric tons/ mil. pers.) |
			Military $/person	Education $/person	Health $/person	MnVA $/person	AgVA $/person				
United States	17,480	26	1,163	927	782	3,325	370	276	899	1,602	4,974
Norway	15,400	13	474	1,023	825	1,890	614	192	4,340	4,833	2,118
United Arab Emirates	14,680	17	1,341	339	153	1,939		203	7,071	5,319	3,894
Sweden	13,160	19	395	1,039	1,092	2,485	457	143	4,436	3,892	1,934
Finland	12,160	15	206	730	738	2,490	1,027	165	3,338	3,130	3,029

Notes: See table 3.2C.

Table 3.7A Dimensions of growth: Ranked by GNP
Group VI: GNP > population > area

	Population % global	Area % global	GNP % global	MnVA % global	AgVA % global	CEC % global	Exports % global	Imports % global	Carbon emissions % global
Japan	2.490	0.283	10.307	16.547	8.849	4.771	10.114	5.869	3.877
West Germany	1.248	0.189	4.861	8.444	2.542	3.735	11.677	8.792	2.820
France	1.135	0.416	3.924	5.211	3.998	2.306	5.996	5.954	1.489
United Kingdom	1.162	0.186	3.323	4.249	1.474	3.276	5.131	5.812	2.516
Italy	1.172	0.229	3.231	3.935	3.666	1.996	4.694	4.576	1.437
Spain	0.793	0.384	1.243	1.880	2.050	0.924	1.305	1.613	0.755
East Germany	0.340	0.082	1.239			1.445	1.331	1.261	1.398
Netherlands	0.299	0.031	0.967	0.966	1.025	1.136	3.812	3.464	0.531
Czechoslovakia	0.318	0.097	0.951			1.060	0.982	0.969	0.996
Romania	0.469	0.181	0.912			1.126	0.602	0.526	0.845
Switzerland	0.133	0.031	0.759			0.277	1.798	1.888	0.174
Belgium	0.203	0.024	0.604	0.778	0.394	0.599	3.306	3.159	0.402
Austria	0.156	0.064	0.502	0.766	0.446	0.327	1.086	1.201	0.219
Denmark	0.105	0.033	0.425	0.407	0.572	0.296	1.022	1.053	0.259
Bulgaria	0.184	0.084	0.404			0.571	0.641	0.628	0.497
Hong Kong	0.111	0.001	0.247	0.282	0.023		1.701	1.627	0.105
Greece	0.205	0.100	0.243	0.228	0.854	0.264	0.271	0.522	0.243
Israel	0.088	0.016	0.176		0.126	0.119	0.342	0.494	0.110
Kuwait	0.037	0.014	0.165	0.069		0.160	0.354	0.269	0.124
Singapore	0.053	0.001	0.127	0.181	0.017	0.117	1.079	1.174	0.135
Ireland	0.074	0.053	0.121	0.029	0.450	0.141	0.607	0.535	0.119
Trinidad and Tobago	0.025	0.004	0.042	0.022	0.038	0.099	0.066	0.062	0.074

Notes: See table 3.2A.

less dense (26 persons per square kilometer), but consumes much more energy and produces more carbon dioxide—they appear to have achieved at least modest technological and energy-use efficiencies together with relatively low levels of per capita carbon emissions.

To the extent that GNP per capita is regarded as an indicator of development, Switzerland—a relatively "dense" industrialized country (never an empire)—ranks relatively high among group VI countries, i.e., low in per capita energy consumption and production of carbon dioxide per capita. Similarly, an even denser Japan (323 persons per square kilometer), with a high GNP per capita and a slightly lower level of energy consumption per capita, had a 1987 level of carbon dioxide per capita that was not much higher.

Much the same can be said of other group VI countries—France, the Netherlands, Belgium, and Italy. Given their population densities and limited domestic resource bases, the quality-of-life indicators for these countries, from Cyprus to Japan, are also favorable. Their numbers are in sharp contrast, however, with those of the two oil-producing countries, Kuwait and Bahrain. None of the major industrialized states in group VI allocates more to military expenditures than to education or health. In regard to political rights and civil liberties, all "top" group VI countries (with one exception) are assessed at the 1/1 level. The single exception is France, with a 1/2 assessment. The lower-ranking countries in group VI include Greece (1/2), Israel (2/2), and Bahrain (6/5).

The profiles of group VI countries are notably different from those of countries in groups I through V in that their GNP levels are high (especially in Japan and Germany)—both absolutely and per capita—compared with their populations, which are also high relative to their areas (only 585 square kilometers for the city-state of Singapore). As an indicator of domestic resource availabilities (bases), area is clearly a constraining factor in the group VI profiles, but by industrialization (and/or the building of financial institutions, as in Switzerland) the more technologically advanced of these countries have succeeded in achieving and maintaining high export levels in order to pay for high import levels and thus to compensate for limited domestic resource bases.

To summarize, table 3.8 lists the countries in each of the six profile groups derived empirically for 1987. It is essential to stress that over time the positions of countries (both *within* and *across* profiles) change

Table 3.7B Dimensions of development: Ranked by GNP per capita
Group VI: GNP > population > area

	GNP per capita ($/pers.)	Government expenditure			Life expectancy (years)	Infant mortality (per 1000)	Political rights	Civil liberties
		Military % global	Education % global	Health % global				
Switzerland	17,680	0.252	0.735	1.246	77	7	1	1
Kuwait	13,890	0.164	0.148	0.013	73	19	6	5
Japan	12,840	1.841	10.292	12.003	78	6	1	1
Denmark	12,600	0.161	0.652	0.560	75	8	1	1
West Germany	12,080	2,659	4.374	7.343	75	9	1	2
East Germany	11,295	0.844	0.737	0.602	72	9	7	6
France	10,720	2.811	4.754	6.397	77	8	1	2
Netherlands	10,020	0.513	1.253	1.696	77	8	1	1
Austria	9,990	0.113	0.609	0.641	74	10	1	1
Czechoslovakia	9,284	0.496	0.496	0.685	70	14	7	6
Belgium	9,230	0.330	0.679	0.824	75	10	1	1
United Kingdom	8,870	2.970	3.556	4.299	75	9	1	1
Italy	8,550	1.414	2.827	3.790	77	10	1	1
Singapore	7,410	0.117	0.127	0.038	73	9	4	5
Hong Kong	6,910				76	8		
Bulgaria	6,800	0.189	0.260	0.227	72	15	7	7
Israel	6,210	0.599	0.257	0.087	75	12	2	2
Romania	6,026	0.167	0.220	0.271	71	26	7	7
Trinidad and Tobago	5,360	0.008	0.047	0.029	70	21	1	2
Ireland	5,070	0.040	0.170	0.230	74	9	1	1
Spain	4,860	0.537	0.856	1.384	76	10	1	2
Greece	3,680	0.305	0.152	0.252	76	12	2	2

Notes: See table 3.2B.

Table 3.7C Per capita dimensions: Ranked by GNP per capita
Group VI: GNP > population > area

| | GNP per capita ($/pers.) | Population density (pers./km²) | Government expenditure | | | MnVA $/person | AgVA $/person | CEC (petajoules/ mil. pers.) | Exports $/person | Imports $/person | Carbon emissions (thous. metric tons/ mil. pers.) |
			Military $/person	Education $/person	Health $/person						
Switzerland	17,680	159	331	854	1,209			115	5,765	6,314	1,766
Kuwait	13,890	100	779	620	44	919		240	4,102	3,247	4,563
Japan	12,840	327	129	640	623	3,252	507	106	1,735	1,050	2,108
Denmark	12,600	119	270	966	692	1,908	780	157	4,175	4,486	3,353
West Germany	12,080	245	372	542	761	3,311	290	166	3,996	3,138	3,059
East Germany	11,295	154	433	335	229			235	1,670	1,651	5,561
France	10,720	101	433	648	728	2,246	502	113	2,255	2,336	1,775
Netherlands	10,020	356	300	648	733	1,580	488	210	5,441	5,157	2,402
Austria	9,990	90	127	605	532	2,408	408	116	2,977	3,435	1,905
Czechoslovakia	9,284	121	273	242	279			185	1,320	1,358	4,246
Belgium	9,230	319	284	518	525	1,876	277	164	6,959	6,935	2,681
United Kingdom	8,870	231	447	474	478	1,790	181	156	1,886	2,228	2,931
Italy	8,550	190	211	373	418	1,643	446	94	1,710	1,739	1,659
Singapore	7,410	2,600	385	368	93	1,658	46	121	8,652	9,812	3,423
Hong Kong	6,910	5,400	0	0		1,248	29	999	6,563	6,549	1,280
Bulgaria	6,800	81	179	218	159			171	1,483	1,517	3,644
Israel	6,210	205	1,188	451	128		204	75	1,660	2,497	1,691
Romania	6,026	96	62	72	75			133	548	499	2,437
Trinidad and Tobago	5,360	240	53	297	153	430	218	223	1,147	1,129	4,065
Ireland	5,070	51	96	357	404	193	869	106	3,516	3,228	2,183
Spain	4,860	77	118	167	226	1,160	368	65	703	906	1,288
Greece	3,680	76	260	115	159	545	594	71	565	1,135	1,603

See table 3.2C.

as a result of changes in growth and development. The broader task of our research program, therefore, is to examine these changes—and their environmental implications. Figures 3.3–3.8 show, in graphic terms, six countries at roughly the "top" and "bottom" of each profile group to illustrate the differences in size and scale *within* and *across* profile groups.

Policy Paradox

Compared with the overall challenge of this book, our intent in this chapter was limited. Our purpose here was to present a theoretically and empirically derived approach to the analysis of socioeconomic observations that appear to be relevant to the apparent contradictions between economic and political growth, development, and stability, on the one hand, and environmental sustainability on the other. In the longer run, our concern is for providing the theoretical and empirical underpinnings necessary for the analysis of economic, political, and environmental decision and policy making on national, international, and global levels through time.

In framing the profiles, this chapter has addressed the potential contradictions that exist between the achievement of environmental sustainability within national, international, and global economies, on the one hand, and the growth and development that are indispensable for achieving and maintaining economic, political, and social stability, on the other. This paradox is salient in modern societies, in which the undeniable benefits derived from applications of technology, energy in various forms, and other natural resources are increasingly balanced against consequent ecological debits. Each increment of growth and development appears to exact costs in resource depletion, pollution, and other forms of degradation. Conversely, serious efforts undertaken to protect the environment are perceived as threats to agricultural and industrial production, commercial enterprises, employment, and the general welfare as it is conventionally defined.

Systematic analysis of these apparent contradictions is constrained by the extent to which serious investigations must draw upon the knowledge and skills of diverse disciplines from physics, chemistry, meteorology, and biology to economics and political science. Also relevant are the

Table 3.8 Country profiles, 1986

Group I	Group II	Group III	Group IV	Group V	Group VI
Brazil	China	South Korea	Soviet Union	United States	Japan
Iran	India	Poland	Canada	Sweden	West
Argentina	Mexico	Yugoslavia	Australia	Norway	Germany
South Africa	Indonesia	Portugal	Saudi Arabia	Finland	France
Algeria	Nigeria	Hungary	New	United Arab	United
Venezuela	Turkey	North Korea	Zealand	Emirates	Kingdom
Colombia	Thailand	Cuba	Libya	Iceland	Italy
Peru	Iraq	El Salvador	Oman		Spain
Chile	Egypt	Jamaica			East Germany
Ecuador	Pakistan	Lebanon			Netherlands
Cameroon	Philippines	Mauritius			Czechoslovakia
Côte d'Ivoire	Malaysia				Romania
Sudan	Syria				Switzerland
Kenya	Bangladesh				Belgium
Tanzania	Morocco				Austria
Uruguay	Viet Nam				Denmark
Jordan	Tunisia				Bulgaria
Zimbabwe	Guatemala				Hong Kong
Ethiopia	Burma				Greece
Panama	Sri Lanka				Israel
Zaire	Ghana				Kuwait
Angola	Dominican				Singapore
Bolivia	Republic				Ireland
Paraguay	Yemen				Trinidad and
Gabon	Costa Rica				Tobago
Afghanistan	Uganda				
Mozambique	Honduras				
Senegal	Albania				
Nicaragua	Nepal				
Papua New	Haiti				
Guinea	Rwanda				
Madagascar	Malawi				
Zambia	Sierra Leone				
Congo	Burundi				
Niger	Benin				
Guinea	Togo				
Mongolia	Lesotho				
Somalia					
Mali					
Burkina Faso					
Liberia					
Yemen, People's					
Democratic					
Republic of					
Botswana					
Chad					
Central African					
Republic					
Mauritania					
Laos					
Bhutan					

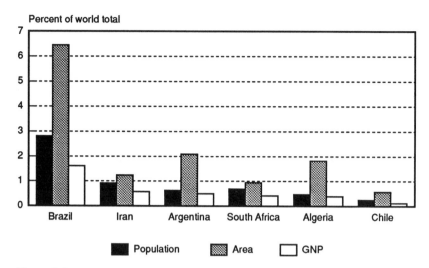

Figure 3.3
Group I: Area > Population > GNP
Source: Data in Tables 3.3–3.8.

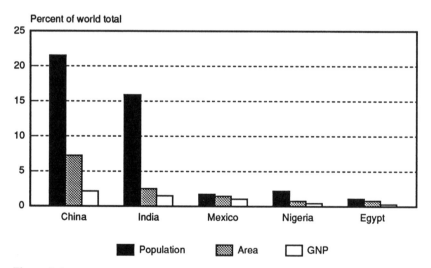

Figure 3.4
Group II: Population > Area > GNP
Source: Data in Tables 3.3–3.8.

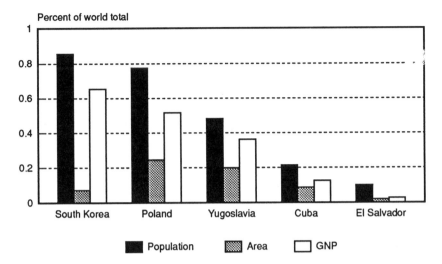

Figure 3.5
Group III: Population > GNP > Area
Source: Data in Tables 3.3–3.8.

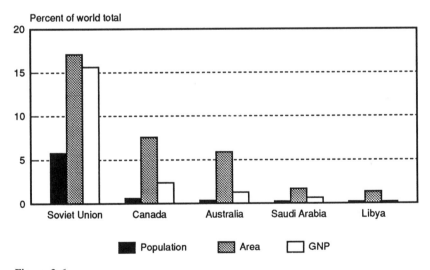

Figure 3.6
Group IV: Area > GNP > Population
Source: Data in Tables 3.3–3.8.

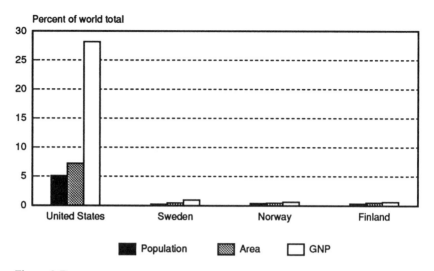

Figure 3.7
Group V: GNP > Area > Population
Source: Data in Tables 3.3–3.8.

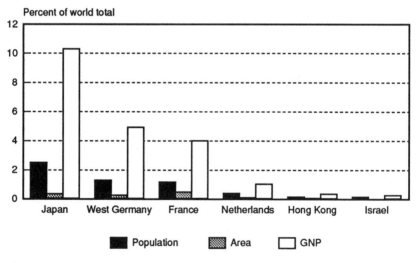

Figure 3.8
Group VI: GNP > Population > Area
Source: Data in Tables 3.3–3.8.

uneven quality and availability of data required by these disciplines if progress is to be achieved. In the formulation and execution of policy, relatively objective paradoxes of this sort tend to emerge as subjective decision- and policy-making dilemmas with contradictory horns around which polarized coalitions (developers and environmentalists, for example) tend to rally and organize. Both the characteristics and the salience of such polarities differ in different contexts.

Managing Change: Two Development/Environment Paths
Two main growth and development pathways emerge from this empirical perspective and from the uneven growth and development of the three master variables, population, resources, and technology: *Path A.* Considered sequentially, countries in Groups I → IV → V describe a pathway, starting from countries like Brazil and Argentina and progressing through two profile transitions as technology first "overtakes" populations (best represented by Iceland, Canada, and Australia) and subsequently overtakes resource bases represented by Norway, the United States, and Sweden). *Path B.* Also traced sequentially, countries in Groups II → III → VI describe a different pathway, starting from China, India, and Mexico and progressing through two profile transitions as technology first outpaces resource bases (as in Portugal and the Republic of Korea) and subsequently outpaces population (as Switzerland, Japan, and Germany). Although the orientation of these pathways is primarily directed toward economic, political, and social growth and development, the right-hand columns in each of the tables and figures in this chapter provide clues to the environmental implications.

A simplified schematic of the paths to profile alteration is presented in figure 3.9. The ways in which profiles may change as a function of growth in (a) population or (b) GNP are shown in figure 3.9. Note again that GNP is used as a surrogate for technology and that area (and material imports) is a proxy for resources—with all the caveats and qualifications in mind.

There are two ways in which political behavior and public policy shape such transformations. The first is the outcome of the aggregate of all of the bargaining, leveraging, and other interactions that have resulted from the activities, through time, of individuals and organizations within a state in pursuit of their undifferentiated interests without formal artic-

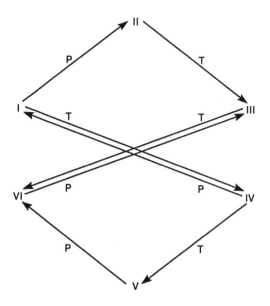

Paths generated by rising technology: Paths generated by rising population:

I ——▶ IV ——▶ V   IV ——▶ I ——▶ II

II ——▶ III ——▶ VI   V ——▶ VI ——▶ III

Dynamics of profile change

Notes: I: Resources   > Population   > Technology
       II: Population   > Resources   > Technology
       III: Population   > Technology   > Resources
       IV: Resources   > Technology   > Population
       V: Technology > Resources   > Population
       VI: Technology > Population   > Resources

Source: MIT Program on Global Accord: International Relations and Global Environment. Prepared by Jan Sundgren.

Figure 3.9
Dynamics of profile change

ulation or framing of relevant policy. The other possibility amounts to the converse—that is, the transformations that are attributable to policy formulations and implementations undertaken precisely in order to achieve intended outcomes or transformation (as in the case of Japan from the Meiji Restoration). These two paths bear directly on the *endogenization* of the master variables, the context of dynamic analysis over time. Population, resources, and technology can be "modeled" as growing "normally," depending on their previous values and current investments, or they can be altered more radically, through effective policy intervention (immigration, importation, innovation, etc.) or a combination of both. In essence, therefore, while we have treated the master variables as independent variables or dependent variables (as the case may be), how they assume these characteristics is in itself both an empirical question and a policy issue.

Left to largely undirected, largely conscious trial-and-error adaptation, over many generations countries might "learn," however painfully, to sustain the local and global environments upon which their welfare depends. However, with a deeper awareness of how we and our organizations (including states) threaten these environments, we might succeed in reducing the "pain" and other costs in decades rather than generations or centuries. Here are a few over-simplified and (until time series analyses have been undertaken) highly tentative future strategies for countries on each of the two pathways:

Path A. Allow population to grow along the I → IV → V pathway only to the extent that energy-efficient technologies and resource availabilities develop well in advance of the numbers of people and are sufficient to ensure social welfare and quality of life. It is critically important to avoid the artificial "development" patterns associated with some of the oil-rich nations, along with organizational and management dysfunctions such as those in Yugoslavia and the former USSR, and the resource and waste profligacy of the United States. In these terms the more advanced countries in groups IV and V need to focus on the development of technological and resource efficiencies both within their own borders and worldwide.

Path B. With respect to countries on the II → III → VI path, group II and III countries need to constrain population growth sharply but acceler-

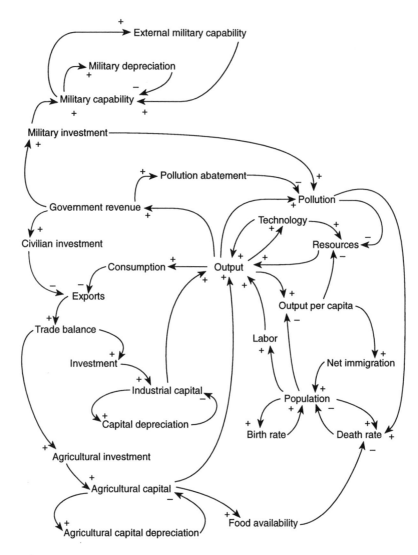

Figure 3.10
Dynamic feedback relations: Some illustrations
Source: Based on Choucri and Bousfield (1978) and Lichtman (1988).

ate technological advancement while expanding resource availabilities domestically by developing appropriate knowledge and skills and externally through worldwide trade. Heavy emphasis needs to be placed on the development or importation of energy-efficient technologies and resources. Meanwhile, national and global environments alike will benefit to the extent that group VI nations join relatively advanced group IV and V countries in assuming primary global responsibility for the speedy facilitation and distribution of technological and resource efficiencies and demographic stabilization both domestically and worldwide.

Figures 3.9A and 3.9B thus show schematically the alternative potential pathways of growth and development across profiles. The stylized paths in Figures 3.9A and 3.9B are presented for illustrative purposes only to show how profile transformations can take place.

For all countries and their components, pending time series analysis, the profile approach suggests the need to (1) accelerate resource efficient technological development in advance of population growth; (2) pursue stable balances between economics and demographics; (3) grant high priority to the development of energy-efficient and energy-saving technologies and resources; (4) develop and systematically monitor more sophisticated environmental and quality-of-life indicators; and, correspondingly, (5a) establish and maintain local, national, and global institutions in order to accelerate environmental/economic development and sustainability, and (5b) respond with "firehose" measures when indicators signal or preferably forewarn of a negative trend. The next challenge is to develop a dynamic model of these changes (Laird 1972; Choucri, Laird, and Meadows 1972; Choucri and Bousfield 1978; Litchman 1988) along the lines of figure 3.10.

Notes

1. The dynamic representation in figure 21.2 in Choucri and Bousfield 1978 (p. 314) provides the basis for figure 3.10 in this chapter.

2. Implicit here is the need to incorporate the pervasive environmental dimension relative to conditions of complex interdependence. See Keohane and Nye 1989 as a basis for international institutional responses. See Alker 1977 for a comprehensive conceptual approach to the notion of interdependence and Choucri 1976 for a detailed empirical analysis of international interdependence in the area of energy.

3. Initially we set out to identify the immediate structural outcomes—the specific

profiles of individual states—resulting from unevenness, in times series, of the master variable indicators of each. Conceptually, each individual profile could be envisaged as an instantaneous photograph (or X ray) of the population/technology/resource access structure of a particular state at a particular cross section of time. In time series, however, the "snapshot" becomes a cinematic unfolding as a given state (with measurable growth and "sizes" of master variables) pursues its own particular paths of growth and development or transformation (or relative decline).

4

The Rise of Global Ecopolitics

Hayward R. Alker, Jr. and Peter M. Haas

In a scholarly book on international political responses to global environmental challenges, a brief look at pre-1992 efforts similar to our own is appropriate. Consistent with the organizing framework of the present volume (Chapter 1 of this volume, especially table 1.1), our retrospective look at humankind's intellectual and political relationships with nature will include both conservative (geopolitical), reformative, and transformative (ecopolitical) scholarly perspectives on the issues of global change. We shall also pay special attention to the ways in which scientifically shaped environmental policy concerns have actually been expressed in and through international economic, social, and political institutions.

The Ecological Foci of Our Review

Thinking Ecologically

Our review is based on two fundamental premises, the first of which is our belief that global changes in our natural surroundings must be reunderstood *ecologically*, i.e., in the terms of an inclusive, post-Darwinian, interdisciplinary science of the relationships of the earth's living beings with their environment. This conception fulfills Ernst Haeckel's field-constituting, but now somewhat dated, definition of *ecology* as

. . . the body of knowledge concerning the economy of nature—the investigation of the total relations of the animal both to its inorganic and to its organic environment; including above all, its friendly and inimical relations with those animals and plants with which it comes directly or indirectly into contact—in a word, ecology is the study of all those complex interrelations referred to by Darwin as the conditions of the struggle for existence. (Haeckel 1866).[1]

Our first premise leads one to wonder if this apparently conservative conception of ecology can be reconciled, more than a century later, with the ecologically transformative views of the Brundtland Commission (World Commission on Environment and Development [WCED]) in *Our Common Future*, its preparatory report for the 1992 United Nations Conference on Environment and Development (UNCED) conference. This report provocatively proffers ecological principles such as that viewing "the Earth as an organism whose health depends on the health of all its parts" (WCED 1987, 1), a holistic view closer to Durkheim or Teilhard de Chardin[2] than to Charles Darwin! Cutting across conventional distinctions between centrally planned and market-oriented countries or developed and developing countries, *Our Common Future* further asserts, "We all depend on one biosphere for sustaining our lives" (p. 7).

These views lead the Commission to call for *sustainable development,* which is defined as "development that meets the needs of the present without compromising the ability of future generations to meet their own needs" (WCED 1987, 27). Here, *needs* include the essential, or basic, needs of the world's poor; a need to preserve the common biospheric bases of renewable human fulfillment is also suggested.

These goals do not sound at all like "the survival of the fittest"! More conservatively, technological and organizational "limits" affecting the utilization of environmental resources are also acknowledged in the Brundtland report, as well as limits on the ability of "the biosphere to absorb the effects of human activities" (WCED 1987, 43).[3] To argue that these contrasting conceptions of ecology can be better understood and then at least partly reconciled, we shall rely below on the path-breaking biogeochemical and historical scholarship of Vladimir Vernadsky.

As a preview of this coherence-preserving possibility, we mention here an interdisciplinary research program proposed by a committee of social scientists concerned with both the global and local aspects of environmental change. Harold Jacobson and Martin Price (1990, 16) have usefully distinguished two types of global change processes affecting environmental commons: "those that take place [unevenly] *across* the globe [italics ours], such as loss of agricultural land through desertification, loss of biodiversity, and increases in acid deposition" and "those that take place *throughout* a global system [italics ours], including modifications of the climate system as a result of the buildup of greenhouse gases and the depletion of the stratospheric ozone layer." "Across-the-globe" processes more immediately connect up in our minds with unequally distributed Darwinian "conditions of the struggle for existence"; the latter, more holistic, change processes "throughout a global system" usually refer to more recently recognized and pervasive phenomena with the capacity to threaten humankind, and other species, as a whole. "Throughout-the-globe" changes have been given provocative, post-Darwinian ecological interpretations in Vernadsky's research on the earth's inhabitable envelope, the biosphere.

Rethinking Ecopolitical Alternatives

The second grounding premise of this chapter is our belief that while differing ecological orientations toward public policy questions may be meaningfully correlated with well-known political-economic "Left/Center/Right" differences, they do not reduce to them; they may even transform them. Choucri's "transformative/reformative/conservative" axis well catches this ambivalence: We can interpret these words in terms of socioeconomic hierarchies or in terms of human-environmental relationships.

We might similarly contrast "technological optimists" versus "Malthusian" or "prudent pessimists" (Alker and Tickner 1977, 29; Clark 1986, 8; Costanza 1989, 2f.), "Cornucopians versus Malthusians" (Haas 1992), or "Deep Ecology versus Frontier Economics" (Colby 1990a).[4] Thus we need to recognize that scholars trained in liberal economic theorizing are now fundamentally challenging the commitment to growth, at least as it has previously been defined. For example, Daly (1990) attacks Brundtland on this point, preferring an alternative of ecologically sustainable development.[5] Whatever their phraseology, these contrasts resonate with different sides of a much earlier debate alternatively described either in "Marx versus Malthus" (Galtung 1973) or "Smith versus Malthus" terms. (Clark 1986, citing Kates and Burton 1986).

Perhaps the best, or most fundamental, way of contrasting ecological and political alignments is to call attention to their distinctive ontological perspectives, i.e., their different fundamental concepts of the nature, variety, and inter/intra relationships of different forms of animate and inanimate being. Progressive thinkers of the nineteenth century tended to agree with traditional Western religious views placing the human species over and above nature, while they disagreed on the existence or relevance of a divine being to biological understanding. Darwin's onto-logical treatment of humankind as a superior part of nature was differ-ently interpreted both by "liberal" or "progressive" social scientists who wanted to segment off the realms of their disciplinary specializations from ontologically inferior, micro- and macro-biological considerations and by "conservative" and racist variants of social Darwinists.

Those whom Haas (1991) calls "philosophical holists" and whom Colby (1990a and 1990b, following Naess) describes as "deep ecolo-gists" now go further than Darwin in describing our environmental interdependence. They ask why our concern for promoting and protect-ing human life does not extend equally to other species, including those with which we share coevolutionary or symbiotic relationships with, or subsumptively to, the biosphere or the earth itself.

The preoccupation of ecologists with "limits" to available resources or to population growth can also be seen to have gone through several stages of increasing biological and geographical scope (Clark 1986, 9). Whereas Malthus was greatly concerned with the economic and political needs of the landed aristocracy and the limited productivity of British agriculture, quasi-Darwinian geopoliticians of the turn of the century worried about the limits to growth in the mineral, animal, and energy resources of aristocrats, empires, industries, races, or the human species. Late twentieth-century ecologists more frequently study limits in the globe's renewable resources and the biosphere's protective or threatening roles (such as climate change and ozone holes). Contemporary deep ecologists often think of the earth as a living organism, define it as an irreplaceable resource of biodiversity, and identify with a variety of living species besides *Homo sapiens*. Ontologically, these newer concerns with limits challenge our presuppositions about the natural hierarchy of forms of life on earth.

Geopolitics vs. Ecopolitics before, between, and during the World Wars

Regarding previous scholars who researched global environmental change, we shall first briefly comment on Malthus's demographic and political-economic theorizing (especially Malthus 1986, originally 1798); the evolutionary ecological theorizing of Darwin and Wallace (Darwin 1958, originally 1859, which gives Wallace credit for the codiscovery of the relevance of Malthusian mechanisms for species evolution); Marx's critical reformulations of Darwin and his rejection of Malthus (Parsons 1977); the writings of the early environmental naturalists Gilbert White (1789) and George Perkins Marsh (1864); and the geopolitical writings of political geographers such as Ratzel, Haushofer, Mahan, and Mackinder, who were enthralled by Darwinian collective self-understandings (see Dikshit 1982, Parker 1985, Taylor 1989, and Alker 1990a for overlapping treatments).

In order to sharpen our current understandings of environmental politics at the global level, we shall focus on a contrast between the extremely influential geopolitical applications of Malthus's and Darwin's ideas—doubtless some of which they would have objected to—with the proto-ecopolitical thinking of the early conservationists. In the late nineteenth century and the first half of the twentieth century, we shall argue, geopolitics easily upstaged global ecopolitics.

The Malthusian-Darwinian evolutionary doctrine of "geometric [population] increase," "natural selection," and "the survival of the fittest"— the last phrase, accepted by Darwin, suggested by the famous social Darwinist Herbert Spencer—fell on fertile, well-prepared soil. The competitive, expansionary, modern practice of seeking dominance over a femininely gendered "nature" (including "inferior" peoples and resource bases anywhere around the globe) is now generally seen as symptomatic of an age of European (and European-imitative) imperialisms. Although the developmental trajectory of this modern impulse is still being debated (and clearly includes trans-European roots), its geographical expression is generally recognized to stretch back at least to fifteenth-, sixteenth-, and seventeenth-century conquests of African coastal areas and most of the Americas by various European states. Subsequent technological revolutions made possible vast industrialized, resource-importing production processes capable of sustaining mobile, high-firepower military forces, which further transformed Europe and the rest of the world.

As a consequence of the development and use of a wide range of these and other new technologies, there occurred in the eighteenth, nineteenth, and twentieth centuries what Robert North (1991, 184f. and 214f., citing Modelski) calls the globalization of international society and of war. Without having sufficient space here to argue the point in detail, we nonetheless suggest that social Darwinist biological, economic, and political self-understandings were extraordinarily powerful sources, in the later nineteenth and early twentieth centuries, of "scientifically" rationalizing and justifying such expansionary processes.

This growth-linked interest in domination conflicted sharply with the conservationists' ecologically sensitive historical warnings, with the ironic result that the limited success of Victorian-era international conservationist measures often had an imperial tinge.[6] It also produced competitive reactions by "peripheral" powers in North America, on the Eurasian land mass, and on the East Asian periphery that would transform twentieth-century world politics.

Contrast in scope and influence the ecologically oriented international organizational applications of the conservationist ideas of Marsh, Gilbert White, Muir, or Pinchot (see McCormick 1991, Ch. 1) or their more distant predecessors (Glacken 1967). Although the American conservationist movement, like those in several other European countries or colonies, did have several national or regional conferences in the first decades of the twentieth century, President Theodore Roosevelt's ambitious effort in 1908 and 1909 to have a world conservation congress at The Hague was called off, even though fifty-eight countries had received invitations. Roosevelt's successors, until after the Second World War, appear to have had little interest in conservation or in Pinchot's governmental conservationist efforts (McCormick 1991). However, Marsh inspired various conservationists, especially those concerned about forests; with help from their geneticist colleagues, they slowly developed specific, scientifically oriented environmental research programs.

But neither quasi-Darwinian geopolitics nor Marshian ecopolitics, founded in highly contrastive views of the human-nature relationship, achieved scientific reformulations acceptable to, or constitutive of, a global ecoscience. Thus, for scientific, political, and philosophical reasons, neither formed the basis for a cooperative global politics of environmental utilization, conservation, preservation, or transformation—especially one that would include on an equal economic basis patriotic scholars from post-colonial societies. We must therefore look elsewhere, as we shall do below in discussing Vernadsky's and Braudel's work, for inter-war and post-war progress in globally oriented ecological research and its application to global environmental change.

Global Ecological Politics in the Era of Soviet-American Rivalry

Overlapping with, but perceptively later than, this creative but imperialistic epoch is a recognizable period of globalistic, transformative developments of Darwinian ecological ideas shaped by the ideological and geopolitical antagonisms of Soviet-American rivalry. Although the Great Power-linked geopolitical thought of Haushofer, Mahan, and Mackinder continued to be influential in the first half of the present century, the success of the Soviet Revolution of 1917 dramatically introduced a fundamentally new dimension of state-supported theorizing, ideology, and political-economic practice into world politics (Levin 1972).

As ecopolitically suggestive features of this aspect of twentieth-century ecopolitics we shall focus on Vernadsky's revolutionary theories of the geosphere, the biosphere, and the noosphere; Braudel's post-Marxist world histories; and the "limits-to-growth" advocates of the early 1970s, seen as reacting both to radical egalitarian ideas and to the expansionary growth processes of capitalist societies.[7] These three visionary yet richly detailed accounts of global environmental change were all developed in a period in which liberal capitalism, Soviet socialism, and other ideologies battled for the hearts and souls of "nonaligned" or "Third World" nations and their citizens. Moreover, Vernadsky's awesome scientific innovations suggest that we should label him as a Marxist "Darwin of the biosphere" whose neo-Malthusian counterpart we shall also find in the "limits-to-growth" debate.

Vernadsky's Integrative Research on the Geosphere, the Biosphere, and the Noosphere

With roots in both the Malthusian-Darwinian-Marxist literature and earlier environmentalism, Vladimir Vernadsky's book (1929) on the biosphere heralded a transformation in the evolutionary understanding of the earth's recent history. Indeed, to show how both the holistic/ global and the Marxist-Darwinian-Malthusian branches of evolutionary ecological thought can be integrated, below we shall review Vernadsky's more recent theories of the geosphere, the biosphere, and the noosphere and, more briefly, his self-reflective work on the history of science (Vernadsky 1945; Tagliagambe 1983; Clark and Munn 1986; Yanshin and Yanshina 1988; "Reconciling the Sociosphere and the Biosphere" 1989).

A Materialist Science of the Geosphere.   Let us start with the geochemical bases of Vernadsky's conception of the geosphere. Like Darwin, Vernadsky saw everything geological—minerals, rocks, liquids, and gaseous masses of the planet and its atmosphere—in terms of its origins, which he soon, in a Marshian spirit, came to recognize included many prior activities of living organisms. Materialistically and quantitatively inclined, he ascertained the elemental and chemical composition of the earth's fluids and solids. These were seen to cohere in four different interpenetrated processes, each of which was the result of geophysical movements and chemical equilibria: atomic elements and their compounds in minerals, rocks, liquids and gases; the often very different elements and compounds contained in living organisms; the elements contained in high-pressure magmas; and rare trace elements. *Geospheres* are earth envelopes between which such chemical elements migrate.[8] *Geochemistry* is the discipline Vernadsky helped create, which studies the reactive and distributional histories of such elements on or beneath the surface of the earth (Yanshin and Yanshina 1988, 287).[9]

Physical and chemical reductionism had great payoffs for Vernadsky. A key move was his reduction of "life" to "living matter," which could be measured in terms of weight, chemical composition, and embodied energy.[10] All the chemical elements were reclassified by Vernadsky into six groups according to the roles they played in the geochemical history of the earth's crust. Moreover, from related chemical analyses he made empirical sense of the Lamarckean view (Vernadsky 1945, 7) that living matter was the creator of the main rocks of this planet. Much less obviously than oil shale, the granitic envelope, which has not been found on the moon or on Venus, was genealogically reinterpreted to be the geospherical residue of past biospheres. Especially stunning was Vernadsky's analytical conclusion that "the Earth's atmosphere with its main gases, oxygen, nitrogen, and carbon dioxide, was created by life" (Tagliagambe 1983, 526).[11]

The Interactions of the Geosphere and the Biosphere. Like the geosphere, to which it is inseparably related, the *biosphere* is a thin envelope of the earth's crust and atmosphere, an analytically distinguished subsystem of the earth system within which life naturally occurs. In making sense of this concept and its uses, it may be helpful to think of Vernadsky as the Darwin of the biosphere. Like Darwin's world of species, the biosphere is characterized by a close nutritional, respirational, or physical-chemical interrelationship[12] between all living organisms. It, too, is seen by Vernadsky in terms of its origins, descent, or processual genealogy, as "both a creation of the sun and a product of the Earth processes" whereby cosmic rays are transformed into various forms of (usable) energy. Vernadsky and his followers focused on the role and magnitudes of unicellular marine algae and tropical forests in making such transformations.

We see here an even more contemporary, scientifically based "rewriting" of the Great Chain of Being (Lovejoy 1936): Whereas Darwin had replaced God with man as the top of that chain, Vernadsky in effect encompasses humanity within the rest of living matter, the biosphere, and the earth itself. The systemic unity, being, and reality of the biosphere are due to its cosmic function of metabolically and physicochemically transforming solar energy into physical and chemical forms. Vernadsky identifies life with the entire system of energetic transformations in the biosphere, within which all organisms, including man, are described as "a function of the biosphere in its determined space-time" as monadlike "condensations." Indeed, rephrasing Darwin and Wallace, Vernadsky says, "The evolutionary process is a characteristic only of living matter," which "*is proceeding in a definite direction*" (Vernadsky 1945, 6ff.).

But whereas Darwin emphasized hierarchy and parasitic dependencies resulting from the struggle for survival, Vernadsky's material, holistic vision also emphasizes symbiosis, coevolutionary adaptation ("coadaptation" was a less hierarchical term which Darwin did use), and interdependence. Along with his biosocialistic commitments to the "biological unity and equality of all men" (Vernadsky 1945, 8),[13] his technical-scientific optimism, and his transformative version of Darwinian materialism, Vernadsky had a real commitment to the preservation of species diversity. Rather than praise the extinction brought on by the struggle for existence, he argues that ecologically induced evolutionary development "represents a harmonious whole made up of numerous trophic links. The destruction of a single species of organism disrupts these links and can entail the extinction of other species, not to mention the diminution of the genetic pool of living nature" (Yanshin and Yanshina 1988, 292).

Vernadsky (1945, 1) said, "Man tends to increase the size of the biosphere." With this optimistic claim, we see an instantiation of Marx's technologically optimistic image of human technological and individual development.[14] If one puts the earth first, the rapid transformation of the globe brought about by human beings suggests that they have the chance of collectively directing the future evolutions of the biosphere. The ontological implication is one of an evolving envelope of higher possibilities of being!

The Historical Development of the Noosphere. We at last come to the realm of concerted human social and political practices, the realm in which ecologically understood global change and international relations meet. For Vernadsky the *noosphere,* etymologically the sphere of the mind, is the inseparable but analytically distinguished part of the biosphere where humankind collectively and rationally works for the sustainable development of itself in balance with the rest of the biosphere. Without going into the essential, and disaggregated, political details, he refers to the "reconstruction of the biosphere in the interests of freely thinking humanity as a single totality" (Vernadsky 1945, 9; compare Jantsch and Waddington 1976; Levins and Lewontin 1982; Simberloff 1982).

Vernadsky's Dialectical Histories of Science. Vernadsky was well aware of the titanic struggles associated with World Wars I and II, well traveled in European scientific circles for his time, and proficient in the scientific literatures of several languages. But his most comprehensive investigations of transnational social activities seem to have been in the proto-noospheric realm of the history of science. In a quasi-Kuhnian fashion, he was especially interested in the dialectical dynamics of paradigm-transcending scientific revolutions, with which his own work had given him personal acquaintance.

The previously cited sources (especially Tagliagambe 1983) suggest that Vernadsky knew how the present state of science is intimately connected to previous ways of understanding the past. When the history of science provides metalinguistic systems appropriate for better understanding one's own scientific period, science history itself contributes to improved collective self-understandings. When alternative histories of the past are conceivable and alternative possible histories of the future are suggested, one can argue that mankind is entering the noosphere. With this evolved understanding of the noosphere, Vernadsky seems to have discovered the possible historicity—the time-ordered collective self-understandings—of a globalized world society. He found global historicity in the competing genealogical narratives offered by ecologically sensitive scholars of global change.

Braudelian Post-Marxist Histories of Global Change

Though Vernadsky's contributions will certainly survive the end of the Cold War and the dissolution of the Soviet Union as the world has known it, Soviet treatises on world politics and economics are less likely to be seen as texts of enduring scholarly value. For further contributions to, and revisions in, a Marxian wave of environmental thought, we now turn[15] to the writings of a holistic, post-Marxist, French school of history associated for decades with a famous journal, *Annales d'Histoire Economique et Sociale*, founded by Lucien Febvre[16] and Marc Bloch in Strasbourg in 1929. The school's most illustrious alumnus, and our focal concern, is Fernand Braudel (1976, 1980, 1981–84).

Braudel's greatest achievement is his convincing reformulation and presentation of "the history of the long, even of the very long time span, of the *longue durée*." Historians in the decades of the 1920s and 1930s had already structured European history in terms of Kondratieff cycles of growth and stagnation. In the third volume of his magnum opus, entitled in French *Le Temps du Monde,* Braudel extends such arguments and integrates these forty-five- to sixty-year cycles with even larger secular trends of a century or more and an explosive growth in world productivity from about 1750 until at least the 1970s (Braudel 1981–84, III, 71–88). Earlier (p. 17f.) he has written, "[W]orld time . . . might be said to concentrate above all [regions] on a kind of super-structure of world history: It represents a crowning achievement, created and supported by forces at work underneath it, although in turn its weight has an effect upon the base."

In a passage favorably citing eighteenth- and early nineteenth-century cultural historians, including Ranke and Burckhardt, Braudel argues (1980, 29) for the validity of their insights, now conceived as truths or laws of the *longue durée:* "If one accepts that this going beyond the short span has been the most precious, because the most rare, of historiographical achievements during the past hundred years, then one understands the preeminent role of the history of institutions, of religions, of civilizations, and . . . the ground-breaking role of the studies devoted to classical antiquities" (1980, 29). The authors of this chapter have shared Braudel's recognition (1980, 209f.) that "civilizations are realities of the extremely *longue durée.* They are not mortal . . ., endlessly readapting themselves to their destiny, exceed[ing] in longevity any other collective reality."

Thus recognizing the contributions of classical studies, but consistent with his materialistic roots, Braudel rejects the adequacy of intellectually, spiritually, or metaphysically predetermined cultural histories. Spengler or Toynbee developed their suggestive but flawed civilizational histories independent of a careful study of their civilization's economic and social bases and their dialogical interchanges with other civilizations, which have produced "a rich common basis" of world civilization, things such as writing, numbers, mathematical functions, and steam power, which mankind "will not be able to forget" (Braudel 1980, 189–201, quoting Margaret Mead). "And if it is absurd to neglect the superstructure," Braudel continues (pp. 205f.) "it is no less so to neglect . . . the infrastructure. . . . [W]e . . . need . . . to go hand in hand with a Toynbee or a Lucien Febvre on the one side and on the other with sociologists, anthropologists, economists, and even Marxists."

Similarly, Braudel's holistic, synthetic approach rejects a priori metaphysical frameworks, such as cultural or civilizational "ages" (as proposed by Vico and Comte), Spencer's "phases" of constraint and liberty, Durkheim's organic and mechanical successive solidarities, Ratzel's growing populational densities, Marx's famous materialistic stages, and Spengler's or Toynbee's "rigid schemes" (Braudel 1980, 201). Yet Braudel allows recombined and revised uses of any such interpretive or explanatory ideas where appropriate.

Thus Braudel accepts the Spencerian-Darwinian-Marxist metaphor of socioeconomic evolution, but argues that there are "several kinds of evolution, which may rival, assist, or at times contradict one another," and "several economies" as well. Lying underneath the easily visible, "transparent" mechanisms of production and exchange linked to rural agricultural activities, fairs, workshops, banks, and "spontaneously developing" markets, he says, "there is another, shadowy zone" (Braudel 1981–84, I, 23). And later: "This rich zone, like a layer covering the earth, I have called . . . *material life or material civilization*" (Braudel 1981–84, II, 600). It is a world of peoples, towns and cities, necessities and luxuries of consumption, technologies of printing, energy production, transport, and war.

This multilayered conception of economic life suggests a radical post-Marxian reformulation of the meaning, nature, and viability of capitalism. Just as Braudel fundamentally redefined the limiting envelope of Marxist "base" structures to include an action-constraining "envelope" slowly evolving, extremely pervasive practices and geocultural contexts of "material civilization" (1981–84, I, 24f.), he introduces a superior limit to marketplace economics. A "second shadowy zone" Braudel sees as "hovering above the sunlit world of the market economy, and constituting its upper limit so to speak, represents the favoured domain of capitalism" (1981–84, II, 455–57). This domain is speculative, multinational or transnational; and involves long-distance trade which exhibits von Thunen's exploitively linked core, semi-periphery and periphery geographical zones in a world of big business and superprofits "distinct from the market economy" (Braudel 1981–84, III, 619–32).

This historically engendered, three-tiered layering of evolutionary processes is the basis of Braudel's original title, *Civilisation, Economie et Capitalisme: XVe–XVIIIe Siecle;* of the three-volume division of his work; and of his attempts to gain insights concerning the sources of, and prospects for, the industrial world. Contrary to Marx, Braudel asserts that earlier forms of material civilization are extraordinarily persistent or inertial, and "capitalism as a system has every chance of surviving" because of its grounding in enduring material-civilizational systems of social inequality; with Marx (and against Malthus), "every thesis in favour of social inequality is another argument for [continued] capitalism" (Braudel 1981–84, III, 624). Similarly, it "would . . . be a mistake to imagine capitalism as something that developed in a series of stages or leaps—from mercantile capitalism to industrial capitalism to finance capitalism . . . The whole panoply of forms of capitalism— commercial, industrial, banking—war already deployed in thirteenth-century Florence" (Braudel 1981–84, III, 621).

Multiple contradictions across levels are observed, such as that between "capitalism . . . and its antithesis, the 'non-capitalism' of the lower level" (Braudel 1981–84, III, 630). There are also the rather Malthusian "limits of the possible," a narrow "envelope" due to "inadequate food supplies, a population that was too big or too small for its resources, low productivity of labour, and the slow progress [of the pre-industrial era] in controlling nature" within the material civilization of the pre-industrial West. These limits did not really change until "innovation and revolution along the borderline between possible and impossible came with the nineteenth century and the changed face of the world" (Braudel 1981–84, I, 27).

From an analysis of these contradictory developments, a process we have seen alternatively described as imperialism or the globalization of international society and war, Braudel concludes that the "history of the world between about 1400 and 1850–1950 is one of an ancient parity [between Europe and Asia] collapsing under the weight of a multisecular distortion, whose beginnings go back to the late fifteenth century." The "machine revolution" was "not merely an instrument of competition" but "a weapon of domination and destruction of foreign competition." Using the geopolitical terminology of the Cold War era, he cites Paul Bairoch's statistical evidence to support these claims demonstrate the accelerating economic growth of European nations ahead of the rest of the world: In 1800, western Europe reached the [per capita GNP] figure of $213 [1960 U.S. dollars] higher than that of the "Third World" of the time—about $200. China reached $228 in 1800, but declined to

$204 in 1860. But the "figure for western Europe as measured in 1976, is $2325, whereas China—despite recent recovery—is only $369, and the Third World as a whole is at about $355, far behind the developed nations" (Braudel 1981–84, III, 534f.).

Neo-Malthusians and Their Critics in the Limits-to-Growth Debate

We have seen how Braudel's cultural, social, and economic history has filled in many of the layered ways in which humankind has structured and transformed the biosphere. His post-Marxist, reformist conclusion politically supported the transformative call in the 1960s and 1970s of the post- and anti-colonial majority of states in the United Nations for an anti-exploitive, redistributive New International Economic Order. In the aftermath of the American-Vietnamese War, similar conclusions from a variety of neo-Marxist writings on the exploitive structure of the world economy were much discussed, e.g. Cardoso and Faletto 1979, originally 1971; Amin 1974; and Wallerstein 1974, 1978. One might expect conservatives in the advanced industrial countries of "the free world" to wish for a new Malthus, returned from the grave!

A neo-Malthusian claim of equality preventing, globally constraining "limits to growth" had already appeared in a chapter title of a computer analysis of world dynamics written by an MIT professor of management (Forrester 1971a), much amplified by the work of his students (D. H. Meadows et al. 1972). Their arguments could be described as neo-Malthusian critiques of resource-intensive egalitarian growth practices in both the socialist and capitalist spheres. Ridiculed by leftist writers such as Galtung (1973) for the way such representations obfuscated class conflicts, this literature nonetheless resonated, we now know, with popular, middle-class, and elite concerns on both sides of the Iron Curtain. Reasons for popular concern included a decade of concern about nuclear fallout, the spread of industrial pollution (including acid rain), salination problems, highly publicized oil spills, the apparent exhaustion of the post–World War II economic boom, environment-stressing pressures from poor and rich populations in both "advanced" and "developing" countries, and the dawn of an era when alternative complex nonlinear global systems models could be computer simulated by scholars around the world.

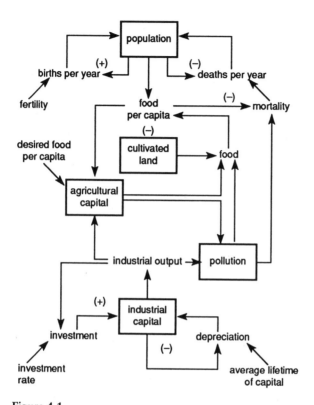

Figure 4.1
Feedback loops of population, capital, agriculture, and pollution
Note: Some of the interconnections between population and industrial capital
operate through agricultural capital, cultivated land, and pollution. Each arrow
indicates a causal relationship, which may be immediate or delayed, large or
small, positive or negative, depending on the assumptions included in each model
run.
Source: Donella H. Meadows. In D. H. Meadows et al. 1972. Reprinted by
permission of the author.

Figure 4.1 summarizes some of the rather Malthusian (but sometimes more complexly specified) demographic and technological assumptions of the MIT modelers. Population growth is governed by an exponential/ geometric birth rate and a negative mortality rate; food shortages, age, resource exhaustion, pollution, and crowding are the potential long-term killers. Somehow the deleterious or constructive effects of politicians, of "moral restraint," of wars, and of improved technologies for pollution abatement, renewable resource utilization, and population growth abatement are treated as implicitly contained within the model's "limits," its feedback loops, and its parameters.[17]

Within the Systems Dynamics group at MIT in the early 1970s, debate about the future predicted by this and alternative models was focused on whether drastic reduction in world population around the years 2020 to 2040 would occur or whether draconian policies aimed at stopping population growth and capital growth would allow for a smoother, poorer, but asymptotically stable demographic future.

More broadly within MIT, and globally, policy positions polarized along lines similar to those evoked by Malthus's early writings. With respect to the enormous challenge by the material aspirations of the economically underdeveloped world, positions included veiled advocacy of battlefield "triage" of the irreparably underdeveloped liberal variants of technological optimism, neo-Marxist technological optimism (in the Soviet Union and the Latin American Bariloche Group), as well as intermediate reformist positions like those of Mesarovic and Pestel (1974) and their associates.

We shall make only two main points about these debates here. First of all, our expectation that conservative/reformist/transformative axes might have different meanings socioeconomically and environmentally speaking is realized in the limits-to-growth debates of the 1970s. Thus the "technological optimist" pole that earlier contained Smith, Ricardo, and Marx had now split into capitalist versus socialist camps; the same could be said regarding radical writers, since several socialist analysts, in particular Heilbroner and Dumont, showed signs of technological pessimism.[18] Certain precursors of Soviet "new thinking" similarly recognized environmental issues to be "global" ones transcending international class conflicts (Soviet Political Science Association 1985).

Secondly, just as Braudel (1980, 42–47) was quite interested in the new forms of "social mathematics," so Cold War-driven developments in computer capacities and the limits-to-growth controversies gave a cumulative impetus to systems modeling as a way of quantitatively and qualitatively clarifying (and partly empirically testing) deeply ideological/geopolitical assumptions about world developments.

We conclude this section of our review by approvingly quoting from a remarkably self-observant, self-critical review published by the world modelers themselves ten years after *The Limits to Growth* appeared. They derive twelve general lessons about the world shared by the scholars of seven rather different modeling groups, the first four of which conclusions we recall below:

1. There is no known physical or technical reason why basic needs cannot be supplied for all the world's people into the foreseeable future. These needs are not being met now because of social and political structures, values, norms, and world views, not because of absolute physical scarcities.
2. Population and physical (material) capital cannot grow forever on a finite planet.
3. There is no reliable, complete information about the degree to which earth's physical environment can absorb and meet the needs of further growth . . . a great deal of partial information, which optimists read optimistically and pessimists read pessimistically.
4. Continuing "business-as-usual" policies through the next few decades will not lead to a desirable future—or even to meeting basic human needs; it will result in an increasing gap between the rich and the poor, problems with resource availability and environmental destruction, and worsening economic conditions for most people (Meadows, Richardson, and Bruckmann 1982, xviii.).

Malthus too (1970, 249f.) included within his mature reflections humankind's "vast mass of responsibility" for ameliorating the vices and misery of their species.

Geopolitics versus Ecopolitics—Again

In the world of international organizations, whole books have been written about environmental collaboration since 1945, e.g., McCormick 1991 and Young 1989a. Surely the globally collaborative work of UNESCO's 1968 Biosphere Conference (allied with its Man and the Biosphere program and the Global Environmental Monitoring System were important achievements of the Cold War era. The treaty-regulated halting of atmospheric nuclear tests by the superpowers must also be mentioned as an important early Cold War-era achievement, as well as an evolving, partial agreement between Soviet/Russian and Western atmospheric scientists about the holistic perils of "nuclear winter." We speculate that the scientific community in the Soviet Union that was responsible for carrying and transmitting Vernadsky's scientific achievements helped legitimate Soviet Bloc participation in and contributions to such activities.

But the creation of a globally oriented United Nations Environment Program (UNEP) at the 1972 Stockholm UN Conference on the Human Environment was probably the most important institutional consequence of increased concern with global environmental change in the Cold War era. Scholars associated with various sides of the "limits-to-growth" debate gave advice to the UNEP Secretariat. Previewed by Ward and Dubois (1972) and furthered by widespread, if uneven, concerns with oil spills, deforestation, salination, desertification, and other environmental problems, UNEP's importance was not accurately measured by its modest size or even more modest budget. Nor were its attempts to redefine environmental concerns in ways largely compatible with the developmental priorities of Third World countries unappreciated.

Rather, a better measure of institutionalized responses to increased popular environmental concerns across the globe was the coming into existence of environmental protection agencies and ministries across the globe. Because it transcended Northern and Southern, Communist and capitalist, Islamic and Jewish differences and was located at the core of the Mediterranean world, the Mediterranean Action Plan (Haas 1990a) has been one of the most important regional spinoffs of UNEP in this regard.

In a summary, metaphorical fashion, we may say that the second wave of globally oriented environmental thinking produced more substantial, but somewhat parallel, results when compared to the first. If British social Darwinist reformism may be said to have been the dominant, most widely felt current in the first wave of global environmental thought, the Russian Revolution and a reformed or post-Marxist radical, globally oriented tradition of systems thinking was the central new force of the second, which was evident even in the work of MIT's neo-

Malthusian modelers. Both optimistic leftist transformative currents and rightist technologically and developmentally pessimistic currents existed within this "wave."

Given that Cold War containment ultimately proved successful in resisting (and reversing) Communism's major political force, with an attendant diminishing in importance of contested Third World "sites," one could summarize these results in Braudelian terms as evidence of the persistent superior strength of the earlier wave's scholarly and political formations as they rippled back from North American shores. Thus the geopolitics of containing Communism[19] largely won out over the ecopolitics of global planetary responsibilities which, except for the brief if spectacular sunset of Soviet "new thinking," lacked an authoritative voice on the world scene.

Two Research Directions for the Post–Cold War World

Only the beginnings of a post–Cold War era of interdisciplinary ecological research are likely to have been easily visible to distant observers of the UNCED conference; therefore, more futuristically, we shall also summarize two research clusters shaping views expressed there. The first is a Northern-oriented, interdisciplinary research program on the "sustainable development of the biosphere"; the second is an overlapping but Southern-oriented mixture of research programs on the "sustainable development" of the nations of the world.

Interpreting the UN Conference on the Environment and Development as a genuinely post–Cold War event requires us to sketch the scholarly and political wave of environmental concerns shaping its deliberations and implementational concerns. We choose to outline two such ambitious, synthetic research clusters that are capable of shaping the next wave of scholarly thinking and policy concern regarding global environmental change (but see also Fujii 1990). Although both clusters of effort include contributions from the different regions of the world, it may still be fair to describe the first as primarily a globalistic, Northern-focused effort on sustainable development *throughout* the biosphere and the second as an effort by Northern and Southern scholars to reconceptualize "sustainable development" *across* the biosphere in ways consonant with the primary developmental interests of the less developed countries.

Research on the Sustainable Development of the Biosphere

Recognizing that "[h]umanity is . . . entering an era of chronic, large-scale, and extremely complex *syndromes* of interdependence between the global economy and the world environment," on the first page of the first of two related volumes, William Clark enunciates that a "major challenge of the coming decades is to learn how long-term, large-scale interactions between environment and development can be better managed to increase the prospects for ecologically sustainable improvements in human well-being" (Clark 1986, 5). Because these two volumes (Clark and Munn 1986 and Turner et al. 1990) have together probably done the most productive interdisciplinary work capable of informing and effectively criticizing, from a post–Cold War perspective, internationally sanctioned actions or inaction concerning global environmental change (see also Johnston and Clark 1982), we shall focus on them here. As "scientific holists" (Haas 1991), only Clark, Munn, and Turner adequately presage the scope of our own ecopolitically oriented review of changes in, throughout, and across, the biosphere.

What will serve as a unifying framework for stimulating scientific research and findings that very different states, transnational private actors, and international organizations can act on is by no means clear; but respectful attention to the valid contributions of different scholarly approaches should surely help. The above account of Vernadsky's global ecoscience—one highly suitable in 1945 for an emergent state-socialist superpower—should help clarify the synthetic geneology and knowledge-enhancing progress of the volumes by Clark, Munn, and Turner. The title of the first of these volumes, *Sustainable Development of the Biosphere*—and our use of it to label the research program of Clark and Munn—reflects Vernadsky's influence; the title of the second, *The Earth as Transformed by Human Action,* pays homage to Marsh's 1864 volume. Clark's metaphor of the earth as a garden that needs careful tending in order for it to remain usefully productive is a masterful synthesis of these two themes (Clark 1986). Our review will emphasize several integrative and cumulative contributions of the "sustainable development of the biosphere" research program.

Like *The Limits to Growth,* the Clark and Munn volume gives considerable space to neo-Malthusian arguments about population change.

We also find a fascinating empirical exploration of the population dynamics of several geographically dispersed regional systems from the more or less distant past in the volume by Turner et al.[20] Clearly the message the authors wish to convey is that their scholarship will be open but cautious, i.e., balanced, with respect to ideologically linked demographic, environmental, or economic issues.

A second contribution attempts to broaden Vernadsky's measurements of the biosphere, more systematically operationalize Marsh's environmental concerns, and define a related interdisciplinary research program. After showing that both deforestation and declines in terrestrial vertebrate diversity are very early aspects of environmental degradation processes, a chapter in the Turner volume by Kates, Turner, and Clark (1990) presents a trend analysis with respect to measurable biospheric concentrations. It concludes that water withdrawals; floral diversity; carbon, nitrogen, and phosphorus releases; and sediment flows are recent and accelerating changes in the biosphere. This preliminary set of findings cries for further analysis both globally and locally using both old and new (including satellite-based) measuring practices. Indeed, entire chapters in the volume by Turner et al. are devoted to one or a few of the biospheric components joined to a systematically organized set of regional studies organized in a South-North agrarian industrial advanced industrial typology amplified by attention to differences in population densities across the globe.

In the volume by Turner et al., historical time scales are mostly shaped to the consequences of fossil fuel-based industries and population growth—expected to reach ten billion people by 2050—on the biosphere. (See also Kates and Burton 1986.) Consonant with Braudel-Bairoch findings, these impacts get labeled "The Great Transformation" (Kates, Turner, Clark 1990), a title borrowed and transformed from Karl Polanyi's earlier work on the political and economic character of the Industrial Revolution. Adams (1990) wrote a particularly provocative essay in the volume by Turner et al. concerning the implications highlighted by an alternative five-century framework associated with the European diaspora and the birth of the modern world economy—a millennial framework that suggests pondering why a European rather than a Mediterranean or Asian perspective should be used to organize so much of the world's recent history.

Third, the volumes by Clark, Munn, and Turner further differentiate the components of the various interacting realms that Vernadsky's tripartite division of earth processes suggests—a geosphere, within which are found a biosphere and a noosphere.[21] As Toynbee, Braudel, many geographers and most critics of the early world models have suggested, these include a much more inclusive orientation toward the ecological and economic aspects of cultural systems in a realm that has come to be called the sociosphere ("Reconciling the Sociosphere and the Biosphere" 1989). Many of the chapters of the Clark, Munn, and Turner volumes detail linkages between the biosphere and the sociosphere.[22] This enhanced conception allows the concept of the noosphere to represent a special domain within the sociosphere—i.e., institutionalized forms of global, ecological, and historical self-understanding and action, as Vernadsky originally intended.

Within the sociosphere, Clark and Turner are particularly open minded regarding the roles of international relations variables. These include the role of center-periphery differences in the world economy, phenomena at the center of the second wave of global ecological thought that are still very much with us today in a somewhat different form— e.g., UNCED's focus on environment *and* development. The Clark, Munn, and Turner volumes also point to the possibilities and difficulties of international regime formation and the provocative transnational culturally oriented literature of ecofeminism.[23]

Fourth, Clark, Turner, and their associates take Vernadsky's vision of global historicity seriously; theirs appears to be a synthesis of conservative, reformist, and transformative managerial concerns. This occurs in two ways in the earlier volume: besides a provocative discussion of expected and unexpected surprises in environmental management, there is an especially flexible appreciation of the use of gaming and simulation or global modeling techniques as alternatives to future surprises. In a situation in which so much research on climate change/global warming and the solar radiation effects of more methane, lots of carbon dioxide, and lethal chlorofluorocarbons need continuing investigation, this methodological orientation is clearly salutory. Adams's visionary retrospective (1990) in Turner et al. suggests how this research contributes to the building of a noosphere.

Ecological-Economic Research on Sustainable Development

Stimulated by UNCED, the work of UNEP, and ecological writings in and before the "limits-to-growth debate" (work summarily reported in Daly 1973), a much more loosely clustered set of research approaches has focused on local or regional problems of development across the biosphere, particularly in developing countries.[24] What distinguishes these newer ecological-economic approaches is that they take the ecological dimension seriously enough to re-define conventional conservative, reformative, or transformative approaches to economic development. Characteristically, they start from the recognition that environmental change and development are inextricably linked. With different mixes of optimism and pessimism they discuss synergisms and trade-offs in development planning and practice.

Alternative Environmental Development Paradigms.   Taken from Colby 1990a, with citations that go back at least to Daly's earlier work, Figure 4.2 suggests the most general way in which a Vernadskean perspective on the biosphere has re-shaped thinking about growth and development. Economic questions concerning the renewability of households and firms need to be re-defined within a larger biospherical systems conception. Whether the focus is on biomass management in agro-industrial systems design (Colby 1990, 26, presenting the ideas of Sachs and Silk) or the re-design of specific high-energy, environmentally threatening, industrial refining systems (Ayres 1989), ecologically sensitive economists and engineers are conscious of the underutilized solar-based outer limits of renewable energy sources. And they are in the process of re-defining the measurement of the economic value of nonrenewable resources, the "real value added" of pollution-generating production processes, and the "exploitation" of human and other natural resources.

Colby (1990, 8) further differentiates among the "paradigms" for environmental management in development on the basis of their thematic foci and dominant imperatives and threats, their images of human-nature relationships, their prevalent property and payment regimes, their allocations of primary responsibilities for development and management, and their environmental management methodologies, technologies and strategies. (See also Costanza ed. 1991 and Chapter 5 of this volume).

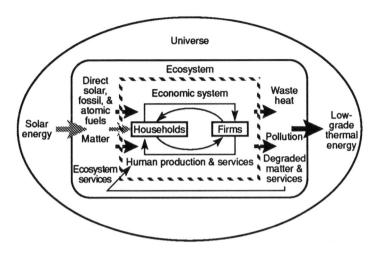

Figure 4.2
Economic production from a biophysical perspective
Note: A continuous input of high-quality/low-entropy fuels, varying-entropy materials ("natural" resources), and ecosystem services enter the economic system from the larger ecosystem. The economy then uses the fuels to upgrade the natural resources, driving the circular flow between households and firms in the process. The fuel, materials, and services are degraded and returned to the ecosystem as low-quality, high-entropy heat and matter and impaired ecosystem process functioning.
Source: Colby 1990a. Excerpts of this dissertation are available in Colby 1991. Reprinted by permission of the author.

Early strongly anthropocentric liberal and later Marxist versions of "frontier economics" are grouped together and contrasted with a bio-centric "deep ecology" paradigm that emphasizes decentralized growth-avoiding back-to-nature schemes. Intermediate "environmental protection," "resource management," and (now possibly emerging) "eco-development" paradigms are described as well in ontological, intellectual, methodological, and policy-oriented terms. If Marshian trade-offs, Muir-style conservation, and public environmental regulation efforts characterize the "environmental protection" paradigm, "sustainability," a modified anthropocentric orientation, global commons law, "polluter pays" regulations, and ecological re-definitions of economic value are salient features of Colby's "resource management" scheme. He speculates that an ecocentric "eco-development" paradigm is becoming current, emphasizing more comprehensively re-defined ecological and economic regimes, "pollution prevention pays" principles, and newer interdisciplinary analytic bases such as ecological economics, biophysical economics, and open system dynamics.

The Latin American and Caribbean Agenda for UNCED. Because it provocatively suggests how earlier transformative New International Economic Order themes are being rewritten in environmental terms, we reprint Figure 4.3 here (with permission from LACCDE (no date, 18).) Besides showing how open systems thinking methodologies (like those of the Clark, Munn, and Turner volumes) are concretely applied, it introduces us to transformative Southern perspectives on ecopolitical issues. The figure comes from a larger report prepared by a group at the Bariloche Foundation in Argentina, an earlier contributor to the "limits-to-growth" debate.

From a cumulative perspective, note particularly how many of the concrete problems suggested by the limits-to-growth debate, the biospheric research program of the Clark, Munn, and Turner volumes, and the much discussed Agenda 21 document are included in the heavily boxed set of environmental problems. Characteristically for new-wave ecological economic analyses, economic and environmental variables are treated as highly interconnected. The transformative implications of deteriorating terms of exchange, of increased indebtedness, and of technological dependence are also suggested.

Perhaps the most challenging aspect of the report by the Latin American and Caribbean Commission on Development and Environment (LACCDE) is its treatment of issues of responsibility. Early on it points out that "poverty is both the cause and the result of environmental degradation (LACCDE no date, 2f.). The model of development employed by the already industrialized countries and adopted by the Latin and Caribbean countries "appears less viable with each passing day" (p. 1); "a half century of flawed development has produced total stagnation for those of us in Latin America" (p. 5). Less developed countries have become dumping grounds for others' wastes; Central America has "the highest worldwide per capita use of pesticides," resulting in "19,000 pesticide poisonings over a five-year period" (p. 7).

Because of their often predatory use of nonrenewable resources in both the North and the South, many of them plundered, and an unequal resulting pattern of deforestation, "the industrialized countries have incurred an ecological debt with the world. This carries an obligation now to support development in order that it may not aggravate delicate conservation and environmental balances resulting from past neglect" (LACCDE no date, viii). Just as Agarwal and Narain (1991) challenge the World Resources Institute's figures on the relative share of India's and China's carbon dioxide production, so the Latin American and Caribbean Commission challenges developed countries, the primary beneficiaries of the industrial revolution, to pay for the accumulated effects of their wrongdoings (which the authors later admit involved the complicity of certain Latin and Caribbean states as well). Against this background, common to contemporary and emergent North-South ecopolitics, a call is made for a new global agreement, a new commitment to sustainable development.

Conclusions

Are there some larger lessons contained in our attempted periodization of two hundred years of research and practice concerning global environmental change? Our reconstructive journeys into the history of global change research and practice have been, at least for us, surprisingly successful.

The Roots of the Present in the Past

First of all, we have been struck by the number of coherent and continuing strains of thought that have emerged in the preparation of the present chapter. For example, Malthusian population-resource economics and the naturalistic environmentalism of Gilbert White and George Perkins Marsh were two pre-Darwinian roots that showed new modes of expression in subsequent conservative thought on the limits to growth. Here our use of "conservative" is intended to catch the previously described ambiguity of Choucri's "conservative/reformative/transformative" axis of ecopolitical orientations. Similarly, even our brief rehearsal of Darwin and Marx's materialist evolutionary thinking linked it to Vernadsky's transformative theorizing about the geosphere, biosphere, and noosphere; to Braudel's post-Marxist ecological history; and

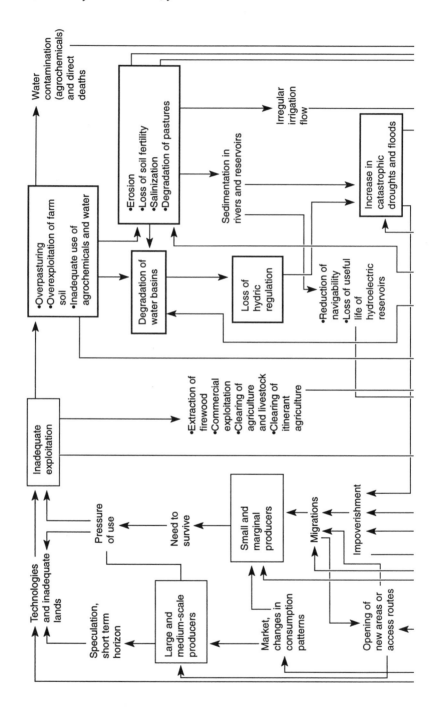

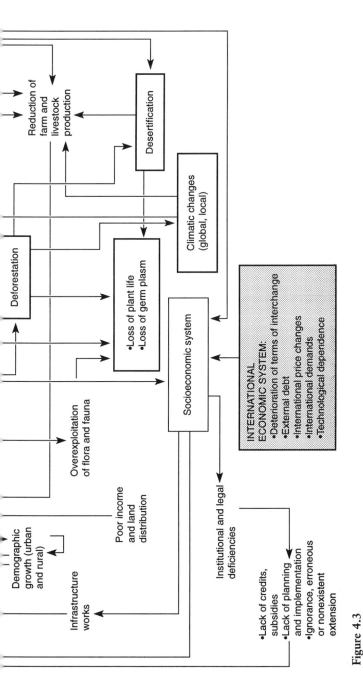

Figure 4.3
Simplified diagram of principal factors and relationships of environmental problems and land use
Guide: The causal relationships are represented by arrows, the principal environmental problems by rectangles with thick borders, and the extra-regional factors by a shaded rectangle.
Source: *Our Own Agenda.* Copyright 1989 by Ecological Systems Analysis Group (ESAG), Villegas 369, Office 3B, 8400 San Carlos de Bariloche, Rio Negro, Argentina. Reprinted by permission of Ecological Systems Analysis Group and its director, Dr. Manuel Winograd.

to the transformative thrust of Latin American radicalism concerning sustainable national development.

The Emergence of Synthetic Concepts, Frameworks and Inter-Disciplinary Research Paradigms for Gauging Ecopolitical Change

The majestic synthesis of concerns in Clark and Munn 1986 and Turner et al. 1990 cannot be appreciated without a knowledge of these roots. Like Fujii (1990) and the Bariloche study we have momentarily glimpsed, they suggest a useful framework, major dimensions, and some of the probable linkages needed to describe international environmental issues. Indeed, as we have repeatedly seen, over the last two hundred years scholarly and popular conceptions of the natural environment and its relationship to human activities have been transformed, including the recognition of multiple overlapping processes with different time scales and disparate implications for the analysis and regulatory reform of global change.[25] In short, many heterogeneous yet interrelated social and ecological factors have become endogenized into collectively shared and empirically researchable visions of international environmental politics. Ecological research paradigms have extended and deepened their scope to include environmental relations within, across, and throughout the biosphere.

No less provocative, but not yet as cumulative, have been the ways development economists have begun to link environmental degradation and sustainability questions with non-liberal economic theories of growth and development. Ironically, in the post–Cold War era, the ceteris paribus assumptions separating environmental, social, economic, and political realms in liberal thought have come unstuck. Alternate ecopolitical world pictures are emerging that are more biologically integrated.

The Dialectical Quality of Progress in Global Environmental Science and Political Practice

Our three overlapping periods also allow for a dialectical, progressive reconstruction of most of the historical episodes of theorizing and application that we have presented (and some, but not all, of their countercurrents). Different fusions of Enlightenment science, industrial-technological revolution, an expansionary wave of global capitalism, imperial competition, social Darwinism, and European-American geopolitics provided the principle energies of our first "wave" of theory and practice.

Darwinian re-definitions of the biological unity of nature, of humans, and of other animals (see Ritvo 1987 for a fascinating and suggestive account) have had some longer-term consequences. Holistic collective ecological self-understandings gradually helped re-define for many those systems of interaction and identity formation that must be preserved as part of humankind's environmental commons. Notions of "ecological science" and "the environment," as well as their corresponding disciplinary boundaries and ontological foundations, also evolved.

Three "second-wave" moments of such rethinking have been highlighted above. First, Braudel's post-Marxist, Annales-inspired, ecologically sensitive multilayered reconceptualization of material civilization, market economics, capitalism, and world politics in the early modern era suggests a rich variety of middle and longer-term cyclic and developmental systems and processes shaping human identifications and purposes throughout the globe. If capitalist political economy represents a layer of human experience most impressively embodying the freedom of some to choose, it has also been associated with a widening gap in standards of living between commercial and industrial Northern countries and their less developed, exploited Southern peripheries. Patterns of ecologically grounded material civilization and attendant systems of social stratification are changing more slowly than class structures, usually exercising powerful constraints on the political autonomy of states and nations.

Second, Vernadsky's breathtaking scientific revolution in biogeochemistry and the post-Darwinian ecological reconceptualizations of the biosphere that it inspired suggest new ways of endogenizing the consequences for humanity as a whole of the climatic, economic, and civilizational fluctuations that Marsh and Braudel, among others, have begun to explore on a regional or interregional basis. As a result, the scope and depth of holistic ecological thinking concerning processes at work throughout the globe significantly increased. Third, the neo-Malthusian proponents of limits to growth in the early 1970s provoked ideologically charged controversies that echoed, but eventually improved upon, earlier debates. Global systems thinking was a prominent feature of their reconceptualizations. The widely attended UN Conference on the Human Environment, resulting in the formation of the United Nations Environment Program, was perhaps the most important environmentally relevant organizational achievement of this period.

If the thesis and antithesis periods of our story overlap and suggest subsequent, partially synthetic developments arising out of the contradictions within each period, the dominant character of our third, post–Cold War, period of global environmental thought and practice has not fully emerged. The UNCED conference, and the institutions it legitimizes, should be an important early expression of the emerging changes in collective self-understanding associated with our "third wave" of ecopolitical thought and practice.

We have tried to sketch both the scientific and political parameters of a twenty-first–century ecopolitical contest between technological optimists and ecological pessimists, between pro-Southern redistributive developmentalists, development-oriented global holists, and privatistic Northern conservatives divided between post-Malthusian pessimists and neo-Smithean optimists over the seriousness of environmental threats to their own narrowly defined security.

The Rise of Global Ecopolitics

Our brief review suggests the existence of considerable, but dialectical, progress in the interdisciplinary scope, scientific depth, global scale, and popular comprehension of ecological thought, combined with a lagged but impressive increase in the scope and impact of institutional responses to holistic ecological concerns. In some ways this new ecopolitical way of understanding humanity's environmental commons will be considered a fulfillment of Enlightenment ideals, in other ways a post-modernist transformation of them. Together these findings justify our forecast of a new era in which global ecopolitics will define many of the terms, if not the practices, of world politics. Because North-South tensions are likely to be a salient conservative geopolitical feature of this new era, incompletely echoing the imperialism and Cold War antagonisms of earlier times, the transformational accomplishments of ecopolitics must await detailed future investigations. In the meantime, ecopolitically motivated scholars and activists have much to do regarding the naturally and politically possible.

Our account has shown a rather rapidly emerging, if still incomplete and controversial, transformation in the discourse and debates of global environmental politics. Combined with globally thinking, locally acting environmental movements and the work of environmentally concerned international and transnational organizations in the public and private spheres, publicists, educators, and scientists have transformed the terms of public environmental debate across the globe, and some environmentally sensitive practices as well. This complex, discursive, and practical transformation we call "the rise of global ecopolitics."

The Ecopolitical Challenge to Growth-Oriented Modernity

One reason for writing the above highly selective reviews of the "science" and "politics" of global environmental change has been to clarify the challenges to "science and politics as usual," at least as these have been understood in the anti-Communist Western world.[26] It turns out that conventional Western liberal Realist—or neo-Realist (as in Keohane 1986)—worldviews also paint an inadequate picture of the world we live in and our relationships to it. The concepts and theories reviewed here help to both globally and transnationally re-define the conventional historically grounded focus of international relations research on nation-states as the essential units of analysis.

We have also seen how contemporary ecologically oriented scientists have helped ontologically re-define influential hierarchical images of human-nature relationships. If Kant's enlightened critiques helped weaken or break the metaphysical hold on Western philosophical consciousness of the Great Chain of Being (but see Friedman 1988, Lakoff and Turner 1989, and Alker 1989), Darwin's natural fitness hierarchies helped replace God with Nature in popular understandings of natural phenomena. Recent research on "sustaining the biosphere" and "sustainable development" goes even further to challenge the human-centered ontological, epistemological, historical, and practical presuppositions of growth-oriented modernity. Much of Northern-style environmental change research is grounded in more egalitarian, holistic, and symbiotic ontologies that fundamentally re-define the older hierarchies of natural being usually associated with the development of the modern era.

Ironically, the great-grandchildren of the Enlightenment and the Industrial Revolution have begun to challenge their underlying ideal of unlimited growth and progress. We have thus seen multiparadigmatic research orientations standing before, or spreading across, a modernity/ post-modernity continental divide in the history of world politics.

The Persistence of Geopolitics: the North-South Dimension of Ecopolitics

Nonetheless, the rise of global ecopolitics and its successes have not, and cannot be, fully separated from the geopolitics of the imperial and the Cold War eras. Although it is not adequately describable as a return to the imperial/colonial world, contemporary global ecopolitics reflects somewhat analogous North-South geopolitical differences, as pre-UNCED differences within recent biosphere-oriented sustainable development research have shown. Domestically oriented policymakers still exhibit highly ambivalent and contradictory relationships with a cluster of increasingly coherent transnational ecologically oriented epistemic communities. Because we have contrasted economically improvable environmental problems such as poverty-induced environmental degradation, acid rain, and biodiversity that are visible across the globe with problems occurring throughout the earth system, such as ozone depletion and global warming, North-South differences between, and within, recently visible research clusters should have become clearer.

Meeting the Practical Challenges of Ecopolitics

We are also interested in meeting the practical challenges ecopolitics presents to the contemporary world. Given the difficulty of reconciling growth, development, and sustainability goals, this may involve stretching the limits of the possible concerning sustainable development of, within, and across the biosphere. In a world where the United States is playing a leading military role but where economic difficulties distract it from the economic leadership one might expect, its environmental ambivalence and its anti-redistributive positions on issues of economic development have made progress towards reaching either variant of "sustainable development" especially difficult. (See Stern, Young, and Druckman 1992 for a start in this direction.)

But change in the shared self-understandings of citizens within the most economically developed countries (including, but not limited to, the United States) is not all that is needed. The increases in wealth achieved by Japan, oil-rich states, and the newly industrialized countries have not extended to most other Latin, African, Asian, and East European states. When "development" is such an illusive goal, "sustainable development" appears to be only harder; blaming the developed world is an almost irresistible, if inadequate, political response.

Neither the ineffectiveness of most international conservationist programs before 1945, nor the extraordinary costliness of world-level geopolitical struggles, nor the limited, highly restricted success of the Montreal Protocol is an adequate precedent for ecopolitical change. Value convergence, shared goals, and political will are required, as are appropriate technical knowledge and convergent scientific understanding among differently situated scientific research communities.

As many "reflectivist" scholars of international institutions have argued,[27] innovative policy-shaping ideas are likely to be accepted when they help justify preexisting political ends, regulate or order extant power-serving networks, or limit challenges to the constitutive principles of both domestic or international systemic orders. But as Braudel and the Clark, Munn, and Turner volumes have shown, these principles themselves may reflect different layerings of practice, themselves changing at different speeds. In the aftermath of the Cold War and the collapse of the Soviet Union, such principles now include reasserted national sovereignty attributions, commitments to market economics, and capitalistic property relationships.

But the "victory" of the West reveals contradictory developments as well. A rapidly changing international division of labor, the fusion and transfer of sovereignty taking place in evidently successful European common market institutions, the breakdown of traditional liberal ceteris paribus assumptions, and the rise in salience of trans-border ecopolitical issues do not suggest a return to the Darwinian era. Within these changing, contradictory, and sometimes amorphous constraints, reformist ecopolitical innovation is, can be, and should be taking place.

Notes

Drafted by the first coauthor, this paper is a product of a decade of continuing, sometimes intense, and we hope productive conversations between its coauthors, who can no longer fully discriminate responsibility for its main arguments. We wish to thank all the participants in the present volume, especially the editor, for their helpful comments on an earlier draft. A version of that draft was presented at the 1991 Annual Meeting of the Mexican Association for International Studies.

1. The English language translation of Haeckel's definition is taken from McIntosh (1985, 7ff.). Haeckel's influential, monistic, pantheistic, neo-Lamarkean, eugenic natural philosophy is reviewed in Bramwell (1989, Ch. 3).

2. The noted French Catholic philosopher, geologist, and paleontologist, who attended Vladimir Vernadsky's Paris lectures in the 1920s on the geosphere and the biosphere and developed a religious conception of the noosphere. He argued that man's biological, social, and spiritual evolution were continuing, and convergent.

3. The "deepening interconnections" of "[e]conomics and ecology" are cited as the "central justification for the establishment of the Commission" on pp. 27f. An influential commentator, Daly (1990, 1), sharply distinguishes between *sustainable development* and *sustainable growth; growth* refers to natural increases "in size by the addition of material through assimilation or accretion," while *development* denotes the expansion or realization of potentialities, the achieving of "a fuller, greater, or better state." Daly hopes that "the glaring contradiction of a world economy growing by a factor of 5 or 10 and at the same time respecting ecological limits, which was present but subdued in the Report [will] be resolved in future discussion."

4. Typically, optimists advocate "new" forms of "growth," "symbiosis," "niche development," or "adaptability," perhaps democratically undertaken by new or more able social groups or formerly oppressed classes. Typically they make claims of bountiful resource availability, made possible by humankind's boundless technological ingenuity. Pessimists disagree, stressing inexorable "limits," "checks," "scarcities," or "natural necessities."

5. Costanza et al. (1990) abstracts nearly two hundred scholarly works on this theme; the journal *Ecological Economics* is equally relevant.

6. McCormick (1991, 18) links the Society for the Preservation of the Wild Fauna of the Empire to its hunter sponsors, nicknamed by their contemporaries "penitent butchers." Similarly, the early London Zoological Society served to symbolize the conquest and appropriation of nature and to scientifically glorify the extent and power of the British Empire. "[A]dmission was restricted, at least in the intention of the society's council, to visitors belonging to the classes that produced officers, administrators, and commercial entrepreneurs. The nature of their interest in the animals was inveterately described as scientific . . . and allied it to the project of intellectual appropriation that often shadowed the extension of English political influence" (Ritvo 1987, 210).

7. We recommend Dikshit 1982, Parker 1985 (Chs. 8 and 9), Ferri 1986, Taylor 1989, and Wallerstein 1991 for discussions of Cold War geopolitics, a subject unfortunately omitted from our text.

8. We here—and subsequently, without further attribution—quote and para-phrase Tagliagambe 1983; this four-component list and the associated definition of geospheres occurs on his pp. 525ff.

9. Seen through the Darwinian, materialist lenses of biogeochemistry, the solar-energy-transformative capacities of the earth's biomass come to the focus of our attention. Hence "Pasteur was correct in regarding the preponderance of opti-cally active compounds as the most characteristic general property of living matter; this idea is of immense importance" (Vernadsky 1945, 2).

10. Note the Darwinian materialism: "Living matter is the totality of living organisms. This is nothing other than the scientific . . . generalization of . . . indisputable facts. The concept of 'life' always overflows the bounds of the concept 'living matter' into the realms of philosophy, folklore, religion, and artistic creation—all connotations that are no longer present in 'living matter'" (Yanshin and Yanshina 1988, 289).

11. From this perspective it is only a few (rather controversial) additional steps to L. E. Lovelock and Lynn Margulis's consistent reformulation of the Gaia hypothesis in terms of negentropic atmospheric homeostasis (Lovelock and Mar-gulis 1973; Lovelock 1979). The later work argues that feedbacks from living matter to the atmosphere have maintained an average earth temperature of 10 to 20 degrees Celsius, which is supportive of life (p. 21).

12. Working from a negentropy framework like that of figure 4.2, Robert U. Ayres similarly suggests thinking of "both the biosphere and the industrial economy as systems for the transformation of materials." He suggests an evo-lution-like process in increasing the sustainability, through recycling, of "our industrial metabolism, the energy- and value-yielding process essential to eco-nomic development" (Ayres 1989).

13. The replay of socialist versus capitalist ideological themes is also evident in Lynn Margulis's indictment of "big science" prerogatives given to DNA research (rather than to ecological studies of forest habitats, for example). She points out that "predation, photosynthesis, communication, social organization, motion" all occurred in bacteria, that the main source of evolutionary novelty is the acquisition of symbionts, symbiosis, rather than "the accumulation of chance mutations." She says her critics "wallow in their zoological, capitalistic, com-petitive, cost benefit interpretation of Darwin" (Margulis no date; Mann 1991).

14. Similarly, Kenneth Boulding claims that "adaptability is the capacity to expand niches or to find new niches;" and he imaginatively critiques Darwin's "unfortunate" Spencerian "metaphors" (Boulding 1978, 110f.).

15. Ecologically sensitive alternatives one might also want to consider at this point include those proposed by Renouvin and Duroselle (1967), the many books of the Sprouts (including Sprout and Sprout 1965), and developments in lateral pressure theory, including those described by Choucri and North (1975) and Ashley (1980).

16. "Febvre insisted that at the basis of every civilization are its vital, endless repeated links with the environment, links which it creates or rather has to recreate throughout its long destiny, all those elementary and seemingly primitive relationships with the soil, the vegetation, the animal population, endemic dis-eases . . ." (Braudel 1980, 206).

17. Although the MIT modelers were criticized by liberals and leftists as omitting a variety of adaptive feedback processes, systems dynamics modeling practices did allow the re-specification of thought models like the one sketched in figure

4.1 in ways that prevented the ominous rapid future drops in population and welfare that the neo-Malthusians projected. See Alker and Tickner 1977; Cole 1977; Cole and Miles 1978; Meadows, Richardson, and Bruckmann 1982; Ashley 1983; and Hughes 1985.

18. Both Cole and Miles (1978, 61) and Hughes (1985, 48) suggest what we would call "North versus South" cum "East versus West" geopolitical configurations for the variety of futures studies stimulated by *Limits to Growth*, alignments quite characteristic of the Cold War era (Alker and Russett 1965). Both sources use as their "North-South" axis "no-limits" "technical optimists" versus "limits"-sensitive "Malthusian pessimists." Their "East versus West" axis is given variant classical liberal to reformist to radical/Marxist/dependency theory interpretations. Forrester gets a high "North West" characterization in both studies.

19. Our selective review has paid scant attention to the largely Realist scholarly literature of Cold War international politics which in the West has usually treated population, technology, resources, and their geographic distributions as limiting or enabling elements of national power and has advocated geopolitical "containment" and "deterrence" goals vis a vis Communist states.

20. T. M. Whitmore et al. (1990, 25–39) offers a variety of growth alternatives but concludes that, on the basis of past, smaller-scale regional evidence, quite sharp (but not necessarily Malthusian) downturns have frequently occurred.

21. Clark (1986, 15, citing Bretherton) has a graph of "The relations among biological, chemical and geophysical in the biosphere." He has also provided us with an even more complex version, sketching out relationships between atmospheric physics, ocean dynamics, terrestrial surface moisture/energy balances, marine biogeochemistry, stratospheric chemistry and dynamics, terrestrial ecosystems, and tropospheric chemistry taken from Earth System Sciences Committee 1986.

22. Without attempting complex graphics beyond those of Choucri's figure 1.2 (Choucri this volume) and those cited in the previous footnotes, it may be helpful to suggest the development of a schematization built on the following:

biosphere   sociosphere
(including the   (including the economic,
geosphere)   cultural, and historical)

Both interactive and identity-changing "inner-active" relationships could be distinguished within the arrows linking these two overlapping but analytically distinguished spheres. Anthropogenic sources of biospheric change could be seen as part of the impacts of the sociosphere on the biosphere. Path-dependent, lagged effects in the physical, chemical, and biological realms of the biosphere/geosphere could be compared and contrasted with changes in national, regional, or global ecological-historical self-consciousness historicity phenomena seen to occur in the realm of the sociosphere.

23. See the references to Braudel and Wallerstein in Clark 1986, plus H. A. Regier and G. L. Baskerville, "Sustainable Redevelopment of Regional Ecosystems Degraded by Exploitive Development," chapter 3, and G. Majone, "International Institutions and the Environment," chapter 12, in Clark and Munn 1986. Also note Merchant's ecofeminist account of environmental transformations in Turner et al. 1990.

24. Daly and Cobb 1989 and Costanza et al. 1990 are good summary references written from primarily Northern, ecological-economic perspectives. As representatives of a vast growing body of recent literature being prepared for UNCED discussions we mention here three more "Southern" treatments of some of the same issues: Latin American and Caribbean Commission on Development and Environment, no date; Agarwal and Narain 1991; and Colby and Sagasti's contribution to the present volume.

25. The chapters by Rothenberg and Brown Weiss in this volume build on this changed recognition of phenomena and time scales relevant to international action.

26. Thomas Homer-Dixon's contribution to this volume develops this line of thought as well.

27. Our language here partly derives from Haas 1992; see also Adler and Haas 1992.

II

Actors and Processes

5
Eco-Development and Perspectives on Global Change from Developing Countries

Francisco R. Sagasti and Michael E. Colby

The New Context of Development and Environmental Change

Development efforts during the 1990s will confront an increasingly complex and heterogeneous set of situations. Whereas ten or twenty years ago we could speak of developing countries as a whole, this is no longer possible, for differences between and within these countries have been continuously growing. We will begin by exploring some emerging features of the global context, address a few common misconceptions about climate change, and then delve more deeply into various developing country perspectives and approaches and their implications for attempts to resolve the apparent global change/global environment and development dilemmas.

A Fractured Global Order

All "developed" (hereafter, "industrial") and "developing" countries face the context of a turbulent period of modern history which will force us to adapt our mindsets, organizing concepts, and resulting approaches to action. Several major clusters of changes characterize what has been called a fractured global order, with patterns and systems characterizing the old order having been replaced or transformed into different ones (Sagasti 1989):

• *a rapidly shifting political environment:* a post-bipolar world in which East-West differences no longer matter as much as they did in the last few decades; the spread of political pluralism, participation, and democratic movements on all continents; and a reduction in the political control of nation-states over economic, social, environmental, and technological phenomena.

• *transformations in the patterns of world economic interdependence:* the globalization of financial markets; the emergence of the Pacific rim as the world's largest trading area; the shift from commodities trade to high-technology services and manufactured products; economic union in western Europe; conversion to market economies in eastern Europe and the former Soviet Union; economic turmoil in the Middle East; the Latin America debt crisis; and the decline of Africa.

• *cultural transformations:* the growth of religious fundamentalism as a political force; tension between pressures to homogenize values and aspirations versus the desire to preserve cultural identity; and the emergence of moral and ethical issues at the forefront of choices about both inter- and intragenerational equity, particularly in relation to the environment, income distribution, and the elimination of poverty.[1]

• *the accelerating pace and increasing complexity of scientific advances and technological change:* advances in computer science and informatics have changed the way new scientific knowledge is generated, which has in turn made the process of technological innovation more rapid and systematic, but also more difficult and costly for developing countries.

• *the challenge of environmental sustainability:* poverty and population growth in developing countries can be seen as both causes and effects of environmental/resource degradation, while the effects of excessive, often wasteful resource consumption habits in the industrial countries on poorer countries receives little attention. Climate patterns are not the only type of global environmental change putting future generations' livelihoods and quality of life at risk: The extinction of genetic resources in the form of biodiversity, stratospheric ozone depletion, the spread of toxic chemicals, and deforestation, among others, are now global issues.[2] Major social adaptations and perhaps changes in lifestyles will be essential in both groups of countries in order to ensure ecological stability and economic prosperity in the coming decades.

A Frazzled Global Climate

Juxtaposed with this political, economic, and social context is the physical context of impending global climate change and its uncertain ecological and economic consequences.[3] Climate change is often referred to as "global warming" or "the greenhouse effect." While these terms may be useful metaphors at the global level, policy discussions are often based on misunderstandings of potentially far-reaching consequence.

By *frazzled* we essentially mean confused or semi-chaotic (compared to what we are accustomed to). The full consequences of the impending new regime are very uncertain; change may already be starting to happen, but we cannot say for sure. First, while the overall trend appears to be one of global warming, this trend is very difficult to "prove" statistically given climatic variability, the shortness of the monitoring record, and non-uniform change over the planet. Furthermore, what is significant according to statistical (or economic; e.g., Nordhaus 1990) theory may not coincide with what is significant in terms of climatological, ecological, or social realities.

Second, regional changes in climate may be more important than global changes, particularly in terms of economic effects. Some areas may even get cooler while others get warmer, with the aggregate average showing little or no change. The rise in sea level accompanying polar or overall warming will have much more severe effects in low-lying and island countries than on others; the same would be true for the effects of storms.

Third, and perhaps most important in the short to medium term, is the likelihood that deviations from familiar climatic patterns will become greater. This means that severe, unusual events (hurricanes, floods, precipitation patterns, monsoon seasons, and droughts) will probably become both more extreme and more common.

Our social and institutional systems are unprepared for this combination of a "fractured global order" (resulting from the array of political, cultural, economic, and scientific changes) and a "frazzled global climate" (due to physical and ecological changes).[4]

Developing World Perspectives on Global Change

Three different types of information provide a cross-view of what is often considered a "typical" developing country perspective on global change, environment, and development. First, some daunting economic statistics and actual living conditions indicate a fundamental trend of increasing economic polarization in the world. The per capita gross national product (GNP) averaged only U.S. $330 in the thirty-five "low-income" developing countries in 1989 ($350 for China and India) versus $19,090 in the nineteen nations in the Organization for Economic Cooperation and Development (OECD)—more than fifty-five times as much. In terms of land area, the two groups cover comparable portions of the earth, 36.7 million square kilometers for the poor countries and 31.2 million square kilometers for the OECD nations, but the population of the poor countries outnumbers that of the OECD nations by a factor of four (and climbing), now three billion to three-fourths of a billion, respectively. By comparison, the fifty-five "middle-income" countries averaged $2,040 per capita GNP, with a total population of 1.1 billion in an area of 40.4 million square kilometers. In the 1980s, annual inflation averaged 9.1 percent in the poor countries versus 4.3 percent in the OECD nations and 73.0 percent in the middle-income group. Sub-Saharan Africa's per capita food production declined by 5 percent in the 1980s (World Bank 1991, 204–205, 211).

Scott Willis' 1989 "Yo! Amigo!!" editorial cartoon[5] is now perhaps one of the most reproduced political cartoons of all time. It depicts a developed country "fatcat" yelling through the sunroof of his gas-guzzling, carbon dioxide- and smog-emitting limousine at a peasant who is brandishing an ax toward a tree (while the latter's donkey watches). The fat cat says, "Yo! Amigo!! We need that tree to protect us from the greenhouse effect." Whether the peasant's purpose in cutting the tree is to clear some land to grow food for his family, to burn as energy to cook that food, to clear a pasture for export cattle (for fast-food hamburgers) or to export the tree to an industrial country in the form of raw logs, chopsticks, construction forms, or plywood veneer does not appear to matter to the Northerner.

Third, a recent paper by Agarwal and Narain (1990), of the Centre for Science and Environment (CSE) in New Delhi, picks up on this theme as it charges that estimates by the Washington-based World Resources Institute (WRI) of different countries' actual and permissible contributions to the atmospheric buildup of greenhouse gases are biased against developing countries (WRI 1990). WRI (and, by extension, all policy analysts from industrial countries) is in essence accused of unfairly blaming poor countries, especially China, India, and Brazil, for the resulting warming trend. The industrial countries are charged with "environmental colonialism," trying to control how fundamental resources such as forests and energy are used in the poor countries, perhaps even forcing them to forego development in order to save the world from the greenhouse effect, which is actually so far a result of industrial countries' practices.[6]

This "typical" perspective serves to illustrate that many developing countries have a host of other priorities that compete with responding to climate change. *Global change* means a variety of additional things to these countries, many of which are more immediately pressing than preparing for a change in climate. Deeply felt poverty is pervasive, the terms of trade for their raw materials have been in decline for years, their abilities to feed themselves are declining, an assortment of local and regional natural resource crises (e.g., soil erosion, deforestation, water shortages, desertification), and even more conventional pollution issues (such as the pollution of urban air and water) are often far worse than those experienced in industrial nations in recent years. So the threat of climate change often seems a rather distant one to policymakers and citizens alike from developing countries. There is a dearth of financial resources with which to deal with any of these issues, as net financial transfers to many developing countries have been negative in the past few years, with more going back to the lenders than is newly disbursed (World Bank 1989).

Southern Divergences
A careful reading of Agarwal and Narain's own statistics for the portion of greenhouse gases that currently come from developing versus industrial countries (9 percent versus 91 percent, respectively) shows a more complex picture, however. They assert that there is solidarity among the less developed countries on this issue, but their data indicates heterogeneity. The United States and Canada come off looking much more the villains, but so do Brazil, Saudi Arabia, Colombia, and Côte d'Ivoire. India, China, and Indonesia do not appear so dastardly, but neither do Japan and France. Thus, while WRI is accused of bias in favor of North America, CSE might be accused of its own pro-Asia leanings. Others (e.g., Pachuari 1990 and Monastersky 1991) fall in between WRI's figures (47.4 percent versus 52.6 percent) and CSE's.

Furthermore, not all developing countries share what we have called the "typical" view. At an international conference in Chantilly, Virginia to launch negotiations on a climate treaty in February 1991, an alliance of twenty-eight small island nations from the Pacific, Caribbean, and Mediterranean injected a sense of urgency into talks because the anticipated sea rise that would come with global warming would have such

severe effects on them: Some islands (and cultures) would literally disappear under water (Monastersky 1991). Similar, mainland but low-
lying Bangladesh would be hit with a triple whammy adding to already
severe floods: Sea rise and consequent river backup could inundate large
areas of the country, cyclones from the Bay of Bengal could get more
severe or frequent, and rainfall and river runoff from Himalayan snow-
melt might increase (Brammer 1989). The new influence of this group
of previously very minor players in international politics may be ascribed
to the fact that this alliance was based on homogeneous, unambiguous
interests and benefited from some astute advice on how to organize
themselves. It is also a harbinger of dramatic change in how international
relations are conducted—what Alker and Haas in chapter 4 of this
volume call a shift from "geopolitics" to "ecopolitics"—which will have
consequences for institutional systems.[7]

Meanwhile, the positions of other large developing countries are evolving. At the same conference, Brazil, Mexico, and Pakistan are reported
to have taken stands that begin to approach those of the industrial
countries. The Pakistani delegate, for instance, indicated that while his
country has the economic and moral right to seek development and
industrialized countries bear the greatest responsibility for the present
threat, Pakistan would nonetheless attempt to limit its contribution to
climate change problems as it develops (Monastersky 1991, 201).

Three lessons emerge from these different developing country
perspectives:

• Data analysis is commonly affected by politics and worldviews, with
volitional purposes affecting any attempt to devise comprehensive indices. There is a need for evolution in the underlying concepts that guide
thinking about relationships between data analysis, international politics
and policy, and environmental management and development in general.
• The G77 will not speak in unison with a single "developing country"
perspective on global change after all, and it is necessary to go beyond
stereotypes. In some cases developing countries will be rivals on the issue
rather than allies. This might be considered another indicator of the
"fractured global order."
• And clearly, more research and careful analysis in this area are needed
(in conjunction with the cautionary note about the interaction between
data and politics.

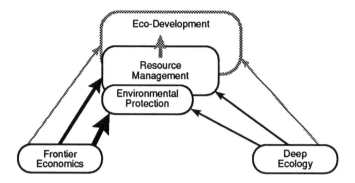

Figure 5.1
The evolution of environment-development paradigms
Note: The vertical scale represents the progression in time from one paradigm
to the next going upward; the horizontal scale indicates the positions of the
upper three paradigms on a spectrum between the diametrically opposed frontier
economics and deep ecology paradigms. The sizes of the boxes roughly signify
the degree of inclusiveness or integration of social, ecological, and economic
systems in the definition of the development and organization of human societies.
Non-solid lines indicate the hypothesized future.
Sources: Colby 1990a, 1991.

Five Paradigms of Environmental Management in Development

The issue of global change, as explained above, fits into a larger issue
the world is just starting to seriously grapple with: the overall relationship between environmental management and development. It is not just
physical or economic circumstances that determine policy positions or
perspectives on environmental issues. General views about the relationship between human society and nature and how to govern it have a
major impact, coloring people's perceptions of issues, the evidence they
give credence to, their estimations of importance, the methods of analysis
they consider acceptable, and, not least, the solutions they favor.

   Figure 5.1 depicts an "evolutionary tree" of five paradigms of the
relationship between environmental management and development as
presented earlier by Colby (1990a, 1991). The concepts and concerns
of the first three paradigms are firmly rooted in the philosophy and
experience of Western industrial countries.

   Frontier economics is characterized by the view that the environment
consists of limitless resources and that economic growth may be disem-

bodied from nature. Nature is conceived as a mechanism that exists to serve humans, and subject to improvement by them, or as an adversary to be conquered (e.g., Francis Bacon). Thus, society engineers nature for its own purposes, often attempting to replace it altogether (e.g., "green revolution" agriculture and flood control on the Mississippi and Yangtze rivers). This results in at best a laissez faire economic policy regarding environmental quality and natural resources (Barnett and Morse 1963) and, at worst, the active promotion of their destruction (as in the cutting of tropical rainforests in the 1970s and 1980s). Many nations adopt(ed) this view as a necessary but minor evil that is justified by the need for economic growth. Human population growth is considered good, enabling economies of scale and greater cultural inventiveness (Simon and Kahn 1984).

Deep ecology takes the opposite view, that humans are subservient to nature, which provides for them. Society must therefore adapt itself to nature (e.g., Callenbach 1975; Devall and Sessions 1985; Goldsmith 1988). Other species have value equal to that of humans. The earth's resources are finite, and therefore human consumption and economic growth, conceived of as intrinsically ecologically harmful, must be constrained to a level that ensures harmony with nature. Modern technology is sometimes seen as one root of ecological evil because of its power to transform or destroy nature on a much larger scale than ever before. Rousseau's romantic notion of the "noble savage" depicts the ideal relationship between humans and nature. Human population must be reduced in order to preserve as much wilderness as possible.

Environmental protection began in the 1960s, mainly as a response to pollution in the industrial countries (e.g., Carson 1962). It relies on legal regulations (proscriptions or prescriptions, such as remedial technological add-on solutions to specific problems) to trade off amenity values of the environment against economic growth in the short term, primarily to protect human health and a few species of special interest (Friedman 1988). Promoting development and regulating its "externalities" are separate responsibilities, so that different institutions in government are often pursuing conflicting goals, or at least inefficient means of achieving them. After-the-fact damage control prevails, while little is done to modify development goals and activities themselves to prevent the externalities in the first place. Environmental quality is considered a luxury value that rich people (or countries) can afford to buy, but it is a low priority for the poor.

Resource management expands the traditional application of economic principles for allocating scarce factors of production to include biophysical resources. It recognizes the linkages between the sustainability of economic activities and natural resources and trades the cross-sectoral impacts of resource degradation off against each other (Barney 1980; Clark and Munn 1986; WCED 1987). The environment is a fragile resource for society that must be actively managed to achieve "sustainability," a constraint for "green growth." The market mechanism of getting the prices right, an element of the "polluter pays" principle (Beckerman 1975, 90) is preferred over legal regulation (finessing the fact that just as much, if not more, legal work may be involved). Controlling population growth in the poor countries (especially those that supply raw natural resources to the rich countries) reemerges as a major concern, as it drives increased consumption of resources. In essence, ecology is being economized. While many of the issues driving Resource Management come from developing countries, the concepts and logic used to think about them still come from the industrial countries' traditions.

Eco-development attempts to integrate social factors and goals with long-term economic and ecological ones, striving for the "co-development" of society and the environment by actively restructuring the economy according to both ecological and equity criteria (e.g., Riddell 1981; Glaeser 1984; Sachs 1984; Norgaard 1988; Daly and Cobb 1989). The first criterion means ecologizing economics and engineering—designing human society with its environment for the benefit of both using self-designing ecosystems as a primary tool—rather than economizing and engineering ecology (Mitsch and Jørgensen 1989). The second means basing development activities on the participation of communities in goal setting, design, and benefit sharing. Synergism rather than trade-offs ("balance") is sought between production technologies to conserve the resilience of and options for development of all three systems (economic, ecological, and social). Proactive, visionary leadership rather than reactive, incremental management is paramount. Eco-Development is the first paradigm of environmental management in development which is based equally on the experiences, philosophies, needs, and logic of developing and industrial countries.

Table 5.1 summarizes many of the differences between these five paradigms along several "dimensions," such as their dominant imperatives, perceived threats, main themes, property regimes, responsibility for management, technologies and strategies, analytic tools and planning methodologies, and flaws.

Paradigms in Transition

We view environmental protection as a transitory phase made necessary by the tensions inherent in the overly reductionistic, short-term view of frontier economics. Debate about sustainable development is now open; it should be remembered that sustainable development is an idealistic goal, not a strategy. It is a sort of vague "motherhood" or mission statement for the planet, but it does not specify how we are to accomplish the mission. It appears that two competing strategic paradigms of how to achieve sustainable development are emerging: Resource Management and Eco-Development. Both are more inclusive, more realistic, and less polarized replacements for the frontier economics and deep ecology paradigms (see also Lele 1991).

Both Resource Management and Eco-Development will be needed for some time. At the present, their boundary is a bit fuzzy. Some of their technological solutions appear quite similar, but Eco-Development would go much further toward the use of ecological principles in the proactive design criteria for production and service technologies. Their degree of social/political integration and their approaches to social participation, equity, action, and diversity are crucial areas of distinction. Because it is based more equally on ideas and experiences from developing as well as industrial countries and because of its explicit concern for equity, Eco-Development should be more acceptable to poor people—of both industrial and developing countries—than Resource Management.

The preceding discussion has been primarily descriptive. At this point, we would like to shift to a more normative (advocative) stance focusing on the strategies of Eco-Development for dealing with global change.

Eco-Development as an Integrated Strategy for the Future

Historical Background

The concept of Eco-Development began to be formulated in the 1970s as an alternative to conventional growth-imperative models in an attempt to explicitly incorporate cultural, social, and ecological goals into development (Sachs 1974). The Founex conference laid the groundwork for the 1972 Stockholm Conference, which created the United Nations Environment Program (UNEP), an early advocate of Eco-Development. The explicit inclusion of the satisfaction of basic needs and the principles of self-sufficiency and participation were subsequently added as criteria for Eco-Development (the 1974 Cocoyoc Declaration; Glaeser 1984; Wisner 1988). Another motivation was the desire of Third World peoples for a new style of development more appropriate to their cultures, climates, and styles of thinking than that of the Western industrial cultures (Cocoyoc 1974; Riddell 1981; Sardar 1988). While Eco-Development recognizes the need for economic growth, it also recognizes the need to be much more particular about exactly what it is that is growing—in many cases it should *not* be the material and energy intensity of an economy—and that growth that must be of qualitatively very different nature from that which has been pursued in conventional economic development approaches.

In most developing countries, a large proportion of the populations derive their livelihoods not from the market economy, but from the relatively invisible (to economic measures) survival economy of natural resources (Bandyopadhyay and Shiva 1988). Sustenance and basic needs satisfaction are the organizing principles for natural resource use in the survival economy, while profits and capital accumulation are the organizing principles for natural resource use in the market economy.

Ecological Economics

Ecological and Economic Scale. One fundamental problem that remains for Resource Management is the fact that one can manage the parts of a system "optimally" to maximize sustainable production and still drive it to a point of breakdown or rapid change by damaging those parts' larger environmental context (the dust bowl of the American

Table 5.1 Basic distinctions between five paradigms of environmental management in development

Paradigm: Dimension	Frontier Economics (FE)	Environmental Protection (EP)
Dominant imperative	"Progress," as infinite economic growth and prosperity	"Trade-offs," as in ecology versus economic growth
Human-Nature relationship	Very strong anthropocentric	Strong anthropocentric
Dominant threats	Hunger, poverty, disease, "natural disasters"	Health impacts of pollution, endangered species
Main themes	Open access/free goods; exploitation of infinite natural resources	Remedial/defensive; "legalize ecology" as economic externality
Prevalent property regimes	Privatization (neoclassical) or nationalization (Marxist) of all property	Privatization dominant; some public parks set aside
Who pays?	Property owners (public at large; especially poor)	Income tax payers (public at large)
Responsibility for development and management	Property owners (individuals or state)	Fragmentation: development decentralized, management centralized
Fundamental flaws	Creative but mechanistic; no awareness of reliance on ecological balance	Defined by FE in reaction to DE; lacks vision of abundance

Resource Management (RM)	Eco-Development (ED)	Deep Ecology (DE)
"Sustainability" as necessary constraint for "green growth"	Co-developing humans and nature; redefine "security"	"Eco-topia": anti-growth, constrained harmony with nature
Modified anthropocentric	Ecocentric ?	Biocentric
Resource degradation; poverty, population growth	Ecological uncertainty; global change	Ecosystem collapse; "unnatural" disasters
Global efficiency; "economize ecology"; interdependence	Generative restructuring; "ecologize economy" and social system; sophisticated symbiosis	Back to nature; "biospecies equality"; simple symbiosis
Global Commons Law (GCL) for conservation of oceans, atmosphere, climate, biodiversity	GCL plus local common and private property regimes for intra- and inter-generational equity and stewardship	Private plus common property set aside for preservation
"Polluter pays" (producers and consumers); tradable emissions permits	"Pollution prevention pays"; income-indexed environmental taxes	Avoid costs by foregoing development
Toward integration across multiple levels of government (federal/state/local)	Private/public institutional innovations and redefinition of roles	Largely decentralized but integrated design and management
Downplays social factors; subtly mechanistic; doesn't handle uncertainty	May generate false security; magnitude of changes requires new consciousness	Defined in reaction to FE; organic but not creative; how reduce population?

Table 5.1   (continued)

Paradigm: Dimension	Frontier Economics (FE)	Environmental Protection (EP)
Environmental management technologies and strategies	Industrial agriculture: high inputs of energy, biocides, nutrients, and water; monocultures and mechanized production; fossil energy; pollution dispersal; unregulated waste disposal; high population growth; "free markets"	"End-of-the-pipe" clean-up, or "business as usual— plus a treatment plant"; "command and control"; Market Regulation: some prohibition or limits, repair, and set-asides, mainly focusing on protection of human health, "land doctoring," environmental impact statements
Analytic/modeling and planning methodologies	Neoclassical or Marxist: closed economic aystems: reversible equilibria, production limited by man-made factors, natural factors not accounted for. Net present value maximization cost-benefit analysis of tangible goods and services	Neoclassical plus: environmental impact assessment after design; optimum pollution levels; equation of willingness to pay and compensation principles

Resource Management (RM)	Eco-Development (ED)	Deep Ecology (DE)
Impact assessment and risk management, pollution reduction, energy efficiency, renewable resource/conservation strategies, restoration ecology, population stabilization, and technology-enhanced carrying capacity, some structural adjustment	Uncertainty (resilience) management, industrial ecology eco-technologies, e.g: renewable energy, waste/resource cycling for throughput reduction, agro-forestry, low input agriculture, extractive forest reserves; population stabilization and enhanced capacity as for RM	Stability management; reduced scale of market economy (including trade); low technology; simple material needs; non-dominating science; indigenous technology systems; "intrinsic values"; population reduction
Neoclassical plus: include natural capital; true (Hicksian) income maximization in UN System of National Accounts; increased, freer trade; ecosystem and social health monitoring; linkages between population, poverty, and environment	Ecological economics: biophysical-economic open systems dynamics; sociotechnical and ecosystem process design; integration of social, economic, and ecological criteria for technology; trade and capital flow regulated based on community goals and management; equity in land distribution; geophysiology	Grassroots bioregional planning; multiple cultural systems; conservation of cultural and biological diversity; autonomy

Midwest in the 1930s comes to mind, as do the attempts to "train" the Mississippi and now the Brahmaputra River) (World Bank 1990).

Ecological health requires longer-term management of adaptability, resilience, and uncertainty to reduce the occurrence of "surprises" caused by crossing over unknown ecological thresholds. Thus, management flexibility and ecological uncertainty must be integrated into economic modeling and planning mechanisms; current techniques of risk management are of limited use in complex, tightly coupled systems in which discontinuous change becomes more likely (Perrow 1984; Perrings 1987).

These concerns are related to the issue of the "scale" of the economy in the ecosystem (Foy and Daly 1989). Ecological and economic communities are coming to be viewed as smaller, faster-changing subsystems embedded within larger, (normally) slower-changing systems that environ them (Norton 1990). Traditional economic calculus does not integrate across these different spatial levels and time dimensions; what is needed is a new kind of multi-level, multi-criteria systems analysis-synthesis.

Ecological and Economic Distribution.   Another problem for Resource Management is that of distribution: the social consequences of how efficiency is achieved. Do these social consequences feed back to ecological and even economic consequences? Many believe the answer is yes (e.g., Korten 1990). The question of sustainability can be viewed as one of intergenerational equity, with serious legal and economic (Norgaard 1991) implications.[8] The distribution of land tenure rights has major effects on the conservation of forests, or on desertification, for instance (e.g., Cronon 1983). Neither absentee owners nor short-term tenants care much whether land is used so as to ensure its future usability. The very poor, with no surplus in man-made capital, must use up their natural capital to survive today or they won't be around tomorrow to worry about what is left (Foy and Daly 1989). If the economic pie is cut in such a way that most workers cannot buy the products of their own labor, there will not be much of an economy. There are efficient allocations of resources at any number of different balances in their distribution; the proper distribution cannot be decided on economic or engineering grounds alone (Norgaard 1991).

One can extend this argument to equity between nations, as well as within them. First, industrial countries are often major consumers of developing countries' natural resources. Now that tropical forests are becoming scarce, the North is raising a hue and cry, telling the South not to cuts its trees because the North needs them for a greenhouse gas sink and a supply of genetic resources for multinational drug and seed companies. Eco-development also attempts to incorporate the cultural equity concerns raised in the various schools of deep ecology. Greater recognition is given to indigenous knowledge and experience in the management of human-ecosystem interactions. Using Eco-Development principles, ecologically sound common property regimes would be maintained and perhaps replicated (Berkes 1989; Bromley and Cernea 1989).

Ecologizing Trade Regimes. Differences between the environmental standards of trading nations have had many deleterious effects on the environment as well as complicating international business, such as motivating the migration of polluting industries. They have also made it possible for consumers in industrial countries to continue to make disproportionate contributions to resource depletion and environmental degradation in the world through the products they import while living under the illusion that someone else was responsible because the damage occurred far away (e.g., South Americans burning down the rainforests to raise beef or coca, or Southeast Asians logging their forests for export to Japan). "Free trade agreements" may exacerbate environmental problems in some countries, and in fact environmental concerns are supposed to be the one issue that can override free trade policies between European Community countries after 1992.

New national legislation has been proposed in the United States to compel transnational corporations to conform their foreign production, service, and disposal operations to the environmental protection and resource conservation standards of whichever nation, their home base or their foreign hosts, are stricter. Such an approach would signal a dramatic change in international environmental law. The United States' Foreign Corrupt Practices Act (FCPA) is one potential model. It could be argued, however, that this would be an "imperialistic" extension of the United States' legalistic Environmental Protection approach that would infringe on the sovereignty of other nations to regulate business within their borders as they see fit.

A new economic argument for limitations on international trade has been offered by Herman Daly and John Cobb in their book *For The Common Good* (1989, Ch. 11). They discuss the principle of comparative advantage, its use in the promotion of free trade, and the resultant impacts on environment and community. Comparative advantage has long been assumed to lead to mutual benefit from trade. Daly and Cobb argue that since the basic assumption underlying comparative advantage, the international immobility of capital, is not valid in the modern world, absolute advantage (profitability) rather than comparative advantage governs investment decisions, to the widespread detriment of workers, communities, and the environment of the disadvantaged nation.[9] The rich get richer, and the poor get poorer.

The conditions leading to the Global Convention on Transboundary Movement of Hazardous Wastes can be seen as a case for this argument. International trade in hazardous wastes due to the appearance of "comparative advantage" was in the not-so-long run detrimental to the interests of the "importing" communities. The national internalization of the costs of producing wastes is the only truly equitable solution, and even if it costs more in the short term, it will lead to more rapid changes in production technologies that result in cleaner development, possibly worldwide.

Eco-Logic for Development: Beyond Trade-Offs to Synergy

It is easy to think of environmental management simply as a remedial cost, and therefore to focus on trade-offs between different resource allocations. However, there are great economic and social benefits, not just environmental or aesthetic ones, that would accrue from the types of sophisticated symbioses between ecosystems and economies that a re-definition of development along the lines of Eco-Development would help to promote.

For example, one of the major factors contributing to the "economic miracles" of post-war West Germany and Japan is that fact that they were forced to completely rebuild their economic infrastructures with new, state-of-the-art technological production systems and innovative ways of organizing the social (human) factors of production. While the

United States had almost no serious economic competition in the first couple decades after the war because its production systems had not been destroyed, its industries eventually suffered in the newly competitive world marketplace of the 1970s and 1980s. This was at least in part because the technological and social aspects of its production systems were inefficient and outdated (Passmore and Sherwood 1978; Piore and Sabel 1984). Paradoxically, one frequently hears the claim today that investing in energy efficiency for the sake of environmental protection will make the United States less competitive! It is no accident that the most economically efficient economies of today's world are among the most energetically efficient ones (Colby 1990c).

It is quite likely that in restructuring socio-technical systems of production along the lines of Eco-Development, new "eco-technologies" will bring comparative advantages that will help to make those economies that are quickest and most effective at undertaking it more competitive and prosperous in the long run rather than less so. Taiwan and Singapore are examples of newly industrialized nations which, like Japan, have been spurred by increasingly stiff environmental regulations due to severe pollution problems at home and, as a result, are finding expanding export markets for environment-cleaning exports ("Growth Can Be Green" 1989).

High technology is not the only path to new "green exports"; markets are also growing for ecologically sound agricultural products whose harvest does not cause degradation in the first place (e.g., agro-ecosystems including "green manure" and vegetative barriers to control water flow and soil erosion in Central America and India (Bunch 1985; see also the discussion of forests and extractive reserves below). Many of the eco-technologies described by Mitsch and Jørgensen (1989) involve using or copying natural ecosystems to perform functions we have previously used mechanical construction and/or chemical processes to accomplish—sludge disposal, wastewater recycling, the creation of integrated fishponds and man-made wetlands, etc. Examples where developing countries have pioneered ecological engineering include biogas production and the treatment/utilization of wastewater in China (Mitsch and Jørgensen 1989) and integrated experiments on rural agro-industrial system design in Brazil and China (Sachs and Silk 1988).

In sum, it is possible that some developing countries might be able to "leapfrog" over the cosmetic but expensive Environmental Protection phase of environmental management and development to a much more efficient and sustainable, as well as self-defined, path of Eco-Development. The following section will discuss the implications of some of these principles of Eco-Development for policies aimed at responding to global change, with special reference to the needs of developing countries.

Implications for Policy Response to Global Change from Developing Countries' Perspectives

Macro-Strategic Options

We have discussed the political, economic, and social context of global change (the "fractured global order") and the importance of the conceptual framework(s) one brings to thinking about the issue. There are three fundamental strategic options for responding to the threat of global climate change, and they can be directly linked to respective paradigms of the relationship between environmental management and development: do nothing now, and adapt to change as needed if it happens (e.g., Frontier Economics and Environmental Protection); postpone change by introducing the easier, "no regrets" reforms, such as energy efficiency (Resource Management); and make a more aggressive attempt to minimize or prevent global climate change by promoting strong criteria for redesigning economies to ensure compatibility with ecosystem functions (Eco-Development).

Strategic Mechanisms

Three basic mechanisms for intervention to implement a chosen macro-strategy will be discussed: regulation, tradable permits, and environmental taxation. All three require unprecedented international cooperation, in the form of new agreements and possibly new institutions (see Part Four of the volume).

Regulation.   There has been a movement in the past decade to lionize the virtues of the private sector and castigate the state/government as a brake on development. This too is a simplification, especially when it comes to environmental management and planning for the future vis a vis climate change. It is well known that there is no such thing as a perfectly functioning market. Another politically unpopular truism would be that there is no such thing as free trade. Societies have norms that regulate markets—and trade—in myriad ways, whether they are codified in law or not:

Put simply, governments need to do less in those areas where markets work, or can be made to work, reasonably well. At the same time governments need to do more in those areas where markets alone cannot be relied upon. Government intervention to protect the environment is necessary for sustainable development. In addition to air and water pollution, sustained development is threatened by the depletion of forests, soil, village ponds, and pastures. Appropriate policies include proper pricing of resources, clearer property rights and resource ownership, taxes and controls on pollution, and investment in production alternatives. . . . Market reforms can also help to protect the environment. But specific environmental actions are needed (World Bank 1991, 9).

The German experience in mandating technological change to reduce acid rain has proven to be far less costly than economists' predictions, and far more time-efficient than their favored market mechanisms (Schärer 1990). Industry sometimes does prefer regulation to economic measures. No clear alternatives to the trade ban on chlorofluorocarbons (CFCs) in the updated Montreal Protocol (Benedick 1991) or the Hazardous Wastes Convention have been found to deal with the free-rider problem. Some mechanism for harmonizing (without simply watering down) national environmental regulations is required. In many circumstances, direct resource management policies that integrate social costs and imperatives are needed.

Tradable Emissions Permits. Tradable emissions (pollution) permits are a preferred tool of Resource Management that are derived from the "polluter pays" principle and aimed at capturing market forces for more efficient environmental management. Unfortunately, such permits do not adequately incorporate ecological uncertainty and social equity issues. They not only create a market for "bads"; they also create new property regimes, as in the right to pollute. Once new property rights have been created (a politically very sticky allocation problem in its own right), they are very difficult to take away (Knetsch and Sinden 1984; Knetsch

1989). But given the extreme uncertainties involved in calculating sustainable levels of pollution or even resource harvests (Walters 1986), it is likely that permit levels would need to be changed further down the road. The common suggestion for dealing with this, annual auctions of permits, would create an extremely uncertain business climate, making it even more difficult for businesses to plan for the long term. Futures markets for permits might reduce this problem. It is likely, however, that tradable permits would be the most expensive approach to administer and enforce because of the need for intensive monitoring and regulation of the trading market. They would be extremely difficult to use in most developing countries.

Environmental Taxes.   Gradually ecologizing tax codes can be revenue neutral (if desired) by decreasing taxes on activities that should be encouraged—labor (especially in the lower income brackets), saving, investing, recycling resources, increasing efficiency, protecting ecosystem functions, etc.—while simultaneously increasing taxes on activities we want to discourage, such as resource extraction, polluting activities, the creation of waste in packaging, etc. These "eco-taxes" can be thought of as "global commons users' fees." They can be implemented in a way that is not socially regressive either intranationally or internationally (see Table 5.2; Colby 1990b). Implementation and enforcement are far simpler than for tradable permits (via prices), and thus eco-taxes are more appropriate for developing countries. The main difficulty, besides the idea of new taxes in general, is the uncertainty over the price elasticity of the discouraged activities—how much reduction would occur for a given price increase. Table 5.3 compares the pros and cons of tradable permits versus eco-taxes.

Key Problem Areas

Population
The population boom in developing countries is again attracting the attention of the Resource Managers from the industrial countries. Population is a vital issue for sustainable development. If developing countries' populations continue to grow, the pressure on their ecosystems

Table 5.2   International Indexing Suggestions for Greenhouse Gas Taxes

---

In general, *all* greenhouse gases (CO_2, CFCs, CH_4, N_2O, etc.) should be indexed according to their relative heat-trapping potential per molecule.

The resulting taxes on energy sources (fossil fuels and renewables) should then be subindexed according to their carbon dioxide-equivalent release per unit of usable energy obtained.

Provide tax relief for low-income people whose energy consumption is inelastic and who can least afford the increased cost. For instance, the standard income tax deduction should be raised considerably so that the energy-greenhouse gas tax serves its purpose as a consumption disincentive without unduly penalizing the poor. In effect, this would give everyone a right to use a certain amount of energy for subsistence purposes unpenalized.

CO_2, CFCs, and possibly other greenhouse gas taxes could be indexed according to a nation's past and current contributions to the accumulation of climate-changing gases (a higher percentage meaning a higher tax rate).

An alternative would be to index according to a nation's percentage of current annual total (global) emissions (a higher percentage meaning a higher tax rate).

Another alternative is indexing according to national per capita emissions.

Any greenhouse gas taxes should be introduced gradually, with preannounced schedules by which they would increase and a preannounced date for review of the success of the program and reassessment of the need for further emissions reductions in the light of new information.

Source: Colby 1990b.

and renewable resources, already severe in many cases, will get worse. If their per capita energy use also grows, as currently expected (needed), their greenhouse gas emissions will mushroom (see "Energy" below, and Chapters 1 and 2). Care must be taken with using the per-capita criterion in allocating emissions permits or indexing taxes so as not to create a disincentive for countries to reduce population growth.

In addition, northern resource managers should remember that population is only one third of an equation: It is population size times per capita consumption that determines the biophysical scale of an economy—a population's overall affect on the environment—not just population size by itself (Daly 1989). Choice of technology plays a major role in determining per capita consumption. Currently, one average person from an industrial country consumes up to fifty times as much material and energy as an average person from a developing country.

Table 5.3 Tradable Permits versus Environmental Taxes: Some Pros and Cons

	Pros	Cons
Tradable permits	Maximize efficiency across aggregate economy (equalize marginal costs of emissions reductions). Set absolute emissions limits (and sometimes resource consumption) while still providing incentives to emit/use less. Increase cost-sharing possibilities. Very good for reallocating property rights that have already been formally distributed but are inefficiently used (e.g., distribution of water from agriculture to cities for domestic use).	Highest administrative costs, reduced net efficiency gains. Uncertainty over ecologically sustainable levels and decreased flexibility to adjust for new knowledge due to formalization of property regimes. How to distribute initial quotas? Inter- and intra-national equity issue; might penalize those who've already become cleaner or haven't had an opportunity to develop yet. Yearly auctions would create an uncertain business climate. Market in bads, with potential for hoarding, monopolization, etc.—also reduces efficiency.
Environmental taxes	Simpler (less costly) to administer. More flexible adjustment due to new knowledge. Not subject to uncertainty over sustainable levels, so more dynamic. Continuous incentive to improve both input and output sides of production/consumption. More options to steer entire economy in ecological directions while reducing perverse steering effects. Greater equity; coalition building for global environmental issues; trust fund for redistribution to poor/clean technologies transfer. Less disruptive—can be implemented gradually to allow planning/reduce shock.	No absolute limits (but we don't know what these should be anyway). Equal per-unit cost for pollution, but unequal marginal costs of reductions in emissions. Uncertainty about sufficient price signals needed to encourage direct investment in clean technologies, which is more efficient. More radical change; perhaps more difficult politically.

Source: Colby 1990b.

Energy

Current projections show fossil energy consumption in developing countries mushrooming perhaps as much as tenfold in the next few decades to fuel the five- to ten-fold expansion of their economies that was calculated by the Brundtland Commission (WCED 1987) as necessary to support their expanding populations. At current rates of conversion of energy into economic output, this is very likely impossible for economic, ecological, and purely physical reasons; a 1990 World Bank study estimated that meeting such power needs via conventional centralized stations would require an annual investment of $100 billion, only a fraction of which is available. Moreover, such a capital-intensive route requires what most of these countries have least of (capital) and needs the least what they have most of (labor).

Nevertheless, it is a pernicious myth that combating the greenhouse effect will require great grim sacrifice (Meadows 1989). Improving environmental management and efficiency doesn't necessarily sacrifice the economy or jobs; there is evidence that it in fact creates more jobs (Bezdek, Wendling, and Jones 1989) and improves international competitiveness. There are some trade-offs, but, even more important, there are also a lot of synergetic benefits. It is no accident that the two most robust economies of the 1980s—Japan and West Germany—are among the most energetically efficient advanced economies and have the highest consumer prices for fossil fuels.

Least-cost energy planning techniques have shown that energy services can be obtained much less expensively by investing in efficiency and conservation than in new generating capacity, while also avoiding pollution clean-up expenses ("negawatts" are more valuable than megawatts). By becoming much more efficient, developing economies should be able to develop with much less than the projected growth in the throughput of energy and greenhouse gases. Many of the new, cleaner, and more efficient technologies—motors, appliances, and, perhaps especially, small biogas turbines, photovoltaics, hydrogen, and wind-power—are particularly suitable to developing countries where they have more sunlight that can be captured directly or through photosynthesis and where alternative technologies face less competition from large established centralized power grids. There is a potentially huge market there for more efficient, clean technologies.

Forestry

Conventional agriculture and livestock husbandry on ex-tropical forest land are often unsustainable. The logic of frontier economics has long held that the "jungle" is not productive enough to support significant numbers of people with a high quality of life. But new archaeological research is indicating that the Amazon forest did support sizable sophisticated cultures before the arrival of Europeans (Gibbons 1990). Economically productive land does not have to be a pasture, a planted field, a resort, an industrial park, or a residential suburb thereof. The remnants of those ancient cultures, plus groups of "rubber tappers" who moved into the forest a century ago, are beginning to show that the forest can be more valuable economically left standing than cut, with all its vital ecological-cum-economic functions maintained in the bargain (Peters, Gentry, and Mendelsohn 1989).

The idea of "extractive reserves" in which the seasonal products of plants (e.g., fruits, nuts, resins) rather than the plants themselves are extracted and where the natural fauna of the forest (e.g., iguanas) can be husbanded with equal if not greater output than cattle (Cohn 1989) is emerging as a new model for development in tropical forests. It is better adapted to the ecosystem in which it occurs, takes advantage of local cultural knowledge of that ecosystem's functions and productivity, and thereby allows diverse cultures to survive, develop, and in fact prosper.

Coordinating National and International Responses

It is obvious that an unprecedented degree of international cooperation and coordination is required for dealing with global change. Economic incentives and policies, legal regulations, financing, technology development and diffusion,[10] and intellectual property rights are among the fields over each of which there are numerous positions and interests in need of resolution. This would be daunting on the scale of a single nation focusing only on the concerns of those generations alive today. Now we must include all nations in various stages of development—"established industrial" countries (OECD), "newly industrial" countries (e.g., the "Pacific tigers"), "transforming" (ex-Soviet Bloc) countries, "stirring giants" (e.g., China, Brazil, India, Indonesia, Mexico, and Nigeria), and the "have nots" (Fri and Cooper 1991)—and weigh the interests of future generations perhaps equally with the interests of the present generation (Chapters 9, 10 and 11 of this book). Innovation along all of these fronts will be required (see Part IV of this volume).

Financing

Although many of the efficient, clean technologies will save more in the long run, they tend to cost more up front than old ones. One cannot and should not expect developing countries to pay higher costs in the near term to import these technologies to combat a problem they did not create while foregoing less expensive domestic alternatives or foregoing development itself. The industrial countries that caused the problem must be willing to provide softer loans and grants (more patient capital) to bridge the gaps in costs between cleaner, more efficient technologies and the conventional alternatives, as they recently agreed to do for CFC replacements. The new Global Environment Facility administered by the World Bank, UNDP, and UNEP is a step in the right direction, but much more will be needed. This facility also runs the risks of compartmentalization: Because it exists, more traditional financing mechanisms may feel less pressure to change business as usual. See Part IV of this volume for more information.

Incentive Allocation/Indexing

Tradable emissions permits and emissions taxes have already been mentioned as two mechanisms to support such financing requirements. Debt-for-nature swaps are another, but they may have inherent limits in scope and are subject to the ecological imperialism charge. Permits and taxes raise complicated questions of allocation and/or indexing between nations that will require great skill—and will—to negotiate (e.g., Richards 1991). We have suggested some guidelines for equitable tax indexing, though the distribution of the proceeds will be complicated nonetheless. Similar principles could guide emissions allocation if that mechanism were used, but the initial allocation formulas are still likely to be very divisive politically.

Technology and Intellectual Property

The accelerating pace and increasing complexity (not to mention cost) of scientific advances and technological change pose very difficult challenges for many developing nations (see Chapter 8 in this volume). It is hard enough to promote the development of needed technologies; it is still harder to ensure their diffusion to the people who need them most, particularly if they cannot afford to buy them. Industrial corporations are loath to give away expensive technologies they have developed with great effort.[11] Unfortunately, they are also often loath to pay fair prices for the basic resources that go into those technologies, supplies of which they want the developing countries to conserve for them (e.g., the genetic resources of tropical biodiversity). The seriousness of global change—in terms of climate as well as biological resources—gives both the private and public sectors of technology-rich nations a special opportunity and a particular responsibility to engage in an ambitious, well-conceived program for transferring appropriate environmental knowledge and equipment to less technologically endowed nations (Fri and Cooper 1991).

Conclusions: The Challenge for Strategic Leadership

Many of the actions and policies that would adjust the world economy to slow down climate change also make sense on other grounds, providing multiple benefits. They would make economies more efficient, provide new jobs, and make implementing countries more competitive internationally (by becoming more efficient and by becoming the first to produce the products that others need and want to buy) while reducing pollution, conserving resources for future generations, and enabling a more equitable distribution of wealth for present populations. These conditions make development more effective and more lasting.

The challenges of responding to the risks of global climate change can be seen as opportunities for creating a sustainable, desirable future, not just as threats to the status quo or current ill-conceived visions of the future. Clearly, finding the capital to make the required investments in re-tooling and developing a new infrastructure is a challenge. But finding the courage needed to do so may be the ultimate challenge for everyone.

Notes

Dr. Francisco Sagasti is currently senior advisor in the External Affairs and Policy Review Departments of The World Bank in Washington, D.C. Dr. Michael Colby is founder of Eco-Development Associates, an international network of consultants in strategic planning, environmental management, and sustainable development based in Arlington, Virginia.

1. See chapters 9, 10, and 11 of this volume on the economic and legal aspects of intergenerational equity.

2. See chapter 2 of this book on the physical dimensions of global change.

3. As documented with various pertinent statistics in chapters 1 and 2 of this volume.

4. Parts III and IV of this book will address some of the important steps in social and institutional evolution required by this new context.

5. *San Jose Mercury News,* reprinted in the September 1989 issue of *Scientific American;* and Agarwal and Narain 1990, among many places.

6. An example that has already been put in practice is the use of "carbon offsets," whereby a North American power utility plants fast-growing trees in Central America as a sink for the carbon dioxide it will release over its thirty-year lifetime of burning fossil fuels. This raises questions such as What happens to the peasants who might have used that land to feed their families? Was a natural, biologically rich, and diverse forest cut down to make way for the faster-growing trees? What other environmental problems does this exacerbate? What happens if the seedlings die (surely the power plant won't be de-commissioned)?

7. See chapter 4 and Part IV of this volume.

8. See chapter 10 of this book on legal aspects and chapters 9 and 11 on the economics of intergenerational equity.

9. Such prominent economists as Adam Smith, David Ricardo, and John Maynard Keynes saw the immobility of capital to be in the community and national interest (Daly and Cobb 1989, 209–216). Only when national boundaries play an important role, such as limiting capital and labor mobility, does the principle of comparative advantage replace that of absolute advantage.

10. See chapter 7 of this volume on science and technology as sources of change.

11. See chapter 6 on multinational corporations and the global environment.

6

Multinational Corporations and the Global Environment

Nazli Choucri

Private firms operating across national boundaries have dominated international business since the end of the last century. Changing international realities—politics, economics, technology, finance, and investments—have forced changes in both the structure and function of cross-border enterprises. Formidable growth in the scale and scope of corporate activities has accentuated both the *need* for change and the *consequences* of change. The rapid growth in the global economy since World War II has created unprecedented alterations in ways of doing business. Now environmental factors generate new challenges for corporate activities, shaping new constraints as well as new opportunities.

This chapter (1) illustrates the environmental implications of corporate activities worldwide; (2) draws upon the theory of lateral pressure to illustrate some generic features of the growth, expansion, and increased complexities of international investments and related transactions; (3) examines corporate activities in three industries—oil, chemicals, and construction—to show environment/technology linkages and the emergence of awareness, patterns of response, and consequences for corporate planning; and (4) presents a synthesis of new imperatives for corporate environmental linkages in terms of theory, policy, and practice.

Generation and Transmission of Effluents

The uneven growth and development of states—while often supporting economic and political stability—also contribute to a wide range of effluents that threaten environmental balances (see chapters 1 and 3 of this volume). International investments and transactions (trade, overseas production, and associated activities) that are undertaken primarily for economic purposes also serve as conduits for effluence generation, energy use, excessive carbon emission, and the transmission of pollution and other forms of environmental degradation throughout the global system—all in the course of pursuing legitimate economic and business transactions. Environmental problems of this sort are traced largely to normal economic activities—exploration, extraction, production, distribution, consumption, and disposal of both wastes and products (Walter 1982, 23; North 1990).

Agents and Institutions
The generation of effluence and depletion mechanisms is basically inadvertent in that it is a concomitant material aspect of the development paradoxes that shape development-environment relationships (see chapter 3 of this volume). These paradoxes may assume different characteristics (forms and types) as different institutions serve as agents in the distribution of effluents. As used here, *agents* refers to technologies (mechanical and organizational knowledge, skills, designs, tools, machines, and processes) and to resources and goods (fuels, herbicides, insecticides, and other materials) that are environmentally depleting and/or degrading. Such effects can, and normally do, occur at both ends of relevant international transactions (i.e., exports, imports, and associated exchanges.) And in this context, by *institutions* we mean the organized collectivities (formal and informal), characterized by regular and routinized forms of activities, rules, and regulations, through which the actions generating international transactions (production, trade, investment, consumption, etc.) are undertaken.

Earlier we referred to the border-crossing activities and interests of states, and their populations and institutions, as manifestations of lateral pressure (Choucri and North 1975, 16–19 and 1989, 294–297; North 1990, 21–24). The political map of the world—a fairly simple and conventional device delineating "sovereign" entities—may help us to visualize some of the critical issues that are involved when agents of pollution and other forms of degradation cross borders that jurisdictionally separate one country from another. This reference to the map is to remind ourselves that the depletion-pollution-degradation process normally occurs, to some degree, on both ends of every transaction.

Environmental effects on the exporting country include resource depletions and degradation associated with product manufacturing, use, and
transportation, whereas environmental impacts on the importing country
are likely to be attributable to consumption, storage, domestic distribution, and end-use effects.

Are these issues matters of trade, of investment, of finance? Should
they be viewed in the context of trade theory, investment theory, management, and finance? As Rubin and Graham (1982, 62) properly note,
there are tight interconnections among both the empirical realities and
the theoretical perspectives. Compelling stories about the human sources
of transmission and distribution of depleting and degrading agents into
and across the international system are already becoming legendary.
Illustrative is the exporting worldwide—including, sometimes especially,
to developing countries—by the United States and other industrialized
countries of three prominent categories of enterprise: chemical plants
producing highly toxic goods (asbestos, herbicides, pesticides, plastics,
and so on); those involving heavy metals (copper, lead, and the like);
and automobiles, trucks, tractors, and other machines that generate
highly polluting emissions (UNCTC 1988, 230). Also relevant is the
adoption by the newly industrialized countries of the same type of
polluting and environmentally detrimental industries learned or imported from the industrial countries.

These processes are becoming considerably more complex as a function of the worldwide process of growth. As countries grow and develop,
their total international transactions tend to expand. "Third-World
multinationals" refers to the corporate structure and activities that originate in developing countries. There is every indication that multinational
corporations (MNCs) from developing countries behave more or less
like those of industrial countries (Lall 1983, 2–18). As global producers,
distributors, and consumers—from all national origins—multinational
companies play powerful roles both in the creation of environment as
an issue and in the shaping of investment-environment relationships.

Environmental Accounting
While accepted forms of environmental accounting are still at early
stages of formalization, it is clear that environmental costs are exacted
with most economic exchanges and that some form of measuring device

must be developed. When extensive patterns of effluence and emission are generated locally, these impacts may aggregate and translate into global-level impacts. Under such circumstances the environmental accounting problem becomes more complex, especially in the absence of an operational view of the global system that integrates natural and social systems and reflects ecological decision systems (see figure 1.6).

Clearly, there are numerous difficulties associated with efforts to analyze relationships between the exporting and importing of resources, goods, and services (the purview of economics and finance) and the agents of environmental depletion and degradation that in effect are inadvertently generated and transmitted from one country to another as trade and financial exchanges occur. The quality of environmental data available from many countries is generally much more suspect than that of the economic data, thereby making it all the more difficult to consider specific causal relationships.[1] Underlying this venture, however, is the extraordinary difficulty confronted by anyone who attempts to assign cost/benefit values to the actions of depleting and degrading agents and to balance these values against the economic costs and benefits with which they are associated. (Even more compelling are the implications for intertemporal and intergenerational effects. See Chapters 10, 11, 12 of this volume).

Multinationals in Practice

We begin with three facts: (1) Since multinational corporations conduct most of the world's economic activity, they are the major environmental actors as producers, managers, and distributors of goods and services; (2) by necessity, these firms are generic polluters as they engage in a wide range of hazardous and pollution-intensive activities; and (3) corporations are also central to the "solution." Global enterprises are the major technological innovators, the institutions of technological change, and agents of commercialization for new technology (both organizational and mechanical) worldwide.

Because MNCs serve as the major innovators and the transmitters of technology, as well as often being both the sources and the diffusers of commercial ideas, their involvement in the active search for solutions is necessary—but certainly not sufficient (Schmidheiny 1992). Their actions and strategies are crucial in determining the overall dimensions of the environmental landscape or, as we point out later on, the environmental aspects of "organizational fields" for firms (Fligstein 1990). It is the corporations—their technological capabilities and edge—that will shape new modes of economic performance.

Scale and Scope

Clearly, industrial countries account for almost all multinational corporate activities overall. In 1980–81 the United States accounted for 28 percent of all direct investment abroad, in contrast to 65 percent in 1965–69. At the same time Japan's share grew from 2 percent to 7.5 percent of all global investments. Concurrently the largest magnet for corporate investments outside the country of origin is the United States. Together the United States and Canada were recipients of 25 percent of the stock of foreign investment in 1980. That figure was roughly similar to that of all the developing countries hosting foreign investors (which stands at 27 percent). Europe as a whole also attracted about 27 percent of the global total. While the shifts in corporate activities worldwide may have important market implications, environmental consequences remain unaffected by who pollutes. However, how much they pollute and why are obviously not neutral with respect to global economic, political, or legislative effects, as will be noted further along.

Recurrent debates as to whether the size of firms affects external investments remain unresolved. On the one hand is the argument that firm size is a significant factor; on the other is the argument that size does not affect the propensity to expand. Based on a survey of six hundred international firms with sales over $1 billion, the United Nations Center on Transnational Corporations (UNCTC) found no relationship between firm size and share of foreign sales relative to total sales. But there is a threshold: Attaining a certain size is necessary before external expansion can take place; once that threshold is reached, size is no longer a significant factor.

By contrast, there is a significant positive relationship between the size of a firm's domestic market and the propensity to expand outward: The larger the size of the domestic market, the greater the constraints on further expansion of size and the higher the propensity for expansion. In lateral pressure terms, expansion processes are shaped by the con-

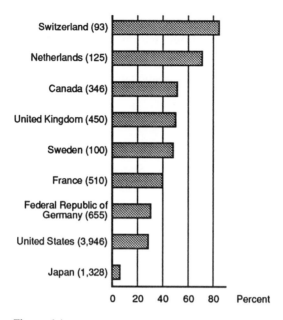

Figure 6.1
TNCs in the "Billion Dollar Club": relationship between foreign content of sales and size of home market, 1985
Source: U.N. Center on Transnational Corporations 1988.
Note: The amounts given in parentheses are the figures in billions of U.S. dollars for the country's GDP in 1985.

straints on activities within national boundaries, which in turn propel extended expansion abroad. The UNCTC analyses appear to confirm such a hypothesis with respect to firms in the "billion-dollar club" (UNCTC 1988, 35). The smaller the size of the domestic market relative to the capabilities and output of the firm, the greater the propensity for outward expansion. A rough indication of this relationship is seen in figure 6.1.

Environmental and Empirical Evidence
Industrial activity anywhere and of any sort has the inevitable conse-quence of generating effluents of various types. According to the UNCTC five trends appear noteworthy with respect to the environmental con-sequences of international investments (UNCTC 1985, 47). Together they may provide a sense of broad tendencies upon which more specific

hypotheses can be framed about the interrelationship between corporate and environmental action.

First, there are notable differences between sources of process pollution and those of product pollution—each with distinct patterns, agents, and effects. Process pollution problems are generated by the chemical, iron and steel, petroleum, and pulp and paper industries, among others; product polluters are concentrated in the agriculture, automotive, and tobacco industries, among others. Such differences have been determined on the basis of patterns of pollution control expenditures that point to significant distinctions between product and process pollution.

Second, there is a notable trend in the shift in location—away from developed countries and toward developing countries. This trend toward production in developing countries is due mainly to growth and industrialization in developing countries rather than to conscious efforts by private agents to relocate activities of corporations in industrial countries beyond their own borders and into jurisdictions of developing countries. The proposition that relocation of activities is driven by avoidance of environmental legislation has not been refuted by recent trends (Walter 1975, 129–30).

Third, shifts in the location of investments and corporate activities overseas cannot to date be attributed solely (or even largely) to differences in national environmental policies. It is reasonable to expect that the more stringent the environmental policies may be in a particular country, the less attractive that country may appear to be to foreign direct investors. As of 1988, however, "pollution havens" had not yet become apparent.

Fourth, shifts in corporate location of activities—from more to less developed nations—are notably attributable to policies of site exclusion rather than to movement to world environmental legislation. Then, although shifts in location to exclude industrial activities from densely populated areas are evident in Japan, Denmark, and Holland, among others, site exclusion in itself is a significant determinant of the lateral mobility of industrial activities. The greater the exclusion based on site characteristics, the greater is the likelihood that industries will relocate elsewhere. There appear to be no consistent patterns indicating where "elsewhere" is likely to be.

Fifth, shifts in responsibility for pollution management are becoming increasingly apparent. The locus of final responsibility appears to move away from corporate headquarters, or operations in the home country, and toward overseas locations. This means that more responsibility is assumed in the field—in the host country and on site—rather than in corporate management at the center. This type of shift is reinforced by the trends in developing countries for national operations to assume greater control of their own industrial and manufacturing sectors rather than to perpetuate reliance on foreign companies.

Environmental Investments
In practice, to date the multinational corporations have shown little environmental responsiveness. With regard to the United States, table 6.1 shows the historical trends of domestic and overseas pollution control expenditures in relation to total capital spending over a ten-year period, 1970–1980, by U.S. firms with foreign operations, by industry. This was an important decade as it pre-dated the surge of environmental legislation in the United States. In 1980, gross annual costs for pollution abatement as a share of the total value of shipments was negligible. Based on U.S. Bureau of Census data, the average for all industries stood at .0043, a rather minuscule share. Of the nineteen major industries examined, primary metal industries showed the largest percentage of pollution expenditures relative to the value of shipments, namely .0125 percent (UNCTC 1988, 100). All of this reflects the marginal corporate response to environmental degradation due to industrial activities.

More recent trends in investments for the control of pollution by U.S. industry are presented in table 6.2. Expenditures targeted to the control of air, water, and solid waste pollution (as percentages of capital spending) are presented in table 6.3. There is evidence of increased environmental responsiveness.

Environmental Legislation
The nature of the relationship between environmental laws and investment patterns remains ambiguous. The strengthening of environmental laws does not in itself determine investment patterns, nor does it serve

Table 6.1 Domestic and overseas pollution control expenditures as a percentage of total capital spending by United States firms with foreign operations

Industry[1]	1970 U.S.	1970 O/S	1971 U.S.	1971 O/S	1972 U.S.	1972 O/S	1973 U.S.	1973 O/S	1974 U.S.	1974 O/S	1975 U.S.[2]	1975 O/S	1976 U.S.[2]	1976 O/S	1977 U.S.[2,3]	1977 O/S	1980 U.S.[2,3]	1980 O/S[4]
Iron and steel and nonferrous metals	9.2	1.8	11.5	2.0	13.8	9.5	14.8	3.7	18.8	10.3	21.2	9.8	20.4	15.0	15.4	8.5	12.2	—
Fabricated metals	4.3	2.5	7.1	1.8	7.3	2.3	7.2	2.8	5.6	3.0	10.8	4.9	11.2	4.4	6.2	3.0	17.2	—
Stone, clay, and glass	6.4	3.0	13.2	7.2	9.6	4.5	9.0	6.5	17.5	2.9	17.6	8.0	9.0	4.6	7.5	5.0	9.7	—
Chemicals	4.9	5.8	8.2	3.2	10.9	7.6	10.2	5.9	7.3	3.9	8.9	5.3	12.3	5.5	11.8	6.1	13.5	—
Paper and pulp	9.3	4.2	20.6	8.7	23.3	8.1	22.8	6.2	16.6	9.7	21.9	11.8	25.7	7.9	25.8	5.7	13.0	—
Rubber	5.3	3.2	5.4	1.1	5.8	1.1	6.2	3.1	3.0	2.2	4.8	2.6	5.7	2.7	7.3	3.9	8.3	—
Petroleum	6.0	1.9	9.0	5.6	10.7	8.3	12.7	7.4	7.2	5.3	12.8	5.1	7.5	4.5	6.4	4.7	6.6	—
Mining	6.1	3.5	2.8	2.1	5.1	1.5	7.6	4.8	7.0	1.8	8.2	3.9	6.9	6.2	7.0	12.7	5.2	—

Source: United Nations Center on Transnational Corporations 1985. Data reprinted with permission.
U.S.: domestic operations.
O/S: overseas operations.
1. Industry classification is the same for the United States and overseas, except as follows: iron and steel plus nonferrous metals for the United States (primary metals for overseas); fabricated metals for the United States (fabricated metals plus instruments for overseas).
2. Including solid waste.
3. Planned.
4. No data available.

Table 6.2   Investments for pollution control (millions of dollars)

	Level			Percentage change	
	1988[1]	1989	1990	1989	1990
Blast furnaces, steel works	520	725	542	39.4	−25.3
Nonferrous metals	210	213	212	1.2	0.0
Electrical machinery	200	202	203	1.1	0.4
Nonelectrical machinery	180	169	170	−6.1	0.9
Motor vehicles	370	679	802	83.6	18.1
Aircraft	110	133	131	20.6	−1.3
Fabricated metals	130	169	196	30.0	15.8
Stone, clay, and glass	200	265	274	32.7	3.2
Other durables[2]	440	440	435	0.0	−1.2
TOTAL DURABLES	2,360	2,995	2,965	26.9	−1.0
Chemicals	1,260	1,361	1,375	8.0	1.0
Paper	720	1,172	1,144	62.8	−2.4
Rubber and plastic	60	73	78	21.9	6.8
Petroleum	1,650	1,619	1,662	−1.9	2.7
Food including beverages	320	287	287	−10.4	0.1
Textiles	30	40	40	34.0	−1.7
Other nondurables	100	200	200	100.0	0.0
TOTAL NONDURABLES	4,140	4,752	4,785	14.8	0.7
ALL MANUFACTURING	6,510	7,747	7,750	19.0	0.0
Mining	180	178	178	−0.9	−0.5
Railroads	20	20	20	1.6	0.0
Air transportation	30	28	29	−8.0	5.8
Other transportation	50	44	88	−12.6	100.3
Electric utilities	1,710	2,154	2,329	26.0	8.1
Gas and other utilities	40	40	40	−0.2	−0.6
Communications[3]	100	101	102	0.8	1.2
Trade and services[4]	380	363	362	−4.4	−0.3
ALL NONMANUFACTURING	2,510	2,928	3,147	16.7	7.5
ALL BUSINESS	9,020	10,676	10,897	18.4	2.1

1. U.S. Department of Commerce, Bureau of Economic Analysis estimates.
2. Includes instruments.
3. Consists of communication; construction; social services and membership organizations; and forestry, fisheries, and agricultural services.
4. Consists of wholesale and retail trade; finance and insurance; personal business services (excluding construction); and real estate.
Source: DRI/McGraw-Hill, *22nd Annual DRI/McGraw-Hill Survey of Pollution Control Expenditures, 1988–90,* Lexington, Mass.: Data Resources, Inc., August 1989, p. 2.

as a clear deterrent in corporate strategy. This is especially noteworthy with respect to the United States. Some of the strongest environmental laws are in the United States, and this country ranks first as a recipient of foreign direct investment. This case in itself belies simple linkages between environmental laws and the location of foreign direct investments.

The record of U.S. environmental legislation presented in figure 6.2 reveals the trends in such legislation. A stable (flat) response to emerging environmental problems is evident throughout the better part of one hundred years. From 1895 to 1960 or so, environmental regulations were modest in number and scope. The surge after 1960 was accompanied by a shift in content—from technical controls to financial allocations. The Superfund Amendment of 1990, the last datum in table 6.4, was largely financial relative to the contents of earlier legislation. The surge of regulation over the past twenty years shows little sign of abatement.

By tracing legislative patterns over time—and shifts in the contents of legislation—we can infer, even predict, the types of business responses to these trends. We are likely to see more rather than less regulation of private activities at all levels. Multinational firms as well as national, state, and local enterprises will be faced with more rather than less pressure for compliance with environmental regulations and legislation. In chapter 12 we will see how similar the patterns are with respect to the scale, content, and scope of multilateral environmental treaties binding sovereign states. In chapter 15 these trends are presented in graphic form; here we note only the increasing salience of environmental legislation for corporate management.

Multinationals in Theory

Theoretical perspectives of the institutions of the multinational corporations (MNCs) can be viewed roughly through three disciplinary lenses, each reflecting different intellectual and policy traditions: (1) international relations analyses in political science, (2) market analyses in economics, and (3) organizational theory in business and management. They all reflect inherent biases, and none effectively addresses environment-investment linkages.

Table 6.3 Pollution control expenditures: air, water, and solid waste (percent of capital spending)

	1988			1989			1990		
	Air	Water	Solid waste	Air	Water	Solid waste	Air	Water	Solid waste
Blast furnaces, steel works	4.7	3.1	0.8	7.8	3.0	0.9	6.7	2.5	0.5
Nonferrous metals	4.0	2.5	1.1	3.5	2.2	1.0	3.5	2.2	1.0
Electrical machinery	0.3	0.6	0.2	0.3	0.5	0.2	0.3	0.6	0.2
Nonelectrical machinery	0.2	0.7	0.2	0.2	0.7	0.2	0.2	0.7	0.2
Motor vehicles	1.1	1.4	0.9	0.9	2.3	1.2	0.5	3.1	1.2
Aircraft	0.6	1.5	1.2	0.6	1.5	1.2	0.6	1.5	1.2
Fabricated metals	0.7	2.3	0.2	0.7	2.6	0.3	0.7	2.7	0.3
Stone, clay and glass	1.7	1.1	2.5	2.0	1.6	2.5	2.3	1.6	2.6
Other durables	1.5	1.1	0.7	0.9	1.3	0.4	0.8	1.3	0.5
TOTAL DURABLES	1.2	1.2	0.6	1.2	1.4	0.6	1.1	1.6	0.6
Chemicals	2.3	2.7	1.6	2.2	2.3	1.3	2.2	2.3	1.3
Paper	3.8	0.9	1.6	5.0	0.8	1.6	4.9	0.8	1.4
Rubber and plastic	0.8	0.8	0.3	0.5	1.1	0.1	0.8	1.2	0.2
Petroleum	3.0	4.2	1.1	3.2	4.3	1.0	3.0	4.2	1.0
Food including beverages	0.8	1.4	0.2	0.6	1.0	0.2	0.7	1.1	0.2
Textiles	0.9	0.5	0.5	0.9	0.4	0.4	1.3	0.6	0.6
Other nondurables	0.2	0.3	0.1	0.2	0.7	0.0	0.2	0.8	0.1
TOTAL NONDURABLES	1.9	2.0	0.9	2.1	1.8	0.8	2.1	1.9	0.8
ALL MANUFACTURING	1.6	1.6	0.7	1.7	1.6	0.7	1.6	1.7	0.7
Mining	0.6	0.6	0.2	0.5	0.6	0.2	0.5	0.6	0.2

Table 6.3 (continued)

	1988			1989			1990		
	Air	Water	Solid waste	Air	Water	Solid waste	Air	Water	Solid waste
Railroads	0.0	0.3	0.0	0.0	0.2	0.0	0.0	0.3	0.0
Air transportation	0.0	0.0	0.3	0.0	0.0	0.3	0.0	0.0	0.3
Other transportation	0.1	0.6	0.0	0.1	0.4	0.0	0.1	0.5	0.0
Electric utilities	3.5	1.2	0.7	3.5	1.3	1.6	3.5	1.7	1.6
Gas and other utilities	0.1	0.2	0.0	0.1	0.2	0.0	0.1	0.2	0.0
Communications	0.1	0.1	0.1	0.1	0.1	0.1	0.1	0.1	0.1
Trade and services	0.1	0.0	0.1	0.1	0.0	0.1	0.1	0.0	0.1
ALL NONMANUFACTURING	0.4	0.2	0.1	0.4	0.2	0.2	0.4	0.2	0.2
ALL BUSINESS	0.8	0.7	0.4	0.9	0.7	0.4	0.8	0.8	0.4

Source: DRI/McGraw-Hill, *22nd Annual DRI/McGraw-Hill Survey of Pollution Control Expenditures, 1988–90*, Lexington, Mass.: Data Resources, Inc., August 1989, p. 7.

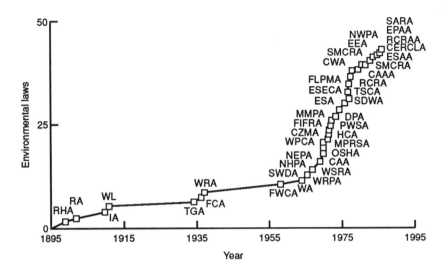

Figure 6.2
Growth in the number of U.S. environmental laws
Note: Acronyms refer to specific laws.
Source: Nazli Choucri. "The Technology Frontier: Responses to Environmental Challenges," prepared for the Dräger Foundation Malente Symposium IX: The ECO-Nomic Revolution—Challenge and Opportunity for the 21st Century, Timmendorfer Strand, Germany, November 18–20, 1991, reprinted with permission from *Technology and Environment,* edited by Jesse H. Ausubel and Hedy E. Sladovich, 1989. Washington, D.C.: National Academy Press, p. 101. Copyright by the National Academy of Sciences.

Environment in MNC Theory

Remarkable as it may be, to date case studies of the multinationals from any of the three perspectives make no reference to environmental or ecological factors or to the environmental consequences—intended and/ or unintended—of corporate activities and investments. However, even if dominant theories of corporate behavior do not address environmental effects, they may help highlight environmental implications. For example, product-cycle theory might imply that developing countries may host greater pollution since they operate with older technology. So, too, the environmental factor might become central to a firm's "organizational field" (defined below), and to its priorities for research and development (R&D).

Table 6.4   Growth in the number of U.S. environmental laws

1899 River and Harbors Act (RHA)	1974 Deepwater Port Act (DPA)
1902 Reclamation Act (RA)	1974 Safe Drinking Water Act
1910 Insecticide Act (IA)	(SDWA)
1911 Weeks Law (WL)	1974 Energy Supply and Environ-
1934 Taylor Graring Act (TGA)	mental Coordination Act
1937 Flood Control Act (FCA)	(ESECA)
1937 Wildlife Restoration Act	1976 Toxic Substances Control Act
(WRA)	(TSCA)
1958 Fish and Wildlife Coordination	1976 Federal Land Policy and Man-
Act (FWCA)	agement Act (FLPMA)
1964 Wilderness Act (WA)	1976 Resource Conservation and Re-
1965 Solid Waste Disposal Act	covery Act (RCRA)
(SWDA)	1977 Clean Air Act Amendments
1965 Water Resources Planning Act	(CAAA)
(WRPA)	1977 Clean Water Act (CWA)
1966 National Historic Preservation	1977 Surface Mining Control and
Act (NHPA)	Reclamation Act (SMCRA)
1968 Wild and Scenic Rivers Act	1977 Soil and Water Resources Con-
(WSRA)	servation Act (SWRCA)
1969 National Environmental Policy	1978 Endangered Species Act
Act (NEPA)	Amendments (ESAA)
1970 Clean Air Act (CAA)	1978 Environmental Education Act
1970 Occupational Safety and	(EEA)
Health Act (OSHA)	1980 Comprehensive Environmental
1972 Water Pollution Control Act	Response Compensation and
(WPCA)	Liability Act (CERCLA)
1972 Marine Protection, Research	1982 Nuclear Waste Policy Act
and Sanctuaries Act (MPRSA)	(NWPA)
1972 Coastal Zone Management Act	1984 Resource Conservation and Re-
(CZMA)	covery Act Amendments
1972 Home Control Act (HCA)	(RCRAA)
1972 Federal Insecticide, Fungicide	1984 Environmental Programs and
and Rodenticide Act (FIFRA)	Assistance Act (EPAA)
1972 Parks and Waterways Safety	1986 Safe Drinking Water Act
Act (PWSA)	Amendments (SDWAA)
1972 Marine Mammal Protection	1986 Superfund Amendments and
Act (MMPA)	Reorganization Act (SARA)
1973 Endangered Species Act (ESA)	

Note: This is an illustrative, not an exhaustive, list. Nonetheless, the basic trend is confirmed when we consider the *entire* record of environmental legislation in the United States.

Source: Reprinted with permission from *Technology and Environment*, edited by Jesse H. Ausubel and Hedy E. Sladovich, 1989. Washington, D.C.: National Academy Press, p. 101. Copyright by the National Academy of Sciences.

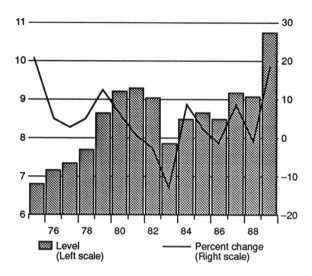

Figure 6.3
Pollution control spending by all businesses (billions of dollars)
Source: DRI/McGraw-Hill, *22nd Annual DRI/McGraw-Hill Survey of Pollution Control Expenditures, 1988–90,* Lexington, Mass.: Data Resources, Inc., August 1989, p. 1.

It is a historical and intellectual fact that theories of multinational corporate behavior have evolved devoid of an environmental context or concern for environmental variables. It is as if private investments and actions crossing borders are neutral relative to environmental, ecological, or atmospheric impacts—at any level of social organization. While this type of "environmental neutrality" is prominent in most forms of social theory, it is especially stark for theories addressing collectivities known as multinational corporations. To date *all* theories of the MNCs ignore the impacts of corporate activities on the natural environment and on ecological balances. Indeed, the term "natural environment" is never cited in the indexes of volumes on the multinational corporations or international political economy. (See Gilpin 1987 as an example of this typical omission.)

States and Trade

The conventional state-centric focus in the study of international relations has all but obscured international realities of contending and powerful privately owned enterprises that can exert strong influences on national behavior. Private actors tend to shape international relations in ways that cannot be well explained by resorting to theories of the state, or of international systems, or of international processes. While this limitation is generally recognized, few theoretical efforts have been made to address the practice of foreign direct investment. Efforts in that direction are largely descriptive syntheses of ideas on corporate behavior (Gilpin 1987) or case studies of contending power and influence (Rodman 1988). The MNCs are either completely ignored (in state-centric power-based theories) or are assumed to play a nebulous role at best (such as the erosion of sovereignty), to interact with internal political forces (such as colluding with anti-democratic local forces at the expense of the national economy), or to serve as instruments for enhancing dominant relations (as in structural theories of imperialism, control, and domination).

Nonetheless, at least three propositions about MNC activities emerge in the international relations literature:

First, multinationals are seen as both instruments of state behavior and as institutions shaping state actions. The influence goes both ways, so to speak, but the conditions and relative weight of directionality are underspecified. Does state legislation affect corporate action (Ausubel and Victor 1992)? Or, alternatively, can and do corporations influence state actions and legislation to "level the playing field" (Choucri 1990)?

Second, in parts of the international relations literature, multinational corporations are seen as dominating and shaping the politics of "host" countries (Gilpin 1975, 1987). A wide range of influences are posited, as are types of resulting conflicts between foreign corporations and national governments serving as hosts.

Third, multinationals shape tastes, influence preferences, and effectively create demands for new products and new processes. In this way the MNCs affect the demand side of the economic equation in host countries and help to leverage their own responses by shaping the supply side as well.

Environmental factors associated with these three factors—as causes, intervening variables, or consequences—are entirely ignored in the international relations literature.

Trade and Markets

In economics the analysis of corporate behavior is grounded in trade theory. In principle, the practice of free trade versus exchange through operations of multinational firms are posed as logical alternatives in response to market conditions. In the best of all possible worlds, free trade generates optimal exchanges for all parties. Only when exporting or licensing is not feasible (for a variety of reasons) is the decision of a firm to move production outside the jurisdiction of the country of origin considered to be a reasoned alternative. When trade is not possible, principles of efficiency are safeguarded by changes in the form, modes, and location of production (Rugman, Lecraw, and Booth 1985, 97–98). Production overseas becomes the best among the options for reaching and shaping foreign markets.

In a world of perfect competition—with differentiated markets, no barriers to trade, and costless information—trade is the only type of international exchange (Kindleberger 1969, 13).[2] From an economic perspective, however, multinationals are important because they respond to market imperfections that impede free trade, and therefore they are important economic actors. Kindleberger's work, popularly known as the "market imperfections" paradigm—focusing on imperfections in goods markets, factor markets, economies of scale, and government-imposed regulations—has been further extended and modified (Calvet 1981) in recognition of an increasingly globalized marketplace.

In this connection, MNC activities are viewed as a response to market imperfections due to four sets of factors: (1) market conditions, (2) government regulations, (3) market structure, and (4) market failure. Calvet noted that the justification and logic for the expansion of production and operations overseas increase from (1) to (4), as does the justification for the horizontal expansion of firms' organizations (Calvet 1981, 44). It is this "push" logic that provides the connection between economic and market-based theories of the firm and lateral pressure theory discussed below.

Markets and Firms

The managerial perspective of MNC behavior shifts the focus from the market and its properties to the firm and its characteristics. Recent work on industrial organizations extends the initial focus on MNCs as economic actors by addressing their role in a global marketplace. But the shift is limited; MNCs' behavior is viewed in terms of reducing transaction costs rather than as being the result of other, more complex, mixes of incentives and pressures. And the industrial organization perspective does not consider the consequences of MNCs' responses to new incentives and pressures. Among the most pressing of such new factors are environmental considerations.

Traditionally the management literature has centered on three concerns: one was the product life-cycle type of explanation, introduced and popularized by Vernon (1966); a second emphasized the responsiveness of MNCs to local conditions—customs, legislation, tastes, and market structures; and a third focused on scale and scope in the manufacturing and distribution of goods. (See Porter 1990 and Bartlett and Ghoshal 1989). Increasingly all three concerns have been converging, largely due to the effects of either new technology and technology competition or increased competitiveness, in all aspects of the global marketplace. Recent developments in both the theory and practice of MNCs' organization and behavior focus on explanations of the type, location, and scale of activities at each stage of the production process. The notion of the globalization of business reflects this convergence and the development of new directions of corporate theory (Lessard and Antonelli 1990). But to date environmental concerns have remained singularly ignored.

Viewed from the perspective of the firm rather than the state or the market both the globalization of business and increased organizational complexity are generally explained by three requisites for effective performance—appropriability, internalization, and diversification.[3] Together they indicate why a firm chooses production (of the whole or parts of its output) outside its jurisdiction of origin rather than the use of contractual mechanisms, such as licensing or other arrangements. They are also central to explanations of firms' performance and success. To the extent that firms respond to market opportunities and/or constraints due to greater awareness of and concern for environmental factors, it will be by anchoring behavior to environment in terms of these three core requisites. Indeed, from a broader environmental perspective, these three factors can be framed as useful policy guides from which managers can plan for environmental factors and incorporate them into their decisions.

Decisions and Environment

Actions and decisions of individual managers determine corporate policy within the firm's "organizational field" (Fligstein 1990, 5–11). Organizational fields, defined as the policy spaces within which decisions are made about the actions of firms, are in practice determined by characteristic features of product lines, industry, and the sizes of firm. Certainly, managers (and analysts) appreciate that corporate activities cannot be seen independently of the state. The state provides "rules of the game"; and the state is a central actor, both directly and indirectly. As a direct actor the state undertakes investments—influences state-firm interactions, invests in activities, holds title and ownership, and intervenes in economic activity (i.e., via taxes and public expenditures, and so on). As an indirect actor, the state shapes the political atmosphere and the business climate.

A firm's organizational field is conditioned by the state and by "the rules by which actions in the economy are carried out" (Fligstein 1990, 8). As Fligstein notes (1990, 12), "The *state* and the *organizational field* constitute the firm's external unit." The power struggle within firms determines who controls and makes key decisions on behalf of the firm. The power struggle *between* firms determines which firms (activities, industries, economic sectors) expand, how they expand, and by how much.

Environment and environmental legislation are increasingly becoming relevant to corporate behavior, interjecting new constraints that may significantly affect both the nature and the conduct of multinational firms. Following the scheme in figure 1.1 of chapter 1, environmental legislation has become a set of parameters within which firms are expected to operate. Firms can influence these rules, or they can bypass them—or firms can move their operations to other locations that are less environmentally stringent. In the United States, for example, environmental legislation illustrates the dominance of environmental controls. These controls are stronger in the United States than in other industrial countries, and they may be forerunners of trends worldwide.

It seems increasingly evident that corporate organization and activities are becoming increasingly influenced by environmental awareness, legislation, and litigation. Since the role of knowledge and technology (both organizational and mechanical) is critical to all industries and to their operations, environment bears on considerations pertaining to appropriability, internalization, and diversification.

Lateral Pressure Theory of Corporate Behavior

When applied to the entity of the multinational corporation, the theory of lateral pressure appears to be best positioned to clarify the environmental effects of both operations and applications and thus to remedy the weaknesses of the other theoretical perspectives. Designed explicitly to integrate political, economic, and environmental factors (see chapter 1), the theory provides a "handle" on the interconnections of human decisions and ecological systems (chapter 3). Further in this chapter we refine the lateral pressure theory to address interactions between private and public entities—i.e., firms and states.

Corporate theory highlights an underlying logic of lateral pressure: the propensity of firms from one country to engage in direct outward investment—placing production outside its own national jurisdictions—will vary according to the level of development and technological capabilities of that country (Dunning 1988, 14). And as indicated earlier, different profiles of states are associated with different types and forms of effluents. The same is generally applicable to the entity of the multinational corporation (Fligstein 1990).

Growth and Expansion: Linkages between States and Firms
In specifying the sources and potential consequences of the process of growth and expansion, the theory of lateral pressure is highly complementary to paradigms of corporate growth and expansion (based on Dunning, 1988, among others). From a developmental and transformative perspective, the corporate investment and expansion paths follow a logic analogous to that embedded in the profiles of states (see chapter 3). In Dunning's terms—and consistent with the theory of lateral pressure—a sequence of corporate expansion outside the borders of the country of origin can be framed both historically and developmentally.

The sequence of corporate expansion yields a dynamic approach to corporate growth and expansion that is related to the level of growth and development of the home state. Where the theory of lateral pressure is considerably more explicit than the conventional business and management literature is with regard to the *direction* of corporate expansion and the *consequences* in terms of differentials in growth and development (and capabilities) between the home and host countries.

Drawing on MNC theory and refining lateral pressure theory, the corporate-state growth and development process can be roughly characterized in sequential terms as follows. In early phases of development a country will generate neither outward nor inward MNC activity due largely to limited technology and limited institutional and organizational capability. In essence, poor countries such as those at the bottom of Group I (in terms of the groupings in chapter 3) would have limited MNC activities, if any. As investments are made domestically and the infrastructure improves, the demand in the home country for intermediate products will grow, leading to the expansion of import demand and to active imports. The ability to import is of course contingent on the ability to pay for imports. Hence exports are essential. This is a generic aspect of the development process. However, at that stage of development the agents and organizations responsible for undertaking and for initiating trade will normally be of small size, with limited capacity. So institutional capacities will be limited, as will the ability to engage in external transactions.

Over time, as a country grows and develops sufficiently so as to generate its own corporate activities and extend its own sovereign ownership over production and operations, external activities become more common. At this stage the choice of investment and related economic activities and transactions will reflect economic conditions in the home country (prevailing factor endowments) and its profile characteristics (interactions of technology, resources, and population attributes). Gradually, through its private organizations, a country generates a wide range of cross-border activities and may even become a net outward investor.

The number of listed domestic companies for countries with "developed" and "emergent" markets in table 6.5 shows very clearly the development of internal entrepreneurial capability—with allowance made for differences in the quality and type of capability. The more "developed" the country is, the greater are its entrepreneurial capabilities. Each of the country names is preceded by a profile designation as defined in chapter 3.

Further reference to some empirical observations will shed light on the dynamic processes described here, their implications for state profiles, and expansion and external investments as a function of growth and development. Table 6.6 shows a rough distribution of equity market indicators by developed and developing countries and their profiles.

Table 6.7 shows market capitalization by country (and profile type) from 1980 to 1988. "Developed" markets are distinguished from "emerging" markets. (This designation applies to size of equity markets, not level of economic development.)

As the advantages that led to a country's initial outward expansion become more firm-specific and less country-specific and the organizational responses of the firm become more firm-oriented and less home country-based, domestic constraints become less binding and corporate activities abroad expand significantly. Accordingly, it will be the capabilities of the firms, rather than the power and profile of the home country, that will become more significant in shaping corporate activities abroad. This means that the initial conditions that lead to the growth and development of the country in the first place and generate corporate expansion abroad improve and shape the development and expansion of the firm itself. Concurrently, then, corporations make investment decisions on the basis of broader regional, international, and even global market and strategic bases rather than on the basis of economic conditions, endowments, or the profile of the home country.

In this process the dynamics of lateral pressure of the "sovereign" entity may support and reinforce the processes of expansion abroad for corporate entities. The firm's strategies become nearly independent of the state's profile, although synergism may remain. If the level and composition of environmental discharges are concomitant with the type and extent of economic activity, then economic expansions mean the spreading of effluence. At each stage of this developmental process, the country-corporate relationship changes in type and form. Whether there is an empirical relationship between state profile (Groups I–IV), on the one hand, and stages in the development of MNC activities abroad as related to the developmental level of the home country, on the other, is

Table 6.5 Number of listed domestic companies by profile group

	1980	1981	1982	1983	1984	1985	1986	1987	1988
Developed markets									
Group I:									
South Africa	481	475	470	464	470	462	536	838	754
Group IV:									
New Zealand	—	—	—	—	237	317	339	361	297
Group V:									
Australia	1,007	982	931	930	1,009	1,028	1,162	1,528	1,303
Canada	731	771	759	808	943	912	1,034	1,147	1,145
Finland	—	—	—	48	52	50	49	49	66
Norway	117	109	112	113	140	156	149	146	130
Sweden	103	130	138	145	159	164	154	157	142
United States	6,251	6,866	6,834	7,722	7,977	8,022	8,403	7,181	6,680
Group VI:									
Austria	66	63	62	62	63	64	74	69	74
Belgium	225	218	212	204	197	192	191	192	186
Denmark	218	219	206	211	231	243	274	277	291
France	586	568	535	518	504	489	482	650	646
Germany	459	456	450	442	449	472	492	507	609
Hong Kong	137	158	—	—	—	260	248	276	282
Israel	117	136	212	258	269	267	255	283	265
Italy	134	132	138	138	143	147	184	204	211
Japan	1,402	1,412	1,427	1,441	1,444	1,829	2,549	1,912	1,571
Netherlands	214	202	216	215	263	232	219	248	232
Singapore	103	103	112	118	121	122	122	127	132
Spain	496	490	448	394	375	334	312	327	368

Table 6.5 (continued)

	1980	1981	1982	1983	1984	1985	1986	1987	1988
Switzerland	118	121	119	120	121	131	145	166	161
United Kingdom	2,655	2,403	2,279	2,217	2,171	2,116	2,106	2,135	2,054
Not ranked:									
Luxembourg	74	80	88	102	134	175	253	364	422
Subtotal	15,694	16,094	15,748	16,670	17,472	18,184	19,732	19,144	18,021
Emerging markets									
Group I:									
Argentina	278	263	248	238	236	227	217	206	186
Brazil (São Paulo)	426	477	493	505	522	541	592	590	589
Chile	265	242	212	214	208	228	231	209	205
Colombia	—	—	193	196	180	102	99	96	86
Jordan	71	72	86	95	103	104	103	101	106
Kenya	54	55	54	54	54	54	53	53	55
Peru	103	133	144	150	157	159	177	197	236
Venezuela	—	—	98	—	116	108	108	110	60
Zimbabwe	62	62	62	60	56	55	53	53	53
Group II:									
Bangladesh	22	25	28	43	56	69	78	85	101
Costa Rica	13	19	24	32	41	51	61	71	76
Egypt (Cairo)	62	64	112	154	258	317	387	430	483[1]
India	2,265	2,114	3,358	3,118	3,882	4,344	5,460	6,017	6,000
Indonesia	6	8	14	19	24	24	24	24	24
Malaysia	182	187	194	204	217	222	223	232	238
Mexico	271	240	215	174	178	188	166	233	255

Table 6.5 (continued)

	1980	1981	1982	1983	1984	1985	1986	1987	1988
Morocco	78	75	78	76	77	76	76	76	71
Nigeria	90	93	93	93	93	96	99	100	102
Pakistan	314	311	326	327	347	362	361	379	404
Philippines	195	190	200	208	149	138	130	138	141
Sri Lanka	—	—	—	—	—	171	171	168	176
Thailand	77	80	81	88	96	100	98	125	141
Turkey	—	—	314	—	373	—	40	50	50
Group III:									
Jamaica	38	36	35	36	36	38	40	43	44
Korea	352	343	334	328	336	342	355	389	502
Portugal	25	23	26	25	23	24	40	143	171
Group VI:									
Greece	116	111	113	113	114	114	114	116	119
Kuwait	—	—	—	—	—	55	70	64	65
Trinidad and Tobago	—	29	34	34	36	36	33	33	33
Not ranked:									
Taiwan, China	102	107	113	119	123	127	130	141	163
Subtotal	5,467	5,359	7,282	6,703	8,091	8,472	9,789	10,672	10,935
Total	21,161	21,453	23,030	23,373	25,563	26,656	29,521	29,816	28,956

1. Estimated.
— Not available.
Source: Adapted from International Financial Corporation 1988.
Note: Profile groups are defined in chapter 3. See table 3.1.

Table 6.6   Equity market indicators, 1987, by profile group

Country	Average market capitalization[1] (percentage of GNP)	Turnover ratio[2] (percentage of average capitalization)	Number of companies listed
High-income countries			
Group V:			
United States	58	93	7,181
Group VI:			
Japan	92	93	1,912
United Kingdom	80	72	2,135
Germany, Federal Republic of	21	161	507
France	18	56	650
Developing countries			
Group I:			
Jordan	60	15	101
Chile	27	11	209
Zimbabwe	10	4	53
Brazil	7	43	590
Venezuela	7	8	110
Colombia	3	8	96
Argentina	2	16	206
Group II:			
Mexico	8	159	233
Philippines	7	62	138
India	6[3]	19[c]	6,017
Malaysia	58	23	232
Nigeria	4	1	100
Pakistan	5	9	379
Thailand	9	114	125
Turkey	3	6	50
Group III:			
Korea, Republic of	19	111	389
Portugal	10	44	143
Group VI:			
Greece	5	18	116

1. Average market capitalization is a five-quarter average of the total value of listed stock, based on year-end data, assuming constant exponential growth during the year.
2. Turnover ratio is the value of stocks actually traded as a percentage of the average total value of listed stock.
3. Bombay exchange.
Source: Adapted from World Bank 1989, 109.
Note: Profile groups are defined in chapter 3. See table 3.1.

Table 6.7 Market capitalization (in millions of U.S. dollars) by profile group

	1980	1981	1982	1983	1984	1985	1986	1987	1988
Developed markets									
Group I:									
South Africa	100,000	74,900	77,800	82,800	53,400	55,439	102,652	128,663	126,094
Group IV:									
New Zealand	—	—	—	—	6,161	8,761	22,215	15,713	13,200
Group V:									
Australia	59,700	54,400	41,500	59,600	49,900	59,877	94,035	171,783	183,483
Canada	118,300	105,500	103,500	140,600	134,700	147,000	166,300	218,817	241,880
Finland	—	—	2,759	4,134	4,167	5,855	11,692	19,698	30,179
Norway	3,190	3,334	2,396	4,597	5,793	10,063	10,122	11,818	14,332
Sweden	12,900	17,200	18,600	30,200	25,700	37,296	63,354	70,564	100,083
United States	1,448,120	1,333,385	1,520,167	1,898,063	1,862,945	2,324,646	2,636,598	2,588,890	2,793,816
Group VI:									
Austria	2,000	1,600	1,500	1,500	1,500	4,602	6,656	7,411	8,862
Belgium	10,000	8,400	8,500	10,800	12,200	20,871	37,337	41,377	58,920
Denmark	5,400	6,200	5,500	10,600	7,600	15,096	16,284	20,181	30,178
France	54,600	38,100	28,000	38,100	41,100	79,000	149,500	172,048	244,833
Germany	71,700	62,600	68,900	82,600	78,400	183,765	257,677	213,166	251,777
Hong Kong	39,104	38,912	18,784	17,095	23,602	34,504	53,789	54,088	74,377
Israel	4,828	6,972	15,894	5,083	6,120	7,626	9,884	12,001	5,458
Italy	25,300	24,000	19,900	20,900	25,700	58,502	140,249	119,559	135,428
Japan	370,200	417,000	417,400	545,800	644,400	910,000	1,841,785	2,802,956	3,816,908
Netherlands	29,300	23,000	25,700	33,700	31,100	59,363	83,714	86,240	113,565
Singapore	24,418	34,808	31,235	15,525	12,247	11,069	16,620	17,931	24,049
Spain	16,600	16,700	11,100	10,900	13,200	19,000	48,922	71,188	174,869
Switzerland	37,600	35,200	36,800	42,500	38,700	90,000	132,400	128,527	140,527
United Kingdom	205,200	180,600	196,200	225,800	242,700	328,000	439,500	680,721	771,206
Unranked:									
Luxembourg	4,017	4,457	4,686	5,799	6,648	12,658	26,163	38,277	44,808
Subtotal	2,642,477	2,487,268	2,656,821	3,286,696	3,327,983	4,482,993	6,367,448	7,691,617	9,398,832

Table 6.7 (continued)

	1980	1981	1982	1983	1984	1985	1986	1987	1988
Emerging markets									
Group I:									
Argentina	3,864	2,056	974	1,386	1,171	2,037	1,591	1,519	2,025
Brazil (São Paulo)	9,160	12,598	10,249	15,102	28,995	42,768	42,096	16,900	32,149
Chile	9,400	7,050	4,395	2,599	2,106	2,012	4,062	5,341	6,849
Colombia	1,605	1,399	1,322	857	762	416	822	1,255	1,145
Jordan	1,605	2,457	2,845	2,713	2,188	2,454	2,839	2,643	2,233
Kenya	—	—	—	—	—	—	—	—	24
Peru	—	1,371	685	546	397	760	2,322	831	—
Venezuela	2,657	2,441	2,415	2,792	—	1,128	1,510	2,278	1,816
Zimbabwe	1,456	—	355	265	176	360	410	718	774
Group II:									
Bangladesh	27	30	34	48	87	113	186	405	430
Costa Rica	—	—	—	118	156	195	246	—	—
Egypt (Cairo)	246	216	654	1,106	1,691	1,382	1,716	1,826	1,760
India (Bombay)	7,585	11,802[1]	11,497[1]	8,510	8,018	14,364	13,588	14,480	23,845
Indonesia	63	74	144	101	85	117	81	68	253
Malaysia	12,395	15,300	13,903	22,798	19,401	16,229	15,065	18,531	23,318
Mexico	12,994	10,100	1,719	3,004	3,661	4,163	5,952	12,674	23,630
Nigeria	3,118	3,010	1,458	2,970	3,191	2,743	1,112	974	960
Pakistan	643	864	877	1,126	1,226	1,370	1,710	1,960	2,460
Morocco	441	377	292	253	236	255	279	357	446
Philippines	3,478	1,738	1,981	1,389	834	669	2,008	2,948	4,280
Sri Lanka	—	—	—	—	—	365	421	608	471
Thailand	1,206	1,003	1,260	1,488	1,720	1,856	2,878	5,485	8,811
Turkey	477	511	952	968	956	—	935	3,221	1,135
Group III:									
Jamaica	54	127	177	113	142	266	536	631	796

Table 6.7 (continued)

	1980	1981	1982	1983	1984	1985	1986	1987	1988
Korea	3,829	4,224	4,408	4,387	6,223	7,381	13,924	32,905	94,238
Portugal	191	156	92	84	73	192	748	8,857	7,172
Group VI:									
Greece	3,016	2,266	1,923	964	766	765	1,129	4,464	4,285
Kuwait	—	—	—	—	—	—	10,108	14,196	11,836
Trinidad and Tobago	—	1,175	1,357	1,011	843	463	374	388	268
Unranked:									
Taiwan, China	6,082	5,312	5,086	7,599	9,889	10,432	15,367	48,634	120,017
Subtotal	85,592	87,657	71,054	84,297	94,993	115,255	144,015	205,097	377,426
Total	2,728,069	2,574,925	2,727,875	3,370,993	3,422,976	4,598,248	6,511,463	7,896,714	9,776,258

Source: Adapted from International Financial Corporation 1988.
Note: Profile groups are defined in chapter 3. See table 3.1.1.
1. Estimated.
— Not available.

a question with both theoretical and empirical properties. At issue are the interactions between firm and state as their respective capabilities expand.

Refining the theory of lateral pressure to explain the activities of multinational enterprises, it appears plausible that propensity to invest outward or to host the investment of others inside national jurisdictions generates a range of hypotheses about the propensity of private actors to extend their commercial activities worldwide. These bear upon the generic elements of lateral pressure inherent in the behavior of firms within their organizational fields. These elements have led to the altered global business context, creating new corporate strategies and structures, and to new modes of interaction between government and business.

Among the most compelling propositions drawn from the logic indicated above regarding trade, market, importation, and foreign operations are those pertaining to the "master variables," economic conditions, and institutional capability. Here we extract from the literature four types of propositions. These are as follows: (1) The higher the level of technology in a country, the larger will be the skilled population and the greater will be the propensities for outward corporate activities; (2) the greater the extent of market failures at home, the greater will be the propensities for expansion abroad; (3) the more advanced the level of technology in a society, the greater will be the trend toward the establishment of specialized capabilities; (4) the more specialized functions and capabilities that are developed in a country, the more likely it is that corporate activities will expand beyond the country's borders; and (5) the more developed the institutional capabilities in a country are (such as the prevailing contractual systems), the greater will be the ease with which propensities for expansion abroad are realized.

In table 6.8 is shown the distribution of direct investment flows—both outward and inward—in two paths of time, 1975–80 and 1981–85. Instructive in these figures is the complexity of directionality: Flows go "both ways," but "outward" flows are greater for developed countries and "inward" flows are greater for developing countries. These patterns are entirely consistent with what would be predicted by the lateral pressure theory of corporate activities.

These patterns are further confirmed in tables 6.9 and 6.10, which show the distribution of the world stock of direct investment abroad—outward and inward—at five points in time from 1960 to 1984. Again, both the industrial countries and their profile designations are indicated.

Implicit in these propositions are the dynamics of growth and development (of size and capability, of adjustments and of transformations). The more developed these processes are, the greater are the propensities for corporate expansion abroad. Central to these processes is the fact that patterns of industrial activities and the locations of activities represent, and are congruent with, the prevailing profile groupings. As a generic process, growth entails economic expansion; both growth and expansion have the inevitable and invariable concomitant effect of generating effluence. By contrast, development—defined in terms of profile transformation—allows for the potential decoupling of the historical trends in effluence-growth linkages and draws attention to both the need for and prospects of effluence-minimizing technological changes and institutional adjustments. Such prospects would then serve to break the close, and to date seemingly inevitable, link between growth and environmental degradation.

From a corporate perspective these connections point to the importance of incorporating (and internalizing) environmental strategy and pollution abatement policies and expenditures within the frame of the firm's own strategic mandate. As more firms—from a wider range of countries—extend their behavior laterally, the need for internalization of environmental factors increases. (This issue is discussed below.) In the longer run this reorientation of corporate concerns, such as internalizing environmental factors, may be more important by far than efforts to control or directly regulate sources of either process or product pollution.

The Environment in Three Global Industries

This section looks at the environment as a factor in the petroleum, chemical, and construction industries worldwide. These industries have been chosen for analysis here based on four criteria: First, they are central, even essential, to industrial processes everywhere—to the maintenance of industrial capacity and to the growth of new capacity—at all levels of economic development worldwide; second, activities within

Table 6.8 Distribution of international direct investment flows by major source and host countries (percentage share)

	Outward capital flows		Inward capital flows	
	1975–80	1981–85	1975–80	1981–85
All countries*	100.0	100.0	100.0	100.0
Developed countries	*98.8*	*96.6*	*75.5*	*75.2*
Group I:				
South Africa	0.5	0.4	−0.3	0.4
Group IV:				
Canada[1]	5.2	8.8	2.8	−0.5
Australia and New Zealand	0.9	3.0	5.1	4.3
Group V:				
United States[2]	44.2 a)	19.3 a)	25.8	39.5
Group VI:				
Japan[1]	5.7	11.4	0.5	0.7
Europe:	*42.3*	*53.7*	*41.6*	*30.8*
Group V:				
Sweden	1.5	2.3	0.3	0.3
Group VI:				
France[1]	4.9	6.2	7.0	4.5
Germany	8.3	7.7	3.5	2.1
Italy[1]	1.1	3.8	1.9	2.2
Netherlands[1]	7.3	8.6	3.8	2.7
Switzerland	—	2.5	—	1.1
United Kingdom	16.8	19.5	13.1	8.6
Unranked:				
Belgium-Luxembourg[1]	1.4	0.4	4.0	26.8
Other European Countries[1]	0.6	1.2	3.8	2.8
Developing countries[1]	*1.2*	*3.4*	*24.5*	*24.8*

Source: Adapted from U.S. Department of Commerce, International Trade Administration 1988.

*Profile groups are defined in chapter 3. See table 3.1.

1. Outward and inward capital flows for the countries shown, and for a number of other European and developing countries not shown separately, do not include reinvested earnings. Belgium and Luxembourg, Malaysia and Singapore do not identify reinvested earnings on direct investment separately from total investment income. The Netherlands does not collect reinvested earnings data for the banking industry. If reinvested earnings data were available for these countries, their shares would be higher.

2. Net capital inflows from U.S. direct investment in Netherlands Antilles finance affiliates for the years 1977–85 are excluded.

Table 6.9 World stock of direct outward investment abroad by region or major country of origin (billions of U.S. dollars or percentage)

	Amount					Percentage distribution					Average annual rates of growth			
	1960	1967	1973	1980	1984	1960	1967	1973	1980	1984	1960–67	1967–73	1973–80	1980–84
All countries	67.7	112.3	211.1	516.7	698.7	100.0	100.0	100.0	100.0	100.0	7.5	11.1	13.6	3.7
Developed countries	*67.0*	*109.3*	*205.0*	*503.4*	*580.4*	*99.0*	*97.3*	*97.1*	*97.4*	*97.0*	*7.2*	*11.1*	*13.7*	*3.6*
Group I:														
South Africa	1.3	2.0	2.1	5.9	3.6	1.9	1.8	1.0	1.1	0.6	6.3	0.8	15.3	–11.6
Group IV:														
Canada f)	2.5	3.7	7.8	22.6	31.6	3.7	3.3	3.7	4.4	5.3	5.8	13.2	16.4	8.7
Australia and New Zealand	0.2	0.4	1.1	2.6	5.7	0.3	0.4	0.5	0.5	0.9	10.4	18.4	13.1	21.7
Group V:														
United States[1]	31.9	56.6	101.3	220.2	236.6	47.1	50.4	48.0	42.6	39.5	8.5	10.2	11.7	1.8
Group VI:														
Japan[2,7]	0.5	1.5	10.3	19.6	37.9	0.7	1.3	4.9	3.8	6.3	17.0	37.9	9.6	17.9
Europe:	*30.6*	*45.1*	*82.4*	*232.5*	*265.0*	*45.2*	*40.2*	*39.0*	*45.0*	*44.3*	*5.7*	*10.6*	*16.0*	*3.3*
Group V:														
Sweden	0.4	1.7	3.0	7.2	11.0	0.6	1.5	1.4	1.4	1.8	23.0	9.9	13.3	11.2
Group VI:														
France[2]	4.1	6.0	8.8	20.8	31.9	6.1	5.3	4.2	4.0	5.3	5.6	6.6	13.1	11.3
Germany[3]	0.8	3.0	11.9	43.1	46.2	1.2	2.7	5.6	8.3	7.7	20.8	25.4	20.2	1.8
Italy	1.1	2.1	3.2	7.0	11.9	1.6	1.9	1.5	1.4	2.0	9.7	7.3	11.8	14.2
Netherlands[2]	7.0	11.0	15.8	42.4	40.6	10.3	9.8	7.5	8.2	6.8	6.7	6.2	15.1	–1.1
Switzerland[4]	2.3	2.5	7.1	22.4	25.5	3.4	2.2	3.4	4.3	4.2	1.2	19.0	17.8	3.3
United Kingdom[5]	12.4	15.8	27.5	80.7	85.4	18.3	14.1	13.0	15.6	14.3	3.5	9.7	16.6	1.4
Unranked:														
Belgium, Luxembourg[2]	1.3	1.3	1.8	4.8	5.5	1.9	1.2	0.9	0.9	0.9	0.0	5.6	15.0	3.5

Table 6.9 (continued)

	Amount					Percentage distribution					Average annual rates of growth			
	1960	1967	1973	1980	1984	1960	1967	1973	1980	1984	1960–67	1967–73	1973–80	1980–84
Other European countries[2]	1.2	1.7	3.3	4.1	7.0	1.8	1.5	1.6	0.8	1.2	5.1	11.7	3.1	14.3
Developing countries[2,8]	0.7	3.0	6.1	13.3	18.2	1.0	2.7	2.9	2.6	3.0	23.1	12.6	11.8	9.8

Source: Adapted from U.S. Department of Commerce, International Trade Administration 1988.

Note: Profile groups are defined in chapter 3. See table 3.1. Detail may not add to totals because of rounding. Year-end exchange rates were used to convert stocks or stock estimates valued in local currencies or SDRs into U.S. dollars.

1. Data for 1980 and 1984 exclude the negative U.S. direct investment position in the Netherlands Antilles finance industry.

2. Among developed countries, Belgium, France, Luxembourg, several other European countries not shown separately, and Japan do not collect reinvested earnings data. The Netherlands does not collect reinvested earnings data for the banking industry. Also, a number of developing countries do not collect reinvested earnings data. If reinvested earnings were included, the stocks for those countries would be higher.

3. Beginning with 1976 and for subsequent years, data used are "statistics on levels" for both primary and secondary investment as compiled and published by the Deutsche Bundesbank. Data for years prior to 1976 are commonly referred to as "special statistics" published by the Ministry of Economics.

4. Data back to 1960 have been revised by the Union Bank of Switzerland to more accurately reflect its estimates (based on sample data) of Swiss direct investment abroad.

5. Data include banking beginning with 1976. Prior to 1979, investment in insurance companies is for the United States only. Beginning with 1979, data include investment by oil companies, insurance companies, and investment in real estate, all of which were previously excluded.

6. Direct investment abroad by Canadian banks is not included.

7. Beginning with 1976 and for subsequent years, data used are direct investment external assets (which exclude reinvested earnings) as compiled and published by the Bank of Japan. Data for years prior to 1976 are "approvals basis data" from the Ministry of Finance.

8. Stock estimate for developing countries includes adjustment for Kuwait. Outward direct investment flows from Kuwait have been adjusted to 2,253 million SDRs in 1981, 506 million SDRs in 1982, and 659 million SDRs in 1984. The data for Kuwait were adjusted based on U.S. data showing direct investment capital inflows to the United States from Kuwait.

Table 6.10 World stock of direct inward investment abroad by region or major country of origin (billions of U.S. dollars or percentage)

	Amount				Percentage distribution				Average annual rates of growth		
	1967	1973	1980	1984	1967	1973	1980	1984	1967–73	1973–80	1980–84
All countries*	105.4	207.6	490.6	602.6	100.0	100.0	100.0	100.0	11.9	13.1	5.3
Developed countries	*73.2*	*153.7*	*379.9*	*448.7*	*69.4*	*74.0*	*77.4*	*74.4*	*13.2*	*13.8*	*4.2*
Group I:											
South Africa	7.2	8.1	16.4	16.0	6.8	3.9	3.3	2.7	2.0	10.6	−0.1
Group IV:											
Canada	19.2	33.0	51.6	61.9	18.2	15.9	10.5	10.3	9.4	6.6	4.7
Australia, New Zealand	4.9	10.5	15.5	19.0	4.6	5.1	3.2	3.2	13.5	5.7	5.2
Group V:											
United States	9.9	20.6	83.0	164.6	9.4	9.9	16.9	27.3	13.0	22.0	18.7
Group VI:											
Japan[1,2]	0.6	1.6	3.3	4.5	0.6	0.8	0.7	0.7	17.8	10.9	8.1
Europe:	*31.4*	*79.9*	*210.1*	*182.7*	*29.8*	*38.5*	*42.8*	*30.3*	*16.8*	*14.8*	*−3.4*
Group V:											
Sweden	0.5	1.0	1.7	1.2	0.5	0.5	0.3	0.2	12.2	7.9	−8.3
Group VI:											
France[1]	3.0	6.5	21.1	16.0	2.8	3.1	4.3	2.7	13.8	18.3	−6.7
Germany[3]	3.6	13.1	47.9	35.8	3.4	6.3	9.8	5.9	24.0	20.3	−7.0
Italy	2.6	7.8	8.9	9.3	2.5	3.8	1.8	1.5	20.0	1.9	1.1
Netherlands[1]	4.9	7.6	19.2	16.4	4.6	3.7	3.9	2.7	7.6	14.2	−3.9
Switzerland[4]	2.1	4.3	14.3	13.1	2.0	2.1	2.9	2.2	12.7	18.7	−2.2
United Kingdom[5]	7.9	24.1	60.2	47.1	7.5	11.6	12.3	7.8	20.4	14.0	−6.0
Unranked:											
Belgium, Luxembourg[1]	1.4	3.8	8.2	7.3	1.3	1.8	1.7	1.2	18.1	11.6	−2.9

Table 6.10 (continued)

	Amount				Percentage distribution				Average annual rates of growth		
	1967	1973	1980	1984	1967	1973	1980	1984	1967–73	1973–80	1980–84
Other European countries[1]	4.1	8.5	21.2	31.5	3.9	4.1	4.3	5.2	12.9	13.9	10.4
Developing countries[1,6]	32.2	53.9	110.7	153.9	30.6	26.0	22.6	25.5	9.0	10.8	8.6

Source: Adapted from U.S. Department of Commerce, International Trade Administration 1988.

Note: Profile groups are defined in chapter 3. See table 3.1.

Detail may not add to totals because of rounding. Year-end exchange rates were used to convert stocks or stock estimates value in local currencies or SDRs into U.S. dollars.

1. Among developed countries, Belgium, France, Luxembourg, several other European countries not shown separately, and Japan do not collect reinvested earnings data. The Netherlands does not collect reinvested earnings data for the banking industry. Also, a number of developing countries do not collect reinvested earnings data. If reinvested earnings were included, the stocks for those countries would be higher.

2. Beginning with 1976 and for subsequent years, data used are direct investment external liabilities (which exclude reinvested earnings) as compiled and published by the Bank of Japan. Data for years prior to 1976 are "approvals basis data" from the Ministry of Finance.

3. Beginning with 1976 and for subsequent years, data used are "statistics on levels" for both primary and secondary investment as compiled and published by the Deutsche Bundesbank. Data for years prior to 1976 are commonly referred to as "special statistics" published by the Ministry of Economics.

4. Data back to 1960 have been revised by the Union Bank of Switzerland to more accurately reflect its estimates (based on sample data) of Swiss direct investment abroad.

5. Data include banking beginning with 1976. Prior to 1979, investment in insurance companies is for the United States only. Beginning with 1979, data include investment by oil companies, insurance companies, and investment in real estate, all of which were previously excluded.

6. Data for inward direct investment flows to Saudi Arabia as published by the IMF for the years 1979–84 were not used in this table to estimate the stock of inward direct investment in OPEC countries in 1980 or 1984. Instead, these flows were estimated based on outward direct investment flows to Saudi Arabia from major source countries, as compiled from major source country data. Inward direct investment flows to Saudi Arabia were estimated at (in millions of SDRs) 1,662 in 1979; −2,480 in 1980; −317 in 1981; −1 in 1982; 891 in 1983; and 349 in 1984.

each industry entail both process pollution and product pollution at each phase in the respective production process; third, to a large extent these three industries are interdependent, with their respective products and processes contingent on the products and processes of the others; and fourth, all three industries represent ubiquitous processes in the modern era.

Almost overnight, global companies have confronted concerns well beyond the pale of conventional strategic planning—concerns that were certainly not the subject of traditional education in business schools or schools of management. The challenge for the MNCs is not whether to respond to the new business context, but how; it is not whether such action will reshape competition, but how fast and how effectively it will do so. This is true across the board, in all sectors and in all facets of international and, increasingly, global business. To the extent that firms act voluntarily, they will maintain the advantage of being able to choose their responses and identify their options.[4] To the extent that environmental practices become regulated, legislated, and controlled, the companies will find themselves on the defensive and their activities bounded by external conditions.

Constrained by Market Signals: Oil

For a long time the oil industry was insulated from any significant constraint on operations or on policy—either by governments or by private groups. The nearly total absence of environmental codes in overseas exploration and development, let alone transport by ship or land, gave the industry free rein. All that has begun to change. The public at large is now concerned about such mishaps as spills, which are inherent to the transport of oil given prevailing practices. In the United States alone, on the average a spill occurs each day. Reliable worldwide totals of oil and related hazardous spills are difficult to find (Mills and Graves 1986), but the evidence suggests a relative decrease of the total number of spills throughout the decade of the 1980s.

Global oil enterprises will find themselves increasingly engaged in public relations wars with potentially high legislative and regulatory stakes. The hazards to the corporate bottom lines are obvious: Higher environmental standards could well bite into profits. But what are the opportunities associated with this new reality? Exxon, Texaco, and

Chevron, among others, have charged remarkably high environmental costs against profits—a new fact of corporate life. Phillips Petroleum's token donation of $625,000 over five years to preserve wetlands in the Southwest may be illustrative of things to come, with environmental strategies including preventing damage as well as repairing it. And Conoco, a subsidiary of DuPont, recently ordered two double-hull tankers designed to reduce the extent of oil spills. These incidents all represent departures from traditional practice for this industry.

There are business opportunities well beyond those for public relations firms and clean-up technology. Such opportunities involve creating and shaping markets at the technological frontier in each phase of the oil industry—from exploration to transportation and utilization. Both on-the-shelf and beyond-the-horizon technologies are beginning to play a role—and, most particularly, technologies designed to reduce effluents, wastes, and byproducts in the extraction, production, and consumption processes. Will such moves reshape the competitive arena? In retrospect, the petroleum industry has traditionally responded well to market signals—for example, by exploring new kinds of contracts when the negotiation power of host countries has grown. In the same manner, the development of voluntary environmental codes and guidelines by the industry could preempt the most demanding legislative constraints.

The Dual Role of Technology: Chemicals

Like the oil industry, the chemical industry faces ubiquitous environmental problems, but global chemical companies are positioned more precariously than oil companies with respect to the environment. They are already subject to international regulations sanctioned by formal intergovernmental agreement. Accidents have mobilized the chemical industry. The 1984 Union Carbide blast at the Bhopal pesticide plant dramatized the potential environmental consequences of the industry. Bhopal drew attention to the wide span of hazardous chemical operations and highlighted Union Carbide's weak environmental protection policies. In a business climate already strained because of a massive 1976 chemical explosion at a factory in Seveso, Italy, that was owned by the Swiss firm Hoffmann-La Roche, Bhopal augured poorly for the whole industry. The Seveso blast, grossly mismanaged by Italian authorities, was not reported until twenty-seven hours after it happened, and then as a "herbicide cloud." Waste disposal was contracted to a French firm. Transmission mechanisms were poorly understood or vastly understated. The toxic materials surfaced in France seven years later.

Chemical companies are essential to technological solutions of environmental problems. They are by far the most visible multinationals in ongoing international deliberations on the regulation and management of effluents. Two landmark events of international deliberation, the Basel Convention and the Montreal Protocol, are illustrative of emerging trends (see chapters 12, 13, and 14 of this volume). The Basel Convention should best be seen as a regulatory response to prevailing "free" market conditions. Against the background of rapidly growing trade in hazardous materials, the Basel Convention sought at a minimum to devise rules for transactions in hazardous wastes and byproducts. Over the past decade the number of countries that either import or export hazardous wastes has grown dramatically. About three million tons of toxic waste cross European boundaries annually.

The former West Germany exported its wastes to the former East Germany. Now the Federal Republic of Germany finds itself in the anomalous position of having to clean up these same sites. And while efforts to handle hazardous waste problems at first focused on reducing exports to developing countries from industrial nations, the transport of wastes among industrial states is also extensive. In the United States, about 80 percent of our wastes is shipped to Canada and Mexico. Great Britain has continually increased its imports of hazardous wastes—thus belying the rather simplistic view that it is always the rich countries that dump their wastes onto the territories of poor countries.

The chemical industry is now confronted with both international directives and national regulation to control and phase out the production of ozone-depleting chlorofluorocarbons (CFCs). While industrial societies are the principal consumers of CFCs, exports to developing countries are coming under scrutiny—with or without the participation or full consent of potential "buyers." It appears that the international community is no longer willing to permit the unrestricted production or diffusion of, and transactions in, materials and chemicals that are fully recognized as hazardous to natural or social environments.

The 1987 Montreal Protocol to reduce CFC use is of global significance both in recognizing a class of environmental problems and in establishing the need for worldwide efforts to resolve them. The gradual shift from adversarial to cooperative negotiation is one of the most significant aspects of the entire process. The large chemical companies played a major role in that process. Of these DuPont was clearly in the forefront (Benedick 1991). In 1990 the protocol was revised and more countries signed it, suggesting an expanded role for intergovernmental agreements of this sort.

Private nongovernmental organizations (NGOs) are more central to the ongoing process of CFC/ozone-related negotiations than they were to the deliberations leading to the Basel Convention. The participants in the informal, but critical, discussions leading to the Montreal Protocol included fifty-five states and many transnational public interest groups and scientific organizations, as well as formal regional and international institutions and chemical companies, notably DuPont. Although the formal signatories were national governments, the direct and indirect participants in the emerging bargaining, negotiation, leveraging, and counterleveraging varied in size, interest, representation, national jurisdiction, and institutional affiliation. In this respect the protocol is unprecedented in the scale, scope, and variety of the actors engaged in the bargaining process. Chemical companies could neither ignore nor control such strong alignments of interests. These alignments consisted of too many parties that in the aggregate were becoming too influential.

As the CFC/ozone issue shows, technological innovation is two-edged: It can generate both hazardous and less hazardous alternatives. For example, a joint venture between DuPont and Merck, announced in July 1990, presages business as well as environmental opportunities in the chemical industry. Merck, the world's largest pharmaceutical company, has a reputation for environmental responsiveness. DuPont and Merck could jointly develop a strategy to influence regulatory standards for the chemical industry worldwide. If they do not, others will do it for them. Whatever the outcome of efforts like that of DuPont and Merck, the prospects are improved that growing concern for codes, protocols, and environmental responsiveness could make the search for and relocation of wastes to places with lax environmental laws difficult, if not impossible. Depending on the industry, the issues, and the companies involved, the result may well be the creation of something of a "level playing field." This would mean that global companies would all be subject to generic constraints. Under these conditions only a foolhardy CEO would limit attention to the environmental dimensions of corporate activity (Choucri 1990). Underlying these concerns is a fundamental problem. Conventional accounting methods ignore the environmental costs of resource depletion and degradation. As indicated in chapters 9, 10, and 11, good intentions are not sufficient unless corporations and consumers alike have access to more rigorous cost-benefit and inter-generational time discounting analyses applicable to natural as well as social environments. Additionally, data from such record-keeping should facilitate the search for more energy-efficient production processes, technologies, and resource uses.

Managing Built Environments: Construction
The construction industry's dilemma is in many ways even more stark than that of either the oil or the chemical industry. The problem is this: By definition, building physical structures means dislocating natural systems. All facets of the construction industry clash with nature, from the harvesting of building materials to site preparation, transportation, actual construction, and the disposal of residual materials. Dislocations cannot be avoided; at best they can be managed and minimized.

In industrial societies construction has already changed the environment in major ways. Here the challenge is to repair, upgrade, and expand structures without significantly altering the environment further. But for developing countries the problem is just beginning, and it is in these markets that the industry envisages its most extensive expansion. International environmental groups are already braced for encounters with global construction. In the confrontation between those who desire to build and those who oppose it, the governments of developing nations will be in a precarious position: They must develop their infrastructures but cannot be viewed as declaring war on nature.

These governments are already beginning to seek a way out by exploring the bargaining possibilities inherent in environmental protection. For example, a wide range of debt-for-nature swaps are reducing the burden of past financial commitments and may free resources to meet more immediate social needs. Similarly, nature-for-technology swaps may be negotiated to facilitate access to less polluting technologies. This is especially important in the area of energy, where the potential for conservation and the development of more efficient technology is extensive. In developing countries such efforts may target the reduction of both carbon emissions and the rate of deforestation.

Still, the construction industry has yet to think seriously about the environment, remarkable as that may be in an industry whose purpose is to transform natural systems into built ones. But the environment is clearly becoming a salient factor in strategic planning for the construction industry. Like the oil industry, construction faces important opportunities for staying ahead of environmental constraints and for shaping the way in which national and international bodies address these issues. It may well be that pollution prevention would pay for itself by reducing the need for waste disposal. At a minimum it could reduce liabilities.

In sum, the crucial equation connecting business and the environment in these three industries is this: Consumer protection legislation plus emerging environmental protection ethos plus precedents for payments to pollution victims equals increased liability costs (Choucri 1991, 40).

The Environment Factor in Corporate Strategy

If a firm is to compete effectively in an increasingly competitive global market, it cannot misread the signals of the growing environmental ethos and conduct business as usual. But while governments, public interest groups, and international organizations are searching for institutional innovation and adaptation in this area, global corporations, with few exceptions, have generally failed to develop a strategy for dealing with the environment. We conclude this chapter by discussing matters of theory and practice.

New Directions in Theory

Internalizing the Globalization Process. Against a background of development in the theory of corporate behavior and the practice of corporate expansion, adjustments to environment in three industries—oil, chemicals, and construction—reveal new trends in global business. These trends have important implications for environmental policy and environmental management. Informed in part by recent surveys of market changes (Lessard and Antonelli 1990, 15–17), trends in these three industries have contributed to new corporate responses designed to manage the hazards of enhanced environmental concerns.

First is the globalization of competition in terms of integration of markets and increased specialization of production. Driven by a global trend toward reduced barriers to trade, competition shifts to production and to all associated activities. In this context, responding to imperatives of environment (of a highly uncertain nature) constitutes both a challenge and a constraint. The quest for appropriability, internalization, and diversification extends to environmental products and pollution management technologies. Since such markets are still at early stages of development, the globalization of competition will accelerate that process of market formation.

Second is a corollary of global competition—namely, greater parity in technological capability and in environmental protection processes and procedures. A certain standardization of responses may eventually evolve as the international community seeks to develop shared understandings and shared strategies toward environmental management. Prospects for corporate flight from environmental legislation—in terms of relocating investment and production capabilities into regions, countries, or markets with weaker environmental controls—may be dampened to the extent that a degree of global environmental consensus emerges.

Third is a new, but countervailing, role for national governments. On the one hand is a trend toward decreased government investments in markets (privatization); on the other hand is a trend toward an enhanced government role in regulation (environmental legislation). The corporate community is thus confronted by both reduced constraints of one sort and increased constraints of another.

New Strategic Outlook.   With the public demanding accountability and more government intervention in the offing, how will each industry manage potential embarrassments? How can firms minimize, manage, or channel government intervention? And most pressing of all, how will they take advantage of the changing business environment? First, global firms are beginning to appreciate the pressures they are under to be environmentally responsible over the long run. This environmental sensitivity may no longer be viewed solely as a posture of convenience or as a way to maximize short-run profits. This flexibility may facilitate the renegotiation of agreements and encourage international deliberation on other related environmental issues. Further, the increased acceptance of the "polluter pays principle" (PPP) in international forums puts added pressures on the multinationals. MNCs will be able to respond only if they have responsible environmental strategies that adopt a longer-term perspective, extending beyond concerns regarding the maximization of profit in the short run.

Second, the marketing challenge—once limited to identifying a product—now extends to explaining what a company will do about the environmental consequences of its activities and how it will protect the natural environment. Managing an inquisitive and possibly hostile public must be part of maintaining a positive image, but public relations without environmental action will surely backfire. Third, global corporations are beginning to appreciate the business opportunity inherent in environmental sensitivity. One case is DuPont's accelerated R&D on replacements for CFCs. This is an interim measure that will buy goodwill for DuPont for some time. In the oil industry the Norwegian firm Norsk Hydro argued that it was making a strong claim for sound environmental management. Since it also enjoyed some of the goodwill accruing to Norway for its sensitivity to the environment, such claims could translate into augmented goodwill. But at some point the company will be called upon to show evidence of performance, not simply of intent.

Fourth, firms might increasingly find it necessary to identify appropriate environmental niches. For example, World Envirotech, a U.S. subsidiary of the Kubotu Corporation of Japan, has found a niche in offering to dispose of refuse left after treating sewage. Adopting an aggressive approach to marketing waste treatment technology in the United States, World Envirotech creates opportunities and reaps goodwill. Finally, firms are shaping and will shape the creation of new markets for environmentally sensitive products and processes. How rapidly a firm understands and addresses the changing norms and values regarding the environment will in part define its competitive edge. Companies must decide whether they will impede or preempt, prevent or participate in international efforts to develop effective global environmental strategies.

New Directions in Practice

The symmetry between theory and practice is seldom perfect. Three new directions in strategy appear to be salient in corporate practices. All three are institutional in character and are therefore likely to have more long-term significance. These are (1) establishing a corporate consortium for environmental management, (2) developing financial systems for environmental investments, and (3) strengthening the "technology triangle."

Establishing a Corporate Consortium for Environmental Management. Retaining a competitive edge in an era of increasing environmental awareness will be a formidable challenge. The "soft technologies" of management need to be improved, updated, and tuned. Industry will continue to be on the defensive unless it buttresses environmental management and corporate organizational charts reflect environmental priorities. Risk assessments and contingent responses to hazards must be routine. With large multinationals uniquely positioned to frame public policy, a good offense may be the best defense. Shaping public policy is good business—providing it is done with a modicum of ethics. Unless the multinationals develop a strategy for influencing policy, they will be reduced to responding directly to outraged citizens. The legal implications are obvious, and the precedents of cross-jurisdictional litigation are numerous. Developing networks for access to specialized services in environmental products and processes may reduce both the risk and the pain for all firms. New alliances may also force governments to make regulation rational.

Under these circumstances the case for establishing a "corporate consortium on the environment" seems powerful. The goal of a consortium would be to help level the environmental playing field and keep competition where it should be: focused on energy-efficient, material-saving technology, improved management skills, and the creation and shaping of environmentally sensitive markets. In the case of environmental concerns, the shared predicaments outweigh by far the idiosyncratic risks. The rules of global investments are changing, and it is in the joint interest of global firms to make the new rules provide the best markets. Because markets function efficiently and serve social objectives only given stable and well-understood norms, corporations must strive to help steer global deliberations toward clarity and consistency. Preserving the planet's natural assets could become sound business practice as surely as it is already excellent public relations (Choucri 1991b).

Developing Financial Systems for Environmental Investments. Numerous proposals have been put forward for financing environmental investments, for "clean-up" as well as for new facilities. The establishment of the Global Environmental Facility, an international overture involving the United Nations Environment Program, the United Nations Development Program, and the World Bank (and managed by the World Bank), is an institutional step of significant proportions. While the issue of finance is clearly crucial, equally important are the institutional mechanisms necessary to ensure the effective utilization of global funds and to guarantee fiscal and operational responsibility. Here we address such institutional requisites, leaving aside the dual issues of the true costs of environmental management and the mechanisms for securing needed finance.

Following the analysis in Lessard and Perotti (1990) of the essential features for an effective financial system at the national level, we extend their analysis by arguing that analogous logics pertain to the institutional requisites for the effective management of global funds targeted to environmental purposes. They identify five requisites. These are risk intermediation, risk diversification, risk mitigation, incentive creation, and contract enforcement. To these must be added, in our view, two other requisites that are fundamental to global financial transactions: norm development and compliance and monitoring. These factors are defined as requisites because they must be construed as processes that require behavioral and institutional adjustments (the nature of which is beyond the scope of this chapter). Even if treated as a checklist, they can help define the conditions necessary for the effective management of financial resources targeted for environmental protection.

Strengthening the Technology Triangle. If the international community's experience with large-scale science and technology enterprises has taught us anything, it is that value added can be accrued by facilitating linkages among the core institutions bearing on the generation of new knowledge for both scientific and commercial purposes. In industrial societies these linkages are embedded in what has become known as the "technology triangle" (Choucri 1989). In developing countries both the need and the underlying requisites for establishing and marketing a "technology triangle" have been widely recognized (Ramesh and Weiss 1971, 139, 169).

The *technology triangle* refers to robust linkages between three sets of crucial actors influencing innovation and technological change: (1) government, which influences policy and public expenditures; (2) business and industry, which influence government policies and are the commercial innovators and translators of ideas into the marketplace both nationally and internationally; and (3) research institutions and universities, which are the generators of new ideas and embody both the quality and the quantity of a society's human capital (Choucri 1984; 1991).

The essence of the technology triangle is that each party assumes particular responsibilities whose effective discharge is contingent on the effectiveness of the others (Choucri 1991b). In many countries government serves as the source of large-scale financial resources for new research ventures and for sustaining existing ventures when necessary. Business is the ultimate user of ideas generated by professionals in the knowledge industry (the universities and the scientific institutions). These professionals are dependent on both—one for resources, science and technology, and research targeted to national needs; the other for access to the demand side, those that will utilize the output of the universities in terms of human capability as well as organizational and mechanical processes.

In areas in which uncertainties are legion and the risks are extensive— as in all environmental management spheres—the triangle may play an especially important role. In the United States this triangle is relatively well established. It is considered an important and legitimate mechanism of technological change and, to a large extent, desirable by all three parties. In Europe the linkages are generally weaker. In Japan the linkages are strong largely between government and industry. In developing countries neither the technology triangle nor its individual components may even be recognized as significant factors for enhancing national capability.

The logic for stressing the technology triangle as an institutional mechanism for accelerating "appropriate" technological change both nationally and internationally is embedded in the overall deployment of a country's intellectual and business assets. The closer the linkages, the greater the information transmitted and the greater the efficiency in knowledge generation, and in its application, management, and diffusion on a worldwide basis.

Notes

1. The National Reports prepared for UNCED 92 constitute important steps in the direction of unifying environmental description, assessment, and accounting.
2. To Kindleberger (1969) is due the credit for the first survey of theoretical MNCs, which focuses on the MNCs as collectivities in roles as economic actors. This focus on MNCs as economic actors is further due to Hymer's seminal theories that locate MNCs within the realm of industrial organizations rather than that of foreign direct investment. The Kindleberger-Hymer theses provide the basis of an economic theory of cross-border firm activities.
3. *Appropriability* refers to accruing return on investments associated with advancing technology. *Internalization* refers to the ability of the firm to retain the advantage of knowledge and skills. *Diversification* refers to the internalization of financial activities and transactions within the firm, driven by a recognition of imperfections in financial markets.
4. Groups such as the Business Council for Sustainable Development (BCSD) and the International Chamber of Commerce (ICC) have directed their efforts toward formulating "principles" for corporate environmental responsibility.

7

Science and Technology: The Sources of Change

Eugene B. Skolnikoff

Science and Technology: Source and Saviour

Science and technology are inextricably entwined with environmental change as causes, as potential solutions, as calibrators, and as the basis of assessments. The driving forces that determine the direction of the evolution of science and technology and the nature of the scientific and technological enterprises are thus essential pieces of the overall environmental puzzle.

The growth in wealth and population that the world has experienced since the beginning of the scientific age, and particularly since the Industrial Revolution, would not have taken place absent the knowledge produced through scientific and technological research and development (R&D). In turn, the scientific and technological system that produced the knowledge has grown to become a central factor in the development of society as nations have committed increasing resources to the conduct of R&D. It has also become a central element in international politics. This growth in wealth and population has had an increasing impact on the natural environment through second-order, usually unanticipated, effects. The result has been local, regional, and now global consequences, many of which are considered to be undesirable.

Concern over these effects has now become a serious political and social issue within and among nations. But the double-edged character of science and technology is ubiquitous: Not only do the applications of scientific and technological knowledge lead to significant problems along with the benefits they bestow; they also provide the essential elements for avoiding or ameliorating those problems. At least as important, they are critical for assessing just what those problems are and how they may be confronted. The world would not know it had a global environmental issue arising from greenhouse gases or the use of chlorofluorocarbons (CFCs) if it were not for the research of the scientific community.

Science and technology are, in essence, both dependent and independent variables; they are products of the system and, at the same time, forces on the system. The reasons for and consequences of that relationship need to be understood if the influence of science and technology, and the means of influencing science and technology, are to be used to achieve environmental policy goals. This complex role of science and technology—as causal agents, as consequences, and as intervening factors—is the focus of this chapter.

The Science and Technology System

The Evolution of Technology[1]

The overall magnitude of the resource commitment that is being made to science and technology today has grown to substantial levels, whether it is considered in absolute terms or as a proportion of national income.[2] The total worldwide funding for R&D in 1989 was roughly in the range of $450 to $500 billion per year, the overwhelming proportion expended by the industrialized nations.[3] The United States accounted for close to $140 billion, Western Europe and Canada about $90 billion, and Japan in excess of $50 billion (OECD 1991a, 52–53). The commitment of the former Soviet Union is hard to estimate, but can conservatively be assumed to have equaled that of the United States at $140 billion.[4] The rest of the world made up the difference, most represented by the larger developing countries and the rapidly growing nations of East Asia. The relatively small scale of R&D carried out by or in the developing countries, not much more than 5 percent of the total, is an indicator of how important it will be to stimulate the development of indigenous R&D if the transfer of technology necessary that is essential for preventing or ameliorating environmental change in the future is to be successful.

The total resources for R&D, and the purposes for which they are allocated, may change with the end of the Cold War and the disarray in Russia and its sister republics, but the order of magnitude will change little while the absolute amounts continue to grow, possibly more slowly. This is the scale of the scientific and technological system in place, counting only the R&D portion, that will have an impact on environmental change long into the future.

The scientific and technological system around the world is shaped by both public and private funding. The split varies enormously among nations, with essentially all the expenditures being from the public treasuries in socialist countries, roughly 50/50 public/private in the United States, while less than 20 percent comes from public funds in Japan.

The majority of funding worldwide for R&D goes to the applied and development portion of the spectrum, those R&D activities determined largely by the end use contemplated rather than by the advancement of knowledge. A rough rule of thumb is that in advanced countries in the neighborhood of 15% to 20% of the total of public funds for R&D, and considerably less of industrial funds, are for basic research, for which the possible end applications are not directly relevant to the setting of specific research objectives. Thus, approximately 85% of the total funding for R&D (higher in less technologically advanced countries) is for applied research and development, for which the goals are known in advance. Other public policies in addition to direct funding influence technological development, including regulations (which are particularly relevant to environment policies), tax credits or charges, guaranteed loans, tariff protection, and other policy mechanisms. These, too, are primarily intended to bring technologies with specific characteristics or capabilities into existence. They are goal-oriented, defined by the goals of the society, the government, or the entrepreneur.

In other words, most new technology that emerges is a direct product of a political and industrial process that defines what technologies are needed or wanted; estimates costs, benefits, and feasibility; and then allocates resources or develops policies designed to bring them into existence. Almost all technology the world must assimilate, or cope with, is thus a product of calculated decisions made in existing policy processes. Technological change does not result from mindless evolution outside the control or influence of human decision and choice. Harvey Brooks (1980, 68–70) suggests that biological evolution can be used as an appropriate metaphor for the whole process. This is not a perfect analogy, but one that offers valuable insights and a suggestive intellectual framework.

Brooks starts by equating genetic inheritance to the inherent logic of technological development and natural biological selection to decision mechanisms for technology (prominently including the market). Just as the natural environment leads to selection in species evolution, so the socioeconomic environment, including competing technologies, determines the evolution of a given technology. As in biological systems, technological selection is exercised through millions of decentralized and uncoordinated decisions. Conscious choice in technological evolution, for example, by means of government regulation or public investment to produce particular technologies, is analogous to intervention in biological systems through artificial selection. In both cases, man has learned how to intervene in the environment so as to direct evolution in desired directions. But the ability to bring about desired change is limited by the internal logic of technological evolution, just as intervention in biological evolution is limited by the laws of genetics and by what already exists. Thus, to a first approximation, the technologies that result from the technological enterprise are a product of human choices made at many different points of the innovation process, but always constrained by the state of knowledge at the time and by the internal logic of the technological system.

It is the decentralized nature of innumerable choices—in the development process or in the marketplace—with each made on the basis of different and localized considerations, that limits control over the direction of technological development and gives the appearance of a technological momentum that is outside human governance. A parallel and coupled conclusion can be drawn about environmental change, as the effects of innumerable small decentralized decisions, often with regard to the application of technology, each with minor environmental effects, can accumulate to have major widespread consequences (see Chapters 1, 2, and 3 of this volume).

The Role of Governments

Science and Technology Policy. From having an erratic and rather distant role in the development of science and technology in earlier centuries, governments have now become crucial to the determination of the direction and pace of scientific and technological advance. The extent of their importance varies among countries according to the form of political structure, the level of development of science and technology, and the degree of policy dependence on technology. In socialist countries the government has been by far the dominant influence, while in capitalist countries the private sector has a major role, sometimes in rough alliance with government as in France and Germany, sometimes far larger than the role of government but strongly influenced by it as in Japan, sometimes more independently, as in the United States. In developing countries it is typically government that seeks to develop the direction of national science and technology policy, in part because of the substantial government presence in the economy and in part because of the relative absence of a technologically strong private sector.

The primary objectives of government are the protection and advancement of the interests of the state and its citizens as defined by the political process in place; so, necessarily, is government support for science and technology in the service of state and citizens. That can mean many things in many different contexts, and usually implies a mixture of purposes requiring trade-offs among various conflicting objectives. To the extent governments are involved, the scientific and technological enterprises are thus necessarily tied to national goals, and the processes of technological development will be biased toward those goals. This is most evident in the national security area, but increasingly in economic affairs as well in the context of international economic competition. It is also relevant to subjects such as space, agriculture, and health and to the many fields affected by regulatory and other policies intended to serve particular domestic purposes. The pace of development of technology designed to serve environmental needs will thus be heavily determined by the policy decisions of individual national governments. There is nothing inherently conspiratorial or pathological about that process; it is a generic part of the science and technology system.

The national basis of decision making generates two other consequences. First, it imparts a powerful national identification to science and technology, defining in national/domestic terms the interest of the state in their strength and productivity and implicitly underlining the element of competition in the international arena. Second, the national base binds the enterprises to the policy and decision processes of individual nations, and thus to particular political structures, to the idiosyncrasies of national attitudes and budgets, and to the perspectives of a single country. Thus, the policy processes dealing with science and technology and the enterprises that encompass them remain predominantly national even if progress in science and technology and in their applications inexorably moves toward international and even global effects.

The pattern of evolution of technology is not necessarily common across national borders, for in practice countries tend to have rather different policy styles with regard to science and technology, with resulting disparate influence on technological development. Henry Ergas, in his comparative studies of economic policies in countries of the Organization for Economic Cooperation and Development (OECD), describes three strategies that most Western industrial countries adopt (Ergas 1987)[5]: (1) a "mission-oriented" strategy characterized by a focus on a small number of technologies of particular strategic importance, with centralized decision making and commitment of resources to achieve those technologies (the United States, the United Kingdom, and France share this strategy); (2) a "diffusion-oriented" strategy characterized by decentralized policies and reliance on diffuse decision making that can keep up with, and take advantage of, radical innovations occurring elsewhere (Germany, Sweden, and Switzerland are primarily diffusion-oriented in their science and technology policies); and (3) a strategy, exemplified by Japan, that combines both of the others in a unique blend that sets that nation apart.

Developing countries, and socialist countries as well, by and large follow a diffusion-oriented strategy by default as they are rarely in a position to move in advance of the progress in the technologically advanced Western countries. Concentrating the support for science and technology to achieve technologies of large strategic importance, which is characteristic of mission-oriented countries, will necessarily have effects on the pattern of technology that results. This can be seen most clearly in the national security area, where defense objectives aiming at the latest in technological capabilities have had such great prominence in the funding of R&D in the United States, the United Kingdom, and France. The norm is to emphasize new weapons capabilities and to anticipate all possible developments that might be accessible to others, as opposed to the refinement of existing capabilities. As a result, maximum rate of change and technical sophistication tend to be the goals of weapons systems development, and thus of resulting technologies.

The roots of this attitude lie deep in military history when new technologies periodically revolutionized warfare and gave strategic advantage, often decisive, to the nation that first mastered the technology. Though the military did not always welcome new technologies (to put it mildly), the experience in World War II was convincing, as radar, missiles, and finally the nuclear bomb showed the advantage that leadership in technology could bring. The 1991 Gulf War was seen as a further validation of the significance of a technological advantage in conventional as well as strategic weapons. The same pattern can be observed in the support for the occasional large project, such as the Apollo moon landing or the magnetic fusion program, in which some governments have taken on large-scale technology-forcing roles that used to be chiefly restricted to the security area. The pattern is also evident in the civilian economies in those countries, with emphasis placed on seeking innovative new products or processes as a way to capture commercial markets.

Thus, *mission-oriented* nations have a general characteristic of seeking radical technological developments in public technological applications such as defense or space, but also in commercial fields hoping to base new industries on new technologies. In effect, a strong "technology-push" policy and attitude is the result, with the state of the art, rather than specific need or cost, the basis for the setting of technological development goals. Diffusion-oriented countries are less likely to push technological development in radical directions; rather they emphasize incremental adaptation to technological change. In the process, they will more typically focus on factors such as cost, scope of services provided, reliability, and quality. These, it must be noted, can be critical determinants of commercial success in industries, particularly in high-technology fields in which challengers adept at incremental improvements of new technologies can have an advantage over the innovator with regard to cost, quality, and reliability. Since it is more likely that technologies that serve environmental goals will be incremental improvements on existing technologies rather than radical innovations, those nations that are better attuned to pursuing incremental strategies will be in a better position to respond to the opportunities and to profit from the results.

Other Government Policies. Governmental influence on the nature of technological evolution is not restricted to science and technology policies. Regulation, the setting of standards, taxation, and trade restrictions have also become powerful technology-forcing agents. Standards set by governments or agreed to in international negotiations can determine the design and economic returns of new technologies, such as high-definition television, or of massive technological systems, such as integrated information networks. Environmental regulations are now becoming a steadily more important example of regulations that create an incentive for developing new technologies to meet mandated needs. And the growth and broadened interpretation of product and environmental liability rules can stimulate the development of "safe" technologies and of the means to anticipate problems caused by undesirable technological externalities.

Recent public attention to the environment has not—at least not in the United States and most Western countries—created a climate sufficient to compel substantial commitment of government funds that would accelerate the rate of change of environmentally related technology. Other government policies have had an important effect, but the provision of public funds directly for the development of environmental technologies remains low. Japan appears to be the exception, as that government has taken steps to organize industrial efforts and has invested public funds in the expectation of a substantial market in environmental technology (Swinbanks 1991).

Industrial Incentives
For industry in market economies, the prospect of profits in the marketplace is the primary influence on the funding of R&D. As a result, the dominant forces affecting the evolution of commercial technology would presumably be characterized as "market pull" rather than "technology push," with decentralized decisions by consumers creating the market. Since the market cannot be aware of new technological possibilities before they are introduced, it could be expected that gradual rather than rapid evolution would be the norm. It is a much more compli-

cated process than that, however, and one that varies among nations. There are several generalizations that are important for their bearing on the character of emerging technology. Nathan Rosenberg identifies three primary historical inducements to technological change in industry, all in the context of expectation of profit: correcting imbalances in technology (improving one part of a system to compensate for obvious and costly limitations in another); avoiding vulnerability to labor disruption (substituting technology for labor); and protecting against disaster (insulating against cutoff of supplies or catastrophic technological failure) (Rosenberg 1976).

We would add three other, more recent, inducements that stem from the changed makeup of the incentives and rewards that affect the scientific and technological enterprises. First is the growing role of governmental regulatory, taxation and related policies that directly or indirectly affect technology. Barely in existence before this century, that influence on technological evolution is now substantial, and bound to grow, especially in environmentally related areas. Pollution controls on automobiles and electricity-generating power plants are excellent examples of environmental regulations that have served as stimuli for technological development to reduce effluent pollution. A substantial tax on fossil fuel combustion would have similar effects on the development of technologies for improving the efficiency of consumption of fossil fuels, or for finding economically viable alternatives.

Second is the expectation of substantial government procurement, particularly in the defense area. That expectation has led to the commitment of R&D funds and resources by industry to developments corresponding to the objectives of the defense establishment, that is, to push technological capabilities in specific areas ahead as far and as fast as possible. The ever-closer marriage of science and technology within industry contributes to that process. It is unlikely that environmental interests would ever replace or come close to defense interests as a source of government procurement. But to the extent they did, industrial commitment to the development of environmental technology would be correspondingly enhanced.

Third is the emphasis on innovation that now characterizes high-technology industry, in the context of a marketplace that provides large rewards for rapid change in high-technology products. In fact, the dominant corporate strategy for those industries most involved in high technology—computers and communications in particular—can be best described as maximizing the rate of innovation in a competitive market environment (MIT Symposium 1988). To the extent that an industrial commitment to rapidly changing environmental technology emerges and takes on the characteristics of high-technology industries, probably far in the future if at all, pressures for rapid change and innovation will correspondingly become relevant to that industrial segment as well.

In sum, there is a new emphasis in some industrial sectors on the development of technology before identification of need—a technology-push factor in the evolution of technology that encourages innovation as a primary goal, with utility, cost, and other decision elements considered only after the outlines of the technological possibilities become clear. There have been examples in the past of the development of new technologies that had little relevance to a perceived need. Until recently, however, most were not deployed, simply became the knowledge base for other, later innovations, or were forgotten. But this is surely the first era in history in which there is heavy investment in the development of new technology with little knowledge at the outset of what will be its ultimate market value.

Other goals of course also influence private sector interest in technology. To survive, all industries, especially those in a highly competitive environment, must be concerned with factors such as cost, scope of services provided, reliability, quality and, increasingly, environmental effects. This is true even in industry in mission-oriented economies, though in those such factors do not typically receive as much attention as in economies dominated by a diffusion-oriented strategy. In all countries, however, a substantial portion of private sector R&D—not easily quantifiable—is devoted to improving or expanding those qualities in a company's product mix.

Note that in the countries with command economies, the influences on the setting of technological goals and the expenditure of R&D funds as a whole more nearly parallel that for government funds in the West. However, the generally lagging scientific and technological capacity in command economies have tended to mean they are primarily users of technology developed in the West, and only rarely serious contributors in technological evolution. The costs of that situation to those countries in their domestic economies, in environmental deterioration, and in global competition are now so apparent as to have been a major contribution to the changes that have taken place in Eastern Europe, China, and what had been the Soviet Union.

Factors within Science and Technology
The influences on the scientific and technological system just described come from outside; there are also many factors within the system itself that affect the evolutionary process, and thus the character of the technologies that emerge. Some have always been present; some are new or of altered significance because of the greatly changed nature of the system and the influences on it.

Technological Optimism. The spectacular advances in technology in recent years have contributed to the view that science and technology are crucial means for coping with the problems that surround us. Notwithstanding the companion dark side that sees technology as the source of many problems, this has led to the increased commitment of R&D resources for the achievement of specific public and private objectives. This optimism at times leads to the view that there are few constraints on technological possibilities, that technology can be designed to solve all problems or reach all goals, if only enough resources in money or manpower are allocated. New "Manhattan Projects" are often proposed as the best route to a cure for the planet's or human maladies. That cry has not been absent in environmental matters as well.

The reality, of course, is rather different. Harking back to the evolutionary metaphor, possible technologies are always conditioned by the state of knowledge and by the internal logic of technological evolution, just as intervention in biological evolution is conditioned by existing varieties and the laws of genetics. The internal structure of the system shapes what that system can produce or generate. At the fundamental level, some technological capabilities are simply barred by physical principles: communication at greater than the speed of light, for example. Wishful thinking about the desirability of overcoming underlying laws of nature may be common, but is unavailing. Surprises in scientific research are inevitable, but technology cannot be planned on the assumption that new scientific knowledge will disprove existing physical laws. Even if fundamental principles are not at stake, some desired technologies may require materials, or knowledge, or calculations that are not available based on the present knowledge base, and cannot be assumed ever will be. It is evident that many technologies that would be advantageous on environmental grounds are of this character.

On more subtle grounds, many technological goals require a degree of systems integration to perform complex tasks that proves to be difficult or unrealizable in practice, and whose successful accomplishment can not be assured in advance. The more demanding the requirement for such systems integration, the greater will be the uncertainty and the lower the probability that the system will function as desired. The Strategic Defense Initiative as it was originally proposed (the construction of something equivalent to an astrodome over the United States that would be impervious to missiles) was a rather extreme example of such a technological objective that would have had, if it had ever been built, unprecedented requirements for systems integration. Paradoxically, excessive optimism about the short-run uses of a new technology often coexists with conservatism and lack of vision about the long run. The transistor, for example, was widely touted as a much superior replacement for the vacuum tube when it was developed, with no inkling of the much more astounding capabilities of integrated circuits that transistors were to make possible.

Movement of Information.   A second important factor affecting technological evolution is the pattern of movement of scientific and technological information. The pattern is not fundamentally different from the past. But the scale of the scientific and technological enterprises, the spectacular advances in communication and transportation technologies, and the development of large, closely-knit worldwide communities of scientists, have greatly increased the volume of transfer that takes place, the cross linkages among fields, and the synergistic interaction of technologies with each other.[6]

Scientific information generally moves through open channels, with unimpeded communication of results essential for the effective cumulation of knowledge. The principles of openness are reflected in the values and norms of the scientific community that date from its Baconian origins. There have been attempts at various times to restrict the flow of scientific information, especially for national security reasons during the cold war. Such restrictions tend to be only marginally effective, and are likely to be counterproductive both for security and for science (NRC Reports 1982, 1987). Attempts at restriction are likely to emerge again, however, as technologies with significant economic potential become increasingly science-intensive. Signs of that are evident in advocacy of restrictions on access of foreign scientists to research at American universities, or to strategic areas of basic research, such as semiconductors or superconductivity (MIT Faculty Study 1991). Environmental technologies will probably be little affected by policies attempting to restrict underlying science, unless the technologies become heavily science-dependent and economically important.

Information about technology, compared with information about science, is more susceptible to control, with considerable effectiveness possible in limiting its availability for a period of time. But eventually there can be few secrets, even in technology. The more radical and fundamental an innovation, the harder it is to prevent others from finding out about it and reproducing it, independently if necessary. In fact, it is the incremental innovation built on fundamental concepts that is often easier to protect from competitors than the concepts themselves because it involves more implicit know-how. This is often called "embedded" knowledge, a product of experience rather than codified technological development.

Thus, the essential technological information necessary for widespread technological evolution is ultimately available to all who seek it and have the necessary resources and competence to identify and understand it. The requirement for competence at the receiving end of technological information is a critical factor in effective transfer of technology, and is particularly relevant to the development and diffusion of technology for environmental purposes that must be applied in countries with inadequate scientific and technological capability. Indigenous capacity in science and technology will be a crucial element in the future ability of the international community to deal with environmental degradation that reaches beyond national borders.

The inevitable spread of technological information does not deter nations from approaching technology as a national, even a nationalistic, enterprise. In practice, short-term technological advantage can convey important benefits to the state or industry, especially economic benefits in fast-moving high-technology areas. Over time, technological advantage becomes harder to maintain as knowledge spreads, and as technological competence irresistibly develops in other nations. Leadership can be maintained, but it must be done through accomplishment, rather than ultimately futile attempts to deny knowledge to others. The inevitable spread of information also means that it is essentially impossible to prevent the development somewhere, sometime, of feasible technologies for which there is strong motivation.[7] Ironically, attempts to limit deployment of some technologies, for example through arms control agreements, can increase the incentives for development of related technologies that are not excluded by the agreement and that in the end may devalue the worth of the agreement.

Synergism among Technologies. The above factors lead to a third factor that is of increasing importance in the system: unplanned and unexpected synergistic effects among technologies. Synergism is a generic feature of technological development, but the now much larger scale of the scientific and technological enterprises, the dispersed nature of decision making for them, and the rapid diffusion of information all combine to produce often unexpected, and at times highly significant, new technological opportunities. Development efforts aimed at increasing the sensitivity and performance of radio telescopes had major applications in commercial high-fidelity equipment; advances in solid-state electronics for commercial purposes made possible equipment miniaturization that in turn greatly enhanced the feasibility as well as the capability of ballistic missiles; rapid progress in genetic technology with health applications in mind, might prove to have applications as well in alternative energy or food systems, with significant environmental impact. New technologies, whatever their source, can have applications far from the original purposes for which they were developed, adding to the element of surprise and unpredictability in the evolution of technology and its applications.

From Fundamental Knowledge to Application. The closer relationship between basic scientific fields and potential technological applications, however, is a factor that is making it more feasible than in the past to influence the direction of technological evolution through the support for basic science. The explosive nature of progress in molecular biology, for example, will over time have major effects on the control of disease and on the productivity and externalities of agriculture; advances in the physics of materials, such as those related to superconductivity, will one day have large economic impact in energy applications; developments in pure mathematics will affect computer designs and the development of global circulation models; and advances in fields such as the atmospheric sciences will be of central importance in recognizing and dealing with global environmental problems. Many environmental problems are at the frontier of knowledge—determination of risks to humans of low dosages of toxic chemicals, understanding of ocean absorption of carbon from the atmosphere, elaboration of how environmental factors influence the genetic structure of humans and plants at the cellular level—so that the development of environmental technology will also be able to be influenced by how support for basic science is allocated.

The exact nature of the discoveries, or how or when they will result in usable applications, cannot be foreseen. But the general proposition that advances in some fields of science will have a relatively direct route to their application in technology, sometimes with large and rapid financial gains, is of increasing validity. One notable effect, among many, is to encourage more investment, and ultimately a faster pace of change in "hot" scientific fields and in their related technologies. Another is to make basic research more relevant to the goals of nations than in the past. As environmental issues become more politically salient, so too will the emphasis on environmentally related research likely increase.

In addition, as many technologies have become more scientific dependent—that is, embodying proportionally more direct scientific knowledge—the relation between laboratory and application has necessarily also become closer. This, too, increases the relevance of basic research to national goals. This change in the relationship of fundamental knowledge to technology does not mean that scientific surprise is any less likely. Scientific theory attempts to build upon known facts and accepted ideas to hypothesize yet unknown or unobserved relationships or phenomena. But those hypotheses cannot take account of that which has not yet been imagined, so that prediction and actuality have often turned out to be strikingly different. The revolution in physics in this century that developed entirely new concepts of the quantum structure of matter was not foreseen by scientists of earlier eras. Yet it was that knowledge that made possible many of the technologies we are grappling with today including, most vividly, nuclear weapons.

The discovery in 1986 of superconductivity at higher temperatures than previously thought possible, with the physics of the phenomenon still incompletely understood, was another, less dramatic, example of the inability to anticipate new scientific knowledge. The discovery galvanized the scientific community in that and neighboring fields; it opened new questions for exploration and understanding and may well trigger expansion of knowledge over a much broader expanse. It will also, quite certainly, produce economic advantage for those able to translate the knowledge into successful technological application.

At times, nature also seems capricious in ways that are not predictable in advance. The number of neutrons emitted in the fission process under bombardment, for example, is a product of the detailed and complex processes taking place during fission rather than a fundamental property of nuclear physics; it could have been different without changing the basic theoretical model of the nucleus (Smyth 1945). If that number had been too low to sustain a nuclear chain reaction, uranium-based nuclear weapons would not have been possible, though the rest of nuclear physics would have been little affected.

Thus, notwithstanding the steadily closer relationship between the laboratory and technological application, there is no way to anticipate all or even most advances in scientific knowledge; surprise is inevitable. This fundamental unpredictability is particularly relevant for those environmental issues about which too little is known to rule out the existence of nonlinear relationships. Atmospheric or oceanic current models, for example, are based on measurements and interactions that are assumed to be continuous in the absence of contrary evidence or experience. However, threshold effects may exist that are not predictable on the basis of the equations being used, yet cannot be ruled out. The probability of their occurrence may be small, but are not calculable. The result is the ineradicable possibility of surprise or irreversibility in large-scale environmental phenomena. These possibilities must be taken into account in the making of policy, a remarkably difficult task when little is known and large issues are at stake.

Pace of Change.   Considering all the expansionary elements in the scientific and technological enterprises, it would seem to be a reasonable proposition that the rate of change in science and technology and their applications is steadily accelerating, that, as a result, society will have to cope with an ever-increasing flood of technology-induced innovation. Qualitative experience would seem to support the impression; rhetoric usually assumes it to be true. But, the proposition is not as certain as it appears. The time between laboratory and commercial application of new discoveries is not necessarily different now from what it was in previous centuries. The transistor, laser, and computer all took decades to have appreciable impact on industry, while some inventions, such as the telephone in the nineteenth century, were widely and quickly adopted.[8] New developments in biotechnology are also slow in reaching the marketplace, and it is not at all clear that the discoveries of higher-temperature superconductors will find their way into widespread commercial use any more rapidly. The increase in the speed of communication during the nineteenth century was actually proportionally very much greater than comparable increases in the twentieth century; in 1800 information could move no faster than a horse could travel, and by 1900 it could move at the speed of light.

As Rosenberg correctly argues, the lag between the demonstration of technical feasibility and commercialization is accounted for by both technical and economic factors. That is, the time it takes for a new technology to emerge on the market depends on the need for related technical advances (e.g., acceptable production techniques) and the economics of the marketplace (e.g., the relative cost of alternative products already available).[9] There is no "automatic" time lag applicable to all inventions.

The justification for the proposition of accelerating change, and for the common acceptance of its validity, lies elsewhere. One contributing factor arises from the relative steady-state nature of mankind's early history, with progress in understanding the physical world and in the development of technology concentrated in the last six centuries, and primarily in the last. Another is a result of the breadth and the scale of today's scientific and technological enterprises, rather than the pace of change within any given segment. Advances come across a much broader front than in previous eras, with correspondingly greater opportunities for synergism within science and technology and much more extensive and complex interactions with society. Similarly, the institutionalization of innovation drives the system at a faster pace, offering larger rewards for development and implementation of new technology. And finally, the increase in scale of many other attributes of society, in particular population and wealth, when coupled with new developments in science and technology, create more evident and more widespread changes and problems that impinge on human consciousness. AIDS and global environmental change are especially good illustrations.

Social Effects of Scientific and Technological Change

Outlining the nature of the system that leads to technological development does not determine the social effects to which those developments will give rise—a subject well beyond the scope of this chapter. However, a few observations about anticipating the societal effects of the scientific and technological enterprises are in order. First, technology alone is never the sole cause of societal change. Change comes about through a complex interaction of many variables, of which technology is only one. In fact, technology itself is a product of interacting factors that encompass more variables than the strictly technological.

Second, the choices made regarding R&D by both government and industry tend to be rather closely tied to the narrow objectives to be served, without extensive consideration of the broader consequences that may result when the technologies are applied. Some unplanned consequences are rapidly visible. Others, often the most important, build slowly and may emerge in areas quite different from the original applications for which the technology was developed. Examples are legion: effect of the use of fiber optics communications on the demand for copper; the dependence on foreign sources of oil resulting from the scale of the use of the automobile; the role of CFCs in the destruction of the ozone layer; the change in sexual mores as a result of the introduction and widespread use of birth control technologies; and the global environmental effects of energy dependence on fossil fuel.

Third, for these unanticipated consequences, it is the interaction of technology with other social factors, usually in gradual increments that can obscure the scale of the changes under way, that bring about the overall social impact. Technology alone does not cause these effects, but in an important sense it makes them possible. Fourth, the unpredictability of these societal consequences has a different character than the unpredictability that accompanies scientific research. For science, the unpredictability stems from the inability to know that which has not yet been discovered, perhaps not yet even thought about. For social change, the unpredictability stems from the complexity of the interaction of many variables, and the indeterminacy of the behavior of those variables that depend on human reaction. It is the distinction between the unexpected discovery that the super stability of CFCs that made them so valuable could break down in the upper atmosphere, and the emergence of the automobile as a major cause of urban pollution when at the time of its introduction it was hailed as the cure for the dangerous pollution caused by horses.

Conclusion: Patterns of Outcomes and Effects

The science and technology system that has evolved is thus one that is dedicated to expanding knowledge and stimulating change in technology for the purpose of enhancing capabilities and performance. The incentives and the structure that make the system work in this way are now institutionalized in the scientific and technological enterprises themselves and in their surrounding economic and social setting. The result is a stream of technological outcomes that contribute to a steady, sometimes spectacular, growth in the capability to carry out new tasks, and to perform existing tasks at a faster rate, at a greater (or much shorter) distance, with greater precision, with higher quality, with greater efficiency, with fewer people, at lower cost, with more power, and with other enhanced characteristics.

Can some of the first-order societal effects that will flow from these technological outcomes be identified, even at high levels of generality? There are important pitfalls in making such generalizations or in predicting social consequences at all, but patterns can be seen that can provide a sense both of the ways continuing technological change will affect the environment and the ways technology can be manipulated to affect the environment in desired directions. In presenting these generalizations, it must be remembered that technological change is not uniform across fields nor independent of policy, so that disaggregation by fields or by differences among nations (e.g., in taxation or regulatory policy) can bring about significant differences in the nature of technological development, and thus in the implications for the environment.

Broader Opportunities, Choice, and Flexibility

A consequence of expanding capabilities is that the horizons of choice are expanded for individuals, organizations, industries, and governments. The promise that science and technology offer to cure disease, to solve pressing needs, to reduce or eliminate environmental degradation, to multiply availability of necessities or develop substitutes for them, to provide new services (often on a global scale), or to achieve many other varied dramatic goals creates increasingly wide options for policy in all societies. Obviously, this enhanced capability is of great and growing importance for society as it comes to grips with environmental problems.

Growing Internationalization and Globalization

Two effects are at work here. As technology is developed that expands limits of size, distance, and power, it becomes increasingly international in its reach, either because it must be deployed in an international setting, such as space systems, or because its effects have unavoidable international impact, such as atomic weapons, nuclear power, or communications technology. A second effect stems from the cumulative externalities of countless small decisions about technology that integrate over time and space to build implications broader than national entities. Concerns over global warming or destruction of the ozone layer, both stemming from effluents of widely used and essential technologies, are obvious examples. A critical consequence of both effects is the very much more rapid and effective diffusion of information on a global basis, and the increased difficulty for governments to prevent the diffusion of knowledge of events or of ideas.

Growth of Large Technological Systems

As capabilities expand, it becomes possible and efficient, often necessary, to link technologies in increasingly large systems, now increasingly international in scope. Once the systems are in place, however, the sunk costs and fixed installations tend to reduce flexibility since change can only come slowly and with substantial cost. The global energy system, now so wedded to fossil fuels, provides an apt and forbidding illustration of a massive system, with major environmental implications, that can only be altered slowly and over many years.

Interlocking of Societies and of Economies

The result of expanding technological systems and internationalization of technology is an increased interlocking of national economies and societies. This is, of course, one of the most widely remarked international effects of technology, usually labelled interdependence. Examples are endless, but so is the rhetoric. In relation to the environment, issues such as climate change, ozone depletion, the effects of nuclear accidents, regulations that force changes in imports, acid rain, and countless others demonstrate the new levels of interdependence across borders.

Alteration of Factor Endowments

Technological change, occurring both in new systems and in the evolution of existing technology, means that the factor inputs that determine, among other things, the costs of manufacturing processes or the demand for raw materials or energy, will be correspondingly changing. Indeed, one of the characteristics of continued technological development is to bring down, often dramatically, the costs of the inputs required for a particular function, as R&D leads to expanded output per unit of input. Technological advance that alters factor costs is not a new phenomenon, but the continuousness and breadth of change in technology introduces a fluidity to factor costs, and hence factor endowments, that in turn mean continuing change in the economic potential of states and in their economic relationships to each other. It will also mean varying economic ability of states to cope with environmental degradation as changes in factor costs affect the wealth of states in differential ways, most often favoring the technologically advanced industrial states over the weaker developing nations.

Diffusion of Physical Power and Capability

The growing ability to package usable explosive power with large yields in small packages that are able to be delivered with high accuracy at a distance at low effective cost and supported by the spread of technological information, represents technological development that makes all but inevitable the diffusion of physical power to nations, to insurgents, to groups, or even to individuals. Actual or prospective nuclear proliferation is an obvious example; the devastating use of shoulder-fired Stinger antiaircraft missiles by Afghan rebels or the acquisition of Scud missiles by Iraq are at least as striking, for they dramatize how widespread is the availability of new high-technology weapons that have significant military effects.

Physical power need not imply only power that is used for military purposes; the ability of nations or corporations to carry out activities on a scale that has direct environmental effects on other nations, or on global conditions, is also growing. The plans (now suspended) to reverse the flow of Arctic rivers in the Soviet Union, the consequences of nuclear power accidents such as Chernobyl, or the destruction of the Amazon rain forest show that continuing trend. The widespread environmental damage resulting from the Persian Gulf War in 1991 vividly demonstrates the growing scale of the dangers.

Increased Science-Dependence of Technology
The closer relation of technology to the products of the basic research laboratory means, among other implications, that the health of science and the results of fundamental research have greater significance for technological progress and the economic competitiveness of nations than at any time in the past. It will also mean that the development of technologies to cope with environmental conditions will benefit from the development of new knowledge through basic research, rather than being dependent solely on the application of existing knowledge.

Increased Complexity and Uncertainty
Synergisms, the increased sophistication of science and technology, and inevitable uncertainties in the development processes imply that technological outcomes and their societal interactions are certain to be complex and impossible to foresee in detail. This adds to the difficulty of assessing the consequences of the interaction of technology with social variables, but also provides hope (but not the certainty) that presently unforeseen knowledge and technology may prove to be applicable and effective in coping with issues such as those of the environment.

Discovering Problems and Causes

One important outcome of science and technology comes not from the development and application of new physical technology, but rather from the design of analytical methodologies for probing complex issues, from the expanded research to understand the causes of change, and from the ability to construct complex models to forecast future conditions. These capabilities will continue to find unrealized problems, challenge desirable goals by detailing undesirable consequence, raise the need for potentially costly measures to deal with issues not yet observable in daily life, and complicate public issues with analyses not readily accessible except to experts. There are no clearer examples of this than the global environmental issues of ozone depletion and possible global warming, both discovered only through research, not by the measurement of effects.

Change Made Permanent

The institutionalization of scientific and technological development in government and industry guarantees that the technological environment, and thus the social environment, will never be static. New capabilities, new opportunities, altered competitive balances, unexpected problems, and full-blown surprises will continue to lead to changes in the structure of societies and of issues, not least in those affecting the natural environment.

Increased Societal Significance of Science and Technology

The manifold interactions of science and technology with the social system have had the effect of increasing their importance in the functioning of society and in the policy processes concerned with its governance. Science and technology have become part of almost all issues of social affairs, sometimes only a minor part, sometimes of central importance. They are significant factors relevant to the making of policy in a great many areas of policy, not the least in the environmental relationships with which this volume is primarily concerned.

These first-order effects of the scientific and technological enterprises will continue as long as science and technology are supported by society in roughly the manner and at the scale that they are today and as long as they are injected into an economic and social system similar in fundamentals to that of today. In this way, the outcomes of the scientific and technological system will continue to function as though they were independent variables, affecting society and the natural environment through their innumerable interactions with human affairs, some predictable, others unexpected or incalculable. But science and technology will also continue to be dependent variables, perhaps constrained by new notions of "acceptable" technology engendered by environmental concerns, and able to be targeted for policy goals to meet the needs posed by global environmental change. In innumerable and inseparable ways, the scientific and technological enterprises are directly relevant to the global environmental commons.

The outputs of the enterprises are important causal factors in undesirable environmental change just as they are necessary elements of the means to identify, ameliorate, or deter such change. Environmental policy as a whole cannot be fully planned or undertaken without including an understanding of the driving forces, internal and external, that determine the workings of those enterprises.

Notes

This chapter has been adapted from *The Elusive Transformation: Science, Technology and the Evolution of International Politics* (Princeton: Princeton University Press). Publication is scheduled for 1993.

1. Precise definitions of *science* and *technology* will not be attempted here. For the purposes of this chapter, *science* is the knowledge of how and why things are as they are. *Technology* is the knowledge of how to fulfill certain human purposes in a specifiable and reproducible way, implying considerably more than a piece of hardware alone. Note that the boundary between science and technology is not at all clear, nor is there a simple linear progression from one to the other. Rather, the relation between them is complex and contains many feedback paths. Until recently, science was more likely to depend on the prior development of technology rather than the reverse.

2. Precision in these figures is not possible, notwithstanding the extensive data bases in some countries, for the data is bedeviled by problems of definition, perspective, and simple absence of information. It is also possible that commitments as they were at the end of the 1980s could undergo revision in the future as a result of the dramatic collapse of the threat from the East. Economic constraints (recessions or worse) and other slow-moving changes in social preferences are likely to have a larger impact on R&D expenditures than the alteration in the security threat.

3. Science and technology activities as a whole are much larger than this, for they would include items such as production, application, and marketing of technology not captured in R&D data. Only the latter are available, and in any case are the most relevant to the development of new technology.

4. Figures for the former Soviet Union are not only difficult to obtain, but are subject to many uncertainties, including the appropriate exchange rate to use. Loren Graham has estimated expenditures on science (presumably basic and applied research) as averaging more than 26 billion rubles per year in the early 1980s (Graham 1987). That would be approximately $40 billion at official rates, implying total R&D expenditures of some $120 billion at that time, assuming that basic and applied research is about one-third of the total, as it is for government funding in the United States.

5. The material in the following paragraphs is drawn from this seminal work.

6. For a current model of innovation that relies heavily on the "chain-linked" model of repeated interactions between science and technology, see Kline and Rosenberg 1986.

7. The progress Iraq made toward developing nuclear weapons is an unfortunate illustration (Broad 1991, 1; Smith 1991, 22; Albright and Hibbs 1991, 14–23).

8. Fagan 1975; White 1962.

9. Noted in *Technology, Trade, and the U.S. Economy,* (Washington, DC: National Academy of Sciences, p. 23).

8

Environmental Challenges and Managerial Responses: A Decision Perspective

Garry D. Brewer

Introduction

Managers in every conceivable kind of organization, in virtually every corner of the world, increasingly encounter problems they have seldom if ever faced before. While certainly differing in their details, these new problems are remarkably similar in their origins, difficulty, and urgency. Their origins are coupled to the natural environment, often to unexpectedly large or rapid changes emanating from it. Usually the changes, on inspection and analysis of them, are traced to human decisions made years before and for then perfectly rational reasons. The cumulative effects of what were once seemingly innocent or harmless acts loom larger with each passing day (White 1967). The difficulties in understanding and coming to grips with the effects grow in consequence and challenge decisionmakers around the world as never before. These challenges are managerial, a traditional business view now widening in scope to include all of planet earth (Clark 1989).

New Decision Context

Business tools and knowledge must be supplemented by a collection of environmental knowledge and skills that enable managers to create safe workplaces, manage hazardous and toxic materials responsibly, and resolve environmental policy conflicts, ideally without costly litigation. Those who are environmentally aware in business know that their companies' success depends on taking the lead rather than waiting to react to events in environmental management.

Sensitive managers realize that business success increasingly requires an integrated approach that is based on several disciplines and capable of providing multiple viewpoints of the same problem. In dealing with popular fears and mistrust, as many in the energy and natural resource sectors must do, a consistent lesson of the last decade is *never ignore perceptions,* however unreasonable they appear. In the often emotional, even highly charged, arena of environmental disputes, perception may just as well be treated as the reality, for politically it usually is.

Two parallel lessons many in business have learned the hard way, as "business as usual" slowly adapts, make the point differently. Just as there is no "away" where waste can be thrown and forgotten, there is actually little to be gained by minimal, grudging, or tardy compliance with environmental regulations. Going to jail is no longer unthinkable for those who fail to comply. On the positive side, there may even be profits for those who take entrepreneurial risks by growing "green" businesses.

Traditional management skills remain as necessary as ever, but they are no longer enough. A collection of environmental ideas, skills, and sensibilities needs to be acquired and nurtured throughout all businesses. These new demands do not stop with commerce, although their urgency is readily apparent there. Environmental knowledge is sorely needed to improve the understanding and practice of decisionmakers in the public and not-for-profit sectors as well (National Research Council 1986, I).

This chapter adopts a decision perspective. What makes environmental problems different from other management problems? How do these differences conspire to undermine traditional decision and management forms and to challenge decisionmakers everywhere? (Coates 1991). The challenges come as failures of definition and understanding, mismatches in place and time, and in anyone's capacity to know—to separate causes from consequences or longer-range effects. The analytic perspective then shifts to focus on the extreme differences separating scientists and scholars in essential environmental disciplines, which range from oceanography and climatology to anthropology, economics, and law. Never has there been greater call for the integration and synthesis of knowledge, the success and progress of which seems, contradictorily, possible mainly by fragmentation into increasingly disconnected specializations (See Chapter 1 of this volume).

Clear thinking is required to establish and clarify our research and practical goals and objectives. Priorities must be set based on the expected added value to be gained by developing and deploying this or that new device to observe and measure the world around us. Just as the world defies dependable replication in our most elaborate models of it, so, too, are we limited in our capacities to observe and measure. We need to be very clear in deciding what we eventually measure and why. On the face of it, deciding to measure aspects of the environment posing evident threats or harm to human health might be one approach. But, to vividly illustrate the prior claim of intellectual fragmentation, imagine how unlikely it would be to encounter an epidemiologist or environmental health specialist hard at work on a problem shared with an oceanographer or global change modeler.

Much is made by those who fear for the environment—or, quite literally, the fate of the world—about what "decisionmakers" need to know and do to reverse our course and save the planet. Close inspection of these demands seldom answers the crucial question here: "Who are these awful people whose decisions lead us to ruin?" The answer is "All of us," of course, but even trying to talk to one another about our problems, much less resolving who must do what about them, proves most difficult. Even closer inspection, presuming one can correctly identify and then talk to "the decisionmaker," almost always reveals that person's institutional means to do very much are inappropriate, inadequate, or just plain inept.

Litigation versus Science
Other powerful factors seemingly limit the clarifying and rationalizing reach of scientific inquiry into essential environmental matters. The aftermath of the *Exxon Valdez* disaster in Prince William Sound provided one of the greatest scientific opportunities around, especially for anyone wanting to discover what really happens to a luxuriant ecosystem just insulted by ten million gallons of sour crude oil. Some of that knowledge has been bought, captured by warring bands of litigants. Some will never be created, and many with both interest and skill have struck the Faustian bargain of taking money for their talent, speaking only when spoken to and just in a court of law.

The clash between litigation and science occurs in other arenas, such as the testing of substances for human safety and effects, or in the case of so-called toxic or other tort liabilities. Plea bargains or out-of-court settlements, with "normal" sealing of records from public view, do little to advance science, or even common knowledge, about our environment. Running counter to this trend to cut or close off essential science and scientists are emerging opportunities to open matters up. Threats to human well-being, for instance, register irrespective of race or place. The more politicized the environment in this fashion, the more one expects popular demand "to know" to mount and thus open up knowledge-creating possibilities.

Environmental Problems and Decision Making

Environmental problems push conventional analytic, decision, and management means hard, often well beyond their effective capacities. Salient characteristics of environmental problems may account for the lack of managerial success and define challenges for decisionmaking at all levels of analysis and for institutions everywhere.

Science Is Essential

An environmental problem will contain large amounts of scientific information, often drawn from several different disciplines or fields, and seldom organized in ways meant to convey clearly either the nature of the problem or its implications. Specialization by its very nature means efficient communication among its adherents, but there are gains and challenging losses from such seeming efficiency. The dual challenges are these: We must know where to look and what to ask for. We must discover who in the scientific community is trustworthy, especially where knowledge is newly emerging, partly verified, or contentious. And we must be ready with the "So what?" series of inquiries needed to collect, organize, and translate numerous scientific "facts" into a more meaningful composite or whole. With precious few exceptions, scientists themselves are usually unable or unwilling to collect, organize, and translate. They are neither trained nor rewarded for doing so.

Science Is Scarce

More is probably known about the back side of the moon than about what goes on in the average swamp. Even what constitutes a swamp or, rather, defines a "wetland," can be raised as matters of scientific debate having extraordinary implications for decision. Beyond simple definition rise clouds of uncertainty and controversy about how a wetland works, what is good for it and bad, how much or how little of it is needed, or why anyone should even care in the first place. The image of a swamp usefully represents an ecosystem or process, most all of which are or readily become central components in an environmental problem (Hall and Day 1977).

Natural systems are often highly variable, in the same place over time and in different places for apparently comparable systems (Orians 1975). Managed ecosystems can be at least as problematic. Consider the following: The natural history of different fishes that have been unaffected by human predation comes to us from historical evidence gleaned over long periods of time (Steele and Henderson 1984). Some species are long-lived in localized communities exhibiting stable size; others live briefly, scattered and in highly variable total amounts. Natural relationships between different species, as for predator and prey, are not so well known or understood (Rothschild 1981). Most biological representations or models of fish populations consider just one species as it moves through time. Even in well measured fisheries, such as the North Sea and off Georges Bank, the imprecision of estimates has been used as an excuse to allow ruinous practices to continue. Poor fisheries management around the world provides additional testimony on this point (Rothschild 1983; May 1985).

Even where the science appears to be solid and reliable, it may not be enough or even appropriate. To the extent we understand them, physical laws are relatively solid and dependable. They include properties such as hot and cold, the movement of fluids, and the composition of matter. We do not know how the oceans circulate or how much carbon dioxide they contain, both critical kinds of information bearing on the overheated debate about "global warming" (Wunsch 1984). We do somewhat better in our concepts of atmospheric processes, but predicting the weather accurately is at best a two- to three-day bet. It is therefore hard to get excited about forecasts of an atmospheric Armageddon even when they are spelled out "by the numbers" and with attendant scientific gravity (Erlich et al. 1984; SCOPE 1986; Smith 1985, 1986; Singer 1985; Kerr 1985; National Research Council 1985b).

The other side of the issue of scarce scientific information—where "scarcity" can be taken to be nonexistence, unreliability, or imprecision—is doing nothing. But taking no action in the face of an unfolding environmental problem can itself be consequential. For example, the result of not limiting the escape of Freon and similar compounds into the atmosphere is further degradation of the earth's protective ozone layer. Loss of this layer, in turn, translates directly into greater incidence and prevalence of human skin cancers, which have different rates and effects for different parts of the world, different races, ages, and even social and economic groups (Benedict 1991).

Doing something, when one is faced with scientific uncertainty and incompleteness of information, may not be appropriate either, especially if the acts turn out to make matters worse or to have no consequence save spending money. Efforts to conceive and apply trial-and-error decision making to capture relevant information generated by perturbing and observing a system are one form of notable and appropriate response under these circumstances. The term "adaptive management" identifies one such effort (Walters 1986; K. N. Lee 1989).

Time and Space
Essential aspects of time and space characterizing environmental problems do not conform to usual institutional and managerial means. Everyone cares much more about the here and now than the typically discounted future (See Chapter 9 of this volume). And, depending on the rate of discount, uncaringness may occur quite soon indeed, for instance in something less than the number of days until the next election (Norgaard and Howarth 1991; Quirk and Terasawa 1987).

Environmental problems unfold according to natural, not human, clocks, where relevant time may be measured in decades or centuries. The mismatches between human and natural imperatives are consequential for decision making. Time itself becomes a factor for debate. Among the right groups of scientists, passionate debate can be sparked over the issue of timing for global warming, ozone depletion, sea level rise and coastal subsidence, or many other natural processes. The extreme differences in opinion may span millennia, while the locus of opinion may converge on something such as, "Within thirty to fifty years the earth will experience an average warming of two degrees Celsius." At that distant temporal remove, is it any wonder that politicians, and the public whose opinions they aim to reflect, could not care less?

There is, in effect, little meaningful interpretation of the scientific facts, and what little does communicate is readily discounted by those synchronized to political and economic, not natural, clocks. And since environmental problems show scant regard for boundaries humans have erected to govern and manage themselves, that fact is particularly relevant. Think, for example, of the range, difficulty, and complexity of challenges that confront managers of the multiple jurisdictions affecting a polluted river system, watershed, or national park such as the Danube, the Great Lakes, or Yellowstone (National Parks and Conservation Association 1989).

Synergisms and Thresholds

Environmental problems are often the consequence of various innocent, incremental, inconsequential acts which, when taken or added together, produce results unexpected and far out of proportion to the norm. The acts could have happened long ago, or they could even be far removed from the place where the unusual effects eventually occur. Sometimes a modest or even routine act, considered all alone, will in retrospect be the proverbial "straw to break the camel's back" (see Chapter 1 of this volume). Ecologists have terms to describe such occurrences: cumulative effects, synergisms and catalysts, tight coupling, and thresholds (Holling 1973). Each partly portrays important aspects of environmental systems seldom considered for decision by traditional managers. All together strongly suggest different concepts and essential information no manager can for long deny or ignore. The "tyranny of small decisions," a concept of enormous scope and power, captures the matter well (Odum 1982).

Ecological knowledge is seldom capable of providing specific answers to crucial questions, particularly in specific circumstances (Wilson 1988; Wilson 1989; Solbrig 1991). How many species can be extinguished before an ecosystem's resilience and adaptability are imperiled? How much diversity is required to sustain life? But ecological knowledge does provide sensitivities and cautions. The sensitivities are to our limited understanding of complex biological, geological, and chemical processes and systems, and the cautions are to tread more lightly on the planet and to hedge bets by not taking excessive risks of crossing a threshold beyond which recovery may not occur (National Research Council 1986). The basic messages are hardly new, although as the price of ignoring them becomes both evident and frightening, the time becomes right for them to be repeated and learned (Marsh 1874).

Environment and Institutions

Several large and complex ecosystems—some in grave distress—illustrate the mismatches and inconsistencies between natural systems and human means to manage or coexist with them. How many authorities affect the environmental quality of the Greater Yellowstone Ecosystem? The Rhine River? The Mediterranean Sea? These numbers must be large; they may even be enormous (National Parks and Conservation Association 1989; Brouwer et al. 1991; Haas 1990a). But how large? And, of these institutions, which have relatively greater or lesser effects? And does it matter? If so, to whom and how? If not, why not? These questions are infrequently posed and, when they are, it is typically in the midst of an environmental crisis—an eventuality seemingly required to catch the attentions of and to motivate decisionmakers everywhere. It is also an event that, by its definition, leaves precious little time to identify, collect, and interpret the available scientific information one needs to identify ways of responding to manage in crisis (Haas 1992).

Gaps, Mismatched Impedances, and Immiscibility

Environmental degradation and crisis highlight the crucial differences— gaps, separations, and conflicts—between scientists and others having special knowledge, relevant competence, and managerial responsibility. A rough sense of the matter is that critical components needed to sense environmental problems sooner and more systematically often in fact exist. However, the parts are seldom connected or, when they are, the results fail to harmonize or mix. Specialization and fragmentation in the sciences themselves help explain the problem, as do differences in the scale and magnitude of the parts of the world that different disciplines observe and measure.

Specialization and Fragmentation

Progress in science proceeds as many different individuals learn and know more and more about less and less. Specialization is necessitated by the sheer vastness and bulk of what there is to discover and know. Paradoxically, the dreamed-of payoffs from the growing number of initiatives in global change and earth systems science require extraordinary integration of the sciences, a task only a few have lately identified and begun to comprehend (Clark and Munn 1986).

Doubts exist, however, about prospects for the integration and improvement of scientific information and political and economic institutions, which are necessary conditions to secure wise and timely choices. For instance, unprecedented efforts to observe and measure global biogeochemical processes hold hope for a revolution in our capacity to monitor and know the present and future consequences of human acts. These efforts seem worthwhile considering the consequences of passing over a threshold or otherwise harming such processes. Human life itself could be imperiled. Unfortunately, a striking aspect of this fact gathering is the near-absence of interest or input from others except earth and atmospheric scientists. Dimensions of the "human environment" are only just now being identified or defined and their importance understood (Stern, Young, and Druckman 1992).

Curiously, this deficiency stems not nearly so much from any exclusionary designs by natural scientists—climatologists, geologists, geophysicists, oceanographers, and the like—as from the considerable unconcern of the individuals within the human and social sciences and the incapacity of these disciplines to engage or contribute. This point is being made simultaneously, and often fiercely, in fields as far removed as ecology and economics (Hall 1991; Costanza 1991; Norgaard 1992) and public health (J. A. Lee 1985). In a most provocative and accusatory way Dryzek describes the matter with a *Titanic* metaphor:

Many ecologists are aware of icebergs in the vicinity, and seek to avoid them. Most economists would be more concerned with ensuring a utility-maximizing arrangement of deck chairs. Most political scientists would worry about whether their methods for analyzing the voting behavior of the people in the deck chairs were scientific. The trouble is that the iceberg-avoidance task is left to those with scant knowledge of the political-economic systems, who consequently produce naive, sweeping, and erroneous analyses. Icebergs merit more serious attention. (Dryzek 1987, ix)

One need not accept the vivid imagery here to still agree with the metaphorical point: The gradual cumulative effects of disciplinary specialization have had many unhelpful consequences in the increasingly related realms of environmental science and management. Severe disconnections exist within the sciences and between the sciences and the institutions and leadership they must learn to serve.

Scale Effects

Large differences in the scale of observation inhibit the ready integration of the sciences encompassing interactions between land, sea, and air (Kerr 1988a). The problem is not trivial, even though technical means are close at hand to help its resolution. One of the more prominent and promising of these is large-scale modeling of the global climate, an impossibility in the time prior to earth-observing satellites and supercomputers (Schneider 1987).

The global scale of such models results in their being both data poor and theory-driven, which is to say that they rely heavily on general physical principles and relate only incidentally to specific places and times in the world (Gates 1985). So, for instance, a result quite typically would refer to a global average in temperature or its expected implications for sea levels and precipitation, also averaged and aggregated at the global level. Regional-scale models dimensioned in terms of thousands of kilometers are coming more into use as observation and measurement challenges are resolved. Severe weaknesses will exist in addressing interconnections between land, sea, and air. John Steele, former director of the Woods Hole Oceanographic Institution, summarizes the problem well:

We have entered a period where the study of the earth as a total system is within the reach of our technical and scientific capabilities. Further, an understanding of the interactions of earth, sea, and air is a practical social necessity. These interactions encompass physical, chemical, and biological factors. The biological or ecological components are critical not only as parts of these processes but as a major and direct impact on man of the consequences of global changes in the system. Yet, the possible nature and direction of ecological change are the most difficult aspects to predict and to relate to the other, physical and chemical processes. (Steele 1987, 1–2)

Popular confusion, including that among notable decisionmakers, is a commonplace under these basic, limiting conditions of scientific knowledge. From a politician's standpoint, regardless of what they may think or believe, *doing nothing* is the predictable and sensible best course. Doing nothing, however, is itself a decision with implications and consequences. One of those is to request more study and research. Sorting out confusions, trying to make sense, and translating what it all might mean—when and for whom—increasingly become matters for high-level assemblies of specialists, often convened into committees and panels by the National Academy of Sciences or interagency or intergovernmental authorities (National Research Council 1991; Schneider 1991; Nitze 1990). By the time matters get to this point, however, it is little wonder that popular and political attentions wander. These are problems of immediate import for those entrusted with decision and managerial responsibilities. The significance of these matters demands that the struggle be joined and the job of better fitting science to society be done by someone soon (Pool 1990).

The Clash of Cultures

One observer has characterized the problems of scientific fragmentation and resultant poor communication not so much as a clash or conflict, but more as an elementary failure to mix. Wooster (1987) describes "immiscible investigators" whose cultural differences explain the oil-and-water relationships that exist between oceanographers, meteorologists, and fishery scientists. Failure to mix is at least in part due to some fundamentally different ways each specialized group views the world (Brewer 1983a). It may also be attributed to different opinions, attitudes, and beliefs about the environment they hold both individually and collectively (Bhatti 1988). Whatever the origins in specific circumstances, these differences between specialists can be cause for confusion and even cynicism between rulers and the ruled. The energy crises of the 1970s have been analyzed in just these terms (Brunner and Vivian 1980).

Discovering and resolving these problems undoubtedly involve social and behavioral scientists, very few of whom know enough about the essential sciences or the scientists to contribute meaningfully—and many of whom do not even particularly care. Exceptions fortunately point the way, although no coherent body of theory or insight exists to inform the work (Schnaiberg 1977; Ezrahi 1990). Such exceptions are also seldom rewarded in practice. Crash programs simply to define the human dimensions of global change are indicative, long overdue, and most welcome (Stern, Young, and Druckman 1992).

Model Simple and Think Complex

Big is not necessarily better, especially with regard to problems no one genuinely understands. The fact that a result and its associated decision, managerial, and policy conclusions emanate from a big computer model guarantees very little. Few control what goes in and what comes out of a model, and even fewer understand what the results might mean (Brewer 1983b). Our experiences in these matters with the energy crises a decade ago hold many pertinent lessons for the coming greenhouse decade (Greenberger et al. 1983). Among these lessons several stand out prominently: In many situations a pencil and paper plus a hand calculator may be as powerful as a Cray super-computer (Keepin 1984). Paying attention to the institutional context, including the culture and incentives that make it work, may be a better guide to policy and decision behavior than all the tables, charts, graphs, and "proofs" in the world (Wynne 1984; Nelson 1974). Models constructed from theory alone, or nearly so, are far less likely to mean much than those built in real circumstances to solve real problems; this holds at least as well for ecology and energy (Hall and Day 1977; Hall 1991; Norgaard 1992; Ascher 1978) as it does for economics (Costanza 1991; Holden, 1990). And finally, never pay much attention to anyone who begins a sentence with "The model says" and concludes it with "therefore we should," as this person probably believes that the model's right and the world isn't (Dickson 1985).

These general insights specifically hold for the management of oil spills, where the pooled judgment of many different experts, if sharpened by real-time information from the site, can lead to effective short- and medium-term projections of transport, fate, and even effect (National Research Council 1985a). Having adequate baseline information, including information about the human environment, is also essential to determine initially what is most valuable and at risk and thus most worthy of protection. Baselines eventually help to assess damages by providing a standard against which physical, ecological, and human losses can be measured (National Research Council 1989a). Failure in any of these information aspects has essentially halted oil development and production in environmentally sensitive locales (National Research Council 1989–90).

What to Measure and Why

Technical means exist to observe and measure the world, quite literally. Indeed a scientific revolution unlike any in human history may well be in the offing; strong claims to this general end are now routinely heard (International Council of Scientific Unions 1990; World Climate Research Program 1991). To a large extent the technical means are directly tied to advances in satellite-borne instruments and the computers on the ground required to collect, reduce or fuse, and disseminate the flood of raw data expected in coming years. Simply because something can be monitored is not sufficient reason to do so, a critical point to consider when various groups of scientists seek to measure what interests them (Izrael and Munn 1986). Driven by scientific imperatives alone, "more" is always "better" when it comes to collecting data. At the very least, budgetary considerations provide a constraint on such scientific enthusiasms.

Particularly inadequate are existing and planned means to deal with the flood of data expected in nearly every scientific vision of the future. The problem, referred to as "data glut," is extremely serious. The basic claims of Dennis Kneale, in an investigative report for the *Wall Street Journal*, if correct, are indicative: "The U.S. has spent billions on space exploration the past two decades, searching out the secrets of the moon and Venus, or Mars, Jupiter and Saturn and galaxies beyond. But the little known secret is that scientists have looked at only 10% of the data that spacecraft have sent back to earth. They have closely analyzed only 1% of the mountain of tape" (Kneale 1988, 1). Most of the data is recorded on tapes and then stored in what Kneale refers to as "tape landfills." Simple cataloguing has not even been done. "Over 60% haven't even been located or catalogued," Kneale says. Nearly a decade lapsed between the initial satellite readings that ozone in Antarctica was rapidly depleting and someone's recognition of the facts. "The hole in the ozone . . . showed up 10 years ago [1978] in raw data from the Nimbus 7 satellite. Yet no one ever sifted it out of the tangle of tape" (Kneale 1988, 33).

Many in the scientific community are quick to assert that the problem is under control—or, in effect, it is "no problem." Assurances such as those offered by scientists in the World Climate Research Program are typical and illustrative. The following is from their recent report, *The Global Climate Observing System:* "In addition to the need to make additional observations, the *ad hoc* group recognized that the GCOS [Global Climate Observing System] must incorporate appropriate support mechanisms for the collection, processing, archiving, and distribution of data and products" (World Climate Research Program 1991, 7). The main means cited to achieve these goals is a nonexistent Earth Observing System Data and Information System (EOSDIS), about which little has been considered, planned, or budgeted.

There are two main sources of skepticism. One is technical and the other political. The technical side involves sheer volumes of data never before seen or handled. It also involves the first truly international effort of its type, with numerous and different satellites and systems from the United States, the former Soviet Union, France, India, and Japan contributing to the flood. Data transmission rates from a single spacecraft in 1974 were about 1000 bits of data per second. By 1980 this rate had increased to 50,000 bits per second. By 1995, with either NASA's space station or some version of the Earth Observing System, the rates could top 200 million bits per second. The political side is based on the historical unwillingness of funding agencies to "waste" money on unexciting support activities such as data cataloguing and management, computer model documentation, or other software requirements (Moore 1989).

What is to be done? Several different but complementary strategies can be imagined to help resolve the what and why of measurement. Being imaginative—as in modeling simply and continuing to think creatively—is certainly a possibility. Specific efforts by Verstraete and Dickinson to identify the minimum essential information needed to characterize desertification and to relate this in turn to General Circulation Models (GCMs) on a global scale point the way to large data efficiencies and management economies. One need not measure everything if the essentials have been identified by careful and linked theoretical and empirical field work (Verstraete and Dickinson 1986; Verstraete and Pinty 1990).

Placing human beings directly in the picture is another strategy. Where are the greatest risks to humans and over what time frames as a consequence of global and environmental changes? Similarly, where are most humans at risk? With this approach some kinds of natural processes and certain locations stand out for more intense measurement concern. In the case of a global rise in sea level, this approach would recommend a selective focus on places such as New Orleans, Alexandria in Egypt, and Bangladesh. In the case of ozone depletion, it would pinpoint fair-skinned people in the high latitudes or any other populations at high risk for skin cancers. Areas of great population and intense agricultural activity, particularly if supported by irrigation, would be another focal point to observe and measure. Rising temperatures should mean less precipitation, more demand for irrigation, and increasing risk of desert encroachment (Verstraete 1986). Under the human conditions just specified, one ought to be highly motivated to begin finding out.

This approach necessarily involves specialists from human health professions such as human epidemiology, environmental health, toxicology, demography, and probably a few more to help focus on the high-value locales of at-risk populations (J. A. Lee 1985; Brewer 1989).

Since concerns and fears about human health and environmental matters are growing in importance, added political support may be marshaled to pursue scientific means to clarify and help resolve these matters (Freudenberg 1988). Where human perception of risk and rational assessment of the same risk do not match, powerful political forces are often unleashed. The formidable difficulties that the differences between perception and assessment of risk present to managers in all segments of modern society constitute an additional reason to link the human environment directly to the biogeochemical one. Among the many difficulties are managing risk perceptions (Fischoff 1985; Sandman 1986) and discovering appropriate communication means to inform and manage human populations made erratic by fears for their lives (National Research Council 1989b; Covello and Slovic 1987).

Continuing to fund hundreds of research projects and dozens of megabuck programs, all in pursuit of knowledge about global change, is both wasteful and unacceptable if human causes and implications are not weighed in from the beginning. At the moment, they are not (National Research Council 1989a; Stern, Young, and Druckman 1992). And no strategy appears in the offing. Decisions about what to measure may be forced by budgetary constraints. The recent experience of NASA in setting priorities and calibrating its technical dreams with fiscal reality provides both insight and a possible model for what might be done (Wheelon 1989). A group of qualified scientists was enlisted to make hard budgetary choices; the more common alternative is to have accountants and politicians do it. How the jobs of setting priorities and making measurement choices are eventually accomplished will be important and open to considerable debate. Having to make choices is beyond doubt.

Decisionmakers

The question "Who decides?" about matters of global change is usually answered by default or exhortation—if it is even raised at all. Elected officials, high-level federal bureaucrats, and captains of industry are, though usually unspecified, all likely suspects. Sometimes a particular individual will be cited, as in something like: "John Sununu doesn't believe in global change, so we have to convince him," or some such. It is far more sensible and productive to think of every human being as a potential decisionmaker. By extension, one might think of every existing and future human being as a manager, responsible for dealing with environmental challenges.

Concern for the future, often expressed overdramatically in doomsday terms, can be managed quite directly by vesting a share of decision making in imagined generations to come (Bailey 1989; Clark 1986). The concept of intergenerational equity is an analogous line of thought and argument whose realization is stunted by the political expediency of "benefits now for my constituents, and costs later paid by everyone" (See Chapters 9, 10, and 11 of this volume). This linked problem of *time* and *decision* obviously must be examined and an appropriate decision frame adopted.

A new decision frame is also recommended for spatial reasons. An ecosystem is not equivalent to, does not map on, a congressional district—or many other environmentally potent political jurisdictions, for that matter. As a consequence one should expect considerable institutional experimentation in the future as many different kinds of decisionmakers search out sensible and effective ways to deal with or manage ecosystem-based problems. The worldwide increase in the number of nongovernmental organizations or NGOs is indicative of such experimentation and an emerging trend around the world. It draws its strength from the ineffectiveness of traditional authorities and the conventional and limiting bounds of legal jurisdictions across the international system. If an ecosystem is not the same as a conventional jurisdiction, then deciding what it is, in fact, takes on some importance. Bounding an ecosystem is not a simple matter.

Ecosystems as Decision Contexts

A consistent sense of what constitutes general classes of ecosystems and how those classes pertain to particular locations on earth must be developed. The critical importance of tying the general to the specific cannot be overstated, especially where political pressures mount to "redefine," as has happened for "wetlands" in the United States in 1991. Stability in definition is required for longer-term biological treatments, e.g., mitigation, replanting, channeling, and reclamation. Biological standards, including baselines from which all subsequent progress can be assessed, must be stable. If the definitions or baselines are not clearly spelled out or do not exist, plans cannot be made or performance evaluated. If the biological conditions and frameworks are not carefully spelled out and consistently defended, there is little reason to expect longer-term plans or programs to succeed. Political expediencies and short-run economic planning horizons will.

From a bureaucratic standpoint, small-scale ecosystems may be more successful than large ones. Scalar effects could thus favor timidity in system boundary definition. By contrast, if something like a small watershed infiltrated with nuclear waste is defined as an ecosystem for purposes of cleanup, failure, and at very high costs, may still result because the nature of the task remains so formidable. Whatever the specific outcome and consequences, scalar effects in ecosystem definition will likely be an important policy matter. The logical natural boundary definitions may reduce chances of managerial success from a bureaucratic or political standpoint. This reality is a powerful constraint on effective policy from an environmental standpoint.

To an organization or policy specialist, the issues are elementary; but they point out some obvious basic problems few ecosystem management proponents seem to know exist. The broader issue of creating means and fora for experts, specialists, and those with constituted authority to interact is thus brought back to our attention. Just as there are few chances for an ecologist to cooperate with a political scientist, so there are few moments for any environmental specialist to inform a politician.

One added issue regarding "decisionmakers" emerges as the world and the United States adjust to life with a lessened threat of nuclear war. The scientists and other expert specialists whose lives and livelihoods were tied to the prevention and prosecution of that war are looking for new employment (Pool 1991). Some will find or invent it within existing institutions. The Department of Defense recently created an office for an Assistant Secretary of the Environment. The weapons-building Department of Energy confronts monumental cleanup and rehabilitation tasks at virtually all of its facilities, and is beginning to make amends. None of these developments is of as great a concern as the huge study and analysis bureaucracy created and sustained during the nuclear era to advise and support the Pentagon. For more than enough of it, scientific validation was often equated with making the customer happy, a consequence reflected in the common name of these bureaucrats and private analysts, "Beltway Bandits," whose transformation from red, white, and blue to green one ought to fear (Brewer and Shubik 1979). Focusing attention on the specific concern about whether science and scientific expertise will flourish is crucial if we are to manage our environmental challenges.

Facing the Challenges with More Information or Less?

The distinctive nature of environmental problems defines numerous and difficult observation and measurement requirements. Ways of assembling and representing the data thus generated, in terms of models and other analytic forms, likewise direct one's attention to pressing information needs. The importance of new information was never doubted. Problematic is whether essential, even critical, environmental information will flow freely and in a timely fashion to decisionmakers. Available evidence is in itself hardly determinative. Some of it is actually discouraging, although encouraging opportunities exist as well.

Less Information: The Legal Context

One encounters repeated instances in which nonscientific considerations simply overpower efforts to observe, measure, and learn about environmental problems, including those related to human health. For example, litigation surrounding assignment of damages due to the *Exxon Valdez* spill essentially cut off all normal scientific activity and, in so doing, wasted a unique opportunity to learn about ecosystem responses to a monumental environmental insult. Litigation related to cases of commercial product hazards, toxicity, workplace risks, industrial emissions and discharges, contaminated sites, and so forth usually result in restricted information flow as well. Science as a general enterprise is impeded as a consequence. Decisionmakers in circumstances closely comparable to those kept secret are unable to benefit or learn. In each of these and subsequent environmental challenges, the managerial responses are unlikely to be well informed for lack of essential scientific information and knowledge.

The March 1989 disaster at Bligh Reef in Prince William Sound, in which the *Exxon Valdez* ran aground and spilled over 240 thousand barrels of Alaska crude into one of the richest ecosystems on earth, presented scientists with a remarkable learning opportunity that was largely foregone because of the huge stakes involved in the damage assessment. Soon after the accident, according to Lisa Busch in an article in *Science,* Alaska's attorney general issued a series of memos to "state scientists ordering them to keep their data on the spill under wraps." The point of this was "to prevent Exxon from gaining the upper hand in the litigation that was shaping up from the moment the *Valdez* ran aground" (Busch 1991, 772). Secrecy has its own costs, not the least of which in this case are uncertainties over the long-term damage to Prince William Sound, health risks imposed on workers involved in the cleanup, and whether different kinds of cleanup worked or were needed at all (Roberts 1989b; Lancaster 1991; Barinaga 1989). As Jim Gibeaut, chief science coordinator for the spill response team, puts it, "Without damage-assessment data, the environment suffers . . . [so] how do we know what cleanup efforts would do more harm than good?" (Busch 1991, 772) The answer is unstated but obvious: We don't. We will also never know if the reported $2 billion Exxon spent did anything more than help clean up the corporation's soiled reputation.

This accident demonstrated two general negative effects on improved information generation and flow that occur when litigation takes priority over science: First, existing and baseline data are not widely shared. Second, impediments to free communication among scientific experts increase duplication of effort, reduce the integration of information from different specialists, and open up multiple opportunities for dispute and conflict. The sum is diminished capacity to respond to comparable environmental challenges in the future. "Confidentiality is an integral part of the civil litigation process, and plays an essential role in fostering the resolution of disputes from start to finish" (A. R. Miller 1991, 66). Judges, those directly charged to resolve the disputes, "generally lack the scientific or medical expertise needed to evaluate properly the complex data and theories routinely implicated when health and safety are at issue" (A. R. Miller 1991, 68). Obtaining that expertise, in the current litigious circumstances, is a significant challenge, as can be attested by two chastened scientists brought to trial in an important and long-drawn-out Hudson River power plant case:

New scientific knowledge or truth rarely emerges during a trial; the most scientists can hope for is to preserve their objectivity and professional dignity. In the Hudson River power case, scientists found their normally reasonable differences becoming polarized, strident, and disrespectful under the pressures of trial procedures, and the regulatory hearing never achieved a resolution of the issues. . . . An adversarial judicial procedure seems an unsuitable means of resolving issues that are both highly controversial and highly technical. (Christensen and Klauda 1988, 307)

Resolving the matter obviously has implications far wider than specific technical decisions might imply, e.g., trying to decide if a new power plant's heated water outflow will harm Hudson River striped bass or calculating the penalties to be paid for each sea otter killed by oil spilled in Prince William Sound. One implication is political; it fixes quickly on the public's mistrust and suspicion of its leaders where environmental, safety, and health matters are concerned (W. Schneider 1989). The effects of other implications include individual indecisiveness (Solomon 1990), apparent institutional incapacity to cope (Olson 1991), and social immobility.

More Information: The Strategic Context

If improved information generation and use are ingredients essential to improve environmental problem solving, then their pursuit along unconventional paths is certainly in order. At the very least, efforts must be made to think as creatively as possible. The following two directives—thoughts—are offered in this spirit.

First, cooperation with the political entities that emerge from the former Soviet Union could very well result in more and better information about the world's environmental status. For historical reasons related to both cultural and technological differences between the Soviet Union and the United States, the Soviets have produced many more and simpler satellites for intelligence and communications purposes. The United States has always excelled relative to the Soviets in satellite data management: collection, fusion, reduction, and dissemination. These capabilities reside primarily in the intelligence community, not the unclassified scientific one discussed earlier in terms of "data glut." A premium placed on real-time acquisition and interpretation, which are critical to timely decision making in a nuclear war setting, drove these capabilities. The United States, in contrast to the Soviets, historically tended to collect its observational assets into a relatively few very expensive platforms. "Gold plating" is the common term applied to this weapons philosophy and its extension into satellite reconnaissance. The philosophy persists in the Earth Observing Systems program of NASA, which employs a few expensive multipurpose satellites to keep track of life on Earth.

If many of the environmental problems one anticipates flowing from global change are first manifested as local anomalies, as in a sea level rise in Bangladesh or ozone depletions in places other than the polar regions, for instance, a capacity to put small, inexpensive observational platforms in place quickly will be highly advantageous. Similarly, episodic events such as large forest fires or oil spills could be managed more effectively with fast-reaction observations from space. A kind of cooperation is necessary in the interests of more, more timely, and better refined information for environmental management purposes. The Soviets have certain comparative advantages, and we have their complement, presuming that experience from the classified realm, including technical wherewithal, can be re-directed to peaceful environmental purposes.

A second directive also implicates the former Soviet Union, but in very different ways. The Soviets have large quantities of essential natural resources, including oil and gas, forest products, and minerals. As would be expected, given their present economic turmoil nearly all these resources are poorly utilized. Lagging technology, inadequate capitalization, poor personnel training, and worse maintenance of facilities all take their inevitable toll (Browning 1991). Natural gas in particular appears to be especially abundant and promising (Stokes 1991). The quid pro quo is basic and ensures some kind of deal in coming months. The former Soviets need capital and technology, both generally and specifically to resurrect their oil and gas industry. Energy corporations need dependable supplies of product, especially if the associated environmental risks are low enough to be tolerable. Engaging international oil and gas corporations in exploration, development, and production in what used to be the Soviet Union takes pressure off of many environmentally sensitive areas where attentions are presently focused. It offers hope for more production of natural gas, the least offensive of the petroleum fuels, and for some bolstering of the disastrous Soviet economy.

The key aspects of each of these directives are as follows: Unlikely cooperation and a demand to be more expansive and creative will enhance our efforts to meet and manage environmental challenges.

Conclusion

This chapter focuses on matters of decision and management. By defining environmental problems as fundamentally different and their resultant challenges as more difficult than "conventional" ones managers have dealt with through time, the importance of science and scientific information stands out clearly: They are essential. Decisionmakers and managers must learn to focus intently on environmental problems to highlight their informational aspects. Having done so, adjustments to conventional managerial methods at least become imaginable. Without focus, imagination, and adjustment, however, no one should expect to overcome the challenges of global change.

III

Economics and Law

9

Economic Perspective on Time Comparisons: Evaluation of Time Discounting

Jerome Rothenberg

Introduction

Global climate change involves deep intertemporal and intergenerational issues to a unique degree. These issues are serious obstacles to constructive international action. Briefly, the long, accumulative—and therefore effectively irreversible—process by which human activities are believed to influence change in global climate makes it possible to warn against such dangers long before they actually occur, and therefore makes it possible in principle to prevent their happening at all. But by the same token it makes for a very long lag between the time when preventive action is taken and when its effects are experienced. The climatic changes now being warned against will not damage anyone now alive or, essentially, their direct descendants. If present trends in human-generated greenhouse gas emissions continue undisturbed, then it is remote generations from the present that will be progressively damaged, and the more distant, the greater the damage. Yet present ameliorative action imposes considerable real costs on the present generation. So no one now living gains personally from preventive action; indeed, everyone loses nontrivially, and only remote future generations gain.

So present preventive policy involves a considerable transfer of real well-being from the present generation to future generations (as an offset to the prospect of considerable damages which present actions will impose on those same generations). But nations differ widely in their willingness to make such sacrifices. Many have unfulfilled present needs of such urgency that no further sacrifice of present interests can be contemplated. This constitutes a grave obstacle to present preventive

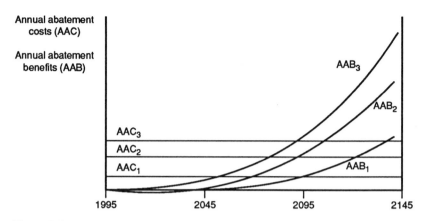

Figure 9.1
Illustrative time profile of climate changes

policy because a second major feature of the climate change mechanism is that greenhouse gas emissions from anywhere on earth become equally part of the atmospheric reservoir that influences climate: Emissions have global externalities. No one nation or small group of nations can achieve effective prevention by their own efforts. Much of the globe's population must coordinate preventive action for the effort to be effective towards anyone's interests.

Under these conditions, can preventive policy interventions be attractive? Conventional project evaluation makes events at different times comparable by time discounting everything to a common discounted present value. This allows for scalar comparability and consistency in comparing projects with very different time profiles of benefits and costs. The discounting operation has a persuasive empirical-normative attractiveness that is not lightly to be discarded. But conventional time discounting has extreme consequences for global climate policy.

Present knowledge about global climate change involves huge uncertainties. Even so, some gross characteristics of the time shape of benefits and costs from preventive actions seem clear. Abatement now incurs considerable costs that vary with the degree of abatement. Benefits are the decreased damages due to climate change that result from decreasing the extent of that change. Figure 9.1 shows this gross time shape for three simple potential cost scenarios and three potential benefit scenarios. In all cost scenarios, costs begin immediately, are nontrivial, and continue essentially level thereafter (by assumption). Grossly consistent with the spirit of many empirical estimates, without abatement of emissions climate change is negligible for at least 50 years, then rises thereafter, probably at an increasing rate, and possibly becoming quite high beyond 150 or so years. Then induced human damage will trace out a similar path. Abatement benefits amounting to some proportion of these damages would roughly track the same time pattern. In the figure are three benefit trajectories that are possible given the large uncertainties associated with damages due to climate change, showing that annual costs exceed annual benefits until between 65 and 140 years into the future, depending on the scenario pair, and an increasing reversal thereafter. Given widespread concern over possible large future damages, we want our abatement policy evaluation to be sensitive to this. It will not, however, be sensitive under conventional discounting. Far events have exponentially declining weights relative to near events, so near-future costs dominate far-future benefits so much that very large benefit differences in the far future make little difference in the net present discounted sum—even with unrealistically low discount rates. This is primarily due to the extremely long impact lags of the climate change process.

Conventional discounting will typically generate negative net benefits for all preventive abatement policies: They are not worth their costs, no matter how large the absolute benefits may be in the far future. This makes such evaluation insensitive to differences in outcomes that most other interested parties believe make a difference for policy decisions. The use of such evaluational techniques would essentially exclude economists from current debates on public policy here. Can the relevance of economic insights be preserved by using a different method to compare outcomes that are widely separated in time from one another?

Consider what is involved. Our argument implies that every present-generation abater loses and members of far-future generations gain most. An abatement policy is therefore transfer of a gift from the present generation to far-future generations (to offset a comparable transfer of damages due to climate change). Let us simplify to put the issue in relief. Assume that a one-time gift is to be given to humans living at various times in the future. How much would members of the present generation be willing to pay now to give a gift of $1,000 to people living 50 years from now, 100 years from now, 200 years from now? The gain to the

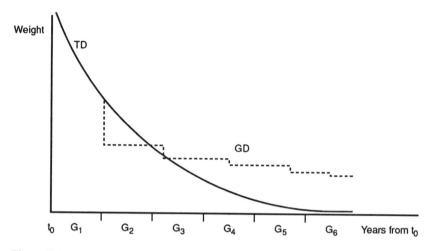

Figure 9.2
Period weights: intertemporal and intergenerational discounting
where t is time in years; G_1, G_2, etc., are generations, with G_1 the present
generation; TD is the intertemporal discounting function ——— ; and GD is
the intergenerational discounting funtion ---- .

present generation is only vicarious and occurs here and now; no waiting
is involved. Conventional time discounting provides an answer based on
the costs involved in postponing consumption and the prospective net
productivity gains involved in using resources for investment. A typical
pattern is shown in figure 9.2: a smooth negative exponential decline
(TD) that is very low by 100 years from now and near zero by 150
years and thereafter. Yet figure 9.1 shows that the period beyond 100
years is critical to what is at stake in abatement.

How reasonable is this pattern of evaluation of the future for the
present generation? Consider the gift transfer from generation one to
generation five. How much would generation one (present) find it worth
to amass by the end of its lifetime for direct transfer via abatement to
generation five, such that it is indifferent between that transfer and an
increase in wealth by generation five equal to $1,000? Neither consumer
impatience nor the productivity of capital—the twin justifications for
time discounting—is involved in this calculation. The transfer occurs at
the end of generation one's lifetime, so the individuals cannot be impatient for the gift to reach its recipients since the former will be dead:
They should be indifferent on that score as to how long a delay is

involved. Similarly, no productivity of capital is involved: Since the transfer is *direct* via abatement at the end of generation one's lifetime, there is no further augmentation of its magnitude between the time it leaves generation one and arrives at generation five, so the extent of the delay does not cause any increase in the gift through time.

The latter factor is involved in *indirect* transfers from generation one to generation five—i.e., generation one amasses capital and gives it to generation two for the latter to invest it productively and hand the total to generation three for the same process, with the cumulatively augmented total finally handed directly by generation four to generation five. Time discounting would be appropriate here if generation one could be sure that its intentions with regard to generation five would be exactly heeded by the intermediate generations. But generation one cannot impose its intentions on the generations that follow; the indirect route to generation five is covered with uncertainty. Therefore the size of generation one's transfer reflects not only the pure evaluation of what a hypothetical gain by generation five is worth to generation one, but the mixed-in expectations by the latter of what the intermediate generations would do with generation one's transfer along its indirect journey. A pure evaluative comparison requires the direct transfer; and in this neither impatience nor productivity is involved, so time preference is not inherently relevant.

Probably more inherently relevant to the evaluation of this intergenerational gift than the year of receipt is the degree of empathic closeness between the two generations: How similar are they in values, tastes, and lifestyles? As the future recedes, present perceptions tend to treat whole generations as single homogeneous entities. The degree of empathic closeness would seem to be more tolerably measured by the number of generations separating the present from any particular future period than by the number of years between them.

Figure 9.2 shows a hypothetical set of weights based on intergenerational empathy—the *GD* function—in comparison with time discount weights (*TD*). It is discontinuous, breaking at each generational boundary.[1] Its first segment, (G_1), the remaining lifetime of the present generation, coincides with *TD*. There is a modest drop to segment G_2, comprised of the present generation's direct biological descendants, a long drop to segment G_3, but thereafter more modest further drops to later generations, showing the gradual blurring of perceptions about more remote generations. In G_1 gratification is direct, but beyond G_1 all gratification is vicarious only—and therefore presumably less valuable to G_1. The welfare of G_2 is in a real sense a direct extension of the welfare of individuals in G_1. There is no such direct link between G_1 and generations after G_2. The large drop from G_2 to G_3 shows this. What is important for our present purposes is that beyond G_2, if G_1 has empathy for G_3 it is not likely to be much less for G_4 and even G_5. The step function GD declines only slowly beyond G_2.

The upshot of this informal argument is that beyond 60 or so years into the future—and progressively so in the crucial interval of 100 to 200 years—GD is significantly above TD. Even as far away as 200 years, the GD weights are nontrivial while the TD weights are effectively zero. So big differences in scenarios in that remote interval can have big differences in policy evaluation. Two factors account for the difference in weights: (1) the GD weight is constant for each whole generation, while the TD weights decline throughout it, and (2) remote future blurring leads to smaller losses of empathy for successive generations under GD than is seen in the constant rate of loss represented by TD (except of course when TD nears zero).

Generation weights can potentially give remote future events significant influence in policy evaluation. Their possible use suggests that we distinguish between intertemporal comparisons and intergenerational comparisons, the former for events that predominantly fall within the lifetime of a single generation, the latter for events separated by generational lifetimes. Our chief focus is the latter. This does not mean, however, that generational weighting automatically constitutes the most preferred alternative to time discounting for such comparisons. While not inherently relevant, time discounting may nonetheless turn out to have more attractive features than all alternative approaches. An explicit examination of the claims of different approaches is therefore needed. Chapter 11 provides such an examination.

The balance of this chapter appraises the value of time discounting for making intertemporal and intergenerational comparisons. It finds serious weaknesses in the performance of intergenerational comparisons.

Accordingly, Chapter 11 examines six alternative approaches to treating intergenerational issues more appropriately and selects a mix of elements from them to constitute a more satisfactory overall approach. It then discusses the implication for using this chosen approach to enhance the adoption and implementation of global climate policies in the international context that is essential to achieve effective action. While the explicit focus of this volume as a whole is the issue of global climate change, the substance of the analysis applies to the much broader class of issues that involve long time lags, either backward or forward.

Summary of Time-Lag Issues in Global Climate Change Policy

This brief sketch of the schematics of climate change and its control suggests several propositions. First, The effect of greenhouse emissions on climate is a "stock pollution" process, not a "flow pollution" process. It is not annual flows, but reservoirs accumulated from these flows over time, that actually influence weather. This distinction points up effective irreversibilities both in taking and in failing to take, present actions. Second, there may be very long time lags between flow changes and resulting changes in climate—both where flows are not moderated by policy interventions and where they are.

Third, the amount of climatic change possible under zero policy intervention will not necessarily reach a moderate limiting degree or plateau sometime during the next century. Progressive change can conceivably continue through future centuries, and possibly at an increasing rate. As it does, progressively more serious damage beyond inconvenience and modest production and consumption dislocations can occur. Major threats to basic ecological systems and the fundamental life-support processes that make human life on the planet viable may well be possible. Quantitative predictions are subject to various large uncertainties. Fourth, if human interests in the far future matter to humans in the present, then very big stakes may be involved: the damages (costs) possible in the absence of offsetting action and the gains possible via offsetting action. But such concerns are technically relevant to the present because of the very long lead times empirically needed to offset or prevent those future damages.

Fifth, preventive abatement is a matter not of a one-period change in greenhouse gas emissions, but of an indefinitely continuing series of period-by-period emissions modifications. An abatement policy is a continuing series of cost-incurring emissions modifications. Sixth, because of global externalities involved in the radiative forcing function of greenhouse gases, everyone in the present population is a part of the cause of prospective climate change. No group's emissions can be targeted as having any particular spatial impact: A nation cannot unilaterally have more than an insignificant effect on its own future climate, even with radical modification of its activities. Effective climate modification for any nation requires the compatible modification of behavior by most nations.

Seventh, no member of the present generation stands to benefit directly from present abatement activities or from abatement or adaptation investments. Direct descendants of the present generation could benefit only trivially from such present efforts. If they continued such efforts as part of a continuing intergenerational abatement policy, they too could suffer direct negative benefits. In sum, policy intervention in the present represents actions on behalf of *future* interests; to be effective for such interests, they must be internationally pervasive. But the significant stakes refer to futures well beyond the direct and indirect *personal* interests of the present population; and both the absolute and net costs of making a real difference in these far-future stakes are quite large. How are such public policy situations evaluated by our conventional appraisal techniques? We shall answer this question next.

Discounting and Intertemporal Evaluation: Conditions for Optimality

Multiperiod projects are conventionally evaluated by converting each anticipated dated cost and benefit into a present discounted value and then obtaining the algebraic sum of all such converted entries to determine the present discounted value. Our interest here is in how such discounting reflects and influences the willingness to sacrifice present interests to future interests. In comparing the claims of present and future interests, we begin by examining the conditions under which the present discounted value as an investment criterion generates an optimal use of resources.

Case I: Single-Generation Homogeneous Population

The simplest case of discounting that promotes an optimal intertemporal allocation of resources is that in which only a single generation of fixed size is involved. The individuals of this generation are homogeneous in age, tastes, and endowments and have the same lifetime duration, which is known with certainty. All investments have a lifetime less than or equal to the human lifetime. Investment postpones present consumption—want gratification—in favor of future consumption. The amount of increase of future consumption that is made possible depends on the investment's rate of return. Offsetting this is the impatience with postponing want gratification. Good things are wanted as soon as possible; bad things are wanted delayed as long as possible. "Impatience" is usually heavily associated with uncertainty as to when one will die, but this is less salient here, so our case excludes it by assuming a known lifetime which exceeds all project lengths. "Impatience" here is assumed to be a psychological characteristic of intertemporal tastes. The inclusion of an uncertain lifetime would strengthen our overall thesis.

Assume that many investment projects of fixed size and equal duration are available, each project having a fixed rate of return, with rates differing for different projects. All members of the population have equal access to them all through the capital market. In figure 9.3 we show both the enhanced future consumption opportunities obtainable by using different total amounts of present resources for investment rather than consumption and the degree of enhancement that the population would require in order to be willing to commit various amounts of resources to investment rather than present consumption. The marginal investment payoff function p shows, for each hypothetical overall investment level, I_i, the maximum rate of return available on the best remaining project if all projects with higher rates of return have already been chosen to constitute the next lower level I_{i-1}. The marginal payoff required function r shows, for each I_i, the lowest rate of return that would be required by lenders as payment for switching away from current consumption the additional resources necessary to adopt the best last investment project involved in going from level I_{i-1} to level I_i.

Lower than $\hat{I}$, the intersection of the two curves, the population could gain a higher enhancement of future consumption from investment than they would require to sacrifice more present consumption. So they would

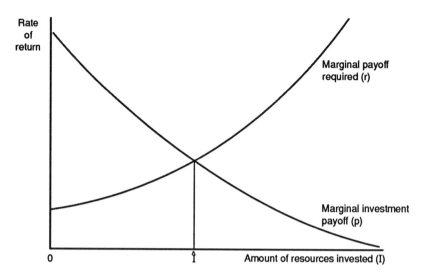

Figure 9.3
Optimal investment: one-generation case

be better off by shifting toward more investment—a greater sacrifice of present interests for future interests. This argument holds everywhere from $I = 0$ to $I = \hat{I}$. Similarly, everywhere above $\hat{I}$ the investment payoff is less than what the population requires to justify that large a sacrifice of present interests to future interests: The population would be better off with less investment, down to level $\hat{I}$. With the perfect capital market we are assuming, that market will in fact gravitate toward $\hat{I}$, thereby achieving a use of resources that represents the best compromise between present and future interests.

Why the capital market moves to $\hat{I}$ and stays there is the point of the discussion. It is because, if investments are evaluated in terms of the criterion of maximization of present net discounted value, investors will want to invest resources in every project for which the rate of return on investment is no less than the market rate of interest. This is roughly mathematically equivalent to discounting costs and gross payoffs from the investment by the market rate of interest as the discount factor, and then investing if that resulting present net discounted value exceeds zero. In our assumed perfect capital market, nothing intervenes between rate of return to the investor and his offer of a price to pay for a loan; similarly, nothing intervenes between required future consumption enhancement for a lender and his asking price for a loan. So the clearing of this market equates for all traders the magnitudes in our graph—and the market equilibrium achieves the optimal intertemporal compromise on resource use.

The compromise here is between present interests and future interests—but they are the interests of the same people. Can an optimal compromise be achieved under discounting where *present* and *future* refer to different populations? Case II explores this premise.

Case II: Multiple Homogeneous Generations with Fungible Durable Capital

We now have a succession of generations with all individuals identical in tastes and personal endowments within and across generations. Again, everyone in the same generation has the same age, and all lifetimes are known with certainty. Now all investment projects are assumed to last beyond the lifetimes of any one generation. All durable and organizational capital is privately owned, and full property rights can be transferred without friction by exchange transactions. Each successive generation overlaps the last period of the former's lifetime, so intergenerational sale of property rights occurs in this overlap period and the sellers still have the alternative opportunities to consume the proceeds or give them to the next generation as bequests. The other assumptions of case I continue to hold here.

Assume that all investment projects produce the same physical goods or services here as in case I. The critical assumption has to do with the value of these commodities to the second generation compared to their value in case I. Our assumptions about population homogeneity—together with an assumption of absence of income effects (i.e., commodity valuation as influenced by per capita well-being)[2] permit us to infer that the second generation will value these commodities as much as the first generation did in case I. Here, however, the second generation cannot consume these commodities unless they buy property rights to them by paying their owners—the first-generation investors—in the last period of the first generation's lifetime. So the first-generation investors obtain *the same purchasing power* here from their investments as in case I, *and at the same time*—via the maturity of the investment in case I and via the selling of property rights to the second generation in case II. First-

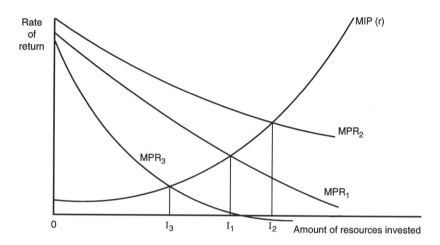

Figure 9.4
Optimal investment: two-generation case
where MPR is the marginal productivity of investment (in effect, the rate of
return on investment).

generation owners, therefore, obtain the same last-period consumption
opportunity relative to their first-period sacrifice in both cases. From
their point of view, the two opportunity functions displayed in figure
9.1 are the same in both cases, so their optimal investment decision,
level $\hat{I}$, is also the same.

Thus, the existence of two consecutive generations does not necessarily
change the optimality properties of present discounted value as an investment criterion. Generation one is equally well off in the two-generation case as in the one-generation case; and the individuals of generation
two receive the same transfer of resource use from period one to their
lifetime as if it had been they themselves who had made the decision in
period one how much resource use should be transferred to generation
two's interests via long-term investment.

The same general principle holds if generation two's valuation of the
commodity differs from that of generation one (See figure 9.4. If MPR_2
$> MPR_1$ (that of figure two), then $\hat{I}_2 > \hat{I}_1$; if $MPR_3 < MRS_1$, then $\hat{I}_3 <$
$\hat{I}_1$. But in all three situations, the amount invested reflects generation
two's valuation of the commodity (because generation one cannot consume it directly during its lifetime), and generation one's degree of
impatience. So an MPR_2 or MPR_3 belonging to generation one would

result in the same investment level whether one or two generations were involved.

Two more variants of case II should be examined: (1) variable maturity investments, where length to maturity is the result of generation one's decision, and (2) of multiple generations with and without variable maturity.

Variable Investment Maturity.   All investments made in period one can be voluntarily redeemed into consumption by generation one in the last period of its lifetime or can be renewed by that generation as an investment to mature in the last period of generation two's lifetime. The individuals of generation one make the decision by comparing what the project's consumption option is worth to them with what generation two offers them to extend the investment. If they choose to terminate the investment during their own lifetime, we simply have case I, and the allocation is optimal directly. If they choose to extend it, then the size of the intertemporal transfer is determined by the common rate of impatience (over the two-generation period) and generation two's valuation of the project output—which is optimal indirectly, as noted above for case II.

Multigenerational Case.   Say there are three generations, and projects can extend into the third generation. Now generation two has a choice of two possibly different valuations: valuation of its own consumption of the project output, or sale of property rights to generation three for its consumption of the later maturing project. If such a sale is preferred, then the original allocation of resources for transfer to the future is based on the value of generation three's consumption compared to the common rate of impatience over the three-generation period; again, given assumed population homogeneity, the choice is optimal indirectly.

Any number of generations can be subsumed under this model by simply linking decisions of later generations to those of earlier generations via sales of property rights to the investment at the common meeting points of successive generations. Thus, generation one is linked to generation five, say, via discretionary sales opportunities between generations one and two, two and three, three and four, and four and five. The same basic principle holds if generations overlap one another.

So, abstracting from frictions, uncertainty of the future, market imperfections, and the differences among generations, the discounting process does not inherently disenfranchise future generations or even discriminate against them. The fact that any gratification is worth less if it comes later than if it comes earlier is not a bias against a later generation, since if the earlier generation lived that long it too would depreciate the later gratification in favor of the earlier and be willing to wait only if waiting augmented gratification enough to offset the time depreciation.

Are there any circumstances, then, under which discounting does inherently discriminates against future generations? We shall answer this question next.

Discounting Optimality and Intergeneration Value Judgments

The simple model presented above was, even beyond its obvious simplifications, meant to be incomplete. In its intergenerational optimality, the intertemporal resource allocations that would maximize the welfare of generation one alone would also "appropriately" represent the interests of the generations that lived in the future by duplicating how generation one itself would have lived in that future. Omitted was the question of how future generations would pay generation one to obtain property rights to capital with a productive life beyond that of generation one—and without which such a "future optimal" scenario would not be possible. New issues are involved in dealing with this question.

We must complicate our two-generation model. First we must assume that, instead of all investment projects being long-lived, only one-period investment projects are possible—like planting a crop each year with seeds produced by last year's crop but not consumed this year. So each period's consumption and the following period's production possibilities are directly competitive and must be re-decided in each period.

Second we must determine how the second generation obtains enough purchasing power—inherently endowed as it is only with its raw labor power—to pay generation one for cross-generational capital as much during the overlap period as the present generation would itself have paid in balancing its own present versus future consumption (assuming a longer life for it).[3] Generation one's valuation of that cross-generation capital would have depended not only on their tastes but also on their overall wealth: their raw labor endowment and all accumulated human and durable physical capital resulting from past investments. Generation two can meet that bid only if generation one donates to them enough purchasing power to raise their wealth to the appropriate level in the overlap period. This can be done by donors in generation one transferring purchasing power to generation two to buy crossover capital from property owners in generation one. Some donors will themselves be property owners—in effect paying for vicarious consumption. These intergenerational grants are the lubricant for that "commercialization" of intergenerational resource allocation that permits the simplified form of optimality within the "self-interest" perspective of the present generation presented above.

The new model variant works as follows. Each year, generation one must choose how much of the fungible output of the preceding period to consume and how much to invest—i.e., plant for next year's crop. The decision is such that the incremental present utility from a particular consumption level—implying a particular present investment level— equals the present discounted utility value of the next period's combined consumption and investment. But the utility significance of that investment level depends, in turn, on the utility valuation twice removed (in terms of present discounted value) of the consumption and investment combination that follows. In like manner, none of these sequential terms of investment can be given a utility significance until the total harvest in the last year of the final generation's lifetime is given a utility value in terms of consumption during that last year. This depends on direct consumption and grant-financed "indirect" consumption via generation two. Once this is determined, the backward conditional linkage gives a total utility value to each year, moving backward from last to first. Thus, each prospective period-one investment level has a present discounted utility level that is higher to the extent that productive investment projects generate annual utility increases greater than the discount rate. The combination of the distribution of project net productivities and the amount that generation one is willing to donate to generation two in the last year of its lifetime help determine how high optimal investment will be in period 1 and thereafter. The larger the grant, the higher will be generation one's overall investment over its lifetime.[4]

This trade-off depends on investment productivities and intergenerational donations, but also on the size of the discount rate and on the rate at which incremental utility of consumption (marginal utility) declines as the total consumption level rises. High investment productivities favor more investment, and larger donations favor more investment. But the higher the discount rate, the higher both of these must be to warrant any given level of investment; thus the total investment level is depressed. Finally, decreasing marginal utility favors more consumption when the overall consumption level is low, but favors less consumption when the overall consumption level is high. Since the drag against investment through discounting means that only projects with substantial net productivities will be enacted, such a chain over time implies a significant growth in income level over time. Diminishing marginal utility decreases the attractiveness of further investment in the late periods, but favors intergenerational donations in the last period at the expense of more consumption.

The intergenerational trade-off in the last period is then dependent, first, on the overall lifetime investment sequence up to that point, which helps determine the total income during the last period. This can be directly consumed or "consumed vicariously" by reinvesting it for an output beyond generation one's lifetime and, via donating adequate residual purchasing power to those of generation two's representatives who are present in this last period, permit generation two to buy the invested capital from generation one, thereby making this investment fungible for the consumption of generation one in the same last period. The discount rate does not affect this trade off, since both direct and indirect consumption options are available in the same last period. The vicarious consumption via donation to generation two occurs in generation one's last period, not in the period after its disappearance. The trade off however, depends significantly on the rate of diminishing marginal utility and the utility worth of vicarious consumption versus direct consumption.

Marginal utility is straightforward and conventional. But vicarious consumption is the critical issue for the present work. What is "vicarious consumption"? It is the bequest motive and an intergenerational altruism. The bequest motive is the feeling that some future humans are a physical-moral extension of oneself; therefore, additions to their well-being are additions to one's own welfare. This motive is strongest for next-generation biological descendants and becomes progressively attenuated for nonadjacent generations. Intergenerational altruism is a feeling of generic responsibility for and empathy with future undesignated humans simply as members of the same species who are unavoidably dependent on some actions of the present generation.

The last-period intergenerational trade-off compares the strength of direct consumption and vicarious consumption, the first qualified by diminishing marginal utility, the second qualified by any degree of selfishness and progressive weakening of empathy for more distant generations. Our model implicitly includes many future generations, all linked to generation two the way successive years are linked together in the consumption-investment trade-off: Later years are encumbered by a cumulative discounting of their interests. What generation one donates to generation two implicitly influences what generation two will donate to generation three, and this, in turn, influences generation three's donation to generation four. So the worth of generation one's vicarious consumption depends partly on how important the whole chain of future generations is to generation one.

How strong is the worth of vicarious consumption? The answer is suggested by the many forms it takes in the real world, contrary to our model's simplifications. Richard B. Howarth (1990b, 20) states that intergenerational transfers "may take many forms, including child care, expenditures on education, investment in new technologies and capital, the transfer of natural resource rights, and bequests of wealth from parents to their immediate offspring. While some transfers are motivated by private altruism, the role for collective transfers through governmental institutions is both theoretically well-founded and readily apparent in public debates over natural resource policy."

The crux of this discussion is that our earlier model's intergenerational optimality requires a trade-off between direct and vicarious consumption such that the utility sequence for generation one will be the same up to the specified last period of its lifetime even if that lifetime should be extended by one period—i.e., its consumption-investment sequence through period m should be the same whether the period $m + 1$ applies directly to generation one or to the next generation. This condition is fulfilled only if the utility attenuation for generation one via diminishing marginal utility exactly balances its utility attenuation via imperfect empathy with future generations. This is a very stringent requirement, and it will generally not hold empirically.

The result is important for three reasons. First, the optimality of intergenerational allocation is not the same as that for intertemporal allocation even where the time interval is the same. Second, this optimality depends on values concerning how worthwhile future generations are to the present generation. Most treatments of allocational properties of present discounted value investment criteria refer only to allocation issues, ignoring or explicitly excluding distributional issues. Our formulation, which tries to make the case for discounting optimality most easily (since it refers only to the evaluational perspective of the present generation rather than to a more inclusive multigenerational criterion), in fact requires a demanding set of distributional values. Third, there are no empirical grounds for supposing that the optimality conditions will in fact be met by a discounting allocational regime. Therefore, in examining below the willingness of the present generation to make the kinds of large remote intergenerational sacrifices involved in taking early preventive action against global climate change, the specific determinants of intergenerational transfers are matters of real priority.

We now turn to a discussion of circumstances in which discounting leads to biased intergenerational allocations.

Intergenerational Biases under Discounting

We have argued that time discounting significantly reduces the relevance of economic analysis to the current international concern and debate over policy for global climate change because it makes policy evaluation nearly insensitive to large differences in damage scenarios for the far future, the only period in which these scenarios diverge greatly. We have also argued that the ineluctable appropriateness of time discounting for making intertemporal comparisons does not in fact hold for intergenerational comparisons. Moreover, in a stringent context (perfect cross-generation commercialization) designed to make intragenerational and intergenerational choices compatible, the required condition is unlikely to be met empirically. So time discounting becomes only one of a number of possible approaches to structuring intergenerational relationships of the sort we are concerned with for global climate policy, and must be explicitly appraised along with the others in terms how well it does so. Conventional criticisms of the standard uses of discounting in investment criteria stress imperfections and distortions in present markets, resource immobilities, market signal defects, critical uncertainties, incentive distortions due to various taxes and subsidies, etc., with the effect that there is no single discount rate that is uniquely appropriate in balancing future opportunities with present sacrifices.[5] These certainly affect our problem, but not in unambiguous, inherently salient ways. Accordingly we shall concentrate on a few deficiencies central to our concern.

Basic is the critical distinction between intertemporal and intergenerational allocation—namely, the distinction between intragenerational choices and intergenerational choices. Intragenerational choices refer to trade-offs by and from the perspective of a relatively fixed population: Critically, the same people take responsibility for their own welfare during the entire effective generation period (a deeper treatment of "generation" will be given in the Appendix to chapter 11). Any uncertainties are their uncertainties, even concerning their future tastes and conditions. They may indeed choose with dynamic inconsistency, inappropriately committing themselves to future circumstances. This empirically real possibility reflects the fact that individuals cannot always be counted on to make future provisions even for themselves. But at least they are arguably best represented by themselves in this endeavor.

Where different, widely separated generations are involved, the present population's ability to represent remotely future populations is considerably weakened. Contrary to our simple model above, the present population has little detailed knowledge about later populations—their tastes, circumstances, lifestyles, or even their numbers. While uncertainties about exogenous circumstances are much the same over a given time interval whether one or more generations are present, uncertainties about such things as tastes and social values differ mightily in the two situations. We remember that accurate predictions are needed for perfect cross-generational commercialization because the optimal flow of investment/consumption trade-offs needed from generation one during its lifetime requires their predictions of what the next generation would be willing to pay for various asset carryovers compared to the present generation's valuation of them. Even if the present generation wanted to represent future generations accurately—for the sake of the latter instead of the former—they would do it poorly. But acting in their own self-interest with respect to the latter via the commercialization of durable property adds another degree of distortion to that representation under imperfect predictability. The interests of future generations will not be well represented—certainly not in an optimal balance with those of the present generation.

Three factors seem especially important in distorting representation: public versus private impatience, distortion of signals due to externalities, and relative versus absolute evaluative perspectives.

Public versus Private Impatience

Public versus private impatience is a familiar problem that has been much dealt with.[6] Conventional evaluation generally takes a private market interest rate as a discount rate to obtain present values of costs and benefits. The market rate reflects all the grounds for individuals' expressed "impatience." In addition to a purely psychological bias for receiving good things early and bad things late, "impatience" reflects various uncertainties about the individuals' circumstances, tastes, moods, etc.—and especially their mortality: Will they even still exist to experience postponed gratifications? In our context of public policy, it is the government, not individuals, that is capable of acting on behalf of the future—indeed, is legitimated to do so. While specific individuals worry whether they will still be alive to enjoy a specific future gain, the government does not in principle have a finite existence: It may legitimately consider itself provisionally immortal. Therefore, a major portion of private impatience need not apply to government custodial action on behalf of the future. The conventional proposition stemming from this distinction is that the appropriate public (social) discount rate is in principle lower than the comparable private discount rate. A lower discount rate raises the evaluational weights on far-future outcomes relative to near-future outcomes compared to a higher rate. Since typical resource uses involve costs incurred early and benefits that come late, the lower social discount rate tilts resource uses toward providing more benefits to farther futures than would the higher private discount rate.

Accordingly some redress of the inadequate representation of future generations can be achieved.

This is an idealized picture of representative government. In actuality government behavior is rarely more future-oriented in its responsibilities. While one could probably say, with Robert Solow (1992), that people sometimes address government "in their capacity as citizens" rather than simply favoring their "private interests," the short timetable of political elections and reelections induces a strong tendency to fit the period of responsibility to the period of the next incumbency. Our analysis, however, is not directed to whether we *will* act "wisely" with respect to the future under various evaluational regimes, but simply to whether those regimes make it easier or more difficult to do so.

Intergenerational Externalities

Externalities are an important source of suboptimality via discounting. Both positive and negative externalities are pervasive, and very important. The two most important positive externalities are accumulations and improvements in knowledge (including knowledge in science and technology) and the development and cross-generational transfer of political, social, and economic institutions. Together these may well have been the predominant source of rising world per capita income over recent centuries. Negative externalities to a large extent involve various forms of degradation of natural resources and the environment: air, water, and land pollution; soil erosion; reduced biological diversity; and aberrations of local climate. Most notable in terms of pervasiveness, multifacetedness, and potential (but unknown seriousness) is global climate change via greenhouse gas emissions.

All these externalities have in common the fact that beneficiaries have no way of paying generators to induce greater supplies, nor do victims have any way of obtaining compensation from or penalizing generators to induce smaller supplies: and benefactors have no way of soliciting compensation for providing benefits, while damagers are not required to compensate victims for causing the damage. Property rights are absent or imperfect to connect these gainer-loser pairs. The relevance of this to our issue is that these resource uses carried out in the present are not linked to commercial transactions whereby good and bad consequences for future populations obtain rewards and punishments for their progenitors. Yet intergenerational optimality in our model rests on the comprehensiveness of perfect commercialization of all crossgeneration effects. This is violated for these externalities. Moreover, unlike deliberate adjacent crossgenerational gifts, where the donors essentially know their own valuation of what they give and believe it to be not much different for the recipients, with these externalities there is rarely even a coarse sense of the size of either positive or negative impacts on the recipients. They are diffuse and hard to measure, and their measurement has no reason to be institutionalized (as would measurements for trading, etc). So these represent resource uses that are very poorly integrated with the present generation's attempts to rationalize even its own intertemporal interests.

What is the net effect of positive and negative effects on the future? This question is impossible to answer. But our purpose here does not require such an answer. Assume the present generation has been reasonably satisfied up to now with its vague sense of the overall effect on the future—indeed, reassured that the bias has been positive on balance in the light of the long trend of rising per capita incomes overall. But now it is made aware for the first time that its actions—in the full flush of affluence—may already constitute a possibly serious threat to the future, and, indeed, that future generations may on related grounds expect lower rather than higher standards of living. Whatever the previous complacency of the present generation about its net responsibility to the future, this may well result in a sense that resource use is more biased against the future than was earlier believed. The new perception of potential global climate externalities seems like a solid ground for holding that a discounting criterion for intergenerational trade offs does not protect society from biasing resource use against the future—at least in the specific context of whether something should be done to avert these specific climatic damages.

Relative versus Absolute Evaluative Perspectives

The most dramatic, but most controversial, weakness of discounting concerns its normative legitimacy. The present discounted value criterion, together with the psychological focus of pure impatience, imply that the period within which a resource decision must be made has a special asymmetric importance in the evaluation of different choice alternatives: Every future event must be expressed in terms of its significance to this one period, and each point in time has an evaluative weight that diminishes as its distance from this focus period lengthens. What is so special about this focus period, the present? Each type of resource use under discussion extends over many periods, and in many of them the affected populations are the same. Let us return to the situation of case I, in which we deal with the lifetime of a single generation, to illuminate this problem in its simplest manifestation.

Assume the fixed population is facing three investment options at time t_1, all of which yield the same total net benefits over the projects' similar lifetimes: A, with level benefits over all periods; B, with rising benefits throughout; and C, with falling benefits throughout. Further, assume to begin with, that the marginal utility of gain is constant and that pure impatience is 5 percent. Then the present discounted value criterion will select C because its highest-weighted periods—those closest to the present—are also those with the highest benefits. Its lowest-benefit periods are those with the lowest weights. B is ranked second. A is ranked third because its highest benefits are given lowest weight and its lowest benefits are given highest weight.

Choosing C at time t_1 satisfies the population's impatience at that time. But it must live through t_2, t_3, and so on to the end of its lifetime, during which it must endure progressively declining returns. In each of those succeeding periods it is impatient to have good things sooner rather than later. But there is no period "later" than one that has already passed. The population's impatience applies both forward and backward in time. Once t_1 has passed, the population is likely to regret its past choice of C. Indeed, this regret will grow as t_1 recedes farther and farther into the past. Yet the regret is expressed by the same population that chose it at t_1. Its choice at t_1 committed it to a whole sequence of outcomes beyond t_1. But was the population at t_1 more qualified, more meritorious at t_1 than later, to be permitted to commit all of its later presents to regretful experience?

What is the normative superiority of the population's momentary present incarnation now over all subsequent "present" incarnations? Perhaps only that it has the momentary power now to make such commitments. Surely foresight should suggest that each present is only temporary and will be succeeded by other presents. If any one of these is accorded special privileges, then all the others may suffer. Intertemporal rationality strongly suggests that instantaneous relative impatience should not be permitted to influence intertemporal choice.

What would constitute intertemporal rationality in this kind of situation? One reasonable candidate is a criterion of minimizing regret over the projects' lifetimes. To see some implications of the use of this criterion, we must enrich the model by assuming diminishing marginal utility of income with a nonlinear functional form that is standard in such models. Then the rising trend of monetary returns of alternative B would carry entries with progressively smaller per-unit utility values. The falling trend of returns of C would carry progressively larger per-unit values. Because of nonlinearity the order of preference would be A, C, then B; i.e., equal intertemporal returns would be most preferred.

Notice that, despite no discounting here, raw outcomes in different years have different evaluative weights—the utility significance of each unit net gain. This criterion is therefore mathematically equivalent to the maximization of undiscounted lifetime utility. This may seem very similar to time discounting since the progressively more distant rising entries for alternative B are progressively discounted into lower and lower weights, but this is not so. The progressively more distant entries of alternative C have progressively higher weights. This is moot anyway, because alternatives with cyclical or otherwise nonmonotonic net returns over time will always receive weights based on their size, not on their remoteness in time from some arbitrary starting point.

Minimum regret, or maximum undiscounted lifetime utility, and other similar variants represent radical departures from maximum present discounted value. All dispense with the normative superiority of a single evaluative focus over the rest of the project's impact lifetime. All impact periods are accorded equal normative weight: The fixed population has an equal right "to be represented" at each and every period of its lifetime. Thus, time discounting is normatively suspect for defectively representing a given population's interests by using an inherently asymmetric perspective: Roughly, it always favors a momentary present over all futures. In so doing, it tempts that population to repeated instances of dynamic inconsistency where past "impatient" choices are systematically regretted after they have been made.

If time discounting gives future periods of the same population inadequate representation, how well can it represent future generations? As argued above, given insight into self-identity and self-control, individuals are assumed to be morally capable of planning for their own lives. Yet despite this, dynamic inconsistencies can well occur. But future generations are much less understood by them (in terms of tastes, lifestyles, and the former's intertemporal preferences) and obtain much less sympathy from the latter for gratifying the later generations' wants than the present generation accords its own future wants. Our normative doubts about the dominance of a momentary present in planning its own future should be magnified greatly where it is used to represent the interests of all future generations. This skepticism holds even if "present" is extended to include the whole lifetime of the "present generation" vis a vis all future generations.

We have intruded value judgments here into an area in which allocative efficiency, not distributive equity, is at issue. But value judgments have already intruded—in the conditions for intergenerational optimality, since the present generation had to compare the importance of its own well-being with that of future generations in choosing optimal bequests. Those value judgments can themselves be judged within the broader perspective of the various generations who will successively wield the sheer de facto power to commit their future generations to the consequences of their resource uses. In this larger context might does not necessarily make right: Possession of the temporary de facto power to influence the future does not necessarily convey normative legitimation of any and all kinds of influence.

In this section we have argued that time discounting nontrivially distorts the decision trade-offs among generations and carries no special normative support for using it despite these difficulties. The distortions of intergenerational issues are especially severe with respect to externalities, matters of expected lifetimes, and changing tastes, lifestyles, and values. The unique context of global climate change combines all of these distortions to an exceptional degree, justifying an examination of other approaches to time comparisons for an evaluation of public policy in the area of global climate change that would do more justice to its special features. In chapter 11 we shall look at some of these alternative approaches.

Notes

1. See chapter 11 and its appendix on generations for a discussion of the meaning and temporal designation of generations.

2. This is somewhat constraining, but the constraint will be minor compared to problems revealed in our deeper analysis of the intertemporal distribution of income levels below.

3. That is, in reality, a trade-off between last-period consumption by the present generation versus a production/consumption flow during the next generation's lifetime.

4. This emphasis on intergenerational grants is quite similar to the comparable emphasis, but quite different model context, in Howarth and Norgaard 1990; Howarth 1990a; and Howarth 1990b.

5. See Schmid 1989; Mishan 1982; Musgrave and Musgrave 1980; and Baumol 1970.

6. See, for example, Mishan 1982; Rosen 1992; Margolin 1963; and Feldstein 1964.

10
Intergenerational Equity: Toward an International Legal Framework

Edith Brown Weiss

Introduction

Sustainable development rests on a commitment to equity with future generations. This ethical and philosophical commitment constrains the inclination to take advantage of our temporary control over the earth's resources in order to use them for our own benefit without careful regard for what we leave for our children or for their descendants. The bias to favor ourselves is embodied in the logic that controls economic decisions over the use of resources in daily life. Recent concern for environmental externalities focuses mainly on the costs we and our contemporaries must bear in polluted air, water, and soils from industrial development; in deforestation; and in other aspects of economic development. While it is intended to ensure that the benefits from a contemplated action exceed its costs and that those who bear these costs are adequately compensated, in practice it operates from the perspective of the present generation. The discount rate ensures that short-term benefits nearly always outweigh long-term costs.[1]

Hence, it is useful to address the issue of sustainability through law and philosophy in addition to economics. Concerns about equity are central in the legal tradition. Law and philosophy provide a basis for analyzing the normative relationship among generations and the instruments for transforming normative values into rights and obligations. Legal instruments provide a means for ensuring that those who hold power follow the ideals of justice held by society. (While there are different schools of jurisprudence, it is not necessary to differentiate them for this chapter.)

Sustainability, which implies intergenerational fairness, is possible if we look at the earth and its resources not only as an investment opportunity but as a trust, passed to us by our ancestors, to be enjoyed and passed on to our descendants for their use.[2] Such a "planetary trust" conveys to us both rights and responsibilities. Most important, it implies that future generations, too, have rights, although these rights have meaning only if we, the living, respect them and if this respect transcends the differences among states, religions, and cultures.[3] The notion that each generation holds the earth as a steward or in trust for its descendants strikes a deep chord with men and women of all cultures, religions, and nationalities. Nearly all human traditions recognize that we, the living, are but sojourners on earth and temporary stewards of its resources.

The theory of intergenerational equity proposed argues that we, the human species, hold the natural environment of our planet in common with all members of our species: past generations, the present generation, and future generations (Weiss 1989). As members of the present generation, we hold the earth in trust for future generations. At the same time, we are beneficiaries entitled to use and benefit from it.[4]

There are two relationships that must shape any theory of intergenerational equity in the context of our natural environment: our relationship to *other generations* of our own species and our relationship to the *natural system* of which we are a part. The human species is integrally linked with other parts of the natural system; we affect and are affected by what happens in the system. We alone among all living creatures have the capacity to shape significantly our relationship to the environment. We can use it on a sustainable basis, or we can degrade environmental quality and deplete the natural resource base. As the most sentient of living creatures, we have a special responsibility to care for the planet.

The second fundamental relationship is that between different generations of the human species.[5] All generations are inherently linked to other generations, past and future, in using the common patrimony of the earth.[6] The theory of intergenerational equity stipulates that all generations have an equal place in relation to the natural system. There is no basis for preferring the present generation over future generations in their use of the planet. This assumption finds deep roots in international law. The preamble to the Universal Declaration of Human Rights begins, "Whereas recognition of the inherent dignity and of the equal and inalienable rights of all members of the human family is the foundation of freedom, justice and peace in the world. . . ." The reference to all members of the human family has a temporal dimension that brings all generations within its scope. The reference to equal and inalienable rights affirms the basic equality of such generations in the human family.

Each generation can and should use the natural system to improve the human condition. Improvements should be conserved for future generations. If one generation degrades the environment severely, however, it will have violated its intergenerational obligations relating to the care of the natural system. In such cases, other generations may have an obligation to restore the robustness of the system, with costs distributed across generations. The anchor of a legal framework is thus the notion of equality as the norm connecting sequential generations in their use and care of the environment. The corollary is the concept of *partnership* between humans and nature and between sequences of humans born.

To define intergenerational equity, it is useful to view the human community as a partnership among all generations. In describing a state as a partnership, Edmund Burke (1790: 140) observed that "as the ends of such a partnership cannot be obtained in many generations, it becomes a partnership not only between those who are living but between those who are living, those who are dead, and those who are to be born." The purpose of human society must be to realize and protect the welfare and well-being of every generation in relation to the planet. This requires sustaining the life-support systems of the planet as well as the ecological processes and the environmental conditions necessary for a healthy and decent human environment (IUCN 1980).

In this partnership, no generation knows beforehand when it will be the living generation, how many members it will have, or even how many generations there will ultimately be. It is useful, then, to take the perspective of a generation that is placed somewhere along the spectrum of time, but does not know in advance where it will be located (Rawls 1971).[7] Such a generation would want to inherit the earth in at least as good condition as it has been in for any previous generation and to have as good access to it as previous generations have had. This requires each generation to pass the planet on in no worse condition than that in which it received it and to provide equitable access to its resources and benefits. Each generation is thus both a trustee for the planet with obligations to care for it and a beneficiary with rights to use it.

While intergenerational equity may be viewed as in conflict with achieving intragenerational equity, the two are consistent and in fact must go together. Members of the present generation have an intergenerational right of equitable access to use and benefit from the planet's resources, which derives from the underlying equality which all generations have with each other in relation to their use of the natural system. Moreover, even the most selfish members of the present generation who care only about their own descendants must, as they extend their time horizon further, increasingly care about the general environment that their descendants will inherit. Since no one country or group of countries alone has the power to ensure a healthy environment, all must cooperate to ensure a robust planet in the future. This means meeting the basic needs of the poor so that they will have both the desire and ability to fulfill their intergenerational obligations to conserve the planet.

To be sure, there are instances where the actions needed to protect the health of the planet for future generations may conflict with the immediate alleviation of poverty, although poverty itself is a primary cause of ecological degradation. In these instances, we need to develop processes for ensuring that the rights of future generations are adequately protected while at the same time addressing poverty as quickly and effectively as possible through appropriate mechanisms.

Foundations of the Theory of Intergenerational Equity

Three distinct foundations provide a robust basis for this legal perspective on equity among generations: (1) philosophical and legal traditions, (2) international law roots, and (3) institutional foundations.

Philosophical and Legal Traditions

Philosophers from diverse cultural traditions have recognized that we are trustees or stewards of the natural environment. This fundamental thesis is also deeply rooted in the legal traditions of the international community. These roots can be found in the common and civil law traditions, in Islamic law, in African customary law, and in Asian non-theistic traditions.

The proposed theory of intergenerational equity finds deep roots in the Islamic attitude toward the relation between humans and nature. Islamic law regards man as having inherited "all resources of life and nature" and having certain religious duties to God in using them. Each generation is entitled to use the resources, but must care for them and pass them to future generations.

The utilization and sustainable use of these resources is, in Islam, the right and privilege of all people. Hence, man should take every precaution to ensure the interests and rights of all others since they are equal partners on earth. Similarly, he should not regard such ownership and such use as restricted to one generation above all other generations. It is rather a joint ownership in which each generation uses and makes the best use of nature, according to its need, without disrupting or upsetting the interests of future generations. (IUCN and Saudi Arabia 1983, 13).

Islamic law supports collective restrictions, which are to be observed under a principle of good faith, and collective rights, which are rights of the community of believers as a whole (Khadduri 1984, 137–39, 219–20, 233–39).

In the Judeo-Christian tradition, God gave the earth to the people he created and to their offspring as an everlasting possession, to be cared for and passed on to each successive generation (Genesis 1:1–31, 17:7–8). This tradition has been carried forward in both the common law and the civil law traditions. The English philosopher John Locke (1690), for example, asserts that, whether by the dictates of natural reason or by God's gift "to Adam and his posterity," mankind holds the world in common. In the civil law tradition, this recognition of the community interest in natural property appears in Germany in the form of social obligations that are inherent in the ownership of private property (Dolzer 1976).

The socialist legal tradition also has roots which recognize that we are only stewards of the earth. Karl Marx, for example, states that all communities, even if taken together, are only possessors or users of the earth, not owners, with obligations to protect and improve it for posterity (Ross and Silk 1987, 67).

According to African customary law we are only tenants on earth, with obligations to past and future generations (Allott 1975, 70). Under the principles of customary land law in Ghana, land is owned by a community that goes on from one generation to the next. A distinguished Ghanian chief said, "I conceive that land belongs to a vast family of whom many are dead, a few are living, and countless host are still unborn" (Ollennu, 1962, 4). The nontheistic traditions of Asia and South Asia, such as Shinto, also stress a respect for nature and our responsibilities to future generations as stewards of this planet. In most instances they call for living in harmony with nature (Stewart-Smith 1987; Northrop 1949).

International Law

The theory of intergenerational equity has a deep basis in international law (Weiss 1989: 25–26). The United Nations Charter, the preamble to the Universal Declaration of Human Rights, the International Covenant on Civil and Political Rights, the Convention on the Prevention and Punishment of the Crime of Genocide, the American Declaration on the Rights and Duties of Man, the Declaration on the Elimination of Discrimination against Women, the Declaration on the Rights of the Child, and many other human rights documents reveal a fundamental belief in the dignity of all members of human society and in an equality of rights that extends in time as well as space. Indeed, if we were to license the present generation to exploit our natural and cultural resources at the expense of the well-being of future generations, we would contradict the purposes of the United Nations Charter and international human rights documents.

Since World War II, states have begun to express concern in international legal instruments for the welfare of future generations and to set forth principles or obligations that are intended to protect and enhance the welfare of both present and future generations. Even the United Nations Charter, drafted in the aftermath of World War II, affirmed the universal concern for the welfare of future generations in its opening paragraph: "We the peoples of the United Nations, determined to save succeeding generations from the scourge of war . . ." (United Nations Charter, 26 June 1945, 59 Stat. 1031).

Concern for justice to future generations regarding the natural environment first emerged in the preparatory meetings for the 1972 Stockholm Conference on the Human Environment. The preamble to the Stockholm Declaration on the Human Environment expressly refers to the objective of protecting the well-being of future generations: "To defend and improve the environment for present and future generations has become an imperative goal for mankind." The concept of protecting the natural environment for future generations was explicitly incorporated in the language of three treaties negotiated more or less contemporaneously with the Stockholm Declaration: the 1972 London Ocean Dumping Convention, the 1973 Convention on International Trade in Endangered Species, and the 1972 Convention Concerning the Protection of the World Cultural and Natural Heritage. The regional seas conventions which were subsequently negotiated under the United Nations Environment Programme (UNEP) carried forward this concern for future generations. Other international agreements of the last two decades have contained language indicating either a concern for the sustainable use of the environment or a concern for future generations, ofttimes by reference to the common heritage of mankind (Weiss 1984, 495, 540–63). The 1982 United Nations World Charter for Nature, while not a binding agreement, explicitly refers to a requirement to protect species and ecosystems for future generations.

Except for the above references to future generations, international law to date has addressed intertemporal issues primarily in the context of relating the present to the past. In public international law, an intertemporal doctrine applies to territorial claims, to certain other rules of customary international law, and to several aspects of treaties. In private international law, it is reflected in questions of choice of time, as in conflict-of-law rules. In public international law, Judge Huber enunciated the intertemporal doctrine in the classic *Island of Palmas Arbitration*,[8] which involved a dispute between the United States and the Netherlands over the sovereignty of the small Pacific island. As described by Judge Huber, the doctrine has two elements: that acts should be judged in light of the law at the time of their creation, and that rights acquired in a valid manner may be lost if they are not maintained in a manner consistent with the changes in international law.

Although most disputes raising the intertemporal doctrine have involved territorial claims, the doctrine is more broadly applicable to other issues in customary international law and to treaties. There are several intertemporal issues raised by treaties: the proper interpretation of a treaty over time, the continuing validity of a treaty in the face of changed circumstances, and retroactive application. The Vienna Convention on the Law of Treaties contains specific provisions addressing these issues, although the doctrine of intertemporal law is not explicitly mentioned. Customary international law doctrines, such as *pacta sunt servanda* and *rebus sic stantibus,* respond to the intertemporal question of the continuing validity of treaties.

Intertemporal issues also arise in the context of procedural rules set by international tribunals and in private international law. They arise primarily as conflicts in time of rules of private international law adopted in a particular country, conflicts in time of rules of intertemporal law of the *lex fori* and *lex causae,* and conflicts of time and space caused by changes in the connecting factor. In the late 1970s, l'Institut de Droit International undertook a comprehensive study of intertemporal problems in private international law, and in 1981 it adopted a resolution setting forth applicable rules to govern intertemporal problems in private international law (l'Institut de Droit International 1982 and 1979; Graveson 1979; Sorensen 1973).

Intertemporal problems are common in national legal systems. Frequently they appear as conflict-of-law questions. The civil law tradition has a well-developed theory of conflict-of-law cases of intertemporal law, which invoke such distinctions as *intertemporal, droit transitoire,* and *conflit mobile,* terms which have no ready equivalents in English or the common law traditions. Temporal issues also arise in countries as tort liability cases. These cases involve claims that nuclear tests conducted for twenty or more years caused subsequent cancers and leukemia in victims,[9] that harmful drugs taken by mothers produced harm to fetuses, or that exposure to toxic substances years previously caused subsequent cancers, other health problems, and environmental damage. Similar issues have arisen at the international level, as governments of Pacific islands have made claims against governments of countries with nuclear weapons for the contamination of their people and their environments by nuclear testing in the Pacific in the 1950s.

Institutional Foundations

The International Court of Justice has long invoked equitable principles in its jurisprudence.[10] There is a long tradition in international law of using principles of equity to interpret documents and reach decisions in order to achieve a just result (Lapidoth 1987; Chattopadhyay 1975). In the World Court's jurisprudence, as Sohn (1984, 303, 308) has noted, the court has clearly distinguished between principles of equity and equity *ex aequo et bono* under Art 38(2) of the court's statute and between equitable principles in international law and equity in domestic law. In the *North Sea Continental Shelf* cases, the court sets forth the classic description of equity:

Whatever the legal reasoning of a court of justice, its decisions must by definition be just, and therefore in that sense equitable. Nevertheless, when mention is made of a court dispensing justice or declaring the law, what is meant is that the decision finds its objective justification in considerations lying not outside but within the rules, and in this field it is precisely a rule of law that calls for the application of equitable principles.

Increasingly equity is being invoked to mean "equitable standards for the allocation and sharing of resources and benefits" (Henkin et al. 1986, 102. See also Thacher 1987; Janis 1983). The Law of the Sea Convention, for example, includes several provisions invoking equity. Article 59 provides that conflicts over the exclusive economic zone are to be "resolved in the light of equity." Agreements delimiting the exclusive economic zone between states and opposite or adjacent coasts must "achieve an equitable solution" based on international law. In addition, the International Law Commission's draft articles on the succession of states in respect to state property, archives, and debt repeatedly invoke "equitable proportions" and "equitable compensation" as the basis for allocating property between a predecessor and a successor state(s).

The use of equity to provide equitable standards for allocating and sharing resources and benefits lays the foundation for developing principles of intergenerational equity. These principles can build upon the increasing use by the International Court of Justice of equitable principles to achieve a result that the court views as fair and just. The World Bank, the International Monetary Fund, and the major international organs of the United Nations system are predicated on notions of equity among states. The concepts and the content differ, but the underlying precepts driving 'development,' 'technical assistance,' and more recently 'sustainability' are ones of providing for present and future generations an acceptable quality of life. The 1992 United Nations Conference on Environment and Development (UNCED) focused on environmentally sustainable economic development, which is an inherently intergenerational issue.

The Theory of Intergenerational Equity: Legal Dimensions

The two crucial dimensions for the theory of intergenerational equity are time and space (in relation to the natural system). They are interconnected and cannot be separated, either conceptually or practically, even for purposes of international public policy.

Three Principles of Equity

Three principles frame intergenerational equity. First, each generation should be required to conserve the diversity of the natural and cultural resource base so that it does not unduly restrict the options available to future generations in solving their problems and satisfying their own values, and it should also be entitled to diversity comparable to that enjoyed by previous generations. This principle is called "conservation of options." It can be accomplished in part by technological innovation that creates substitutes for existing resources or processes for extracting and using them more efficiently.

Second, each generation should be required to maintain the quality of the planet so that it is passed on in no worse condition than that in which it was received, and it should also be entitled to planetary quality comparable to that enjoyed by previous generations. This is the principle of "conservation of quality." It does not mean that the environment either could or should remain largely unchanged; this would be inconsistent with the third principle below. Rather it recognizes that tradeoffs are inevitable and that a framework must be developed in which such balancing can take place. This will require the development of predictive indices of environmental quality, the establishment of baseline measurements, and an integrated monitoring network.

Third, each generation should provide its members with equitable rights of access to the legacy of past generations and should conserve this access for future generations. This is the principle of "conservation of access." It means that members of the present generation have a nondiscriminatory right to use the resources of the planet to improve their own economic and social well-being provided that they do not unreasonably interfere with the access of other members of their generation to do so as well.

Four criteria guide the development of principles of intergenerational equity. First, the principles should encourage equality among generations, neither authorizing the present generation to exploit resources to the exclusion of future generations nor imposing unreasonable burdens on the present generation to meet indeterminate future needs. Second, they should not require one generation to predict the values of future generations. They must give future generations flexibility to achieve their goals according to their own values. Third, they should be reasonably clear in their application to foreseeable situations. Fourth, they should be generally shared by different cultural traditions and be generally acceptable to different economic and political systems.

The proposed principles recognize the right of each generation to use the earth's resources for its own benefit but constrain the actions of the present generation in doing so. Within these constraints they do not dictate how each generation should manage its resources, and they do not require that the present generation predict the preferences of future generations, which would be difficult if not impossible. Rather, they try to ensure a reasonably secure and flexible natural resource base for future generations, which they can use to satisfy their own values and preferences. The principles of options (diversity), quality, and access form the basis of a set of intergenerational obligations and rights, or planetary rights and obligations, that are held by each generation. These rights and obligations derive from each generation's position as part of the intertemporal entity of human society.

Rights and Obligations: Planetary Scope

Planetary intergenerational rights and obligations are integrally linked. The rights are always associated with obligations. They are rights of each generation to receive the planet in no worse condition than did the previous generation, to inherit comparable diversity in the natural and cultural resource bases, and to have equitable access to the use and benefits of the legacy. They represent in the first instance a moral protection of interests that must be transformed into legal rights and obligations.

In the intergenerational dimension, the generations to which the obligations are owed are future generations, while the generations with which the rights are linked are past generations. Thus, the rights of future generations are linked to the obligations of the present generation. In the intragenerational context, planetary obligations and rights exist between members of the present generation. They derive from the intergenerational relationship that each generation shares with those who have come before and those yet to come.

Intergenerational rights of necessity inhere in all generations, whether these be immediately successive generations or ones more distant. There is no theoretical basis for limiting such rights to immediately successive generations. If we were to do so, we would often provide little or no protection to more distant future generations. Nuclear and hazardous waste disposal, the loss of biological diversity, and ozone depletion, for example, have significant effects on the natural heritage of more distant generations.

Intergenerational planetary rights may be regarded as group rights, as distinct from individual rights, in the sense that generations hold these rights as groups in relation to other generations—past, present and future. They exist regardless of the number and identity of individuals making up each generation. When held by members of the present generation, they may acquire attributes of individual rights in the sense that they are identifiable interests of the individuals that the rights protect. However, those interests derive from the fact that those living now are members of the present generation and have rights in relation to other generations to use and benefit from the planet. The remedies for violations of these rights will benefit other members of the generation, not only the individual.[11]

Enforcement of these intergenerational rights is appropriately accomplished by a guardian or representative of future generations as a group, not of future individuals, who are of necessity indeterminate. While the holder of the right may lack the capacity to bring grievances forward and hence depends upon the representative's decision to do so, this inability does not affect the existence of the right or the obligation associated with it.

The question arises whether future generations can have rights. According to this argument, rights can exist only when there are identifiable interests to protect. This would require that we identify individuals who have interests to protect. Since we cannot know who the individuals will be in future generations until they are born, or even how many will exist, they cannot, according to this argument, have rights. But the rights of future generations are not individual rights; rather, they are generational rights in which the interests protected do not depend upon knowing the number or kinds of individuals that may exist in any given future generation.

It can be argued that such rights depend upon knowing at least the number of individuals in the future because if the earth's population continues to grow rapidly, the amount of diversity and degree of quality that must be passed on will be higher than if the population in the future were at the same level or less than it is today. But, if anything, the existence of these generational rights to the planet may constrain the population policies of present and future generations. Whether a generation chooses to meet its obligations by curtailing exploitation, consumption, and waste or by constraining population growth is a decision it must make. The fact that future generations have a generational right to receive the planet in a certain condition puts constraints on the extent to which a present generation can ignore this choice.

Almost every policy decision of government and business affects the composition of future generations, whether or not these decisions are taken to ensure their rights under the principles developed above. Decisions regarding war and peace, economic policy, the relative prosperity of different regions and social groups, transportation, health, and education—all influence the demographics and the composition of future generations by affecting the lives and fortunes of the present generation: who will succeed and prosper, who will marry whom, who will have children, and even who will emigrate (Weiss 1990).

Our planetary obligations to future generations are owed to all the earth's future human inhabitants, whomever they may be. This opens the possibility that all decisions deserve to be scrutinized from the point of view of their impact on future generations. This may lead to the further development of human rights law as a useful and broadly acceptable theoretical underpinning to sustainable resource development. The possibility that intergenerational equity may place limits on our actions is an important new area of human rights research.

Such limitations should be applied very narrowly so that the rights of future generations do not develop into an all-purpose club to beat down proposals for change. But long-term environmental damage is a good place to begin. Future generations have the right to be assured that we will not significantly pollute groundwater, load lake bottoms with toxic wastes, extinguish important habitats and species, or change the world's climate dramatically—all long-term effects that are difficult or impossible to reverse—unless there are extremely compelling reasons to do so that go beyond profitability (Weiss 1990).

There may be key breaking points in our global environmental system beyond which systems will reorganize and substantially change their properties.[12] If we are concerned about future generations, it is important to try to predict these breaking points. More important, the best tool that we could give future generations with which to respond to abrupt changes and reorganizations is a robust planet, which requires conserving a diversity of resources so that future generations have greater flexibility in designing responses.

In Chapter 11 of this book, Rothenberg criticizes the planetary trust theory as idealistic and requiring additional assumptions to accommodate intragenerational equity. In its place, he proposes a model of backward indebtedness. According to this construct, members of the present generation owe a debt to their predecessors in previous generations, which they pay to their successors in the form of investments, over and above those they would make in their own interest, in the robustness and sustainability of the planet. These debts are owed separately by each member of the present generation, but are owed to the successor generations taken collectively. In general, the backward debt is used to pay for the same kind of activities that are obligated by the planetary trust—pollution abatement, development of new resources, etc. An important difference is that irreversible change that threatens the robustness of the planet or depletes resource options is discouraged by insurance premiums rather than by normative rules and procedures.

As Rothenberg points out, both the backward indebtedness and the planetary trust models constrain present consumption so as to ensure the welfare of future generations. In the backward indebtedness model, the obligations of the present generation flow directly from the benefits they have received rather than from a normative structure of stewardship and equality among generations. In the planetary trust model, *intra*generational equity flows not from backward indebtedness, but from the nondiscriminatory access rights of each generation to natural (and cultural) resources.

The backward indebtedness model has the major disadvantage that the obligation on the present generation to conserve resources (to engage in proper resource accounting in making investment decisions) is an extra assumption that is external to the model. It assumes that generations are grateful for their legacy, just as children are grateful to their parents, and will sacrifice for unknown generations even though the past generations are not there to hold them accountable in any way. The world is replete with examples of societies that have cursed their pasts and obliterated remnants of them.

As previously discussed, the notion of stewardship is an integral part of the great world religions and of a variety of legal traditions. As a result, it may find deeper acceptance than the altruistic argument based on benefits received. In most ethical and religious traditions, moreover, obligations to future generations are considered separately from obligations to poor members of the present generation, so that the economic logic of the backward indebtedness model may not contribute to its popular appeal.

As Rothenberg also points out in his careful analysis, all models that require the present generation to constrain its current use of resources to ensure the future sustainability and robustness of the earth suffer from inherent problems of defining, measuring, and judging what and how much is to be sacrificed or conserved and to what end. The main pragmatic value of these constructs is to force people to confront the trade-offs between generations and to provide at least qualitative tools for addressing them. Both models depend on philosophical and moral judgments whose acceptance will depend on the extent to which they find deep resonance among the peoples of the world.

Implementation Strategies

Elsewhere I have proposed eight strategies for implementing intergenerational equity.[13] Four of these are stressed here: the representation of future generations in decision-making processes, including those in the marketplace; intergenerational assessments of the impact of our actions on future generations and their implications for intergenerational equity; the elaboration and codification of intergenerational rights and obligations in relation to the planet and the development of the international legal duties associated with certain activities into legal instruments; and global learning and education to raise the public consciousness of all peoples in all age groups of the need to conserve the planet and our cultural resources for future generations and to encourage public participation in relevant decision-making processes. These strategies can be implemented at the local, national, and international levels.

Representation to Future Generations
While the decisions we make today will determine the initial welfare of future generations, they are not effectively represented in the decision-making processes today. While they may be willing to pay us handsomely to prevent certain actions or to have us undertake others, they have no way of voicing this preference.[14] Representation must take place at several levels: in administrative decision-making, in judicial decision-making, and in the marketplace.

To influence administrative and judicial decisions we can appoint and publicly finance an office that has responsibility for ensuring that the interests of future generations are considered, for ensuring that laws regarding our environment and natural resources are observed, for investigating complaints, and for providing warnings of pending problems. States should be encouraged to give standing in their national courts and administrative bodies to a representative of future generations, who might function as a guardian *ad litem*. Other approaches are to designate an ombudsman for future generations or to appoint commissioners for future generations. These could operate at multiple levels: international, national, regional, and/or local. The World Commission on Environment and Development (1987, 332) recommended that countries consider an ombudsman at the national level.

Future generations are not effectively represented in the marketplace today; they must be. This requires that first we understand the fundamental entitlement among generations correctly. Under the theory proposed in this chapter, future generations have an equal claim with the present generation to use and benefit from the natural environment. Using this premise, the task is then to develop the appropriate mix of economic instruments to achieve the entitlement most efficiently (Norgaard 1991). Proper natural resource accounting is an essential instrument.[15]

Assessment of Impacts on Future Generations
If we are to avoid or mitigate adverse effects on future generations, we must assess the long-term effects of our actions today on them. While under the U.S. National Environmental Policy Act environmental impact statements must consider long-term effects, they do so, if at all, from the perspective of the present generation. In other cases, including the 1992 UN Convention on Environmental Assessment in a Transboundary Context, the consideration of long-term effects is not explicitly required. We need to start from the interests of future generations and ask what the effects of our actions will be on those interests. By starting from the perspective of future generations, we may begin to rectify the present imbalance in impact assessment, which favors the present generation. It may be appropriate to have the private sector, in particular transnational corporations, multilateral banks, and private banks, provide intergenerational impact assessments for activities which will significantly affect the well-being of future generations in relation to their natural environments.

Elaboration and Codification of Intergenerational Rights and Obligations
To encourage cooperation between countries and among communities to fulfill obligations to future generations, it is useful to elaborate and codify as many of the relevant norms of intergenerational equity as possible. Codification reduces the ambiguities about the behavior that is expected of parties. It defines cooperative behavior and distinguishes it from uncooperative behavior. Some of these legal instruments will be nonbinding. Others may be binding or may become binding over time.

To the extent that the norms contained in the instruments represent customary international law, all countries would be bound whether or not they were party to the relevant agreement. Some instruments would be general ones that would articulate intergenerational rights and obligations; others would be directed at the use and conservation of specific resources, such as forests, soils, fresh water and biologically diverse marine areas; still others might facilitate the scientific research and development required to develop alternative resources or to use resources more efficiently.[16]

International regimes, including regional and bilateral ones to manage or to coordinate measures for managing particular natural or cultural resources or activities affecting these resources, are also important. They increase the likelihood of cooperative behavior when there are many participants, as in the international community. They also facilitate the development and exchange of information, make it more difficult for a party to defect since there are costs involved, and may facilitate the development of new norms.

Global Learning and Public Participation

To change the approach that we presently use to address intergenerational concerns may require a new ethos that is planetary in scope and encompasses all generations. Since the well-being of even a community's own future generations depends upon the general planetary environment in which they will live, every community must arguably be concerned about the willingness and the ability of all members of the present generation both to use and to conserve the planet for future generations.

For this to happen means that people need to develop a public consciousness about the issues and to be informed about environmentally sustainable development. The rapid and impressive development of information technologies will make the gathering and dissemination of relevant information much easier and will make such information more accessible. Nongovernmental organizations have already assumed an important role in drawing attention to environment and development issues, in mobilizing communities, and in exerting pressure on decision-makers, whether locally, nationally, or internationally.

Implementing our responsibilities to future generations will be difficult. Our institutions, whether they be international, national, or local, are designed to handle relatively short-term problems of several years' duration. They are for the most part not well suited to address long-range problems, particularly those whose effects may not be felt for a generation or more. Most political systems have a short-term perspective built into them. Powerful political incentives encourage those in positions of power to focus on short-term issues so that they will have tangible results to show. Similarly, private businesses are forced by the workings of the market to take a relatively short-term view. But intergenerational equity is based on a long-term perspective. Achieving it will require adjustments in institutions, economic incentives, legal instruments, public consciousness, and political will.

Notes

This chapter is based on Weiss 1989 and Weiss 1990.

1. For insightful analysis of the shortcomings of our present economic instruments in addressing future generations, see chapter 9 of this book by J. Rothenberg.

2. Some scholars, such as J. Simon (1981), would contend that the concern with future generations is misplaced because technological innovation and infinite resource substitution will ensure the well-being of future generations. However, while improvements in technology and the availability of substitute resources may offset some exhaustion of natural resources, the possibility of real price increases in natural resources to future generations remains. Moreover, our activities pose long-term risks to the health of our planet and, arguably, to our cultural resources. We have no right to assume that technical advances will clean up any mess that we make. There are many examples of people with abundant land resources who reduced a region to desert by misuse, such as by excessive cultivation, and then moved on.

3. This chapter sets forth a theory of intergenerational equity that finds resonance in international legal instruments. There are other approaches to intergenerational equity that are not covered here. For analysis of these, see chapter 11 in this book by J. Rothenberg, and Weiss 1989.

4. The theory also applies to cultural resources, since they form an integral part of the legacy we give to future generations and are linked to our role as a member of the natural system. For application of the theory of intergenerational equity to cultural resources, see Weiss 1989.

5. An anonymous reviewer thoughtfully noted that this assumes that humans share the belief that they are part of a "species being." It may be argued that some social groups deny that human beings share a single destiny, such as those who proffer explicitly racial doctrines or those who espouse social Darwinism and believe that human evolution will lead to further differentiation of species and to the disappearance of "backward" elements. However, the fact that humans themselves try to differentiate among themselves or to use theories of evolution to advance their own ends does not alter the fact that all humans are

part of the natural system and, as such, are inherently linked with those who went before and those who come after in using and caring for it.

6. The theory has been criticized for depending upon a link with improving the human condition and hence being anthropocentric rather than on a moral level with nature itself. See D'Amato 1990, 190. While the theory is concerned with equity among generations in the care and use of the planet, it is explicitly rooted in the recognition that the human species is part of the natural system. This implies great respect for the natural system of which we are a part, but it does not imply that all other living creatures are or should be treated equally. Rather, the human species, as a part of this natural system, has a special obligation to maintain the integrity of the planet so that all generations of humans will be able to enjoy its fruits.

7. Some human communities may, however, contend that they know the final days of existence are approaching and hence that they or certain elites within them have extraordinary rights over the environment. The veil of ignorance is only an analytical tool to facilitate the derivation of principles of intergenerational equity; it does not by itself regulate the behavior of communities. Nor need the assumption be accepted by all communities in order for normative principles to develop that would be intended to guide community behavior, including theirs. O. Young, in Chapter 13 of this book, suggests that maximizing uncertainty may be a more effective way to convince the present generation to consider the future than to ask that they imagine themselves in a veil of ignorance. But whatever the merits of this approach, which arguably may cut against positive actions to protect the environment for future generations as well as in favor of such actions, it does not offer a premise from which to derive principles of intergenerational equity.

8. *Island of Palmas Arbitration* (Netherlands v. U.S.) 2 R. Int. Arb. Awards 831 (1928). The principle has been subsequently applied in a number of cases before the International Court of Justice, including the *Minquier and Ecrehos* case, the *Western Sahara* case, the *North Sea Continental Shelf* cases, and the *Aegean Sea Continental Shelf* case. While the first element of the intertemporal doctrine has been widely accepted as a basic principle, the second has been controversial.

9. For example, 460 cancer and leukemia victims who were infants at the time the United States conducted nuclear tests in Utah and Nevada during the 1950s tried to recover for harm. Allen v. U.S., 527 Fed. Supp. 476 (D. Utah 1981). On 15 October 1990, a new law went into effect which established a $100 million trust fund to provide payment to persons believed harmed by fallout from nuclear testing at the Nevada test site (*New York Times,* 16 October 1990, p. 1, cols 4–5).

10. See in particular the maritime boundary decisions; *North Sea Continental Shelf* cases (Federal Republic of Germany v. Denmark; Federal Republic of Germany v. Netherlands) 1969 I.C.J. 3; *Continental Shelf* case (Tunisia v. Libya) 1982 I.C.J. 18; the case *Concerning the Delimitation of Maritime Boundary of Gulf of Maine* (Canada v. U.S.) 1984 I.D.J. 246; and *Continental Shelf* case (Libya v. Malta) 1985 I.C.J. 13.

11. The temporal dimension may offer a theoretical basis for unifying those human rights that we now consider to be group or social rights and for so-called "new" human rights. Group rights, such as cultural rights, have a temporal dimension since the community inherently extends over time. Theoretically, rights to development, to health, and to the environment can be seen as inter-

generational or intertemporal in that they are rights of access of each generation to use and benefit from our natural and cultural resources.

12. This is consistent with the scientific paradigms expressed in the theories of catastrophe and of the dynamics of complex systems far from equilibrium. For catastrophe theory, see Thom 1983; for the theory of complex systems, see Prigogine and Stengers 1984.

13. Weiss 1989. The others include sustainable use of renewable resources; monitoring; scientific research and technological development to enhance understanding, develop substitutes, and increase exploitation and use efficiency; and maintenance of facilities and services (Weiss 1989, 119–52).

14. See Chapters 9 and 11 in this volume by J. Rothenberg for detailed analysis of this problem and for Rothenberg's distinction between intertemporal issues and intergenerational ones.

15. Rothenberg also emphasizes proper natural resource accounting in his backward indebtedness model (see Chapter 11).

16. For a comprehensive list and cross-referencing of relevant international environmental instruments, see Weiss, Magraw, and Szasz 1992, and for a statistical analysis of multilateral environmental agreements, see Chapter 12 by P. Haas in the present volume.

11

Economic Perspective on Time Comparisons: Alternative Approaches to Time Comparisons

Jerome Rothenberg

Alternative Approaches to Intergenerational Evaluation for Global Climate Policy

This chapter extends the analysis of chapter 9 and specifies six different approaches that systematically give more weight to the well-being of future generations relative to the present generation. They are alternatives to time discounting; they are presented here in order of increasing radical modification of the standard discounting approach. Following a review of each, we then present a strategy for formulating intergenerational and intertemporal comparisons. The six approaches are (1) accounting for natural/environmental capital stocks, (2) making present-based social value judgments about future well-being, (3) decoupling time discounting from generation discounting, (4) placing sustainable development constraints on present resource use, (5) extinguishing each generation's debt to the past, and (6) defining an intertemporal social welfare function through Intergenerational Equity: planetary rights.

Accounting for Natural/Environmental Capital Stocks

Under the labels of environmental/resource accounting or "green" accounting, this approach has been receiving growing attention.[1] Conceptually it is very simple and involves the fewest departures from the conventional resource criterion. The argument is this: Standard measures of net output should, unlike present practice, subtract from the total value of production the complete value of whatever resources are used up in generating it. This is obvious, and it is currently practiced for materials and labor services. For durable capital it takes the form of depreciation of the capital stock; it is done for "net" but not for "gross" versions of output. But other resources contribute to production, notably "environmental resources," for which no such deductions are made, and such omissions misrepresent current well-being and generate dysfunctional incentives about resource use.

Resources closely associated with nature are the missing contributors: soil, water, air, climate and the complex of biosphere processes that grow things and reproduce and transform. Their contribution to human production is generally omitted from the formal accounting of production shares because they are typically not owned, bought, or sold by anyone. Their services are not explicitly paid for. Other such resource depletions are omitted because they are not observed, or they are part of complex interactive processes—as, for example, the effect of deforestation on soil quantity and quality, biological diversity, and even local weather. Still other such resources seem to be ordinary private property, but it is not their diminished quantity that is inadequately measured, but the value of the diminishment.[2]

Another form of environmental resource affects not human production, but human consumption. Human activities affect the quality of air, water, and public spaces. Heavy and/or abusive use of these environments in turn adversely affect human physical and psychological health. Market resource-using activities meant to offset these health effects should be considered real costs of those other—production and consumption—activities just as if productive inputs had been used up in generating them. But they are currently treated as if they added to net human well-being instead of representing a lower-bound measure of additional unregistered diminution of that welfare by other activities.

Omission of these real forms of the using up of environmental capital stocks has two negative effects. First, it overstates current production, giving a false sense of the overall productivity of technology and resources. Formal measure of current "income" implies a productivity net of capital stock losses—i.e., implies that the current level of production can be continued into the future. If, instead, total current production is defectively overstated, then, if all else is equal (technology and conventional resources), future production cannot be maintained at the current level. Second, the threat of future decreases in overall productivity will be overlooked. There will be little advance warning, and the source of the decline will not be understood. No signals will provide information or incentives to generate efforts that can systematically be coordinated (in a decentralized manner) to minimize the decline. Incentives for resource use will then be dysfunctional.

Preliminary studies suggest that rectification would make a considerable difference,[3] so the task is worth the effort. Rectification involves calculating values of decreases in natural resource stocks and in various forms of environmental quality that accompany each period's total production and consumption activities. Resource stock decline plus that portion of environment quality that represents an input into production are subtracted from the total value of production to obtain net current production. Declines in environmental quality that directly affect the quality of consumption or forms of defensive consumption that are required to offset utility losses through disamenities causing ill health, inconvenience, etc., are subtracted from gross consumption spending to obtain total net consumption. The ultimate allocation of the decreases in production value will affect current net consumption via that part of current output that is presently consumed; it will affect future consumption by decreasing the real net investment carried over to augment future production.

This procedure is simple in principle, but difficult in practice. It is difficult both to measure the physical change in stocks and environmental quality and to give a value to these changes. Physical and quality changes are difficult to measure because the input/environmental characteristics whose changes we are referring to are often not discernible in short periods—e.g., soil quality, biological diversity, erosion security, and air and water quality. Such changes will often not be registered in changed market values where the resources are owned. The really important function to be performed by the accounting reform is to connect each activity to the particular combination of stock/environment quality declines that it generates. Only then can the accounting indicate how to mitigate specific declines—i.e., which activities need modification in amount or kind to lessen particularly dangerous kinds of decline.

This cause-and-effect linkage is exceptionally difficult because many of the declines are the result of complex indirect systems of interrelationships among animate and inanimate matter: Specific damages cannot be traced back to their causes, and specific causes cannot be followed forward to the broad complex of their effects. And we have no sharply discerning markets to help us here. A third difficulty applies to the more straightforward types of natural resources: nonrenewable minerals. For known deposits, which are owned, it is straightforward to estimate the total annual extractions. But in each period search activities discover new deposits. The problem for accounting is that only rough estimates can be made of the reserves added to before extensive extraction is carried out. So the net change resulting from extractions and additions in any period is only a rough approximation.

The measurement of the values of these changes may be even more difficult. As with physical change, the problem is partly the frequent absence of developed markets to create expertise in the perception of value changes. The measures are really intended to project changes in overall future productivity and consumption welfare. Three elements are therefore involved for owned resources: (1) how much effort it would take to replace the used-up materials—via growing (for renewables) or new discoveries (for nonrenewables); (2) what percentage of known stocks is represented by present net usage (as a predictor of expected price rises); and (3) with what complementary productive resources (natural and human-made) they are combined in production and with what changes in technology. All three elements are uncertain. For non-owned resources and environmental quality the problems are more difficult still because of the absence of markets, the non-monetary nature of the effects, and the complex indirect systems of interrelationships that the externalities take—all masking what changes have to be assessed.

Accounting reform must be accomplished, but how will this kind of accounting reform affect our central issue, the distribution of well-being among generations? At the least it calls to attention the drag on real output due to the exploitation of nature. Coupled with disaggregated cause-and-effect delineation of the sources of environmental depredation, it can lead to the targeted use of policy instruments to moderate such depredation—decreasing the environment/resource impact of production and consumption activities. If producer and consumer exploiters of nature can be held responsible for decreases in the resource-environment stock, then such new disincentives on resource use will slow down the rate at which these natural resources are exploited, generally on behalf of present gratifications over future gratifications. The result is a general present-to-future tilt to resource orientation.

This tilt is inherently intertemporal rather than intergenerational. Resource use is for the present on behalf of the futures of both the present and future generations. Indeed, much of the tilt is probably exclusively intertemporal and *not* intergenerational. The evaluation of investment projects, with present and future costs and benefits corrected for changes in nature's stocks, is still conducted in terms of present discounted values. So there is no decoupling of year-by-year tradeoffs from generation-by-generation tradeoffs.

Accounting reforms must be implemented for their own sake. They do not by any means fully address the problems we set out to address at the outset, but serious attempts at this partial rectification are warranted. Accordingly, only the resource use-corrected variant of the measure of our activities will be referred to hereafter in seeking more pointed and adequate rectification.

Making Present-Based Social Value Judgments about Future Well-Being
The impacts of various governmental interventions (including zero intervention) with respect to global climate change occur well beyond the expected lifetimes of the present generation and are at most only slightly commercializable for present resource owners. Any discount rate for comparable intertemporal trade-offs derived from private market transactions would reflect the uncertainties and fears and impatiences drawn from the narrow, finite, mortal focus of private individuals. But, as indicated in chapter 9, the responsible agent of intertemporal intervention connected to global climate change is not the individual, but the state. For this agent intertemporal trade-offs can in principle (whatever our experienced reality to the contrary!) reflect the continuing, sober responsibility of a provisionally immortal entity, with broad powers and scope of action that can presumably eliminate or at least modify many of the outcome features that are uncertain to biological individuals. The resulting implicit *social* discount rate is likely to be much different—and lower—than the private discount rate generated in private market transactions.

Since the social discount rate is lower than the corresponding private discount rate, distant outcomes are given more relative weight in the former than in the latter, decreasing the inherent tilt favoring present over future outcomes imparted by discounting. The reduced tilt refers to intertemporal trade-offs generally, not specifically to intergenerational ones, but the interests of future generations do gain. In the case in which resource use commitments generate important intergenerational externalities, this gain for future generations comes at the expense of the direct interests of the present generation. This is because the future's gains cannot be commercialized into sellable private property held by the present generation.

Nonetheless, allocation decisions are still based on the evaluational perspective of the present generation. They must indicate how much a unit of benefit to a future generation is worth to them at the "boundary" where the present generation ends and the next generation begins.[4] This comparison must be made at this boundary in order to avoid gross inconsistencies. If the present population believes that a unit of benefit to a future generation is worth less than a unit of benefit to themselves in general, and the vantage of comparison is made to be the present time, then the value to themselves of that same benefit at the future boundary before the next generation will be its present value discounted at the social discount rate. This present discounted value of a benefit to themselves may well be less than the value to them in general of the benefit going to the next generation. In its last period the present generation would be valuing its own gain at less than that same gain going to the next generation.

The trade-off between the present and future generation should thus be based on comparing how high a boundary period present-generation benefit (B) would have to be to have the same worth as a unit benefit to the present generation at the present time (A) and then how much higher that benefit would have to be than that boundary benefit if it went to the next generation instead of the present generation (C). The lower social discount rate lessens the difference between A and C by lessening the difference between A and B, but any intergenerational discount between B and C remains. Thus the procedure is still present-oriented—with respect both to intertemporal and to intergenerational choice. In practice, discounting with social discount rates often makes no distinction among generations since outcomes are valued solely in terms of when they occur, not to whom. Generational identity is incidental. Substitution of social for private discounting changes only the degree of present/future asymmetry, not its epistemological nature.

The strict intertemporal form just noted is compatible with a number of approaches that explicitly attempt to address intergenerational trade-offs (see below). To permit modifications for specifically intergenerational issues, it is easy to recommend that for intragenerational issues the discounting approach itself be modified by distinguishing between resource uses for which private discount rates are appropriate and those for which social discount rates are appropriate. Social discount rates should be used where appropriate instead of private rates for such intragenerational issues. But how are social discount rates to be discovered, and which resource uses qualify for such treatment?

Here we simply sketch some of the questions related to social discount rates.[5] The first obvious choice of an approximation to "the" social discount rate—as less than the private market rate—is the interest rate on government borrowing. Essentially riskless in comparison to the spectrum of risks associated with private investments, in practice it will be less than the latter. The social intertemporal preference trade-off must take account of the differential risk between public and private future-oriented resource use. But the social balancing of present- and future-oriented resource use must also take into account the various types of future externalities involved in collective public action on behalf of future interests. Among others, one relates to functional complementarities and their coordination; another to sheer large scale. The net impact of all of them is with high probability to make the social rate even lower than the government borrowing rate. But no observable transactions will themselves reveal what it is.[6]

Which kinds of government investments should employ social discounting as opposed to private discounting? There is no reason to expect that only investments concerning global climate change should be subject to the lower social discount rates. Any type of project for which the distinctive features of collective investment are present—scale, coordination, and externalities—should similarly receive this treatment. Global climate policy must thus compete against all other types of public future-oriented activities as well as against private projects with present—and future—orientations. It will have no discounting rate advantage over the former, except possibly where not one, but a set of social discount rates are used, each one appropriate for a different degree of collective decision characteristics. When these collective competitors are numerous and important, social discounting will not impart much exceptional tilt toward future interests on issues of global climate policy.

Decoupling Time Discounting from Generation Discounting
Discounting within and across generations may well reflect different empirical and even normative bases. The informedness of resource use choice might be considerably different between the two, as is the degree to which present choosers could take responsibility for the preferences and welfare of those in some future period or would take such responsibility. If we argue that present and future generations are, in fact, dissimilar enough, then one can decouple the two and treat the comparability over time differently in the two cases:

Within generations. The comparability of time periods is based on conventional time discounting.

Across generations. From the perspective of an earlier of two generations, an outcome occurring at any time during the later generation is treated as occurring in that generation and is discounted by a single intergenerational trade-off: how much a unit gain or loss to that specific later generation is worth to the earlier generation. Viewed from the perspective of the earlier generation, the passage of time within the later generation does not change the terms on which the earlier generation is willing to trade off gains to itself for gains to that later generation. The tradeoff simply concerns how members of the earlier generation feel about the population of the later generation on the average.

For any reference generation (the "present"), the treatment of future generations would involve a generation discount rate (GDR) applicable to each future generation, as follows:

$$GD_i = (GDR_{1i}, GDR_{2i}, GDR_{3i}, \ldots, GDR_{ji} \ldots) \tag{1}$$

all $GDR_{ji} \geq 0$.

Each GDR_{ji} represents a discount rate that would convert a generation j event into its "present-generation i discounted value," $PGDV_{ji}$:

$$PGDV_{ji}(X_j) = \frac{X_j}{1 + GDR_{ji}}. \tag{2}$$

Each GDR_{ji} depends on the degree of sympathy or empathy that members of generation i have for the generation j population.[7] Clearly GDR_{ji} increases with increasing remoteness—just as a conventional time discount factor, $(1 + r)^t$, does with increasing t—but not necessarily linearly.

Early in Chapter 9 we presented an illustrative Generation Discount Rate function (figure 9.2) as a generation step function of elapsed time into the future, and monotonically decreasing with the remoteness of the generation. Within the present generation, however, it is identical with conventional time discounting. The first step decline—from G_1 to G_2—is modest, because direct biological linkage renders strong empathy—vicarious consumption that is an extension of one's own direct consumption. The step from G_2 to G_3 is greater because of a sharp break with direct linkage vis a vis G_1. The further downward steps beyond G_3 are, however, progressively smaller because remoteness progressively blurs vividly expected generation differences: Each becomes abstract, stylized, and the differentiation of empathy has little meat to feed on.[8] The subscript i in the vector GD_i indicates that different reference generations may have different sets of trade-offs for future generations, depending on different degrees of sensitivity based on experience, social values, or culture.

The effect of this approach, which defines both a time discount rate, r_i,[9] and a generation discount vector, GD_i, is that events within the duration of the present generation, i, the generation time interval (GTI_i), are made comparable by present time discounted values, and events that will occur beyond GTI_i in some generation j—say one hundred years away—are made comparable by present-generation discounted values, and these latter are computed from the present period alone, not after first discounting them from the end of the present generation's generation time interval, or this compounded further by discounting all intervening generations as well! Thus, events one hundred years and more away are not automatically discounted to near-zero present values regardless of the size of the future events. For example, event outcome X two hundred years away during generation k has a present value simply given as

$$PGDV(X_k) = \frac{X}{1 + GDR_k} \, . \tag{3}$$

Remote events thus have a present value based on the strength of the present generation's empathetic reach into the future, not on the sheer number of years intervening. With a strong reach events even two hundred years into the future may be of concern to the present generation. This certainly may radically increase the willingness to use resources today toward the interest of future populations. Analytically this approach avoids one of the major defects of the most frequently recommended alternative approach: namely, a radical lowering of the social discount rate.

While our discussion of social rate discounting in the last section suggested that different social rates be used for different kinds of resource uses, most conventional recommendations involve a single social discount rate. If people today cared about circumstances for the generation living 200 years from now, the level of the single social discount rate that would be necessary to give those circumstances nontrivial evaluational standing today would be so low that the evaluation of resource uses with maturities within the present generation's lifetime would be severely biased. Projects judged by that social discount rate would far more heavily favor future net benefits than those judged by the private discount rate and, since projects subject to the two rates are substitutes to some extent, there would be an unavoidable considerable, largely unintended, shift of various resource uses to favor future as against present outcomes within the present generation's lifetime—along with the intended attention to circumstances two hundred years into the future.

Multiple social discount rates may be manageable with modest degrees of remoteness in terms of heavy overall resource use bias, but the global climate issue makes very long remoteness relevant, and for this the rate disparities would be huge and lead to large allocational disruptions. But in the present case, they are not necessary. Returning to our hypothetical example, the present population cares about the generation that will be alive two hundred years from now. The exact number of years separating the two populations is less important than the imaginative grasp of what they might be like. The intensity of the concern is the degree of empathic sensitivity rather than an empirical prediction of circumstance as a strict function of elapsing time, so the active expression of that concern should be in terms of the degree of sympathy with different populations.

Thus, there is no unintended biasing of intertemporal balance during the present generation's lifetime. All intragenerational transactions remain evaluated by conventional time discounting. Intergenerational concern is expressed directly in the measure of that concern—intergenerational trade-offs—without interfering with the direct expression of intragenerational trade-offs. The net effect is that future concern can be much more expeditiously translated into action as a result.

A major difficulty in this approach lies with the definition of generations and the operational spelling out of generation time intervals ($GTIs$). Generations are radically overlapping. New people are born every day; new people die every day; every day the population is literally different. What then constitutes a "generation"? How does one assign any time interval to a particular generation, or any generation to a particular time interval? Some expedient procedure must be adopted if the approach is to be implementable at all.

The practical answer is to recognize the necessity of simplification. We move to simplify in two ways: (1) with a conventional estimate of GTI—some average generation lifetime;[10] (2) with an arbitrary assignment of each time period to the GTI of some generation. So what is designated as a single generation is in reality an assortment of people of different but overlapping ages, and "their" lifetime is one within which the composition of the population is in fact continually changing through births and deaths. The simplification is consistent with the intricate network of shared interrelationships and experiences characteristic of a contemporaneous population.[11]

Note also that at some time period t_0 it is possible, although not probable, for a net benefit thirty years into the future to have a higher present value than the same sized net benefit twenty years into the future. This outcome occurs if (1) twenty years from t_0 were still within the present generation's GTI, while thirty years represented the next generation's GTI, and (2) the intragenerational time discount rate were substantial, while the next generation's welfare meant much to this generation, so the generation discount rate was quite small. This is in contrast to the last section, which called for a reference comparison only in the last period of the present generation's *GTI*, because we accord inter- and intragenerational criteria separate and equal evaluational status due to the empirical reality of a spectrum of intergenerational feelings of solidarity.

In sum it is possible, and indeed useful, to distinguish between intra- and intergenerational preference trade-offs as independent entities and to use different principles to secure comparability over time—principles that have equal status as well as being different. This procedure fits our stated need for a policy evaluation instrument for global climate change intervention. Since it is a more facile way of permitting the present generation (or any reference generation) to express its own preferences about future generations' welfare, it can be employed with any of the modifications of standard discounting that have been examined so far. (We shall see below that it is also compatible with more radical alterations that qualify the autonomy of present-generation preferences.)

Procedurally, for whatever further modifications may be adopted, it is necessary to (1) use conventional time discounting *within* each generation for all types of intertemporal impacts—perfectly marketable or involving externalities; (2) use time discounting also for all fully "commercial" impacts *across* generations;[12] and (3) use generation discounting for partly or wholly noncommercial impacts *across* generations (i.e., when public good aspects or externalities are important).

Placing Sustainable Development Constraints on Present Resource Use
So far, all the approaches have rested on the same fundamental normative principle: Those who control resources have the right to use them in ways that their wants dictate. Questions of efficiency refer only to how well the consequences of these uses accord with what they in fact want. Only those presently alive have that control. The will and wants of those presently alive are asymmetrically salient for the evaluation of resource uses. The will and wants of those who were alive in the past are relevant only through the effect of past contracts they made that hold over into the present; the will and wants of those who will—or may—be alive in the future are relevant only through the self-interest (via sales) and/or altruistic concern of those now alive for them, both of which may tilt resource use toward the future. Whatever modifications to the criteria of intertemporal choice have been discussed so far have

always referred to making the consequences of resource uses more closely reflect these interests. In our remaining discussion we shall drop the normative principle of the dominance of the preferences of that uniquely privileged group, those presently living, including their interests in future groups. The right of those presently alive will not be unqualified; several *normative* constraints on those rights will be examined.

The first constraint relates to sustainable development—a normative principle whose adoption has been widely urged relative to many issues in the fields of natural resources and the environment.[13] This approach states that each generation should use natural resources and the environment to meet their needs only in ways and in degrees that leave the next generation with similar capacity to meet their needs and yet leave unimpaired the ability of still further generations to do likewise, and so on for the whole sequence of generations. In cruder terms, it says that each generation should live off income only and leave capital unimpaired.[14]

This principle dispenses with the notion that the present generation should determine for itself how best to use resources on behalf of the present and the future. It imposes on this present generation and on all future present generations the same constraint *symmetrically*. This present generation thereby loses its special normative status as the "measure of all things." The principle imposes on each generation in its turn the responsibility to serve as steward for the interests of future generations. The normative principle is thus a symmetrical universalistic principle, transcending that of self-interest for de facto control.

There are several consequences of this principle in practice. First, the key resources to be used are natural resources and the environment. The danger regarding the former concerns the exhaustion of nonrenewable resources and the overuse of renewable resources so that the cost of renewing supplies becomes progressively higher over time. The danger regarding the latter concerns the degradation of environmental quality (including the integrity of major ecological systems and biological diversity). A critical unresolved question has to do with what is to be preserved: Is it a stock of general natural capacities and qualities, or an undiminished inventory of large classes of natural resources and environmental qualities as production/consumption inputs,[15] or an undiminished inventory of detailed inputs, or an undiminished overall absolute or per capita productive capability, or a non-decreasing flow of real income per capita? There are many variants of the concept embracing one or more of the above objectives for sustainability, but they differ substantively and have significantly different empirical properties.

The major focus of the literature emphasizes sustainability in terms of natural resource/environmental quality inventories: sustainability as maintenance of input stocks. How are these stocks to be measured? Our earlier discussion of natural resource/environmental quality accounting ("green accounting") addressed the same question. How does one recognize the various stocks and calculate their depreciation with use? In the case of renewable resources, how does one gauge degrees of overuse? One must generate complex input cost/supply functions that account for exploration, discoveries, and facility retirements. For exhaustive resources, estimating undiscovered reserves and the cost of finding and exploiting them is crucial. In what terms does one measure various environmental qualities and their impairment? These are difficult problems.

More basic than these, however, are fundamental conceptual questions. Must some overall total input capacity be preserved, or must it be quantities of specific materials, and, if the latter, how finely must these materials be classified? At stake here is the substitutability of different inputs in production: input substitutability in production of the same outputs, and substitutability for shifts in production mix. Then, too, changing technology calls for different input mixes or different kinds of inputs for the same products, or for different products altogether. Concentration on natural resource inputs may be misplaced, since technology change may make various non-natural resource inputs (e.g., human capital) strong substitutes for natural resources.

The more detailed the list of resources that must all be conserved, the less relevant such conservation is to overall productive capacity, because increasingly numerous types of production and consumption substitution are thereby precluded. Sustainability then becomes progressively less relevant to human welfare over time, and the principle thus less and less attractive overall. If only very broad resource categories are used, problems still remain. Once technological change, exploration, and human capital are recognized as influencing substitution possibilities, input productivities, and overall production possibilities, then investments in all of these must be recognized as activities that create potential productivity. Since their gestation periods are varied, and sometimes long, and their success is uncertain, how are such ongoing activities to be allowed to offset the running down of physical stocks? The net balance of these stocks must be consulted to diagnose and evaluate their state of sustainability.

If broad resource categories are used to represent productive capabilities, then individual resources must be aggregated in terms of their potential contribution to production. The conventional procedure is to do so via their market values. Two problems are especially troublesome here: First, a given resource may have a productive capacity (and market value) of Z_1 in a production regime with technology T_1 and combine with complementary inputs I_1; but in a different contemporaneous regime it may well have a capacity (and market value) Z_2 very different from Z_1. Which is correct? Or must there be a weighted sum of such different values for the variety of contemporaneous regimes? Second, since diagnoses of sustainability or nonsustainability are projections into the future of the results of present trends, can these be accomplished without predicting changes in technology and non-natural resource input availabilities for all these regimes—as well as the results of exploration for natural resources—which present investment activities make variously probable?

In sum, for all its present popularity, sustainability of development is not a precise enough concept to inform its implementability; indeed, given the ambiguities of definition and the complexity of measurement (even were it only for present uncertainty about future tastes and technology[16]), it is bound to be notably vague. Moreover, attempts to shape sustainability with precision closer to welfare possibilities move it considerably away from an emphasis on the use of green accounting to spell out specific constraints on current resource uses. It then more closely resembles the approaches of the next two sections. Accordingly, after those sections we shall return for a critical comparison of the three approaches to attempt to sketch out an attractive strategy.

Extinguishing the Backward Indebtedness of the Present Generation
The sustainable development approach emphasizes the moral obligation the present generation owes to all future generations, but it does not

single out any one generation for this obligation: All are equally subject. This symmetrical proposition implies a basic normative criterion, which can be considered the major structural principle of an intergenerational social welfare function. The intergenerational social welfare function is lexicographic—i.e., overall welfare depends on the absolute levels of income achieved by each generation conditional only on leaving unimpaired the capacity to generate comparable income by the next generation. Expressing the sustainability constraints in terms of the conventional economic terminology of a social welfare function[17] (albeit intergenerational) is not especially illuminating, however, because the only real structure given to it is in effect a set of binary, not multiparty, relationships: constraints on each generation with respect to its successor. In this section we propose a symmetrical, multiparty set of constraints, but these essentially reduce to a string of three-party relationships. Therefore, we shall forego the multiparty terminology of social welfare functions, reserving that to the last approach below, whose core is *multilateralism.*

The normative persuasiveness of the sustainable development proposition depends on the plausibility of the moral obligation owed by each present generation to future generations. The obligation arises as a generalization of the bequest motive, whereby individuals make gifts to the next generation during their lifetimes and will the transfer of their remaining property after their death to their descendants (and to others) in the next generation. These personal, specifically targeted relationships between the donors and heirs can be straightforwardly generalized to everyone in the next generation and to everyone in all future generations as well. Some degree of forward altruism surely exists, but not so broadly, so unmitigatedly, and so pervasively. A fundamental moral principle should rest on a stronger empirical base than this.

This section attempts to build a forward responsibility on what may be more substantial empirical grounds. Its core is the unquestioned debt that members of the present generation owe to the past at the moment of birth and the resulting feeling of gratitude that grows in them during their dependency stage.[18] They are born with raw human potential but no natural resources, no technology, no culture, no institutions. They are gradually given, as a legacy from all previous generations, all four of these: access to enormous amounts and diverse kinds of natural and human capital. They are also given material wealth through donation and inheritance. All they really pay for, or gain by their own efforts, is their efforts to use such access to obtain the physical and human wealth offered to them.

They are born with only raw potential which, if applied in a world without such resources, technology, culture, and institutions stemming from the past—and from nature—would generate income streams far smaller than their actual prospects. Then one can formulate what the present generation owes to all past generations and Nature: the difference between their actual prospects at birth and their hypothetical prospects with no assistance from the legacy given them by all past human generations and nature. We couch this in terms of economic opportunity sets. Each opportunity set is based on a given set of productive resources and technology, and it represents the set of overall output mix possibilities that can be generated from that input and technology set.

In order to express each opportunity set in a single dimension to permit comparison among such sets, we find that mix of outputs on the frontier of the production set that maximizes the total value of output at the initial set of "real" output prices[19] and monetizes it by that same set of "real" output prices. Call this *potential income*. So any individual or group in the present generation owes a debt to the past represented by

$$D_j^i = Y_j^i - Y_j^{i*}, \tag{4}$$

where D_j^i is the debt owed by individual or group i in generation j,

Y_j^i is potential income given i's actual endowment of resources and technology (*actual potential income*), and

Y_j^{i*} is potential income given a resource/technology base that excludes the past's (and nature's) endowment[20] (*"primitive" potential income*).

$$Y_j^i = (\max Y \mid S_j^i (I_j^i, T_j^i), P_j) \tag{5}$$

$$Y_j^{i*} = (\max Y \mid S_j^{i*} (I_j^{i*}, T_j^{i*}), P_j) \tag{6}$$

where S_j^i is the actual production opportunity set available to i with resource set I_j^i and technology T_j^i, and S_j^{i*} is the primitive set with corresponding resources and technology; P, is a vector of "real" output prices.

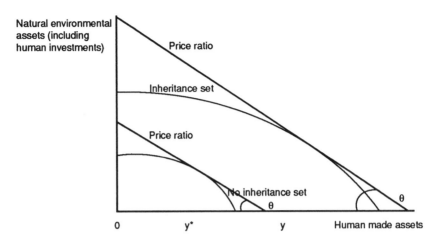

Figure 11.1
Backward indebtedness via opportunity sets
Note: Angle θ is the ratio of human to non-human asset prices; y^* is primitive potential income; y is actual potential income.

$$D_j = \sum_{\text{all } i \in j} D_j^i \tag{7}$$

gives the aggregate indebtedness of generation j.

We can illustrate the debt in convenient simple form (Fig. 11.1).

An important property of this concept of generational indebtedness is that different members and groups (e.g., national populations) may have different amounts of indebtedness given their differential access to resources and technology.

Why and how are these debts to be repaid? We assume the realization of the indebtedness will empirically generate a moral obligation to repay it in some form, a moral obligation that stems from gratitude. This gratitude is empirically abetted by the long dependency period during which much of the transfer is made by and through the agency of the parental generation. The debt cannot be repaid to the past except insofar as the still-living retired parental generation can be subsidized to offset inadequate provision for retirement. Much the larger balance of the original indebtedness can be repaid only by comparable support to future generations, and a "giving back to nature" of what was taken from nature by the generation. The form this support is to take is to assure the next generation a potential income of no less than the predecessor generation (generation j) had at its inception. The mechanism of indebtedness and repayment of debt is as follows:

If generation j leaves a resource/technology base to generation $j + 1$ such that $Y_{j+1} \geq Y_j$, then no further repayment (δ_j) is needed ($\delta_j = 0$). If $Y_{j+1} < Y_j$, then the active repayment needed is

$$D_j \geq \delta_j = Y_j (1 + m_j) - Y_{j+1}, \qquad (8)$$

where m is the population growth rate between generations j and $j + 1$. Thus D_j marks the limit of generation j's responsibility for $j + 1$'s potential income. The significance of the factor $1 + m$ will be discussed below.

How is δ_j to be paid? First, its size is to be estimated during the course of G_j's *GTI* (generation time interval). If δ_j is predicted to be positive, then remedial action on behalf of G_{j+1} is to be taken during (the later part of) G_j's lifetime equal in value to δ_j.

Equation (8) is a payback constraint on G_1. But it is a form of constraint on behalf of G_2. It has much the flavor of the sustainability constraint on any G_1 on behalf of G_2. In practical terms there is much general similarity. But there are important differences. First, the character—and strength—of the normative principle that embeds the two are different. Second, the substantive specifics of what is owed and how it is to be repaid are different (see below).[21] The backward indebtedness orientation involves three active participants—past, present, and future generations. The past-present linkage is the most formidable in attempting to structure a normative context for present-future relations.

Indebtedness and active repayment are couched here in terms of what G_j owes to G_{j+1}. In fact, G_j owes D_j to the whole succession of generations following it but can meet its obligation by means of a $G_j - G_{j+1}$ relationship. This is partly due to the fact that most of G_j's resource/ environmental depredations will in fact affect only G_{j+1}. But some depredations will have longer effects. Our process of global climate change has each G_j negatively impacting generations very remote from G_j. In addition, resource access and environmental quality are affected by significantly nonlinear processes which can lead to effective irreversibilities. It is too costly or even practically impossible for G_{j+1} to remedy some of the damages inherited from G_j. How will these multigeneration impacts be reflected?

Potential income for any generation refers to net output availability (i.e., gross output less the indebtedness that will be owed to the next generation). So if G_j expects to impose costs C_{j+2}^j on G_{j+2}, it must assure for G_{j+1} a gross potential income of $Y_j + C_{j+2}^j$ instead of only Y_j. Thus, active repayment to G_{j+1} is

$$D_j \geq \delta_j = (Y_j + C_{j+2}^j) - Y_{j+1}. \tag{9}$$

If there are multigeneration impacts, then

$$C^j = \sum_{k=1}^{\infty} C_{j+k}^j. \tag{10}$$

Thus, the successor generation is the present generation's link to all of the future, and that successor has its successor playing the same linkage role for its future. All generations are linked together by this binary relationship. But the full constitutive relationship in this model is a trinary relationship: (1) the accumulated past, (2) the present generation, and (3) the next generation.

How is active repayment of debt to be made? As generation j passes through its lifetime (GTI_j), its trends in resource use are projected onto an expected initial situation for G_{j+1}, G_{j+2}, ... If, all other things being equal, this suggests that $\delta_j > 0$ is likely, G_j must undertake preventive/ameliorative/compensatory actions on behalf of G_{j+1}, G_{j+2}, ... These may involve pollution abatement, a decreased rate of usage of scarce exhaustible resources or of overused renewable resources, or compensatory, substitutive ways of increasing overall productivity from the resource base expected to remain by the onset of G_{j+1}. The latter can be accomplished by increasing the base of human-created resources, notably physical and human capital, or improving technology. Such actions under δ_j are to be actions over and above what G_j would have done in its search to maximize its own welfare (by either direct or indirect consumption[22]). Thus, it is a genuine cost to G_j.

This proposal permits "repayment" not only in the same "currency" in which the start-out deficit for G_{j+1} manifests itself, but in substitutive ways as well. If the major focus of global climate policy, for example, is the welfare of future human generations, not the "integrity" of nature, then substitutions that preserve or enhance future human welfare should be acceptable even if they accompany nontrivial changes in natural characteristics.

Explicitly permitting substitutive repayment is due to the fact that the great upward sweep of worldwide per capita income over the last three hundred years, where it has occurred, has not been due to conserving or augmenting the stock of natural resources (or maintaining environmental quality), but to changes in technology and associated increases in human and physical capital. Indeed, these changes have induced large changes in the relative importance of different kinds of natural resources to be used in production—and induced through massive directed exploration, a substantial augmentation of known stocks of many kinds of natural resources despite substantial increases in the rate of their utilization over the period. To require strict, item-by-item constraints on the use of permitted known stocks of resources is to deny human ingenuity the opportunity to improve human welfare by seeking improvements in the most consequence-effective ways and thus to ignore the predominant engine of human improvement during this long period.

The first major emphasis of this repayment approach is to permit major substitutions across natural resources, between natural and human-created resources, and between technology and resources generally. This emphasis is on flexibility. The second is an emphasis on irreversibility. In calculating the amount of G_j's required repayment, if any, the initial stock of resources available to G_{j+1} is converted into total potential productivity by means of the productivity inhering in each resource or each package of resources. Suppose that total productivity has to come from a stock in which the quantity of resource A available has fallen by an amount Z. How much output loss is accounted for by this loss? A good starting estimate would be based on the supposed marginal productivity—reflecting the market price of the resource.

But this price does not reflect what is really at stake. First, the price is based on starting levels of the resource. Where these represent stocks well above exhaustion level (for depletable resources) or are the result of a previous level of use well within easy replenishment (for reproducible resources), prospective levels of use by G_{j+1} do not presage significant rises in price. Then original price is an appropriate estimate of the continuing price for G_{j+1}. If, however, starting stocks are low—the resource is scarce (in either depletable or nondepletable form)—prices might be expected to rise considerably during the course of G_{j+1}'s *GTI:* Significant nonlinearities in the supply price function are to be expected. If stocks are reduced very low, its renewal (for nondepletables) may be practically impossible, and it becomes like a depletable resource—i.e., essentially unavailable.

This is the situation of irreversibility: Resource option has been fore-closed. Since its changing productivity over time is a function not only of a known schedule of effectiveness in combination with other produc-tive inputs (along which schedule firms move depending on supply con-ditions), but also of changes in technology (production methods and new products), then its whole effectiveness schedule may shift drastically. If the resource option is lost, however, the opportunity to take advantage of the improvement is lost. (Of course, technology change may also lower its productivity. What is involved is significant uncertainty.) The present generation must be discouraged from bringing about irreversi-bilities to permit it to take advantage of unexpected large opportunities. This can be done by assigning a price to a scarce resource that adds to the initial price both the expected market rise with precarious use and an insurance premium—a measure of expected regret if the resource should become essentially unavailable—i.e., an option price.

The same treatment is appropriate for green accounting. This back-ward indebtedness approach requires the use of green accounts to enable calculation of the extent of indebtedness and the size of required repay-ments. Price premia for both expected rising supply rices and possible essential exhaustion (irreversibility) are called for in that accounting. As a resource nears significant scarcity its price as a measure of social loss rises significantly, in principle exerting a brake on the further rate of its utilization and inducing a shift in use toward its substitutes. This is the principle of retaining flexibility of options for the future.

Thus, this approach makes possible the observance of two normative/ prudential principles of sustainability: (1) retention of flexibility of op-tions for the present generation and (2) retention of flexibility of options for future generations. Standard treatments of the sustainable develop-ment approach usually sacrifice the first to make the second more fea-sible. The present approach seeks a more even-handed compromise between the two.

Three further issues need to be discussed relative to the backward indebtedness approach: (1) contribution to growth impetus; (2) absolute versus per capita achievements; and (3) treatment of welfare redistribution. Sustainable development and the more radical planetary rights approach (discussed in the next section) stress *similarity of outcomes* for successive generations. Improvements achieved by one generation should be repeatable by the next and secured by the sustainability constraints placed on the former on behalf of the latter. That means that G_j's sacrifice to G_{j+1} must be great enough not only to ensure that G_{j+1} starts from a level no worse than G_j started from, but also to include improvements achieved by G_j during its lifetime (or some representative rate of improvement achieved). Thus G_j is taxed on its growth. As with other taxes, the expected result is to discourage growing to some extent.

The incentive situation is quite otherwise for the backward indebtedness approach. Not only does the success achieved by G_j during its lifetime not add to its indebtedness or its required repayment; it serves to decrease the expected size of required repayment—indeed, significant success makes the probable required repayment zero! A constant strength of the bequest motive is that generations with larger wealth will voluntarily donate more to heirs in the next generation, thereby helping G_{j+1}'s starting situation. The best guarantor of sustainability in the past has been the untrammeled incentive of each generation for economic growth. While greater strains of such growth on resource availability and usability are now perceived, a properly accounted growth is still attractive for human welfare and should not be needlessly sacrificed.

Backward indebtedness is calculated by comparing two initial opportunity sets for the present generation (actual versus primitive opportunity sets), and initial opportunity sets for this generation and its successor. We have not yet highlighted whether these opportunities refer to the absolute aggregative level or the per capita level. Most symmetrical intertemporal welfare functions refer to per capita opportunities or income achievements, not absolute aggregates.

Our treatment is different; Our comparisons refer to absolute aggregates. This treatment has two bases. First, while the present generation can be felt to be responsible for giving the next generation opportunity for something like the same overall resource use that it had, adjusting its absolute income by whatever rate of population increase it is responsible for (the $(1 + m)$ factor in equation (8)) and constrained to enable that latter to be sustainable for the next generation after it as well—i.e., to permit the next generation to be just as responsible for the welfare of its successor, etc.—it cannot really be held responsible for how many extra people the next generation will produce or how many beyond that. The same per capita income with more people beyond the next generation requires a larger initial resource base, and therefore a larger sacrifice by the present generation. This would make the present generation hostage to different anticipated future population growth rates. Yet again the present generation is responsible for its own contribution to population growth (and this constitutes a cost deterrent to such growth), but not for any such choice made, or expected to be made, by the next generation and those beyond it.[23]

The second basis of our treatment is that if indebtedness and repayment were based on per capita opportunities, the present generation would either be forced to predict the next generation's population growth rate on the basis of its own family size preferences or would attempt to select one for that generation to make its contribution either simply determinate or actually favorable to itself. In either case the present generation would be dealing either with what it cannot really know about the different population—or worse, what it has no business attempting to prescribe or influence. The next generation has the right to make its own population growth decision on the basis of its own preferences—but it must then also be responsible for the consequences of that decision (with its own $(1 + m_{j+1})$ factor defining what it owes)! If, for example, given the same resource base for the present and the next generation, a larger population growth rate next generation than this would yield a smaller per capita income later, this decline is entirely the responsibility of the next generation. This is normatively an issue different from the intergenerational obligations we have been talking about.

The final issue concerns how backward indebtedness affects both interpersonal/intergroup welfare distributions within a single generation and such distributions across generations. So far we have emphasized the total indebtedness of the whole generation j to generation $j + 1$ (and through it, to all future generations) and the required aggregate repayment from G_j to G_{j+1}. But our definition of both concepts permits us to disaggregate both debt and required repayment to groups of different degrees of exclusiveness, from a region or nation down to individual households. This is very useful in attempting to deal with the difficult and important issues of welfare distribution within and across generations that abound in resource use and environmental questions, which are of signal importance in public policy for global climate change. Equation (4) expresses backward indebtedness as

$$D_j^i = Y_j^i - Y_j^{i*} \tag{4}$$

where D_j^i is the backward indebtedness of "group" i in generation j. The term Y_j^{i*}, primitive potential income, is essentially constant over the whole generation j, and across generations as well. But Y_j^i varies markedly over households, cities, regions, and nations. So there is a high variance distribution of backward indebtedness within a given generation. On the other hand, the calculation of required repayment, equation (9), modified to include G_j's responsibility for damages beyond G_{j+1}—i.e., C_{j+2}^j—is constant over the whole generation,

(a) $\delta_j = (Y_j + C_{j+2}^j)(1 + m_j) - Y_{j+1};$ \hfill (9)

(b) $\delta_j^i \leq D_j^i,$

except insofar as an equal per capita allocation of the generation aggregate (a) on everyone could easily exceed the individual ceiling (b) for some and fall considerably short for others, thereby failing to raise the necessary total. A more appropriate assignment within a generation would be to exhaust the total with unequal quotas:

$$\delta_j^i = b_i \delta_j \text{ where } b_i = \frac{D_j^i}{D_j}\left(\frac{m_j^i}{m_j}\right). \tag{11}$$

Thus an intergenerational welfare redistribution program inherently functions as an intragenerational redistribution program as well, a progressive one from richer to poorer, as modified by differential contribution to population growth. This is important both for dealing with some fundamental normative issues affecting all questions of intergenerational transfers and for dealing with narrower tactical issues concerned with obtaining agreement on and implementing policies on global climate change.

Defining an Intertemporal Social Welfare Function Through Intergenerational Equity: Planetary Rights

This final approach is the most radical of all. The planetary rights approach of Weiss in Chapter 10 employs a standard of intergenerational comparability that totally dispenses with the uniqueness of any generation.[24] Weiss states:

> The theory of intergenerational equity proposed argues that we, the human species, hold the natural environment of our planet in common with all members of our species: past generations, the present generation, and future generations. As members of the present generation, we hold the earth in trust for future generations. At the same time, we are beneficiaries entitled to use and benefit from it. . . . We can use it on a sustainable basis or we can degrade environmental quality and deplete the natural resource base. As the most sentient of living creatures, we have a special responsibility to care for the planet. . . . Each generation can and should use the natural system to improve the human condition, . . . [and] generations may have an obligation to restore the robustness of the system, with costs distributed across generations.[25]

This normative prescription is given a decisive turn to symmetry by using Rawls's mental game of stochastically placing each potential participant generation in a distributional process in an unpredictable spot in the temporal sequence of generations and asked what behavior it would want the prior generation to have exhibited.[26] Weiss states this in chapter 10: "Such a generation would want to inherit the earth in at least as good condition as it has been in for *any* [my italics] previous generation and to have as good access to it as previous generations have had. This requires each generation to pass the planet on in no worse condition than in which it received it and to provide equitable access to its resources and benefits." Intergenerational and intragenerational equity are not considered in conflict, but "are consistent and in fact must go together."[27]

Intergenerational equity is characterized by three principles: (1) "conservation of options" (conservation of the diversity of natural and cultural resources); (2) "conservation of quality"; and (3) "conservation of access."[28] Implementation of these should stress equality among generations; permit no prior determination by earlier generations of the needs, means, and ends for successor generations (future generation must be accorded "flexibility to achieve their goals according to their own values"); allow for clarity of interpretation when applied to foreseeable situations; and be acceptable to different cultural traditions and economic and political systems.[29]

The three approaches that are willing to displace the ultimate ethical perspective from the "present" generation—sustainable development, backward indebtedness, and now planetary rights—have a great deal in common, emphasizing the temporariness of "presentness" and requiring more concern by the present generation for future generations. But the approaches also differ. The sustainable development approach calls for greater altruism on the part of the present generation for future generations because, as possessors of property rights in the earth, it is for those with power to heed charitably the needs of those without power—a form of noblesse oblige. The backward indebtedness approach does not stress the power of the present generation, nor does it appeal for greater altruism, but rather it stresses that the situation of the present generation stems almost entirely from a free gift from past generations; the present generation is only a poor debtor. Increased aid to future generations is simply the only way this indelible debt can be extinguished. Instead of the present generation's compassion for the future, it is its gratitude to the past that is the operative normative theme.

The planetary rights approach, on the other hand, much more radically shifts normative attention completely away from the present generation. The focus is on all members of the human species equally. All will be part of a present generation sometime, but only briefly, and when that is to be is only a matter of chance. The basic normative principle is that such chance must not affect the life chances of any human being, no matter when that person becomes part of the "present generation."

What the planetary rights approach proposes, therefore, is an intertemporal, intergenerational social welfare function in which the group whose welfare is being measured is the entire human species for all time.[30] The function is entirely symmetrical: As an argument of the function, the welfare of all contemporaneous groups of human beings (generations) should have equal effect on total human welfare. Equality of opportunity for all generations yields the highest total welfare; all departures from equality diminish total human welfare.[31] The strong emphasis on "equal access" for nations, cultural traditions, and other groupings suggests highly equalizing types of constraints.

This chapter seeks a practical approach to modify the methodology of economic evaluation of possible public policies concerning global climate change that is (a) based on a normative foundation which seems more appropriate than what underlies the conventional present discounted value approach, (b) is itself appealing and persuasive, and (c) can generate clear, operational criteria for judging different possible public interventions, including zero intervention. Much as the normative thrust of planetary rights may be appealing intellectually, it is probably not conatively persuasive enough to have a chance to be adopted widely in the near future.

Formulating a Strategy for Intertemporal and Intergenerational Comparisons

Inter- and Intragenerational Time Comparisons

Central to our evaluation of time discounting is the distinction between periods of time within the same generation and between generations. While time discounting within generations, generally a powerful instrument for obtaining temporal comparability, falls short of ensuring intertemporal optimality for various reasons, when comparisons across generations are involved the degree of suboptimality grows markedly and the concept of optimality itself becomes ambiguous. Accordingly, different treatments for the two types of temporal comparison have been warranted. For intragenerational comparisons time discounting is appropriate, but it should be supplemented by a distinction between private (market) discount rates and social discount rates, where the particular social discount rate used for a specific policy area is one that specifically adjusts for the difference in time preference due to the particular intertemporal externalities or risk differentials involved in the type of intertemporal resource uses of that policy area.

A second modification in treatment is necessary for both intra- and intergenerational comparisons. Resource/environmental accounting should be employed in all comparisons. It represents simply a correction of the incomplete conventional gross output (e.g., GNP) accounts, which fail adequately to measure capital usage. Depreciation and depletion of physical, human, resource, and environmental quality capital all should be explicitly measured and subtracted from gross output. The neglect of physical capital depreciation due to measurement problems has been tacitly considered tolerable in the optimistic context of an ever-rising trend of total factor productivity and apparently limitless natural resources. Significant numbers of people forecast—or simply worry about—actual declines in future standards of living. Whether correct or not, such changing human perspectives require more complete accounting to satisfy the much greater sensitivity to issues of real versus imaginary progress.

Resource/environmental accounting is not easier than accounting for the consumption of physical capital. It is much harder. Measuring the stock of such assets in physical terms is extremely difficult, and monitoring its physical changes over time is possibly more difficult. Far more difficult, compared to the measurement of private physical capital, is the attribution of appropriate values (prices) to these assets, since even the sometimes only referential market prices available for physical capital are often nonexistent here. *Prices* here refer to *potential* productivity, not reproduction cost, and the sophistication of the production function that is necessary to impute productivity values, which is so much readier with physical capital, is largely absent here. Add to that the proposed use of "green accounting" largely to predict circumstances in the future, when technology and the availability of complementary resources are only vaguely predictable, and the problem is greater still. Finally, the prospect of exhaustion (for nonrenewable resources) or renewal-crippling overuse (for renewable resources) for some resources (and environments) make the issue of irreversibility important. Green accounting should attempt to place an "option value" surcharge on the "present value" of such resources as an insurance premium to warn against, and deter, unmodified continued use.

With all these extraordinary difficulties, how can one recommend a serious attempt to use green accounting? The present extreme deficiency of any such set of accounts would be fatal for detailed monitoring of ongoing circumstances; but the context for which they are envisioned here concerns only broad long-run trends. For such use even very approximate measures would be importantly illuminating, in contrast to the present near-silence on the matter.

Intergenerational Comparisons and Normative Persuasiveness

We have explored three general approaches to a separate treatment of intergenerational comparisons: the very widely discussed[32] sustainable development approach, Weiss's planetary rights approach, and our (Rothenberg's) backward indebtedness approach. All agree in terms of basic impact. All would loosen the absolute centrality of the present generation's unamended expression of intertemporal preferences as fundamental normative grounds for such comparisons. For all three, such loosening would give greater evaluational standing to the preferences and welfare of future generations relative to the present.

Public acceptance depends on normative and potential persuasiveness, for they all rest on a basic principle designed to supplant that which implicitly sustains the conventional time discounting approach.[33] The sustainable development approach rests on the principle that the present generation is not altruistic enough toward the well-being of future generations (and toward the "integrity of nature"). The planetary rights approach rests on the principle that all human activity ought to be directed to maximizing the total welfare of the human species through all the future, where no contemporaneous (generation) group has any more intrinsic importance than any other; there is no "present generation," only temporary accidental stewardships of the planet's resources. The backward indebtedness approach rests on the principle that the situation of the present generation is overwhelmingly due to the accretion of human advances in the past that have been planted on the present generation as a free gift, and that the present generation is therefore heavily indebted to that past but must extinguish the debt in the only way possible: namely, through comparable support for future generations.

We believe that the planetary rights approach is admirable but probably fatally over-idealistic. The history of the twentieth century does not give much confidence that such an elevated moral position will be seriously entertained today or in the near future. This is especially so if much of the same basic thrust—at least for policy in global climate change—can be secured on the basis of much more limited modifications of conventional normative thinking.

Between sustainable development and backward indebtedness, we believe that appeals to greater altruism may be less effective than designations of indebtedness—i.e., carrying an obligation not because one voluntarily wants to act better or more responsibly toward others, but because one owes it to them in a demonstrable way. The desire to see oneself as good is an important human need. However, to secure that self-regard by continuing genuine costly group-level restraint on behalf of others not yet born does not appear to have been an important avenue of choice for realization to date.

Our preference for backward indebtedness depends more operationally on the substance of implementation. Both the sustainable development and planetary rights approaches emphasize monitoring and goals in terms of available specific types of natural resources and environments. Backward indebtedness, on the other hand, emphasizes overall production and consumption opportunity sets. This difference refers to four kinds of issues.

Nature and Humans   First there is the issue of the "nature" on which any generation is dependent. For the former approaches this is the natural order essentially abstracted from human activity—except for exploitation and spoilage. For the latter, any generation is enormously dependent on how past human activity has modified the environment by means of technological change, new knowledge, elaborately created structures and equipment, coordinative institutions, and explicit forms of control of nature and natural processes (such as medical care and dams and reforestation). A preponderant attention to "natural" natural resources alone is seriously misleading to a concern for future generations.[34]

Range of Permissible Substitutions   This difference in perspective addresses the issue of substitutions among both inputs and outputs. Sustainability does not insist on complete non-substitutability—namely, that every single type of resource stock be maintained at reasonable levels, that no form of living thing be allowed to become extinct—but essentially frowns on the principle of allowing some larger resource classes and life species to decline heavily even if as they are made up for by increases in other classes and species. The degree to which such substitutions are considered tolerable varies among supporters of sustainability, but there are no fixed criteria by which to adjudicate these differences. The most widespread substitution that is desired under this approach is that of substituting the use of renewable resources for the use of nonrenewables.

Backward indebtedness depends fundamentally on the maintenance of comparable opportunity sets, not resources. Opportunity sets are generated not only by resources per se, but by resource qualities—which may be altered both positively and negatively by human action—and by types and amounts of physical and human capital and technology.[35] Any particular mix of consumption goods outputs that emerges from these opportunity sets can be produced with many different combinations of inputs; many different consumption mixes are possible, each one capable of emerging from a great variety of input combinations.

Market signals induce particular input combinations to be most efficient; changes in market signals induce changes in the identity of the most efficient input combinations. Indeed, induced changes not only in natural resource input combinations—resource substitutions—but also across different classes of inputs—human capital and natural resources, technological change and physical capital and natural resources, renewables and nonrenewables—are the dominant manner by which a market economy adjusts in a decentralized way to differing degrees of scarcity at any one time and changes in scarcity over time.

Substitution is the core of market adjustability to the long-run trends we are discussing. Therefore, if primary focus is on the sustainability of human living standards over time, broad substitutability must not only be tolerated, but welcomed. The possibility that uncontrolled substitution will permit widespread exhaustion and extinction is not ruled out, but is made much less likely by our insistence that in the recommended accompanying green accounting of resources,[36] values should be assigned that include a premium for scarcity. Resources with high scarcity would bear prices so high that a cost-minimizing productive sector would significantly decrease its use of them in favor of other resources, capital, labor, or induced technological change. The calculation of indebtedness needing to be repaid by the present generation to the future would show that the continued use of such scarce resources would increase needed repayment far more than production-consumption equivalents that employed less of those resources.

Generational Incentives The third implementational issue concerns productivity incentives for each generation. Backward indebtedness is more growth-oriented than sustainability or planetary rights. The former explicitly relates the indebtedness of any generation to the production/consumption opportunities *at the beginning of its existence*. What a generation does with these opportunities over its lifetime—equal, fall short of, or exceed them—does not affect the size of its indebtedness. Attempts to grow rapidly can increase the size of repayment needed if such growth seriously depletes the resource base. But an offsetting replenishment of the next generation's opportunities is permitted to take many forms, and rapid growth has historically been associated with technological improvements, increased knowledge, and heavy investment in durable plants and equipment—all of which increases the next generation's bequest from the accretion of past accomplishments. If replenishment of varied forms were not permitted and little other than natural resource stocks were consulted, then the sheer high pressure that growth brings to bear on natural resources would act as a brake on growth under the kinds of future-oriented constraints we are considering.

Thus, backward indebtedness does not require the present generation to transfer more wealth to the next generation just because it creates more itself, but only if in creating more it deprives the next generation of its similar initial opportunity to grow in its turn. The present generation is also permitted to offset any incipient disability to the future in whatever way enables it to maximize its present opportunities net of that obligation.

Both other approaches involve a greater emphasis on the sharing of successes by the present generation with future generations. Planetary rights is much more overtly egalitarian in suggesting that all generations share the right to do as well as any. It appears that the present generation's actual achieved standard of living is to be the standard of comparison across generations, not its original opportunities. Sustainability is less overt about this, and there is some ambiguity in the literature on whether it is original or achieved income levels that are to be the basis of intergenerational constraints.

Impediments to growth also appear in the apparently much less tolerant position taken by these approaches to varied substitutions among inputs and outputs. The narrower the permitted classes of substitution offsets to particular resource uses, the more seriously the growth programs of a given generation are likely to be restrained.

Population Growth   Paradoxically, sustainability and planetary rights seem much more tolerant regarding an important element of generational resource use than backward indebtedness. That element is human population size. Most discussions of sustainability, and Weiss's presentation of planetary rights, speak about human opportunities in terms that unmistakably refer to standard of living—i.e., *per capita* opportunities (or income, or consumption). That means that the same standard of living should be counted on by a generation regardless of its size or change of size. Yet increasing population size is guaranteed to impose increasing stress on most natural resources. Both sustainability and planetary rights are either reticent about including population growth in the list of unwarranted resource pressures on the planet or overtly deny earlier generations the right to judge or influence decisions on population size made by later generations. Yet the stringency of constraints on earlier resource use, or the size of the implicit wealth transfers needed from earlier to later generations, will depend on relative population sizes— i.e., on population growth rates—if it is per capita income that is aimed at. For these to be based on decisions that will be made by later generations—but are required to be predicted by the present generation and acted on according—is another form of tax on the present generation's freedom of action. But this, unlike those that we have approvingly discussed to promote general sustainability, is opposite in its effect on sustainability. Population growth must be integrated within the framework of mutual intergenerational responsibility.

Backward indebtedness explicitly integrates population growth by stating the intergenerational responsibility in terms of absolute aggregative opportunity sets adjusted for population increase for which that generation is responsible, but not for subsequent population increases by future generations. Population growth by successor generations is entirely the responsibility of those generations; the latter must take responsibility for the per capita income consequences of their decisions on population growth. If any population growth rate leads to a decline in per capita income given the aggregate resource base available, the responsible generation can neither gain more from the preceding generation nor decrease its responsibility to its successor generation.[37]

Inter- and Intragenerational Distribution   The fifth implementation issue that differentiates backward indebtedness from sustainability and planetary rights concerns income distribution. Backward indebtedness has an attractive built-in redistributional formula. The other approaches are ambiguous as to how distribution essentially fits. Under backward indebtedness we can calculate both the aggregate generation debt (eq. 7) and the debt owed by any group component of the generation (eq. 4). The former compares a generation average (per capita) actual potential income with the generation average primitive potential income. The latter makes the same comparison for any group belonging to the generation: that group's actual versus primitive potential incomes. Thus, well-endowed groups will show higher indebtedness than the generation average, and poorly endowed groups will show lower indebtedness than the generation average. When the actual needed repayment total is determined for the generation as a whole it can be allocated among the members of the generation in accordance with their relative indebtedness, but adjusted by comparative reproduction rates, as given in equation 11:

$$\delta_j^i = b_i \delta_j \text{ where } b_i = \frac{D_j^i}{D_j} \left(\frac{m_j^i}{m_j} \right).$$

This built-in redistributive mechanism is important for two reasons. First, it can strongly contribute to the possibility of obtaining a wide enough multiparty agreement to undertake present public action against global climate change to make such action feasible and attractive overall. At the beginning of Chapter 9 we noted that because of significant global externalities a very large number of nations would have to agree to coordinative action in order to make any nation's action worthwhile. But nations differ greatly in what they feel to be their net stake in successful action, partly because they expect smaller than average benefits (e.g., because of greater impatience), but mostly because they differ much in living standards. Poor countries feel they cannot afford a large transfer to the future when their present is very grim. Wealthy countries feel the joint stakes are very high: They are anxious to pay their share if only the necessary others will do likewise.

The built-in repayment differentials mean that the poor nations need pay less, the rich nations more, than the average: In effect, rich countries would be subsidizing poorer countries to agree to joint action. This is exactly the flexibility needed for negotiation. Moreover, the potential transfers are not simply built on opportunistic bargaining power—which could paralyze bargaining—but rest rather on an inherent normatively plausible structure, and so might well seem "fair." Sustainability and planetary rights do stress the importance of intragenerational equalizing of "access," but they provide no structuring of the formulation and implementation of such redistribution—nor do they provide a ready-made mechanism to accomplish this within the very process of achieving broad acceptance of the program!

The built-in redistribution mechanism makes possible a more general resolution of a deep problem raised by the normative treatment of intergenerational responsibility. All three approaches specify an ethical responsibility for one generation to ensure that its successor generations have real income opportunities no less than it had itself. But within that same generation are groups who have considerably lesser current opportunities than others in the generation. Why does not the same ethical principle of equalizing opportunities not apply within the generation also? If it is answered that it does, but it must be compromised with regard to resulting losses of efficiency, then roughly the same kinds of efficiency losses are involved in ensuring intergeneration equity as well. Indeed, the two forms of equity are competitors for scarce redistributional resources. What is needed is an appropriate mix, or balance, between efforts to achieve the two.

How strong is the impetus to responsibility in intergeneration equity when there is significant incompleteness of intragenerational equity? The backward indebtedness approach makes an explicit contribution to the answer to this question—though it is not thereby fully resolved—by intrinsically integrating the two types of equity via differential intragenerational indebtedness shares in meeting the intergenerational responsibility. The other approaches have no such systematic approach to the problem, despite assertions by their supporters that intragenerational equity is not to be sacrificed just because intergenerational equity is to be pursued. A fuller spelling out of the problem is needed within those approaches.

Postscript: On the Integration of Inter- and Intragenerational Distribution

The author of this chapter has attempted to formulate a resolution of the distributional conflict through an integration of inter- and intragenerational redistributions in a game-theoretic context. A total resolution of this conflict is beyond the scope of the present work because it involves a considerable complicating of the nature of the actions of the different participants, but the character of the resolution does affect the question of how much transfer of real income opportunities will take place between the present and the future. Therefore a brief sketch follows.

First, all individuals are assumed to like improvements in both forms of equity (intra- and intergeneration): The utility function for each individual has positive arguments for both, in addition to a positive argument for a conventional consumption vector. But the strengths of the preferences among the three types of "commodity" differ for different individuals, with some systematic differences accounted for by the individual's income level. All individuals have budget constraints.

Second, intergenerational equity is improved by acting to abate damages on future generations produced by the present generation's activities. The actions of different groups have different marginal effects on such abatement, and their utility costs differ as well for unit abatements. Intragenerational equity is improved by either direct money transfers or by bribes to shift responsibility to others to engage in one's required abatement quota. Individuals donate or receive direct transfers and contract either to shift their own abatement responsibilities to others or to assume others' abatement responsibilities for a money price.

Since intergenerational equity competes with intragenerational equity for the individual's income, the extent of desired intergenerational equity will be less than where no such competition exists. The persuasiveness and particulars of all our future-orientation approaches would be weakened. But the model permits a dual specialization: Those who are poor may have their abatement share paid for by richer ones; those who are more efficient in producing abatement impacts will tend to be contracted with by others to specialize in such actions for them. Insofar as these abatement specialists also tend to be members of the poorer groups, then the contractual transfers increase both forms of equity simultaneously, making them an especially attractive vehicle for achieving both forms of equity.

As a result, more pro-future actions will be undertaken overall: Intragenerational equity considerations will actually augment the degree of future orientation. This is a rather extreme form of comparative advantage which, in favoring specialized roles, increases the overall level of system achievement. That this has empirical relevance in our environmental context is seen in the strategic control that a number of poor countries have over unique constellations of natural resources (rain forests, coal, wetlands, other special habitats, etc). Deals of special conservation or non-use by such countries in exchange for foreign aid to them are increasingly spoken of in the context of adoptable policy for global climate change.

The final word, then, about our intertemporal concern is generalized from the above. The degree of future-orientation may be abetted or hindered within different normative/analytic approaches to evaluation. But such effects are not homogeneous over all or even most of the participants involved. The many differences among these participants will also be likely to affect their unaided degree of concern for the future, as well as the possibility of persuading them to change this concern by appealing to evaluational approaches such as those we have been exploring.

Appendix on Generations

Each individual's lifetime falls into three periods: (1) pre-generation overlap, (2) generation, and (3) post-generation overlap. In the pre-generation overlap period ($\sim$ 15–20 years) the individual is in a dependency situation, making no decisions on resource use, consumption, or intergenerational transfer, but passively acting with such decisions made by parents on her/his behalf. The generation period is that in which the individual makes and engages in the production/resource use decisions: the "working lifetime" of the individual. He/she decides on personal consumption, and makes three kinds of decisions relating to other generations: decisions regarding (1) amount of reproduction (the size of the next generation), (2) wealth transfers to the next (younger) generation— now alive in its dependency period—for their consumption and their development of human capital, and (3) resource uses that determine the future availability of physical and human capital, and future technology.[a] In the post-generation overlap the individual is retired and makes one intergenerational decision: out of current wealth how much to consume and how much to transfer to the next generation—those currently in their "generation stage."

In any given brief time interval, therefore, three generations are alive: the "last generation" in its post-generation stage, the "present generation" in its generation stage, and the next generation in its pre-generation stage. We assume that each individual in the generation stage adopts a coherent rest-of-lifetime resource use plan to avoid dynamic inconsistency: retroactive regret. The plan involves (1) a production/consumption component including the productive use of resources, consumption and saving, size and longevity of physical capital stock, and size and use of human capital stock; (2) early transfers to the next generation while still in the generation stage, include reproduction rate, consumption levels of the next generation, and investment in their early development of human capital; and (3) late transfers to the next generation while the donors are in their post-generation stage and the recipients are in their generation stage, including previously determined wealth (and its longevity and expected productivity via induced technology change) during the post-generation stage, combined with previously determined decisions about consumption levels during that later stage, which together determine the size and character of technology-embodied physical capital available for receipt by the next generation while it is in its generation stage.

---

[a] A possible fourth decision may be made regarding the subsidization of the residual consumption needs of members of the "last generation" who are still living, in a state of retirement, to the extent the latter's own accumulated provision for retirement (via personal savings and quasi-vested public old-age security systems) fall short of perceived "minimum required levels."

Despite the real-world continuous transformation of populations in a spectrum of age groups, our "generation" here can be roughly viewed as making intergenerational decisions that are carried out over a considerable period of time: pure early transfers to the next generation while they are dependent and a mix of pure and commercial late interchanges with that same generation when the donors are in their retirement stage. So intergenerational actions informed by the same generations will be carried out over something like fifty years—despite the fact that the mix of the three simultaneously extant generations changes radically over that interval.

A further stabilizing of the evaluative orientation of intergenerational actions during such long periods is that in a given time period the dependent next generation is being socialized by the current generation, which was in its turn as dependent generation socialized by its then-antecedent generation (its parents). While such socialization is never complete, it certainly slows the rate at which social values toward intergenerational relationships change over time.

This suggested model of generations and time makes possible a reasonable framework within which to think about generations deciding how to treat their own welfare compared to that of other generations. The universal dependency stage that all generations must go through has a special resonance for the kind of intergenerational gratitude and obligation which are the core of the backward indebtedness approach presented in this chapter.

Notes

1. Lutz and El Serafy, 1988; R. Repetto et al., 1989.
2. Both renewable and nonrenewable raw materials are subject to externalities in that quantum effects of certain rates of extraction and/or exploitation on the real cost function of further supply are sometimes poorly dealt with in assigning values to amounts used up.
3. Repetto et al., op. cit.
4. This "boundary" is of course a simplified fiction, as is all talk of the "present generation's" period and the "future generations's" period. This terminology here is a fiction needed to throw into relief the gross features of "differently aged populations." See our elaboration in a model of generations in the Appendix to this chapter.

5. There is a substantial literature on social discount rates. In this space we cannot settle the substantial and unresolved problems of identification and estimation. See the citations in Chapter 9.

6. Estimates must depend on some sense of the empirical magnitude of the various intertemporal externalities involved (with some perhaps negative). How exactly to make such estimates is beyond our scope.

7. We omit all issues concerning the non-homogeneity of the generation i and j populations with respect to this intergenerational evaluation. They are real and potent, but at our present level of generality they would inordinately complicate the analysis.

8. A factor that may increase the declining slope of generation weights beyond G_2 is a belief by the present generation (G_1) that all intervening generations between G_1 and G_i will care for G_i's interests, so less is required to be done by G_1. This in turn is qualified to the extent that the context of evaluation is a unique type of damage being done by G_1 to G_i. Here G_1 might well feel exclusively responsible for helping G_i—especially if a demonstration effect is expected: namely, that unredeemed damage by G_1 against G_i makes each G_{i+1} between G_1 and G_i more likely to be willing to engage in the same kind of unredeemed damage against G_i or any of their successor generations.

9. Indeed, in the general case this can be a year-pair vector of rates. Also:

$$PDV(X_t) = \frac{X_t}{(1 + r_1)(1 + r_2)(1 + r_3) \ldots (1 + r_t)} \, .$$

10. An average life expectancy for each generation, which can change trendwise over time.

11. For a considerable elaboration of a specific model of "generations" that can be used with this approach, see the appendix to this chapter.

12. An asset that generates consumable output later within G_2 will be worth less to G_2 than one that generates the same output earlier in G_2, and therefore G_2 will offer G_1 a lower bid for the former than for the latter.

13. Archibugi and Nijkamp, 1990.

14. There are many formulations of the principle, but most have the gist of the simple form presented here. See, for example, Pearce, Markandya, and Barbier, 1989.

15. Henceforth, we shall treat the direct consumption effects of environmental quality as a form of "production." What we say hereinafter about inputs and production are meant to apply to environmental quality as an input into consumption level.

16. Robert Solow, 1992.

17. A measure of "overall" aggregate welfare as a function of the welfares of the constituent population who make up the relevant group.

18. See the appendix to this chapter.

19. That mix for which the marginal production trade-off for each pair of outputs along the set's frontier—the production-possibility frontier—equals the price ratio between them.

20. Nature's endowment cannot literally be totally excluded. Some conventional minimum contribution of nature is assumed, considerably less supportive than the actual ecological system.

21. The conventional present generation welfare maximization orientation involves a single active participant in the determination of intertemporal effects, namely the—however perpetually myopic—present generation; the sustainable development orientation involves two active participants—the present generation and the future generation(s).

22. Indirect consumption is the result of creating capital with durability beyond G_j's lifetime and selling it to the representatives of G_{j+1} in the overlap period when both generations are present.

23. Of course, the present generation's own "chosen" reproduction rate is a strong influence on the total size of the successive string of generations; indeed, t here is a kind of quasiirreversibility between each present birth and the whole future series of population sizes. The text refers, however, to successive *rates* of population increase, and these can be wholly a matter of responsibility for each future generation.

24. Weiss, 1989; also this book, chapter 10, "Intergenerational Equity: Towards an International Legal Framework."

25. "Intergenerational equity," this book, chapter 10, pp. (2–5 typescript).

26. Op. cit., p. 6 (typescript). This particular proposition is, of course, quite similar to the most general form of the "sustainability" principle; but its source is different, and the larger set of propositions derivable from this approach are more extreme than those derivable from sustainability alone.

27. Loc. cit.

28. Op. cit., p. (20).

29. Op. cit., pp. (20–12).

30. Presumably starting *now*.

31. Weiss argues that intragenerational equity of the symmetric character should apply equally with intergenerational equity. This means that the constituent arguments of the social welfare function are all *individuals* rather than all contemporaneous groups of individuals. We shall speak below about efforts to integrate intragenerational distribution issues with intergenerational distribution issues.

32. This is why we have treated it so briefly.

33. Our evaluation of discounting in Chapter 9 should make clear that time discounting is not value-free or "objective."

34. While it is true that irreversibility may be more of a concern for this latter nature than with human constructs, backward indebtedness attempts to deal with irreversibilities through the resource price premia discussed above. More follows on this.

35. Opportunity sets with respect to environmental quality as directly consumed depend on all of these as well as on the specific consumption good mix that results from production with these production opportunity sets.

36. Biological diversity has always been implicitly included in this term.

37. This does not satisfactorily take care of the population problem. "Investment in population" differs from all other forms of investment in terms of social control of consequences and moral responsibility. Investment in physical and human capital involves a limited productive lifetime, fair predictability of be-

havior over time, and, generally, self-destruction at some finite horizon. The creation of a new human being, in contradistinction, is effectively irreversible: it generates a whole future sequence of other humans over time whose lives cannot be legally terminated and whose reproductive behavior (among others) cannot be closely predicted. Thus there are inherent social externalities of great importance, raising serious questions about social control and moral responsibility.

IV

International Institutions and Systems

12
Evolving International Environmental Law: Changing Practices of National Sovereignty

Peter M. Haas with Jan Sundgren

Countries will have to cede a certain amount of sovereignty in this field for the sake of cooperation.
—François Mitterand, following the Hague Environmental Summit (11 March 1989)

The popular report prepared for the United Nations Conference on the Human Environment (UNCHE) was appropriately titled *Only One Earth* [Ward and Dubos 1972]. Its authors argued that ecological realities made national borders irrelevant for the control of international destiny. More recently international law experts have expressed the hope, perhaps only wistfully, that a new form of collective responsibility is emerging for the collective management of international environmental resources [Goodin 1990; MacNeill, Winsemius, and Yakushiji 1991].

Twenty years after UNCHE, and in the aftermath of its sequel, the United Nations Conference on Environment and Development (UNCED), it is now possible to evaluate the legacy of these conferences. This chapter analyzes the pattern of international treaty making for environmental protection. How has the nature of international law responded to this new array of environmental challenges? How well has it fared in protecting the environment? To what extent are countries superseding sovereignty through the appreciation of global ecological interdependence and the need to devise new forms of collective governance for such a new class of problems? How can such patterns of treaty making be explained?

UNCHE was in fact already part of a long tradition of international environmental treaty making. Yet UNCHE demarcated a new set of international environmental concerns identified in the wake of a number of widely publicized environmental disasters and the emergence of widespread concern about international environmental problems. Since UNCHE the frequency of treaty signings has accelerated. International environmental law now reflects greater attention to international commons problems and a substantive focus on new forms of environmental pollution. These changes are in part the result of new diplomatic techniques with which countries formulate international environmental arrangements. These new processes have led countries to adopt a growing body of law that reflects an ecological understanding of environmental systems as a consequence of the way in which international environmental diplomacy has helped to facilitate the growing influence of authoritative experts responsible for identifying environmental threats and articulating policy and legal responses [Chapter 4 of this book; Haas 1990a; Haas 1990b; Haas 1992].

While the international political system has been grounded on the legal principle of national sovereignty since the Treaty of Westphalia, environmental problems emerge from a class of problems whose solution is particularly difficult within traditional norms and practices of sovereignty [Lang 1986]. The effective management of such problems requires the coordination of international policy. It even requires countries to suppress domestic activities to preserve the environment outside their traditional jurisdictions.

Sovereignty takes two forms. States are guaranteed formal juridical control over *external* affairs relative to other states. They are also guaranteed *internal* autonomy over their own affairs [Beitz 1991; Hinsley 1966; Jackson 190; Poggi 1990]. The first relates to the formal recognition of sources of international authority in joint decision making, the second to a state's discretion over internal policy. Without transforming these fundamental political conditions, many contemporary "realist" and neo-Realist scholars argue, no effective collective environmental protection is possible through traditional treaty making.

Much of current realist-derived writing in international relations is skeptical about the possibility of modifying sovereign practices to the exigencies posed by environmental problems. A conventional Realist understanding of international relations suggests that environmental problems are particularly difficult to resolve collectively. Bargaining is necessary to formulate international agreements, but strong systemic factors exist that inhibit obtaining significant collective benefits. The "logic of collective action" suggests that individual countries will not cooperate on issues that seriously challenge their sovereignty and if they fear that their own costly actions will not be reciprocated. They will not participate if they suspect that others' defections will not be observed, or even if they are not sure that other parties' actions can be effectively monitored [Olson 1965; Olson 1982; for a direct application to environmental problems see Hardin 1968; Underdal 1983]. Arthur Stein notes that "'the tragedy of the commons' exemplifies the dilemma of common interests" [Stein 1983, 129]. Obstacles to collective action are most acute in large groups, where surveillance and monitoring is difficult. Cooperation is easier in small groups, where mutual verification is easier and less expensive. Size is defined largely in terms of the ease of verification and surveillance of a country's actions. William Baumol (1971, 51–52) suggests that seven is the optimal number of members for such a group, and we apply that suggestion below.

Many institutionalist scholars and practicioners are more sanguine about the possiblity of legal solutions to environmental problems. Lynton Caldwell (1990) speaks of leaders recognizing the new ecological interrelationships between problems and correspondingly modifying their behavior [see also Carroll 1988]. Maurice Strong aspired to improve cooperation by reforming the diplomatic process. Under Strong UNCHE developed a new principle for environmental treaty making that was captured by his aphorism "the process is the policy." International law thus becomes a process of developing collectively acceptable rules of collective management [Szasz 1991; Sand 1990]. Even if countries frequently violate their obligations, the international accords establish a benchmark of accountability for governments [Haas, Keohane, and Levy 1993].

The more extensive social choice literature analyzes institutional techniques for promoting cooperation [Young 1989; Ostrom 1990]. Under special conditions a small number of actors—a "k-group"—may be able to obtain sufficient benefits from collective action that they serve as a core group for collective agreements [Schelling 1973; see Sand 1990 for a discussion of "clubs within clubs"]. While k-groups exist for some of these treaties, such as the Thirty Percent Club within the 1979 Long-Range Transboundary Air Pollution Convention (LRTAP) treaty, which now consists of twenty countries out of the thirty-one signing the treaty, it is difficult to evaluate at this degree of abstraction.

This chapter evaluates 132 multilateral environmental treaties signed by 1989.[1] They are drawn from UNEP's *International Register of Environmental Treaties* [UNEP May 1990; texts are available in Kiss 1983 and Rummel-Bulska and Osafo 1991]. Eight treaties were discarded from UNEP's registry of 140 treaties because we determined that they had no significant environmental content.[2] Our coverage does not extend to European Community decisions, bilateral treaties, or the emerging sphere of "soft law" techniques and nonbinding guidelines. [For a broader and more thorough treatment of international environmental law see Weiss, Magrew, and Szasz 1992. On soft law and other styles see Thacher 1991; Sand 1990.] We coded these 132 treaties according to the dimensions specified below. Both the coding sheet and a summary of codings for each treaty is presented in appendix 12.1. This selection contains only entries for successfully concluded multilateral treaties. It is not restricted just to treaties in force; twenty in this selection remain unratified by enough countries to bring them into force. There is a very small percentage of failed international environmental negotiations.

We coded treaties solely for their environmentally relevant aspects. For instance, the 1982 Law of the Sea treaty is coded as a conservation treaty as the environmental sections of the treaty refer to the management of fishery stocks, and the treaty regarding the development of the Lake Chad basin is coded as a conservation treaty because it seeks to conserve fauna and flora. The year 1973 was selected as the break point for analyzing secular trends. It was the year after UNCHE and the first year in which UNEP would have had any significant influence on the treaties it helped to draft. We have found that the choice of year makes little difference for the analysis presented here. Little change results if 1972 or 1974 is chosen as a break point. Only six treaties (4.5 percent of all environmental treaties) were signed in 1973, and they were not distinctively different from those that follow the previous pattern of environmental treaty making. Such changes do not appear until later in the decade.

Secular Trends in Environmental Law

Frequency of Treaty Signing

UNCHE marked a watershed in multilateral environmental treaty signing. From 1920 to 1973 sixty-five multilateral environmental treaties were signed, constituting 49 percent of all recorded multilateral environmental treaties. From 1974 to 1990 sixty-seven treaties were concluded, amounting to 51 percent of the total of treaties. Before UNCHE 1.23 treaties were signed annually. Since UNCHE the pace has accelerated to 4.2 per year, greatly complicating the lives of officials in national environmental ministries who are responsible for monitoring the compliance of their countries and others.

Nature of Environmental Problems Addressed

All international environmental treaties deal with one of two types of environmental problems: (1) protection of physical commons *outside* national control, like the oceans or the atmosphere, and (2) protection of assets or resources that exist *within* a country's territorial control, although the effect of that country's decisions may be felt elsewhere, such as in transboundary pollution problems or the protection of migratory species. Both types of problems affect industrialized and developing countries.

Since UNCHE, international concern with commons problems has increased. While environmental law has long treated commons problems, the relative share of treaties devoted to commons problems grew from 51 percent of all environmental treaties before 1973 to 67 percent during the period since 1973. While commons problems dominate the agenda of international environmental law, accounting for a total of 59 percent of all treaties concluded, few of these actually involve global commons. Many more involve regional commons regulated by the adjacent states, such as regional seas.

International treaty writing has actually shifted away from large-scale treaties since 1973. Before 1973 54 percent of the treaties involved sixteen or more parties, whereas since 1973 only 37 percent of the treaties have involved such large numbers. Medium-sized numbers of parties $(16 > n > 7)$ remained roughly equal between these periods: 23 percent through 1973 and 22 percent since 1973. Before 1973 only 23 percent of the treaties involved small groups, while since 1973 40 percent of the treaties have had fewer than eight signatories, and 48 percent have had fewer than nine signatories.

Global treaties, such as those for various greenhouse gases, may be much more difficult to conclude than these other treaties because of the large number of parties that must be included and whose interests must be satisfied in a successful treaty. UNEP correctly assessed the difficulties of concluding global treaties. In the early 1980s it moved from drafting global principles to focusing on regional issues as a basis of hard and soft law [Petsonk 1990, 362–65].

Substantive Domain of Environmental Treaties
Environmental treaties span a number of subjects. Substantive domains within the environmental sphere include worker protection, conservation and fishery stocks, plant diseases and pest control, frameworks (outlining agendas for action but without specific standards), land-based water pollution (including lakes and rivers), nuclear regulation, oil pollution (operational discharges and accidents), air pollution, marine dumping (deliberate discharge of wastes), and others (including environmental research and treaties falling outside the other categories, such as the convention on the continental shelf and weapons).

Since UNCHE a substantive shift from treaties on conservation to those on pollution control has occurred following the widespread appreciation of humanity's intervention in natural systems [see Chapter 4 of this volume]. Before 1973 37 percent of the environmental treaties dealt with conservation of species, 14 percent with plant diseases and pest control, and 14 percent with other environmental issues. Since 1973 the number of the treaties dealing with conservation has fallen to 25 percent, those dealing with other issues to 4 percent, and those dealing with plant diseases and pest control to 0 percent.

There has been a move to collectively regulate more sophisticated and costly sources of pollution. Controlling air pollution has emerged as a new topic for multilateral international law,[3] and framework treaties have grown in popularity. Air pollution treaties have accounted for 9 percent of the treaties since 1973 (up from 0 percent), treaties dealing with land-based sources of marine pollution grew slightly from 5 percent to 7 percent, and framework treaties grew from 3 percent to 19 percent of all the treaties signed. Treaties dealing with oil pollution control have also grown from 11 percent of the treaties signed through 1973 to 16 percent of the treaties signed since 1973. While oil pollution is not the most serious problem in terms of potential widespread environmental disruption, it is one of the most visible and widely treated of pollution problems. There has been little change in other substantive areas of environmental treaty making. Marine dumping treaties have fallen slightly from 6 percent to 4 percent, treaties dealing with worker protection from environmental hazards have grown from 5 percent to 7 percent, and nuclear regulation and liability treaties have remained constant at 6 percent.

Challenges to National Sovereignty

At the core of environmental problems—as with most other issues in international relations—is the question of national sovereignty. Principle 21 of the Declaration of the United Nations Conference on the Human Environment reads:

States have . . . the sovereign right to exploit their own resources pursuant to their own environmental policies, and the responsibility to ensure that activities within their jurisdiction or control do not cause damage to the environment of other States or of areas beyond the limits of national jurisdiction. (United Nations 1973, 5)

Two measures of sovereignty are applied here. The first relates to the degree to which states agree to regulate their domestic actions for the benefit of others (the internal dimension). Are regulated activities within or outside the territorial borders of the nation-state? This dimension is different from the commons nature of the problem, as the issue of greenhouse gases makes clear. Such emissions take place within territorial borders but degrade a commons. Treaties that regulate both internal and external activities are coded as internal, as internal regulation connotes the greatest challenge to traditional notions of national sovereignty and hence constitutes the greatest change from traditional patterns of international legal activity.

The second measure relates to the degree to which supranational authorities are established with formal control over the exercise of external sovereignty. Do arrangements create significant international obligations and constraints on states' actions relative to other countries?

Table 12.1   Internal controls/total controls

	Before 1973	After 1973
Large n	16 (25%)	20 (29%)
Medium n	10 (16%)	13 (19%)
Small n	10 (16%)	24 (36%)
Total	36 (57%)	57 (84%)

n = number of actors.
Parentheses indicate the percentage of treaties that affected internal sovereignty as a
percentage of all treaties signed during the period.

This measure of sovereignty is coded on the basis of constraints on national choice and codes indicate no constraints, nongovernmental organizations (NGOs) regulate, national governments regulate, national governments must yield information to a supranational authority, supranational authorities conduct their own research, and supranational authorities have the power to enforce treaties.[4]

Since 1973 countries have increasingly demonstrated a willingness to control internal activities, in essence subordinating national political control to international environmental requirements. Through 1973 44 percent of treaties regulated external activities, while 56 percent regulated internal activities. Since 1973 external activities have fallen to 15 percent of the total, with internal controls rising to 85 percent. The extension of territorial limits to two hundred miles converted some external activities to internal, but this shift applies only to conservation and oil pollution. Through 1973 conservation and oil pollution accounted for 38 percent of all internal measures, and together they have accounted for 40 percent of all internal measures since 1973.

Since UNCHE governments have been increasingly willing to sacrifice internal sovereignty. Particularly striking is the large share of internal regulations that have been adopted for problems with large numbers of actors (more than 15). Table 12.1 presents this distribution.

Treaties that strongly challenge internal sovereignty enter into force with roughly the same frequency as those that do not seriously challenge internal sovereignty, as seen in table 12-2.

A clear secular change is evident in the responsibilities assumed at the national level for international or even global resources. Coordinated international environmental policy has not entailed any increase in the

Table 12.2 Relative rates of time for entry into force of sovereignty-threatening treaties

Time for treaties' entry into force	Total treaties	Treaties affecting internal sovereignty
< 2 years	22%	18%
2–5 years	50%	54%
> 5 years	12%	11%
Not in force	15%	17%

level of international integration or constraint on external sovereignty. A slight slowdown is evident in the authority accorded to supranational authorities for the administration of environmental treaties. Before 1973 73 percent relied on national governments to ensure compliance with a treaty, 13 percent required national governments to yield information to a supranational authority, 11 percent allowed supranational authorities to conduct their own research, and 3 percent delegated authority to an international organization to enforce the treaty. In treaties concluded since 1973, 90 percent have required only coordinated regulation by governments, 7 percent have called for national governments to regularly yield information to a supranational authority, and 3 percent have charged international organizations with conducting research.

Impact of Environmental Treaties on Environmental Quality
It is extremely difficult to establish the impact of these treaties on improving the quality of the environment, which is their nominal objective. To the extent that pollution control treaties establish concrete standards, they do so by stipulating emission standards. However, the causal relations between emissions and environmental concentrations are seldom well understood, so that even when measures of environmental concentrations exist, their changes cannot be confidently ascribed to policy actions. Baseline data seldom exist against which to judge recent monitoring reports, and many countries are remiss in collecting and submitting comparable data to international organizations [UNEP 1989; OECD 1991; GESAMP 1990].

Thus, various proxies must be invoked to analyze treaty effectiveness. Three proxies are considered here: (1) the subjective impressions of informed observers about a treaty's effectiveness, (2) whether or not all major polluters or users of a resource are parties to the treaty, and (3) the rapidity of the treaty's entry into force. Other possibilities include changes in levels of national investment in environmental protection, changes in national policies and legislation, and the extent of bureaucratic activity devoted to enforcing environmental treaties and policies.

Only fourteen conservation treaties have been critically appraised in terms of their effectiveness in conserving the species for which they are responsible [Lyster 1985; Birnie 1989; Szekely 1989]. Unfortunately these treaties do not represent any broader subclass of conservation treaties: They cover four of seventeen fisheries regimes and ten of twenty-three nonfisheries species conservation arrangements. Of these treaties, two were deemed to have no impact on conserving species, seven to have little to moderate impact, and five to have a moderate to strong impact.

Forty percent of the treaties coded—only eighty-five were coded for this dimension due to lack of information about major consumers—lack the involvement of a major party. Overall there has been virtually no change in this measure of effectiveness over time: 41 percent of treaties adopted before 1973 had such gaps compared to 39 percent of treaties adopted since 1973. While 50 percent of the marine dumping treaties concluded before 1973 lacked major parties, since 1973 none of the three treaties have lacked the participation of a major coastal dumping country. Of the thirteen framework treaties signed since 1973, 46 percent have lacked a major party. Land-based marine pollution treaties have improved slightly in effectiveness, from 100 percent lacking major parties before 1973 to 80 percent lacking major parties. Oil pollution treaties have improved in their inclusiveness: 71 percent of the treaties concluded before 1973 lacked the participation of a major party, while 33 percent have lacked them since 1973. Fifteen percent of all environmental treaties signed have not yet entered into force. Nine percent of the treaties signed before 1973 are still not yet in force, while 21 percent of the treaties signed since 1973 are not yet in force. This latter number may simply be due to the fact that there is always a lag between a treaty's adoption and its entry into force as countries ratify it through domestic procedures.

Since UNCHE the average lag between a treaty's adoption and its entry into force has fallen. Before 1973, 31 percent of the treaties signed entered into force in under two years (and thus a majority of the countries ratified them quite promptly), 40 percent took two to five years to enter into force, and 20 percent took over five years. Since 1973, 15 percent have entered into force in under two years, 60 percent have taken two to five years, and 4 percent have taken over five years. All treaties signed through 1973 that entered into force had an average lag time of three years before entry into force, while treaties concluded after 1973 have had an average lag time of two years. Since five years have not yet elapsed for many of the more recently concluded treaties, these longitudinal comparisons do not cover a number of treaties still pending ratification.

Realist Explanations of Patterns of Environmental Treaty Making

Realist analysts of international relations rely principally on power and circumstances to explain international cooperation. Power involves diplomatic and other relevant capabilities. Circumstances relate to the array of incentives for cooperation and conflict that face the different parties. The circumstances within which treaties are concluded may play a significant role in their ease of adoption [Oye 1985; Ostrom 1990; Kahler 1992]. Environmental problems are of two types: collaboration games and coordination games. Collaboration games are harder to resolve, as they involve cases in which countries' vital interests are at stake and they have conflicting interests about the problem's resolution. Solutions entail real distributional costs. Most pollution problems entail collaboration games because they involve significant economic costs for compliance, and countries are frequently worried that controlling pollution may entail significant costs, losses of competitiveness for key industries, and challenges to sovereignty; fears about free-riding or chiselling are often pressing. If cheating on an agreement is possible, it was coded as a collaboration game. Table 12.3 indicates the relative difficulty of concluding agreements for different environmental subjects.

Realists propose that the extent to which effective treaties for such hard cases are concluded and enforced is the result of the exercise of power by a dominant country that is capable of compelling others to cooperate and willing to mobilize others' action—a *hegemon*. The United States has possessed these attributes since 1945 and has often played such a leadership role in the period since World War II. Speculation

Table 12.3 Relative difficulty of concluding agreements for different environmental subjects by game type

Environmental subject	Coordination		Collaboration		Total
Air pollution	0	0%	6	100%	6
Conservation	17	41%	24	59%	41
Framework	3	20%	12	80%	15
Land-based water pollution	1	13%	7	88%	8
Marine dumping	1	14%	6	86%	7
Nuclear regulation and liability	7	88%	1	13%	8
Oil pollution	5	28%	13	72%	18
Other	8	67%	4	33%	12
Plant disease/pest control	9	100%	0	0%	9
Worker protection	8	100%	0	0%	8
Total	59	45%	73	55%	132

remains as to whether such leadership is directed toward collective benefits or towards short-term rewards for the United States alone, possibly at the expense of the rest of the world.

Without a global hegemon, cooperation may also occur with the leadership of an issue-specific hegemon. An issue-specific hegemon would suffer disproportionately from the degradation of a shared resource and be able to unilaterally influence the resources' quality or to compel others to act to protect it. Such issue-specific hegemons occur only seldom in the sphere of the environment, because those with issue-specific capability generally lack issue-specific will. Often the largest polluter has the biggest interest in not doing anything rather than organizing pollution control efforts because the costs of changing its behavior will be so high. Domestic pressures may play a role in shaping the will to assume leadership, but these factors lie outside the logic of the collective goods argument.

Easier problems involve coordination games in which countries realize they will benefit from collective action, but consensus is difficult because individual countries are indifferent about which of several options to choose. They may also be reluctant to cooperate because of logistical difficulties, inertia, or whatever. Because the actors are not concerned about chiselling in such matters, cooperation is easier. Thus, one would expect more treaties resulting from coordination games than from collaboration games, which have less need for hegemonic leadership. Cooperation should also occur more frequently regarding issues with smaller numbers of parties involved, where collective interests are more manifest and/or verification and surveillance problems are less daunting.

Table 12.4 presents the distribution of multilateral environmental treaties in terms of coordination and collaboration games and associated political conditions for the conclusion of the environmental treaties.

This distribution confirms that collaboration games are harder to settle without leadership than coordination games; 55 percent of the collaboration games required leadership, whereas only 36 percent of the coordination games required leadership. The hegemon tended to be self-interested as well, and benign leadership was exercised only in cases that were far from national concern, such as conservation cases in which no important national economic or security interests were at stake. Little secular change is evident.

But leadership explains only 36 percent of the coordination games and 55 percent of the collaboration games. Moreover, 25 percent of the large-*n* treaties in collaboration games were concluded without hegemonic or issue-specific leadership.[5] These hard large-*n* cases should be the easiest for the Realists to explain because they dealt with issues that threatened national sovereignty, had a large number of actors, and lacked hegemons. Yet contrary to Realist predictions of failure, treaties were concluded which actually stipulate reasonably stringent standards that will improve environmental quality. This analysis challenges the conventional Realist views based on the collective action logic of international environmental cooperation. Power and circumstance are not compelling explanations for international environmental cooperation.

Our counting rules may overstate the argument only slightly. If small groups are identified as having fewer than nine members (eight or fewer), then two issue hegemony coordination games after 1973 are recorded as small, and three other collaboration games are recorded as small. But, as may be seen in table 12.5, this does not significantly affect the analytic conclusions.

Dynamic Explanations of International Environment Law

A dynamic explanation is necessary to supplement the conventional Realist explanation of international diplomatic behavior. As is seen be-

Table 12.4 Solutions to environmental cooperation games with small groups composed of fewer than eight members

Coordination games

	Through 1973				Post-1973				Total
	$n > 15$	$16 > n > 7$	$n < 8$	Total	$n > 15$	$16 > n > 7$	$n < 8$	Total	Total
Hegemony	10 53%	1 10%	0 0%	11 31%	5 56%	0 0%	1 10%	6 26%	17 29%
Benign	3 16%	0 0%	0 0%	3 8%	2 22%	0 0%	0 0%	2 9%	5 8%
Self-interested	7 37%	1 10%	0 0%	8 22%	3 33%	0 0%	1 10%	4 17%	12 20%
Issue hegemony	0 0%	1 10%	1 14%	2 6%	0 0%	2 50%	0 0%	2 9%	4 7%
Other	9 47%	8 80%	6 86%	23 64%	4 44%	2 50%	9 90%	15 65%	38 64%
Total	19 100%	10 100%	7 100%	36 100%	9 100%	4 100%	10 100%	23 100%	59 100%

Collaboration games

	Through 1973				Post-1973				Total
	$n > 15$	$16 > n > 7$	$n < 8$	Total	$n > 15$	$16 > n > 7$	$n < 8$	Total	Total
Hegemony	10 63%	1 20%	3 38%	14 48%	10 63%	3 27%	2 12%	15 34%	29 40%
Benign	0 0%	0 0%	1 13%	1 3%	2 13%	1 9%	0 0%	3 7%	4 5%
Self-interested	10 63%	1 20%	2 25%	13 45%	8 50%	2 18%	2 12%	12 27%	25 34%
Issue hegemony	1 6%	0 0%	2 25%	3 10%	3 19%	2 18%	3 18%	8 18%	11 15%
Other	5 31%	4 80%	3 38%	12 41%	3 19%	6 55%	12 71%	21 48%	33 45%
Total	16 100%	5 100%	8 100%	29 100%	16 100%	11 100%	17 100%	44 100%	73 100%

Note: Totals may not equal 100% due to rounding errors.

Table 12.5 Solutions to environmental cooperation games with small groups composed of fewer than nine members

Coordination games

	Through 1973				Post-1973				Total
	$n > 15$	$16 > n > 8$	$n < 9$	Total	$n > 15$	$16 > n > 8$	$n < 9$	Total	
Hegemony	10 53%	1 10%	0 0%	11 31%	5 56%	0 0%	1 8%	6 26%	17 29%
Benign	3 16%	0 0%	0 0%	3 8%	2 22%	0 0%	0 0%	2 9%	5 8%
Self-interested	7 37%	1 10%	0 0%	8 22%	3 33%	0 0%	1 8%	4 17%	12 20%
Issue hegemony	0 0%	1 10%	1 14%	2 6%	0 0%	0 0%	2 17%	2 9%	4 7%
Other	9 47%	8 80%	6 86%	23 64%	4 44%	2 100%	9 75%	15 65%	38 64%
Total	19 100%	10 100%	7 100%	36 100%	9 100%	2 100%	12 100%	23 100%	59 100%

Collaboration games

	Through 1973				Post-1973				Total
	$n > 15$	$16 > n > 8$	$n < 9$	Total	$n > 15$	$16 > n > 8$	$n < 9$	Total	
Hegemony	10 63%	1 33%	3 30%	14 48%	10 63%	3 38%	2 10%	15 34%	29 40%
Benign	0 0%	0 0%	1 10%	1 3%	2 13%	1 13%	0 0%	3 7%	4 5%
Self-interested	10 63%	1 33%	2 20%	13 45%	8 50%	2 25%	2 10%	12 27%	25 34%
Issue hegemony	1 6%	0 0%	2 20%	3 10%	3 19%	2 25%	3 15%	8 18%	11 15%
Other	5 31%	2 67%	5 50%	12 41%	3 19%	3 38%	15 75%	21 48%	33 45%
Total	16 100%	3 100%	10 100%	29 100%	16 100%	8 100%	20 100%	44 100%	73 100%

Note: Totals may not equal 100% due to rounding errors.

low, a significant proportion of these international treaties may be explained in light of recent procedural and substantive changes in international environmental diplomacy. A complete explanation of the secular change in environmental treaty making builds from approaches that address diplomatic processes, the diminution of uncertainty, and the application of consensual knowledge to an unfamiliar technical domain. Such new environmental diplomatic techniques have even been usefully applied to hard international environmental problems.

One of the most significant changes in international environmental law has been a procedural innovation in the aftermath of UNCHE. Environmental treaties are not discrete events. The process of international treaty signing has created its own self-reinforcing dynamic. Since UNCHE novel techniques in international environmental diplomacy have given rise to a process of environmental treaty making with its own path-dependent dynamic. This process has two related dimensions. The first is legal. Framework treaties have been used much more frequently for dealing with environmental problems. Eighty-seven percent of all framework treaties have been signed since 1973. In order to sign a framework treaty, states were required to sign at least one corresponding more-stringent protocol. The twenty-three treaties governing ten regional seas that have been signed under UNEP's Regional Seas and Coastal Areas Program fall under this rubric.

The second dimension is a political slippery slope by which states begin with politically easier subjects and progress on to more difficult ones. Many of the drafting exercises were deliberately designed, by UNEP and others, to incorporate such a process. Thirty-two of the sixty-seven treaties signed since 1973 have been part of this slippery slope process, which has been applied to controlling marine pollution from various sources, ozone depletion, and acid rain. The Mediterranean states began by controlling coastal dumping, and over time they progressed to controlling land-based sources of pollution and establishing conservation zones. Globally, in 1985 states adopted a weak framework convention calling for the protection of stratospheric ozone, and in 1987 they adopted a subsequent protocol stipulating stringent cuts in the production and consumption of ozone-depleting chemicals. In 1979 thirty-one advanced industrialized countries adopted a loose umbrella agreement controlling acid rain, followed in 1984 by a protocol establishing a multinational monitoring network, followed by cuts in emissions of sulfur dioxide in 1985 and nitrogen oxides in 1988. The progression to cover new sources of pollution has occurred in several of the regional seas areas as well. North Sea states first cooperated on oil spills (1969), then regulated marine dumping (1972) followed by land-based sources of pollution (1974), and, twelve years later, extended coverage to the air-borne transmission of pollutants landing in the North Sea as well as strengthening earlier dumping controls. Fifty-nine decisions on various land-based sources of pollution had been reached for the North Sea through 1990, and 121 for the Baltic through 1991.

This slippery slope is reinforced by concurrent institutional activities that stress environmental assessment and environmental management supported by institutional measures such as a secretariat and financing. New information about the quality of the environment is developed concurrently with legal discussions about environmental management. Improved scientific understanding generated by the assessment measures provides the impetus for more comprehensive legal measures, and scientists trained in new techniques become partisans for pollution control measures in their respective countries [Thacher 1992]. The technical annexes that are attached to such agreements are constantly subject to expansion and increased stringency as parties gain knowledge about the substances and experience with their control.

This legal process has its own political dimension as well. A side effect of the process of frequent negotiations that stress scientific advice is to invoke the participation of a new constituency for environmental protection. During this process environmental scientists and professionals become involved as experts and advisers to governments and constantly advise them to undertake more stringent and sweeping environmental protection measures [Haas 1990a; Haas 1990b]. NGOs can play an important role in this process, as they can monitor states' compliance with treaties, publicize environmental monitoring data, and press their governments to comply. In fact, the areas in which countries have been most willing to accept limitations on internal sovereignty are those in which such transnational networks of experts have existed: air pollution and framework treaties.

With these changes in focus have come qualitative changes in environmental treaties. A resource management focus is giving way to a growing concern with the management of ecosystems. An incipient move may be afoot to treat ecosystems as the units of international control rather than discrete species or uses of resources. Convention on the Conservation of Antarctic Marine Living Resources (CCAMLR) and conservation treaties that focus on habitats stress an ecosystemic approach to environmental management. The "precautionary principle"— that environmental protection efforts should be undertaken even in the absence of compelling scientific proof of the extent of a problem—was adopted by the North Sea and Baltic regions at the May 1990 Bergen Conference on Sustainable Development and at the November 1990 Second World Climate Conference. While reflecting a more holistic policy perspective, the "anticipatory principle" may also reflect a growing impatience in the north with the pace of international environmental treaty making and the absence of attention paid to compliance.

This substantive reorientation in multilateral environmental law entails a formidable problem for future efforts at environmental lawmaking. To date efforts have focused on regulating discrete uses of the environment. The consequence of twenty (or seventy) years of such ad hocery is to create a set of internally inconsistent standards for the use of the different environmental media. Industries are presented with negative rules regarding emissions into air and water and on land but have few positive obligations regarding their activities. While new technologies may generate less waste than in the past, some form of waste disposal will undoubtedly remain necessary [see Chapter 7 in this volume]. Future lawmaking may call for harmonizing existing law and identifying more rational uses of shared ecosystems in order to prevent economically inefficient uses of environmental resources or inadequate regulatory regimes that do not pay sufficient attention to cross-media environmental effects.

Conclusion

UNCHE unleased new institutional forces. The 1970s and 1980s have seen the gradual creation of a body of international law regulating emissions into all environmental media. As a result of this period of accelerated treaty making, the environment is now irreversibly etched onto the international agenda and increasingly into the annals of international practice and customary international law. Some practices of national sovereignty are eroding in international environmental law. Countries are increasingly acknowledging constraints on domestic policy in order to protect the international environment. Moreover, the threat that national sovereignty may be restrained by international cooperation has not appeared to be a major inhibition to cooperation, although developing countries are still extremely concerned about possible encroachments on their external legal authority [Jackson 1990]. These new practices of sovereignty have emerged without a transformation of the juridical principle of sovereignty or of the international anarchic order within which countries exercise choice. Revolutionary change occurs through reformist means.

Notes

This chapter was written with the support of NSF Grant SES-9010101. We are grateful to M. J. Peterson, Peter Sand and the other authors for comments on previous drafts. Our thanks to Mark Radka and Bret Brown for coding assistance.
1. Not included are the 1989 Sophia Protocol to the 1979 Convention on Long-Range Transport of Air Pollution, the 1989 Basle Convention on the Control of Transboundary Movements of Hazardous Wastes, and the 1990 London Amendments to the 1987 Montreal Ozone Protocol.
2. These are the 1968 European Convention for the Protection of Animals during International Transport, the 1969 European Convention for the Protection of the Archaeological Heritage, the 1976 European Convention for the Protection of Animals Kept for Farming Purposes, the 1979 European Convention for the Protection of Animals for Slaughter, and the 1980 European Outline Convention on Transfrontier Cooperation between Territorial Communities or Authorities.
3. While one of the first pieces of international environmental law regulated the emissions of a smelter in the United States that deposited effluents in Canada, the Trail Smelter, this was a purely bilateral issue.
4. Our thanks to Craig Murphy for suggesting this scale.
5. These cases are the 1949 General Fisheries Agreement for the Mediterranean, the 1959 North East Atlantic Fisheries Agreement, the 1971 Agreement on Tank Arrangements, the 1971 Protection of the Great Barrier Reef, the 1973 Convention on Prevention of Pollution from Ships, the 1979 Treaty on Migratory Species, the 1982 UN Convention on the Law of the Sea, and the 1985 Protocol on Reduction of Sulfur Emissions.

Appendix 12.1. Environmental Treaties Database

Explanations of Variables

1. *Year.* The year in which the treaty was adopted ("Date of adoption" in the UNEP report). All treaties were coded.

2. *Number.* A count of the countries (but not organizations such as the EEC) listed as signatories for each treaty in the UNEP report. For those treaties that have entered into force, the countries listed are those who ratified or acceded to the treaty. For the 20 treaties that have not yet entered into force, the countries listed are those that have signed the treaties. All treaties were coded.

3. *Kind.* The kind of problem the treaty dealt with—the protection of a physical commons outside national control (such as the ocean) or a territorial (within-border) asset or resource (such as an endangered species). All treaties were coded.

4. *Subject.* The subject of the treaty. This variable indicates whether the treaty dealt with framework issues, conservation, oil pollution, marine dumping, land-based water pollution, air pollution, nuclear regulation, worker protection, plant disease and pest control, or other issues. All treaties were coded.

5. *Hegemony.* Universal hegemony: Did the United States ratify the treaty? Every Y (Yes) coding was also coded for whether or not the United States would have had benign reasons to be a hegemon (YB) or purely self-interested reasons (YS).

6. *S1.* The first sovereignty variable: Did the treaty regulate internal (I) or external (E) activities? This variable indicates whether the treaty regulates activities that are within or outside territorial boundaries. This dimension is different from the *kind* variable above, as the emissions of greenhouse gases illustrate. Such emissions take place within borders, but degrade a commons. Treaties that regulate both internal and external activities are coded as internal. One treaty (regarding cooperation in marine fishing, p. 52) was not coded.

7. *S2.* The second sovereignty variable: To what extent did the treaty constrain the national actor? This variable was coded on a six-point scale as follows:

1 = No constraint.
2 = Nongovernmental groups regulate.
3 = National governments regulate.
4 = National governments must yield information to a supranational authority.

5 = A supranational authority conducts its own research.

6 = A supranational authority has power to enforce the treaty.

No treaties received a coding of 1 or 2. One treaty (on the continental shelf, p. 31) was not coded.

8. *IH*. Issue hegemony: Was there a hegemon on the particular issue involved? Issue hegemony requires that a party have both the leverage and the will to compel others to join. Leverage is defined as the ability to inflict concrete damage (and does not include intangibles such as bargaining skill), and will is defined in terms of self-interest (rather than, say, a desire to improve the world). Six treaties were not coded because of insufficient data.

9. *R-type*. Regime-type: Did the treaty address an issue involving common aversions (A) or common interests (I)? The basic criterion is whether or not there is an incentive to chisel, with an issue involving "common interests" being one regarding which chiseling must be overcome. The issue is again whether or not the treaty dealt with some kind of a commons, but with regime-type (as opposed to the commons/territorial distinction), the commons does not have to be a physical space such as the ocean, but can also be (for instance) the stocks of a migratory species. This made it harder to determine whether or not a commons was indeed involved for some treaties (such as the treaty on vicunas). Nevertheless, all treaties were coded. Eleven were commons treaties that involved common aversions, and six were territorial treaties that involved common interests.

10. *Lag*. The length of time between adoption of the treaty and its entry into force. The year of adoption was subtracted from the year of entry into force in the UNEP report, but when the years were the same, the variable was coded as *1*. *0* designates that the treaty is not in force, though this was not explicitly stated for all the treaties with no year of entry into force. All treaties were coded.

11. *Eval Imp*. Evaluated impact. This variable indicates the judgment of observers as to how effective the treaty has been on its target, coded as follows: 1 = no impact, 2 = little to moderate impact, and 3 = moderate to strong impact. Only 14 treaties were coded.

12. *MPM*. Major parties missing: Were there any important parties that were *not* involved in the treaty? Important parties for oil pollution treaties include the United States, Greece, Panama, Liberia, Japan, and the Soviet Union. Eighty-five treaties were coded for this variable.

CODINGS (Treaties in the order of the page number in the UNEP register)

Treaty	Year	Number	Kind
Lead in painting	1921	53	Territorial
Fauna and flora preservation	1933	9	Territorial
Nature preservation in W.H.	1940	19	Territorial
Regulation of whaling	1946	43	Commons
Inter-American trop. tuna	1949	9	Commons
General fisheries for Mediterranean	1949	19	Commons
Protection of birds	1950	10	Territorial
European and Mediterranean plant protection	1951	31	Territorial
Plant protection	1951	92	Territorial
Protection of prawns, etc.	1952	3	Commons
Protocol on fisheries of North Pacific	1978	3	Commons
High-seas fisheries of North Pacific	1952	3	Commons
Prevention of oil pollution	1954	71	Commons
Tank arrangements	1971	27	Commons
Protection of Great Barrier Reef	1971	27	Commons
Plant protection: South East Asia	1956	25	Territorial
Conservation of North Pacific fur seals	1957	4	Commons
Fishing in the Danube	1958	6	Commons
Continental shelf	1958	55	Territorial
Conservation of living resources of high seas	1958	35	Commons
High Seas	1958	58	Commons
North East Atlantic fisheries	1959	19	Commons
Fishing in the Black Sea	1959	3	Commons
Antarctic	1959	32	Commons
Quarantine of plants	1959	10	Territorial
Ionizing radiations	1960	40	Territorial
Third-party liability in nuclear energy	1960	14	Territorial
Supplement to 3rd-party liability in nuclear energy	1963	11	Territorial
Protection of the Moselle	1961	3	Commons
Protection of new varieties of plants	1961	17	Territorial
African migratory locust	1962	16	Territorial
Cooperation in marine fishing	1962	6	Commons
Protection of the Rhine	1963	5	Commons
Civil liability for nuclear damage	1963	10	Territorial
Nuclear weapon tests in the atmosphere	1963	117	Commons
Desert locust in eastern South West Asia	1963	4	Territorial
Development of the Chad Basin	1964	4	Territorial
Exploration of the sea	1964	18	Commons
Desert locust in the Near East	1965	14	Territorial
Conservation of Atlantic tunas	1966	23	Commons
Exploration and use of outer space	1967	76	Commons
Phyto-sanitary convention for Africa	1967	9	Territorial

Subject	Hege-mony	S1	S2	Lag	IH	R-Type	Eval-Eff	MPM
Worker Protection	N	I	3	2	N	A		
Conservation	N	I	3	3	N	A		
Conservation	YB	I	3	2	N	A	1	
Conservation	YS	E	4	2	N	I	2	N
Conservation	YS	E	4	1	Y	I	3	N
Conservation	N	I	5	3	N	I		
Conservation	N	I	3	13	N	A	1	
Plant disease/pest control	N	I	4	2	N	A		
Plant disease/pest control	YS	I	3	1	N	A		
Conservation	N	E	3	1	N	I		N
Conservation	YS	E	3	1	Y	I		Y
Conservation	YS	E	6	1	Y	I		Y
Oil Pollution	YS	E	3	4	N	I		N
Oil Pollution	N	I	3	0	N	I		Y
Oil Pollution	N	E	3	0	N	I		Y
Plant disease/pest control	N	I	3	1	N	A		
Conservation	YS	E	4	1	N	I	2	N
Conservation	N	I	4	1	Y	I		Y
Other	YS	E	0	6	N	A		
Conservation	YS	E	6	8	N	I		Y
Conservation	YS	E	3	4	N	I		
Conservation	N	E	5	4	N	I		N
Conservation	N	I	4	1		I		Y
Other	YS	E	3	2	N	A		N
Plant disease/pest control	N	I	3	1	Y	A		
Worker protection	N	I	3	2	N	A		
Nuclear regulation/liability	N	I	3	8	N	A		
Nuclear regulation/liability	N	I	3	11	N	A		
Land-based water pollution	N	I	5	1	N	I		N
Other	YS	I	3	7	N	A		
Plant disease/pest control	N	I	5	1		A		
Other	N	N	3	1	Y	A		
Land-based water pollution	N	I	5	2	Y	I		N
Nuclear regulation/liability	N	I	3	14	N	A		
Other	YS	E	3	1	N	I		Y
Plant disease/pest control	N	I	3	1		A		
Conservation	N	I	4	0	N	A		N
Other	YS	E	3	4	N	A		
Plant disease/pest control	N	I	3	2		A		
Conservation	YS	E	5	3	N	I		
Framework	YS	E	3	1	N	I		
Plant disease/pest control	N	I	3	0	N	A		

(continued)

Treaty	Year	Number	Kind
Conservation of African natural resources	1968	29	Territorial
Detergents in washing and cleaning products	1968	10	Territorial
Pollution of the North Sea by oil	1969	8	Commons
Living resources of the South East Atlantic	1969	18	Commons
Civil liability for oil pollution damage	1969	63	Territorial
Oil pollution casualties	1969	54	Commons
Marine dumping by other than oil	1973	23	Commons
Hunting and protection of birds	1970	3	Territorial
Desert locust in North West Africa	1970	4	Territorial
Wetlands of international importance	1971	50	Territorial
Amendment of wetlands treaty	1982	35	Territorial
Nuclear weapons on the seabed	1971	80	Commons
Maritime carriage of nuclear material	1971	11	Territorial
Compensation for oil pollution damage	1971	40	Territorial
Protection against benzene poisoning	1971	26	Territorial
Dumping from ships and aircraft	1972	13	Commons
Senegal River development	1972	3	Commons
Antarctic seals	1972	13	Commons
Prohibition of biological and toxin weapons	1972	106	Territorial
Marine pollution by dumping of wastes	1972	65	Commons
Trade in endangered species	1973	96	Territorial
Drought control committee for Sahel	1973	6	Territorial
Living resources in the Baltic Sea	1973	8	Commons
Prevention of pollution from ships	1973	19	Commons
Protocol on pollution from ships convention	1978	53	Commons
Conservation of polar bears	1973	5	Territorial
Protection of environment among Nordics	1974	4	Commons
Marine environment of Baltic Sea area	1974	7	Commons
Marine pollution from land-based sources	1974	12	Commons
Occupational carcinogenic substances	1974	24	Territorial
Protection of Mediterranean from pollution	1976	17	Commons
Protection of Mediterranean from dumping	1976	17	Commons
Protocol on Mediterranean oil emergency	1976	17	Commons
Mediterranean pollution from land-based sources	1980	11	Commons
Mediterranean specially protected areas	1982	12	Commons
Waters of the Mediterranean shores	1976	3	Territorial
Nature in the South Pacific	1976	3	Commons
Protection of Rhine against chemical pollution	1976	5	Commons
Protection of Rhine against chlorides	1976	5	Commons
Hostile use of environmental modeling techniques	1976	52	Territorial
Oil pollution from seabed exploration	1977	6	Territorial
Protection of workers against air pollution	1977	23	Territorial

Subject	Hege-mony	S1	S2	Lag	IH	R-Type	Eval-Eff	MPM
Conservation	N	I	3	1	N	A	2	N
Land-based water pollution	N	I	3	3	N	A		
Oil pollution	N	E	3	1	N	I		N
Conservation	N	E	5	2	Y	I		N
Oil pollution	N	I	3	6	N	A		Y
Oil pollution	YS	E	3	6	N	A		Y
Marine dumping	YS	E	3	10	N	A		Y
Conservation	N	I	3	2	N	A	2	
Plant disease/pest control	N	I	3	1		A		
Conservation	YB	I	3	4	N	A	2	
Conservation	YB	I	3	4	N	A	2	
Other	YS	E	3	1	N	I		Y
Nuclear regulation/liability	N	E	3	4	N	I		Y
Oil pollution	N	I	3	7	N	A		Y
Worker protection	N	I	3	2	N	A		
Marine dumping	N	E	3	2	N	I		N
Framework	N	I	3	0	N	A		N
Conservation	YS	E	3	6	N	A	3	N
Other	YS	I	3	3	N	I		N
Marine dumping	YS	E	3	3	N	I		N
Conservation	YB	E	3	2	N	A	3	
Other	N	I	3	0	N	A		
Conservation	N	I	4	1	N	I		N
Marine dumping	N	E	3	10	N	I		Y
Marine dumping	YS	E	3	5	N	I		N
Conservation	YB	E	3	3	N	I	3	N
Framework	N	I	3	2	N	I		N
Framework	N	I	3	6	N	I		N
Land-based water pollution	N	I	3	4	N	I		N
Worker protection	N	I	3	2	N	A		
Framework	N	I	3	2	Y	I		N
Marine dumping	N	I	3	2	Y	I		N
Oil pollution	N	I	3	2	Y	I		N
Land-based water pollution	N	I	3	3	Y	I		N
Conservation	N	I	3	4	Y	I		N
Other	N	I	5	5	N	A		N
Conservation	N	I	3	0	Y	I		
Land-based water pollution	N	I	3	3	Y	I		N
Land-based water pollution	N	I	4	9	Y	I		N
Other	YS	I	3	2	N	I		
Oil Pollution	N	I	3	0	N	A		
Worker protection	N	I	3	2	N	A		

(continued)

Treaty	Year	Num-ber	Kind
Kuwait convention for protection of marine environment	1978	8	Commons
Protocol to Kuwait convention	1978	8	Commons
Amazonian cooperation	1978	8	Territorial
Cooperation in North West Atlantic fisheries	1978	12	Commons
Migratory species of wild animals	1979	27	Commons
European wildlife and natural habitats	1979	16	Territorial
Physical protection of nuclear material	1979	23	Territorial
Long-range transboundary air pollution	1979	29	Commons
Financing of air pollution program	1984	26	Territorial
Reduction of sulfur emissions	1985	18	Commons
Control of emissions of nitrogen oxides	1988	24	Commons
Management of the vicuna	1979	4	Territorial
Antarctic marine living resources	1980	20	Commons
Future cooperation in North East Atlantic fisheries	1980	10	Commons
Niger Basin Authority and Development Fund	1980	8	Commons
Marine & coastal environments of Western and Central Africa	1981	7	Commons
Combating pollution in emergency	1981	7	Commons
Marine environment of the South East Pacific	1981	4	Commons
South East Pacific oil emergency	1981	5	Commons
Supplemental protocol to South East Pacific oil emergency	1983	5	Commons
Protection of South East Pacific from land-based pollution	1983	4	Commons
Occupational safety and health	1981	9	Territorial
Red Sea and Gulf of Aden environment	1982	4	Commons
Protocol to Red Sea convention	1982	4	Commons
Salmon in the North Atlantic	1982	6	Commons
Benelux nature and landscape protection	1982	3	Territorial
UN convention on the law of the sea	1982	160	Commons
Marine environment of wider Caribbean region	1983	15	Commons
Oil spills in wider Caribbean region	1983	15	Commons
Pollution of the North Sea by oil	1983	8	Commons
Tropical timber agreement	1983	42	Territorial
Protection of the ozone layer	1985	35	Commons
Montreal Protocol on ozone layer	1987	42	Commons
Marine and coastal environments of Eastern Africa	1985	4	Commons
Wild flora and fauna in East Africa	1985	4	Territorial
Marine pollution emergency in East Africa	1985	4	Commons
Occupational health services	1985	6	Territorial

Subject	Hege-mony	S1	S2	Lag	IH	R-Type	Eval-Eff	MPM
Framework	N	I	3	1	N	I		N
Oil pollution	N	I	3	1	N	I		N
Framework	N	I	3	2	Y	A		N
Conservation	N	E	3	1	N	I		Y
Conservation	N	I	3	4	N	I		
Conservation	N	I	3	3	N	A		
Nuclear regulation/liability	YS	I	3	8	N	A		Y
Air pollution	YS	I	3	4	N	I		N
Air pollution	YS	I	3	4	N	I		N
Air pollution	N	I	4	2	N	I		Y
Air pollution	YS	I	3	0	N	I		N
Conservation	N	I	3	3	N	A	3	
Conservation	YB	E	4	2	N	A	2	
Conservation	N	E	3	2	N	I		N
Conservation	N	I	5	2	Y	A		N
Framework	N	I	3	3	N	I		N
Oil pollution	N	I	3	3	N	A		N
Framework	N	I	3	5	N	I		Y
Oil pollution	N	I	3	5	N	I		N
Oil pollution	N	I	3	4	N	I		N
Land-based water pollution	N	I	3	3	N	I		Y
Worker protection	N	I	3	2	N	A		
Framework	N	I	3	3	N	I		Y
Oil pollution	N	I	3	3	N	I		Y
Conservation	YS	E	4	1	Y	I		N
Conservation	N	I	3	1	N	A		N
Framework	N	E	3	0	N	I		Y
Framework	YS	I	3	3	N	I		Y
Oil pollution	YS	I	3	3	N	I		Y
Oil pollution	N	I	3	0	N	I		N
Conservation	YS	I	3	2		I		
Air pollution	YS	I	3	3	Y	I		Y
Air pollution	YS	I	3	2	Y	I		Y
Framework	N	I	3	0	N	I		Y
Conservation	N	I	3	0	N	A		Y
Oil pollution	N	I	3	0	N	I		Y
Worker protection	N	I	3	3	N	A		

(continued)

Treaty	Year	Number	Kind
South Pacific nuclear-free zone	1985	9	Territorial
ASEAN conservation of natural resources	1985	6	Territorial
Safety in the use of asbestos	1986	3	Territorial
Early notification of nuclear accident	1986	31	Territorial
Assistance in case of nuclear accident	1986	25	Territorial
Environment of South Pacific region	1986	13	Commons
Pollution of South Pacific by dumping	1986	19	Commons
Pollution emergencies in South Pacific	1986	19	Commons
Management of Zambezi river system	1987	5	Commons
Antarctic mineral resource activities	1988	6	Commons
Application of Vienna and Paris Conventions	1988	17	Territorial

Subject	Hege-mony	S1	S2	Lag	IH	R-Type	Eval-Eff	MPM
Other	N	I	3	1	N	A		N
Conservation	N	I	3	0	N	A		
Worker protection	N	I	3	3	N	A		
Nuclear regulation/liability	YS	I	4	1	N	A		Y
Nuclear regulation/liability	YS	E	3	1	N	A		Y
Framework	YB	I	3	0	N	I		N
Marine dumping	YB	E	3	0	N	I		N
Oil pollution	YB	I	3	0	N	I		
Conservation	N	I	3	1	N	I		N
Framework	YS	E	3	0	N	A		Y
Nuclear regulation/liability	N	I	3	0	N	A		Y

13
Negotiating an International Climate Regime: The Institutional Bargaining for Environmental Governance

Oran R. Young

Meeting in a suburb of Washington, D.C., for ten days during February 1991, delegates from 102 countries convened the first session of the United Nations Intergovernmental Negotiating Committee on Climate Change (INC).[1] In so doing they launched a process of institutional bargaining designed to produce agreement on the terms of an international convention establishing a regime to regulate human activities that threaten to precipitate major changes in the earth's climate system (Schneider 1991). To the disappointment of some, the opening session of the INC focused largely on matters of organization and procedure; the establishment of a working group on commitments or principles and another on institutional mechanisms became major concerns. But a second session held in Geneva in June, and a third in Nairobi in September, addressed substantive issues.[2] By early 1992 a sense of urgency surrounded these negotiations—not only because scientific projections on climate change suggest that an unchecked buildup of greenhouse gases in the earth's atmosphere could have far-reaching consequences for human welfare, but also because pressure was mounting to produce a fully developed draft convention in time for signature at the United Nations Conference on Environment and Development (UNCED) in Brazil in June 1992.[3]

A study of previous efforts to reach agreement on the terms of international regimes through processes of institutional bargaining reveals a mixed record. Although some initiatives succeed, others fail outright or produce framework agreements that do not evolve into effective institutional arrangements with the passage of time (Young 1989a). Little by little, students of regime formation are piecing together an account of the key determinants of success or failure (Rittberger, ed., 1990; Young and Osherenko, eds., forthcoming). This chapter draws on the results of prior research to shed light on the case of climate change and to offer some advice to those seeking to maximize the prospects for success.

Institutional Bargaining

Participants in the sessions of the INC found themselves engaged in a process of institutional bargaining or, in other words, a set of interactions intended to produce agreement on the terms of a constitutional contract governing behavior relating to climate change over an indefinite period of time (Young 1989b). Unlike the interactions considered in mainstream models of bargaining, institutional bargaining in international society:

• involves several distinct types of actors, including intergovernmental organizations (IGOs) and nongovernmental organizations (NGOs) as well as nation states,

• proceeds in the absence of a fully defined payoff space or utility possibility set, so that the participants do not know at the outset the full extent of the joint gains available to them, and

• centers on efforts to forge consensus on packages of provisions that are acceptable to as many of the participants as possible.

In formal terms, the signatories to constitutional contracts in international society are almost always nation-states. In a sense, therefore, the perspective adopted in this discussion focuses, in the language of chapter 1, on institutional reform in contrast to transformation (see table 1.1). Increasingly, however, nonstate actors play significant roles in the formation of international regimes. An array of United Nations agencies, including the United Nations Environment Programme, the World Meteorological Organization, the Intergovernmental Panel on Climate Change, and the Preparatory Committee of the United Nations Conference on Environment and Development, have not only influenced the conceptualization of climate change as a global concern, but have also become players in the bargaining process currently under way under the auspices of the INC.[4] Even more striking is the evolving role of the NGOs. Today those associated with NGOs have become players in the bargaining process itself. They serve on national delegations, direct the flow of information regarding the probable consequences of institutional options, and advise negotiators acting on behalf of international coalitions as well as individual states.

Those engaged in institutional bargaining ordinarily assume the existence of a contract zone or a range of feasible agreements that all would prefer to an outcome of no agreement; otherwise participants would have little incentive to take such processes seriously. Yet the information available to the parties regarding the scope of the contract zone and the pattern of payoffs likely to flow from specific institutional arrangements is almost always highly imperfect. Although it is reasonable to suppose that negotiators can differentiate clearly between competitive/cooperative relationships and cases of pure cooperation or pure conflict, those negotiating the terms of constitutional contracts at the international level seldom make a sustained effort to perfect their information about payoff structures before negotiations begin. Instead they normally proceed by identifying a small number of key problems, focusing on the development of solutions to these problems, and concerning themselves with the formulation and refinement of negotiating texts that incorporate emerging areas of agreement.

This does not eliminate the distributive element characteristic of all bargaining processes, but it leads to a better balance of integrative and distributive efforts than appears in most conventional models of bargaining (Walton and McKersie 1965). Because the parties do not know the locus of the welfare or Pareto frontier at the outset, they have clear incentives to engage in an exploratory discourse designed to identify mutually beneficial institutional options—in contrast to focusing exclusively on the deployment of bargaining tactics intended to secure the best possible outcomes for themselves.[5] Because they cannot be sure how the streams of benefits and costs flowing from the operation of different institutional arrangements will affect their welfare, individual participants have an incentive to work toward the choice of regimes that will prove acceptable regardless of how they perform in practice. These features of institutional bargaining limit the usefulness of analyses that require precise information ex ante about the structure of the payoff space or the utility possibility set—for example, arguments emphasizing the distinction between coordination problems and collaboration problems or stressing the importance of compliance mechanisms in achieving sustained cooperation in relationships that exhibit the attributes of a prisoner's dilemma (Oye 1986).

Similar observations are in order regarding the impact of the consensus rule in contrast to the majoritarian rules assumed in most conventional models of bargaining. In cases where institutional bargaining involves only two participants, this distinction washes out. Bilateral bargaining cannot produce an agreement unless both parties are prepared to accept the same terms, regardless of the model of bargaining under consideration. Once the number of independent participants grows to three or more (the normal case in institutional bargaining in international society), however, important differences surface. Mainstream models of multiparty bargaining focus on the character of winning coalitions, the processes of coalition formation, and the stability of coalitions once formed.[6] Institutional bargaining, by contrast, emphasizes efforts to form coalitions of the whole or at least to forge a consensus encompassing as many of the participants as possible.

This means that the preferences of individual actors can exert a significant influence on the course of institutional bargaining. While it is sometimes possible simply to ignore the concerns of minor parties articulating extreme demands, the central concerns of major participants must be accommodated. The emphasis on consensus building is so central to institutional bargaining, in fact, that those seeking to devise mutually acceptable formulas often prove willing to make substantial efforts to draw relatively small outlying parties into the consensus. This feature of institutional bargaining has led some observers to conclude that the provisions of constitutional contracts will necessarily reflect the lowest common denominator (Underdal 1980; Sand 1990). But the prominence of imperfect information and the central role of integrative bargaining go some way toward offsetting this conclusion. Although there is little reason to expect that institutional bargaining will alter the underlying interests of the participants, the process can easily lead to a restructuring of initial preferences by providing individual participants with new information and insights regarding the problem at hand and the options available for handling it. Among other things, this opens up influential possibilities for entrepreneurial leadership on the part of individuals capable of persuading participants that their interests will be served by the adoption of arrangements that move well beyond the restricted outcomes associated with the idea of the lowest common denominator.

Power, Ideas, and Interests

The literature on regime formation exhibits a pronounced tendency to focus on single factors in the search for explanations of success and failure in efforts to create institutional arrangements at the international level. Understandable as this tack is for those who value parsimony, it has not met with much success. To understand the prospects for the climate negotiations, we must not only analyze a number of distinct factors but also look at the interactions among them (Young and Osherenko, eds., forthcoming, ch. 7). Three clusters of factors deserve explicit consideration in this context: those dealing with power, ideas, and interests.

The Exercise of Power
Empirical research has discredited the proposition derived from hegemonic stability theory that a dominant power (in the sense of a single actor possessing a preponderance of material resources) is necessary to the achievement of success in the process of regime formation. Charles Kindleberger demonstrated some years ago that dominant powers sometimes fail to exercise their power in the interests of forming institutional arrangements in international society (Kindleberger 1973). Recent research has shown that regimes form in situations where no dominant power is present. With regard to the case of climate change, this is just as well, since no single participant in the process unfolding under the auspices of the INC qualifies as a dominant power.

Leading participants may also find it difficult to translate power in the material sense into bargaining strength or leverage capable of directing processes of institutional bargaining. The history of regime formation is replete with failed efforts on the part of powerful actors to get their way in bargaining over the content of international regimes. Sometimes this leads to a breakdown of the process, as in the case of the deep-seabed mining provisions of the 1982 Law of the Sea Convention, or an agreement to settle for a framework convention with little substantive content, as in the case of the 1985 Vienna Convention on the ozone layer. In other cases it leads to a process in which others succeed in bringing pressure to bear on a powerful actor to accede to their desires, as in the case of the effort to persuade the United States to accept the compensation fund established under the 1990 London amendments to the 1987 Montreal Protocol on Substances that Deplete the Ozone Layer. This, too, raises doubts about any simple application of the theory of hegemonic stability to predict the outcome of the current effort to form a climate regime.

Nonetheless, power is important in institutional bargaining of the type now under way under the auspices of the INC. Given the nature of institutional bargaining, success is likely to depend on the formation of a small number of bargaining blocs. Such blocs can serve several important functions. They provide a mechanism for articulating the major issues at stake in institutional bargaining and ensuring that these issues are taken into account in any bargain struck. Their existence can reduce substantially the rising transaction costs that many analysts regard as a major barrier to success in bargaining involving sizable numbers of parties (Kahler 1992). Because bargaining of this type operates under a consensus rule, interactions among blocs often play a central role in the development of regimes that meet the basic needs of all major interest groups, and are therefore widely accepted as equitable. This is particularly important in cases, such as climate change, where some of the products of a regime's operations are likely to exhibit the attributes of public goods and the implementation of the regime's provisions is likely to prove costly, so that the negotiation of an effective cost-sharing or burden-sharing mechanism is essential.

Although the configuration of blocs in the climate change negotiations remains fluid, several key elements of the bloc politics are already clear (Morrisette and Plantinga 1991). The negotiations in the INC will not amount to a simple replay of the contest between the advanced industrialized countries (as represented by the G-7) and the developing countries (as represented by the G-77) that dominated negotiations over a New International Economic Order (NIEO) a decade and more ago. The industrialized countries have divided into a cautious group led by the United States and a more activist group led by a number of European countries (or the European Community acting on behalf of these countries). The developing countries are separating into a group of newly industrialized countries (NICs), a group of less developed countries that are influential by virtue of their size (for example, Brazil, China, India), and a residual group of less important countries (see chapter 5).

The role of the former socialist states and the former Soviet Union in particular in the climate change negotiations is not yet clear. It seems likely that there will be no socialist bloc in the negotiations over the provisions of a constitutional contract for a climate regime. A newly emerging bloc that has achieved real success within the INC, on the other hand, is the Alliance of Small Island States. This bloc brings together about two dozen island states in the Pacific and Indian Oceans and the Caribbean and Mediterranean Seas, as well as a few others (for example, Bangladesh) likely to be hardest hit by rising sea levels resulting from global warming. Because the concerns of its members are so palpable and because the group has attracted the help of sophisticated advisors from the NGOs, the Alliance of Small Island States has proven effective in the climate negotiations, despite the weakness of its members in material terms.

The climate change negotiations also differ profoundly from the negotiations associated with the NIEO by virtue of the fact that the industrialized countries would find it costly to walk away from the bargaining process, leaving the others to their own devices. There is no way to check global warming without the active participation of the developing countries, and especially large countries such as China (which is exploiting its extensive reserves of coal to fuel its efforts to industrialize) and Brazil (which is critical to the release of carbon resulting from the destruction of moist tropical forests). Nor is it easy for the advanced industrialized countries to persuade developing countries to forego the benefits they themselves acquired through processes involving a heavy reliance on the use of fossil fuels, unless the industrialized countries are willing to make substantial concessions in return for an agreement to follow some other course. Almost certainly efforts to come to terms with climate change at the international level will continue to constitute a major item on the international agenda throughout the 1990s.

The Impact of Ideas

Most observers believe that ideas matter, in the sense that their impact on processes of regime formation is independent of the exercise of power or the interplay of interests. But there is no consensus on the mechanisms through which ideas exert their influence on institutional bargaining. Some have emphasized the role of cognitive convergence, encompassing not only ideas about the causes of important problems but also prescriptions for appropriate solutions. Richard Cooper's account of the battle between the contagonists and the miasmatists during the nineteenth century and the final victory of the former as factors affecting the creation of public health regimes at the international level is suggestive (Cooper 1989). Others have stressed the role of epistemic communities or, in other words, transnational groups of scientists and public officials who share both causal beliefs and prescriptive preferences and who become influential actors in their own right (Adler and Haas 1992).

There is as well a useful distinction between hegemony in the ideational or Gramscian sense and the impact of ideas at the more specific level of day-to-day negotiations. Gramscian hegemony refers to the dominance of an interlocking system of concepts, propositions, and values—an overarching worldview (Cox 1983). While influence of this type is often associated with the actions of an actor that is dominant in the material sense, ideational hegemony may continue and, for that matter, even intensify as the power of the dominant actor declines.

But it is not necessary to focus on such macro-level phenomena, which are inherently difficult to pin down, to observe the impact of ideas on the course of institutional bargaining in an issue area like climate change. There are at least three distinct areas in which ideas appear to be important in shaping the course of institutional bargaining. First and arguably foremost, the global environmental change movement has been important in highlighting the growing significance of anthropogenic change and providing an intellectual framework within which to think systematically about interactions between physical and biological systems on the one hand and human systems on the other (Committee on Global Change 1988). This movement is still in its infancy; there is much that we do not understand about the systemic interactions. Yet the rise of thinking about global environmental change to a position of prominence in the scientific world buttresses the position of those who assert that large-scale environmental issues must be tackled seriously, even in the presence of profound uncertainties regarding the mechanisms at work in specific cases. This development also serves to legitimize the views of those who argue that large-scale environmental issues can only be solved through broadly based international cooperation, a perspective that argues forcefully against any effort on the part of advantaged countries to wall themselves off from environmental degradation elsewhere (Holdgate 1991).

More concretely, the force of ideas is apparent in two separate aspects of the work of the INC itself. To begin with, the Intergovernmental Panel on Climate Change (IPCC), organized and administered jointly by the U.N. Environment Programme and the World Meteorological Organization, was influential in setting the stage for negotiations under the auspices of the INC, both by encouraging scientific consensus on the reality of climate change as a phenomenon to be taken seriously, and by casting the work of the INC as a process of reaching consensus on the provisions of a global climate regime (IPCC 1990). The role of ideas has taken on added significance in connection with the work of the INC precisely because there is so much uncertainty about both the overall course of climate change and the probable impacts of global warming on different parts of the world. To be sure, this has given rise to a battle between those who tend to resolve uncertainties optimistically in favor of lines of thought that minimize the significance of climate change and those who take the opposite tack, pessimistically projecting worst-case scenarios regarding the trajectory and impacts of climate change (Stern, Young, and Drukman, eds., 1992, ch. 4). But these are ultimately clashes of ideas.

It seems clear, then, that the course of institutional bargaining over the content of a climate convention is being molded by ideas, just as it is being shaped by the efforts of negotiating blocs to translate power in the material sense into bargaining leverage in connection with the work of the INC. This does not ensure, as some of those who focus on the role of epistemic communities seem to suggest, that the course of institutional bargaining can be consciously manipulated. The evolution of ideas, such as those that have given rise to the global change movement, is a product of the efforts of many actors responding to a wide variety of stimuli (Hall, ed., 1989). As those who have tried can attest, it is exceedingly difficult to stem the tide of ideas flowing against a particular set of interests or direct such a tide to control the outcome of specific processes of institutional bargaining.

The Interplay of Interests

Interactive decisionmaking among parties pursuing their own interests is never a simple or straightforward process. In virtually every case this process involves an element of competition or conflict that ensures that participants will act to maximize payoffs to themselves and that gives rise to the complications of strategic interaction (Frohlich, Oppenheimer, and Young 1971, ch. 5). In the case of climate change, a number of additional factors contribute to these generic problems associated with the interplay of interests. Because it is critical to draw a wide array of countries into a climate regime, institutional bargaining in this case necessarily involves Southern as well as Northern concerns, which makes it imperative to come to terms with the linkages between environment and development in the negotiations unfolding under the auspices of the INC. Though it may well be true that changes in lifestyle can be implemented without excessive costs to societies in aggregate terms, it is inevitable that they will prove costly to some vested interests within countries that wield considerable influence in domestic political processes (Arthur Miller 1991). And the fact that uncertainties abound regarding the probable course of climate change—some responsible observers remain unconvinced that global warming is a serious problem at all—makes it possible for those who oppose adjustments called for in the name of combatting the greenhouse effect to line up respectable scientific opinion in support of their position.

Small wonder, then, that some commentators have taken to speaking about "the policy gridlock on global warming" (Skolnikoff 1990). But are efforts to form an international climate regime really doomed to failure as a consequence of the operation of these bargaining impediments (Sebenius 1991a)? Studies of the interplay of interests reveal a number of factors that remain relevant in this context.

First and probably foremost is the question of the degree to which the participants approach the negotiations as a process of integrative (in contrast to distributive) bargaining. Given the high degree of uncertainly associated with almost every aspect of climate change, it is apparent that there is great scope for interpretation. There is a wide gap between assessments of climate change that stress systemic concerns and treat global warming as a common problem and calculations that feature the identification of prospective winners and losers and highlight the conflictual potential of this issue (Wallace Stevens 1991). It is worth emphasizing the extent to which most scientists and policymakers have joined forces to focus attention on the common-problem aspect of climate change and to avoid becoming bogged down in battles regarding putative winners and losers. The work of the IPCC during 1989 and 1990 contributed to setting this tone, and the negotiators operating within the INC have carried on, for the most part, in the same vein. None of this guarantees that it will prove possible to make progress toward a climate change convention without running afoul of distributive concerns triggered by a growing preoccupation with the identification of probable winners and losers in the wake of global warming. So far, however, uncertainty has served to soften the problems associated with distributive bargaining.

Uncertainty may also make it difficult for participants in institutional bargaining to make confident predictions about the distributive consequences of alternative institutional arrangements under consideration for inclusion in a climate regime. The resultant "veil of uncertainty" has the effect of increasing interest in the formation of arrangements that can be justified on the grounds of procedural fairness—whatever the nature of the substantive outcomes they produce (Brennan and Buchanan 1985, 28–31). Coupled with the operation of the consensus rule characteristic of institutional bargaining, this has led some analysts to argue that "an effective international agreement to limit [greenhouse gas emissions] will not be undertaken unless the agreement is seen by the participants as fair" (Burtraw and Toman 1991, 1). Of course, this observation may lead skeptics to conclude that the prospects for the formation of any climate regime in the near future are dim. Yet research on regime formation in international society suggests that it would be a mistake to underestimate the potential role of "good" uncertainty in facilitating the efforts of those operating under the auspices of the INC to come to terms on the provisions of an international climate regime (Young and Osherenko, eds., forthcoming).

Other factors associated with the interplay of interests suggest less optimistic conclusions, at least at this stage. It is difficult to identify salient solutions in the sense of focal points around which expectations are likely to converge in the climate change negotiations (Schelling 1960). There is nothing sacred about any particular percentage cuts in greenhouse gas emissions (is there a difference, for example, among 10%, 20%, or 30% in terms of salience?), and a number of common rules regarding what is fair with regard to cost sharing "diverge widely in their prescriptions for an agreement" when applied to the case of climate change (Burtraw and Toman 1991, 27). Nor is the problem of compliance easy to solve. While advances in technology are undoubtedly increasing transparency by improving our capacity to monitor compliance with the rules of international regimes in a relatively unintrusive manner, it would surely be naive to ignore the problems that are likely to arise in achieving compliance with the emission control systems that every member of international society will have to adopt to put a stop to global warming (Chayes and Chayes 1990).

Finally, there is the issue of shocks or crises that are exogenous to the process of institutional bargaining itself. There is little doubt, for example, that the public announcement during 1985 of the Antarctic "ozone hole" played an important role in mobilizing public concern and moving the process of regime formation from the somewhat unimpressive results reflected in the 1985 Vienna Convention to the significant achievements articulated in the 1987 Montreal Protocol (Roan 1989, ch. 8). With all due respect to the heat of the summer of 1988, no exogenous shock comparable to the "ozone hole" has yet surfaced in connection with the effort to establish a global climate regime. Still, given the sensitivity of humans to the weather and the suggestability arising from the absence of knowledge about the mechanisms of climate change, it would be no cause for surprise if exogenous shocks came to play a significant role in shaping the course of institutional bargaining over climate change.

In concluding this discussion of the role of power, ideas, and interests, the importance of individual leadership requires attention. Three types of leadership are central in this context: structural leadership, entrepreneurial leadership, and intellectual leadership (Young 1991). While the structural leader works to translate power in the material sense into bargaining leverage focused on the issue at hand, the entrepreneurial leader deploys negotiating skills to cast issues in ways that facilitate integrative bargaining and to broker interests to build consensus around the choice of a preferred institutional arrangement. The intellectual leader provides systems of thought that offer a coherent analytic framework within which to think about the formation of regimes to deal with international problems.

While the evidence from earlier work on regime formation suggests that leadership is crucial to success in institutional bargaining (Young and Osherenko, eds., forthcoming, ch. 7), the role of leaders in the climate change negotiations is somewhat unclear. Nonetheless, we have begun to profit from intellectual leadership in this realm. Thus, the nesting of climate change into the broader flow of ideas on global environmental change may well prove helpful in providing a basis for thinking systematically about this issue and in influencing negotiators to approach global warming as a common problem rather than a matter to be viewed from a winners-and-losers perspective. The work of the leaders of the IPCC (for example, Bert Bohlin) in articulating the intellectual basis for a climate regime seems particularly important.

When it comes to structural and entrepreneurial leadership, there is less to report. Effective structural leaders have not yet surfaced in the negotiations under way under the auspices of the INC. This is attributable in part to the failure of the United States to push for agreement on the provisions of a climate convention (Simons 1990). Partly it is the result of the inability or unwillingness of others to step forward to fill the vacuum left by the failure of the United States to adopt a constructive position. With regard to entrepreneurial leadership, no one has emerged to assume the role that Koh and others played in the law of the sea negotiations or that Tolba played in the ozone negotiations. The separation of the climate change negotiations from the work of the UNCED PrepCom and from the ongoing efforts of the UN Environment Programme (UNEP) and the World Meteorological Organization (WMO) may prove to be an obstacle to the emergence of entrepreneurial leaders. But this is not to say that capable individuals will not assume this responsibility as the work of the INC progresses.

Normative Concerns

In addition to assessing the probability that a climate regime will form during the near future, we are naturally interested in the shape that such a regime will take both at the outset and over time as a process of institutional evolution unfolds. Part of this interest involves such straightforward matters as the timetable for reducing or phasing out emissions of carbon dioxide and other greenhouse gases and the character of the cost-sharing or burden-sharing mechanisms devised to pay the costs of adjusting to increasingly stringent constraints on these emissions. There are a number of concerns of a broader, normative character that a climate regime may address or that may become subjects of social learning in connection with the operation of such a regime (Nye 1987; E. Haas 1990). This section explores such concerns through an analysis of four intersecting topics: approaches to ecosystems and landscapes, considerations of North/South equity, perspectives on human/environment relations, and ideas of intergenerational equity. These themes are addressed here in declining order in terms of the likelihood that they will be taken seriously in the formation and operation of a climate regime, though there are complexities in each case that make such sweeping judgments hazardous.

Approaches to Ecosystems and Landscapes

The advanced industrialized societies centered in the Northern Hemisphere owe much of their success to patterns of thought that encourage the disaggregation of problems into their component parts and reward efforts to tackle individual issues piecemeal. Such practices have provided the basis for the development and application of technology that is, in many ways, the defining characteristic of modernized systems. Yet the advent of global environmental problems such as ozone depletion, climate change, and the loss of biological diversity has produced growing doubts about the social consequences of these practices, which typically fail to take sufficient notice of the spillovers or externalities arising from the treatment of problems in a disaggregated fashion.

Today we all appreciate the importance of ecological perspectives, which stress interdependencies and linkages among large clusters of factors, in contrast to technological perspectives. The growing influence of the concept of landscapes adds a concern for processes of change in complex ecosystems and highlights path dependence in the trajectories along which such systems move. The complex, path-dependent systems of ecological thinking are not nearly as malleable as the simpler and more circumscribed systems that populate the world of technological thinking. Because it is unreasonable to expect that we can easily manipulate or control global environmental systems in pursuit of human goals, we must be wary of uses of technology that precipitate anthropogenic changes in large physical and biological systems that prove profoundly disruptive (Stern, Young, and Drukman, eds., 1992).

Ecosystems perspectives have been appearing in agreements setting up international regimes for some time (Lyster 1985). As early as 1971, the Ramsar Convention on Wetlands of International Importance Especially as Waterfowl Habitat reflected this trend in its concern for the importance of preserving habitat to protect wildlife. The 1980 Convention on the Conservation of Antarctic Marine Living Resources is predicated squarely on an ecosystems approach.

Does this mean that we can count on general acceptance of ecosystems thinking in the development of a climate regime and on the development of the procedures for environmental accounting needed to translate such thinking into practical measures? Not necessarily. Entrenched modes of thought die slowly, especially when they support the preferences of powerful interest groups. An ecosystems approach will not be welcomed by those (for example, actors who rely on the combustion of fossil fuels to generate electricity or to sustain highly dispersed human settlement patterns) who are likely to find themselves liable for a growing range of unintended or collateral damages as a consequence of the impact of new sensitivities (and new accounting procedures) regarding ecological interdependencies. What is more, states that remain highly sensitive about matters of sovereignty—and this includes many developing countries— are apt to balk at intrusions into their domestic affairs justified in the name of protecting ecosystems that are essential to the support of human life on earth, but that do not conform neatly to the bounds of legal jurisdictions (Hurrell 1992).

Will these obstacles constitute an insuperable barrier to the development of a systems approach within the context of an evolving international climate regime? The answer to this question is almost certainly negative. Systems thinking is an idea whose time has come in our efforts to comprehend global environmental change. Although there will undoubtedly be resistance from some quarters that leads drafters of a climate convention to be somewhat circumspect in the language they use, it is hard to imagine a situation in which the establishment and evolution of an international climate regime does not reflect and rein force the growth of systems thinking in dealing with environmental issues.

Considerations of North/South Equity

Efforts to make use of processes of regime (re)formation to deal with basic questions of equity arising from the disparate circumstances of the advanced industrialized countries of the North and the developing countries of the South have not met with great success. The United States (and several other important players, in a more circumspect fashion) backed away from key provisions of the 1982 Law of the Sea Convention precisely because they became dissatisfied with provisions in Part XI on deep-seabed mining that seemed likely to benefit members of the G-77. The negotiations of the 1970s and early 1980s on various aspects of the NIEO failed because the bargaining process eventually reached a stage at which the advanced industrialized countries preferred to walk away and accept an outcome of no agreement rather than to make more substantial concessions. The ozone regime contains modest concessions to the developing countries together with a compensation fund established under the terms of the 1990 London amendments (Benedick 1991). But the terms of this regime were worked out with little participation on the part of developing countries, and it remains to be seen whether countries like China and India will embrace the arrangement in a wholehearted and sustained fashion.

This is not an encouraging record. Yet there are reasons to expect that institutional bargaining over climate change will follow a different trajectory. This is in part a result of the way in which the problem has been framed. There is no escaping the fact that the increased loading of the earth's atmosphere with greenhouse gases and, especially, carbon dioxide is largely attributable to the behavior of modernized societies (even the destruction of moist tropical forests owes a lot to the actions of investors and consumers located in the North). Nor is it credible to ask developing-country leaders to forego the benefits of industrialization ̶ ̶̶der to contribute to efforts to save large-scale physical and biological   ˡ as a result of the behavior of the affluent in the   e prospect of reaching agreement at the international   of climate change unless all parties take the linkage between environment and development seriously and seek to deal with both agendas in a holistic manner.

The South also has substantial bargaining leverage when it comes to the issue of climate change. China, for example, is already the world's third largest emitter of carbon dioxide and fourth largest emitter of all greenhouse gases combined (World Resources Institute 1990, chs. 1 and 2). Both China and India are poised on the brink of rapid growth in demand for refrigerants and an acceleration of industrial production based on the combustion of fossil fuels. The fate of the world's moist tropical forests lies in the hands of developing countries such as Brazil, Indonesia, and Zaire. To be sure, climate change is likely to affect developing countries as much as, or more than, developed countries, so that the bargaining leverage of the South will rest on threats rather than warnings. Some northerners may doubt the credibility of these threats and advocate a bargaining strategy that offers few concessions to the developing countries.[7] But such a strategy is exceedingly risky. Many people in developing countries are feeling increasingly angry and desperate. Moreover, it is easy for policymakers in these countries to take decisions based on domestic pressures to increase the production of goods and services, with little concern for the impact on global environmental systems. Faced with this prospect, northerners will ignore the demands of the South regarding climate change at their peril.

The roots of this analysis lie in calculations of bargaining strength. But the result is the emergence of an influential body of opinion that takes the environment/development linkage seriously and accepts the proposition that any global bargain about climate change must be accepted by all the major parties as equitable. In the short run, this is likely to result in the establishment of a climate regime that makes explicit provisions for technology transfers, technical training, and additional financial assistance as means of encouraging the developing countries to participate and of assisting those willing to take part to make the economic changes needed to modernize in a way that produces lower levels of greenhouse gas emissions. In the longer term, these initiatives could set in motion a train of events leading to more constructive approaches to the overarching issues of North/South equity that constitute one of the central concerns in international society today.

Perspectives on Human/Environment Relations

Can the issue of climate change play a role in altering the way we think about human/environment relations and precipitating new perspectives on the niche that human beings occupy in the larger scheme of things? We are dealing here with deep-seated and, for the most part, unexamined attitudes and patterns of thought, which are notoriously difficult to change. Nonetheless, the problem of global warming and the international institutions that arise to come to terms with it could well become catalysts for change.

The key to this development lies in the growing realization that human behavior is a critical driving force behind an array of global environmental changes (Stern, Young, and Drukman, eds., 1992). Nowhere is the role of anthropogenic change more apparent or more potentially disruptive than in the case of global warming. The traditional western assumption that natural resources are available to be exploited for human benefit now seems less and less acceptable as a basis for human/environment relations (White 1967). This has led in turn to increasing interest in alternative perspectives such as the idea of stewardship, under which humans would assume a trust responsibility for the welfare of physical and biological systems (Nash 1989), or the idea of biotic citizenship, under which humans would accept a status of equality with other components of the biosphere rather than thinking of themselves as standing apart from and superior to other components (Leopold 1966, 237–264).

Over time, then, it seems probable that we are destined to experience far-reaching changes in the way in which we think about human/environment relations (see chapter 1). But how will this process affect and be affected by the formation of an international climate regime in the near future? As far as the terms of the institutional arrangements themselves go, the emphasis will almost certainly fall on specific, though by no means trivial, provisions designed to enhance the effectiveness of the regime. It is quite possible, for example, that efforts will be made to devise new accounting systems capable of measuring the social as well as private costs and the unintended as well as intended consequences arising from greenhouse gas emissions (Repetto 1989). It is possible also that a system of liability rules will emerge that make humans responsible for damages to physical and biological systems as well as for injuries inflicted on each other (International Law Commission 1990). To the extent that such features are built into a climate regime, this development could set in motion a process that would lead over time to the evolution of a new system of ethics applicable to human/environment relations (Nash 1989).

Beyond this lies the prospect that the effort to deal with climate change will stimulate broader institutional changes intended to alter our behavior. A particularly intriguing suggestion centers on the idea of reconstituting the UN Trusteeship Council to oversee the development and implementation of new ways of thinking about human/environment relations, including the problems of controlling anthropogenic impacts on large physical systems and of preserving both biological and cultural diversity. We should not lose sight of the fact that the climate change negotiations are embedded in a larger flow of events that could well result within the next generation in some far-reaching changes in institutional arrangements governing our interactions with the natural environment.

Ideas of Intergenerational Equity
Much has been written in recent years about the importance of building international regimes to govern human behavior so that members of future generations do not suffer from environmental degradation caused by the actions of those living today (Weiss 1989). This concern, first articulated publicly in the World Conservation Strategy, published in 1980 under the auspices of the International Union for the Conservation of Nature and Natural Resources, became a central theme of *Our Common Future,* the 1987 report of the World Commission on Environment and Development (IUCN 1980; WCED 1987). But what does intergenerational equity require in operational terms, particularly in connection with institutional bargaining over the provisions of an international climate regime?

It is not easy to determine how to proceed in specific cases, even if we are motivated to fulfill the requirements of intergenerational equity (see chapters 9, 10, 11). There is, to begin with, a conceptual problem in specifying the tastes or preferences of members of future generations. These individuals will live in a different world and have preferences molded by different, possibly radically different, life experiences.[8]

There is also the question of devising a usable criterion or standard of intergenerational equity. As Rothenberg and others have pointed out, there are numerous ways to incorporate the legitimate claims of members of future generations into decisionmaking processes about large-scale environmental issues (see chapters 9 and 11, Burtraw and Toman 1991). In general, these procedures yield different prescriptions; in some cases they are based on fundamentally different modes of thinking about the problem.

There are as well political constraints on the process of incorporating the concerns of future generations into institutional bargaining. We encounter here a classic situation in which benefits are likely to accrue to a widely dispersed and, by definition, poorly organized group (that is, the members of future generations), whereas the costs of providing these benefits will fall on a specific group (that is, those living today). Nor is it clear who is authorized to speak for the concerns of future generations in these negotiations. This issue is likely to be approached as a distributive rather than integrative matter in a negotiating environment in which most of the potential beneficiaries are poorly placed to defend or promote their own interests.

Could we devise a process of regime formation that would reduce the extent to which the deck is stacked against the interests of members of future generations? If we were able to simulate a Rawlsian veil of ignorance in these negotiations, the problem would disappear (Rawls 1971). Because those operating under such a veil do not know which generation they belong to, they have a strong incentive to take the issue of intergenerational equity seriously. But as many commentators have noted, this proviso is highly unrealistic. Can the more realistic notion of negotiating under a veil of uncertainty serve just as well in these terms (Brennan and Buchanan 1985)? Although this notion does not yield the obvious solution to the problem of intergenerational equity offered by the concept of a veil of ignorance, it may still prove helpful. Individuals operating under a veil of uncertainty are motivated to establish collective choice procedures that will seem fair, regardless of where they end up in the distribution of payoffs. To the extent that any constitutional contract governing climate change is expected to remain in force indefinitely, its collective choice procedures will apply to the members of future generations as well as to those concerned with the problem today.

In terms of institutional bargaining, this suggests that the most practical way to ensure that the welfare of members of future generations is safeguarded is to act to thicken the veil of uncertainty surrounding the negotiations, rather than running the risk of becoming bogged down in debates of a more substantive nature about criteria or standards of intergenerational equity.

Conclusion

The preceding analysis does not license an unqualified positive prediction concerning the prospects for a climate convention. The INC process has a number of things going for it: the growing influence of the global environmental change movement, an apparent willingness to resist focusing on winners and losers, and an emerging awareness of the importance of the linkage between environment and development. Yet we cannot reject out of hand the argument of those who expect policy gridlock to undermine these negotiations. The negotiating strategies of the blocs that will carry much of the weight in this process of institutional bargaining are still evolving. It is difficult to single out salient solutions to some of the key issues. Vested interests likely to fear the consequences of an international climate regime are strong. It remains to be seen whether structural or entrepreneurial leaders will surface and succeed in playing constructive roles in the negotiations.

Success in producing a climate convention for signature at UNCED would constitute a major step toward establishing a composite (and quantitative) greenhouse gas index, creating a compensation fund to attract meaningful participation on the part of key developing countries, and devising procedures for dealing with technology transfers and technical training.

It might also set in motion an evolutionary process leading to a more comprehensive and effective climate regime over time. Social practices do evolve, often in ways that their founders can neither predict nor control. If the development of a climate regime is accompanied by increasingly influential shifts from technocratic to systems thinking, and from anthropocentric to stewardship or biotic perspectives on human/ environment relations, this incipient institutional arrangement could become a force to be reckoned with in the years to come.

Notes

1. Representatives of eighteen United Nations and other international bodies as well as seventy-seven nongovernmental organizations also participated in the session.

2. A fourth session took place in December, and a fifth session in early 1992.

3. Prepared initially during July and August 1991, this essay was last revised at the beginning of 1992 and edited in August 1992.

4. For a thoughtful account of roles for intergovernmental organizations in processes of regime building, see the chapter by Victor, with Skolnikoff and Chayes in this volume.

5. This is where Krasner's recent account of "life on the Pareto frontier," which assumes extensive knowledge about the payoff possibility set, breaks down (Krasner 1991).

6. In Riker's well-known analysis, for example, the central proposition is that actors in such situations will seek to form "minimum winning coalitions" (Riker 1962).

7. As Schelling pointed out many years ago, there is a difference between a warning, which merely indicates an intended course of action, and a threat, which emphasizes a contingent action that one may be loath to take if the threat fails (Schelling 1960).

8. As Schelling has observed, such transfer payments from present to future generations may well have been the norm rather than the exception through much of human history.

14

Pragmatic Approaches to Regime Building for Complex International Problems

David G. Victor with Abram Chayes and Eugene B. Skolnikoff

Introduction

The community of nations is engaged in a grand enterprise to build a regime that can safeguard the environment of the entire planet. It is an enterprise fraught with uncertainty, with possibly great and controversial costs, and with potentially divisive political implications.

The importance of establishing this regime stems from the global nature of the problem and the small but significant chance that not mitigating and preparing for climate change will have catastrophic consequences. As with many natural hazards (Burton, Kates, and White 1978), the negative consequences of climate change may be disproportionately (but not exclusively) distributed to poor peoples and nations whose needs must therefore command careful attention in the construction and operation of a climate regime. Yet the distribution of costs and benefits over time will be complex and shifting (Ausubel 1991); costs and consequences of mitigating and adapting to climate change will be interwoven with unpredictable socioeconomic systems (COSEPUP 1991).[1] Building a regime to address collectively the climate problem in the face of these uncertainties will require a framework for gathering, assessing, and improving the information on both the climate problem and its socioeconomic context.

That the emissions and impacts of climate change are probably spread long into the future offers the opportunity to make gradually the needed changes from a greenhouse-intensive economy. The earlier this process begins, the lower the ultimate disruption and cost. Yet the reality is that the very nature of the issues involved in climate change will make formal detailed commitments and agreements to allocate the burden of slowing global warming particularly difficult to settle quickly. The integral relationship of everyday individual human activities to eventual global climatic effects, the difficulty of producing rapid change in large-scale systems such as the ecosystem and the socioeconomic system, the uncertainties in almost every aspect of the subject, the unique dependence on science and scientists, the requirement for collective domestic and international action, and the particularly demanding economic and political issues that are raised in relations between industrial and developing nations all conspire to make this one of the more complex, and fascinating, subjects that has ever graced the table of international affairs (Skolnikoff 1990). The practical implications for regime building, however, are considerable tension between the opportunity of beginning a gradual (but decisive) transition to a more greenhouse-benign economy as soon as possible and the reality that negotiating substantive international commitments will be difficult and time-consuming.

The international community is well aware of these requirements and tensions. An impressive set of international activities and negotiations led to the Framework Convention on Climate Change, which was signed at the United Nations Conference on Environment and Development (UNCED) in Brazil in June of 1992. That convention had been under active negotiation in the Intergovernmental Negotiating Committee (INC) established by the UN General Assembly in December 1990 (UNGA 1990), and the INC will continue to serve as an interim secretariat until the convention enters into force.[2] Moreover, ever since the first UN Conference on the Human and Natural Environment in Stockholm in 1972, the international community has been intensively and increasingly engaged in the growing number of environmental issues that, in their causes and effects, extend beyond nation-states. Virtually all of these past and continuing international arrangements are relevant to current and future efforts to slow global warming.

One of the crucial determinants of the success of the climate convention will be the effectiveness of the institutional arrangements for implementing it. The purpose of this chapter is to think through the organizational dimensions of a climate regime by identifying certain core functions that will be needed for the implementation of international policies to control climate change, although the substantive details of such policies are far from clear at present. Such organizational initiatives can help to increase transparency of national policies and thus begin the long process of shaping policies to account for their contributions to global warming.

The transition period from now until the final negotiation and implementation of a substantive, full-blown climate treaty may be quite long. Even the interim between the signing of the initial Framework Convention at UNCED and its effective entry into force and operation could be several years. Our goal is to help ensure that this period is not wasted by needlessly coupling essential organizational initiatives to the inherently more complex and time-consuming substantive details of a climate agreement, such as the negotiation of targets, timetables, and transfers of resources and technology. The proposals we present below are not intended to replace or delay an eventual substantive agreement; on the contrary, they should help ease the process of negotiating and implementing such an agreement.

Our approach differs from the process of institutional bargaining described by Oran Young in the previous chapter (see also Young 1989a and 1989b). Young addresses the process of bargaining over rules and procedures—taking place mainly in the INC and in preparations for UNCED—that comprise the process of regime formation. In contrast, we focus on the organizational arrangements that can serve both the process of regime formation and, eventually, the implementation and operation of a substantive climate regime. Similarly, our organizational approach is different from that of most regime theorists, who have primarily focused on the larger determinants of regime formation (e.g., Ruggie, 1975; Haas, 1980; Krasner 1983), maintenance (e.g., Keohane 1984), and change (e.g., E. B. Haas 1990).

Our organizational approach complements those studies—especially Young's concept of institutional bargaining, which emphasizes the complexity and uncertainty of the bargaining process—as we seek generic organizational characteristics that contribute to the process of regime formation and maintenance for complex, uncertain, and contentious international problems. Our study also contributes to an extensive literature on the nature of decision making in international organizations and the role of such organizations in effectively assisting the process of international cooperation (e.g., Haas 1964; Schachter, Nawaz, and Fried 1971; Cox and Jacobson 1973; Chayes and Chayes 1991; Young 1992). The main difference is that we propose that the capacity to perform many of the core organizational functions can and should be built *before* the process of regime formation is complete.

Regarding table 1.1 of Nazli Choucri's introduction to this volume, our study of pragmatic organizational initiatives is situated in the lower left corner. Our perspective is conservative: We do not propose substantially reforming or transforming the international system. Our domain is the institutional and policy response to global change; the goal of our study is to propose a series of organizational initiatives that can smooth the formation and eventual implementation of substantive agreements to manage global change.

Core Functions

A review of case histories in many areas on international cooperation reveals several core functions that have consistently proved especially useful to the negotiation, implementation, and renegotiation of the substantive terms of cooperation. Because these core functions are generic, they need not wait for more controversial aspects of international negotiation to be settled. However, because we propose building the organizational capacity to carry out these functions in the near term, probably before negotiations reveal the exact shape of a climate treaty, great care must be taken to avoid foreclosing the many possible substantive outcomes. Consequently, in choosing these core functions we have adopted the following four criteria: (1) the function is essential for the negotiation, implementation, and ongoing maintenance of the regime; (2) carrying out the function will help improve the quality and timing of substantive measures, while not presenting an obstacle to reaching such substantive agreements; (3) the function is sufficiently generic that it will usefully contribute to the regime regardless of the wide range of possible substantive outcomes; and (4) the function is common ground; it is not so controversial that our primary purpose— to build the needed organizational capacity as early as possible—is failed because there is no broad consensus on the need for carrying out the function.

At least four core functions for a climate regime can be identified. These are consistent with (but not identical to) the more extensive typologies of functions described by other authors (e.g., Skolnikoff 1972, 13–15, 100–116; Ruggie 1975, 571–74; Jacobson and Kay 1983, 13–18; Archer 1983, ch. 4). The four functions are presented below, organized according to increasing potential controversy. Later in the chapter we will consider how to fulfill these functions and where gaps in the existing capacity may exist. However, here we note that the functions might be implemented in stages, beginning with the least controversial tasks. (Further discussion of these functions, in the context of improving compliance with and the effectiveness of international law, is found in Chayes and Chayes 1991.)

First, coordination of research and periodic assessments of the relevant science are needed for international problems that, like global climate change, have high scientific content. Though scientific research is almost exclusively planned and funded as a national exercise, the historical precedents for useful international coordination are many. In some cases, such as the highly successful International Geophysical Year (IGY) of 1957–58 and the Antarctic Treaty of 1959, research coordination is the central component of international cooperation.[3] In many more cases the coordination (or at least freedom) of research is an integral component of a larger agreement to manage a collective problem. Most agreements to manage shared fisheries or waterways are of this type. The action plan to control pollution in the Mediterranean (Med Plan) both endorsed international scientific research on the Mediterranean Basin and was, itself, partially made possible by an informal network of concerned, informed, and cooperating scientists (P. M. Haas 1990a). In the case of controlling acid rain in Europe, a cooperative research and monitoring effort—the Program for Monitoring and Evaluation of the Long-Range Transmission of Air Pollution in Europe (EMEP)—proved an essential prerequisite for later, substantive agreements to control acid-causing emissions (Sand 1990a; Levy forthcoming).[4]

More recently, the importance of periodic international scientific assessments has been demonstrated. In the case of the Montreal Protocol on Substances that Deplete the Ozone Layer, two assessments sponsored by the United Nations Environment Program (UNEP) and the World Meteorological Organization (WMO) helped to solidify the scientific basis of the international policies under consideration (Benedick 1991). As with the climate case, the ozone depletion issue exists on the international agenda because it was proposed and detected by scientists. For issues such as these that are highly dependent upon scientific assessments, internationally credible science is an especially important basis for subsequent policy action.

In addition, the process of preparing joint, high-quality assessments also helps to build the needed local capacity for governments to conduct their own assessments of the issues. This was clearly demonstrated in the Mediterranean case; as part of the international cooperation framed in the Med Plan, both the technology and the skills needed to monitor and assess water pollution problems were transferred to countries that would otherwise not have had them (P. M. Haas 1990a). Attention to local capacity-building is necessary if developing countries are to participate.

To some degree, entrepreneurial scientists will initiate such assessments on their own. As often stated, scientific knowledge is international and has proved capable of transcending some political barriers and fostering cooperation. But with highly complex policies at stake, international sponsorship appears to have been quite important for international credibility. Indeed, in the ozone depletion case the bulk of the expertise and funding came from a few organizations (including private firms) in only a few industrialized countries. Nonetheless, UNEP and WMO provided the critical international organizational framework; the former also provided formal links to the ongoing policy negotiations taking place under its auspices.

Second, an ongoing forum for negotiations is needed to address issues, such as global climate change, that must be managed over time (rather than solved). Indeed, few international agreements are considered complete when first reached. Both the Antarctic Treaty and the Conference on International Trade in Endangered Species (CITES) have semiannual meetings of the parties to reconsider the terms of the agreement; parties to the Montreal Protocol have met even more frequently. Like the International Monetary Fund (IMF) and World Bank and the General Agreement on Tariffs and Trade (GATT), most international economic arrangements also have a wide variety of ongoing meetings of the parties. Frequently these meetings also include non-member (but interested) states, as well as many nongovernmental organizations (NGOs). In many cases, meetings of the parties have provided a mechanism for non-members to affect the negotiations and, subsequently, become full members of the treaty. For example, the Montreal Protocol has allowed observers from non-signatory states; over time, most of these states that were initially observers have signed and ratified the agreement. This function of ongoing negotiation and management is reflected in periodic decisions, revisions, recommendations, and/or additional protocols produced and approved by the parties.[5]

A third core function is systematic collection, review, and dissemination of data on greenhouse-related emissions. Essentially all international agreements that control discharges of pollutants have required baseline data for negotiating and implementing substantive commitments to control pollution. Once a substantive climate agreement is implemented, this data function can logically evolve to play a role in assessing the overall performance of the regime and verifying compliance (Ausubel and Victor 1992). For example, the "red book" of the International Union for the Conservation of Nature's (IUCN, recently renamed World Conservation Union), a book used to compile scientific research on the populations and status of thousands of endangered and threatened species, partially provides this function for CITES. As the safety of populations change, the parties and secretariat act accordingly and negotiate new control measures for each species; this would not be possible without monitoring and data gathering by IUCN and others.

The collection and dissemination of data can and should be highly synergistic with national scientific research programs. In most cases in which an international authority (e.g., a secretariat) collects and disseminates information, the primary source of monitoring data is self-reporting by the parties (Fischer 1991; GAO 1992). In some cases, the reviewing bodies use other sources that complement or challenge national reports; for example, nongovernmental organizations frequently provide additional sources or assessments of data. In other cases, for example the UN statistical programs, the exclusive source of data is national self-reporting.

As expected, many contentious issues of defining the measured quantities, national secrecy, and accuracy of data typically surface and must be resolved through negotiation with other parties and the secretariat in the context of the treaty. For example, parties to the Montreal Protocol, five years after its first signature, continue to haggle over these types of issues. We do not claim that contentious data issues can or will be fully resolved; rather, a process of reporting, collecting, disseminating, and reviewing data is a good first step in building a shared data set and coming to grips with these inevitable controversies.

A fourth and final core function is the reporting, review, and assessment of national policies relevant to global warming. Any international arrangement to control global warming that focuses only on emissions, for example through goals and timetables for abatement, will be less effective than if the primary focus is on national policy efforts, especially energy policy (e.g., Schelling 1991). Beginning the time-consuming process of building the capacity to conduct international reviews will help establish the relevance and importance of international discussions of national policies and the building of shared views of the problem and responses.[6]

Examples of the effective review and assessment of policies are drawn from several areas. Under the post-war Marshall Plan the United States insisted on the formation of an Organization for European Economic Cooperation (OEEC) to help divide up the aid among the European recipients. The original vision for the OEEC was that, through review and assessment, an integrated European Recovery Plan would be formed out of otherwise separate economic policies. Because of deep divisions among the recipients that the OEEC forum could not fully overcome, the United States still had to play a significant role in dividing the funds; but collective review and assessment through the OEEC did play a constructive role in coordinating national policies, though at a lower level than originally planned. The Organization for Economic Cooperation and Development (OECD), formed in 1960 from the OEEC members plus several others, continues to operate effectively in economic, energy, science and technology, environmental, and other areas through review and assessment. The OECD's directives are not binding, but the legitimacy conferred by a qualified staff and repeated positive experience with review and assessment has helped to build the OECD's role as an effective shaper of otherwise independent national policies. In science and technology policy, the OECD review and assessment process helps nations to see what others do, as well as establishing international norms and leading to special studies on common problems that have been identified in the review process. The operation of the OECD's review and assessment in these areas has improved both the capability of governments to contribute to the review and assessment process (e.g., by providing progressively more useful information in their national reports) and the extent to which relevant international commitments and relationships have been incorporated into the domestic policy-making process.

The pioneer in reporting, review, and assessment activities is the International Labor Organization (ILO). This organization negotiates proposed treaties and adopts recommendations concerning labor legislation and the terms and conditions of employment in member states. The parties are obligated to adopt the treaties and implement domestic legislation. Each party provides a periodic report of the steps it has taken to implement the treaties and recommendations. The reports are examined by a committee of experts, which also investigates the actual state of labor practices in the reporting country. The committee reports its conclusions and comments to the ILO's governing body for discussion at its plenary meetings (Haas 1964; Leary 1992).

Reporting and review are ideally suited for operation in the transition towards a substantive regime. They help to make domestic policies more consistent with the nature of the international problem, and they build norms even in the absence of stringent formal commitments that are typically difficult to reach in the early years of negotiation and regime building. For example, the early years of the IMF saw many nations sign the agreements to stabilize their currencies and make them convertible. However, instead of forcing a timetable for those goals, the agreement allowed countries to "opt out" and move towards stability and convertibility at a pace consistent with other national goals and policies. National reporting and review by IMF officials were part of that transition and gradually helped move countries from "opt out" status to full convertibility (which was reached for the major countries by the early 1960s). IMF review and assessment continues to work in this manner; in addition, the process of regularly assembling, reviewing, and assessing national reports has substantially helped in increasing the expertise within local finance ministries (Chayes 1991).

These four core functions are complementary and necessary for each other. Notably, the reporting, collection, and dissemination of data on emissions and policies provides an important foundation for the other three functions. Scientific research depends critically upon emissions data and policy forecasts; ongoing negotiations depend on the level of current and planned policy efforts; review and assessment begin with primary data on emissions trends and policies; and assessment is most complete when it is done with the latest scientific and policy information from around the world.

All four of these core functions are generic in that they work well with nearly all the different types of substantive climate regimes currently envisioned. At present, the many possible substantive outcomes include but are not limited to (1) a system of mandated but amendable targets and timetables for abatement similar to the approach taken in the Montreal Protocol, (2) a large fund for the transfer of greenhouse-benign technologies, (3) a process of national pledges of abatement and then periodic reviews, (4) a global or regional system of tradable permits, (5) a system of taxes or emissions fees, and (6) a technology-based "best efforts" approach. Regardless of the exact outcomes, all of these and other possible substantive designs would significantly benefit from these core functions, especially if the organizational capacity to fulfill the functions is already fully operating before the substantive measures are agreed to.

Where We Stand

How well will these needed organizational functions be carried out as a climate regime takes shape? Our impression is that the international community is moving swiftly to satisfy the need for the first two functions. Regarding the coordination of research, there is a long tradition of international cooperation in the formation of national research programs in the atmospheric sciences. As a follow-on to its role in organizing the IGY, the International Council of Scientific Unions (ICSU) has been organizing a long-term International Geosphere-Biosphere Program (IGBP), in part to help provide the needed information related to global warming policy.

Directly on the topic of global warming, in 1988 the United Nations Environment Program and the World Meteorological Organization commissioned the Intergovernmental Panel on Climate Change (IPCC) to do a comprehensive assessment of the causes, impacts, and possible policy responses related to anthropogenic climate change. The IPCC met its mandate in the fall of 1990, and its reports provided a basis for the INC and for the global warming-related preparations for UNCED (for the three working group reports, see Houghton, Jenkins, and Ephraums 1990; Tegart, Sheldon, and Griffiths 1990; IPCC Response Strategies Working Group 1991). Presently, follow-up assessments by IPCC panels have been completed and further assessments are under way to keep the negotiators apprised of the latest information, and the Framework Convention establishes an advisory body to assist in this area and to answer specific technical questions. However, there remain some gaps; the needed international social science research programs—in economics and in political and other social sciences—are proceeding but have less extensive experience with such international cooperation.

Regarding the need for a forum and a secretariat for ongoing negotiation and management, the INC occupies this role at present, though its form will likely change after the entry into force of the Framework Convention. However, fulfilling the other two functions appears to be headed for delay through needless conflation of these types of organizational measures with progress on the more controversial aspects of slowing global warming.

Regarding the monitoring and dissemination of data on emissions, there are several national research programs to collect data on concentrations of the major greenhouse gases: carbon dioxide (CO_2), nitrous oxide (N_2O), chlorofluorocarbons (CFCs), methane (CH_4) and some of the precursors of tropospheric ozone (Houghton, Jenkins, and Ephraums 1990, ch. 2). Concentration data, along with existing socioeconomic statistics and a few in situ and laboratory research programs, have been helpful in building inventories of emissions both for the present and historically. Yet for many of the anthropogenic sources and sinks of these gases the uncertainties are high, and it has proven especially difficult to compute accurate inventories at a per-state level of spatial resolution.[7]

The largest contributor to global warming, fossil fuel emissions of carbon dioxide, is luckily among the best understood of the emissions inventories since emissions can be calculated almost directly from fossil fuel consumption data, which is already collected by the UN energy statistical program (Marland et al. 1989). But the UN energy statistics have never been subjected to formal international scrutiny. There are many non-UN sources of energy data, and thus many opportunities exist to improve the shared data set that is used to calculate fossil fuel carbon dioxide emissions. This is an ideal case for gradual improvement through a process of national reporting, review, and assessment.

Confidence is weaker for the primary data sets used to calculate inventories for other greenhouse sources and sinks. In some cases, notably deforestation, the data set needed for accurately computing emissions have not been collected in the past. In virtually all cases, emissions are computed from proxy variables, and better information on the exact relationship between proxies and actual emissions would be very helpful (Victor 1991b). The needed research programs will, of course, take time to produce fruits; in the interim, simple strategies can help avoid paralysis from such poorly understood yet central components of greenhouse policy, for example, proceeding with substantive national policies and international negotiations that focus first on the better known sources and sinks while improving the scientific understanding of the others (Grubb, Victor, and Hope 1991).

Thus there is much activity related to the computation of emissions; a great deal of this data is being collected through existing networks and research programs. But so far there is no sanctioned international organization connected to the climate negotiations that collects and disseminates a single data set and assists with the process of reviewing, challenging, and improving the data.

Regarding the collection and dissemination of information on policies—a combination of the third and fourth functions—there are of course many disparate individuals, organizations, and governments contributing to the debate about global warming; much of the contribution takes the form of healthy critiques of national and international policies and plans. Yet, as with the monitoring and dissemination of emissions data, there is a premium on also having this function formally fulfilled by an organization connected to the negotiation process.

Finally, at this writing there is little movement toward the widespread adoption of the policy review and assessment function. A similar proposal of pledge and review—that is, individual pledges of emissions controls and other policies by states, and then periodic review of progress toward meeting those pledges—gained early support in the negotiations over a climate treaty (Grubb and Steen 1991). But that proposal, because it required substantive pledges, became mired in the other substantive debates since some nations wanted the pledges to be stringent and binding, while others wanted the opposite. The organizational initiatives we envision for review and assessment would require only that experience and expertise in policy review and assessment be developed by a qualified international body, whether or not the exercise of review and assessment is coupled to substantive pledges.

The Framework Convention signed at UNCED (see note 4) establishes a system of reporting of current and forecasted emissions and instructs the Parties to report on relevant policy initiatives. The exact future form and quality of this reporting system are unclear at present. However, it does not appear that there will be regular review and assessment of the reports since the secretariat established under the convention is instructed only to compile and transmit the reports to the conference of the parties and to assist developing countries in compiling the necessary information. Some activist parties as well as NGOs may choose to undertake reviews in some cases. There is an important role for parties or NGOs that wish to take unilateral action by submitting reports of the highest quality to set standards and show the way for other parties.

These gaps—in the collection and dissemination of information on policies, and in policy review and assessment—are especially significant. Without systematically fulfilling these functions there is little framework for the gradual process of ratcheting up national capabilities to contribute to these functions. Similarly, there is little framework for the gradual and regular incorporation of international commitments to slow global warming into national policy choices and discourse. Existing ad hoc arrangements to fulfill these functions are useful, but the regular pattern of intergovernmental reporting, review, and assessment can gradually build an acceptance of international commitments and relationships relevant to climate change.

Some Directions from Here

How can the international community implement the needed organizational initiatives? Here we propose four options to illustrate the choices.

Strengthen UNEP. The logical location for many of these organizational functions is UNEP, perhaps in conjunction with existing UNEP programs—the Global Earth Monitoring System (GEMS) and Global Resource Information Database (GRID)—that already collect and disseminate data on the environment.[8] The main advantage of tapping UNEP is that it already exists and has a favorable reputation. The main disadvantage is that UNEP has little experience with program review and assessment and (most significant) the original vision for UNEP was as a catalyst for environmental policy with limited funding, not as an operating arm of the UN system. Its Nairobi location may make it awkward for UNEP to actively participate in such a large worldwide effort. An additional disadvantage, which applies to many of the options presented here, is that the UN structure may be inflexible and bureaucratic; however, the legitimacy and universality of the UN system probably require that the functions be carried out in large measure through at least some formal UN link (although that need not necessarily be UNEP).

Build the needed expertise out of other arms of the UN system. The WMO has considerable expertise in overseeing data collection and dissemination—as it has done, for example, with weather observations in the highly successful World Weather Watch. Because the WMO is closely involved in the coordination of scientific research, it is ideally suited to ensure that the synergies between scientific research and emissions monitoring are fully realized. Elsewhere in the UN system—for example, in the United Nations Development Program (UNDP), the World Bank, and the IMF—there is considerable experience in monitoring and disseminating information about public policies. The IMF and World Bank, of course, can offer much expertise in program review and assessment. The UNDP is building expertise in environment and development, as is the World Bank through its recently opened Global Environment Facility. The main advantage of this ad hoc approach is that it would help marshal the needed expertise from where it exists within the UN system.

The main disadvantage is that fragmenting the functions across many existing organizations might reduce the ability to do integrated assessments. Perhaps the secretariat or some other body under the Framework Convention could play an effective coordinating role to help avoid fragmentation.

Build a consortium of governmental and nongovernmental organizations to perform the needed functions. The main advantage of such an arrangement is that multiple (and competing) organizations with different allegiances can help ensure that the quality of data sets and policy reviews is maintained at a high level, much as peer review performs the same function in science. The main disadvantage is that governments are unlikely to delegate authority away from government-controlled bodies. We expect, for example, that if NGOs are given a formal role (as in the case of the IUCN and the CITES regime) arrangements will be made to try to retail ultimate authority within governments and governmental organizations.[9]

Establish a new organization. Though any proposal to build a new bureaucracy within the UN (or other international governmental) system will be viewed with skepticism, a small dedicated new organization might be ideally suited to carrying out the needed functions. Such a new organization might be founded under the INC and formally authorized by the Framework Convention on Climate Change and/or its associated legal instruments. Indeed, the convention signed at UNCED establishes new, specialized advisory bodies (see note 2) as well as a secretariat. However, none of these entities has been created with the capacity or mandate to perform the regular review and assessment functions elaborated in this chapter.

Though the situation is highly fluid, as part of UNCED and related processes the international community may be headed for some form of the first option, a significant strengthening of UNEP, although there are many discussions of strengthening and improving the coordination among other organizations, including NGOs and networks of scientific research institutes. However, UNEP has not played a central role in the INC process to negotiate a climate treaty, so its role on matters related to implementing such a treaty (and carrying out the core functions described here) may prove to be quite small. Furthermore, even a larger

UNEP will have many responsibilities, especially since international debates over environment and development have become so fully intertwined; and even a larger UNEP may still limit itself to a catalytic rather than a programmatic role.

Requirements of Organizational Initiatives

Regardless of the exact suite of organizational options chosen, the needed organizational arrangements should be designed and put into place with attention to several requirements that will affect how well the core functions are fulfilled. These requirements have been discussed above and in Chayes and Chayes (1991); they are briefly described below.

A prompt beginning. Links to formal negotiations are important to confer legitimacy on these organizational arrangements, but those links should not be so extensive that they interfere with the essential need to begin carrying out these functions as soon as possible (recognizing that some of these functions are already, to some extent, being fulfilled). The purpose of taking these organizational initiatives is precisely that these measures can be acted upon promptly.

Flexibility. Virtually every international environmental and economic agreement has been subject to change; the complex shifting nature of the issues raised by climate change virtually guarantees that the needed organizational arrangements to serve a climate regime will change considerably in the future (Victor 1991a). Consequently, the content of national reports, types of data sets needed, and character of policy review, among others, will change accordingly. Also, for many countries—especially in the developing world—experience with extensive national reporting and policy review is limited. The organizational arrangements will have to begin modestly and expand in their requirements for reporting only after these states gain more confidence and experience with such systems.[10]

Transparency of every aspect of the organizations that carry out these functions. The record shows that regimes, even without the benefit of binding substantive agreement, can build and enforce norms simply by making individual and national actions transparent. The central position given above to the information-gathering and -monitoring functions reflects the overriding importance of transparency in international environmental regimes. The process of improving the shared international data set and integrating national and international policies is a mechanism by which national actors become more transparent, and norms can be shaped by the international organization(s) that fulfill these functions.

A focus on policy. Unlike many international problems, climate change is a problem whose management will affect virtually every aspect of modern industrial society, especially the consumption of energy. The regime should be built to help pressure and document the transition from a carbon-intensive economy to an economy fueled by cleaner energy sources. Most of all, it should keep the focus on the national policies used to yield this transition. The regime will be much less successful if it is organized around merely tabulating emissions levels and negotiating quotas and timetables for controlling those emissions. The policies that ultimately affect emissions should be the targets for change.

Decentralization. Significant national and private resources for data collection, emissions monitoring, and scientific research on climate change are already in existence and must be put to maximum use. Geographically dispersed and perhaps even competing organizations can best identify and observe the local conditions that are both causes and consequences of global climate change. One of the primary lessons of the IPCC has been the importance, both for the soundness and the credibility of the results, of involving experts from all countries in the assessment process. The process of involving experts from all countries can also help legitimize international assessments within each country and improve the prospects that countries will agree to join future substantive agreements (P. M. Haas 1990a; Levy forthcoming). Decentralization of the core functions may be the best way to ensure wide involvement in carrying them out.

Universality. Climate change is a global phenomenon. The organizational arrangements should therefore permit universal participation while not foreclosing more limited decentralized groupings that may be easier to attain and perhaps more effective for particular tasks. As most notably with the Montreal Protocol, most large multiparty substantive treaties start with a small group of key states and expand outward; the organizational initiatives proposed here can best assist that same process of expansion for a substantive climate treaty, if as many states participate in carrying out the core functions as possible. Broad coverage is also necessary to build a useful data base. However, even if our proposed organizational initiatives are universal (or nearly so), there will still be ample opportunity for substantive actions to take place in smaller, more flexible groups. (Indeed, regional organizations may be best suited to manage many aspects of climate change policy since climate-dependent natural resources (e.g., fisheries and water basins) are primarily regional phenomena.)

Fairness. The effects of global warming and policies to slow global warming are inherently coupled to larger, perennial questions of distributive justice. Fairness (referred to as "equity" by others) is multidimensional, including the familiar North-South division but also many other dimensions—for example, carbon-rich nations (such as petroleum exporters) and the carbon-poor. The organizational arrangements established to serve the formation and implementation of a climate regime must explicitly incorporate the centrality of fairness into their operations. Failing to do so will jeopardize their legitimacy. (The existing organizations, especially those connected to the United Nations, have devoted considerable attention to this issue.)

An emphasis on cooperative rather than intrusive approaches. The ultimate authority in international treaty making is the state, and states are understandably reluctant to cede much authority to international organizations. Thus these proposed organizational arrangements must be made with the realization that wide acceptance will be forthcoming only if the vision for the international organization(s) is as facilitator rather than judge or critic. Even in cases in which the international organization has had much potential authority over the state—for example, the Marshall Plan and the OEEC or the IMF and the World Bank holding funds contingent upon structural adjustment—the organization remains largely a facilitator. If these proposed organizational initiatives are to be pursued as early as possible, there should not be attempts to wrest power from the state.[11] Since these activities, like the UN statistical program, will be based in the first instance on national reporting, they will not intrude on the sovereign prerogatives of participating states.

A significant role for NGOs. As in the field of human rights, in the area of the international environment nongovernmental organizations have played a major part in the formation of policy by identifying priority subjects for international action, producing innovative approaches to public policy, providing thoughtful analyses of environmental trends and other data, and raising public and political consciousness. The organizational arrangements for a climate regime must have multiple points of access so that, in addition to governments, there are ample opportunities for nongovernmental organizations to contribute. At the same time, since NGOs may sometimes be unrepresentative or wedded to particular policy solutions, the international institutions must maintain their own independent operational and decision-making capability.

Expertise. The proposed organizational initiatives must provide a center of credible expertise on the scientific, technical, and policy aspects of climate change. In accordance with the requirement of decentralization, most of the actual work of data gathering, monitoring, and research will be done by existing national, international, and nongovernmental organizations. As noted above, the IPCC experience points to the need for wide involvement in all aspects of the assessment and management of climate change. But there must be a central capability for coordinating the work and the process of review and evaluation. The follow-on functions of policy review, technical assistance, and norm creation also depend on an expert central coordinating and reviewing body.

The exact features of the organizational initiatives, including how the above requirements might be incorporated, is a subject to be negotiated among the parties. Those negotiations and their organizational products should begin as early as possible since they represent a critical investment for more extensive negotiations on the substance of the climate treaty.

Epilogue

The focus in this chapter has been on global climate change; however, our approach to regime formation is clearly applicable elsewhere. When the complexity and controversy of an international problem promises a long delay before substantive measures are implemented, a good early step is to build the organizational capacity to carry out certain core functions. The functions must be chosen so they usefully serve a wide variety of possible substantive outcomes; previous experience with international regime formation and maintenance suggests that activities such as pollution monitoring, building of shared data sets, and national reporting of policies and review are extremely useful for the negotiation and implementation of substantive measures. Building core organizational capacity should begin as early as possible—perhaps long before substantive action is agreed to and implemented—but it must not become a substitute for further substantive measures if they are necessary.

Notes

This paper is based on a series of working papers and workshops on the institutional aspects of international cooperation on climate change organized by Professors Chayes and Skolnikoff as part of a project on institutional arrangements sponsored by the Rockefeller Foundation. David Victor is funded to work on that project through a grant from the U.S. Department of Energy, National Institute for Global Environmental Change. The authors thank the many participants at the workshops for helpful discussions. All of the usual disclaimers apply.

On the basis of those workshops, the authors have also written a shorter essay entitled "A Prompt Start: Implementing the Framework Convention on Climate Change." That essay was circulated widely at the final sessions of the INC and the Preparatory Committee for UNCED, and a resolution in the spirit of "Prompt Start" was adopted by the INC (see note 2 below).

1. The international community recognizes the complex nature of responsibility for causes of and vulnerability to consequences of climate change. The Intergovernmental Negotiation Committee has called for "appropriate commitments," and the United Nations General Assembly regularly points out the special situation of developing countries and the fact that developed countries emit most of the climate-changing gases (e.g., INC 1991; UNGA 1989). However, there is no agreement on a single approach to dividing the burden of controlling future emissions of greenhouse gases (for a review see H. P. Young 1991; Burtraw and Toman 1991).

2. As this chapter went to press, the Framework Convention on Climate Change was opened for signature at UNCED. It will formally enter into force once fifty parties ratify, accept, approve, or accede. Broadly, the convention establishes the following: (1) a framework for future negotiations by establishing a conference of the parties to meet periodically once the convention enters into force; (2) a system of periodic reports to be submitted by the parties regarding current and future emissions of all relevant greenhouse gases; (3) a (small) secretariat to address some administrative and technical needs of the conference of the parties, as well as some subsidiary bodies for scientific advice and to assist in evaluating the performance of the convention and its implementation; and (4) a mechanism for the transfer of financial resources, initially to be entrusted to the Global Environment Facility (which is a pilot funding project of the World Bank, the

United Nations Development Program, and the United Nations Environment Program). The INC also adopted a resolution, to be signed concurrently with the convention at UNCED, that instructs the signatories and an interim secretariat to begin preparation for the first meeting of the conference of the parties as promptly as possible without waiting for the convention to enter into force. The need for this "prompt start" resolution was partially informed by the project that produced this chapter and another report (see unnumbered note above). For the text of the convention see UN General Assembly document A/AC.237/L.14 (including 10 addenda), dated 8 May 1992. For the resolution see UN General Assembly document A/AC.237/L.15, dated 7 May 1992.

3. Other examples in which research coordination is the central component of international cooperation include the many international scientific research programs, such as the Global Atmospheric Research Program (GARP) of the 1960s and 1970s and the International Geosphere-Biosphere Project (IGBP), which is currently underway. Regional scientific cooperation is also commonplace—for example, the coordination of national scientific research programs related to acid rain in Europe to ensure that results were comparable and credible across countries (see Levy forthcoming).

4. Signed by almost every party in the air basin, the 1979 Convention on Long-Range Transboundary Air Pollution (LRTAP) includes a 1984 protocol funding the EMEP program. While the role of EMEP was clearly instrumental, students are unclear to what extent the LRTAP process has been effective; that is, to what extent LRTAP has forced reductions of acid-causing pollutants beyond what states would have done on their own. Even more important, from the policy perspective of increasing the effectiveness of international regimes, are answers to questions regarding which LRTAP mechanisms have been effective and why (see Levy forthcoming). For more on effectiveness see Wettestad and Andresen 1991 and Young 1992.

5. Regular meetings of the parties may also be one of several "ratchet" mechanisms which, over time, de facto result in more stringent (and presumably more effective) management of the problem at hand (for a fuller discussion see Sebenius 1991b). For example, in the GATT, regular meetings of the parties and the system of rounds—whereby each set of negotiations produces a package agreement that builds upon the progress of earlier GATT agreements—has the effect of ratcheting down tariffs and other barriers to trade, although clearly the extent to which the ratchet can be effective depends upon many factors, including domestic protectionist pressures. The GATT system of rounds and package agreements may prove a good model for structuring rounds of climate negotiations (see Victor 1991a).

6. This review and assessment capacity could, at a later date, evolve into the capacity to affect national policies more directly. The self-reporting of policies could produce some form of audit of each nation's policies related to global warming. Through a process of review and assessment both the audit and national policy could be brought into line with accepted international norms. This process would also help to build the norms themselves because it would establish (and, through negotiation, modify) norms of acceptable behavior. For example, the GATT panels—which decide disputes brought before them by GATT members—have played a central role in interpreting and shaping the international norms related to what is meant by "free" trade. (Although GATT panel decisions are not strictly binding, they are closely watched and largely followed.) To different degrees, domestic legal systems operate the same way,

by interpreting general principles and norms through debate and decisions in successive cases.

7. Since international agreements are signed by states—and implemented down to the level of people, plants, cows, etc.—reasonably accurate data at the spatial resolution of states will be essential, since quantitative emissions reports, targets, and/or timetables will probably be on a state-by-state basis (i.e., distinct for each signatory of a greenhouse agreement). For some possible substantive outcomes—such as a global system of emission taxes or tradable permits—an even finer level of spatial resolution will be needed.

8. As with most international data programs, GEMS and GRID are networks and do not, themselves, significantly conduct the monitoring activities that produce the data.

9. In the CITES case, the IUCN's secretariat role is on contract from UNEP; thus, there is governmental and UN authority over the secretariat.

10. Similarly, designing a system of national reporting must accommodate the fact that domestic statistical programs vary in methods, quality, and extent of data collection. While flexibility is needed, one of the main purposes of scientific coordination as well as review and assessment is to establish comparable measuring systems and quality (P. M. Haas 1990a). In the case of greenhouse gas emissions, some efforts to harmonize methodologies are already under way, for example under the auspices of the IPCC and OECD.

11. The extent of intrusive measures permitted will vary across states, depending upon many factors such as domestic institutions and experience with other intrusive international obligations.

V

Conclusion

15

Global Accord: Imperatives for the Twenty-First Century

Nazli Choucri and Robert C. North

Drawing on the preceding chapters, this one provides a perspective on the global system and its components and presents a brief synthesis, which includes a broad integration of the concepts, illustrative data, and analyses put forward in the book as a whole. Additionally, a number of imperatives for research and policy making in the twenty-first century are derived from the earlier chapters.

Three contemporary challenges to humans were identified in Chapter 1. The first arises from close, intensely interactive, and increasingly powerful linkages between forces of the natural environment and human social activities, national characteristics, and international relations. Second is the human decision or behavior problem posed by concepts of—and approaches to—the global environment. This challenge derives from a recognition that the ecological balance of the globe is unintentionally affected by how individuals behave and how groups, institutions, and particular states manage their environments. And third is the institutional challenge pertaining to the identification of an appropriate framework for international cooperation at the global environmental level.

Responses to these challenges have been presented in four parts, which have focused on (1) theoretical and empirical dimensions of global environmental change; (2) the actors and processes involved; (3) evolving law, economics, and intertemporal issues; and (4) international systems and institutions. This chapter, the fifth part of the book, presents an integrated perspective and imperatives for the twenty-first century. The organizational plan for the book (table 1.1) summarized the diverse dimensions and perspectives addressed by the individual chapters. The concerns expressed in this joint effort are of two types: First is the concern with global analysis, which is the subject of our inquiry, and second is the concern with the relevant perspectives or "worldview" implied, implicitly or explicitly, in each of the chapters. The individual chapters are not intended to fit into individual cells in this matrix. Rather, our purpose is to draw attention to the contending underlying intellectual orientations in matters of global environmental change, the policy concern shaped by these orientations, and the modes of institutional responses that emerge as a result.[1] To place the synthesis and conclusion of this volume in theoretical context, however, we will summarize some of the ways in which individuals (and local events), states, and international and global systems are dynamically interconnected.

Human and Physical Dimensions of the Global System

Because of their central relevance to human existence and survivability, population, technology, and resources—presented in chapters 1 and 3 as master variables—are discussed in other chapters as well. There are good reasons for this. The population variable, for example, represents more than mere numbers of people. Inherent in the concept of population are the phenomena of individual human thought, consciousness, imagination, beliefs, feelings, and creativity—to say nothing of needs, wants, demands, and overall (and ever-expanding) productive capabilities (knowledge and skills and technologies) and potentials for transforming energy and other resources into the remarkable accoutrements of modern civilization.

Without these many endowments, the social environment could not exist as distinguishable from (or threatening to) the natural environment. Neither human social systems nor the special environment(s) they create could have emerged without social technologies—the special knowledge and skills that appear to set anthropogenic organizations, activities, and ecological impacts apart from those of other species. In identifying such intricacies, it is not always clear to what extent our efforts are compromised and our conclusions clouded by the reality that we ourselves have emerged from—and are thus an element—of the natural system. Wherever the truth may lie, the fact remains that none of these phenomena, nor other forms of life as we know them, could exist without the resource variable.

It is for all of these reasons that population, technology, and resources are referred to as master variables. They, in turn, are conditioned by uncounted numbers of intervening and dependent variables within the hologram—or the global system of reality—schematically represented by figure 1.6. In this connection, it is important to remind ourselves that, depending on specific functions and the perspective of the observer or analyst, the three master variables—like other variables—can be viewed (and analyzed) as intervening or dependent as well and independent only in the context of a system of complex interrelationships. If there is a case for decomposition, it can be made only for purposes of parsimony and only to integrate the constituent parts with a comprehensive whole. The systems at hand are inherently complex and intensely dynamic.

The Individual as the Source of Organization
Demands, decisions, and actions, strictly construed, originate with individuals in roles that are played out on a multiplicity of organizational levels (and social environments) from family, work team, or other small group to corporations, states, and the international and global systems. A large proportion of such activities are explained and generated by bargaining and leveraging of one kind or another among such individuals in the course of their dealings with each other.

As a reflection of the state, in turn, leadership—the individual leader or the president, prime minister, dictator, or other chief executive—can be envisaged as keeping watch over the country's internal and external environments from a swivel chair and pushing and pulling levers in efforts to achieve and, if possible, maintain something approaching an equilibrium between the two environments. In actuality, of course, a leader is not acting alone. Even a dictator or tyrant must bargain and leverage with his generals, ministers, advisers, enemies, and others; supporting (and unreliable, perhaps challenging) interest groups; and even the populace, of which he may be contemptuous.

Demands circulate throughout the system (unevenly)—as, in response, do energy, other resources, goods, services, benefits, and costs, which tend to cluster around concentrations of capability, influence, and power.

All of these phenomena contribute to the depletion and degradation of energy and other resources across wide landscapes, in a variety of forms and with many consequences. The production and distribution of resource uses and degradations tend to correspond to the generation and distributions of demand, capability, resources, goods, and services—and to concentrate around production and consumption centers. These are generic tendencies.

Worldwide the production, diffusion, and international distributions of resource depletions and degradations generally tend to correspond, in turn, to the distribution of demands, resources, goods, and overall consumption—together with a wide variety and range of depletions and degradations of energy and other resources extending worldwide. The generation of carbon dioxide (CO_2) and other greenhouse gas emissions by human actions is a disturbing manifestation of a broad and interconnected network of environmental uncertainties and potential dislocations.

The International System as a Distributive Mechanism

Interactions and competitiveness among states of disparate capabilities give rise to—and largely drive—the structure and characteristics of the international system, which is shaped and defined to a considerable extent by trade and investment, diplomacy (and international law), and strategic (military, naval, and air) activity—all of which exert powerful impacts on local, national, and global environments. Chapter 6 addresses trade and investment (focusing on multinational corporations), and diplomacy (and international law and regimes) bearing on environmental issues are discussed in chapters 12, 13, and 14. Since none of the chapters deals with international conflict, crises, or war, however, it should be noted in passing that war and preparations for war (including the establishment and maintenance of military, naval, and air bases) are notorious—and, with the development of chemical and nuclear weapons, potentially disastrous—agents of environmental depletion and degradation.

Although primarily driven by economic interests, trade, investment, and the activities of multinational corporations have distributive or disseminating effects that impinge upon local, national, international, and global systems in ways which—partly because of data deficiencies—

have not been adequately investigated. In fact, the rapid globalization of these functions—and the diffusion of structure and organization to perform these functions in the pursuit of desired goals—in recent decades has had the unintended consequences of distributing eminently useful products that are also agents of resource depletion and/or degradation—e.g., industrial chemicals (insecticides, herbicides, solvents, et al.); crude oil and petroleum products (including synthetics and plastics); automobiles, trucks, buses, and tractors); other whole technologies; and weapons of war (not always so unintentionally distributed)—throughout the world.

This is only one side of the story. Trade and investment being historically indispensable to development and social, economic, and political stability, these considerations call attention once again to the tension between growth and development and consequent policy dilemmas. An immediate concern deriving from uneven growth, development, and economic and financial distributions is the dichotomy between North and South, industrial and developing nations, which is explored in chapter 4 and referred to with some frequency in other chapters as well. In fact, as the authors of chapter 5 make clear from the start, the dichotomy concept has become increasingly inappropriate. In recent decades "the accelerating pace and increasing complexity of scientific advances and technological change" have made the process—and the dissemination—of technological and economic innovation "more rapid and systematic, but also more difficult and costly"—and possibly more uneven—for and among developing countries.

At the same time, poverty and population growth in developing countries are both causes and consequences of environmental degradation which, as indicated in chapter 3, tends to be aggravated by the higher levels and broader ranges of energy and other resources required by modern technologies. As if these problems were not sufficiently overburdening, several chapters refer to economic statistics revealing trends in living conditions that point to a widening economic polarization in the world and what Third World writers have referred to as environmental data "biased against developing countries" and a new "environmental colonialism" practiced by industrialized countries.

All of these phenomena occur within—and depend and draw upon—the planet and the natural system it supplies. This means that local, national, and regional programs for environmental regulation and management cannot be fully and effectively operational without some measure of oversight at the global level. In fact, negotiations directed toward a Framework Convention on Climatic Change were already underway in the early 1990s—under the auspices of the Intergovernmental Negotiation Committee (INC) established by the UN General Assembly. And the United Nations Conference on Environment and Development (UNCED) included among its objectives the framing of an Earth Charter and Agenda 21 specifying global priorities for the twenty-first century (chapter 13). All of these factors point to the increasing recognition of local-global linkages and of the need to reach international agreement on environmental management.

Decisions, Outcomes, and Dynamic Feedback

In conventional theory, nation-states have been treated as unitary rational actors seeking to maintain conditions of stable equilibria. But in view of real-life uncertainties deriving from the uneven growth, development, bargaining, and leveraging and subjective decision making referred to above, we tend to discount unitary rational actor and stable equilibria assumptions. Our predisposition, rather, is to conceive of states (through their political systems and their leaders) as continually pursuing elusive equilibria or—at best—maintaining adaptive, continually changing and more or less self-adjusting, "dynamic" equilibria or by trial and error tending toward steady-state processes.

Chapter 2 raises issues similar to some of those identified in chapter 4: How many species can be extinguished before an ecosystem's resilience and adaptability are imperiled? How much diversity is required to sustain life? How, further, does the citizen environmentalist, the corporate executive, or, for that matter, the social scientist address such issues? The reality is that even the trained ecologist is seldom capable of providing certain answers to these crucial questions, particularly in specific circumstances. All too frequently, moreover, the questions are not forcefully addressed until an environmental crisis has occurred. Often, too, it is such a crisis itself that reveals the differences—the gaps, separations, and conflicts—between scientists and others having special knowledge, relevant competencies, and crucial responsibilities (decisionmakers, policy formulators, and bureaucratic managers, for example). How can uncertainties in the "hard" sciences and the perceptions, affects, expectations, suspicions, animosities, and other subjectivities in the "softer" social sciences be dealt with?

Such dynamic feedback relationships, when positive, induce us to continue the behavior at issue or to modify or discontinue if it is negative. As human beings we are also capable, through "feedforward," of complex psychological processing and responding to images, ideas, questions, problems, or issues projected from the present into the future. It is such forms of feedforward that allow us to anticipate, plan for response, and devise the institutional mechanisms for reasonable action. These responses are serious challenges to conventional theory—in the social sciences more broadly defined and, more specifically, in the study of international relations.

Ecopolitics and Ecological Thinking

In reviewing the rise of global ecopolitics since the mid-nineteenth century, chapter 4 presents a main thesis to the effect that the rise of "a genuinely global politics of environmental issues" has been characterized by "a reciprocal, symbiotic, but still contradictory relationship" with a cluster of powerful and highly relevant interdisciplinary research paradigms and programs. An aspect of this relationship pertains to a certain divisiveness that results from the introduction of political issues into the more rigorous and coherent sciences of the natural environment. In line with Vernadsky's concept of "noosphere," this comprehension increasingly encompasses the interconnected but analytically distinguished part of the biosphere where humanity works for the sustainable development in balance with the biosphere as a whole. As Vernadsky saw it, "such an historical phenomenon should be examined as part of a terrestrial *geological* process, rather than merely as a *historical* process." The chapters in this volume are more restrained, but the overall thrust appears to be comparable.

The population, technology, and resource variables referred to in most of the chapters clearly indicate the tight interactions between human beings and the chemical, geological, biological, and other "natural" components of the global system. They also suggest how change and loose analogs of biological evolution reflect and help to explain anthropogenic technological (mechanical, organizational, and institutional) development and consequent impacts on the natural environment. Relevant here are the unevennesses in growth and development processes within and between societies (and states). Central to modern development are the knowledge and skills derived from social learning in general. Also relevant to interconnections of social and natural systems are the distinct pathways of development that appear to be available to (and/or emergent from) countries of different population/technology/resource-availability profiles and grossly disparate capabilities (chapter 3).

Additionally, chapter 4 traces the "evolution of evolutionary thinking" in ways that expose something of a hiatus between the critical linkages inherent in global change (chapter 2) and in growth, development, and environmental change (chapter 3), on the one hand, and, on the other hand, the environmental policy instruments discussed in chapter 5. In this connection, chapter 4 also points to a tendency toward divisiveness that tends to emerge when environmental science confronts environmental politics and management. Both science and technology are double-edged in the sense that "along with the benefits they bestow," they also contribute to serious problems including unintended environmental impacts (chapter 7). Paradoxically, however, it is in science and "new" technology that options for reducing environmental damage are to be found.

Institutional Adaptation and Sociocultural Evolution

Directly relevant to policy formulation and policy response are the concepts and real-world manifestations of institutional development and adaptation or sociocultural evolution, which has been referred to above as an aspect of "the evolution of evolution" idea put forward in chapter 4. Whether derived from trial-and-error social learning, cultural tradition and moral imperative, or "backward indebtedness," intertemporal and intergenerational equity is likely to eventuate and survive as an operational principle only to the extent that it is institutionalized in conjunction with some operational sanctions. There may be an adjunct consideration, however. To the extent that each current generation (including our own as a baseline) can assess the "real" and preferred environmental utilities (developmental), equities (distributional), and their respective costs and benefits, the dynamic system-modeling techniques referred to above should provide us with the capability of monitoring, recording, projecting, and comparing utility and equity balances and trends from region to region and from generation to generation. At this writing, the nations of the world are engaged "in a grand enterprise to build a regime that can safeguard the environment of the whole planet . . . an enterprise fraught with uncertainty, with possibly great and controversial costs, and with potentially divisive political implications" (chapter 13). The divisiveness is due as much to differences in levels of development and socioeconomic, demographic, and technological conditions and capabilities as it is to political and ideological preferences, national priorities, and perceptions of national profile. Fraught with uncertainty, this is an enterprise that "must proceed in timely fashion," however, because the climatic effects of human activities have now reached proportions that may be felt on a worldwide (as well as local) scale. Procedures along these lines should be eminently applicable to a time series study of the (admittedly challengable) profile and growth-development pathway data presented in chapter 3 and relevant to "steering functions," options, incentives, expectations, and other decision-making and management phenomena referred to throughout the entire volume.

Uncertainties and Unpredictabilities

All chapters refer directly or indirectly to uncertainties, unpredictabilities, disintegrative tendencies, and even a certain amount of "chaos" in natural and social environments and in their interactivities. Whether an observer or analyst looks into the past, considers the present, or projects into the future, uncertainties and unpredictabilities are certain to be encountered sooner or later. As in other spheres—research, planning, decision making and policy making—uncertainties and unpredictabilities need to be recognized and taken into account. Chapter 2 refers to a huge array of natural factors that appear to bear upon natural and social forces and thus to influence levels of global energy consumption—and possible levels of global pollution and warming over the next few decades. It goes without saying that these problems are further exacerbated by uncertainties and unpredictabilities in human decision making, policy formation, and program implementation. This problem is exacerbated by very real uncertainties pertaining to the natural environment that remain to be resolved—predicting rates of greenhouse gas emissions and their implications for global warming, for example.

Numbers of other disturbing uncertainties and unpredictabilities are identified in the pages of this book (chapters 1, 2, 3, 4, 5, 6, 8, and 12, among others). As indicated in chapter 12, however, not all uncertainties are "bad." Chapter 2, for example, calls attention to the consideration that nonlinear, uncertain, and unpredictable interactivities often "push" unstable, even disintegrating, organizations or programs into new equilibria. Similarly a society, through its constituent organizations and institutions, may find ways of evading or reducing (if not resolving) difficult paradoxes or dilemmas resulting from a decision-making or policy-forming consensus catalyzed by pressures of uncertainty.

The three master variables raise important uncertainties of their own. This is especially true of the population variable, which includes the known impacts of the numbers of people, their levels of technology (and specific knowledge and skills), and their energy and other resource demands (and what they do with their resources when they obtain them). But also included are the consequences that are unforeseen and unintended—whether due to inadequate information, "irrationalities" of policy or decision, dilemmas of action, or limited scientific or technical (mechanical/engineering) knowledge of skills. Advanced levels of technology (scientific, mechanical, or organizational), in short, can expand human capabilities and widen their horizons of choice, but often the ascertainable problems also increase more or less commensurately (chapter 8). As suggested in chapter 5, the difficulties often emerge from differences in the scale, magnitude, and rates of change among the parts of the world system that different disciplines observe and seek to measure, but they may also result from specializations and fragmentations in the sciences themselves.

A related problem emerges from uncertainties with respect to the junctures in the processes of growth and development at which trend changes can be effected. Difficulties of this kind are exacerbated by the intense interactions, referred to above, that characterize relationships between natural and social (economic, political, strategic, and environmentally oriented) processes. Similar uncertainties emerge from uneven growth and development within and between states. Chapters 3 and 6 focus on some of these essentially structural dynamics (interactions and distributions of populations, technologies, and resource accesses). This perspective should not be allowed to obscure or discount more proximate interventions in the immediate and critical domains of environmental decision making, policy formation, and regulation, but these will be discussed further along.

Intertemporal and Intergenerational Issues: Economics and Law

Some of the threats confronting us—notably possibilities of global warming—are not likely to "damage anyone now alive, nor more than trivially—even most of their direct descendants." No one now living, moreover, "stands to gain personally" by acting (or depriving him- or herself) now. This consideration raises serious questions about the willingness of current (or immediately succeeding) generations to work—or sacrifice—in order to protect the well-being of future generations whom they will never know and cannot even envisage. Yet if such threats persist unabated, more remote generations will be "progressively damaged," and the remoter they are, the greater the damage will be (chapter 9).

Utility versus Equity: Which Should Prevail?
In part, at least, the issue of respecting obligations of the living to the welfare of progeny several generations removed involves a choice between utility and equity (chapters 9 and 11). In pursuit of an international legal framework, chapter 10 presents the achievement and maintenance of the familiar concept of sustainable development resting on a "commitment to equity with future generations." The underlying intent is to constrain "a natural inclination to take advantage of our temporary control over the earth's resources" and use it for our own benefit—even at the expense of future generations. In pursuing any theory of intergenerational equity we must also guard our relationship to the natural system. Sustainability can be achieved and maintained only if we look at the earth and its resources as a trust that our ancestors have passed along for us to enjoy and pass along for the use of our descendants.

In order to define intergenerational equity it is useful to accept the human community as a partnership among all generations wherein each generation inherits the earth in at least as good condition as it had been in for the previous generation and to have as good access to it. Such an approach has roots in the common and civil law traditions of the Judeo-Christian and Islamic traditions and also in African customary law and Asian cultures' nontheistic traditions. There should be no requirement for any generation to predict the basic or core values of future generations.

Finding conventional concepts of sustainable development unsatisfactory, chapter 9 approaches equity by a different route. From the perspective of utility, economists and other evaluators make the costs and benefits of events occurring at different times comparable by discounting them to a common discounted present value basis. The direct applicability of established procedures to matters pertaining to long-term environmental degradation remains subject to great controversy. In this connection, in the real world, given an absence of abatement, damages from climate change would be close to zero for fifty years or so, but would rise thereafter at an accelerating rate and become "very high toward 150 years and, presumably, much higher after that." On the other hand, the annual costs of an abatement program exceed annual benefits for about eighty years into the future, but thereafter (for future generations) benefits exceed costs. But under conventional discounting procedures, understandable concerns about early costs and distant future benefits would be suppressed.

At this point the concept of sustainable development becomes a debatable issue in chapter 9 on the grounds that it depends upon an essentially normative premise. The assumption is that each generation should make use of the environment and its resources only so far as to meet its needs "in ways and in degrees that leave the next generation with similar capacity to meet *its* needs and yet leave unimpaired the ability of still further generations to do likewise, and so on for the whole sequence of generations." Each generation, in short, should "live off income only and leave capital unimpaired."

In effect, this principle imposes on each generation the normative obligation to accept moral responsibility for the interests of future generations—an imperative that "cannot be enforced unless it is voluntarily agreed to by each generation as it assumes de facto control." Additionally, fulfillment of this responsibility raises accounting issues—e.g., if sustainability requires the maintenance of input stocks, how are they to be recognized and measured, and how is their depreciation with use to be calculated? In order to circumvent these complications, chapter 11 introduces the concept of "backward indebtedness," which is founded on "the unquestioned debt that members of the present generation owe to the *past* at the moment of birth." Included in this legacy are the culture, institutions, knowledge and skills, and other forms of "capital" that have been accumulated and passed along by previous generations. How is this debt to be repaid? It cannot be repaid to the past, but only through support to future generations and a "giving back" to nature what "is taken from" nature by the generation. In what form(s) is the debt to be paid? Probably in terms of pollution abatement, protection of scarce and exhaustible resources in favor of resources that are renewable, and the development of more energy-efficient technologies for obtaining, processing, delivering, and using more energy-efficient resources—to name a few.

Asset Management for Sustainable Development
Every country is by definition endowed with a set of attributes and capabilities that together constitute its national assets. Every country controls its assets to one degree or another; however, the countries differ substantially in the type, content, concentration, and control over their national assets. These assets include human capital (population, educated individuals, management skills, etc.), natural resources (energy, agricultural land, raw materials, etc.), financial assets (in various forms), and a whole range of inputs into productive processes (technology broadly defined in its various dimensions and manifestations).

Some of these assets are within national boundaries; others are owned by the sovereign state but are physically located outside national boundaries; still others are owned by nationals of the state but located elsewhere. At issue are matters of ownership as well as those of legal jurisdiction. Every country is confronted with the policy problem of devising the "best" way possible of deploying its national assets in order to meet the needs of present as well as future generations. While the immediate concern for politicians and policymakers is always the present and the short run, none can ignore the longer run and the interests of future progeny.

Together the chapters in this volume point to the importance of envisioning a strategy of sustainable development as one that is tailored to the particular characteristics of each state but that also follows principles that might enhance propensities for sustainability. Once such a strategy is devised, in generic terms, the specifics for each country can be formulated and matters of implementation can be addressed. At this point our concern is with identifying the basic policy principles for enhancing sustainable development.

In the context of the profile concepts, it is clear that different groupings (I to VI) can be described differently with respect to their overall asset configurations (chapter 3). With growth and development, countries may alter the configurations of their national assets and may choose to deploy these differently as their profiles are affected by earlier decisions and developmental policies. An asset management perspective on development forces countries to consider the preservation as well as the expansion of their assets (Leonard 1988). Both preservation and expansion are essential requisites for sustainability. They may also serve as operational guides in the choice of policies. This means that in the choice of policy (in any sector or domain of activity), an important question to be considered is how it may affect preservation versus expansion of (which type of) national assets.

In an asset management perspective the basic priority is the *transformation* of assets from one form to another consistent with the characteristics of individual countries and with their goals and objectives. The content of the assets and the transformations that are required differ from profile to profile and, in the specifics, from country to country. In this connection, for example, for countries in profile group I (resources > population > technology), the general problem is to transform resources (such as oil in the ground) into physical capital (one application of technology) and expand the education base of the population (another application of technology) while at the same time raising the level of knowledge and skills of the population as a whole. By contrast, for countries of the group VI profile (technology > population > resources), the asset management problem involves the transformation of technology, knowledge, and skills into means of greater access to more energy-efficient technologies and resource use. Japan is the prototypical case in the sense that sustainable development will necessitate continued and expanded access to resources (from external sources) by expanded applications of technology and expansion of financial assets derived from investment and related activities.

In sum, every country, industrial as well as developing, is confronted with the need to devise an asset management strategy. Such a strategy would be designed to meet each country's own socioeconomic requirements in a distinctive way that is "customized" to its own conditions for the well-being of present as well as future generations. A good strategy for asset management is a central feature of capacity building. There is no universal prescription. There can be only general principles to guide the well-being of everyone in the international community.

The generic policy problem worldwide then becomes this: how to transform current conditions and the present configuration of national assets into a configuration that can enhance the prospects of survival and protect the interests of both present and future generations. An asset management approach to sustainable development also imposes a norm of equity across states in the international system (Choucri 1992). It frames sustainability in the same general terms for everyone in the sense that all countries, at all levels of development, need to find means of meeting the needs of present generations without undermining the interests of future generations—given the assets available to them, those located within their borders as well as those owned by them or their nationals but located outside national borders. Such challenges must be met on all levels of organization, from individuals, families, and local communities to states (and their major organizational components) and to the international and global systems. An asset management perspective includes the development of assets as well as their effective deployment.

International Law and Treaty Making

The three chapters in Part IV are concerned with the international system and the systems of its institutions—treaty making, international law, and the organization of function-specific international regimes—that most directly bear on issues of international and global environments. Pertinent to these functions are the analyses (quantitative and qualitative) in chapter 12 of international treaty making for environmental protection and the responsiveness of international law "to this array of environmental challenges." Two contributions of chapter 12 are especially notable. First are the discussions on sovereignty, and second are the tables and the wide array of data on environmental realities they capture.

The formalized principle of national sovereignty dates back at least as far as the Treaty of Westphalia (1648), which is historically recognized as formalizing for the first time the concept of international system. Providing a basis for the legal concept of each state's autonomy over its domestic affairs, the concept of sovereignty also includes legal recognition of formal juridical control over a state's relations with other states and over other external affairs such as its authoritative participation (bargaining, leveraging, and coalition formation, for example) in joint decision making within the international system.

As indicated in chapter 12, many conventional Realist and neo-Realist scholars challenge the proposition that states can legally join in collective action for the resolution of environmental depletion or degradation falling beyond the limits of traditional national sovereignty. Other scholars consider this conventional view of sovereignty open to modification—an example of the kinds of adaptation and sociocultural evolution that modern environmental threats (and other contemporary and future exigencies) are likely to require as they become more international and global. In the meantime, the tension between national sovereignty and international interdependence becomes more pronounced as environmental alterations due to human action affect natural environments and their global implications. Not only is the "sovereign" state a reality of international life; it is an essential one: We do not know how to manage and regulate the activities of individuals in the absence of institutional requisites of "sovereign" states.

Chapter 12 traces—and seeks to explain—secular trends in international law and evaluates 132 multinational environmental treaties relevant to environmental issues. All such treaties deal with one of two categories of environmental problems—those pertaining to the protection of the oceans, the atmosphere, and other global "commons" outside national control, and those located or originating within some country's territorial control but exerting an impact elsewhere. All of these issues can be viewed as international in the sense that in effect they extend

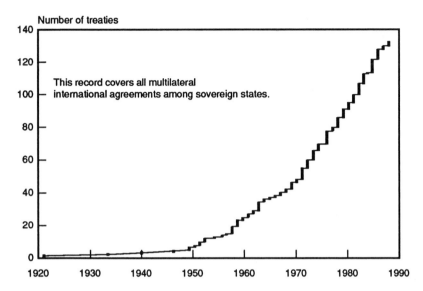

Figure 15.1
International environmental treaties, 1920–1990
Source: Based on compilations by Haas with Sundgren (Chapter 12) and derived from UNEP's International Registry of Environmental Treaties.

beyond national borders and impinge on one or more countries in the international system. To the extent that their impacts are worldwide (or threaten to become worldwide), they become global. In this sense, any country that produces carbon dioxide and other trace gases that rise into the atmosphere can be charged with exerting a global environmental impact.

The trend in international environmental treaty making analyzed in chapter 12 is represented here in figure 15.1. The most compelling factor is the similarity in patterns between legislative responses in the U.S. case (figure 6.2) and those at the international level. Devoid of the power of national law, international agreements nonetheless carry strong weight. Chapter 12 asserts that circumstances relate, in reality, to an array of incentives for cooperation and conflict that face the different parties. Data from the tables of chapter 12, combined with data from the tables of chapter 3, might open possibilities for further analysis and the development and testing of quantitative theories of cooperation in international environmental affairs.

Organization, Policy, and Uncertainty

As the chapters in this volume have shown, the dynamic interaction of social and political systems—shown in figure 1.6—provides a complex context and network of linkages for human dimensions. The point is this: A change at one junction disturbs the entire fabric of interaction, which defines the next (perceived as required) decision. While these are described sequentially for purposes of discussion, decisions and actions—of all kinds—are generally concurrent and simultaneous over and above the sequential (action-reaction) processes.

To the extent that paradoxes, policy dilemmas, and other uncertainties (natural or anthropogenic) impede efforts to regulate human activities contributing to environmental dislocations, chapters 13 and 14 urge organizational initiatives to enhance the transparency of national policies and thus begin the process of shaping effective policies to account for anthropogenic contributions to global warming (and other ecological threats). Such undertakings need to be initiated, in short, well before rates of deterioration and probable outcomes can be assessed at the levels of confidence that might be desired. From a global perspective, appropriate international regimes must be developed now in order to ensure that they are fully operational when they are needed.

Core functions should include the coordination and assessment of relevant science; the provision of an ongoing forum for negotiations; the systematic collection, review, and dissemination of data on emissions; and the review and assessment of national policies relevant to global warming. All four functions are complementary and interactively necessary for the proper function of each. In addition, all are sufficiently generic to work well with most of the different types of substantive climate regimes currently envisioned.

Chapter 15 represents the international community as "moving swiftly" to satisfy the need for the first two functions. In the atmospheric sciences, there is a long tradition of international cooperation in research. Much less progress has been made in the social sciences generally, and social science applications to problems of global warming and other atmospheric problems have barely begun. As indicated in chapter 1, the social sciences developed through a careful and consistent separation of human concerns from natural (environmental) contexts. Then the various dimensions of human activities—social, political, economic, and strategic—were carefully separated from each other and scrutinized, and attendant "theories" of social action emerged. This strategy of fragmented knowledge building, so successful in the past, is no longer adequate, or even minimally effective, in addressing the challenges posed by anthropogenic sources of environmental alteration at all levels of analysis.

Increasingly this challenge of devising responsive strategies has assumed both international and interdisciplinary proportions. The preparatory process for UNCED-92 and the parallel international negotiation on the Framework Convention for Climatic Change were bold experiments for a new international and interdisciplinary duality for global policy. In the early 1990s, for example, the Intergovernmental Negotiating Committee (INC) on Climate Change was performing both forum and secretariat functions. Inasmuch as climate change involves a wide range of environmental and development-related issues, the preparatory processes for UNCED were also contributing to the international deliberations shaping a climate treaty (chapter 13). The secretariat for the Convention on Climate Change was expected then mandated to continue providing secretarial services after the conference had adjourned.

As the opening years of the twenty-first century approach, the need for integrated, fully functioning authoritative and legitimate regimes for managing the global environment becomes increasingly pressing. At the same time, however, the world's economic and political environments are characterized by rapid growth, development, unrest, and, in many places, violence—all deeply rooted in anthropocentric history.

Tumultuous Changes as Context for Policy

Dating from the explorations and colonization of the fifteenth and early sixteenth centuries, Spain, Portugal, England, France, the Netherlands, and other European nation-states rapidly transformed themselves into multinational empires. Thereafter, until World War I, these great overseas imperiums—together with surviving land empires (Chinese, Ottoman, Czarist Russian, and Austro-Hungarian) ruled the world. But the early twentieth century became a historical turning point. In 1912 the Chinese Empire collapsed, and in 1917 the strain of Russian participation in the European conflict triggered the overthrow of the Czar and the establishment of the Soviet regime—in considerable part a reorganization of the empire under new management. By the war's end the Austro-Hungarian empire was dismembered, and the Ottoman Empire gave way to the Turkish Republic.

During the inter-war period the Fascist regime in Italy tried to establish a twentieth century successor to the ancient empire of Rome; the Nazis set out to resurrect and extend the German empire, and Japan expanded its imperial holdings into China and Southeast Asia. These triumphs were short-lived, however, and all three empires were extinguished by the Allied victories of 1945. Within the next few years, the overseas empires of Britain, France, the Netherlands, and other Western European nations were dissolved as their colonies were transformed into independent—for the most part developing—nations (India, Indonesia, Indochina, et al.). Most of Africa was "liberated," as were many island colonies of the Pacific. Many of the former colonies or other remnants of former empires—India, Sri Lanka, Turkey, Iran, Iraq, and numbers of African states—themselves encompass ambitious national ethnic or religious) minorities. Quebec challenges Canada. In northern Ireland the Irish Revolutionary Army opposes British rule with guerrilla tactics; Basque separatists mount a movement in Spain; the former Soviet Union is already dissolved; Yugoslavia has dismembered itself; and so it goes. Whatever its political and economic implications, such widespread fracturing vastly complicates the pursuit of global accord.

This is only one thrust of the times, however. Other seemingly countervailing thrusts point toward regionalization, as in Western Europe, and globalization—phenomena manifested in terms of technological diffusion (including accelerations in communication and transportation), economic interdependence, and strategic security (as evidenced by the "necessity" of keeping nuclear and other weapons of mass destruction under "responsible" control). Further thrusts toward twenty-first century globalization include the threat of ozone depletion, global warming, and a growing recognition that these and other environmental challenges, originating "locally," must be managed globally.

In Pursuit of Global Accord

The record of international environmental treaties presented in chapter 12 is summarized in figure 15.1. The trend speaks for itself. And in conjunction with the record of environmental legislation of the United States (table 6.4), we see evidence of the convergence of national and international responsiveness to environmental legislation.

What are the prospects for developing a global regime capable of regulating human activities that currently threaten to precipitate major changes in the earth's climate system? The current record of initiatives of this kind is somewhat ambiguous, but in recent years research in this direction has identified a number of key determinants of success or failure in this direction. The importance of establishing such a regime derives from the global aspects of the problem and also from the small but significant possibility that not preparing for climate change would have catastrophic consequences (chapter 13). At the core of the task are institutional bargaining, leveraging (positive and negative), and the pay-off structures required for reaching agreements through appropriate regulating procedures (chapter 12) and shaping the bargaining process and evolving norms, including the conception of environmental sustainability and responsibilities to future generations (chapter 10).

Here a distinction needs to be drawn between bargaining approaches to conventional issues of competition and conflict resolution characterized by coalition forming and stabilizing for purposes of "winning" and institutional bargaining, which seeks to establish coalitions of the whole, or at least to develop a consensus involving as many of the countries as feasible. This distinction leads back to the Realist and neo-Realist issues of power and hegemonic stability referred to above. It also draws a sharp contrast between centralized conceptions of global order and consensual/participatory conceptions. Relevant, as indicated in chapter 12, are the considerations that hegemons do not always use their power in the interests of establishing institutional arrangements for "the whole" (or, all too often, for any interest other than their own); hegemons are not always successful in any case; and "regimes can and do form in situations where no dominant power is present."

On the positive side, and perhaps peculiarly relevant for regulating environmental problems, scholars have put forward concepts of institution nesting and networks of specialized international regimes as providing a more promising alternative to hegemonic discipline (see, for example, Koehane 1984, 78–84, 89–92). If there is a new institutional innovation at this point in time, it is the procedure leading to—and emerging from—UNCED-92, which we consider below. The "nesting"/ "networking" is both vertical (within states) and horizontal (across regions and states) as well as governmental and nongovernmental in its institutional context.

But there are additional considerations that also appear to be highly relevant in view of the fact that one "superpower," the United States, is not only a "cautious" champion of environmental causes, but also a major perpetrator of resource depletion and degradation and another superpower, the former Soviet Union, as steward of its vast natural domain has been notably destructive. So far, at least, hegemonic leadership in the environmental domain has been minimal. In this connection, chapter 13 refers positively to the creation of a small number of bargaining entities providing a mechanism for articulating environmental issues at stake and ensuring that ecological threats are dealt with by reducing transaction costs and optimizing applications of the consensus rule in support of the basic needs of all interest groups. In line with these endorsements, there is the possibility of adaptive developments in the bargaining and leveraging function itself.

Central to the establishment of a regime for regulating human activities that threaten the environment (including major changes in the earth's climate system) are advanced processes of institutional bargaining (and adaptations of strategies for reciprocal interaction, such as GRIT and Axelrod's tit-for-tat strategies, for example). Historically, the record of such efforts has been mixed. Participants in institutional bargaining commonly assume the existence of a contract zone or range of feasible agreements that all would prefer over a no-agreement outcome. But reliable information regarding the contract zone and payoff patterns that are likely to emerge from specific institutional arrangements tends to be imperfect at best. In general, those bargaining and leveraging over terms of constitutional contracts at the international level rarely make sustained efforts to improve information about payoff structures before negotiations. The tendency, rather, is to proceed by identifying a small number of key problems and refinement in the negotiating texts to encompass new areas of accord (chapters 12, 13, and 14).

Relevant here is the emphasis placed on the UNCED-92 process of capacity building in order to improve the understanding of local and global environmental problems and to enhance prospects for the identification of effective solutions. Overall, to the extent that capacity building is effective, then it may reduce discrepancy in the power and capability of actors engaged in institutional bargaining.

Emergent Paradigms and Methods of Inquiry
Conventionally, we think of growth, development, and contributory sources of energy or power as production forces, which they are, and decision making and management as option selecting and *steering* functions, which they are. If we use a boat, ship, or other vehicle as a metaphor, we perceive it as propelled by wind (on land by a draft animal) or by an encapsulated natural force such as heated (and expanding) steam, the internal combustion of a fossil fuel, and so on. Also, conventionally, such a vehicle is steered by a different source—a sailor manipulating a long oar from a vessel's stern or manning a tiller or steering wheel, or a driver guiding a draft animal or a motor vehicle.

Certainly societies are not only driven (propelled) by technological advancement and economic growth (production); they are also steered (developed in one "direction" or another, or inclined toward one course of action or another) by the uneven growth (absolute and/or relative to that of other countries) of its master (and other) variables. In different terminology, societies are steered by second differences (changes in the rates of change of their relevant variables). Such changes can be attributable to human decisions (conscious or not), to natural forces (weather, climate, erosion, earthquakes, volcanic eruptions, extinctions of species resulting wholly from natural forces, and so on), or to combinations of natural and anthropogenic phenomena. These considerations widen— and in some respects complicate—the implications of positive and negative feedbacks. And decision and action may influence both the extent and amplitude of feedback.

Recent studies in the physical and biological sciences—and increasingly in economics—have demonstrated the relevance of what have been referred to as nonlinear, disequilibrium dynamics in human (as well as natural) systems characterized by stochastic fluctuations (Sterman 1989, 1–2) and trends toward "self-generating and self-sustaining chaotic oscillations" and unpredictability . . . By analogy, many social and economic systems may, like the weather, not be predictable in the future, even when the full dynamics of the system are known or when the system has no random processes in it (Anderson 1988, 3–4). Such fluctuations and oscillations can be attributed to both "intrinsic mechanisms and external shocks" (Chen 1988, 81).

System dynamics provides ways of linking "hard" uncertainties and "soft" uncertainties in ways that are at least relatively rigorous. It is almost self-evident, for example, that a "real" trend through "real" (elapsed) time can be compared with a "preferred" (subjective) trend and the differences measured. Similar, though admittedly "softer," is the feasibility of projecting an objective trend line (retrospectively established carbon dioxide production, for example) that can be compared with the projection of a preferred trend line and the differences measured (Sterman 1987, 190–209; Choucri 1981; Choucri and Bousfield 1978). However fraught by uncertainties, however, dynamic system approaches may yield more promising outcomes when applied to environmental threats.

Applied to energy markets (and hence to attendant effluence), both market instabilities and adjustments to "normal" conditions may be explained, and modelled, as a function of interactions in a dynamic system (Choucri, Heye, and Lynch 1990). Investments in exploration and development, due to expectations of demand behavior and price paths, influence actual output, hence supplies and thus price—and the resultant supply/demand relations affecting price expectations at the next iteration—and so on.

At issue for performance are decision, policy, and the specification of relations between the estimated parameters and the regimes of behavior—e.g., are the estimated decision rules of the managers "inherently stable, or do they produce limit cycles, period multiples, or chaos?" Variously defined, chaos refers broadly to "complicated, aperiodic, nonlinear dynamic systems . . . sometimes stable, sometimes unstable . . . often creative . . . erratic . . . first high, then low . . . never settling down to a steady state . . . never exactly repeating" (Gleick 1988: 42–43).

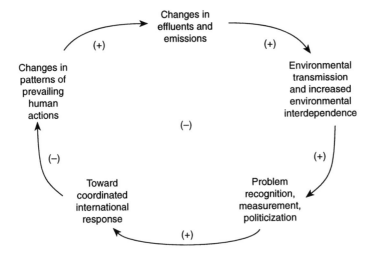

Figure 15.2
Dynamics of Human Action, Environmental Effluences, and Global Accord

In what ways, if any, can this dynamic perspective and attendant system dynamic methodology be useful for framing and analyzing decisions in the context of environmental research and understanding?

Certainly the issues are complex. In this volume we posited a set of dynamic interactions connecting human actions and environmental consequences. Figure 15.2 provides a simplified view of these interactions. The negative sign in the center represents prospects of corrective processes: *if* environmental problems were assessed, and *if* there were appropriate and coordinated international responses, *then* we could expect changes in prevailing patterns of human action and hence alterations (i.e., reductions) in effluence, emission, and pollutants.

The next major challenge for science and for policy is to specify, delineate, and further examine the dynamic processes embedded (and simplified) in figure 15.2. That is most surely an important task for the international community post-Rio.

But there is foundation work that also needs to be done. High on the list (in addition to the need for more and better data) is the development and analysis of time series data along the lines suggested by the national profiles and groupings selectively represented in chapter 3 (for only one year—1986). The object here is to establish to the extent feasible a substructure of levels, rates of change, and second differences over the last four decades. In time series, such country profiles and groups provide a context for "retrospective forecasting" (forecasting over known data) wherein projections from early years can be compared with "real-world" outcomes. (Choucri 1978, 11–15; North 1978, 270–77). It is within such a context and from such an in-depth data base that forecasting into the "real" future can best be undertaken.

Equally fundamental (but not unconnected with the time series data) are the networks of anthropogenic effects that threaten the quality of life in many parts of the globe—water qualities and availabilities, the disappearance of ancient forests, the paving over of agricultural lands, the miles of traffic gridlocks, blankets of urban (and increasingly rural) smog, growing monuments of garbage and trash, and the continuing production of nuclear waste, to mention a few.

The first imperative for the twenty-first century is to recognize the dynamic, multiplicative, transformative, and potentially divisive and constrictive linkages between individuals and their needs, demands, knowledge, and skills, on the one hand, and the implications of their aggregates on the other. More specifically, what we need to get at are the varying ratios of individual needs, demands, and consumption to individual capacities to produce and the multiplicative consequences when these individuals and their demands and productive activities are aggregated. The problems leading into this imperative are elusive. Applied economics and political economy conventionally treat the individual as a source of labor and a potential consumer and taxpayer. The temptation, therefore, when individuals are aggregated, is to conclude that the larger a population is, the more productive (and cheaper) the labor force will be, the stronger the market, and the more extensive the taxable base. These easy assumptions are threatened, if not dispelled, however, (a) when unevennesses among population growth, technological development, and resource availabilities are made explicit; (b) when unevennesses in distributions of knowledge, skills, and capabilities are taken into account; and (c) when the impacts on resources and the other environmental impacts of population growth combined with technological advancement are factored into the calculations.

Issue (a) has already been addressed, and many of the implications of (b)—gross discrepancies in wages and other forms of income, for example—are well known. To the extent that the twenty-first century is characterized by robotics and related applications of automation, however, three possibilities may be exacerbated: Demands for energy and other (possibly rare) resources required for particular operations may increase rapidly; the only workers employable in large numbers may be highly educated specialists; and growing sectors of the populace may become unproductive (the "underclass," drug entrepreneurs, and other contemporary phenomena may be early manifestations) and dependent on unprecedented distributional mechanisms. Issue (c) brings us back to the development-sustainability paradox.

The second imperative, then, is to explore the relationship between the multiplicative potentials of demands and productive potentials, on the one hand, and resource availabilities and costs (depletions or degradations) that are partly additive and partly multiplicative, on the other hand—through time. In order to understand and assess "objective" and changing relationships between processes of growth and development (stability, prosperity, and jobs) and environmental sustainability, both horns of the seeming dilemma need to be clearly and rigorously framed and analyzed through time within the same conceptual, theoretical, and empirical framework. Until this imperative is met and rigorous research is undertaken, rebuttals to the presentation of choices of jobs versus wilderness and owls versus humans are not likely to maintain credibility through the ups and downs of future economic and political cycles. Related, therefore, is the search for ways of integrating and assessing environmental costs and benefits within acceptable accounting procedures.

The third imperative is to formalize evolving international norms for effective responses to environmental challenges. The global norms endemic to the chapters of this volume—legitimacy, equity, volition, and universality (as defined later)—are guides shaping both objectives and the direction of international negotiations for global environmental management. A fourth imperative is to transform what is learned into local, national, international, and global policies, procedures, and actions. This translation problem must be met head on, as authorized by the United Nations General Assembly in 1989. The UNCED and INC preparation processes that have led to the Rio Conference of 1992 were strong efforts in that direction. Nascent efforts to bring representatives of the social and natural sciences into mutual dialogue for improved understanding of interactions among social and natural environments are essential to this process.

Although these general imperatives are for the long run, their pursuit and implementation should not be delayed. At the same time a number of specific imperatives for the management of growth and development—in local, national, international, and global contexts—need to be articulated and implemented. Defining profiles of states, chapter 3 focused on interactions among the master variables—population, resources, and technology. A number of specific policy priorities for each of the six profile groups were identified and predicated within an interactive international system and a global environment; however, many, if not most, of the policy imperatives framed at the state level in chapter 3 are also global issues.

The proposition that populations should be allowed to grow only as technology and resource availabilities proceed in advance of the numbers of people and are sufficient to support increasing such numbers is clearly globally (as well as locally) relevant. As long as technologies and/or resource availabilities in developing countries are severely constrained, populations in developing countries may be expected to attempt emigration to industrialized nations, which may have to confront the risk of becoming less and less capable of absorbing them. Also globally applicable is the proposal that knowledge, skills, and materials pertaining to the management of population concerns should pass freely from industrial to developing societies. In other words, this is an arena in which "protection" or commercial considerations should not necessarily dominate international deliberations toward global accord.

Universally applicable is the clear imperative for the development of technologies, energies, and other resources that are optimally efficient and environmentally "clean." Priorities for the industrialized nations include such developments not only for their own use, but also for use in developing countries. Obversely, of course, industrialized countries need to refrain from exporting to developing countries technologies, resources, and products that are environmentally threatening (and even outlawed for sale and use in the country of origin). And concurrently, connected R & D strategies should be devised to help frame and pursue developmental paths that avoid reproducing environmental degradations of known historical patterns. The balancing of an increasingly scarce (and costly) resource (and/or technology) against another scarce resource (and/or technology) that is slightly less scarce (and costly)—the substitution of nuclear technology and energy for oil technology and energy *prior to the development of an effective solution to the nuclear waste problem,* for example—requires careful analysis and comparisons of environmental costs and benefits.

Some of the most critical imperatives pertain to monitoring environmentally focused and economically and politically relevant time series indicators and performing sustained research including the modeling of alternate futures, that is, making future projections from past trends; generating alternate futures derived experimentally on an "if this, then probably that" basis; and experimentally introducing various different policies (differing rates of change for different indicators) as early steps in the pursuit of optimal balances between economic development and environmental sustainability. In this connection, relevant economic, political, and environmental investigation needs to be integrated to the extent feasible and pursued hand in hand with the other. Interdisciplinarity is often more of a cliche than a reality; but the problems addressed in this volume simply cannot be examined effectively—or solutions rendered—in the absence of insights and exchanges across the diverse disciplines of the social and natural sciences.

Imperatives pertinent to the shaping of legal and institutional dimension of environmental management—issues and actions—include paying close attention on all levels (from the locality to state, international, and global systems) to the development-sustainability paradox. In the meantime, people in all countries and all walks of life need to learn—and contribute to—a body of rule-of-thumb guidelines that could save us from possible delay and immobilization resulting from uncertainties. First of these is to recognize forthwith that the generation of carbon dioxide and other greenhouse gases originates locally and has effects that are local as well as those that are global. Again, an insightful, if homespun, approach to the question is "think globally, act locally." However simple these precepts might seem, the imperatives for their implementation pose daunting challenges.

Toward Global Norms

Meeting crucial challenges and imperatives for the twenty-first century requires framing global norms—those principles essential to guide strategies for environmental viability. All the chapters in this volume, together, point to five strategic norms. These norms are strategic in the sense that they constitute core values that need to be pursued if global accord on environmental management is to be effective.

First is *legitimacy:* Basic responses must be viewed by all actors—governmental and nongovernmental—as legitimate in both content and processes. Since different states of different levels of development generate different types and forms of effluents and emissions and influence natural environments in different ways, the principle of legitimacy is dictated by the ubiquity of both the cause and the consequence of environmental degradation (chapter 3). To the extent that the scale and scope of physical impacts of humans on their natural environments are extensive (chapter 2), then the emerging trend toward global ecopolitics places environmental matters at the core of strategic concerns (chapter 4) and shapes an increasingly salient trend toward internalizing environmental treaty-making (chapters 12, 13, and 14).

Second is *equity:* Policy responses must be viewed as fair and appropriate among countries and across generations (chapters 9, 10, 11). The element of fairness is especially important as developing countries have argued, and will continue to argue, that the "problem" was created in the industrial states and that they should assume the responsibility for "solving" it. Eco-development has as a basic precept framing the policy concerns for the priorities of developing countries (chapter 5). Third is *efficacy:* Approaches and instruments for global environmental management should be effective and pragmatic (chapter 14) rather than strictly "efficient" in narrow economic terms (chapter 9). More important, the efficacy norm would recognize the multidimensional nature of rationality—over and above the technical definition of the term in economic theory, which, by itself, impedes prospects for global accord. Fourth is *volition:* Responses must be voluntary, predicated on a shared recognition of environmental problems based on shared interpretations of scientific evidence and strategies for solution (chapters 7 and 13) rather than on geopolitics or considerations of power and domination.

Fifth is *universality:* Global accord must involve the participation of all actors—governmental and nongovernmental—in that (as with the norm of legitimacy) it is the ubiquity of human action that generates environmental degradation and, therefore, imposes a logic of universality, despite differentials in the scale and scope of degradation at any one point in time. The compelling dynamics of growth and expansion— population growth, technological change, and resource uses—all but guarantee that the developing countries—thus governments, peoples, and nongovernmental organizations—will be the major players in the global environment of the twenty-first century.

These principles constitute crucial norms for the pursuit of global accord in the international community. Together they lead to a critical policy precept: the maintenance of adjustable target priorities in the pursuit of ever more energy-efficient technologies and resources.

Note

1. We leave it to the reader to review each chapter in the context of table 1.1. For the contributors to this volume, the organizational device of that matrix forces us, in this joint venture, to pay explicit attention to the dimensions of interest and perspectives adopted. By way of illustrating the usefulness of this organizational plan for the contributions to this book as we proceeded to frame the intellectual basis for this project, we highlight some examples. The table is to be "read" in terms of any two (or more) combinations of "entries" by dimension and perspective. For example, chapter 1 adopts a society-nature interaction, drawing attention to policy concerns revolving around managing growth processes, and implies both institutional bargaining and novel equity calculations (across nations and across generations). By contrast chapter 7, on science and technology, implies a gradualist intellectual orientation, viewing technology options as a key policy concern and (in conjunction with chapter 14) pragmatic moves as the basic institutional responses.

Bibliography

Adams, R. Mc. 1990. "Foreword: The Relativity of Time and Transformation." In Turner et al. 1990, pp. vii–x.

Adler, Emanuel, and P. M. Haas. 1992. "Epistemic Communities, International Cooperation and World Order: Creating a Reflective Research Program." *International Organization* 46: 367–390.

Agarwal, A., and S. Narain. 1990. "Global Warming in an Unequal World: A Case of Environmental Colonialism." New Delhi: Centre for Science and Environment (CSE).

Albright, David, and Mark Hibbs. 1991. "Iraq's Nuclear Hide-and-Seek." *Bulletin of the Atomic Scientists* (September):14–23.

Alker, Hayward, R., Jr. 1977. "A Methodology for Design Research on Interdependence Alternatives." *International Organization* 31 (1):29–63.

Alker, H. R., Jr. 1989. "World Politics as Ecopolitics." Paper presented at a meeting of the American Political Science Association, September 1989, Atlanta.

Alker, H. R., Jr. 1990a. "Geopolitics vs. Ecopolitics: Geography and the Environment in 20th Century International Thought." Paper read at a meeting of the American Political Science Association, San Francisco.

Alker, H. R., Jr.. 1990b. "Rescuing 'Reason' from the 'Rationalists': Reading Vico, Marx and Weber as Reflective Institutionalists." *Millenium* 19:161–184.

Alker, H. R., Jr., and B. M. Russett. 1965. *World Politics in the General Assembly*. New Haven: Yale University Press.

Alker, H. R., Jr., and J. A. Tickner. 1977. "Some Issues Raised by Previous World Models." In *Problems of World Modeling: Political and Social Implications*, edited by K. W. Deutsch, B. Fritsch, H. Jaguaribe, and S. Markovits. Cambridge: Ballinger.

Allott, A. 1975. *Essays in African Law*. Westport, Conn.: Greenwood Press.

Amin, S. 1974. *Accumulation on a World Scale*. 2 vols. New York: Monthly Review Press.

Anderson, David P. 1988. "Foreword: Chaos in System Dynamics Models." *System Dynamic Review* 4 (1–2):3–4.

Archer, C. 1983. *International Organizations*. London: George Allen and Unwin.

Archibugi, F., and P. Nijkamp, eds. 1990. *Economy and Ecology: Towards Sustainable Development*. Dordrecht: Kluwer Academic Publishers.

Aron, Raymond. 1973. *Peace and War: A Theory of International Relations.* Garden City, N.Y.: Anchor Books.

Arrow, Kenneth J., and Anthony C. Fisher. 1974. "Environmental Preservation, Uncertainty, and Irreversibility." *Quarterly Journal of Economics* 88:312–329.

Ascher, William. 1978. "Energy Forecasting." In *Forecasting,* edited by William Ascher. Baltimore: Johns Hopkins University Press.

Ascher, William. 1981. "The Forecasting Potential of Complex Models." *Policy Sciences* 13:247–267.

Ashley, Richard K. 1980. *The Political Economy of War and Peace: The Sino-Soviet-American Triangle and the Modern Security Problematique.* New York: Nichols Publishing Company.

Ashley, R. K. 1983. "The Eye of Power: The Politics of World Modeling." *International Organization* 37:495–535.

Ausubel, Jesse H. 1991. "A Second Look at the Impacts of Climate Change," *American Scientist* 79:210–221.

Ausubel, Jesse H., and Hedy E. Sladovich, eds. 1989. *Technology and Environment.* Washington, D.C.: National Academy Press.

Ausubel, Jesse H., and David G. Victor. 1992. "Verification of International Environmental Agreements." *Annual Review of Energy and the Environment* 17:1–43.

Axelrod, Robert. 1984. *The Evolution of Cooperation.* New York: Basic Books.

Ayres, R. U. 1989. "Industrial Metabolism." In *Technology and Environment,* edited by J. H. Ausubel and H. E. Sladovich. Washington, D.C.: National Academy Press, pp. 23–49.

Bailey, Ronald. 1989. "Dr. Doom." *Forbes* (October 16).

"Balancing the National Interest: U.S. National Security Export Controls and Global Economic Competition" (the Allen Report). Washington, D.C.: National Academy Press, 1987.

Baldwin, Richard E., and J. David Richardson, eds. *International Trade and Finance.* Boston: Little, Brown.

Bandyopadhyay, J., and V. Shiva. 1988. "Political Economy of Ecology Movements." *Economic and Political Weekly* (June 11, 1988):1223–1232.

Barinaga, Marcia. 1989. "Alaskan Oil Spill: Health Risks Uncovered." *Science* 245:463.

Barnett, H., and C. Morse. 1963. *Scarcity and Growth.* Baltimore: Johns Hopkins Press.

Barney, G., ed. 1980. *Global 2000 Report to the President.* Washington, D.C.: U.S. Council on Environmental Quality.

Bartlett, Chairsopher A., and Sumantra Ghoshal. 1989. *Managing Across Borders: The Transnational Solution.* Boston: Harvard Business School Press.

Baumol, William. 1970. "On the Discount Rate for Public Projects." In *Public Expenditures and Policy Analysis,* edited by R. Haveman and J. Margolis. Chicago: Markham.

Baumol, William J. 1971. *Environmental Protection, International Spillovers and Trade.* Uppsala, Sweden: Almqvist & Wiksell.

Beckerman, W. 1975/90. *Pricing for Pollution.* Hobart Paper 66. London: Institute of Economic Affairs.

Beitz, Charles R. 1991. "Sovereignty and Morality in International Affairs." In *Political Theory Today*, edited by David Held. Stanford: Stanford University Press, pp. 236–254.

Benedick, Richard Elliott. 1989. "Ozone Diplomacy." *Issues in Science and Technology* IV (1):43–50.

Benedick, Richard Elliott. 1990. "Depletion of the Stratospheric Ozone Layer." In *Preserving the Global Environment: The Challenge of Shared Leadership*, edited by Jessica Tuchman Mathews. Proceedings of the Seventy-Seventh American Assembly, April 19–22, Harriman, New York.

Benedick, Richard Elliott. 1991. *Ozone Diplomacy: New Directions in Safeguarding the Planet*. Cambridge, Mass.: Harvard University Press.

Berkes, F., ed. 1989. *Common Property Resources: Ecology and Community-Based Sustainable Development*. London: Belhaven.

Bezdek, R. H., R. M. Wendling, and J. D. Jones. 1989. "The Economic and Employment Effects of Investments in Pollution Abatement and Control Technologies." *Ambio* 18 (5):274–279.

Bhagwati, Jagdish. 1972. *Economics and World Order: From the 1970s to the 1990s*. New York: Macmillan.

Bhatti, Neeloo. 1988. "Acid Rain: A Framework for Political Consensus." In *Dispelling the North American Acid Rain Clouds*. Ph.D. diss. Yale School of Forestry and Environmental Studies, New Haven, Conn.

Biersteker, Thomas J. 1979. *Distortion or Development? Contending Perspectives on the Multinational Corporation*. Cambridge, Mass.: MIT Press.

Bingemer, H. G., and P. J. Crutzen. 1987. "The Production of Methane from Solid Wastes." *Journal of Geophysical Research* 92:2181–2187.

Birnie, Pat W., ed. 1989. "The International Law of Migratory Species." *Natural Resources Journal* 29 (4).

Boughey, A. S., ed. 1973. *Man and the Environment*. 2nd edition. New York: Macmillan.

Boulding, Kenneth E. 1956. *The Image*. Ann Arbor: The University of Michigan Press.

Boulding, K. E. 1978. *Ecodynamics: A New Theory of Societal Evolution*. Beverly Hills: Sage Publications.

Brammer, H. 1989. "Monitoring the Evidence of the Greenhouse Effect and Its Impact on Bangladesh." Paper presented at the International Conference on the Greenhouse Effect and Coastal Areas of Bangladesh (CARDMA), March, Dhaka.

Bramwell, A. 1989. *Ecology in the 20th Century*. New Haven: Yale University Press.

Braudel, F. 1976. *The Mediterranean and the Mediterranean World in the Age of Philip II*. 2 vols. New York: Harpers. (The first French edition was published in 1946 by Libraire Armand Colin).

Braudel, F. 1980. *On History*. Chicago: University of Chicago Press.

Braudel, F. 1981–1984. *Civilization & Capitalism, 15th–18th Century*. 3 Vols. New York: Harper and Row. (The revised French edition, entitled *Civilisation Materielle, Economie et Capitalisme: XV3–XVIII3 Siecle*, was published by Libraire Armand Colin in 1979; the earlier edition began appearing in 1967.)

Brecke, Peter. 1989. "Bibliographies of Global Models." Unpublished manuscript.

Brennan, Geoffrey, and James M. Buchanan. 1985. *The Reason of Rules: Constitutional Political Economy* Cambridge, U.K.: Cambridge University Press.

Brewer, Garry D. 1981. "Where the Twain Meet: Reconciling Science and Politics in Analysis." *Policy Sciences* 13:269–279.

Brewer, Garry D. 1983a. "Elite Viewpoints on Energy." In *Caught Unawares: The Energy Decade in Retrospect,* edited by Martin Greenberger et al. Cambridge, Mass.: Ballinger, pp. 309–344.

Brewer, Garry D. 1983b. "Some Costs and Consequences of Large-Scale Social Systems Modeling." *Behavioral Science* 28:166–185.

Brewer, Garry D. 1986. "Methods for Synthesis: Policy Exercises." In *Sustainable Development of the Biosphere,* edited by W. C. Clark and R. E. Munn. New York: Cambridge University Press, Ch. 17.

Brewer, Garry D. 1989. "Policy Sciences, the Environment, and Public Health." *Health Promotion* 2:227–237.

Brewer, Garry D., and Martin Shubik. 1979. *The War Game: A Critique of Military Problem Solving.* Cambridge, Mass.: Harvard University Press.

Broad, William J. 1991. "Iraqi Atom Effort Exposes Weakness in World Controls." *New York Times* (July 15):1.

Broecker, Wallace. 1987. "Unpleasant Surprises in the Greenhouse?" *Nature* 328 (9 July):123–126.

Bromley, D. W., and M. M. Cernea. 1989. *The Management of Common Property Natural Resources: Some Conceptual and Operational Fallacies.* World Bank Discussion Paper No. 57. Washington, D.C.: The World Bank.

Brooks, Harvey. 1980. "Technology, Evolution and Purpose." In "Modern Technology: Problem or Opportunity?" *Daedalus* 109 (1) (Winter):68–70.

Brooks, Harvey. 1986. "The Typlogy of Surprises in Technology, Insitutions, and Development." In *Sustainable Development of the Biosphere,* edited by W. C. Clark and R. E. Munn. Cambridge: Cambridge University Press.

Brouwer, F. et al., eds. 1991. *Land Use Changes in Europe: Processes of Change, Environmental Transformation, and Future Patterns.* Dordrecht: Kluwer Academic Publishers.

Browning, Graeme. 1991. "The Soviet Far East." *National Journal* 23:2795–2799.

Brunner, Ronald D., and Weston Vivian. 1980. "Citizen Viewpoints on Energy Policy." *Policy Sciences* 12:147–174.

Bunch, Roland. 1985. *Two Ears of Corn: A Guide to People-Centered Agricultural Improvement.* Oklahoma City: World Neighbors.

Burke, E. 1790. "Reflections on the Revolution in France." In *2 Works of Edmund Burke.* London: 1854. Reprint. Irvine, Calif.: Reprint Services, 1987, pp. 130–140.

Burtaw, Dallas, and Michael A. Toman. 1991. *Equity and International Agreements for CO_2 Containment.* Discussion Paper ENR91-07. Washington, D.C.: Resources for the Future.

Burton, Ian. 1989. "Human Dimensions of Global Change: Toward a Research Agenda." In *Greenhouse Warming: Abatement and Adaptation,* edited by Norman J. Rosenberg et al. Washington, D.C.: Resources for the Future.

Burton, I., R. W. Kates, and G. F. White. 1978. *The Environment as Hazard.* New York: Oxford University Press.

Busch, Lisa. 1991. "Science Under Wraps in Prince William Sound." *Science* 252:772–773.

Business Council for Sustainable Development. 1992. *Changing Course.* Cambridge, Mass.: MIT Press.

Caldwell, Lynton K. 1972. *In Defense of the Earth: International Protection of the Biosphere.* Bloomington, Indiana University Press.

Caldwell, Lynton Keith. 1990. *International Environmental Policy.* 2nd edition. Durham, N.C.: Duke University Press.

Callenbach, E. 1975. *Ecotopia.* Berkeley: Banyan Tree.

Calvet, A. L. 1981. "A Synthesis of Foreign Direct Investment Theories and Theories of the Multinational Firm." *Journal of International Business Studies* (Spring/Summer):43–57.

Campbell, Donald. 1969. "Variation and Selective Retention in Socio-Cultural Evolution." In *General Systems,* Vol. 14, edited by Ludwig von Bertalanffy. Ann Arbor: General Systems Research.

Cardoso, F. H., and E. Faletto. 1971. *Dependency and Development in Latin America.* Translation. Berkeley: University of California Press, 1979.

Carroll, John E., ed. 1988. *International Environmental Diplomacy.* Cambridge: Cambridge University Press.

Carson, R. 1962. *Silent Spring.* Boston: Houghton Mifflin.

Central Intelligence Agency (various years). *The World Factbook.* Washington, D.C.: U.S. Government Printing Office.

Chattopadhyay, S. K. 1975. "Equity in International Law: Its Growth and Development." *Georgia Journal of International and Comparative Law,* 5:381–406.

Chayes, Abram. 1991. "Managing the Transition to a Global Warming Regime, or What to Do 'til the Treaty Comes." In *Greenhouse Warming: Negotiating a Global Regime,* edited by J. T. Mathews. Washington: World Resoures Institute.

Chayes, Abram and Antonia H. Chayes. 1991. "Adjustment and Compliance Processes in International Regulatory Regimes," In *Preserving the Global Environment: The Challenge of Shared Leadership,* edited by Jessica Tuchman Mathews. New York: W. W. Norton.

Chen, Ping. 1988. "Empirical and Theoretical Evidence of Economic Chaos." *System Dynamics Review* 4 (1–2):81.

Choucri, Nazli. 1974. *Population Dynamics and International Violence: Propositions, Insights, and Evidence.* Lexington, Mass.: D. C. Heath/Lexington Books.

Choucri, Nazli. 1978. "Key Issues in International Relations Forecasting." In Choucri and Robinson 1978.

Choucri, Nazli. 1989. "The Politicization of Technology Choices." *Business in the Contemporary World* II (1):43–48.

Choucri, Nazli. 1990. "Economic Development, Environment, and Foreign Assistance." Paper presented at the United States Institute of Peace Conference on "Conflict Resolution in the Post-Cold War Third World," October 3–5, Washington, D.C.

Choucri, Nazli. 1991a. "The Global Environment and Multinational Corporations." *Technology Review* (April 1991).

Choucri, Nazli. 1991b. "The Technology Frontier: Responses to Environmental Challenges." In *The ECO-Nomic Revolution—Challenge and Opportunity for the 21st Century.* Proceedings of the Malente Symposium IX, November 18–20, Timmendorfer Strand, Germany: Dräger Foundation.

Choucri, Nazli. 1991c. "A Partnership with Nature." *Construction Business Review* 1 (March/April).

Choucri, Nazli. 1991d. "Resource Constraints as Causes of Conflict." *Ecodecision* (September).

Choucri, Nazli. 1991e. "Policy Parameters for Environmental Protection: National and International." Paper prepared for the Symposium on Global Environment and the Construction Industry, October 21–22, Massachusetts Institute of Technology.

Choucri, Nazli. 1991f. "Development, Environment, and International Assistance." Prepared for UNESCO, Paris.

Choucri, Nazli. 1992. "Technology Transfer." In *Roundtable in Preparation of UNCED '21,* edited by Edeltraud Gammer, Sabine Krings, and Erich Andrlik. Vienna: Vienna Institute for Development and Cooperation.

Choucri, Nazli, and Marie Bousfield. 1978. "Alternative Futures: An Exercise in Forecasting." In *Forecasting in International Relations: Theory, Methods, Problems, Prospects,* edited by Nazli Choucri and Thomas W. Robinson. San Francisco: W. H. Freeman.

Choucri, Nazli, with Vincent Ferraro. 1976. *The International Politics of Energy Interdependence.* Lexington, Mass.: D. C. Heath.

Choucri, Nazli, Peter M. Haas, and Robert C. North. *The State System and the Global Environment.* Forthcoming.

Choucri, Nazli, Christopher Heye, and Michael Lynch. 1990. "Analyzing Oil Production in Developing Countries: A Case Study of Egypt." *The Energy Journal* 11 (3).

Choucri, Nazli, Michael Laird, and Dennis Meadows. 1972. *Resource Scarcity and Foreign Policy: A Simulation Model of International Conflict.* Cambridge, Mass.: MIT: Center for International Studies, C/72–79, March.

Choucri, Nazli, and Robert C. North. 1975. *Nations in Conflict: National Growth and International Violence.* San Francisco: W. H. Freeman and Co.

Choucri, Nazli, and Robert C. North. 1989. "Lateral Pressure in International Relations: Concept and Theory." In *Handbook of War Studies,* edited by Manus I. Midlarsky. Winchester, Mass.: Unwin Hyman, Inc.

Choucri, Nazli, and Robert C. North. 1990. "Global Environmental Change: Uncertainty, Decision, and Policy." Paper prepared for the Annual Meeting of the American Political Science Association, August 30–September 2, San Francisco, California.

Choucri, Nazli, Robert C. North, and Susumu Yamakage. 1992. *The Challenge of Japan Before and After World War II.* Cambridge, Mass.: Routledge.

Choucri, Nazli, and Thomas W. Robinson. 1978. *Forecasting in International Relations: Theory, Methods, Problems, Prospects.* San Francisco: W. H. Freeman.

Choucri, Nazli, with David Scott Ross. 1981. *International Energy Futures: Petroleum Prices, Power, and Payments.* Cambridge, Mass.: MIT Press, 1981.

Christensen, Sigurd W., and Ronald J. Klauda. 1988. "Two Scientists in the

Courtroom: What They Didn't Teach Us in Graduate School." *American Fisheries Society Monograph* 4:307–315.

Clark, William. 1985. *On the Practical Implications of the Carbon Dioxide Question.* Laxenburg, Austria: International Institute of Applied Systems Analysis.

Clark, William C. 1986. "Sustainable Development of the Biosphere." In *Sustainable Development of the Biosphere*, edited by W. C. Clark and R. E. Munn. New York: Cambridge University Press, pp. 5–48.

Clark, William C. 1989. "Managing Planet Earth." *Scientific American* 261 (September):47–54.

Clark, William C., and R. E. Munn, eds. 1986. *Sustainable Development of the Biosphere.* New York: Cambridge University Press.

Coates, Joseph F. 1991. "The Sixteen Sources of Environmental Problems in the 21st Century." *Technological Forecasting and Social Change* 40:87–91.

Cocoyoc Declaration. 1974. From UNEP/UNCTAD Symposium on Patterns of Resource Use, Environment, and Development Strategies, October 8–12, Cocoyoc, Mexico. Reprinted in *International Organization* 29 (Summer 1975):893–901.

Cohn, J. P. 1989. "Iguana Conservation and Economic Development." *BioScience* 39 (6):359–363.

Colby, Michael E. 1990a. "Ecology, Economics, and Social Systems: The Evolution of the Relationship Between Environmental Management and Development." Ph.D. Diss., Wharton School, University of Pennsylvania. Excerpts of this dissertation are available as *Environmental Management in Development: The Evolution of Paradigms.* World Bank Discussion Paper 80. Washington, D.C.: The World Bank.

Colby, M. E. 1990b. "The International Business Climate and the Global Climate Business"." Paper presented at Greenhouse '90: New Technologies, Business Opportunities, and Strategies for Reducing US Greenhouse Gas Emissions Conference, June 19–21, Tysons Corner, Va.

Colby, M. E. 1990c. "Economics and Environmental Management: The Case for Environmental Taxes." Paper presented at ISEE Conference, The Ecological Economics of Sustainability, May 21–23, Washington, D.C.

Colby, M. E. 1991. Environmental Management in Development: The Evolution of Paradigms." *Ecological Economics* 3:193–213.

Cole, S. 1977. *Global Models and the International Economic Order.* Oxford and New York: Pergamon Press for UNITAR.

Cole, S., and I. Miles. 1978. "Assumptions and Methods: Population, Economic Development, Modeling and Technical Change." In Freeman and Jahoda 1978, pp. 51–75.

Committee on Global Change. 1988. *Toward and Understanding of Global Change.* Washington, D.C.: National Academy Press.

Committee on Science, Engineering and Public Policy (COSEPUP), U.S. National Academy of Sciences. 1991. *Policy Implications of Greenhouse Warming.* Washington: National Academy Press.

Cooper, Chester L. 1989. "Epilogue." In *Greenhouse Warming: Abatement and Adaptation,* edited by Norman J. Rosenberg et al. Washington, D.C.: Resources for the Future.

Cooper, Richard N. 1989. "International Cooperation in Public Health as a Prologue to Macroeconomic Cooperation." In *Can Nations Agree? Issues in International Economic Cooperation*, edited by Richard N. Cooper et al. Washington, D.C.: Brookings Institution.

COSEPUP. See Committee on Science, Engineering and Public Policy.

Costanza, R. 1989. "What is Ecological Economics?" *Ecological Economics* I:1–8.

Costanza, R., et al. 1990. *The Ecological Economics of Sustainability: Making Local and Short-Term Goals Consistent with Global and Long-Term Goals.* Environment Working Paper No. 32. Washington, D.C.: World Bank Sector Policy and Research Staff. Selected papers from an associated 1990 conference are scheduled to appear in the journal *Ecological Economics.*

Costanza, Robert, ed. 1991. *Ecological Economics: The Science and Management of Sustainability.* New York: Columbia University Press.

Cottrell, Fred. 1955. *Energy and Society: The Relation Between Energy, Social Change, and Economic Development,* New York: McGraw Hill.

Covello, V. T., and Paul Slovic. 1987. *Risk Communication: A Review of the Literature.* Washington, D.C.: National Science Foundation.

Cox, Robert W. 1983. "Gramsci, Hegemony, and International Relations: An Essay in Method." *Millennium: Journal of International Studies,* 12 (Summer):162–175.

Cox, R. W., and H. K. Jacobson. 1973. *Anatomy of Influence: Decision Making in International Organization.* New Haven: Yale University Press.

Cronon, W. 1983. *Changes in The Land: Indians, Colonists, and the Ecology of New England.* New York: Hill and Wang.

Crutchfield, James, J. Doyne Farmer, and Norman Packard. 1986. "Chaos." *Scientific American,* 255 (December):46–57.

Cyert, Richard M., and James G. March. 1963. *A Behavioral Theory of the Firm.* Englewood Cliffs, N.J.: Prentice Hall.

Daly, H. E. 1973. *Toward a Steady-State Economy.* San Francisco: W. H. Freeman and Company.

Daly, H. E. 1989. "Towards an Environmental Macroeconomics." Washington, D.C.: The World Bank.

Daly, H. E. 1990. "Toward Some Operational Principles of Sustainable Development." *Ecological Economics* 2:1–6.

Daly, H. E., and J. B. Cobb, Jr. 1989. *For the Common Good: Redirecting the Economy Toward Community, the Environment, and a Sustainable Future.* Boston: Beacon Press.

D'Amato, A. 1990. "Do We Owe a Duty to Future Generations to Preserve the Global Environment?" *American Journal of International Law,* 84 (1) (Jan):190–198.

Darmstadter, Joel, and Jae Edmonds. 1989. "Human Development and Carbon Dioxide Emissions: The Current Picture and the Long-Term Prospects." In *Greenhouse Warming: Abatement and Adaptation,* edited by Norman J. Rosenberg et al. Washington, D.C.: Resources for the Future.

Darwin, C. 1958. *Origin of Species.* Everyman's Library edition, introduced by W. R. Thompson. New York: E. P. Dutton & Co. (Originally published in 1859 under its full title: *On the Origin of Species by Means of Natural Selection, or the Preservation of Favored Races in the Struggle for Life.*).

Darwin, C. 1905. *My Life.* London: Chapman and Hall.

Deutsch, K. W. 1966. *Nationalism and Social Communication: An Inquiry into the Foundations of Nationality.* Cambridge, Mass.: MIT Press.

Devall, B., and G. Sessions. 1985. *Deep Ecology: Living As if Nature Mattered.* Salt Lake City: Peregrine Smith Books.

Dicey, A. 1980. *Dicey and Morris on the Conflicts of Law.* 10th edition. London: Stevens.

Dickson, David. 1985. "Global Energy Study Under Fire." *Science* 227 (4 January):34.

Dikshit, R. D. 1982. *Political Geography: A Contemporary Perspective.* New Delhi: Tata McGraw-Hill.

Dolzer, R. 1976. *Property and Environment: The Social Obligation Inherent in Ownership.* Morges, Switzerland: IUCN.

Dorfman, Robert and Nancy S. Dorfman, eds. 1972. *Economics of the Environment.* New York: W. W. Norton & Company, Inc.

Dryzek, John S. 1987. *Rational Ecology: Environment and Political Economy.* London: Basil Blackwell.

Dunning, John H. 1988. "The Eclectic Paradigm of International Production: A Restatement and Some Possible Extensions." *Journal of International Business Studies* (Spring).

Earth System Sciences Committee, NASA Advisory Council. 1986. *Earth System Science Overview: A Program for Global Change.* Washington, D.C.: National Aeronautics and Space Administration.

Ehrlich, Paul, and Anne H. Ehrlich. 1990. *The Population Explosion.* New York: Simon and Schuster.

Ehrlich, Paul, Anne H. Ehrlich, and John P. Holdren. 1977. *Ecoscience: Population, Resources, Environment.* San Francisco: W. H. Freeman.

Ehrlich, Paul, and John Holdren. 1971. "Impact of Population Growth." *Science,* 171 (26 March):1212–1217.

Ehrlich, Paul, et al. 1984. *The Cold and the Dark.* New York: W. W. Norton.

Encyclopedia Britannica. 1980. 15th Edition.

Ergas, Henry, 1987. "Does Technology Policy Matter?" In *Technology and Global Industry: Companies and Nations in the World Economy,* edited by Bruce R. Guile and Harvey Brooks. Washington, D.C.: National Academy Press, pp. 192–245.

Ezrahi, Yaron. 1990. *The Descent of Icarus: Science and the Transformation of Contemporary Democracy.* Cambridge, Mass.: Harvard University Press.

Fagan, M. D., ed. 1975. *A History of Engineering and Science in the Bell System, The Early Years 1875–1925.* New Jersey: Bell Telephone Laboratories, Inc.

FAO. See Food and Agriculture Organization.

Feeney, Griffith, et al. 1989. Recent Fertility Dynamics in China: Results from the 1987 One Percent Population Survey." *Population and Development Review,* 15 (2) (June):297–321.

Feldstein, Martin. 1964. "The Social Time Preference Discount Rate in Cost-Benefit Analysis." *Economic Journal* 74 (June):360–379.

Ferri, A. 1986. "Sui Recenti Sviluppi e Sui Temi Ricorrenti della Geograpfia Politica in Unione Sovietica." *Bollettino Della Societa' Geografica Italiana* Ser. XI, Vol. III:47–80.

Fischer, W. 1991. "The Verification of International Conventions on Protection of the Environment and Common Resources: A Comparative Analysis of the Instruments and Procedures for International Verification with the Example of Thirteen Conventions." Programmgruppe Technologiefolgenforschung, Forschungszentrum Julich.

Fischoff, Baruch. 1985. "Managing Risk Perceptions." *Issues in Science and Technology* 2 (Fall):83–96.

Fisher, Roger, 1981. *Improving Compliance with International Law.* Charlottesville: University Press of Virginia.

Fisher, Roger, and William Ury. 1981. *Getting to Yes.* Boston: Houghton Mifflin.

Fligstein, Neil. 1990. *The Transformation of Corporate Control.* Cambridge, Mass.: Harvard University Press.

Food and Agriculture Organization. 1983. *Fuelwood Supplies in the Developing Countries.* FAO Forestry Paper 42. Rome: FAO.

Food and Agriculture Organization. 1987. *World Fisheries Situation and Outlook.* Rome: FAO.

Forrester, Jay W. 1968. *Principles of Systems.* 2nd edition. Cambridge, Mass.: Wright-Allen Press.

Forrester, J. W. 1971a. *World Dynamics.* Cambridge, Mass.: Wright-Allen Press.

Forrester, Jay. 1971b. "The Counterintuitive Behavior of Social Systems." *Technology Review* 73 (January).

Foy, G., and H. E. Daly. 1989. *Allocation, Distribution and Scale as Determinants of Environmental Degradation: Case Studies of Haiti, El Salvador, and Costa Rica.* Environment Dept. Working Paper No. 19. Washington, D.C.: The World Bank.

Frederick, Kenneth D., and Peter H. Gleick. 1989. "Water Resources and Climate Change." In *Greenhouse Warming: Abatement and Adaptation,* edited by Norman J. Rosenberg et al. Washington, D.C.: Resources for the Future.

Freeman, C., and M. Jahoda. 1978. *World Futures: The Great Debate.* London: Robertson.

Freudenberg, William R. 1988. "Perceived Risk, Real Risk, Social Science and the Art of Probabilistic Risk Assessment." *Science* 242 (7 October):44–49.

Fri, R. W., and C. L. Cooper. 1991. "International Technology Cooperation: A Near-term Approach toward the Long-term Goal." Paper for the Aspen Institute Conference on International Environment Policy and Institutions, July 18–25, Aspen, Colorado.

Friedman, F. B. 1988. *Practical Guide to Environmental Management.* Washington, D.C.: Environmental Law Institute.

Friedman, J. 1988. "Cultural Logics of the Global System." *Theory, Culture & Society* 5:447–460.

Frohlich, Norman, Joe A. Oppenheimer, and Oran R. Young. 1971. *Political Leadership and Collective Goods.* Princeton: Princeton University Press.

Fujii, T. 1990. "Change of Earth Systems." *Seisakugaku: Policy Management.*

Galtung, J. 1973. "The Limits to Growth and Class Politics." *Journal of Peace Research* 17.

GAO. See General Accounting Office.

Gastil, Raymond D. 1988. *Freedom in the World: Political Rights and Civil Liberties.* New York: Freedom House.

Gates, W. L. 1985. "The Use of General Circulation Models in the Analysis of the Ecosystem Impacts of Climatic Change." *Climatic Change* 7:267–284.

General Accounting Office (GAO, U.S.). 1992. *International Environment: International Agreements Are Not Well Monitored.* GAO/RCED-92–43 (January).

GESAMP. 1990. *The State of the Marine Environment.* UNEP Regional Seas Reports and Studies. No. 115. UNEP, 1990.

Gibbons, Ann. 1990. "New View of Early Amazonia." *Science* 248 (22 June):1488–1490.

Gilpin, Robert. 1975. *U.S. Power and the Multinational Corporation: The Political Economy Foreign Direct Investment.* New York: Basic Books.

Gilpin, Robert. 1987. *The Political Economy of International Relations.* Princeton: Princeton University Press.

Glacken, Clarence, J. 1967. *Traces on the Rhodian shore: nature and culture in Western thought from ancient times to the end of the eighteenth century.* Berkeley, CA: University of California Press.

Glaeser, B., ed. 1984. *Ecodevelopment: Concepts, Policies, Strategies.* New York: Pergamon Press.

Gleick, James. 1987. *Chaos: Making of a New Science.* New York: Viking.

Gleick, Peter. 1991. "Water and Conflict." Paper presented to the Project on Environmental Change and Acute Conflict, sponsored by the Peace and Conflict Studies Program of the University of Toronto and the American Academy of Arts and Sciences, June 15–16, Toronto, Canada.

Goldsmith, E. 1988. "The Way: An Ecological Worldview." *The Ecologist* 18 (4/5) 160–185.

Goldstein, Joshua S. 1988. *Long Cycles: Prosperity and War in the Modern Age.* New Haven: Yale University Press.

Goodin, Robert E. 1990. "International Ethics and the Environmental Crisis." *Ethics and International Affairs* 4.

Goodman, Michael R. 1974. *Study Notes in System Dynamics.* Cambridge, Mass.: Wright-Allen Press.

Graedel, Thomas E., and Paul J. Crutzen. 1989. "The Changing Atmosphere." *Scientific American* 261:59–68.

Graham, Loren R. 1987. "Science and Technology Trends in the Soviet Union." Program in Science, Technology and Society, Oct. MIT, Cambridge, Mass.

Graveson, Ronald. 1979. "The Problem of Choice of Time in Private International Law." *Annuaire de l'Institut de Droit International,* Vol. 58, Part I. Basel, Switzerland: S. Korger, pp. 1–96.

Greenberger, Martin, et al. 1983. *Caught Unawares: The Energy Decade in Retrospect.* Cambridge, Mass.: Ballinger.

Grodecki, J. 1975. *International Encyclopedia of Comparative Law,* Volume 3, Chapter 8.

"Growth Can Be Green." 1989. *The Economist* (August 26):12–13.

Grubb, M. J., and N. Steen. 1991. "Pledge and Review Processes: Possible Components of a Climate Convention." London: Royal Institute of International Affairs.

Grubb, M. J., D. G. Victor, and C. Hope. 1991. "Rethinking the Comprehensive Approach to Climate Change," *Nature* 354:348–350.

Grubel, Herbert G. 1976. "Some Effects of Environmental Controls on International Trade: the Heckscher-Ohlin Model." In *Studies in International Environmental Economics*, edited by Ingo Walter. New York: John Wiley and Sons, p. 36.

Haas, Ernst B. 1964. *Beyond the Nation-State: Functionalism and International Organization*. Palo Alto: Stanford University Press.

Haas, Ernst B. 1980. "Why Collaborate? Issue-Linkages and International Regimes." *World Politics* 32:357–405.

Haas, Ernst B. 1990. *When Knowledge Is Power: Three Models of Change in International Organizations*, Berkeley: University of California Press.

Haas, Peter M. 1989. "Do Regimes Matter? Epistemic Communities and Mediterranean Pollution Control." *International Organization* 43:377.

Haas, Peter M. 1990a. *Saving the Mediterranean: The Politics of International Environmental Cooperation*. New York: Columbia University Press.

Haas, Peter M. 1990b. "Obtaining International Environmental Protection through Epistemic Consensus." *Millenium* 19 (3):347–363.

Haas, Peter M., ed. 1992 "Special Issue on Epistemic Communities," *International Organization* 46 (Winter).

Haas, Peter M. 1991. "From Theory to Practice: Ecological Ideas and Environmental Policy." Unpublished manuscript.

Haeckel, E. 1866. *Generelle Morphologie der Organismen*. Berlin: de Gruyter, 1988.

Haggard, Stephan, and Beth A. Simmons. 1987. "Theories of International Regimes." *International Organization* 41:491.

Hall, Charles A. S. 1991. "An Idiosyncratic Assessment of the Role of Mathematical Models in Environmental Sciences." *Environment International* 17:507–517.

Hall, Charles A. S., and J. Day, eds. 1977. *Ecosystem Modeling in Theory and Practice*. New York: Wiley Interscience.

Hall, Peter A., ed. 1989. *The Poltiical Power of Economic Ideas: Keynesianism across Nations*. Princeton: Princeton University Press.

Hammitt, James K., et al. 1986. *Product Uses and Market Trends for Potential Ozone-Depleting Substances, 1985–2000*. The Rand Corporation, No. 3386-EA (May).

Hansen, J., et al. 1988. "Global Climate Changes as Forecast by Goddard Institute of Space Studies Three-Dimensional Model." *Journal of Geophysical Research* 93:9341–9364.

Hansen, Peter. 1989. "Transnational Corporations in World Development: An Overview." *Business in the Contemporary World* 1:74–85.

Hardin, Garret, 1968. "The Tragedy of the Commons." *Science* 163 (13 December).

Henkin, L., et al. 1986. *International Law*. 2nd edition. St. Paul, Minn.: West Publishing Co., p. 102.

Hileman, Bette. 1989. "Global Warming." *Chemical and Engineering News* (March 13):25–44.

Hinsley, F. H. 1966. *Sovereignty.* New York: Basic Books.

Holden, Constance. 1990. "Multidisciplinary Look at a Finite World." *Science* 249 (6 July):18–19.

Holdgate, Martin W. 1991. "The Environment of Tomorrow." *Environment* 33 (July/August):14–20, 40–42.

Holling, C. S. 1973. "Resilience and Stability of Ecological Systems." *Annual Review of Ecology and Systematics* 4:1–23.

Homans, George C. 1961. *Social Behavior in Elementary Forms.* New York: Harcourt Brace.

Homer-Dixon, Thomas F. 1991a. "Environmental Change and Human Security." *Behind the Headlines.* Vol. 48, No. 3. Toronto: Canadian Institute for International Affairs.

Homer-Dixon, Thomas F. 1991b. "On the Threshold: Environmental Changes as Causes of Acute Conflict." *International Security,* 16 (2) (Fall):76–116.

Houghton, J. T., G. J. Jenkins, and J. J. Ephraums, eds. 1990. *Climate Change: The IPCC Scientific Assessment.* New York: Cambridge University Press.

Houghton, J. T., B. A. Callander, and S. K. Varney, eds. 1992. *Climate Change 1992: The Supplementary Report to the IPCC Scientific Assessment.* New York: Cambridge University Press.

Houghton, R. A., et al. 1987. "The Flux of Carbon from Terrestrial Ecosystems to the Atmosphere in 1980 Due to Changes in Land Use: Geographic Distribution of the Global Flux." *Tellus* 39B:122–139.

House of Representatives, Committee on Foreign Affairs, Subcommittee on Europe and the Middle East. 1990. "The Middle East in the 1990s: Middle East Water Issues." Testimony, Tuesday, June 26.

Howarth, Richard B. 1990a. "Economic Theory, Natural Resources, and Intergenerational Equity." Ph.D. diss. University of California, Berkeley.

Howarth, Richard B. 1990b. "Intergenerational Competitive Equilibria under Technological Uncertainty, and an Exhaustive Resource Constraint." Paper presented to the Association for Public Policy Analysis and Management, October, San Francisco.

Howarth, Richard B., and Norgaard, Richard B. 1990. "Intergenerational Resource Rights, Efficiency and Social Optimality." *Land Economics* 66 (1) (February).

Hughes, B. 1985. *World Futures: A Critical Analysis of Alternatives.* Baltimore: Johns Hopkins University Press.

Hurrell, Andrew. 1992. "Brazil and the International Politics of Amazonian Deforestation." In *The International Politics of the Environment: Actors, Interests and Institutions,* edited by Andrew Hurrell and Benedict Kingsbury. Oxford: Oxford University Press. Forthcoming.

Hymer, Stephen. 1960 (1976). *The International Operations of Nations Firms: A Study of Foreign Direct Investment.* Cambridge, Mass.: MIT Press.

Hymer, Stephen. 1972. "The Multinational Corporation and the Law of Uneven Development." In *Economics and World Order: From the 1970s to the 1990s,* edited by Jagdish Bhagwati. New York: Macmillan.

l'Institut de Droit International. 1979. *Annuaire de l'Institut de Droit Internationa.* Vol. 58, Part I. Basel, Switzerland: S. Karger.

l'Institut de Droit International. 1982. *Annuaire de l'Institut de Droit International.* Vol. 59, Part II. Paris: A. Pendone.

Intergovernmental Negotiating Committee (INC). 1991. *Report of the Intergovernmental Negotiating Committee for a Framework Convention on Climate Change on the Work of Its First Session, Held at Washington, D.C. from 4 to 14 February 1991.* UN General Assembly A/AC.237/6, 8 March.

Intergovernmental Panel on Climate Change (IPCC). 1990. *Reports Prepared for IPCC by Working Groups I, II, and III.* United Nations Environmental Program and World Meteorological Organization.

Intergovernmental Panel on Climate Change (IPCC). 1992. *1992 Supplement: Scientific Assessment of Climate Change.* World Meterological Organization and United Nations Environment Programme.

Intergovernmental Panel on Climate Change (IPCC), Response Strategies Working Group (RSWG). 1991. *Climate Change: The IPCC Response Strategies.* Covelo, Calif.: Island Press.

International Council of Scientific Unions. 1990. *Global Change: A Scientific Review.* ICSU and the World Meterological Organization, January.

International Financial Corporation (IFC). 1988. *Emerging Stock Markets Factbook, 1988.* Washington, D.C.: IFC.

International Law Commission. 1990. *Report of the International Law Commission on the Work of its Forty-Second Session.* New York: United Nations General Assembly, Forty-Fifth Session Official Records, Supplement No. 10 (A/45/10).

International Union for Conservation of Nature and Natural Resources (IUCN). 1980. *World Conservation Strategy: Living Resource Conservation for Sustainable Development.* Gland, Switzerland: IUCN.

International Union for Conservation of Nature and Natural Resources (IUCN) and Saudi Arabia. 1983. *Islamic Principles For the Conservation of the Natural Environment.* Gland, Switzerland: IUCN and Saudi Arabia.

IUCN. See International Union for Conservation of Nature and Natural Resources.

IPCC. See Intergovernmental Panel on Climate Change.

Izrael, Yu. A., and R. E. Munn. 1986. "Monitoring the Environment and Renewable Resources." In *Sustainable Development of the Biosphere,* edited by William C. Clark and R. E. Munn. New York: Cambridge University Press, Chapter 13.

Jackson, Robert H. 1990. *Quasi-States: Sovereignty, International Relations, and the Third World.* Cambridge: Cambridge University Press.

Jacobson, H. K., and D. A. Kay. 1983. "A Framework for Analysis." In *Environmental Protection: The International Dimension,* edited by D. A. Kay and H. K. Jacobson. Totowa, NJ: Allanheld, Osmun.

Jacobson, H. K., and M. F. Price for the ISCC Standing Committee on the Human Dimensions of Global Change 1990. *A Framework for Research on the Human Dimensions of Global Environmental Change.* Paris: International Social Science Council.

Janis, M. 1983. "The Ambiguity of Equity in International Law." *Brooklyn Journal International Law.* 9:7–34.

Jantsch, E., and C. H. Waddington, eds. 1976. *Evolution and Consciousness: Human Systems in Transition.* Reading, Mass.: Addison-Wesley.

Johnson, Harry G. 1970. "The Efficiency and Welfare Implications of the International Corporation." In *The International Corporation,* edited by C. P. Kindleberger. Cambridge, Mass.: Massachusetts Institute of Technology Press.

Johnson, Harry G. 1972. "Political Economy Aspects of International Monetary Reform." *Journal of International Economics* 2:401–423.

Johnston, F. F., and W. C. Clark. 1982. *Redesigning Rural Development: A Strategic Perspective.* Baltimore: Johns Hopkins University Press.

Kahler, Miles. 1992. "Multilateralism with Small and Large Numbers." *International Organization,* 46 (3):681–708.

Kates, R. W., and I. Burton. 1986. "The Great Climacteric 1798–2048: Transition to a Just and Sustainable Human Environment." In *Geography, Resources and Environment. Vol. 2: Essays on Themes From the Work of G. F. White,* edited by R. W. Kates and I. Burton. Chicago: University of Chicago Press.

Kates, R. W., B. L. Turner, and W. C. Clark. 1990. "The Great Transformation." In Turner et al. 1990, pp. 1–17.

Keepin, Bill. 1984. "A Technical Appraisal of the IIASA Energy Scenarios." *Policy Sciences* 17:199–275.

Keepin, Bill. 1986. "Review of Global Energy and Carbon Dioxide Projections." *Annual Review of Energy,* Vol. 11:357–392.

Kelfkens, Bert, Frank de Gruijl, and Jan van der Leun. 1990. "Ozone Depletion and Increase in Annual Carcinogenic Ultraviolet Dose." *Photochemistry and Photobiology,* 52 (4):819–823.

Kennan, G. F. 1958. *Soviet-American Relations, 1917–1920. Vol. II: The Decision to Intervene.* Princeton: Princeton University Press.

Keohane, Robert O. 1984. *After Hegemony: Cooperation and Discord in the World Political Economy.* Princeton: Princeton University Press.

Keohane, Robert O., ed. 1986. *Neorealism and Its Critics.* New York: Columbia University Press.

Keohane, R. O. 1988. "International Institutions: Two Approaches." *International Studies Quarterly* 32:379–396.

Keohane, Robert O., and Joseph Nye. 1987. "Power and Interdependence Revisited." *International Organization* 41:725.

Keohane, Robert, and Joseph S. Nye, Jr. 1989. *Power and Interdependence: World Politics in Transition.* 2nd edition. Boston: Little, Brown.

Kerr, Richard A. 1985. "Nuclear Winter Won't Blow Away." *Science* 228 (12 April):163.

Kerr, Richard A. 1988a. "Linking Earth, Ocean and Air at the AGU." *Science* 239:259–260.

Kerr, Richard A. 1988b. "Is the Greenhouse Here?" *Science* 239:559–561.

Kerr, Richard A. 1989. "Hansen vs. the World on the Greenhouse Threat." *Science* 244:1041–1043.

Kerr, Richard A. 1990. "New Greenhouse Report Puts Down Dissenters." *Science* 249:481–482.

Keyfitz, Nathan. 1983. *Can Knowledge Improve Forecasts?* International Institute for Applied Systems Analysis Publication No. RR-83-05, Laxenburg, Austria. Reprinted *Scenarios of Socioeconomic Development for Studies of Global Environmental Change: A Critical Review,* edited by F. L. Toth, E. Hizsnyik, and W. C. Clark. Laxenburg, Austria: International Institute for Applied Systems Analysis, 1989.

Keyfitz, Nathan. 1989. "The Growing Human Population." *Scientific American* 261:118–135.

Keyfitz, Nathan. 1990. "Population Growth Can Prevent the Development That Would Slow Population Growth." In *Preserving the Global Environment: The Challenge of Shared Leadership,* edited by Jessica Tuchman Mathews. Proceedings of the Seventy-Seventh American Assembly, Harriman, 1990. New York, April 19–22.

Khadduri, M. 1984. *The Islamic Conception of Justice.* Baltimore: Johns Hopkins University Press.

Kindleberger, Charles P. 1962. *Foreign Trade and the National Economy.* New Haven: Yale University Press.

Kindleberger, C. P. 1969. *American Business Abroad: Six Essays on Direct Investment.* New Haven: Yale University Press.

Kindleberger, C. P., ed. 1970. *The International Corporation.* Cambridge, Mass.: Massachusetts Institute of Technology Press.

Kindleberger, Charles P. 1973. *The World in Depression 1929–1939.* Berkeley: University of California Press.

Kindlegerger, C. P. 1974. "The Theory of Direct Investment." In *International Trade and Finance,* edited by Richard E. Baldwin and J. David Richardson. Boston: Little, Brown.

Kiss, Alexandre Charles, ed. 1983. *Selected Multilateral Treaties in the Field of the Environment.* Nairobi: United Nations Environment Programme.

Kline, Stephen J., and Nathan Rosenberg. 1986. "An Overview of Innovation." In *The Positive Sum Strategy: Harnessing Technology for Economic Growth,* edited by Ralph Landau and Nathan Rosenberg. Washington, D.C.: National Academy Press, pp. 275–305.

Kneale, Dennis. 1988. "Into the Void." *The Wall Street Journal* (January 12):1, 33.

Knetsch, J. L. 1989. "Environmental Policy Implications of Disparities between Willingness to Pay and Compensation Demanded Measures of Values." Paper presented at the World Bank Seminar on Economic Analysis of Environmental Issues, May 1989, Washington, D.C.

Knetsch, J. L., and J. A. Sinden. 1984. "Willingness to Pay and Compensation Demanded: Experimental Evidence of an Unexpected Disparity in Measures of Value." *Quarterly Journal of Economics* XCIX:507–521.

Kondratieff, Nicolai. 1984. *The Long Wave Cycle.* New York: Richardson & Snyder.

Korten, D. C. 1990. *Getting to the 21st Century: Voluntary Action and the Global Agenda.* Hartford, Conn.: Kumarian Press.

Kraft, Michael E., and Norman J. Vig. 1988. *Technology and Politics.* Durham, N.C.: Duke University Press.

Krasner, Stephen D. 1982. "Regimes and the Limits of Realism: Regimes as Autonomous Variables." *International Organization* 36 (2) (Spring).

Krasner, Stephen D., ed. 1983. *International Regimes.* Ithaca, N.Y.: Cornell University Press.

Krasner, Stephen D. 1984. "Review Article: Approaches to the State: Alternative Conceptions and Historical Dynamics." *Comparative Politics* 16:223–246.

Krasner, Stephen D. 1991. "Global Communications and National Power: Life on the Pareto Frontier." *World Politics* 43 (April):336–366.

Kuznets, Simon. 1966. *Modern Economic Growth: Rate, Structure, and Spread.* New Haven: Yale University Press.

LACCD. See Latin American and Caribbean Commission on Development and Environment.

Laird, Michael W. 1972. *Natural Resources and International Conflict: A Japanese Case Study.* M.S. thesis, Alfred P. Sloan School of Management, Massachusetts Institute of Technology, Cambridge, Mass.

Lakoff, G., and M. Turner. 1989. *More than Cool Reason: A Field Guide to Poetic Metaphor.* Chicago: Chicago University Press.

Lall, Sanjaya. 1983. *The New Multinationals: The Spread of Third World Enterprise.* New York: John Wiley & Sons.

Lancaster, John. 1991. "Long-Term Damage Seen from Exxon Valdez Spill." *Washington Post* (February 21):A-1, A-7.

Lang, Winfried. 1986. "Environmental Protection: The Challenge for International Law." *Journal of World Trade Law* 20 (5):489–496.

Lapidoth, R. 1987. "Equity in International Law." *Proceedings.* Annual Meeting of the American Society of International Law. Washington, D.C.: American Society of International Law, pp. 138–147.

Lasswell, Harold D. 1958. *Politics: Who Gets What, When and How.* New York: McGraw-Hill.

Latin American and Caribbean Commission on Development and Environment. No date. *Our Own Agenda.* Washington, D.C., and New York: Inter-American Development Bank and United Nations Development Program. From internal evidence the publication date was either late 1990 or 1991.

Leary, V. A. 1992. "Survey of Existing International Agreements and Instruments: Working Environment." United Nations Conference on Environment and Development, Research Paper No. 31 (January).

Lee, J. A. 1985. *The Environment, Public Health, and Human Ecology.* Baltimore: Johns Hopkins University Press.

Lee, Kai N. 1989. "The Columbia River: Experimenting with Sustainability." *Environment* 31:6–11, 30–33.

Lee, Thomas. 1989. "Advanced Fossil Fuel Systems and Beyond." In *Technology and Environment,* edited by Jesse Ausubel and Hedy Sladovich. Washington, D.C.: National Academy Press, pp. 114–136.

Lele, S. M. 1991. "Sustainable Development: A Critical Review." *World Development* 19 (6):607–621.

Leonard, Herman. 1988. "Asset Management and Budgetary Policy." Working Paper. CMT International, Cambridge, Mass.

Leonard, Jeffrey. 1989. "Overview." In *Environment and the Poor: Development Strategies for a Common Agenda.* New Brunswick, N.J.: Transaction.

Leopold, Aldo. 1966. *A Sand County Almanac, with Essays on Conservation from Round River.* New York: Ballantine Books.

Lerner, Jean, et al. 1988. "Methane Emissions from Animals: A Global High-Resolution Database." *Global Biogeochemical Cycles* 2:139–156.

Lessard, Donald, and Cristiano Antonelli, eds. 1990. *Managing the Globalization of Business.* Milan: Editoriale Scientifica s.r.l., Parts I, II, and V.

Lessard, Donald, and Enrico Perotti. 1990. "Moving Toward 1992: Managing the Internationalization of Ownership and Corporate Finance." In *Managing the Globalization of Business,* edited by Donald Lessard and Cristiano Antonelli. Milan: Editoriale Scientifica s.r.l.

Levin, N. G. 1972. *Woodrow Wilson and the Paris Peace Conference.* 2nd edition. Lexington, Mass.: D. C. Heath.

Levins, R., and R. Lewontin. 1982. "Dialectics and Reductionism in Ecology." In Saarlinen 1982, pp. 107–138.

Levy, Jack S. 1983. *War in the Modern Great Power System, 1495–1975.* Lexington: University Press of Kentucky.

Levy, M. A. n.d. "European Acid Rain: The Power of Tote-Board Diplomacy." In *Institutions for the Earth: Sources of Effective International Environmental Protection,* edited by P. M. Haas, R. O. Keohane, and M. A. Levy. Cambridge, Mass.: MIT Press. Forthcoming.

Litchman, Scott. 1988. *Enhancing the Design of a System Dynamics Model for "Lateral Pressure".* B.S. thesis, Department of Electrical Engineering and Computer Science, Massachusetts Institute of Technology, Cambridge, Mass.

Locke, John. 1690. "An Essay Concerning the True Original, Extent and End of Civil Government." *Second Treatise on Civil Government.* In *Social Contract,* 2nd edition, edited by Sir Ernest Barker. London: Oxford University Press, 1979, para. 25, 31, 33, and 37.

Longstreth, Janice. 1989. "Overview of the Potential Health Effects Associated with Ozone Depletion." In *Coping with Climate Change: Proceedings of the Second North American Conference on Preparing for Climate Change,* edited by John Topping, Jr., Washington, D.C.: The Climate Institute, pp. 163–167.

Lovejoy, A. 1936. *The Great Chain of Being.* Cambridge: Harvard University Press.

Lovelock, L. E. 1979. *Gaia: A New Look at Life on Earth.* New York: Oxford University Press.

Lovelock, L. E., and L. Margulis. 1973. "Atmospheric Homoeostasis by and for the Biosphere: the Gaia Hypothesis. *Tellus* 26.

Lutz, Ernst, and Salah El Serafy. 1988. *Environmental and Resource Accounting: An Overview.* The World Bank, Environmental Department Working Paper #6, June.

Lyman, Francesca, et al. 1990. *The Greenhouse Trap.* Boston: The Beacon Press.

Lyster, Simon. 1985. *International Wildlife Law: An Analysis of Treaties Concerned with the Conservation of Wildlife.* Cambridge: Grotius Publications Ltd.

MacNeill, Jim, Pieter Winsemius, and Taizo Yakushiji. 1991. *Beyond Interdependence.* New York: Oxford University Press.

Makhijani, Arjun, Amanda Bickel, and Annie Makhijani. 1990. "Still Working on the Ozone Hole." *Technology Review* (May/June):53–59.

Malthus, T. R. 1970. *An Essay on the Principle of Population and A Summary View of the Principle of Population.* Edited with an introduction by Antony Flew. Hammondsworth: Penguin.

Malthus, T. R. 1798. *An Essay on the Principle of Population.* The first edition (1798), and the sixth edition (1826) with variant readings from the second edition (1803). *The Works of Thomas Robert Malthus.* 3 vols. Edited by E. A. Wrigley and D. Souden. London: William Pickering.

Manibog, Fernando. 1984. "Improved Cooking Stoves in Developing Countries: Problems and Opportunities." *Annual Review of Energy* 9:199–227.

Mann, C. 1991. "Lynn Margulis: Science's Unruly Earth Mother," *Science* 252 (19 April 1991):378–381.

Manzer, L. E. 1990. "The CFC-Ozone Issue: Progress on the Development of Alternatives to CFCs." *Science* 249:31–35.

Maoz, Zeev, and Dan S. Felsenthal. 1987. "Self-Binding Commitments, the Inducement of Trust, Social Choice, and the Theory of International Cooperation." *International Studies Quarterly* 31:177–200.

Margolin, Stephen. 1963. "The Social Rate of Discount and the Optimal Rate of Investment." *Quarterly Journal of Economics* (February).

Marland, G. et al. 1989. *Estimates of CO_2 Emissions from Fossil Fuel Burning and Cement Manufacturing, Based on the United Nations Energy Statistics and the U.S. Bureau of Mines Cement Manufacturing Data,* ORNL/CDIAC-25, NDP-030 (Oak Ridge, Tenn.: Oak Ridge National Laboratory, Carbon Dioxide Information and Analysis Center). Updated data are also available.

Marsh, G. P. 1874. *The Earth As Modified by Human Action.* New York: Scribners, Armstrong.

Marsh, G. P. 1965. *Man and Nature, Or Physical Geography as Modified by Human Action.* Edited by David Lowenthal. Cambridge: Belknap Press of Harvard University Press.

Marshall, Eliot. 1989. "Valdez: The Predicted Oil Spill." *Science* 244:20–21.

Marshall (George C.) Institute. 1989. *Scientific Perspectives on the Greenhouse Problem.* Washington, D.C.: G. C. Marshall Institute.

Marx, K. 1963–1971. *Theories of Surplus-Value, Volume IV of Capital.* 3 volumes. Moscow: Progress Publishers.

Mathews, Jessica Tuchman. 1991. *Preserving the Global Environment: The Challenge of Shared Leadership.* Proceedings of the Seventy-Seventh American Assembly, April 19–22, Harriman, New York.

May, Robert E., ed. 1985. *Exploitation of Marine Communities.* New York: Springer-Verlag.

Mayr, Ernst. 1976. *Evolution and the Diversity of Life.* Cambridge: Belknap Press.

McClain, David. 1983. "Foreign Direct Investment in the United States: Old Currents, 'New Waves,' and the Theory of Direct Investment." In *The Multinational Corporation in the 1980s,* edited by Charles P. Kindleberger and David Audretsch. Cambridge, Mass.: MIT Press, pp. 278–333.

McCormick, R. 1991. *Reclaiming Paradise: The Global Environmental Movement.* Bloomington: Indiana University Press.

McIntosh, R. 1985. *The Background of Ecology.* Cambridge, England: Cambridge University Press.

McKibben, W. 1989. *The End of Nature.* New York: Random House.

McNicoll, Geoffrey. 1984. "Consequences of Rapid Population Growth: An Overview and Assessment." *Population and Development Review* 10 (2) (1984):177–240.

Meadows, D. H. 1989. "Clouds of Dispute Cover Global Warming." *Los Angeles Times* (October 15):M1.

Meadows, D. H., et al. 1972. *The Limits to Growth.* New York: Potomac Associates.

Meadows, D. H., J. Richardson, and G. Bruckmann. 1982. *Groping in the Dark: The First Decade of Global Modeling.* New York: John Wiley & Sons.

Mesarovic, M. D., and E. Pestel. 1974. *Mankind at the Turning Point.* New York: Dutton.

Miller, Allan. 1991. "Economic Models and Policy on Global Warming." *Environment* 33 (July/August):3–5, 43–44.

Miller, Arthur R. 1991. "Private Lives or Public Access?" *ABA Journal* (August):65–68.

Mills, Edwin S., and Philip E. Graves. 1986. *The Economics of Environmental Quality,* 2nd edition. New York: W. W. Norton & Company.

Mishan, E. J. 1982. *Benefit-Cost Analysis.* 3rd edition. London: George Allen and Unwin.

MIT Faculty Study Group. 1991. *The International Relationships of MIT in a Technologically Competitive World,* May, Cambridge, Mass.

MIT Symposium on World Telecommunications Policy, In Tribute to Ithiel de Sola Pool. 1988. *Proceedings,* January 27–28.

Mitsch, W. J. and S. E. Jørgensen, eds., 1989. *Ecological Engineering: An Introduction to Ecotechnology.* New York: Wiley Interscience.

Monastersky, R. 1991. "Time for Action." *Science News* 139 (13):200–202.

Moore, David H. 1989. "A Budget-Constrained NASA Program for the 1990s." In *Space Policy Reconsidered,* edited by Radford Byerly, Jr. Boulder, Colo.: Westview Press, Ch. 1.

Morris. 1984. *The Conflict of Laws.* 3rd edition. London: Stevens.

Morrisette, Peter M., and Andrew J. Plantinga. 1991. "The Global Warming Issue: Viewpoints of Different Countries." *Resources* 103 (Spring):2–6.

Musgrave, R. A., and Peggy B. Musgrave. 1980. *Public Finance in Theory and Practice.* 3rd edition. New York: McGraw-Hill.

Nagel, Stuart S., ed. 1990. "Global Policy Studies." *International Political Science Review* 11.

Nash, Roderick Frazier. 1989. *The Rights of Nature: A History of Environmental Ethics.* Madison: University of Wisconsin Press.

National Parks and Conservation Association. 1989. *National Parks: From Vignettes to a Global View.* Washington, D.C.: NPCA.

National Research Council. 1982. *Scientific Communication and National Security.* Washington, D.C.: National Academy Press.

National Research Council. 1985a. *Oil in the Sea.* Washington, D.C.: National Academy Press.

National Research Council. 1985b. *The Effects on the Atmosphere of a Major Nuclear Exchange.* Washington, D.C.: National Academy Press.

National Research Council. 1986. *Ecological Knowledge and Environmental Problem Solving.* Washington, D.C.: National Academy Press, Part I.

National Research Council. 1987. *Balancing the National Interest: U.S. National Security Export Controls and Global Economic Competition.* Washington, D.C.: National Academy Press.

National Research Council. 1989. *Improving Risk Communication.* Washington, D.C.: National Academy Press.

National Research Council. 1989. *The Adequacy of Environmental Information for Outer Continental Shelf Oil and Gas Decisions.* Washington, D.C.: National Academy Press.

National Research Council. 1989–90. "Environmental Data Lacking for Oil and Gas Leasing." *NewsReport* 40 (December–1990):2–4.

National Research Council. 1991. *Policy Implications of Greenhouse Warming.* Washington, D.C.: National Academy Press.

Nelson, Richard. 1974. "Intellectualizing about the Moon-Ghetto Metaphor." *Policy Sciences* 5 (December):375–414.

Nitze, William A. 1990. "A Proposed Structure for an International Convention on Climate Change." *Science* 249:607–608.

Nordhaus, William D. 1990. "Count Before You Leap." *The Economist* (July 7):21–24.

Norgaard, R. B. 1988. "Sustainable Development: A Co-Evolutionary View." *Futures* 20 (6):606–620.

Norgaard, R. B. 1991. *Sustainability as Intergenerational Equity: The Challenge to Economic Thought and Practice.* World Bank Internal Discussion Paper, Asia Regional Series No. IDP 97, Washington, D.C.

Norgaard, Richard B. 1992. "Environmental Science as a Social Process." *Environmental Monitoring and Assessment* 16.

Norgaard, Richard B., and Richard B. Howarth. 1991. "Sustainability and Discounting the Future." In *Ecological Economics: The Science and Management of Sustainability,* edited by Robert Costanza. New York: Columbia University Press, Ch. 7.

North, Robert C. 1978. "Some Observations on Forecasting Based on Lessons from Retrospective Analysis." In *Forecasting in International Relations: Theory, Methods, Problems, Prospects,* edited by Nazli Choucri and Thomas W. Robinson. San Francisco: W. H. Freeman.

North, Robert C. 1990. *War, Peace, Survival: Global Politics and Conceptual Synthesis.* Boulder: Westview.

Northrop, F. S. C. 1949. *The Meeting of East and West.* Woodbridge, Conn.: Oxbow.

Norton, B. G. 1990. "Context and Hierarchy in Aldo Leopold's Theory of Environmental Management." *Ecological Economics* 2:119–127.

Nye, Joseph S., Jr. 1987. "Nuclear Learning and U.S.-Soviet Security Regimes." *International Organization* 41 (Summer):371–402.

Odum, Eugene P. 1971. *Fundamentals of Ecology.* 3rd ed. Philadelphia: W. B. Saunders Company.

Odum, W. E. 1982. "Environmental Degradation and the Tyranny of Small Decisions." *BioScience* 32:728–729.

OECD. See Organization for Economic Cooperation and Development.

Ollennu, Nii Amaa. 1962. *Principles of Customary Land Law in Ghana.* London: Sweet and Maxwell.

Olson, Mancur. 1965. *The Logic of Collective Action.* Cambridge: Harvard University Press.

Olson, Mancur. 1982. *The Rise and Decline of Nations: Economic Growth, Stagflation, and Social Rigidities.* New Haven, Conn.: Yale University Press.

Olson, Walter K. 1991. *The Litigation Explosion: What Happened When America Unleashed the Lawsuit.* New York: E. P. Dutton.

Organization for Economic Cooperation and Development. 1991a. *OECD in Figures: Supplement to the OECD Observer.* Paris: OECD Publications, No. 170, June/July.

Organization for Economic Cooperation and Development. 1991b. *The State of the Environment.* Paris: OECD Publications.

Orians, Gordon H. 1975. "Diversity, Stability, and Maturity in Natural Ecosystems." In *Unifying Concepts in Ecology,* edited by W. H. Van Dobben and R. H. Lowe-McConnell. The Hague: W. Junk, pp. 139–150.

Osgood, Charles E. 1962. *An Alternative to War or Surrender.* Urbana: University of Illinois Press.

Ostrom, Elinor. 1990. *Governing the Commons: The Evolution of Institutions for Collective Action.* Cambridge: Cambridge University Press.

Oye, Kenneth A. 1986. "Explaining Cooperation under Anarchy: Hypotheses and Strategies." In *Cooperation under Anarchy,* edited by Kenneth A. Oye. Princeton, N.J.: Princeton University Press, pp. 1–24.

Oye, Kenneth, ed. 1985. *Cooperation Under Anarchy.* Princeton, N.J.: Princeton University Press.

Oye, Kenneth. 1990. *The World Political Economy in the 1930s and 1980s: Economic Discrimination and Political Exchange.* Princeton, N.J.: Princeton University Press.

Pachuari, R. K. 1990. "Energy Efficiency in Developing Countries, Policy Options and the Poverty Dilemma." *Natural Resources Forum* 319–325.

Parker, G. 1985. *Western Geopolitical Thought in the Twentieth Century.* London: Croom Helm.

Parry, M. L. 1986. "Some Implications of Climatic Change for Human Development." In *Sustainable Development of the Biosphere,* edited by William Clark and R. E. Munn. Cambridge, U.K.: Cambridge University Press, pp. 378–407.

Parry, M. L., T. R. Carter, and N. T. Konijn, eds. 1989. *The Impact of Climatic Variations on Agriculture. Volume 1: Assessments in Cool Temperate and Cold Regions; Volume 2: Assessments in Semi-arid Regions.* Dordrecht, Netherlands: Kluwer.

Passmore, W. A., and J. J. Sherwood. 1978. *Sociotechnical Systems: A Sourcebook.* San Diego, Calif.: University Associates.

Pearce, David, Anil Markandya, and Edward B. Barbier. 1989. *Blueprint for a Green Economy Annex: Sustainable Development—A Gallery of Definitions.* London: Earthscan Publications.

Pearson, Charles. 1982. "An Environmental Code of Conduct for Multinational Companies?" In Rubin and Graham, eds., pp. 154–160.

Perrings, C. 1987. *Economy and Environment: A Theoretical Essay on the Interdependence of Economic and Environmental Systems.* Cambridge, U.K.: Cambridge University Press.

Perrow, C. 1984. *Normal Accidents: Living with High-Risk Technologies.* New York: Basic Books.

Peters, C. M., A. H. Gentry, and R. O. Mendelsohn. 1989. "Valuation of an Amazonian Rainforest." *Nature* 339:655–656.

Peterson, Susan, and John Teal. 1986. "Ocean Fisheries as a Factor in Strategic Policy and Action." In *Global Resources and International Conflict: Environmental Factors in Strategic Policy and Action,* edited by Arthur Westing. New York: Oxford University Press.

Petsonk, Carol Annette. 1990. "The Role of the United Nations Environment Programme (UNEP) in the Development of International Environmental Law." *American University Journal of International Law and Policy* 5:351–391.

Piore, M. J., and C. F. Sabel. 1984. *The Second Industrial Divide: Possibilities for Prosperity.* New York: Basic Books.

Pirages, Dennis. 1978. *Global Ecopolitics: The New Context for International Relations.* North Scituate, Mass.: Duxbury Press.

Pirages, Dennis. 1989. *Global Technopolitics: The International Politics of Technology and Resources.* Pacific Grove, Calif.: Brooks/Cole Publishing Company.

Poggi, Gianfranco. 1990. *The State: Its Nature, Development and Prospects.* Stanford: Stanford University Press.

Pool, Robert. 1990. "Struggling To Do Science for Society." *Science* 248:672–673.

Pool, Robert. 1991. "U.S. National Labs Face Changing Roles." *Nature* 353 (5 September):6–7.

Porter, Gareth, and Delfin Ganapin, Jr. 1988. *Resources, Population, and the Philippines' Future: A Case Study.* WRI Paper No. 4. Washington, D.C.: World Resources Institute.

Porter, Michael E. 1980. *Competitive Strategy: Techniques for Analyzing Industries and Competitors.* New York: The Free Press.

Porter, Michael E., ed. 1986. *Competition in Global Industries.* Boston: Harvard Business School Press.

Porter, Michael E. 1990. *The Competitive Advantage of Nations.* New York: The Free Press.

Portney, Paul R. 1989. "Assessing and Managing the Risks of Climate Change." In *Greenhouse Warming: Abatement and Adaptation,* edited by Norman J. Rosenberg et al. Washington, D.C.: Resources for the Future.

Prigogine, I., and I. Stengers. 1984. *Order Out of Chaos: Man's New Dialogue With Nature,* New York: Bantam.

Quirk, James P., and Katsuaki L. Terasawa. 1987. *The Choice of Discount Rate Applicable to Government Resource Use.* Santa Monica, Calif.: The RAND Corporation, R-3464.

Raiffa, Howard. 1982. *The Art and Science of Negotiation.* Cambridge, Mass.: The Belknap Press of Harvard University Press.

Ramesh, Jairam, and Charles Weiss, eds. 1971. *Mobilizing Technology for World Development.* New York: Praeger Special Studies.

Rawls, John. 1971. *A Theory of Justice.* Cambridge: Harvard University Press.

"Reconciling the Sociosphere and the Biosphere." 1989. *International Social Science Journal* XLI (121).

Renouvin, Pierre, and Jean-Baptiste Duroselle. 1967. *Introduction to the History of International Relations.* Trans. Frederick A. Praeger, Inc. New York: Frederick A. Praeger Publishers.

Repetto, Robert. 1989. "Balance-Sheet Erosion—How to Account for the Loss of Natural Resources." *International Environmental Affairs* 1 (Spring):103–137.

Repetto, R., et al. 1989. *Wasting Assets: Natural Resources in the National Income Accounts.* World Resources Institute, June.

Revelle, Roger R. 1989. "Thoughts on Abatement and Adaptation." In *Greenhouse Warming: Abatement and Adaptation,* edited by Norman J. Rosenberg et al. Washington, D.C.: Resources for the Future.

Richards, K. 1991. "Outline of Issues for Tradable Permits in the Global Climate Convention." Report made to Environmental Defense Fund, June 13.

Riddell, R. 1981. *Ecodevelopment: Economics, Ecology, and Development: An Alternative to Growth Imperative Models.* London: Gower.

Riker, William H. 1962 (1982). *The Theory of Political Coalitions.* New Haven, Conn.: Yale University Press.

Rittberger, Volker, ed. 1990. *International Regimes in East-West Politics.* New York: Pinter Publishers.

Ritvo, H. 1987. *The Animal Estate: The English and Other Creatures in the Victorian Age.* Cambridge, Mass.: Harvard University Press.

Roan, Sharon L. 1989. *Ozone Crisis: The 15-Year Evolution of a Sudden Global Emergency.* New York: John Wiley and Sons.

Roberts, Leslie. 1989a. "Long, Slow Recovery Predicted for Alaska." *Science* 224 (7 April):22–24.

Roberts, Leslie. 1989b. "How Fast Can Trees Migrate?" *Science* 243:735–737.

Rodman, Kenneth A. 1988. *Sanctity Versus Sovereignty: the United States and the Nationalization of Natural Resource Investments.* New York: Columbia University Press.

Rosen, Harvey S. 1992. *Public Finance.* 3rd edition. Homewood, Illinois: Irwin.

Rosenau, James N. 1969. *Linkage Politics.* New York: Free Press.

Rosenberg, Nathan. 1976. *Perspectives on Technology.* Cambridge, U.K.: Cambridge University Press.

Rosenberg, Norman J. et al., eds. 1989. *Greenhouse Warming: Abatement and Adaptation.* Washington, D.C.: Resources for the Future.

Ross, L., and M. Silk. 1987. *Environmental Law and Policy in the People's Republic of China.* New York: Quorum Books.

Rothschild, Brian J. 1981. "More Food from the Sea?" *BioScience* 31 (March):216–222.

Rothschild, Brian J., ed. 1983. *Global Fisheries.* New York: Springer-Verlag.

Rubin, Seymour J., and Thomas R. Graham, eds. 1982. *Environment and Trade:*

the Relation of International Trade and Environmental Policy. Totowa, N.J.: Allanheld, Osmun.

Ruggie, J. G. 1975. "International Responses to Technology: Concepts and Trends." *International Organization* 29:557–583.

Rugman, A. M., D. J. Lecraw, and L. D. Booth. 1985. *International Business: Firm and Environment.* New York: McGraw Hill.

Rummel-Bulska, Iwona, and Seth Osafo, eds. 1991. *Selected Multilateral Treaties in the Field of the Environment,* Volume 2. Cambridge: Grotius Publications.

Saarinen, E., ed. 1982. *Conceptual Issues in Ecology.* Dordrecht: Reidel.

Sachs, I. 1974. "Environment and Styles of Development." *Environment in Africa* 1 (1):9–35.

Sachs, I. 1984. "The Strategies of Ecodevelopment." *Ceres* 17 (4):17–21.

Sadik, Nafis. 1990. *The State of World Population 1990.* New York: United Nations Population Fund.

Sadik, Nafis. 1991. *The State of World Population 1991.* New York: United Nations Population Fund.

Sagasti, Francisco R. 1989. "International Cooperation in a Fractured Global Order." Address to the UNESCO Colloquium on the Future of International Cooperation in Science and Technology for Development, June 14–16, Paris.

Sand, Peter. 1990a. "Regional Approaches to Transboundary Air Pollution." In *Energy: Production, Consumption and Consequences,* edited by J. L. Helm. Washington: National Academy Press.

Sand, Peter H. 1990b. *Lessons Learned in Global Environmental Governance.* Washington, D.C.: World Resources Institute.

Sandman, Peter M. 1986. *Explaining Environmental Risk.* Washington, D.C.: Environmental Protection Agency, Office of Toxic Substances, November.

Sardar, Z., ed. 1988. *The Revenge of Athena: Science, Exploitation and the Third World.* New York: Mansell.

Schachter, O., M. Nawaz, and J. Fried. 1971. *Toward Wider Acceptance of UN Treaties.* New York: Arno Press for United Nations Institute for Training and Research.

Schärer, Bernd. 1990. West German Umwelt Bundesamt, Berlin. Paper presented at U.S. EPA, March 12.

Schelling, Thomas C. 1960. *The Strategy of Conflict.* Cambridge, Mass.: Harvard University Press.

Schelling, Thomas C. 1973. "Hockey Helmets, Concealed Weapons, and Daylight Saving." *Journal of Conflict Resolution* 17 (3):381–428.

Schelling, T. C. 1991. Statement to Subcommittee on Energy and Power, U.S. House of Representatives, 19 June.

Schmid, A. Allan. 1989. *Benefits-Cost Analysis.* Boulder, Colorado: Westview Press.

Schmidheiny, Stephan, with the Business Council for Sustainable Development. 1992. *Changing Course.* Cambridge, Mass.: MIT Press.

Schnaiberg, A. 1977. "Obstacles to Environmental Research by Scientists and Technologists: A Social Structural Analysis." *Social Problems* 24:500–520.

Schneider, Keith. 1991. "U.S. to Negotiate Steps on Warming." *New York Times* (15 February):A7.

Schneider, Stephen H. 1987. "Climate Modeling." *Scientific American* 256:72–80.

Schneider, Stephen H. 1989a. "The Greenhouse Effect: Science and Policy." *Science* 243:771–781.

Schneider, Stephen H. 1989b. "The Changing Climate." *Scientific American* 261:70–79.

Schneider, Stephen H. 1990a. *Global Warming: Are We Entering the Greenhouse Century?* New York: Vintage Books.

Schneider, Stephen H. 1990b. "The Global Warming Debate Heats Up: An Analysis and Perspective." *Bulletin of the American Meterological Society* 71:1292–1304.

Schneider, Stephen H. 1991. "Three Reports of the Intergovernmental Panel on Climate Change." *Environment* 33:25–30.

Schneider, Stephen H., and Norman J. Rosenberg. 1989. "The Greenhouse Effect: Its Causes, Possible Impacts, and Associated Uncertainties." In *Greenhouse Warming: Abatement and Adaptation,* edited by Norman J. Rosenberg et al. Washington, D.C.: Resources for the Future.

Schneider, William. 1989. "Welcome to the Greening of America." *National Journal* 21 (May 27):1334.

Scientific Committee on Problems of the Environment (SCOPE). 1986. *Environmental Consequences of Nuclear War.* New York: John Wiley & Sons.

"Scientific Communication and National Security" (the Corson Report). Washington, D.C.: National Academy Press, 1982.

Sebenius, James K. 1983. "Negotiation Arithmetic: Adding and Subtracting Issues and Parties." *International Organization* 37:281–316.

Sebenius, James K. 1991a. "Negotiating a Regime to Control Global Warming." In *Greenhouse Warming,* edited by Jessica Tuchman Mathews et al. Washington, D.C.: World Resources Institute, pp. 69–98.

Sebenius, J. K. 1991b. "Designing Negotiations Toward a New Regime: The Case of Global Warming," *International Security* 15:110–148.

Sedjo, Roger A., and Allen M. Solomon. 1989. "Climate and Forests." In *Greenhouse Warming: Abatement and Adaptation,* edited by Norman J. Rosenberg et al. Washington, D.C.: Resources for the Future.

Shimizu, H. 1986. "The Self-Organization of Semantic Information in Biosystems." In *Information and Its Functions.* Proceedings of the Symposium '86. Tokyo: Institute of Journalism and Communication Studies, University of Tokyo.

Simberloff, D. 1982. "A Succession of Paradigms in Ecology: Essentialism to Materialism and Probablism." In Saarinen 1982, pp. 63–100.

Simon, Julian. 1981. *The Ultimate Resource.* Princeton: Princeton University Press.

Simon, J. L., and H. Kahn. 1984. *The Resourceful Earth.* New York: Basil Blackwell.

Simons, Marlise. 1990. "U.S. View Prevails at Climate Parley." *New York Times* (8 November):A9.

Singer, S. Fred. 1985. "On a 'Nuclear Winter.'" *Science* 227 (25 January):356, 358, 360, 362.

Sivard, Ruth Leger. 1989. *World Military and Social Expenditures 1989*. 13th edition. Washington, D.C.: World Priorities.

Skolnikoff, Eugene B. 1972. *The International Imperatives of Technology: Technological Development and the International Political System*. University of California at Berkeley, Institute of International Studies, Research Series #16.

Skolnikoff, Eugene B. 1990. "The Policy Gridlock on Global Warming." *Foreign Policy* 79:77–93.

Smil, Vaclav. 1987. *Energy, Food, Environment: Realities, Myths, Options*. Oxford: Oxford University Press.

Smil, Vaclav. 1990. "Planetary Warming: Realities and Responses." *Population and Development Review* 16 (1) (March).

Smith, R. Jeffrey. 1985. "DOD Says 'Nuclear Winter' Bolsters Its Plans." *Science* 227 (15 March):1320.

Smith, R. Jeffrey. 1986. "DOD Declines to Consider Impact of Nuclear Winter." *Science* 232 (30 May):1088–1089.

Smith, R. Jeffrey. 1991. "Grim Lessons for the World in Iraq's Secret Nuclear Program." *The Washington Post National Weekly Edition* (Aug. 19–25):22.

Smyth, Henry de Wolf. 1945. *Atomic Energy for Military Purposes: The Official Report on the Development of the Atomic Bomb Under the Auspices of the United States Government*. Princeton: Princeton University Press.

Snidal, Duncan. 1985. "Coordination versus Prisoners' Dilemma: Implications for International Cooperation and Regimes." *American Political Science Review* 79:923–942.

Sohn, L. 1984. "The Role of Equity in the Jurisprudence of the International Court of Justice." In *Melanges Georges Perrin*, edited by B. Dutoit and E. Grisel. Lausanne: Payot.

Solbrig, Otto T., ed. 1991. *From Genes to Ecosystems: A Research Agenda for Biodiversity*. Cambridge, Mass.: IUBS.

Solomon, Burt. 1990. "Save the Coast or Drill for Oil? Ex-Oilman Bush Debates Himself." *National Journal* 22 (March 10):589–590.

Solow, Robert. 1992. Personal communications with Jerome Rothenberg.

Sorensen, M. Max. 1973. "Le Problem du Droit Intertemporal dans l'Orde International." *l'Annuaire de l'Institut de Droit International*, Vol. 55, Part I. Basel, Switzerland: S. Karger, pp. 1–114.

Soviet Political Sciences Association. 1985. *Global Problems of Mankind and the State*. Problems of the Contemporary World, No. 116. Moscow: USSR Academy of Sciences.

Sprout, Harold. 1962. *Foundations of International Politics*. Princeton, N.J.: Van Nostrand.

Sprout, H., and Margaret Sprout. 1965. *The Ecological Perspective on Human Affairs with Special Reference to International Politics*. Princeton, N.J.: Princeton University Press.

Steele, John H. 1987. "Global Ecosystem Dynamics: Comparison of Terrestrial and Marine Systems." Woods Hole, Mass.: WHOI, 11/23/87.

Steele, John H., and E. W. Henderson. 1984. "Modelling Long-Term Fluctuations in Fish Stocks." *Science* 224:985–987.

Stein, Arthur A. 1983. "Coordination and Collaboration." In *International Regimes,* edited by Stephen D. Krasner. Ithaca, N.Y.: Cornell University Press.

Sterman, John D. 1987. "System Simulation: Expectation Formation in Behavioral Simulation Models." *Behavioral Science* 32:190–209.

Sterman, John D. 1988. "Deterministic Chaos in Models of Human Behavior: Methodological Issues and Experimental Results." *Systemic Dynamics Review* 4 (1–2):161–175.

Sterman, John D. 1989. "Deterministic Chaos in an Experimental Economic System." *Journal of Economic Behavior and Organization* 12:1-28.

Stern, Paul C., Oran R. Young, and Daniel Druckman, eds. 1992. *Global Environmental Change: Understanding the Human Dimensions.* Washington, D.C.: National Academy Press.

Stevens, Wallace K. 1991. "In a Warming World, Who Comes Out Ahead?" *New York Times* (5 February):C1.

Stevens, William. 1991. "Ozone Loss Over the U.S. Is Found To Be Twice as Bad as Predicted." *The New York Times* (April 5):A1.

Stewart-Smith, Geoffrey. 1987. *In the Shadow of Fujisan.* New York: Viking Penguin.

Stokes, Bruce. 1991. "Soviet Oil Not a Salve," *National Journal* 23 (November 16):2809–2812.

Stone, J. 1961. *The Province and Function of Law.* Cambridge, Mass.: Harvard University Press.

Swinbanks, David. 1991. "Going for 'Green Technology.'" *Nature* 350 (March 28):266–267.

Szasz, Paul C. 1991. "The Role of International Law." *Evaluation Review* 15 (1):7–26.

Szekely, Alberto. 1989. "Yellow-Fin Tuna." in Birnie 1989.

Tagliagambe, S. 1983. "The Originality and Importance of Vernadsky's Ideas." *Scientia, Rivista Internazionali di Sintesi* 118:505–535.

Taylor, Lance. 1983. *Structuralist Macroeconomics: Applicable Models for the Third World.* New York: Basic Books, Inc.

Taylor, P. J. 1989. *Political Geography: World-Economy, Nation-State and Locality.* 2nd edition. Harlow, Essex: Longman.

Tegart, W. J. McG., G. W. Sheldon, and D. C. Griffiths, eds. 1990. *Climate Change: The IPCC Impacts Assessment.* Canberra: Australian Government Publishing Service.

Thacher, P. 1987. "Equity Under Change." *Proceedings.* Annual Meeting of the American Society of International Law. Washington, D.C.: American Society of International Law, pp. 133–138.

Thacher, Peter S. 1989. "Institutional Options for Management of the Global Environment and Commons." Preliminary paper for the World Federation of United Nations Associations Project on Global Security and Risk Management.

Thacher, Peter S. 1991. "Multilateral Cooperation and Global Change," *Journal of International Affairs* (Winter 1991) Vol. 44, No. 2.

Thacher, Peter S. 1992. "The Mediterranean: A New Approach to Marine Pollution." In *International Environmental Negotiations,* edited by Gunnar Sjostedt. Laxenburg, Austria: International Institute for Applied Systems Analysis.

Thom, R. 1983. *Mathematical Models of Morphogenesis*. New York: Prentice-Hall.

Thompson, William R. 1983. "World Wars, Global Wars, and the Cool Hand Luke Syndrome." *International Studies Quarterly* 27 (3):369–74.

Tollison, Robert D., and Thomas D. Willett. 1979. "An Economic Theory of Mutually Advantageous Issue Linkages in International Relations." *International Organization* 33:425–449.

Toon, Owen and Richard Turco. 1991. "Polar Stratospheric Clouds and Ozone Depletion." *Scientific American* (6) (June):68–77.

Toth, F. L., E. Hizsnyik, and W. C. Clark, eds. 1989. *Scenarios of Socioeconomic Development for Studies of Global Environmental Change: A Critical Review*. Laxenberg, Austria: International Institute for Applied Systems Analysis.

Turner, B. L., II, et al., eds. 1990. *The Earth as Transformed by Human Action: Global and Regional Changes in the Biosphere over the Past 300 Years*. Cambridge, U.K.: Cambridge University Press and Clark University.

Ugarte, A. P. 1981. *Introduction to Geopolitics*. Santiago, Chile: Editorial Andres Bello.

UNCTC. See United Nations Center and Transnational Corporation.

Underdal, Arild. 1980. *The Politics of International Fisheries Management: The Case of the Northeast Atlantic*. Oslo: Universitetsforlaget.

Underdal, Arild. 1983. "Causes of Negotiations 'Failure.'" *European Journal of Political Research* 11:183–195.

UNEP. See United Nations Environment Program.

UNGA. See United Nations General Assembly.

United Nations. 1973. *Report of the United Nations Conference on the Human Environment*. Stockholm, June 5–16, 1972.

United Nations. 1980. *Interrelations: Resources, Environment, Population and Development*. New York: United Nations.

United Nations. 1986. *Demographic Yearbook*. New York: United Nations.

United Nations. 1989. *World Population at the Turn of the Century*. New York: United Nations Population Studies No. 111, Publication E.89.XIII.2.

United Nations Center on Transnational Corporations. 1985. *Environmental Aspects of the Activities of Transnational Corporations: A Survey*. New York: United Nations Publications ST/CTC/55.

United Nations Center on Transnational Corporations. 1988. *Transnational Corporations in World Development: Trends and Prospects*. New York: United Nations Publications ST/CTC/89.

United Nations Environment Program. 1989. *Environmental Data Report*. 2nd edition. Oxford: Blackwell Reference.

United Nations General Assembly (UNGA). 1989. "Protection of Global Climate for Present and Future Generations of Mankind" Resolution A/RES/44/207 (22 December).

United Nations General Assembly (UNGA). 1990. "Protection of Global Climate for Present and Future Generations of Mankind" Resolution A/RES/45/212 (21 December).

U.S. Department of Commerce, International Trade Administration. 1988. *In-*

ternational Direct Investment: Global Trends and the U.S. Role. Washington, D.C.

U.S. Dept of Energy (DOE), Energy Information Administration. 1989. International Energy Outlook 1989, Projections to 2000. Washington, D.C.: U.S. DOE.

United States Environmental Protection Agency. 1989. "Policy Options for Stabilizing Global Climate." Report to Congress, February.

Vernadsky, V. I. 1929. La Biosphere. Paris: Felix Alcan.

Vernadsky, V. I. 1945. "The Biosphere and the Noosphere." American Scientist 33:1–12.

Vernon, Raymond. 1966. "International Investment and International Trade in the Product Cycle." Quarterly Journal of Economics 80 (2):190–207.

Vernon, Raymond. 1971. Sovereignty at Bay. New York: Basic Books.

Vernon, Raymond. 1974. "The Location of Economic Activity." In Economic Analysis and the Multinational Enterprise, edited by John H. Dunning. London: George Allen & Unwin.

Verstraete, Michel M. 1986. "Defining Desertification: A Review." Climatic Change 9:5–18.

Verstraete, Michel M., and Robert E. Dickinson. 1986. "Modeling Surface Processes in Atmospheric Circulation Models." Annales Geophysical 4:357–64.

Verstraete, Michel M., and B. Pinty. 1990. "The Potential Contribution of Satellite Remote Sensing to the Understanding of Arid Lands Processes." In Vegetation and Climate Interactions in Semi-Arid Regions, edited by A. Henderson-Sellars and A. J. Pittman. Dordrecht: Kluwer Academic Publishers.

Victor, David G. 1990. "Calculating Greenhouse Budgets." Nature 347:431.

Victor, D. G. 1991a. "How to Slow Global Warming," Nature 349:451–456.

Victor, D. G. 1991b. "Limits of Market-Based Strategies for Slowing Global Warming: The Case of Tradeable Permits." Policy Sciences 24:199–222.

Wallerstein, I. 1974, 1978, 1989. The Modern World-System, Vols. I, II, III. New York and San Diego: Academic Press.

Wallerstein, I. 1991. Geopolitics and Geoculture: Essays on the Changing World-System. Cambridge, U.K.: Cambridge University Press; Paris: Editions de La Maison des Sciences de l'Homme.

Walter, Ingo. 1975. International Economics of Pollution. New York: John Wiley & Sons.

Walter, Ingo. 1982. "Environmentally Induced Industrial Relocation to Developing Countries." In Environment and Trade: the Relation of International Trade and Environmental Policy, edited by Seymour J. Rubin and R. Graham. Totowa, N.J.: Allanhead, Osmun.

Walters, Carl. 1986. Adaptive Management of Renewable Resources. New York: Macmillan.

Walton, Richard E., and Robert B. McKersie. 1965. A Behavioral Theory of Labor Negotiations: An Analysis of a Social Interaction System. New York: McGraw-Hill.

Waltz, Kenneth N. 1959. Man, the State, and War. New York: Columbia University Press.

Ward, Barbara, and Rene Dubos. 1972. *Only One Earth*. Harmondsworth: Penguin.

Warrick, Richard, and William Riebsame. 1981. "Societal Response to CO_2-Induced Climate Change: Opportunities for Research." *Climatic Change* 3 (4):387–428.

Washington, Warren M., and Gerald A. Meehl. 1989. "Climate Sensitivity Due to Increased CO_2: Experiments with a Coupled Atmosphere and Ocean General Circulation Model." *Climate Dynamics* 4:1–38.

Watson, R. and P. Watson. 1969. *Man and Nature: An Anthropological Essay in Human Ecology*. New York: Harcourt, Brace and World.

WCED. See World Commission on Environment and Development.

Weiss, Edith Brown. 1984. "The Planetary Trust: Conservation and Intergenerational Equity." *Ecology Law Quarterly* 11 (4):495–581.

Weiss, Edith Brown. 1989. *In Fairness to Future Generations: International Law, Common Patrimony, and Intergenerational Equity*. Dobbs Ferry, N.Y.: Transnational and United Nations University.

Weiss, Edith Brown. 1990. "Our Rights and Obligations to Future Generations for the Environment." *American Journal International Law* 1 (84):190–212.

Weiss, Edith Brown, Daniel B. Magraw, and Paul C. Szasz. 1992. *International Environmental Law: Basic Instruments and References*. Dobbs Ferry, N.Y.: Transnational Publishers.

Wettestad, J., and S. Andresen. 1991. "The Effectiveness of International Resource Cooperation: Some Preliminary Findings." Fridtjof Nansens Institutt, Lysaker, Norway, R:007–1991.

Wheelon, Albert D. 1989. "Toward a New Space Policy." In *Space Policy Reconsidered*, edited by Radford Byerly, Jr. Boulder, Colo.: Westview Press, Ch. 3.

White, Lynn, Jr. 1962. *Medieval Technology and Social Change*. Oxford: Oxford University Press.

White, Lynn, Jr. 1967. "The Historical Roots of Our Ecologic Crisis." *Science* 155 (10 March):1203–1207.

White, Robert M. 1990. "The Great Climate Debate." *Scientific American* 263:36–43.

Whitmore, T. M., et al. 1990. "Long-Term Population Change." In Turner et al. 1990, pp. 25–39.

Wicks, George, and Dennis Bickford. 1989. "Doing Something About High-Level Nuclear Waste." *Technology Review* (November/December):51–58.

Wijkman, Per Magnus. 1982. "Managing the Global Commons." *International Organization* 36:511.

Willums, Jan-Olaf, ed. 1990. *The Greening of Enterprise: Business Leaders Speak Out*. Paper presented at the Industry Forum on Environment, 10–11 May, Bergen, Norway. ICC Publication No. 487E. Aurskog, Norway: International Chamber of Commerce, in cooperation with the Nordic Confederations of Industry.

Wilson, Edward O., ed. 1988. *Biodiversity*. Washington, D.C.: National Academy Press.

Wilson, Edward O. 1989. "Threats to Biodiversity." *Scientific American*, 261 (3):108–116.

Wisner, B. 1988. *Power and Need in Africa: Basic Human Needs and Development Policies.* London: Earthscan.

Woodwell, G. M., et al. 1983. "Global Deforestation: Contribution to Atmospheric Carbon Dioxide." *Science* 222:1081–1086.

Wooster, Warren. 1987. "Immiscible Investigators." *BioScience* 37 (November):728–730.

World Bank. 1988. *World Development Report 1988.* New York: Oxford University Press.

World Bank. 1989. *World Debt Tables, 1985–89.* New York: UN Dept. of Public Information.

World Bank. 1990. "Flood Control in Bangladesh: A Plan for Action." Technical paper no. 119, Asia Region Technical Dept. Washington, D.C.: World Bank.

World Bank. 1991. *World Development Report 1991.* New York: Oxford University Press.

World Climate Research Program. 1991. *The Global Climate Observing System.* Winchester, U.K.: Joint Scientific Committee, SCRP, January.

World Commission on Environment and Development (WCED). 1987. *Our Common Future.* New York: Oxford University Press.

World Meteorological Organization (WMO). 1986. *Atmospheric Ozone: 1985.* Global Ozone Research and Monitoring Project Report #16.

World Meteorological Organization (WMO). 1990. *Scientific Assessment of Stratospheric Ozone: 1989,* Global Ozone Research and Monitoring Project Report #20.

World Resources Institute (WRI). 1989. *World Resources 1988–89.* New York: Basic Books.

World Resources Institute (WRI). 1990. *World Resources 1990–91.* New York: Oxford University Press.

World Resources Institute, International Institute for Environment and Development, and United Nations Environment Program. 1988. *World Resources 1988–89.* New York: Basic Books.

World Resources Institute and United Nations Environment Program. 1990. *World Resources 1990–91.* New York: Oxford University Press, 1990.

Worrest, Robert et al. 1989. "Potential Impact of Stratospheric Ozone Depletion on Marine Ecosystems." In *Coping with Climate Change: Proceedings of the Second North American Conference on Preparing for Climate Change,* edited by John Topping, Jr. Washington, D.C.: The Climate Institute, pp. 256–262.

WRI. See World Resource Institute.

Wunsch, Carl. 1984. "The Ocean Circulation in Climate." In *The Global Climate,* edited by John T. Houghton. Cambridge, U.K.: Cambridge University Press.

Wynne, Brian. 1984. "The Institutional Context of Science, Models, and Policy." *Policy Sciences* 17 (November):277–320.

Yanshin, A. L., and F. T. Yanshina. 1988. "The Scientific Heritage of Vladimir Vernadsky." *Impact of Science on Society* 38:283–296.

Young, H. P. 1991. "Sharing the Burden of Global Warming." Equity and Global Climate Change Discussion Paper, University of Maryland at College Park, School of Public Affairs.

Young, Oran R., ed. 1975. *Bargaining: Formal Theories of Negotiation.* Urbana, Illinois: University of Chicago Press.

Young, Oran R. 1989a. *International Cooperation: Building Regimes for Natural Resources and the Environment.* Ithaca, N.Y.: Cornell University Press.

Young, Oran R. 1989b. "The Politics of International Regime Formation: Managing Natural Resources and the Environment." *International Organization* 43:349–375.

Young, Oran R. 1991. "Political Leadership and Regime Formation: On the Development of Institutions in International Society." *International Organization* 45 (Summer):281–308.

Young, Oran R. 1992. "The Effectiveness of International Institutions: Hard Cases and Critical Variables." In *Governance without Government: Change and Order in World Politics,* edited by J. N. Rosenau and E.-O. Czempiel. New York: Cambridge University Press.

Young, Oran R. and Gail Osherenko, eds. Forthcoming. *The Politics of International Regime Formation: Lessons from Arctic Cases.* Ithaca: Cornell University Press.

Index

industrial, 96, 147, 418
management of, 211–212, 458
transmission of, 206, 207
treaties on, 406–407, 409, 416–417, 419n3
Population, 67, 69, 71, 148(fig.),
478, 479, 483, 486. *See also* Generations; Population density
Population density, 108
and development, 96, 106, 113
and GNP, 81, 85, 89–91(table),
101, 112(table), 117(table),
121(table)
Population growth, 8–9, 14(fig.), 32,
45, 46, 56, 60, 64n8, 65n11, 78,
108, 129, 137, 149, 170n17, 176,
178, 180, 255, 345, 373, 378,
388–389, 396–397n37, 481
changes in, 24, 127, 153–154
country profiles and, 73, 76, 124–126(figs.)
future, 327–328
future consumption and, 315–316
growth and, 82–84(table), 93–94(table), 103(table), 114(table),
118(table)
homogeneous, 315–320
impacts of, 47, 48, 49, 62
and organizational development,
10–11
and resource management, 196–197
and resources, 106–107, 110
and technology, 13–14, 68–69, 95,
113
Portugal, 102, 106, 127, 495
Poverty, 95, 176, 179
and environmental degradation,
158, 166, 190, 336, 481
Power, 70
in negotiations, 435–437
purchasing, 317, 320, 321
technology and, 275–276
treaty enforcement, 411–412
Preparatory Committee of the United
Nations Conference on Environment and Development (UNCED
PrepCom), 432, 443

Price, Martin, 134–135
Prince William Sound, 283, 299, 300
Private sector, 27, 194–195, 264, 349
Product-cycle theory, 220
Product disposal, 206
Production, 25, 45, 85, 115,
157(fig.), 225, 226, 248, 499
technological restructuring of, 192–193
Productivity, 108, 375, 376, 478, 502
and capital stocks, 356–357
incentives for, 387–388
substitutability in, 368–369
Profile groups, 231(table)
changes in, 119, 122, 127–129
defining, 75–76
domestic companies in, 228–230(table)
IV, 106–110
V, 110–115
measuring, 80–81
I, 80–92
VI, 115–122
III, 101–106
II, 92–101
Profiles, 74(fig.), 485
components, 76–78
country, 72–75, 123(table), 504
Program for Monitoring and Evaluation of the Long-Range Transmission of Air Pollution in Europe
(EMEP), 457, 473n4
Property, 167, 202, 326, 370
Property rights, 195, 319, 327, 381
Public consciousness, 348, 350–351
Public relations, 243

Qatar, 113
Qualities of life, 69, 79, 101, 106,
110, 115, 129, 131

Radiation, ultraviolet, 53, 63
R&D. *See* Research and development
Ramsar Convention on Wetlands of
International Importance Especially as Waterfowl Habitat, 445
Ranke, Leopold von, 144